STUDY GUIDE
TO ACCOMPANY
McCONNELL AND BRUE

Macroeconomics

STUDY GUIDE
TO ACCOMPANY
McCONNELL AND BRUE

Macroeconomics

THIRTEENTH EDITION

William B. Walstad
Professor of Economics
University of Nebraska—Lincoln

Robert C. Bingham
Late Professor of Economics
Kent State University

McGraw-Hill, Inc.
New York • St. Louis • San Francisco • Auckland • Bogotá • Caracas
Lisbon • London • Madrid • Mexico City • Milan • Montreal • New Delhi
San Juan • Singapore • Sydney • Tokyo • Toronto

Study Guide to Accompany McConnell and Brue:
Macroeconomics

Copyright © 1996, 1993, 1990 by McGraw-Hill, Inc. All rights reserved.
Portions of this text have been taken from the *Study Guide to Accompany*
McConnell and Brue: Economics, Thirteenth Edition. Copyright © 1996 by
McGraw-Hill, Inc. All rights reserved. Printed in the United States of America.
Except as permitted under the United States Copyright Act of 1976, no part of
this publication may be reproduced or distributed in any form or by any
means, or stored in a data base or retrieval system, without the prior written
permission of the publisher.

3 4 5 6 7 8 9 0 MAL MAL 9 0 9 8 7 6

ISBN 0-07-046822-2

This book was set in Helvetica by York Graphic Services, Inc.
The editors were Lucille H. Sutton and Joseph F. Murphy;
the designer was Joseph A. Piliero;
the production supervisor was Annette Mayeski.
Malloy Lithographing, Inc., was printer and binder.

About the Authors

William B. Walstad is a professor of economics at the University of Nebraska—Lincoln where he directs the Center for Economic Education and the National Center for Research in Economic Education. He received his Ph.D. degree from the University of Minnesota. Professor Walstad has been honored with a Distinguished Teaching Award at Nebraska. He also received the Henry H. Villard Research Award for his published research in economic education. He co-edited *The Principles of Economics Course: A Handbook for Instructors* (McGraw-Hill) and developed three national tests in economics. He serves as an associate editor of the *Journal of Economic Education*.

Robert C. Bingham was an undergraduate student at DePauw University and obtained M.A. and Ph.D. degrees from Northwestern University. He taught at the University of Nebraska—Lincoln where he was a colleague of Professor McConnell before coming to Kent State University from which he retired in 1985. He was the author of several other study guides and supplements for the principles of economics courses.

To
Karen, Laura, and Kristin

Contents

How to Use the Study Guide to Learn Economics

This **Study Guide** is designed to help you read and understand Campbell R. McConnell and Stanley L. Brue's textbook, **Macroeconomics,** Thirteenth Edition. If used properly, a guide can be a great aid to you in what is probably your first course in economics.

No one pretends that the study of economics is easy, but it can be made easier. Of course a study guide will not do your work for you, and its use is no substitute for reading the text. You must be willing to read the text, spend time on the subject, and work at learning if you wish to understand economics.

Many students do read their text and work hard on their economics course and still fail to learn the subject. This is because principles of economics is a new subject for them, and they have had no previous experience in learning economics. They want to learn but do not know just how to go about it. Here is where the **Study Guide** can help. Let us first see what the **Study Guide** contains and then how to use it.

■ WHAT THE STUDY GUIDE IS

The **Study Guide** contains forty chapters—one for each chapter in the text and a **glossary.** Each **Study Guide** chapter has eleven sections. The first five sections identify and explain the basic content and concepts in each chapter.

1. An **introduction** explains what is in the chapter of the text and how it is related to material in earlier and later chapters. It points out topics to which you should give special attention, and reemphasizes difficult or important principles and facts.

2. A **checklist** tells you the things you should be able to do when you have finished the chapter.

3. A **chapter outline** shows how the chapter is organized and summarizes briefly the essential points made in the chapter.

4. A list of the **important terms** found in the chapter points out what you must be able to define in order to understand the material in the chapter. A definition of each of these terms will be found in the glossary at the end of the **Study Guide.**

5. Selected **hints and tips** are given for each chapter to help you master the material and to make connections with any previous discussion of a topic.

The next six sections of the **Study Guide** allow you to **self-test** your understanding of the chapter material.

6. **Fill-in questions** (short-answer and list questions) help you to learn and remember the important generalizations and facts in the chapter.

7. **True-false questions** can be used to test your understanding of the material in the chapter.

8. **Multiple-choice questions** also give you a chance to check your knowledge of the chapter content and to prepare for this type of course examination.

9. **Problems** assist you in learning and understanding economic concepts by requiring different skills—drawing a graph, completing a table, or finding relationships—to solve the problems.

10. **Short answer and essay questions** can be used to test yourself, to identify important questions in the chapter, and to prepare for examinations.

11. **Answers** to fill-in questions, to the problems and projects, to true-false questions, and to the multiple-choice questions are found at the end of each chapter. You are also given the references to the specific pages in the textbook for each true-false, multiple-choice, and short answer or essay question.

■ HOW TO STUDY AND LEARN WITH THE HELP OF THE STUDY GUIDE

1. **Read and outline.** For best results, quickly read the introduction, outline, list of terms, and checklist in the **Study Guide** before you read the chapter in the text. Then read the chapter in the text slowly and keep one eye on the **Study Guide** outline and the list of terms. The outline contains only the major points in the chapter. Highlight the chapter as you read it by identifying the major **and the minor** points and by placing outline numbers or letters (such as I or A or 1 or a) in the margins. Circle the important terms. When you have completed the chapter, you will have the chapter outlined and it will give you a set of notes on the chapter. Be careful to highlight or underline only the really important or summary statements.

2. *Review and reread.* After you have read the chapter in the text once, return to the introduction, outline, and list of terms in the ***Study Guide.*** Reread the introduction and outline. Does everything there make sense? If not, go to the text and reread the topics that you do not remember well or that still confuse you. Look at the outline. Try to recall each of the minor topics or points that were contained in the text under each of the major points in the outline. When you come to the list of terms go over them one by one. Define or explain each to yourself and then look for the definition of the term either in the text chapter or in the glossary. Compare your own definition or explanation with that in the text or glossary. The quick way to find the definition of a term in the text is to look in the index of the text for the page or pages on which that term or concept is mentioned. Make any correction or change in your own definition or explanation that is necessary.

3. *Test and check answers.* When you have done all this, you will have a general idea of what is in the text chapter. Now take a look at the fill-in questions, true-false questions, multiple-choice questions, and problems. Tackle each of these four sections one at a time, using the following procedure. (**1**) Answer as many questions as you can without looking in the text or in the answer section. (**2**) Check the text for whatever help you need. It is a good idea to do more than merely look for answers in the text. Reread any section for which you were not able to answer questions. (**3**) Then consult the answer section at the end of the chapter for the correct answers and reread any section of the text for which you missed questions. (See the text page references that are given with the answer to each true-false or multiple-choice question.)

The questions in these four sections are not all of equal difficulty. Do not expect to get them all right the first time. Some are designed to pinpoint things of importance which you will probably miss the first time you read the text and to get you to read about them again. None of the questions is unimportant. Even those that have no definite answers will bring you to grips with many important economic questions and increase your understanding of economic principles and problems.

The short answer and essay questions cover the major points in the chapter. For some of the easier questions all you may do is mentally outline your answer. For the more difficult questions you may want to write out a brief outline of the answer or a full answer. Do not avoid the difficult questions just because they are more work. Answering these questions is often the most valuable work a student can do toward acquiring an understanding of economic relationships and principles.

Although no answers are given in the ***Study Guide*** to the short answer and essay questions, the answer section does list page references in the text for each question. You are ***strongly*** encouraged to read those text pages for an explanation to the question or for better insight into the question content.

4. *Double check.* Before you turn to the next chapter in the text and ***Study Guide,*** return to the checklist. If you cannot honestly check off each of the items in the list, you have not learned what the author of the text and of this ***Study Guide*** hoped you would learn.

■ SOME FINAL WORDS

Perhaps the method of using the ***Study Guide*** outlined above seems like a lot of work. It is! Study and learning necessarily entail work on your part. This is a fact you must accept if you are to learn economics.

After you have used the ***Study Guide*** to study three or four chapters, you will find that some sections are of more value to you than others. Let your own experience determine how you will use it. But do not discontinue use of the ***Study Guide*** after three or four chapters merely because you are not sure whether it is helping you. ***Stick with it.***

In addition to the material in the ***Study Guide,*** there are questions at the end of each chapter in the text. Some of these questions are similar to questions in the ***Study Guide,*** but none is identical. It will be worthwhile for you to examine all the questions at the end of each chapter and to work out or outline answers for them. Students who have trouble with the problems in the ***Study Guide*** will find the end-of-chapter problems useful in determining whether they have actually mastered their difficulties.

■ ACKNOWLEDGMENTS

The late Professor Robert Bingham prepared the first ten editions of the ***Study Guide.*** He worked with great care and wanted the ***Study Guide*** to be a valuable aid for students. Many past users of the ***Study Guide*** will attest to his success. Although Professor Bingham did not participate directly in this revision, his work remains a major contribution to this edition.

I also wish to acknowledge other help I received. Campbell McConnell and Stanley Brue offered many helpful comments for the revision. Professor Thomas Phelps of Pierce College and Professor Janet West of the University of Nebraska–Omaha provided many good suggestions in their reviews of the previous edition of the ***Study Guide.*** George Langelett, a graduate student at Nebraska, helped me check the self-test questions. Another graduate student, Wayne Edwards, identified the textbook pages in the answers. Students in my principles of economics classes offered many good comments and suggestions. Sharon Nemeth was of invaluable assistance in proofing the manuscript. Finally, the team at McGraw-Hill, especially Lucille Sutton, Victoria Richardson, Michael Elia, and Edwin Hanson, gave me great assistance with the editorial and production work. Despite the many contributions from others, all responsibility for errors and omissions is mine.

William B. Walstad

Macroeconomics

CHAPTER 1

The Nature and Method of Economics

Chapter 1 introduces you to economics—the study of how people decide how to use scarce productive resources to satisfy material wants. Knowledge of economics is important because it is essential for well-informed citizenship and it has many practical applications to personal decisions. The purpose of this chapter is to explain the nature of the subject and to describe the methods that economists use to study economic questions.

Economists use three different approaches to examine economic topics. **Descriptive economics** is the gathering of relevant facts about an economic problem. **Economic theory** or economic analysis involves the derivation of principles using inductive or deductive methods. **Policy economics** entails the formulation of policies or recommended solutions to economic problems.

The heart of the chapter is the discussion of economic principles in the economic theory section. Economic principles are generalizations. Because the economist cannot employ laboratory experiments to test the generalizations, these principles are always imprecise and subject to exceptions. Economics is a science but it is not an exact science. Economic principles are also simplifications—approximations of a complex world—and both the formulation and application of these principles present many opportunities for making serious mistakes. Economic principles are not the answers to economic questions but are tools—intellectual tools—for analyzing **microeconomic** and **macroeconomic** problems and for finding solutions to these problems.

The choice of an economic policy depends on economic principles **and** on the value judgments and weights given to economic goals. Here we move from economic theory and positive economics, which investigates **what is,** to normative economics, which incorporates subjective or value-laden views of **what ought to be.** Many of the apparent disagreements among economists are over normative policy issues and involve deciding which economic goals for our economy are most important in making the case for a policy solution.

Clear thinking about economic questions requires that the beginning student avoid many pitfalls. Errors of commission and omission can occur from bias, loaded terminology, imprecise definitions, fallacies of composition, and causation fallacies. Awareness of these pitfalls will help you think more objectively about economic issues.

The last section of the chapter describes the three key features of the economic perspective. First, the economic perspective recognizes that all choices involve costs. Second, it incorporates the view that people make decisions that reflect their rational self-interest when achieving a goal. Third, it shows how people weigh the marginal benefits against marginal costs when making decisions. You will develop a better understanding of these features and the meaning of the economic perspective as you read about the microeconomic and macroeconomic decisions in this book.

■ CHECKLIST

When you have studied this chapter you should be able to:

☐ Write a formal definition of economics.
☐ Give two good reasons for studying economics.
☐ Define descriptive economics, economic theory, and policy economics.
☐ Distinguish between induction and deduction in economic reasoning.
☐ Explain what an economic principle is and how economic principles are obtained.
☐ Discuss how economic principles are generalizations and abstractions.
☐ Explain what the "other things equal" (**ceteris paribus**) assumption is and why this assumption is employed in economics.
☐ Distinguish between macroeconomics and microeconomics.
☐ List the three steps in formulating economic policy.
☐ Identify eight economic goals that are widely accepted for our own and many other societies.
☐ State four significant points about economic goals.
☐ Give examples of positive and normative economics.
☐ Recognize the "pitfalls to objective thinking" when confronted with examples of them.
☐ Describe the three key features of an economic perspective.

☐ Give examples of the application of an economic perspective.

■ CHAPTER OUTLINE

1. Economics is concerned with the efficient use of limited productive resources to achieve the maximum satisfaction of human material wants.

2. Citizens in a democracy must understand elementary economics to comprehend the present-day problems of their society and to make intelligent decisions when they vote. Economics is an academic rather than a vocational subject, but a knowledge of it is valuable to business executives, consumers, and workers.

3. Economists gather relevant facts to develop economic principles that may be used to formulate policies which will solve economic problems.
  a. *Descriptive economics* is the gathering of relevant facts about the production, exchange, and consumption of goods and services.
  b. *Economic theory* is the analysis of the facts and the derivation of economic principles.
  (1) To obtain and test their principles economists use both the *inductive* and the *deductive* methods.
  (2) Economic principles are also called laws, theories, and models.
  (3) Each of these principles is a generalization.
  (4) Economists employ the *ceteris paribus* (or "other things equal") assumption to obtain these generalizations.
  (5) These principles are also abstractions from reality.
  (6) Economists can derive principles about economic behavior at the *macroeconomic* or *microeconomic* level of analysis.
  c. *Policy economics* is the combination of economic principles and economic values (or goals) to influence economic events.
  (1) The three steps in creating an economic policy designed to achieve an economic goal involve defining the goal, identifying the effects of alternative policies, and evaluating the results.
  (2) There are eight major economic goals that are often important to consider—economic growth, full employment, economic efficiency, price level stability, economic freedom, equitable distribution of income, economic security, and a balance of trade.
  (3) Economic goals can be complementary or conflicting and involve tradeoffs; issues related to goal interpretation or setting priorities can cause problems.
  (4) Values are the judgments people make about what is desirable (good, just) and what is undesirable (bad, unjust).
  (5) Positive economics concerns *what is,* or the scientific analysis of economic behavior; normative economics suggests *what ought to be* in offering answers to policy questions.

4. Objective thinking in the study and use of economic principles requires strict application of the rules of logic in which personal emotions are irrelevant, if not detrimental. The pitfalls encountered by beginning students in studying and applying economic principles include:
  a. bias of preconceived beliefs not warranted by facts;
  b. loaded terminology or the use of terms in a way which appeals to emotion and leads to a nonobjective analysis of the issues;
  c. the definition of terms by economists in ways which may not be the same as the ways in which these terms are more commonly used;
  d. the fallacy of composition or the assumption that what is true of the part is necessarily true of the whole.

5. There are two causation fallacies to remember:
  a. The *post hoc* fallacy is the mistaken belief that when one event precedes another, the first event is the cause of the second; and,
  b. confusing correlation with causation.

6. The economic perspective has three interrelated features.
  a. It recognizes scarcity requires choice, and that all choices entail a cost.
  b. It views people as rational decision-makers who make choices based on their self-interest.
  c. It uses marginal analysis to assess how the marginal costs of a decision compare with the marginal benefits.

■ IMPORTANT TERMS

Economics	Macroeconomics
Descriptive economics	Microeconomics
Economic theory (analysis)	Policy economics
Induction	Economic goals
Deduction	Tradeoffs
Economic principles (law) or generalizations	Positive and normative statements
Economic model	Fallacy of composition
Abstraction	*Post hoc, ergo propter hoc* fallacy
"Other things equal" (*ceteris paribus*) assumption	Correlation and causation
	Economic perspective

■ HINTS AND TIPS

1. The chapter introduces important pairs of terms: inductive and deductive reasoning; microeconomics and macroeconomics; and positive economics and normative economics. Make sure you understand what each pair means.

2. Objective thinking about economic problems is difficult and requires that you be able to recognize the major pitfalls—loaded terminology, inaccurate definitions, fallacy of composition, **post hoc** fallacy, and confusing correlation with causation. One way for you to remember these pitfalls is to associate each one with a practical example.

3. The economic perspective presented in the last section of the chapter has three features related to decision-making—scarcity and the necessity of choice, rational self-interest in decision-making, and the marginal analysis of the costs and benefits of decisions. Although these features may seem strange to you at first, they are central to the economic thinking used to examine decisions and problems throughout the book.

SELF-TEST

■ **FILL-IN QUESTIONS**

1. Economics as a subject:
a. Is, first of all, the study of the

_____ ,

_____ ,

and _____
of the material goods and services that satisfy human wants.
b. But, more formally, it is concerned with the efficient

use of _____ productive resources to

achieve the _____ satisfaction of these wants.

2. An understanding of economics is essential if we are

to be well-informed _____ and it has many
personal applications even though it is an academic and

not a _____ subject.

3. The gathering of relevant facts is the part of the

economics called _____ economics.

4. Economic _____ involves deriving general principles about the economic behavior of people and institutions.

5. When economists develop economic principles from

studying facts, they are using the _____

method; whereas the _____ method uses facts to test the validity of hypotheses or economic theories.

6. Economic principles are also called _____ .

These principles are _____

about people's economic behavior and as such necessar-

ily involve _____ from reality.

7. Economists know that the amount consumers spend for goods and services in any year depends upon their after-tax income in that year and several factors other than their income. To look at the relationship between the spending and income of consumers, economists often assume that these other factors are constant and do not change; and when economists do this they make the

_____ assumption.

8. Macroeconomics is concerned with the _____

output of the economy and the _____ level
of prices, while microeconomics is concerned with output

in a(n) _____

_____

and the price of a(n) _____

9. The formulation of recommended solutions or remedies for economic problems is referred to as

_____

economics.

10. The three steps in the formulation of economic policy

are: (1) stating of economic _____ ; (2) assessing

the policy _____ ; and (3) conducting an

_____ of policy effectiveness.

11. Eight widely accepted economic goals in the United States are the following:

a. _____

b. _____

c. _____

d. _____

e. _____

f. _____

g. _____

h. _____

12. Increases in economic growth that promote full employment would be an example of a set of (conflicting,

complementary) _____ economic goals.
Efforts to achieve an equitable distribution of income that reduce economic efficiency and growth would be an ex-

ample of a set of _____ economic goals.

13. There are two different types of statements that can be made about economic topics. A (positive, normative)

_____ statement explains **what is** by offering a scientific proposition about economic behavior that is based on economic theory and facts. A _____ statement includes a value judgment about an economic policy or the economy that suggests **what ought to be.** Many of the reported disagreements among economists usually involve _____ statements.

14. There are many pitfalls to straight thinking in economics. For example, the statement that "what is good for the individual is also good for the group" may not be correct because of the fallacy of _____. The person who believes that "washing a car will cause it to rain tomorrow" is expressing a _____ fallacy.

15. The economic perspective has three interrelated features: (1) It recognizes that _____ requires choice, and that all choices entail a cost; (2) people are _____ decision-makers who make choices based on their self-interest; and (3) weighing the costs and benefits of an economic decision is based on _____ analysis.

■ TRUE-FALSE QUESTIONS

Circle the T if the statement is true; the F if it is false.

1. Economics deals with the activities by which humans can earn a living and improve their standard of living.   **T F**

2. Economics is academic and of little value because it does not teach the student how to earn a living.   **T F**

3. Gathering the relevant economic facts from which economic principles are derived is called economic analysis.   **T F**

4. The deductive method is the scientific method and the method used to derive economic principles from economic facts.   **T F**

5. Economic principles enable us to predict the economic consequences of many human actions.   **T F**

6. In economics the terms "law," "principle," "theory," and "model" mean essentially the same thing.   **T F**

7. The "other things equal" or **ceteris paribus** assumption is made in order to simplify the reasoning process.   **T F**

8. Microeconomic analysis is concerned with the performance of the economy as a whole or its major aggregates.   **T F**

9. The first step in the formulation of an economic policy, the statement of goals, may be an occasion for disagreement because different people may have different and conflicting goals to be achieved.   **T F**

10. Once a single goal or end has been determined as the sole objective of economic policy, there is seldom any question of which policy to adopt to achieve that goal.   **T F**

11. One of the widely (though not universally) accepted economic goals of Americans is an equal distribution of income.   **T F**

12. A tradeoff is a situation where some of one economic goal is sacrificed to obtain some of another economic goal.   **T F**

13. When value judgments are made about the economy or economic policy, this is referred to as positive economics.   **T F**

14. The statement that "the legal minimum wage should be raised to give working people a decent income" is an example of a normative statement.   **T F**

15. If you speak of "capital" to most people, they understand you to be referring to money. The economist, therefore, is obligated to use the term "capital" to mean money.   **T F**

16. The **post hoc, ergo propter hoc** fallacy is the belief that "what is true for the individual or part of a group is necessarily true for the group or whole."   **T F**

17. A person who concludes that more education increases incomes may be confusing correlation with causation.   **T F**

18. From an economic perspective, "there is no such thing as a free lunch."   **T F**

19. Rational self-interest is the same thing as being selfish.   **T F**

20. The economic perspective views individuals or institutions as making rational choices based on the marginal analysis of the costs and benefits of decisions.   **T F**

■ MULTIPLE-CHOICE QUESTIONS

Circle the letter that corresponds to the best answer.

1. What statement would be the best one to use to complete a short definition of economics? "Economics is the study of:
   (a) how business produces goods and services."
   (b) the efficient use of scarce productive resources."
   (c) the equitable distribution of society's income and wealth."
   (d) the printing and circulation of money in the economy."

2. Economics is a practical field of study in several ways. Which one of the following is *not* an element of its practicality?

(a) every person affects and is affected by the operation of the economy

(b) every person has to earn a living in some manner, and economics develops skills and trains the student in the art of making a living

(c) every person in a democracy is confronted with its political problems, many of which are economic in nature

(d) every person who understands the overall operation of the economy is in a better position to solve personal economic problems

3. When economic principles or theories are developed from factual evidence, this method of economic reasoning is called:

(a) descriptive economics

(b) hypothesis testing

(c) deduction

(d) induction

4. The development of an economic theory and the testing of this theory by an appeal to facts is:

(a) induction

(b) deduction

(c) policy economics

(d) normative economics

5. Knowing that as the price of a commodity rises the quantity of the commodity sold decreases and that the imposition of a higher tax on a commodity increases its price, the economist concludes that if a government increases the tax on gasoline, less gasoline will be sold. This is an example of:

(a) prediction

(b) control

(c) policy

(d) the fallacy of composition

6. One economic principle states that the lower the price of a commodity, the greater will be the quantity of the commodity which consumers will wish to purchase. On the basis of this principle *alone,* it can be concluded that:

(a) if the price of raincoats falls, more raincoats will be purchased by consumers

(b) if the price of raincoats falls, a consumer will purchase two instead of one

(c) if the price of raincoats falls and there are no important changes in the other factors affecting their demand, the public will probably purchase a greater quantity of raincoats than it did at the higher price

(d) if more raincoats are purchased this month than last month, it is because the price of raincoats has fallen

7. An economic model is *not*:

(a) an ideal type of economy or an economic policy for which we ought to strive to achieve

(b) a tool which the economist employs in order to predict

(c) one or a collection of economic principles

(d) an explanation of how the economy or a part of the economy functions in its essential details

8. The economist sometimes assumes that "other things are held constant" when studying an economic problem. This statement would best be an example of:

(a) the *post hoc, ergo propter hoc* fallacy

(b) the fallacy of composition

(c) deductive reasoning

(d) *ceteris paribus*

9. When we look at the whole economy or its major aggregates, our analysis would be at the level of:

(a) microeconomics

(b) macroeconomics

(c) positive economics

(d) normative economics

10. Which of the following would be studied in *microeconomics*?

(a) the output of the entire economy

(b) the total number of workers employed in the United States

(c) the general level of prices in the American economy

(d) the output and price of wheat in the United States

11. Which of the following economic goals is subject to reasonably accurate measurement?

(a) economic security

(b) full employment

(c) economic freedom

(d) an equitable distribution of income

12. To say that two economic goals are conflicting means that:

(a) there is a tradeoff in the achievement of the goals

(b) these goals are not accepted as goals

(c) the achievement of one of the goals results in the achievement of the other

(d) it is possible to quantify both goals

13. Which economic goal is associated with the idea that we want to get the maximum benefits at the minimum cost from the limited productive resources which are available?

(a) full employment

(b) economic growth

(c) economic security

(d) economic efficiency

14. If economic growth tends to produce a more equitable distribution of income among people in a nation, then this relationship between the two economic goals appears to be:

(a) deductive
(b) conflicting
(c) complementary
(d) mutually exclusive

15. Which one of the following is a normative economic statement?
(a) the consumer price index rose 5.6% last month
(b) the unemployment rate of 6.8% is too high
(c) the average rate of interest on loan is 8.6%
(d) the economy grew at an annual rate of 2.6%

16. Sandra states that "there is a high correlation between consumption and income." Arthur replies that it occurs because "people consume too much of their income and don't save enough."
(a) both Sandra's and Arthur's statements are positive
(b) both Sandra's and Arthur's statements are normative
(c) Sandra's statement is positive and Arthur's statement is normative
(d) Sandra's statement is normative and Arthur's statement is positive

17. During World War II the United States employed price control to prevent inflation; this was referred to as "a fascist and arbitrary restriction of economic freedom" by some and as "a necessary and democratic means of preventing ruinous inflation" by others. Both labels are examples of:
(a) economic bias
(b) the fallacy of composition
(c) the misuse of commonsense definitions
(d) loaded terminology

18. If an individual determines to save a larger percentage of his/her income he/she will no doubt be able to save more. To reason, therefore, that if all individuals determine to save a larger percentage of their incomes they will be able to save more is an example of:
(a) the *post hoc, ergo propter hoc* fallacy
(b) the fallacy of composition
(c) economic bias
(d) using loaded terminology

19. The government increases its expenditures for road-construction equipment and later the average price of this equipment falls. The reason that the lower price was due to the increase in government expenditures may be an example of:
(a) the *post hoc, ergo propter hoc* fallacy
(b) the fallacy of composition
(c) imprecise definition
(d) using loaded terminology

20. One of the major features of the economic perspective that is described in the text is:
(a) equating rational self-interest with selfishness
(b) comparing of marginal benefits with marginal costs

(c) the validity of normative economics for decision-making
(d) the recognition of the abundance of economic resources

■ **PROBLEMS**

1. *News report:* "The Russian demand for wheat in the United States increased and caused the price of wheat in the United States to rise." This is a *specific* instance of a more *general* economic principle. Of which economic *generalization* is this a particular example? _____
_____
_____

2. Below are four statements. Each of them is an example of one of the pitfalls frequently encountered in the study of economics. Indicate in the space following each statement the type of pitfall involved.
  a. "Investment in stocks and bonds is the only way to build real capital assets." _____
  b. "An unemployed worker can find a job if he looks diligently and conscientiously for employment; therefore, all unemployed workers can find employment if they are diligent and conscientious in looking for a job."
  _____
  c. *McConnell:* "Regulation of public utilities in the United States is an immoral and unconscionable interference with the God-given right of private property and, as you know, old chum, there is no private property in the communist nations." *Brue:* "It is far from that, my boy. You know perfectly well that it is an attempt to limit the unmitigated avarice of mammoth corporations in order, as the Constitution commands, to promote the general welfare of a democratic America." _____
  _____
  d. "The stock market crash of 1929 was followed by and resulted in 10 years of Depression."_____
  _____

3. Below is a list of economic statements. Indicate in the space to the right of each whether they are positive (P) or normative (N). Then in the last four lines below, write two of your own examples of positive statements and two examples of normative economic statements.
  a. New York City should control the rental price of apartments. _____
  b. Consumer prices rose at an annual rate of 5% last year. _____
  c. Most people who are unemployed are just too lazy to work. _____
  d. Generally speaking, if you lower the price of a product, people will buy more of that product. _____

e. The profits of drug companies are too large and ought to be used to conduct research on new medicines. _____

f. Government should do more to help the poor. _____

g. _____ P

h. _____ P

i. _____ N

j. _____ N

■ SHORT ANSWER AND ESSAY QUESTIONS

1. Define economics in both a less and a more sophisticated way. In your latter definition, explain the meaning of "resources" and "wants."

2. What are the principal reasons for studying economics?

3. Define the terms induction and deduction and give an example of each.

4. Define and explain the relationships between descriptive economics, economic theory, and applied economics.

5. What is the relationship between facts and theory?

6. What is a "laboratory experiment under controlled conditions"? Does the science of economics have any kind of laboratory? Why do economists employ the "other things equal" assumption?

7. Why are economic principles and models necessarily generalizations and abstract?

8. What does it mean to say that economic principles can be used for prediction?

9. Explain the difference between macroeconomics and microeconomics.

10. What procedure should be followed in formulating sound economic policies?

11. Of the eight economic goals listed in the text, which one would you *rank* first, second, third, etc.? Would you add any other goals to this list? If economic goals 2 and 4 were conflicting, which goal would you prefer? Why? If goals 1 and 5 were conflicting, which would you prefer? Why?

12. How can the concept "tradeoffs" be applied to the discussion of economic goals? Give an example.

13. Why do economists disagree?

14. What are some current examples of positive economic statements and normative economic statements?

15. Explain each of the following:
(a) fallacy of composition;
(b) loaded terminology;

(c) the *post hoc, ergo propter hoc* fallacy.

16. Use an example to describe how correlation differs from causation.

17. What are the three interrelated features of the economic perspective?

18. What is the economic meaning of the statement "there is no such thing as a free lunch"?

19. What is the difference between rational self-interest and selfishness?

20. How do economists use marginal analysis?

ANSWERS

Chapter 1 The Nature and Method of Economics

FILL-IN QUESTIONS

1. a. production, distribution, consumption;
   b. limited (scarce), maximum
2. citizens, vocational
3. descriptive
4. theory
5. inductive, deductive
6. laws (or theories or models), generalizations, abstractions
7. "other things equal" (*ceteris paribus*)
8. total, general, individual industry, particular product
9. policy
10. goals, options, evaluation
11. *a.* economic growth; *b.* full employment; *c.* economic efficiency; *d.* price stability; *e.* economic freedom; *f.* equitable distribution of income; *g.* economic security; *h.* balance of trade
12. complementary, conflicting
13. positive, normative, normative
14. composition; *post hoc, ergo propter hoc*
15. scarcity, rational, marginal

TRUE-FALSE QUESTIONS*

1. T, p. 1	**6.** T, p. 4	**11.** F, p. 6	**16.** F, p. 9
2. F, pp. 2-3	**7.** T, p. 4-5	**12.** T, p. 7	**17.** T, p. 9
3. F, p. 3	**8.** F, p. 5	**13.** F, pp. 7-8	**18.** T, p. 9
4. F, p. 4	**9.** T, p. 7	**14.** T, pp. 7-8	**19.** F, p.10
5. T, pp. 4-5	**10.** F, pp. 6-7	**15.** F, p. 8	**20.** T, pp. 10-11

MULTIPLE-CHOICE QUESTIONS

1. b, pp. 1-2	**6.** c, pp. 4-5	**11.** b, p. 6	**16.** c, pp. 7-8
2. b, pp. 2-3	**7.** a, p. 4	**12.** a, p. 7	**17.** d, p. 8
3. d, p. 3	**8.** d, pp. 4-5	**13.** d, p. 6	**18.** b, pp. 8-9
4. b, p. 3	**9.** b, p. 5	**14.** c, p. 7	**19.** a, pp. 8-9
5. a, pp. 4-5	**10.** d, p. 5	**15.** b, pp. 7-8	**20.** b, p. 11

PROBLEMS

1. An increase in the demand for an economic good will cause the price of that good to rise.

2. *a.* definitions; *b.* the fallacy of composition; *c.* loaded terminology; *d.* the **post hoc, ergo propter hoc** fallacy.

3. *a.* N; *b.* P; *c.* N; *d.* P; *e.* N; *f.* N

*Page references are for the textbook.

SHORT ANSWER AND ESSAY QUESTIONS

Appendix to Chapter 1 Graphs and Their Meaning

This appendix provides an introduction to graphing in economics. Graphs help illustrate and simplify the economic theories and models that will be presented throughout this book. The old saying that "a picture is worth a thousand words" applies to economics; graphs are the way that economists "picture" relationships between economic variables.

You will need to master the basics of graphing if these "pictures" are to be of any help to you. The appendix explains how to achieve that mastery. It begins by showing you how to construct a graph from a table of data on two variables, such as income and consumption. Economists usually, but not always, place the *independent* variable (income) on the horizontal axis and the *dependent* variable (consumption) on the vertical axis of the graph. Once the data points are plotted and a line drawn to connect the plotted points, you can determine whether there is a *direct* or an *inverse* relationship between the variables. Identifying a direct and an inverse relationship between variables is an essential skill that will be used repeatedly in this book.

Information from data in graphs and tables can be written in an equation. This work involves determining the *slope* and *intercept* from a straight line in a graph or data in a table. Using values for the slope and intercept, you can write a *linear* equation that will enable you to calculate what the dependent variable would be for a given level of the independent variable.

Some graphs used in the book are *nonlinear.* With nonlinear curves, the slope of the line is no longer constant throughout but varies as one moves along the curve. This slope can be estimated at a point by determining the slope of a straight line that is drawn tangent to the curve at that point. Similar calculations can be made for other points to see how the slope changes along the curve.

■ APPENDIX CHECKLIST

When you have studied this appendix you should be able to:

☐ Explain why economists use graphs.
☐ Construct a graph of two variables using the numerical data from a table.
☐ Make a table with two variables from data on a graph.
☐ Distinguish between a direct and an inverse relationship when given data on two variables.

☐ Identify dependent and independent variables in economic examples and graphs.
☐ Describe how economists use the *ceteris paribus* assumption in two-variable graphing.
☐ Calculate the slope of a straight line between two points.
☐ List three comments that can be made about the slopes of lines.
☐ Determine the vertical intercept for a straight line in a two-variable graph.
☐ Write a linear equation using the slope of a line and the vertical intercept; when given values for the independent variable, determine values for the independent variable.
☐ Estimate the slope of a nonlinear curve at a point using a line that is tangent to the curve at that point.

■ APPENDIX OUTLINE

1. Graphs illustrate the relationship between variables to give economists and students another means, in addition to verbal explanation, of understanding economic phenomena. Graphs serve as an aid in describing economic theories and models.

2. The construction of a simple graph involves the plotting of numerical data about two variables from a table.
   a. Each graph has a horizontal and a vertical axis that can be labeled for each variable and then scaled for the range of the data point that will be measured on the axis.
   b. Data points are plotted on the graph by drawing perpendiculars from the scaled points on the two axes to the place on the graph where the perpendiculars intersect.
   c. A line or curve can then be drawn to connect the points plotted on the graph.

3. A graph provides information about relationships between variables.
   a. A line that is upward sloping to the right on a graph indicates that there is a positive or *direct* relationship between two variables: an increase in one is associated with an increase in the other; a decrease in one is associated with a decrease in the other.
   b. A line that is downward sloping to the right means that there is a negative or *inverse* relationship between the two variables because the variables are changing in opposite directions: an increase in one is associated with a decrease in the other; a decrease in one is associated with an increase in the other.

4. Economists are often concerned with determining cause and effect in economic events.
   a. A dependent variable changes (increases or decreases) because of a change in another variable.
   b. An independent variable produces or "causes" the change in the dependent variable.

c. In a graph, mathematicians place an independent variable on the horizontal axis and a dependent variable on the vertical axis; economists are more arbitrary about which variable is placed on an axis.

5. Economic graphs are simplifications of economic relationships. When graphs are plotted, there is usually an implicit assumption made that all other factors are being held constant. This "other things equal" or *ceteris paribus* assumption is used to simplify the analysis so the study can focus on the two variables of interest.

6. The *slope* of a straight line in a two-variable graph is the ratio of the vertical change to the horizontal change between two points.
   a. A *positive* slope indicates that the relationship between the two variables is *direct.*
   b. A *negative* slope indicates that there is an *inverse* relationship between the two variables.
   c. Three other comments can be made about line slopes. They:
   (1) are affected by the *measurement units* for either variable;
   (2) measure *marginal* changes; and
   (3) can be *infinite* (line parallel to vertical axis) or *zero* (line parallel to horizontal axis).

7. The vertical *intercept* of a straight line in a two-variable graph is where the line intersects the vertical axis of the graph.

8. The slope and intercept of a straight line can be expressed in the form of a *linear equation.* This equation is written as $y = a + bx$. Once the values for the intercept (a) and the slope (b) are calculated, then given any value of the independent variable (x), the value of the dependent variable (y) can be determined.

9. The slope of a straight line is constant, but the slope of a nonlinear curve changes throughout. To estimate the slope of a nonlinear curve at a point, the slope of a line tangent to the curve at that point is calculated.

■ IMPORTANT TERMS

Vertical and horizontal axes

Direct (positive) and inverse (negative) relationships

Dependent and independent variables

Slope of a line

Vertical intercept

Linear equation

Nonlinear curve

Tangent

■ HINTS AND TIPS

1. This appendix will help you understand the graphs and problems presented throughout the book. Don't skip reading the appendix or working on the self-test questions and problems in this study guide. The time you invest now will pay off in improved understanding in later chapters. Graphing is a basic skill for economic analysis.

2. Positive and negative relationships in graphs often confuse students. To overcome this confusion, draw a two-variable graph with a positive slope and another two-variable graph with a negative slope. In each graph, show what happens to the value of one variable when there is a change in the value of the other variable.

3. A straight line in a two-variable graph can be expressed in an equation. Make sure you know how to interpret each part of the linear equation.

SELF-TEST

■ FILL-IN QUESTIONS

1. The relationship between two economic variables can be visualized with the aid of a two-dimensional graph.

   a. Customarily, the (dependent, independent) _____ _____ variable is placed on the horizontal axis and the _____ variable is placed on the vertical axis. The _____ variable is said to change because of a change in the _____ variable.

   b. The vertical and horizontal (scales, ranges) _____ on the graph are calibrated to reflect the _____ of values in a table of data points on which the graph is based.

   c. Other variables, beyond the two in the graph, that might affect the economic relationship are assumed to be (changing, held constant) _____.

Ceteris paribus also means that other variables are

_____

2. The graph of a straight line that slopes downward to the right indicates that there is (a direct, an inverse) _____ relationship between the two variables. A graph of a straight line that slopes upward to the right tells us that the relationship is (direct, inverse) _____. When the value of one variable increases and the value of the other variable increases, then the relationship is _____; when the value of one increases, while the other decreases, the relationship is _____

3. The slope of a straight line between two points is defined as the ratio of the (vertical, horizontal) _____ change to the _____ change. When two variables move in the same direction, the slope will be (negative, positive) _____; when the variables move in opposite directions the slope will be _____. The point at which the line meets the vertical axis is called the _____

4. We can express the graph of a straight line with a linear equation that can be written as *y = a + bx.*

   a. *a* is the (slope, intercept) _____ and *b* is the _____

   b. *y* is the (dependent, independent) _____ variable and *x* is the _____ variable.

   c. If *a* was 2, *b* was 4, and *x* was 5, then *y* would be _____. If the value of *x* changed to 7, then *y* would be _____. If the value of *x* changed to 3, then *y* would be _____

5. The slope of a (straight line, nonlinear curve) _____ is constant throughout; the slope of a _____ varies from point to point. An estimate of the slope of a nonlinear curve at a point can be made by calculating the slope of a straight line that is _____ to the point on the curve.

■ **TRUE-FALSE QUESTIONS**

Circle the T if the statement is true; the F if it is false.

   1. Graphs are designed by economists to confuse students and the public.   **T   F**

   2. If the straight line on a two-variable graph is downward sloping to the right, then there is a positive relationship between the two variables.   **T   F**

   3. A variable that changes as a consequence of a change in another variable is considered to be a dependent variable.   **T   F**

   4. Economists always put the independent variable on the horizontal axis and the dependent variable on the vertical axis of a two-variable graph.   **T   F**

   5. *Ceteris paribus* means that other variables are changing at the same time.   **T   F**

   6. In the ratio for the calculation of the slope of a straight line, the vertical change is in the numerator and the horizontal change is in the denominator.   **T   F**

   7. If the slope of the linear relationship between consumption and income was .90, then it tells us that for every $1 increase in income there will be a $.90 increase in consumption.   **T   F**

   8. The slope of a straight line in a two-variable graph will *not* be affected by the choice of the units for either variable.   **T   F**

   9. The slopes of lines measure marginal changes.   **T   F**

   10. The absence of a relationship between a change in the price of variable *A* and the quantity of variable *B* would be described by a line parallel to the horizontal axis.   **T   F**

   11. A line with an infinite slope in a two-variable graph is parallel to the horizontal axis.   **T   F**

   12. In a two-variable graph, income is graphed on the vertical axis and the quantity of snow is graphed on the horizontal axis. If income was completely unrelated to the quantity of snow, then this unrelatedness would be represented by a line parallel to the vertical axis.   **T   F**

   13. If a linear equation was $y = 10 + 5x$, the vertical intercept is 5.   **T   F**

   14. When a line is tangent to a nonlinear curve, then it intersects the curve at a particular point.   **T   F**

   15. If the slope of a straight line on a two-variable (*x,y*) graph was .5 and the vertical intercept was 5, then a value of 10 for *x* means *y* is also 10.   **T   F**

   16. A slope of -4 for a straight line in a two-variable graph indicates that there is an inverse relationship between the two variables.   **T   F**

   17. If *x* is an independent variable and *y* is a dependent variable, then a change in *y* results in a change in *x.*   **T   F**

   18. An upward slope for a straight line that is tangent to a nonlinear curve would indicate that the slope of the line is positive.   **T   F**

   19. If one pair of *x, y* points was (13, 10) and the other was (8, 20), then the slope of the straight line between the two sets of points in the two-variable graph, with *x* on the horizontal axis and *y* on the vertical axis, would be 2.   **T   F**

   20. When the value of *x* is 2, a value of 10 for *y* would be calculated from a linear equation of $y = -2 + 6x$.   **T   F**

■ **MULTIPLE-CHOICE QUESTIONS**

Circle the letter that corresponds to the best answer.

   1. If an increase in one variable is associated with a decrease in another variable, then we can conclude that the variables are:

(a) nonlinear
(b) directly related
(c) inversely related
(d) positively related

2. The ratio of the absolute vertical change to the absolute horizontal change between two points of a straight line is the:
(a) slope
(b) vertical intercept
(c) horizontal intercept
(d) point of tangency

3. There are two sets of *x, y* points on a straight line in a two-variable graph with *y* on the vertical axis and *x* on the horizontal axis. If one set of points was (0, 5) and the other set (5, 20), the linear equation for the line would be:
(a) $y = 5x$
(b) $y = 5 + 3x$
(c) $y = 5 + 15x$
(d) $y = 5 + .33x$

4. In a two-variable graph of data on the price and quantity of a product, economists place:
(a) price on the horizontal axis because it is the independent variable and quantity on the vertical axis because it is the dependent variable
(b) price on the vertical axis because it is the dependent variable and quantity on the horizontal because it is the independent variable
(c) price on the vertical axis even though it is the independent variable and quantity on the horizontal axis even though it is the dependent variable
(d) price on the horizontal axis even though it is the dependent variable and quantity on the vertical axis even though it is the independent variable

5. In a two-dimensional graph of the relationship between two economic variables, an assumption is usually made that:
(a) both variables are linear
(b) both variables are nonlinear
(c) other variables are held constant
(d) other variables are permitted to change

6. When the slope of a straight line to a point tangent to a nonlinear curve is zero, then the straight line is:
(a) vertical
(b) horizontal
(c) upward sloping
(d) downward sloping

*The next four questions (**7, 8, 9,** and **10**) are based on the following four data sets. In each set, the independent variable is in the left column and the dependent variable is in the right column.*

(1)		(2)		(3)		(4)	
A	B	C	D	E	F	G	H
0	1	0	12	4	5	0	4
3	2	5	8	6	10	1	3
6	3	10	4	8	15	2	2
9	4	15	0	10	20	3	1

7. There is an inverse relationship between the independent and dependent variable in data sets:
(a) 1 and 4
(b) 2 and 3
(c) 1 and 3
(d) 2 and 4

8. The vertical intercept is 4 in data set:
(a) 1
(b) 2
(c) 3
(d) 4

9. The linear equation for data set 1 is:
(a) $B = 3A$
(b) $B = 1 + 3A$
(c) $B = 1 + .33A$
(d) $A = 1 + .33B$

10. The linear equation for data set 2 is:
(a) $C = 12 - 1.25D$
(b) $D = 12 + 1.25C$
(c) $D = 12 - .80C$
(d) $C = 12 - .80D$

*Answer the next four questions (**11, 12, 13,** and **14**) on the basis of the following diagram.*

11. The variables *A* and *B* are:
(a) positively related
(b) negatively related
(c) indirectly related
(d) nonlinear

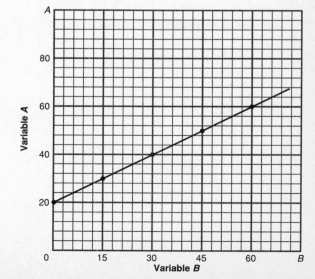

12. The slope of the line is:
(a) .33
(b) .67
(c) 1.50
(d) 3.00

13. The vertical intercept is:
(a) 80
(b) 60
(c) 40
(d) 20

14. The linear equation for the slope of the line is:
(a) $A = 20 + .33B$
(b) $B = 20 + .33A$
(c) $A = 20 + .67B$
(d) $B = 20 + .67A$

Answer the next three questions (15, 16, and 17) on the basis of the following diagram.

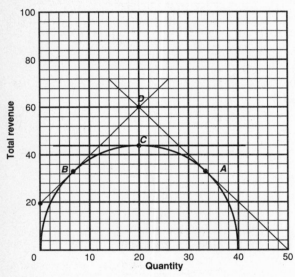

15. The slope of the line tangent to the curve at point **A** is:
(a) 2
(b) −2
(c) −1.5
(d) −0.5

16. The slope of the line tangent to the curve at point **B** is:
(a) −2
(b) 2
(c) 3
(d) 0.5

17. The slope of the line tangent to the curve at point **C** is:
(a) −1
(b) 1
(c) 0
(d) undefined

18. Assume that the relationship between concert ticket prices and attendance is expressed in the equation $P = 25 - 1.25Q$, where **P** equals ticket price and **Q** equals concert attendance in thousands of people. On the basis of this equation, it can be said that:
(a) more people will attend the concert when the price is high compared to when the price is low
(b) if 12,000 people attended the concert, then the ticket price was $10
(c) if 18,000 people attend the concert, then entry into the concert was free
(d) an increase in ticket price by $5 reduces concert attendance by 1,000 people

19. If you know that the equation relating consumption (**C**) to income (**Y**) is $C = \$7,500 + .2Y$, then:
(a) consumption is inversely related to income
(b) consumption is the independent variable and income is the dependent variable
(c) if income is $15,000, then consumption is $10,500
(d) if consumption is $30,000, then income is $10,000

20. If the dependent variable changes by 22 units when the independent variable changes by 12 units, then the slope of the line is:
(a) 0.56
(b) 1.83
(c) 2.00
(d) 3.27

■ **PROBLEMS**

1. Next are three exercises in making graphs. On the graphs plot the economic relationships contained in each exercise. Be sure to label each axis of the graph and to indicate the unit measurement and scale used on each axis.

a. Graph national income on the horizontal axis and consumption expenditures on the vertical axis; connect the seven points and label the curve "Consumption Schedule." The relationship between national income and consumption expenditures is a(n) (direct, inverse)

_____ one and the Consumption Schedule

a(n) (up-, down-) _____ sloping curve.

National income, billions of dollars	Consumption expenditures, billions of dollars
$ 600	$ 600
700	640
800	780
900	870
1000	960
1100	1050
1200	1140

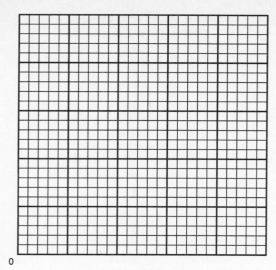

0

b. Graph investment expenditures on the horizontal axis and the rate of interest on the vertical axis; connect the seven points and label the curve "Investment Schedule." The relationship between the rate of interest and investment expenditures is a(n) (direct, inverse) _____ one and the Investment

Schedule a(n) (up-, down-) _____ sloping curve.

Rate of interest, %	Investment expenditures, billions of dollars
8	$220
7	280
6	330
5	370
4	400
3	420
2	430

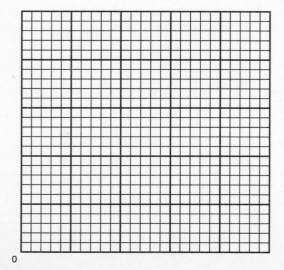

0

c. Graph average salary on the horizontal axis and wine consumption on the vertical axis; connect the seven points.

Average salary, American college professors	Annual per capita wine consumption in liters
$52,000	11.5
53,000	11.6
54,000	11.7
55,000	11.8
56,000	11.9
57,000	22.0
58,000	22.1

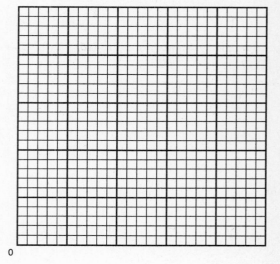

0

(1) The average salary of a college professor and wine consumption (are, are not) _____ **correlated.** The higher average salary (is, is not) _____ the **cause** of the greater consumption of wine.

(2) The relationship between the two variables may be purely _____; or, as is more likely, both the higher salaries and the greater consumption of wine may be the result of the higher _____ in the American economy.

2. This question is based on the graph in the top left column of the next page.
  a. Construct a table for points **A-I** from the data shown in the graph.
  b. According to economists, price is the (independent, dependent) _____ variable and quantity is the _____ variable.
  c. Write a linear equation that summarizes the data.

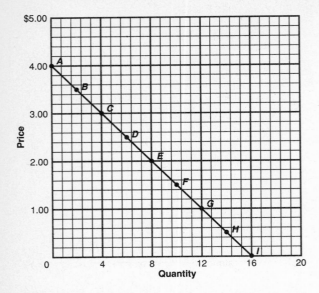

3. The following three sets of data each show the relationship between an independent variable and a dependent variable. For each set, the independent variable is in the left column and the dependent variable is in the right column.

(1)		(2)		(3)	
A	B	C	D	E	F
0	10	0	100	0	20
10	30	10	75	50	40
20	50	20	50	100	60
30	70	30	25	150	80
40	90	40	0	200	100

a. Write an equation that summarizes the data for each set: (1), (2), and (3).
b. State whether each data set shows a positive or inverse relationship between the two variables.

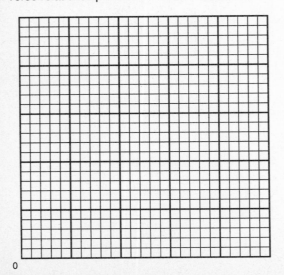

c. Graph data sets 1 and 2 on the graph. Use the same horizontal scale for both sets of independent variables and the same vertical scale for both sets of dependent variables.

4. This problem is based on the following graph.

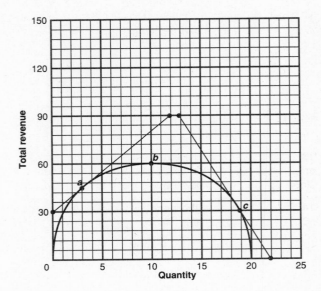

a. The slope of the straight line through point **a** is?
b. The slope of the straight line through point **b** is?
c. The slope of the straight line through point **c** is?

■ SHORT ANSWER AND ESSAY QUESTIONS

1. Why do economists use graphs in their work?

2. Give two examples of a graph that illustrates the relationship between two economic variables.

3. What does the slope tell you about a straight line? How would you interpret a slope of 4? A slope of −2? A slope of .5? A slope of −.25?

4. If the vertical intercept increases in value but the slope of a straight line stays the same, what happens to the graph of the line? If the vertical intercept decreases in value, what will happen to the line?

5. How do you interpret a vertical line on a two-variable graph? How do you interpret a horizontal line?

6. When you know that the price and quantity of a product are inversely related, what does this tell you about the slope of a line? What do you know about the slope when the two variables are positively related?

7. Which variable is the dependent and which is the independent in the following economic statement: "A decrease in business taxes had a positive effect on investment spending."

8. How do you tell the difference between a dependent and independent variable when examining economic relationships?

9. Why is an assumption made that all other variables are held constant when we construct a two-variable graph of the price and quantity of a product?

10. How do mathematicians and economists differ at times in the way that they construct two-dimensional graphs? Give an example.

11. How is the slope of a straight line in a two-variable graph affected by the choice of the units for either variable? Explain and give an example.

12. What is the relationship between the slopes of lines and marginal analysis?

13. Describe a case where a straight line in a two-variable graph would have an infinite slope and a case where the slope of a line would be zero.

14. If you know that the equation relating consumption (C) to income (Y) is $C = 10,000 + 5Y$, then what would consumption be when income is $5,000? Construct an income-consumption table for five different levels of income.

15. How do the slopes of a straight line and a nonlinear curve differ? How do you estimate the slope of a nonlinear curve?

ANSWERS

Appendix to Chapter 1 Graphs and Their Meaning

FILL-IN QUESTIONS

1. *a.* independent, dependent, dependent, independent; *b.* scales, ranges; *c.* held constant, held constant
2. inverse, direct, direct, inverse
3. vertical, horizontal, positive, negative, vertical intercept
4. *a.* intercept, slope; *b.* dependent, independent; *c.* 22, 30, 14
5. straight line, nonlinear curve, tangent

TRUE-FALSE QUESTIONS

1. F, p. 14	**6.** T, p. 16	**11.** F, p. 17	**16.** T, pp. 16-17
2. F, p. 15	**7.** T, pp. 16-17	**12.** F, p. 17	**17.** F, p. 16
3. T, p. 16	**8.** F, p. 17	**13.** F, p. 17	**18.** T, p. 18
4. F, p. 16	**9.** T, p. 17	**14.** F, p. 18	**19.** F, pp. 16-17
5. F, p. 16	**10.** F, p. 17	**15.** T, p. 17	**20.** T, p. 17

MULTIPLE-CHOICE QUESTIONS

1. *c*, p. 15	**6.** *b*, pp. 16;18	**11.** *a*, p. 15	**16.** *b*, p. 18
2. *a*, p. 15	**7.** *d*, p. 15	**12.** *b*, p. 16	**17.** *c*, p. 17
3. *b*, pp. 16-17	**8.** *d*, p. 17	**13.** *d*, p. 17	**18.** *b*, p. 17
4. *c*, p. 16	**9.** *c*, p. 17	**14.** *c*, p. 17	**19.** *c*, p. 17
5. *c*, p. 16	**10.** *c*, p. 17	**15.** *b*, p. 18	**20.** *b*, p. 16

PROBLEMS

1. *a.* direct, up-; *b.* inverse, down-; *c.* (1) are, is not; (2) coincidental, incomes (standard of living, or some other such answer)
2. *a.*

Point	Price	Quantity
A	$4.00	0
B	3.50	2
C	3.00	4
D	2.50	6
E	2.00	8
F	1.50	10
G	1.00	12
H	.50	14
I	.00	16

b. independent, dependent; *c.* $P = 4.00 - .25Q$
3. *a.* (1) $B = 10 + 2A$; (2) $D = 100 - 2.5C$; (3) $F = 20 + .4E$; *b.* (1) positive; (2) inverse; (3) positive
4. *a.* 5; *b.* 0; *c.* −10

■ SHORT ANSWER AND ESSAY QUESTIONS

1. p. 14	**5.** pp. 16-17	**9.** p. 16	**13.** p. 17
2. p. 16	**6.** p. 15	**10.** p. 16	**14.** p. 17
3. pp. 16-17	**7.** p. 16	**11.** p. 17	**15.** p. 18
4. p. 17	**8.** p. 16	**12.** p. 17	

CHAPTER 2

The Economizing Problem

The aim of Chapter 2 is to explain the central problem of economics. The problem is that resources—the ultimate means of satisfying material wants—are scarce **relative** to the insatiable wants of society. Economics as a science is the study of the various aspects of the behavior of society in its effort to allocate the scarce resources—land, labor, capital, and entrepreneurial ability–in order to satisfy as best it can its unlimited desire for consumption.

Economics is called the science of efficiency. To understand what efficiency means, however, you must first define its two characteristics—**full employment** and **full production.** Full employment means that all productive resources that are available to the economy should be being used. Full production requires that two types of efficiency—allocative and productive–are being achieved. Allocative efficiency means that resources are being devoted to the optimal product mix for society. Productive efficiency entails producing this optimal product mix in the least-costly way.

The production possibilities table and graph are used in this chapter to discuss the major concerns of economics. The production possibilities model is a valuable device for illustrating the meaning of many concepts defined in the chapter—scarcity, choice, the law of increasing opportunity cost, allocative and productive efficiency, unemployment, and economic growth. It can also be applied to many real economic situations involving budgeting, wartime production, discrimination, productivity, economic growth comparisons, environmental protection, international trade, famine, and central planning. This basic economic model is the first and one of the most important ones presented in the text that you will be using to understand the economic world.

Every economy is faced with the problem of scarce resources and has to find ways to respond to the economic problem. No economy answers the problem in the same way that another economy does. Between the extremes of pure (or laissez faire) capitalism and the command economy (communism) are various economic systems; all these systems are different devices—different methods of organization—for finding an answer to the economic problem of relative scarcity. Chapters 3 through 6 will explain in greater detail how the United States economy is organized and operates to address the economizing problem.

The circular-flow-of-income model (or diagram) is a device which illustrates for a capitalistic economy the relation between households and businesses, the flow of money and economic goods and services between households and businesses, their dual role as buyers and sellers, and the two basic types of markets essential to the capitalistic process.

■ **CHECKLIST**

When you have studied this chapter you should be able to:

☐ Write a definition of economics that incorporates the relationship between resources and wants.
☐ Identify four types of economic resources.
☐ Describe the resource payments made in return for each economic resource.
☐ Explain why full employment and full production are necessary for the efficient use of resources.
☐ Distinguish between allocative efficiency and productive efficiency.
☐ State the four assumptions made when a production possibilities table or curve is constructed.
☐ Construct a production possibilities curve when you are given the appropriate data.
☐ Define opportunity cost and utilize a production possibilities curve to explain the concept.
☐ State the law of increasing opportunity costs.
☐ Explain the economic rationale for the law of increasing opportunity cost.
☐ Use marginal analysis to define allocative efficiency.
☐ Explain how allocative efficiency determines the optimal point on a production possibilities curve.
☐ Use a production possibilities curve to illustrate unemployment and productive inefficiency and economic growth.
☐ Give nine different examples of the application of the production possibilities model.
☐ Define pure capitalism, command economy, and traditional economy.
☐ Use two characteristics to compare and contrast pure capitalism with a command economy.

☐ Explain why many economies can be described as mixed economic systems.
☐ Draw the circular flow diagram; and correctly label the real and money flows and the two major types of markets.

■ **CHAPTER OUTLINE**

1. The bases upon which the study of economics rests are two facts.

a. Society's material wants are unlimited.

b. The economic resources which are the ultimate means of satisfying these wants are scarce in relation to the wants.

(1) Economic resources are classified as land, capital, labor, and entrepreneurial ability.

(2) The payments received by those who provide the economy with these four resources are rental income, interest income, wages, and profits, respectively.

(3) Because these resources are scarce (or limited) the output that the economy is able to produce is also limited.

2. Economics, then, is the study of how society's scarce resources are used (administered) to obtain the greatest satisfaction of its material wants.

a. To be efficient in the use of its resource an economy must achieve both *full employment* and *full production.* Full production implies that there are

(1) *allocative efficiency,* which means that resources are devoted to those goods most wanted by society; and

(2) *productive efficiency,* which means goods and services are being produced in the least-costly way.

b. The production possibilities table indicates the alternative combinations of goods and services an economy is capable of producing when it has achieved full employment and full production.

(1) The four assumptions that are usually made when a production possibilities table is constructed is that there are economic efficiency, fixed resources, fixed technology, and two products being considered.

(2) The table illustrates the fundamental choice every society must make: what quantity of each product it wants produced.

c. The data contained in the production possibilities table can be plotted on a graph to obtain a production possibilities curve.

d. The opportunity cost of producing an additional unit of one product is the amounts of other products that are sacrificed; and the law of increasing opportunity costs is that the opportunity cost of producing additional units of a product increases as more of that product is produced.

(1) The law of increasing opportunity costs results in a production possibilities curve that is concave (from the origin).

(2) The opportunity cost of producing additional units of a product increases as more of the product is produced because resources are not completely adaptable to alternative uses.

e. Allocative efficiency means that resources are being devoted to the optimal product mix for society. This optimal mix is determined by assessing marginal costs and benefits.

(1) The marginal cost curve for a product rises because of the law of increasing opportunity costs; the marginal benefit curve falls because of the consumption of a product yields less and less satisfaction.

(2) There will be *underallocation* of resources to production of a product when the marginal benefit is greater than the marginal cost, and *overallocation* when the marginal cost is greater than the marginal benefit.

(3) Allocative efficiency is achieved when the marginal cost of a product equals the marginal benefit of a product.

3. Different outcomes will occur when assumptions underlying the production possibilities model are relaxed.

a. The economy may be operating at a point inside the production possibilities curve if the assumption of full production and productive efficiency no longer holds. In this case, there will be an unemployment of resources and production will not occur in the least-costly way.

b. The production possibilities curve can move outward if the assumption of fixed resources or the assumption of no technological change is dropped. Economic growth occurs when there is an expansion in the quantity and quality of resources, or when there is technological advancement.

c. The combination of goods and services an economy chooses to produce today helps determine its production possibilities in the future.

4. There are many applications of the production possibilities model. These examples include the budgeting of time between work and leisure, society's production of war goods or consumer goods, discrimination, inefficient use of resources, the slowdown in productivity, investment, and economic growth, tradeoffs in environmental protection, international trade, famine, and the problems with a centrally planned economy.

5. Different economic systems differ in the way they respond to the economizing problem.

a. At one extreme is pure capitalism, which relies upon the private ownership of its economic resources and the market system.

b. At the other extreme, the command economy uses the public ownership of its resources and central planning.

c. Economies in the real world lie between these two extremes and are hybrid systems.

d. Some less-developed nations have traditional (or customary) economies which are shaped by the customs and traditions of the society.

6. The circular flow model is a device used to clarify the relationships between households and business firms in a purely capitalistic economy.

   a. In resource markets households supply and firms demand resources and in product markets the firms supply and households demand products. Households use the incomes they obtain from supplying resources to purchase the goods and services produced by the firms; and in the economy there is a real flow of resources and products and a money flow of incomes and expenditures.

   b. The circular flow model has several limitations.

■ IMPORTANT TERMS

The economizing problem	Production possibilities curve
Unlimited wants	Optimal product mix
Scarce resources	Opportunity cost
Land, capital, labor, and entrepreneurial ability	Law of increasing opportunity costs
Factors of production	Unemployment
Investment	Economic growth
Consumer goods	Pure (laissez faire) capitalism
Capital goods	
Real capital	Command economy (communism)
Money (financial) capital	Authoritarian capitalism
Rental income, interest income, wages, and profit	Market socialism
Utility	Traditional (customary) economies
Economics	Circular flow model
Economic efficiency	Households
Full employment	Resource market
Full production	Product market
Allocative efficiency	
Productive efficiency	
Production possibilities table	

■ HINTS AND TIPS

1. Chapter 2 presents a number of economic definitions and classifications. Spend time learning these definitions *now.* They will be used in later chapters, and it will be necessary for you to know them if you are to understand what follows.

2. The production possibilities graph is a simple and extremely useful economic model. Practice your under-

standing of it by using it to explain the following economic concepts—scarcity, choice, opportunity cost, the law of increasing opportunity costs, full employment, full production, productive efficiency, allocative efficiency, unemployment, and economic growth.

3. Opportunity cost is always measured in terms of a foregone alternative. From a production possibilities table, you can easily calculate how many units of one product you forgo when you get another unit of a product. The ratio of what you forgo to what you get measures the opportunity cost of a choice in a production possibilities table.

SELF-TEST

■ FILL-IN QUESTIONS

1. The economizing problem arises because society's material wants are (limited, unlimited) _____ and economic resources are _____

2. The four types of resources are:

   a. _____

   b. _____

   c. _____

   d. _____

3. The property resources are _____ and _____. The human resources are _____ and _____

4. Both consumer goods and capital goods satisfy human wants. The consumer goods satisfy these wants (directly, indirectly) _____ and the capital goods satisfy them _____

5. The incomes of individuals are received from supplying resources. Four types of incomes are _____, _____, _____, and _____

6. Economics can be defined as _____ _____ _____ _____

7. Economic efficiency requires full (employment, allocation) _____ so that all available resources can be used, and that there be full (production, distribution) _____ so that the employed resources contribute to the maximum satisfaction of material wants.

8. Full production implies that two types of efficiency are achieved: resources are devoted to the production of the mix of goods and services that are most wanted by society, or that there is (allocative, productive) _____ efficiency; and, the goods and services will be produced in the least-costly way, or that there will be _____ efficiency.

9. When a production possibilities table or curve is constructed, four assumptions are made. These assumptions are:

a. _____

b. _____

c. _____

d. _____

10. Below is a production possibilities curve for tractors and suits of clothing.

a. If the economy moves from point **A** to point **B** it will produce (more, fewer) _____ tractors and (more, fewer)_____ suits of clothing.

b. If the economy is producing at point **X,** some of the resources of the economy are either_____ or _____

c. If the economy moves from point **X** to point **B** (more, fewer) _____ tractors and (more, fewer) _____ suits will be produced.

d. If the economy is to produce at point **Y,** it must either _____ or _____

11. Allocative efficiency is determined by assessing the marginal costs and benefits of the output from the allocation of resources to production.

a. The marginal cost curve for a product rises because of increasing (satisfaction, opportunity costs) _____, and the marginal benefit curve falls because of less _____ from the additional consumption of a product.

b. When the marginal benefit is greater than the marginal cost, there will be (over, under) _____ -allocation of resources to the production of a product, but when the marginal cost is greater than the marginal benefit there will be an _____ -allocation.

c. Optimal allocation of resources occurs when the marginal costs of the product output are (greater than, less than, equal to) _____ the marginal benefits.

12. The quantity of other goods and services an economy must go without in order to produce more low-cost housing is the_____ of producing the additional low-cost housing.

13. The more an economy consumes of its current production, the (more, less) _____ it will be capable of producing in future years if other things are equal.

14. In:

a. pure capitalism property resources are (publicly, privately) _____ owned and the means employed to direct and coordinate economic activity is the_____ system.

b. a command economy the property resources are (publicly, privately) _____ owned and the coordinating device is central _____

15. In the circular flow model:

a. Households are demanders and businesses are suppliers in the _____ markets; and businesses are demanders and households are suppliers of the _____ markets of the economy.

b. The two flows are called the _____ flow and the _____ flow.

c. The expenditures made by businesses are a _____ to them and become the_____ of households.

■ TRUE-FALSE QUESTIONS

Circle the T if the statement is true; the F if it is false.

1. The conflict between the scarce material wants of society and its unlimited economic resources gives rise to the economizing problem.   **T   F**

2. The wants with which economics is concerned include only those wants which can be satisfied by goods and services.   **T   F**

3. Money is a resource and is classified as "capital."
                                                                  T   F

4. Profit is the reward paid to those who provide the economy with capital.   **T   F**

5. Resources are scarce because society's material wants are unlimited and productive resources are limited.   **T   F**

6. Economic efficiency requires that there be both full employment of resources and full production.   **T   F**

7. Allocative efficiency means that goods and services are being produced by society in the least-costly way.
                                                                  T   F

8. Only allocative efficiency is necessary for there to be full production.   **T   F**

9. The opportunity cost of producing antipollution devices is the other goods and services the economy is unable to produce because it has decided to produce these devices.   **T   F**

10. The opportunity cost of producing a good tends to increase as more of it is produced because resources less suitable to its production must be employed.   **T   F**

11. Drawing a production possibilities curve concave to the origin is the geometric way of stating the law of increasing opportunity costs.   **T   F**

12. Allocative efficiency is determined by assessing the marginal costs and benefits of the output from the allocation of resources to production.   **T   F**

13. The marginal cost curve for a product rises because of increasing satisfaction from the consumption of the product.   **T   F**

14. Given full employment and full production, it is not possible for an economy capable of producing just two goods to increase its production of both.   **T   F**

15. Economic growth means an increase in the ability of an economy to produce goods and services; and it is shown by a movement of the production possibilities to the right.   **T   F**

16. The more capital goods an economy produces today, the greater will be the total output of all goods it can produce in the future, other things being equal.   **T   F**

17. It is economically desirable for a nation to have unemployed resources at the outset of a war because it can increase its production of military goods without having to decrease its production of civilian goods.   **T   F**

18. Communism is characterized by the private ownership of resources and the use of a system of markets and prices to coordinate and direct economic activity.   **T   F**

19. In the circular flow model, the household functions on the demand side of the resource and product markets.
                                                                  T   F

20. One of the limitations of the simple model of the circular flow is that flows of output and income are constant.   **T   F**

■ MULTIPLE-CHOICE QUESTIONS

Circle the letter that corresponds to the best answer.

1. Which is the correct match of an economic resource and payment for that resource?
  (a) land and wages
  (b) labor and interest income
  (c) capital and rental income
  (d) entrepreneurial ability and profit

2. An "innovator" is defined as an entrepreneur who:
  (a) makes basic policy decisions in a business firm
  (b) combines factors of production to produce a good or service
  (c) invents a new product or process for producing a product
  (d) introduces new products on the market or employs a new method to produce a product

3. An economy is efficient when it has achieved:
  (a) full employment
  (b) full production
  (c) either full employment or full production
  (d) both full employment and full production

4. Allocative and productive efficiency are conditions that best characterize:
  (a) full employment
  (b) full production
  (c) pure capitalism
  (d) command economy

5. When a production possibilities schedule is written (or a production possibilities curve is drawn) four assumptions are made. Which of the following is *not* one of those assumptions?

(a) only two products are produced
(b) the nation is not at war
(c) the economy has both full employment and full production
(d) the quantities of all resources available to the economy are fixed

Answer the next four questions (6, 7, 8, and 9) based on the following graph.

6. At point **A** on the production possibilities curve in the following illustration:

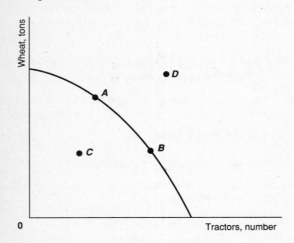

(a) wheat production is inefficient
(b) tractor production is inefficient
(c) the economy is employing all its resources
(d) the economy is not employing all its resources

7. Unemployment and production inefficiency would best be represented in the graph by point:
(a) **A**
(b) **B**
(c) **C**
(d) **D**

8. The choice of point **B** over point **A** as the optimal product-mix for society would be based on:
(a) productive efficiency
(b) full employment of resources
(c) the law of increasing opportunity costs
(d) a comparison of marginal costs and benefits

9. Economic growth could be represented by:
(a) a movement from point **A** to point **B**
(b) a movement from point **B** to point **A**
(c) a shift in the production possibilities curve out to point **C**
(d) a shift in the production possibilities curve out to point **D**

10. The production possibilities curve is:
(a) concave
(b) convex
(c) linear
(d) positive

11. What is the economic rationale for the law of increasing opportunity cost?
(a) full production and full employment of resources has not been achieved
(b) economic resources are not completely adaptable to alternative uses
(c) economic growth is being limited by the pace of technological advancement
(d) an economy's present choice of output is determined by fixed technology and fixed resources

12. If there is an increase in the resources available within the economy:
(a) more goods and services will be produced in the economy
(b) the economy will be capable of producing more goods and services
(c) the standard of living in the economy will rise
(d) the technological efficiency of the economy will improve

13. If the production possibilities curve below moves from position **A** to position **B,** then:
(a) the economy has increased the efficiency with which it produces wheat
(b) the economy has increased the efficiency with which it produces tractors
(c) the economy has put previously idle resources to work
(d) the economy has gone from full employment to less-than-full employment

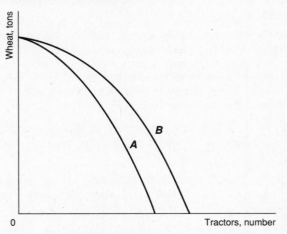

14. Which would be the best example of allocative efficiency? When society devoted resources to the production of:
(a) slide rules instead of hand-held calculators
(b) horse-drawn carriages instead of automobiles
(c) word processors instead of manual typewriters
(d) long-play records instead of compact discs or cassettes

15. Which situation would most likely shift the production possibilities curve for a nation in an outward direction?
  (a) deterioration in product quality
  (b) reductions in the supply of resources
  (c) increases in technological advances
  (d) rising levels of discrimination

16. The opportunity cost of a new public stadium is the:
  (a) money cost of hiring guards and staff for the new stadium
  (b) cost of constructing the new stadium in a future year
  (c) change in the real estate tax rate to pay off the new stadium
  (d) other goods and services that must be sacrificed to construct the new stadium

17. Which situation would most likely cause a nation's production possibilities curve to shift inward?
  (a) investing more resources in new plants and equipment
  (b) eliminating discrimination based on race and ethnic background
  (c) increasing international trade or incurring a trade deficit
  (d) going to war with another nation and suffering a major defeat

18. The combination of products in society's production possibilities table which is the most-valued or optimal is determined:
  (a) at the midpoint of the production possibilities table
  (b) at the endpoint of the production possibilities table
  (c) where the marginal benefits equal marginal costs
  (d) where the opportunity costs are maximized

19. The underallocation of resources by society to the production of a product means that the:
  (a) marginal benefit is greater than the marginal cost
  (b) marginal benefit is less than the marginal cost
  (c) opportunity cost of production is rising
  (d) consumption of the product is falling

Answer the next three questions (20, 21, and 22) on the basis of the data given in the following production possibilities table.

	Production possibilities (alternatives)					
	A	B	C	D	E	F
Capital goods	100	95	85	70	50	0
Consumer goods	0	100	180	240	280	300

20. The choice of alternative B compared with alternative D would tend to promote:
  (a) a slower rate of economic growth
  (b) a faster rate of economic growth
  (c) increased consumption in the present
  (d) central economic planning

21. If the economy is producing at production alternative D, the opportunity cost of 40 more units of consumer goods is about:
  (a) 5 units of capital goods
  (b) 10 units of capital goods
  (c) 15 units of capital goods
  (d) 20 units of capital goods

22. In the table, the law of increasing opportunity costs is suggested by the fact that:
  (a) greater and greater quantities of consumer goods must be given up to get more capital goods
  (b) smaller and smaller quantities of consumer goods must be given up to get more capital goods
  (c) capital goods are relatively more scarce than consumer goods
  (d) the production possibilities curve will eventually shift outward as the economy expands

23. The private ownership of property resources and use of the market system to direct and coordinate economic activity is characteristic of:
  (a) pure capitalism
  (b) the command economy
  (c) market socialism
  (d) the traditional economy

24. The two kinds of markets found in the circular flow model are:
  (a) the real and the money markets
  (b) the real and the product markets
  (c) the money and the resource markets
  (d) the product and the resource markets

25. In the circular flow model businesses:
  (a) demand both products and resources
  (b) supply both products and resources
  (c) demand products and supply resources
  (d) supply products and demand resources

■ **PROBLEMS**

1. Below is a list of resources. Indicate in the space to the right of each whether the resource is land (LD), capital (C), labor (LR), entrepreneurial ability (EA), or some combinations of these.

  a. Fishing grounds in the North Atlantic _____

  b. A cash register in a retail store _____

  c. Uranium deposits in Canada _____

  d. An irrigation ditch in Nebraska _____

  e. The work performed by the late Henry Ford _____

  f. The oxygen breathed by human beings _____

  g. An IBM plant in Rochester, Minnesota _____

  h. The food on the shelf of a grocery store _____

i. The work done by a robot at an auto plant _____

j. The tasks accomplished in perfecting a new computer for commercial sales _____

k. A carpenter building a house _____

2. A production possibilities table for two commodities, wheat and automobiles, is found below. The table is constructed employing the usual assumptions. Wheat is measured in units of 100,000 bushels and automobiles in units of 100,000.

Combination	Wheat	Automobiles
A	0	7
B	7	6
C	13	5
D	18	4
E	22	3
F	25	2
G	27	1
H	28	0

a. Follow the general rules for making graphs (see Chapter 1); plot the data from the table on the graph below to obtain a production possibilities curve. Place wheat on the vertical axis and automobiles on the horizontal axis.

b. Fill in the table below showing the opportunity cost per unit of producing the 1st through the 7th automobile.

Automobiles	Cost of production
1st	_____
2d	_____
3d	_____
4th	_____
5th	_____
6th	_____
7th	_____

3. The graph at the top of the next page is a production possibilities curve. Draw on this graph:

a. A production possibilities curve which indicates greater efficiency in the production of good A.

b. A production possibilities curve which indicates greater efficiency in the production of good B.

c. A production possibilities curve which indicates an increase in the resources available to the economy.

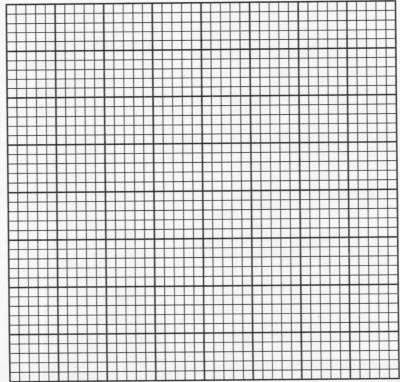

0

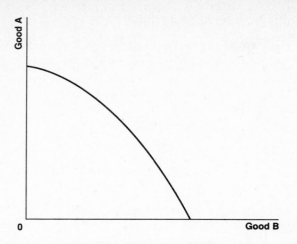

4. Below is a list of economic goods. Indicate in the space to the right of each whether the good is a consumer good (CON), a capital good (CAP), or that it depends (DEP) upon who is using it and for what purpose.

a. An automobile _____

b. A tractor _____

c. A taxicab _____

d. A house _____

e. A factory building _____

f. An office building _____

g. An ironing board _____

h. A refrigerator _____

i. A telephone _____

j. A quart of a soft drink _____

k. A cash register _____

l. A screwdriver _____

5. In the circular flow diagram below, the upper pair of flows (*a* and *b*) represent the resource market and the lower pair (*c* and *d*) the product market.

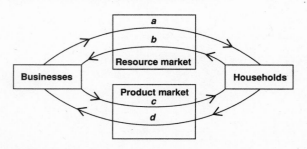

Supply labels or explanations for each of the four flows:

a. _____

b. _____

c. _____

d. _____

■ SHORT ANSWER AND ESSAY QUESTIONS

1. Explain what is meant by the "economizing problem." Why are resources scarce?

2. In what sense are wants satiable and in what sense are they insatiable?

3. What are the four economic resources? How is each of these resources defined?

4. What is the income earned by each economic resource?

5. When is a society economically efficient? What is meant by "full production" and how does it differ from "full employment"?

6. Explain why full production implies both allocative and productive efficiency.

7. What four assumptions are made in drawing a production possibilities curve or schedule?

8. What is opportunity cost? Give an example.

9. What is the law of increasing opportunity cost? Why do costs increase?

10. What determines the optimal product-mix for society's production possibilities?

11. How do technological advance and an increased supply of resources in the economy affect the production possibilities curve or schedule?

12. What is the important relationship between the ***composition*** of the economy's current output and the ***location*** of future production possibilities curves?

13. Describe some real-world applications of the production possibilities curve.

14. Pure capitalism and the command economy differ in two important ways. Compare these two economic systems with each other and with authoritarian capitalism and market socialism.

15. In the circular-flow-of-income model:
(a) What two markets are involved?
(b) What roles do households play in each of these markets?
(c) What roles do businesses play in each of these markets?
(d) What two income flows are pictured in money terms? In real terms?
(e) What two expenditure flows are pictured in money terms? In real terms?

ANSWERS

Chapter 2 The Economizing Problem

FILL-IN QUESTIONS

1. unlimited, limited

2. land or raw materials, capital, labor, entrepreneurial ability (any order)

3. land, capital (any order); labor, entrepreneurial ability (any order)

4. directly, indirectly

5. rental income, interest income, wages, profits

6. the social science concerned with the problem of using or administering scarce resources to attain maximum fulfillment of unlimited wants

7. employment, production

8. allocative, productive

9. *a.* the economy is operating at full employment and full production; *b.* the available supplies of the factors of production are fixed; *c.* technology does not change during the course of the analysis; *d.* the economy produces only two products

10. *a.* fewer, more; *b.* unemployed, underemployed; *c.* more, more; *d.* increase resource supplies, improve its technology

11. *a.* opportunity costs, satisfaction; *b.* under, over; *c.* equal to

12. opportunity cost

13. less

14. *a.* privately, market; *b.* publicly, planning

15. *a.* product, resource; *b.* real, money (either order); *c.* cost, income

TRUE-FALSE QUESTIONS

1. F, pp. 21-22	**6.** T, p. 24	**11.** T, p. 26	**16.** T, pp. 30-31
2. T, pp. 21-22	**7.** F, p. 24	**12.** T, pp. 27-28	**17.** F, p. 31
3. F, p. 22	**8.** F, p. 24	**13.** F, pp. 27-28	**18.** F, pp. 33-34
4. F, p. 23	**9.** T, p. 26	**14.** T, pp. 25-26	**19.** T, p. 35
5. T, pp. 21-22	**10.** T, p. 26	**15.** T, p. 28	**20.** F, p. 37

MULTIPLE-CHOICE QUESTIONS

1. *d,* p. 23	**8.** *d,* pp. 26-27	**15.** *c,* pp. 29-31	**22.** *a,* p. 26
2. *d,* p. 23	**9.** *d,* p. 30	**16.** *d,* p. 26	**23.** *a,* p. 33
3. *d,* p. 24	**10.** *a,* p. 26	**17.** *d,* p. 32	**24.** *d,* pp. 34-35
4. *b,* p. 24	**11.** *b,* p. 26	**18.** *c,* p. 27	**25.** *d,* p. 35
5. *b,* pp. 24-25	**12.** *b,* p. 29	**19.** *a,* p. 27	
6. *c,* p. 26	**13.** *b,* pp. 29-30	**20.** *b,* pp. 30-31	
7. *c,* p. 26	**14.** *c,* p. 24	**21.** *d,* pp. 25-26	

PROBLEMS

1. *a.* land; *b.* C; *c.* land; *d.* C; *e.* EA; *f.* land; *g.* C; *h.* C; *i.* C; *j.* EA; *k.* labor

2. *b.* 1, 2, 3, 4, 5, 6, 7 units of wheat

4. *a.* DEP; *b.* CAP; *c.* CAP; *d.* DEP; *e.* CAP; *f.* CAP; *g.* DEP; *h.* DEP; *i.* DEP; *j.* DEP; *k.* CAP; *l.* DEP

5. *a.* money income payments (wages, rent, interest, and profit); *b.* services or resources (land, labor, capital, and entrepreneurial ability); *c.* goods and services; *d.* expenditures for goods and services

SHORT ANSWER AND ESSAY QUESTIONS

1. pp. 21-22	**5.** pp. 23-24	**9.** p. 26	**13.** pp. 31-33
2. pp. 21-22	**6.** p. 24	**10.** pp. 27-28	**14.** pp. 33-34
3. pp. 22-23	**7.** pp. 24-25	**11.** pp. 29-30	**15.** pp. 34-35
4. p. 23	**8.** p. 26	**12.** pp. 30-31	

Understanding Individual Markets: Demand and Supply

Chapter 3 is an introduction to the most fundamental tools of economic analysis: demand and supply. If you are to progress successfully into the later chapters it is essential that you understand what is meant by demand and supply and how to use these powerful tools.

Demand and supply are simply "boxes" or categories into which all the forces and factors that affect the price and the quantity of a good bought and sold in a competitive market can conveniently be placed. Demand and supply determine price and quantity exchange and it is necessary to see **why** and **how** they do this.

Many students never do understand demand and supply because they never learn to **define** demand and supply **exactly** and because they never learn (1) what is meant by an increase or decrease in demand or supply, (2) the important distinctions between "demand" and "quantity demanded" and between "supply" and "quantity supplied," (3) the equally important distinctions between an increase (or decrease) in demand and an increase (or decrease) in quantity demanded and between an increase (or decrease) in supply and an increase (or decrease) in quantity supplied.

Having learned these, however, it is no great trick to comprehend the so-called "law of supply and demand." The equilibrium price—that is, the price which will tend to prevail in the market as long as demand and supply do not change—is simply the price at which **quantity demanded** and **quantity supplied** are equal. The quantity bought and sold in the market (the equilibrium quantity) is the quantity demanded and supplied at the equilibrium price. If you can determine the equilibrium price and quantity under one set of demand and supply conditions, you can determine them under any other set and so will be able to analyze for yourself the effects of changes in demand and supply upon equilibrium price and quantity.

The chapter includes a brief examination of the factors that determine demand and supply and of the ways in which changes in these determinants will affect and cause changes in demand and supply. A graphic method is employed in this analysis in order to facilitate an understanding of demand and supply, equilibrium price and quantity, changes in demand and supply, and the resulting changes in equilibrium price and quantity. In addition to under-standing the **specific** definitions of demand and supply, it is necessary to understand the two counterparts of demand and supply: the demand **curve** and the supply **curve.** These are simply graphic (or geometric) representations of the same data contained in the schedules of demand and supply.

You will use supply and demand over and over again. It will turn out to be as important to you in economics as jet propulsion is to the pilot of a Boeing 767. You can't get off the ground without it.

■ **CHECKLIST**

When you have studied this chapter you should be able to:

☐ Define a market.
☐ Define demand and state the law of demand.
☐ Graph the demand curve when you are given a demand schedule.
☐ Explain the difference between individual and market demand.
☐ List the major nonprice determinants of demand and explain how each one shifts the demand curve.
☐ Distinguish between a change in demand and a change in the quantity demanded.
☐ Define supply and state the law of supply.
☐ Graph the supply curve when you are given a supply schedule.
☐ List the major nonprice determinants of supply and explain how each shifts the supply curve.
☐ Distinguish between a change in supply and a change in the quantity supplied.
☐ Determine when you are given the demand for and the supply of a good what the equilibrium price and the equilibrium quantity will be.
☐ Explain why the price of a good and the amount of the good bought and sold in a competitive market will be the equilibrium price and the equilibrium quantity, respectively.
☐ Predict the effects of changes in demand and supply on equilibrium price and equilibrium quantity; and on the prices of substitute and complementary goods.

☐ Explain the meaning of the rationing function of prices.

☐ Explain why violations of the "other things equal" assumption may cause confusion about the validity of the laws of demand and supply.

■ **CHAPTER OUTLINE**

1. A market is any institution or mechanism that brings together the buyers and the sellers of a particular good or service; and in this chapter it is assumed that markets are purely competitive.

2. Demand is a schedule of prices and the quantities which buyers would purchase at each of these prices during some period of time.

a. As price rises, other things being equal, buyers will purchase smaller quantities, and as price falls they will purchase larger quantities; this is the law of demand.

b. The demand curve is a graphic representation of demand and the law of demand.

c. Market (or total) demand for a good is a summation of the demands of all individuals in the market for that good.

d. The demand for a good depends upon the tastes, income, and expectations of buyers; the number of buyers in the market; and the prices of related goods.

e. A change (either an increase or a decrease) in demand is caused by a change in any of the factors (in **d**) which determine demand, and means that the demand schedule and demand curve have changed.

f. A change in demand and a change in the quantity demanded are **not** the same thing.

3. Supply is a schedule of prices and the quantities which sellers will offer to sell at each of these prices during some period of time.

a. The law of supply means, other things being equal, that as the price of the good rises larger quantities will be offered for sale, and that as the price of the good falls smaller quantities will be offered for sale.

b. The supply curve is a graphic representation of supply and the law of supply; the market supply of a good is the sum of the supplies of all sellers of the good.

c. The supply of a good depends upon the techniques used to produce it, the prices of the resources employed in its production, the extent to which it is taxed or subsidized, the prices of other goods which might be produced, the price expectations of sellers, and the number of sellers of the product.

d. Supply will change when any of these determinants of supply changes; a change in supply is a change in the entire supply schedule or curve.

e. A change in supply must be distinguished from a change in quantity supplied.

4. The market or equilibrium price of a commodity is that price at which quantity demanded and quantity supplied are equal; and the quantity exchanged in the market (the equilibrium quantity) is equal to the quantity demanded and supplied at the equilibrium price.

a. The rationing function of price is the elimination of shortages and surpluses of the commodity.

b. A change in demand, supply, or both changes both the equilibrium price and the equilibrium quantity in specific ways.

c. In resource markets suppliers are households and demanders are business firms, and in product markets suppliers are business firms and demanders are householders; and supply and demand are useful in the analysis of prices and quantities exchanged in both types of markets.

d. When demand and supply schedules (or curves) are drawn up it is assumed that all the nonprice determinants of demand and supply remain unchanged.

■ **IMPORTANT TERMS**

Market	**Inferior good**
Demand schedule	**Substitute (competing)**
Law of demand	**goods**
Diminishing marginal utility	**Complementary goods**
Quantity demanded	**Supply schedule**
Income effect	**Quantity supplied**
Substitution effect	**Law of supply**
Demand curve	**Supply curve**
Individual demand	**Nonprice determinant of**
Total or market demand	**supply**
Nonprice determinant of demand	**Increase (or decrease) in supply**
Increase (or decrease) in demand	**Equilibrium price**
Normal (superior) good	**Equilibrium quantity**
	Rationing function of prices

■ **HINTS AND TIPS**

1. This chapter is the most important one in the book. Make sure you spend extra time on it and master the material. If you do, there will be a long-term payoff because it will make it much easier for you to understand the applications in later chapters.

2. One mistake that students often make is to confuse a **change in demand** with a **change in quantity demanded.** A change in demand causes the entire demand curve to **shift,** whereas a change in quantity demanded is simply a **movement** along an existing demand curve.

3. It is strongly recommended that you draw supply and demand graphs as you work on supply and demand problems so that you can see a picture of what happens when demand shifts, supply shifts, or both demand and supply shift.

4. Make a chart and related graphs that show the *eight* possible outcomes from changes in demand and supply. Figure 3–6 in the text illustrates the *four single shift* outcomes:

(1) *D*↑: *P*↑, *Q*↑ (3) *S*↑: *P*↓, *Q*↑
(2) *D*↓: *P*↓, *Q*↓ (4) *S*↓: *P*↑, *Q*↓

There are *four shift combinations* that are described on pages 51–54 of the text. Make a figure to illustrate each combination.

(1) *S*↑, *D*↓: *P*↓, *Q*? (3) *S*↑, *D*↑: *P*?, *Q*↑
(2) *S*↓, *D*↑: *P*↑, *Q*? (4) *S*↓, *D*↓: *P*?, *Q*↓

SELF-TEST

■ **FILL-IN QUESTIONS**

1. A market is the institution or mechanism that brings together the _____ and the _____ of a particular good or service.

2. In resource markets prices are determined by the demand decisions of (business firms, households) _____ and the supply decisions of _____

3. In product markets prices are determined by demand decisions of _____ and the supply decisions of_____

4. The relationship between price and quantity in the demand schedule is a(n) (direct, inverse) _____ _____ relationship; in the supply schedule the relationship is a(n) _____ one.

5. The added satisfaction or pleasure obtained by a consumer from additional units of a product decreases as her or his consumption of the product increases. This phenomenon is called _____

6. A consumer tends to buy more of a product as its price falls because:
  a. The purchasing power of the consumer is increased and the consumer tends to buy more of this product (and of other products); this is called the (income, substitution) _____ effect;
  b. The product becomes less expensive relative to similar products and the consumer tends to buy more of this and less of the similar products; and this is called the _____ effect.

7. When demand or supply is graphed, price is placed on the (horizontal, vertical) _____ axis and quantity on the _____ axis.

8. The change from an individual to a market demand schedule involves _____ the quantities demanded by each consumer at the various possible _____

9. When the price of one product and the demand for another product are directly related, the two products are called (substitutes, complements) _____; however, when the price of one product and the demand for another product are inversely related, the two products are called _____

10. When a consumer demand schedule or curve is drawn up, it is assumed that five factors that determine demand are fixed and constant. These five determinants of consumer demand are:
  a. _____
  b. _____
  c. _____
  d. _____
  e. _____

11. A decrease in demand means that consumers will buy (larger, smaller) _____ quantities at every price, or will pay (more, less) _____ for the same quantities.

12. A change in income or in the price of another product will result in a change in the (demand for, quantity demanded of) _____ _____ the given product, while a change in the price the given product will result in _____the given product.

13. An increase in supply means that producers will make and be willing to sell (larger, smaller) _____ quantities at every price, or will want to be paid (more, less) _____ for the same quantities.

14. A change in resource prices or the prices of other goods that could be produced will result in a change in the (supply, quantity supplied) _____ of the given product, but a change in the price of the given product will result in a change in the _____

15. The fundamental factors which determine the supply of any commodity in the product market are:

a. _____

b. _____

c. _____

d. _____

e. _____

f. _____

16. The equilibrium price of a commodity is the price at

which _____

_____

17. If quantity demanded exceeds quantity supplied,

price is (above, below) _____
the equilibrium price; and the (shortage, surplus)

_____ will cause the price to (rise, fall)

_____

18. In the spaces below each of the following, indicate the effect [*increase* (+), *decrease* (-), or *indeterminate* (?)] upon equilibrium price (**P**) and equilibrium quantity (**Q**) of each of these changes in demand and/or supply.

                                                          P   **Q**

a. Increase in demand, supply constant   ____ ____

b. Increase in supply, demand constant   ____ ____

c. Decrease in demand, supply constant   ____ ____

d. Decrease in supply, demand constant   ____ ____

e. Increase in demand, increase in supply ____ ____

f. Increase in demand, decrease in supply____ ____

g. Decrease in demand, decrease in ____ ____
supply

h. Decrease in demand, increase in supply____ ____

19. If supply and demand establish a price for a good such that there is no shortage or surplus of the good, then

price is successfully performing its _____

20. To assume that all the nonprice determinants of demand and supply do not change is to employ the

_____ assumption.

■ **TRUE-FALSE QUESTIONS**

Circle the T if the statement is true; the F if it is false.

1. A market is any arrangement that brings the buyers and sellers of a particular good or service together. **T F**

2. Demand is the amount of a commodity or service which a buyer will purchase at a particular price.   **T F**

3. The law of demand states that as price increases, other things being equal, the quantity of the product demanded increases.   **T F**

4. The law of diminishing marginal utility is one explanation for why there is an inverse relationship between price and quantity demanded.   **T F**

5. The substitution effect suggests that, at a lower price, you have the incentive to substitute the more expensive product for similar products which are relatively less expensive.   **T F**

6. There is no difference between individual demand schedules and the market demand schedule for a product.
                                                              T F

7. In graphing supply and demand schedules, supply is put on the horizontal axis and demand on the vertical axis.   **T F**

8. If price falls, there will be an increase in demand.
                                                              T F

9. If the demand curve moves from D_1 to D_2 in the graph shown below, demand has increased.   **T F**

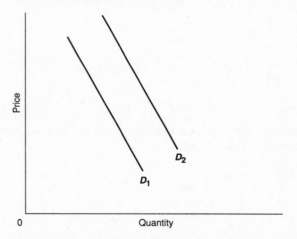

10. A fall in the price of a good will cause the demand for goods which are substitutes for it to increase.   **T F**

11. If two goods are complementary, an increase in the price of one will cause the demand for the other to increase.   **T F**

12. A change in income will cause a change in the quantity demanded for a product, but it will not change the demand for the product.   **T F**

13. Supply is a schedule which shows the amounts of a product a producer can make in a limited time period.
                                                              T F

14. A change in resource prices is a factor that will cause a change in supply. **T F**

15. An increase in the prices of other goods that could be made by producers will increase the supply of the current product that the producer is making. **T F**

16. A change in supply means that there is a movement along an existing supply curve. **T F**

17. If the market price of a commodity is for a time below its equilibrium price, the market price will tend to rise because demand will decrease and supply will increase. **T F**

18. The equilibrium price of a good is the price at which the demand and the supply of the good are equal. **T F**

19. The rationing function of prices is the elimination of shortages and surpluses. **T F**

20. Economists often make the assumption of "other things equal" to hold constant the effects of other factors when examining the relationship between price and quantity demanded. **T F**

■ **MULTIPLE-CHOICE QUESTIONS**

Circle the letter that corresponds to the best answer.

1. The markets examined in this chapte. are:
(a) purely competitive markets
(b) markets for goods and services
(c) markets for products and resources
(d) all of the above

2. A schedule which shows the various amounts of a product consumers are willing and able to purchase at each price in a series of possible prices during a specified period of time is called:
(a) supply
(b) demand
(c) quantity supplied
(d) quantity demanded

3. The reason for the law of demand can best be explained in terms of:
(a) supply
(b) complementary goods
(c) the rationing function of prices
(d) diminishing marginal utility

4. Assume that in a competitive market video tape players (VCRs) double in price. What will most likely happen in that market to the equilibrium price and quantity of video tapes?
(a) price will increase; quantity will decrease
(b) price will decrease; quantity will increase
(c) price will decrease; quantity will decrease
(d) price will increase; quantity will increase

5. Given the following individuals' demand schedules for product X, and assuming these are the only three consumers of X, which set of prices and output levels below will be on the market demand curve for this product?

Price X	Consumer 1 Q_{dx}	Consumer 2 Q_{dx}	Consumer 3 Q_{dx}
$5	1	2	0
4	2	4	0
3	3	6	1
2	4	8	2
1	5	10	3

(a) ($5, 2); ($1, 10)
(b) ($5, 3); ($1, 18)
(c) ($4, 6); ($2, 12)
(d) ($4, 0); ($1, 3)

6. The income of a consumer decreases and his/her demand for a particular good increases. It can be concluded that the good is:
(a) normal
(b) inferior
(c) a substitute
(d) a complement

7. Which of the following could cause a decrease in consumer demand for product X?
(a) a decrease in consumer income
(b) an increase in the prices of goods which are good substitutes for product X
(c) an increase in the price which consumers expect will prevail for product X in the future
(d) a decrease in the supply of product X

8. If two goods are substitutes for each other, an increase in the price of one will necessarily:
(a) decrease the demand for the other
(b) increase the demand for the other
(c) decrease the quantity demanded of the other
(d) increase the quantity demanded of the other

9. If two products, A and B, are complements, then:
(a) an increase in the price of A will decrease the demand for B
(b) an increase in the price of A will increase the demand for B
(c) an increase in the price of A will have no significant effect on the price of B
(d) a decrease in the price of A will decrease the demand for B

10. If two products, X and Y, are independent goods, then:
(a) an increase in the price of X will significantly increase the demand for Y
(b) an increase in the price of Y will significantly increase the demand for X

(c) an increase in the price of Y will have no significant effect on the demand for X

(d) a decrease in the price of X will significantly increase the demand for Y

11. The law of supply states that, other things being constant, as price increases:
(a) supply increases
(b) supply decreases
(c) quantity supplied increases
(d) quantity supplied decreases

12. If the supply curve moves from S_1 to S_2 on the graph below, there has been:
(a) an increase in supply
(b) a decrease in supply
(c) an increase in quantity supplied
(d) a decrease in quantity supplied

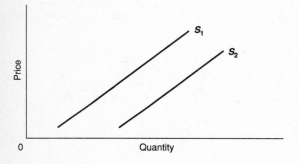

13. A decrease in the price of a product would most likely be caused by:
(a) an increase in business taxes
(b) an increase in consumer incomes
(c) a decrease in resource costs for production
(d) a decrease in the price of a complementary good

14. Which of the following could **not** cause an increase in the supply of cotton?
(a) an increase in the price of cotton
(b) improvements in the art of producing cotton
(c) a decrease in the price of the machinery and tools employed in cotton production
(d) a decrease in the price of corn

15. When government sets the price of a good and that price is below the equilibrium price the result will be:
(a) a surplus of the good
(b) a shortage of the good
(c) an increase in the demand for the good
(d) a decrease in the supply of the good

The next three questions (16, 17, and 18) refer to the following table. Consider the following supply and demand schedules for corn.

Price	Quantity demanded	Quantity supplied
$20	395	200
22	375	250
24	350	290
26	320	320
28	280	345
30	235	365

16. The equilibrium price in this market is:
(a) $22
(b) $24
(c) $26
(d) $28

17. An increase in the cost of labor lowers the quantity supplied by 65 units at each price. The new equilibrium price would be:
(a) $22
(b) $24
(c) $26
(d) $28

18. If the quantity demanded increases by 130 units, then the new equilibrium quantity will be:
(a) 290
(b) 320
(c) 345
(d) 365

19. A decrease in supply and a decrease in demand will:
(a) increase price and decrease the quantity exchanged
(b) decrease price and increase the quantity exchanged
(c) increase price and affect the quantity exchanged in an indeterminate way
(d) affect price in an indeterminate way and decrease the quantity exchanged

20. An increase in demand and a decrease in supply will:
(a) increase price and increase the quantity exchanged
(b) decrease price and decrease the quantity exchanged
(c) increase price and the effect upon quantity exchanged will be indeterminate
(d) decrease price and the effect upon quantity exchanged will be indeterminate

21. An increase in supply and an increase in demand will:
(a) increase price and increase the quantity exchanged
(b) decrease price and increase the quantity exchanged
(c) affect price in an indeterminate way and decrease the quantity exchanged
(d) affect price in an indeterminate way and increase the quantity exchanged

22. A cold spell in Florida devastates the orange crop. As a result, California oranges command a higher price. Which of the following statements best explains the situation?

(a) the supply of Florida potatoes decreased, causing the supply of California oranges to increase and their price to increase

(b) the supply of Florida oranges decreased, causing their price to increase and the demand for California oranges to increase

(c) the supply of Florida oranges decreased, causing the supply of California oranges to decrease and their price to increase

(d) the demand for Florida oranges decreased, causing a greater demand for California oranges and an increase in their price

The next three questions (23, 24, and 25) are based on the following graph showing the market supply and demand for a product.

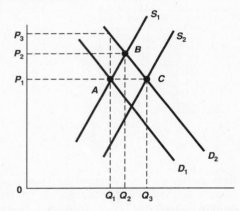

23. A movement from point **B** to point **C** on demand curve **D₂** would most likely be caused by an increase in:

(a) consumer incomes
(b) product price
(c) prices of related goods
(d) number of buyers

24. If the market equilibrium was at point **B,** but the price of the product was set at **P₁**, then there would be a:

(a) surplus of $Q_3 - Q_1$
(b) shortage of $Q_3 - Q_1$
(c) surplus of $Q_1 - Q_2$
(d) shortage of $Q_2 - Q_1$

25. Assume that the market is initially in equilibrium where **D₁** and **S₁** intersect. If consumer incomes increased and the technology for making the product improved, then new equilibrium would be at:

(a) P_1 and Q_1
(b) P_2 and Q_2
(c) P_1 and Q_3
(d) P_3 and Q_1

■ PROBLEMS

1. Using the demand schedule below, plot the demand curve on the *graph on the next page.* Label the axes and indicate for each axis the units being used to measure price and quantity.

Price	Quantity demanded, 1,000 bushels of soybeans
$7.20	10
7.00	15
6.80	20
6.60	25
6.40	30
6.20	35

a. Plot the supply schedule which follows on the same graph.

Price	Quantity supplied, 1,000 bushels of soybeans
$7.20	40
7.00	35
6.80	30
6.60	25
6.40	20
6.20	15

b. The equilibrium price of soybeans will be $_____

c. How many thousand bushels of soybeans will

be exchanged at this price?_____

d. Indicate clearly on the graph the equilibrium price and quantity by drawing lines from the intersection of the supply and demand curves to the price and quantity axes.

e. If the Federal government supported a price of $7.00 per bushel there would be a (shortage, surplus)

_____ of _____ bushels of soybeans.

2. The demand schedules of three individuals (Robert, Charles, and Lynn) for loaves of bread are shown in the table below. Assuming there are only three buyers of bread, draw up the total or market demand schedule for bread.

Price	Quantity demanded, loaves of bread			Total
	Robert	Charles	Lynn	
$.40	1	4	0	_____
.36	3	5	1	_____
.32	6	6	5	_____
.28	10	7	10	_____
.24	15	8	16	_____

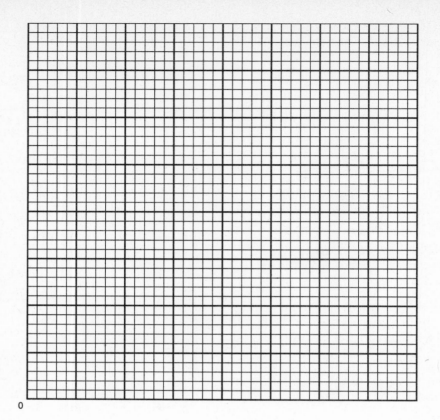

0

3. Below is a demand schedule for bushels of apples. In columns 3 and 4 insert *any* new figures for quantity which represent in column 3 an increase in demand and in column 4 a decrease in demand.

(1) Price	(2) Quantity demanded	(3) Demand increases	(4) Demand decreases
$6.00	400	_____	_____
5.90	500	_____	_____
5.80	600	_____	_____
5.70	700	_____	_____
5.60	800	_____	_____
5.50	900	_____	_____

4. Assume that O'Rourke has, when his income is $100 per week, the demand schedule for good A shown in columns 1 and 2 of the following table and the demand schedule for good B shown in columns 4 and 5. Assume that the prices of A and B are $.80 and $5, respectively.

Demand for A (per week)			Demand for B (per week)		
(1) Price	(2) Quantity demanded	(3) Quantity demanded	(4) Price	(5) Quantity demanded	(6) Quantity demanded
$.90	10	0	$5.00	4	7
.85	20	10	4.50	5	8
.80	30	20	4.00	6	9
.75	40	30	3.50	7	10
.70	50	40	3.00	8	11
.65	60	50	2.50	9	12
.60	70	60	2.00	10	13

a. How much A will O'Rourke buy? _____

How much B? _____

b. Suppose that, as a consequence of a $10 increase in O'Rourke's weekly income, the quantities demanded of A become those shown in column 3 and the quantities demanded of B become those shown in column 6.

(1) How much A will he now buy? _____

How much B? _____

(2) Good A is (normal, inferior) _____

(3) Good B is _____

5. The market demand for good X is shown in columns 1 and 2 of the table below. Assume the price of X to be $2 and constant.

(1)	(2)	(3)	(4)
Price	Quantity demanded	Quantity demanded	Quantity demanded
$2.40	1,600	1,500	1,700
2.30	1,650	1,550	1,750
2.20	1,750	1,650	1,850
2.10	1,900	1,800	2,000
2.00	2,100	2,000	2,200
1.90	2,350	2,250	2,450
1.80	2,650	2,550	2,750

a. If as the price of good Y rises from $1.25 to $1.35 the quantities demanded of good X become those shown in column 3, it can be concluded that X and Y are (substitute, complementary) _____ goods.

b. If as the price of good Y rises from $1.25 to $1.35 the quantities of good X become those shown in column 4, it can be concluded that X and Y are _____ _____ goods.

6. In a local market for hamburger on a given date, each of 300 identical sellers of hamburger has the following supply schedule.

(1)	(2)	(3)
Price	Quantity supplied— one seller, lb.	Quantity supplied— all sellers, lb.
$2.05	150	_____
2.00	110	_____
1.95	75	_____
1.90	45	_____
1.85	20	_____
1.80	0	_____

a. In column 3 construct the market supply schedule for hamburger.

b. Below is the market demand schedule for hamburger on the same date and in the same local market as that given above.

Price	Quantity demanded, lb.
$2.05	28,000
2.00	31,000
1.95	36,000
1.90	42,000
1.85	49,000
1.80	57,000

If the Federal government sets a price on hamburger at $1.90 a pound the result would be a (shortage, surplus)

_____

of _____ pounds of hamburger in this market.

7. Each of the following events would tend to increase or decrease either the demand for or the supply of computer games and, as a result, increase or decrease the price of these games. In the first blank indicate the effect upon demand or supply (increase, decrease); and in the second indicate the effect on price (increase, decrease).

a. It becomes known that a local department store is going to have a sale on these games three months from now. _____ ;

b. The workers who produce the games go on strike for over two months. _____ ;

c. The workers in the industry receive a $1.00 an hour wage increase. _____ ;

d. The average price of movie tickets increases. _____ ; _____

e. The firms producing the games undertake to produce a large volume of missile components for the Defense Department. _____ ;

f. It is announced by a private research institute that children who have taken to playing computer games also improve their grades in school. _____ ;

g. Because of the use of mass-production techniques, the amount of labor necessary to produce a game decreases. _____ ;

h. The price of computers increases. _____ ;

i. The average consumer believes that a shortage of games is developing in the economy. _____ ;

j. The Federal government imposes a $5 per game tax upon the manufacturers of computer games. ___ _____ ; _____

■ SHORT ANSWER AND ESSAY QUESTIONS

1. What is a market? Define it and give examples.

2. Define demand and the law of demand.

3. What are three possible explanations for the inverse relationship between price and quantity demanded?

4. Two decades ago, the price of coffee in the United States rose significantly as a result of bad weather in coffee-producing regions. Use the income effect and the substitution effect concepts to explain why the quantity of coffee demanded in the United Sates significantly decreased.

5. Use the diminishing marginal utility concept to explain why the quantity demanded of a product will tend to rise when the price of the product falls.

6. What is the difference between individual and market demand? What is the relationship between these two types of demand?

7. Explain the difference between an increase in demand and an increase in the quantity demanded.

8. What are the factors that cause a change in demand? Use supply and demand graphs to illustrate what happens to price and quantity when demand increases.

9. How are inferior, normal, and superior goods defined? What is the relationship between these goods and changes in income?

10. Why does the effect of a change in the price of related goods depend on whether a good is a substitute or complement? What are substitutes and complements?

11. A newspaper reports that "blue jeans have become even more popular and are now the standard clothing that people wear for both play and work." How will this change affect the demand and supply of blue jeans? What will happen to the price and quantity of blue jeans sold in the market? Explain and use a supply and demand graph to illustrate your answer.

12. What is meant by the term supply? What is the law of supply?

13. Supply does not remain constant for long because the factors which determine supply change. What are these factors? How do changes in them affect supply?

14. Explain the difference between an increase in supply and an increase in the quantity supplied.

15. Describe and illustrate with a supply and demand graph the effect of an increase in supply on price and quantity. Do the same for a decrease in supply.

16. The U.S. Congress passes a law that raises the excise tax on gasoline by $1.00 per gallon. What effect will this change have on the demand and supply of gasoline? What will happen to gasoline price and quantity? Explain and use a supply and demand graph to illustrate your answer.

17. What is the relationship between the price of a product and a shortage of the product? What is the relationship between the price of a product and surplus of the product?

18. Given the demand for and the supply of a commodity, what price will be the equilibrium price of this commodity? Explain why this price will tend to prevail in the market and why higher (lower) prices, if they do exist temporarily, will tend to fall (rise).

19. Analyze the following quotation and explain the fallacies contained in it: "An increase in demand will cause price to rise; with a rise in price, supply will increase and the increase in supply will push price down. Therefore, an increase in demand results in little change in price because supply will increase also."

20. What is meant by the "rationing function of prices"?

ANSWERS

Chapter 3 Understanding Individual Markets: Demand and Supply

FILL-IN QUESTIONS

1. buyers (demanders), sellers (suppliers) (either order)

2. business firms, households

3. households, business firms

4. inverse, direct

5. diminishing marginal utility

6. *a.* income; *b.* substitution

7. vertical, horizontal

8. summing (or adding), prices

9. substitutes, complements

10. *a.* the tastes or preferences of consumers; *b.* the number of consumers in the market; *c.* the money income of consumers; *d.* the prices of related goods; *e.* consumer expectations with respect to future prices and incomes

11. smaller, less

12. demand for, a change in the quantity demanded of the product

13. larger, more

14. supply, quantity supplied

15. *a.* the technique of production; *b.* resource prices; *c.* taxes and subsidies; *d.* prices of other goods; *e.* price expectations; *f.* the number of sellers in the market

16. quantity demanded and quantity supplied are equal

17. below, shortage, rise

18. *a.* +, +; *b.* −, +; *c.* −, −; *d.* +, −; *e.* ?, +; *f.* +, ?; *g.* ?, −; *h.* −, ?

19. rationing function

20. other things being equal

TRUE-FALSE QUESTIONS

1. T, p. 39	**8.** F, pp. 41-42	**15.** F, p. 48
2. F, pp. 39-40	**9.** T, p. 43	**16.** F, pp. 48-49
3. F, p. 40	**10.** F, p. 44	**17.** F, pp. 50-51
4. T, pp. 40-41	**11.** F, p. 44	**18.** F, p. 50
5. F, p. 41	**12.** F, p. 45	**19.** T, p. 50
6. F, p. 42	**13.** F, p. 46	**20.** T, p. 53
7. F, pp. 41-42	**14.** T, p. 47	

MULTIPLE-CHOICE QUESTIONS

1. *d*, p. 39	**10.** *c*, p. 44	**19.** *d*, p. 53
2. *b*, pp. 39-40	**11.** *c*, p. 46	**20.** *c*, p. 52
3. *d*, pp. 40-41	**12.** *a*, p. 47	**21.** *d*, p. 53
4. *c*, p. 44	**13.** *c*, p. 47	**22.** *b*, p. 53
5. *b*, p. 42	**14.** *a*, pp. 47-48	**23.** *b*, p. 47
6. *b*, p. 44	**15.** *b*, pp. 49-50	**24.** *b*, pp. 49-51
7. *a*, p. 44	**16.** *c*, p. 49	**25.** *c*, p. 53
8. *b*, p. 44	**17.** *d*, pp. 47-49	
9. *a*, p. 44	**18.** *d*, pp. 42-43; 51	

PROBLEMS

1. *b.* 6.60; *c.* 25,000; *e.* surplus, 20,000

2. Total: 5, 9, 17, 27, 39

3. Each quantity in column 3 is greater than in column 2, and each quantity in column 4 is less than in column 2.

4. *a.* 30, 4; *b.* (1) 20, 7; (2) inferior; (3) normal (superior)

5. *a.* complementary; *b.* substitute

6. *a.* 45,000; 33,000; 22,500; 13,500; 6,000; 0 *b.* shortage, 28,500

7. *a.* decrease demand, decrease price; *b.* decrease supply, increase price; *c.* decrease supply, increase price; *d.* increase demand, increase price; *e.* decrease supply, increase price; *f.* increase demand, increase price; *g.* increase supply, decrease price; *h.* decrease demand, decrease price, *i.* increase demand, increase price; *j.* decrease supply, increase price

SHORT ANSWER AND ESSAY QUESTIONS

1. p. 39	**8.** pp. 43-45	**15.** p. 52
2. pp. 39-40	**9.** p. 44	**16.** pp. 48, 52
3. pp. 40-41	**10.** p. 44	**17.** pp. 49-50
4. p. 41	**11.** pp. 43-45	**18.** pp. 50-52
5. pp. 40-41	**12.** p. 46	**19.** pp. 50-52
6. p. 42	**13.** pp. 47-48	**20.** p. 50
7. p. 45	**14.** pp. 48-49	

CHAPTER 4

Pure Capitalism and the Market System

Chapter 4 describes the characteristics of pure capitalism, identifies three practices found in all modern economies, and offers a detailed explanation of the operation of the market system.

The first part of Chapter 4 describes the ideological and institutional characteristics of pure capitalism. In a pure capitalist system, most of the resources are owned by its citizens, who are free to use them as they wish in their own self-interest; prices and markets serve to express the self-interests of resource owners, consumers, and business firms; and competition serves to regulate self-interest—to prevent the self-interest of any person or any group from working to the disadvantage of the economy as a whole and to make self-interest work for the benefit of the entire economy.

The three practices of all modern economies are the employment of large amounts of capital, extensive specialization, and the use of money. Economies use capital and engage in specialization because it is a more efficient use of their resources; it results in larger total output and the greater satisfaction of wants. But when workers, business firms, and regions within an economy specialize they become dependent on each other for the goods and services they do not produce for themselves. To obtain these goods and services they must engage in trade. Trade is made more convenient by using money as a medium of exchange.

The latter part of Chapter 4 describes the operation of the competitive market system. There are Five Fundamental Questions that any economic system must answer in attempting to use its scarce resources to satisfy its material wants. The five questions or problems are: (1) How much output is to be produced? (2) What is to be produced? (3) How is the output to be produced? (4) Who is to receive the output? (5) Can the economic system adapt to change? Only the last four questions will be discussed in this chapter. Answers to the first question will await the presentation of material on macroeconomics.

The explanation of how the market system finds answers to the last four of the Five Fundamental Questions is only an approximation—a simplified version or a model—of the methods actually employed by the American economy. Yet this simple model, like all good models, contains enough realism to be truthful and is general enough to be understandable. If the aims of this chapter are accomplished, you can begin to understand the market system and methods employed by our economy to solve the economizing problem presented in Chapter 2.

■ CHECKLIST

☐ Identify the six important institutional or ideological characteristics of capitalism.
☐ Describe the significance of property rights in capitalism.
☐ Distinguish between freedom of enterprise and freedom of choice.
☐ Explain why self-interest is a driving force of capitalism.
☐ Identify two features of competition.
☐ Explain why capitalism is a market economy.
☐ Describe size of government in capitalism.
☐ List three characteristics of all modern economies.
☐ Explain why the production of capital goods entails roundabout production.
☐ Discuss how specialization improves efficiency.
☐ Describe the advantages of money over barter for the exchange of goods and services.
☐ Identify the Five Fundamental Questions.
☐ Explain how a competitive market system determines what will be produced.
☐ Distinguish between normal profit and economic profit.
☐ Predict what will happen to the price charged by and the output of a prosperous and an unprosperous industry; and explain why these events will occur.
☐ Explain how production is organized in a competitive market system.
☐ Find the least-costly combination of resources when you are given the technological data and the prices of the resources.
☐ Explain how a competitive market system determines the distribution of total output.
☐ Describe the guiding function of prices to accommodate change in the competitive market system.
☐ Explain how the competitive market system initiates change by fostering technological advances and capital accumulation.

☐ State how the "invisible hand" in the competitive market system tends to promote public or social interests.
☐ List three virtues of the competitive market system.

■ **CHAPTER OUTLINE**

1. The United States economy is not pure capitalism, but it is a close approximation of pure capitalism. Pure capitalism has the following six peculiarities that distinguish it from other economic systems.

a. Private individuals and organizations own and control their property resources by means of the institution of private property.

b. These individuals and organizations possess both the freedom of enterprise and the freedom of choice.

c. Each of them is motivated largely by self-interest.

d. Competition prevents them as buyers and sellers from exploiting others.

e. Markets and prices (the market system) are used to communicate and coordinate the decisions of buyers and sellers.

f. The role of government is limited in a competitive and capitalistic economy.

2. In common with other advanced economies of the world, the American economy has three major characteristics.

a. It employs complicated and advanced methods of production and large amounts of capital equipment to produce goods and services efficiently.

b. It is a highly specialized economy; and this specialization increases the productive efficiency of the economy.

c. It also uses money extensively to facilitate trade and specialization.

3. There are Five Fundamental Questions which must be answered by every economic system:

(1) How much output is to be produced?
(2) What is to be produced?
(3) How is output to be produced?
(4) Who is to receive the output?
(5) Can the economic system adapt to change?

4. The system of prices and markets and the choices of households and business firms furnish the economy with answers to the last four Fundamental Questions.

a. The demands of consumers for products and the desires of business firms to maximize their profits determine what and how much of each product is produced (and its price).

b. The desires of business firms to maximize profits by keeping their costs of production as low as possible guide them to employ the most efficient techniques of production and determine their demands for and prices of the various resources; competition forces them to use the most efficient techniques and ensures that only the most efficient will be able to stay in business.

c. With resource prices determined, the money income of each household is determined; and with product prices determined, the quantity of goods and services which these money incomes will buy is determined.

d. The market system is able to accommodate itself to changes in consumer tastes, technology, and resource supplies.

(1) The desires of business firms for maximum profits and competition lead the economy to make the appropriate adjustments in the way it uses its resources.

(2) Competition and the desire to increase profits promote both better techniques of production and capital accumulation.

e. Competition in the economy compels firms seeking to promote their own interests to promote (as though led by an "invisible hand") the best interest of society as a whole: an allocation of resources appropriate to consumer wants, production by the most efficient means, and the lowest possible prices.

5. The market system has been praised for its merits. The two economic virtues of the system are the *efficient* use of resources and the *incentives* for productive economic activity. A noneconomic virtue is the personal *freedom* allowed by the market system.

■ **IMPORTANT TERMS**

Private property	Normal profit
Self-interest	Economic cost
Competition	Economic profit
Market	Expanding (prosperous)
Freedom of choice	industry
Freedom of enterprise	Declining (unprosperous)
Roundabout production	industry
Specialization	Dollar votes
Division of labor	Consumer sovereignty
Money	Derived demand
Medium of exchange	Guiding function of prices
Barter	Self-limiting adjustment
Coincidence of wants	Technological advance
Five Fundamental	Capital accumulation
Questions	Invisible hand

■ **HINTS AND TIPS**

1. The "Operation of the Market System" is both the most important part of this chapter and the part you will find most difficult. If you will try to understand how the American system of prices and markets finds answers for each of the four basic questions by examining them *individually* and in the order in which they are presented, you will more easily understand how the market system as a whole operates. Actually the market system finds answers for all these questions simultaneously, but it is much simpler to consider them as if they were separate questions.

2. Be sure to understand the *importance* and *role* of each of the following in the operation of the market system: (1) the rationing and directing functions of prices, (2) the profit motive of business firms, (3) the entry into and exodus of firms from industries, (4) competition, and (5) consumer sovereignty.

SELF-TEST

■ **FILL-IN QUESTIONS**

1. The ownership of property resources by private individuals and organizations is the institution of _____ _____

2. Two basic freedoms encountered in a capitalistic economy are the freedom of _____ and _____

3. Self-interest means that each economic unit attempts to _____; this self-interest might work to the disadvantage of the economy as a whole if it were not regulated and constrained by _____

4. According to the economist, competition is present if two conditions prevail; these two conditions are:

   a. _____
   _____
   b. _____
   _____

5. If the number of buyers and sellers in a market is large, no single buyer or seller is able to _____ the price of the commodity bought and sold in that market.

6. In a capitalistic economy individual buyers communicate their demands and individual sellers communicate their supplies in the _____ of the economy; and their decisions are coordinated by the _____ determined there by demand and supply.

7. In the ideology of pure capitalism government is assigned (no, a limited, an extensive) _____ role.

8. Modern economies make extensive use of capital goods and engage in roundabout production because it is more _____ than direct production.

9. Modern economies practice specialization and the division of labor because the self-sufficient producer or worker tends to be a(n) _____ one.

10. In modern economies money functions chiefly as a(n) _____

11. Barter between two individuals will take place only if there is a(n) _____

12. List the Five Fundamental Questions which every economy must answer.

   a. _____
   b. _____
   c. _____
   d. _____
   e. _____

13. The competitive market system is a mechanism for both _____ the decisions of producers and households and _____ these decisions.

14. A *normal* profit (is, is not) _____ an economic cost because it is a payment that (must, need not) _____ be paid to (workers, landowners, suppliers of capital goods, entrepreneurs) _____ but a *pure* (or *economic*) profit (is, is not) _____ an economic cost because it (must, need not) _____ be paid to them to obtain and retain the services they provide to the firm.

15. Pure or economic profits are equal to the total _____ of a firm less its total _____

16. Business firms tend to produce those products from which they can obtain:

   a. at least a (pure, normal) _____ profit; and
   b. the maximum _____ profit.

17. If firms in an industry are obtaining economic profits, firms will (enter, leave) _____ the industry, the price of the industry's product will (rise, fall) _____, the industry will employ (more, fewer) _____ resources, produce a (larger, smaller) _____ output, and the industry's economic profits will (increase, decrease) _____ until they are equal to _____

18. Consumers:

a. vote with their _____ for the production of a good or service when they buy that good or service;

b. are said, because firms are motivated by their desire for profits to produce the goods and services consumers vote for in this way, to be (dependent, sovereign) _____ ;

c. (restrict, expand) _____ the freedom of firms and resource suppliers.

19. Because firms are interested in obtaining the largest economic profits possible the technique they select to produce a product is the one that enables them to produce that product in the least _____ly way.

20. In determining how the total output of the economy will be divided among its households the market system is involved in two ways:

a. it determines the money _____ each of the households receives; and

b. it determines the _____ they have to pay for each of the goods and services produced.

21. In industrial economies:
a. the changes which occur almost continuously are changes in consumer _____ , in _____ , and in the supplies of _____ ;
b. to make the adjustments in the way it uses its resources that are appropriate to these changes a market economy allows price to perform its _____ function.

22. The competitive market system tends to foster technological change.
a. The incentive for a firm to be the first to employ a new and improved technique of production or to produce a new and better product is a greater economic _____ ;
b. and the incentive for other firms to follow its lead is the avoidance of _____

23. The entrepreneur uses money which is obtained either from _____ or from _____ to acquire capital goods.

24. If the market system is competitive, there is an identity of _____ interests and the _____ interest; firms seem to be

guided by an _____ to allocate the economy's resources efficiently.

25. The two economic arguments for a market system are that it promotes _____ use of resources and that it uses _____ to direct economic activity. One noneconomic argument for the market system is that it allows for personal _____

■ **TRUE-FALSE QUESTIONS**

Circle the T if the statement is true; the F if it is false.

1. The United States economy can correctly be called "pure capitalism." **T F**

2. There are in the United States legal limits to the right of private property. **T F**

3. The freedom of business firms to produce a particular consumer good is always limited by the desires of consumers for that good. **T F**

4. The pursuit of economic self-interest is the same thing as selfishness. **T F**

5. When a market is competitive the individual sellers of the commodity are unable to reduce the supply of the commodity enough to drive its price upward. **T F**

6. A gas station is an example of a market. **T F**

7. The employment of capital to produce goods and services requires that there be "roundabout production" but it is more efficient than "direct" production. **T F**

8. Increasing the amount of specialization in an economy generally leads to the more efficient use of its resources. **T F**

9. One way that human specialization can be achieved is through a division of labor in productive activity. **T F**

10. Money is a device for facilitating the exchange of goods and services. **T F**

11. "Coincidence of wants" means that two persons desire to acquire the same good or service. **T F**

12. Cigarettes may serve as money if sellers are generally willing to accept them as money. **T F**

13. One of the Five Fundamental Questions is who will control the output. **T F**

14. Business firms try to maximize their normal profits. **T F**

15. Industries in which economic profits are earned by the firms in the industry will attract the entry of new firms into the industry. **T F**

16. If firms have sufficient time to enter industries, the economic profits of an industry will tend to disappear.
T F

17. Business firms are really only free to produce whatever they want in any way they wish if they do not want to maximize profits or to minimize losses. **T F**

18. To say that the demand for a resource is a derived demand means that it depends upon the demands for the products the resource is used to produce. **T F**

19. Resources will tend to be used in those industries capable of earning normal or economic profits. **T F**

20. Economic efficiency requires that a given output of a good or service be produced in the least costly way.
T F

21. If the market price of resource A decreases, firms will tend to employ smaller quantities of resource A. **T F**

22. Changes in the tastes of consumers are reflected in changes in consumer demand for products. **T F**

23. The incentive which the market system provides to induce technological improvement is the opportunity for economic profits. **T F**

24. The tendency for individuals pursuing their own self-interests to bring about results which are in the best interest of society as a whole is often called the "invisible hand." **T F**

25. A basic economic argument for the market system is that it promotes an efficient allocation of resources.
T F

■ **MULTIPLE-CHOICE QUESTIONS**

Circle the letter that corresponds to the best answer.

1. Which of the following is one of the characteristics of capitalism?
(a) selfishness
(b) central economic planning
(c) private property
(d) limited choice

2. Maximization of profits appears to be in the self-interest of:
(a) business firms
(b) landowners
(c) workers
(d) consumers

3. Which of the following is a characteristic of competition as the economist sees it?
(a) the widespread diffusion of economic power
(b) a small number of buyers in product markets
(c) several sellers of all products

(d) the relatively difficult entry into and exit from industries by producers

4. To decide how to use its scarce resources to satisfy human wants pure capitalism relies on:
(a) central planning
(b) roundabout production
(c) a price system
(d) the coincidence of wants

5. In pure capitalism, the role of government is best described as:
(a) nonexistent
(b) limited
(c) significant
(d) extensive

6. In an economy in which there are full employment and full production, constant amounts of resources, and unchanging technology:
(a) increasing the production of capital goods requires an increase in the production of consumer goods
(b) decreasing the production of capital goods necessitates a decrease in the production of consumer goods
(c) increasing the production of capital goods is impossible
(d) increasing the production of capital goods requires a decrease in the production of consumer goods

7. When workers specialize in various tasks to produce a commodity, the situation is referred to as:
(a) double coincidence of wants
(b) roundabout production
(c) freedom of choice
(d) division of labor

8. Which of the following is *not* a necessary consequence of specialization?
(a) people will use money
(b) people will engage in trade
(c) people will be dependent upon each other
(d) people will produce more of some things than they would produce in the absence of specialization

9. The competitive market system is a method of:
(a) communicating and synchronizing the decisions of consumers, producers, and resource suppliers
(b) centrally planning economic decisions
(c) promoting productive efficiency, but not allocative efficiency
(d) promoting allocative efficiency, but not productive efficiency

10. Which of the following best defines economic costs?
(a) total payments made to workers, landowners, suppliers of capital, and entrepreneurs
(b) only total payments made to workers, landowners, suppliers of capital, and entrepreneurs which must be paid to obtain the services of their resources

(c) total payments made to workers, landowners, suppliers of capital, and entrepreneurs less normal profits
(d) total payments made to workers, landowners, suppliers of capital, and entrepreneurs plus normal profits

11. If less-than-normal profits are being earned by the firms in an industry, the consequences will be that:
(a) lower-priced resources will be drawn into the industry
(b) firms will leave the industry, causing the price of the industry's product to fall
(c) firms will leave the industry, causing the price of the industry's product to rise
(d) the price of the industry's product will fall and thereby cause the demand for the product to increase

12. Which of the following would necessarily result, sooner or later, from a decrease in consumer demand for a product?
(a) a decrease in the profits of firms in the industry
(b) an increase in the output of the industry
(c) an increase in the supply of the product
(d) an increase in the prices of resources employed by the firms in the industry

13. If firm A does not employ the most "efficient" or least costly method of production, which of the following will **not** be a consequence?
(a) firm A will fail to earn the greatest profit possible
(b) other firms in the industry will be able to sell the product at lower prices
(c) new firms will enter the industry and sell the product at a lower price than that at which firm A now sells it
(d) firm A will be spending less on resources and hiring fewer resources than it otherwise would

Answer the next two questions (14 and 15) on the basis of the following information.

Suppose 50 units of product X can be produced by employing just labor and capital in the four ways shown below. Assume the prices of labor and capital are $5 and $4, respectively.

	A	B	C	D
Labor	1	2	3	4
Capital	5	3	2	1

14. Which technique is economically most efficient in producing product X?
(a) A
(b) B
(c) C
(d) D

15. If the price of product X is $1.00, then the firm will realize:
(a) an economic profit of $28
(b) an economic profit of $27
(c) an economic profit of $26
(d) an economic profit of $25

16. Which of the following is **not** a factor in determining the share of the total output of the economy received by any household?
(a) the price at which the household sells its resources
(b) the quantities of resources which the household sells
(c) the tastes of the household
(d) the prices which the household must pay to buy products

17. If an increase in the demand for a product and the resulting rise in the price of the product cause the supply of the product, the size of the industry producing the product, and the amounts of resources devoted to its production to expand, price is successfully performing its:
(a) guiding function
(b) rationing function
(c) medium-of-exchange function
(d) standard-of-value function

18. In a capitalistic economy characterized by competition, if one firm introduces a new and better method of production, other firms will be forced to adopt the improved technique:
(a) to avoid less-than-normal profits
(b) to obtain economic profits
(c) to prevent the price of the product from falling
(d) to prevent the price of the product from rising

19. Which of the following would be an indication that competition does not exist in an industry?
(a) less-than-normal profits in the industry
(b) inability of the firms in the industry to expand
(c) inability of firms to enter the industry
(d) wages lower than the average wage in the economy paid to workers in the industry

20. The chief economic virtue of the competitive market system remains that of:
(a) allowing extensive personal freedom
(b) efficiently allocating resources
(c) providing an equitable distribution of income
(d) eliminating the need for decision-making

■ **PROBLEMS**

1. Assume that a firm can produce **either** product A, product B, or product C with the resources it currently employs. These resources cost the firm a total of $50 per week. Assume, for the purposes of the problem, that the firm's employment of resources cannot be changed. The market prices of and the quantities of A, B, and C these resources will produce per week are given below. Compute the firm's profit when it produces A, B, or C; and enter these profits in the table below.

Product	Market price	Output	Economic profit
A	$7.00	8	$_____
B	4.50	10	_____
C	.25	240	_____

   a. Which product will the firm produce? _____

   b. If the price of A rose to $8, the firm would _____

_____

(Hint: You will have to recompute the firm's profit from the production of A.)

   c. If the firm were producing A and selling it at a price of $8, what would tend to happen to the number of firms producing A?

_____

2. Suppose that a firm can produce 100 units of product X by combining labor, land, capital, and entrepreneurial ability in three different ways. If it can hire labor at $2 per unit, land at $3 per unit, capital at $5 per unit, and entrepreneurship at $10 per unit; and if the amounts of the resources required by the three methods of producing 100 units of product X are indicated in the table, answer the questions below it.

Resource	Method 1	Method 2	Method 3
Labor	8	13	10
Land	4	3	3
Capital	4	2	4
Entrepreneurship	1	1	1

   a. Which method is the least expensive way of producing 100 units of X?_____

   b. If X sells for 70 cents per unit, what is the economic profit of the firm? $_____

   c. If the price of labor should rise from $2 to $3 per unit and if the price of X is 70 cents,

   (1) the firm's use of:

Labor would change from _____ to _____

Land would change from _____ to _____

Capital would change from _____ to _____
Entrepreneurship would not change.

   (2) The firm's economic profit would change from

$_____ to $_____

■ SHORT ANSWER AND ESSAY QUESTIONS

  1. Explain the several elements—institutions and assumptions—embodied in pure capitalism.

  2. What do each of the following seek if they pursue their own self-interest? Consumers, resource owners, and business firms.

  3. Explain what economists mean by competition. Why is it important to have competition in an economy whose members are motivated by self-interest?

  4. What are the advantages of "indirect" or "roundabout" production?

  5. How does an economy benefit from specialization and the division of labor?

  6. What disadvantages are there to specialization and the division of labor?

  7. What is money? What important function does it perform? Explain how money performs this function and how it overcomes the disadvantages associated with barter.

  8. Why are people willing to accept paper money in exchange for the goods and services which they sell?

  9. What are the Five Fundamental Questions?

  10. In what way do the desires of entrepreneurs to obtain economic profits and to avoid losses make consumer sovereignty effective?

  11. Why is the ability of firms to enter industries which are prosperous important to the effective functioning of competition?

  12. Explain *in detail* how an increase in the consumer demand for a product will result in more of the product being produced and in more resources being allocated to its production.

  13. To what extent are firms "free" to produce what they wish by methods which they choose? Do resource owners have freedom to use their resources as they wish?

  14. What are the two important functions of prices? Explain the difference between these two functions.

  15. Households use the dollars obtained by selling resource services to "vote" for the production of consumer goods and services. Who "votes" for the production of capital goods, why do they "vote" for capital-goods production, and where do they obtain the dollars needed to cast these "votes"?

16. What is meant when it is said that competition is the mechanism which "controls" the market system? How does competition do this?

17. "An invisible hand operates to identify private and public interests." What are private interests and what is the public interest?

18. What is it that leads the economy to operate as if it were directed by an invisible hand?

19. If the basic economic decisions are not made in a capitalistic economy by a central authority, how are they made?

20. Describe three virtues of the market system.

ANSWERS

Chapter 4 Pure Capitalism and the Market System

FILL-IN QUESTIONS

1. private property

2. enterprise, choice

3. do what is best for itself, competition

4. *a.* large numbers of independently acting buyers and sellers operating in the markets; *b.* freedom of buyers and sellers to enter or leave these markets

5. control (rig, effect)

6. markets, price

7. a limited

8. efficient

9. inefficient

10. medium of exchange

11. coincidence of wants

12. *a.* at what level to utilize resources in the productive process; *b.* what collection of goods and services best satisfies its wants; *c.* how to produce this total output; *d.* how to divide this output among the various economic units of the economy; *e.* how to make the responses required to remain efficient over time

13. communicating, synchronizing (coordinating)

14. is, must, entrepreneurs, is not, need not

15. revenues, costs

16. *a.* normal; *b.* pure (economic)

17. enter, fall, more, larger, decrease, zero

18. *a.* dollars; *b.* sovereign; *c.* restrict

19. cost

20. *a.* income; *b.* prices

21. *a.* preferences (tastes), technology, resources; *b.* guiding

22. *a.* profit; *b.* losses (bankruptcy)

23. profits, borrowed funds

24. private, public (social), invisible hand

25. efficient, incentives, freedom

TRUE-FALSE QUESTIONS

1. F, p. 58	**8.** T, p. 62	**15.** T, p. 65	**22.** T, p. 68
2. T, pp. 58-59	**9.** T, p. 62	**16.** T, p. 65	**23.** T, p. 69
3. T, p. 59	**10.** T, pp. 62-63	**17.** T, p. 66	**24.** T, pp. 69-70
4. F, p. 59	**11.** F, pp. 62-63	**18.** T, p. 66	**25.** T, p. 70
5. T, pp. 59-60	**12.** T, p. 63	**19.** T, pp. 66-67	
6. T, p. 60	**13.** F, p. 64	**20.** T, p. 67	
7. T, p. 61	**14.** F, p. 65	**21.** F, p. 67	

MULTIPLE-CHOICE QUESTIONS

1. *c*, pp. 58-59	**6.** *d*, p. 61	**11.** *c*, pp. 65-66	**16.** *c*, pp. 67-68
2. *a*, p. 59	**7.** *d*, p. 62	**12.** *d*, pp. 65-66	**17.** *a*, p. 68
3. *a*, pp. 59-60	**8.** *a*, p. 62	**13.** *d*, p. 67	**18.** *a*, p. 69
4. *c*, pp. 59-60	**9.** *a*, p. 64	**14.** *b*, p. 67	**19.** *c*, pp. 69-70
5. *b*, p. 61	**10.** *b*, p. 65	**15.** *a*, pp. 65, 67	**20.** *b*, p. 70

PROBLEMS

1. $6, − $5, $10; *a.* C; *b.* produce A and have an economic profit of $14; *c.* it would increase

2. *a.* method 2; *b.* 15; *c.* (1) 13, 8; 3, 4; 2, 4; (2) 15, 4

SHORT ANSWER AND ESSAY QUESTIONS

1. p. 58	**6.** pp. 62-64	**11.** pp. 65-66	**16.** pp. 69-70
2. p. 59	**7.** pp. 62-64	**12.** pp. 65-66	**17.** pp. 69-70
3. pp. 59-60	**8.** pp. 62-64	**13.** pp. 66-67	**18.** pp. 69-70
4. p. 61	**9.** p. 64	**14.** pp. 68-69	**19.** pp. 69-70
5. p. 61	**10.** pp. 65-66	**15.** p. 69	**20.** p. 70

CHAPTER 5

The Mixed Economy: Private and Public Sectors

In the American economy, there are private sectors and a public sector. The first part of Chapter 5 discusses the private sectors: the 96 million households, the roughly 20 million business firms in the country, and our trade with other nations in the foreign sector. The second part of Chapter 5 deals with the public sector of the economy: the Federal, state, and local governments found in the United States. These two parts will acquaint you with a few of the facts relevant to an understanding of our economy.

Chapter 5 begins with an examination of the households of the economy, the distribution of income in the United States, and the uses to which the households put their incomes. Two different distributions of income are examined. American households earn five kinds of income and receive transfer payments. The way in which the total personal income received by all American households is divided among the five types of earned income and transfer payments is called the *functional distribution.* The way in which the total personal income received by all households is distributed among the various income classes is called the *personal* distribution of income. Attention should be concentrated on the *general* facts of income distribution (not the exact figures), the conclusions which are drawn from these general facts, and the definitions of the new terms employed. In the examination of the different uses households make of their incomes, several new terms and concepts are introduced; and figures are employed in the discussion. Again, attention should be paid to the generalizations and to the new terms.

Business firms of the United States are the next focus of the chapter. It is apparent that what most characterizes American business is the differences among firms insofar as their size and legal form are concerned, as well as in the products they produce. You should note the distinctions between a proprietorship, a partnership, and a corporation and the advantages and disadvantages of each. Also, big business is an important characteristic of the American economy because corporations account for the major source of production in the economy. This "bigness" may restrict competition in the economy and require government intervention as discussed later in the chapter.

Chapter 5 introduces you to the five basic functions performed by the Federal, state, and local governments in America's mixed capitalistic economy. This is an examination of the role of government (the public sector) in an economy which is neither a purely planned nor a purely market-type economy. The discussion points out the degree and the ways in which government causes the American economy to differ from pure capitalism. The chapter does not attempt to list all the *specific* ways in which government affects the behavior of the economy. Instead it provides a *general* classification of the tasks performed by government.

This part of the chapter begins by discussing the two major functions of government. First, the legal and social framework for the operation of the market system is provided by government. Second, government actions can be taken to maintain competition in the economy. In addition, the chapter explains how government influences the market system in three other ways: by redistributing wealth and income; altering domestic output; and stabilizing the economy.

The chapter also returns to the circular flow model that was first presented in Chapter 2. The model has now been modified to include government along with businesses and households. The addition of government changes the real and monetary flows in the model. The twelve linkages among the household, business, and government sectors in the model are described in detail.

The facts of public-sector or government finance in the United States presented in the final sections of Chapter 5 center on two questions: Where do governments get their incomes? On what do they spend these incomes?

The organization of the government finance discussion is relatively simple. First, the trends for taxes collected and expenditures made by all levels of government—Federal, state, and local—are examined briefly. Second, a closer look is taken at the major items upon which the Federal government spends its income, the principal taxes it levies to obtain its income, and the relative importance of these taxes. Third, the chapter looks at the major expenditures of and the major taxes of the state and the local governments, and at fiscal federalism.

■ CHECKLIST

When you have studied this chapter you should be able to:

☐ Define and distinguish between a functional and a personal distribution of income.

☐ State the relative size of the five sources of personal income in the functional distribution.

☐ List the three uses to which households put their personal incomes and state the relative size of each.

☐ Distinguish among durable goods, nondurable goods, and services.

☐ Explain the differences among a plant, a firm, and an industry; and between limited and unlimited liability.

☐ State the advantages and disadvantages of the three legal forms of business enterprise.

☐ Report the relative importance of each of the legal forms of business enterprise in the American economy.

☐ Cite evidence to indicate that large corporations dominate the economy.

☐ Explain in one or two sentences why the American economy is *mixed* rather than *pure* capitalism.

☐ Enumerate the five economic functions of government in the United States and explain the difference between the purpose of the first two and the purpose of the last three functions.

☐ Define monopoly and explain why government wishes to prevent monopoly and to preserve competition in the economy.

☐ Explain why government feels it should redistribute income and list the three principal policies it employs for this purpose.

☐ Define a spillover cost and a spillover benefit; explain why a competitive market fails to allocate resources efficiently when there are spillovers; and list the things government may do to reduce spillovers and improve the allocation of resources.

☐ Define a public good and a private good and explain how government goes about reallocating resources from the production of private to the production of public goods.

☐ Draw a circular flow diagram that includes businesses, households, and government; label all the flows in the diagram; and use the diagram to explain how government alters the distribution of income, the allocation of resources, and the level of activity in the economy.

☐ List the five causes of the historical expansion and the present size of government tax revenues and expenditures.

☐ Explain the differences between government purchases and transfer payments and the effect of each of these two kinds of expenditures on the composition of the national output.

☐ Describe the three largest categories of expenditures and the two greatest sources of revenue of the Federal government.

☐ Define and explain the difference between the marginal and the average tax rate.

☐ Describe the progressivity of the Federal personal income tax.

☐ List the two largest sources of tax revenue and the four largest types of expenditures of state governments; also list the largest single source of tax revenue and the largest category of expenditures of local governments.

■ CHAPTER OUTLINE

1. Households play a dual role in the economy. They supply the economy with resources, and they purchase the greatest share of the goods and services produced by the economy. They obtain their personal incomes in exchange for the resources they furnish the economy and from the transfer payments they receive from government.

   a. The functional distribution of income indicates the way in which total personal income is divided among the five sources of earned income (wages and salaries, proprietors' income, corporate profits, interest, and rents) and transfer payments.

   b. The personal distribution of income indicates the way in which total personal income is divided among households in different income classes.

2. Households use their incomes to purchase consumer goods, to pay taxes, and to accumulate savings.

   a. Personal taxes constitute a deduction from a household's personal income; what remains after taxes can be either saved or spent.

   b. Saving is what a household does not spend of its after-tax income.

   c. Households spend for durable goods, nondurable goods, and services.

3. The business population of the American economy consists of many imperfectly defined and overlapping industries; business firms which operate one or more plants and produce one or more products are the components of these industries.

4. The three principal legal forms of organization of firms are the proprietorship, the partnership, and the corporation; each form has special characteristics, advantages, and disadvantages. The form of organization which any business firm should adopt depends primarily upon the amount of money capital it will require to carry on its business. Although the proprietorship is numerically dominant in the United States, the corporation accounts for the major portion of the economy's output.

5. Large corporations are a characteristic of the American economy and dominate many of its industries.

6. The American economy is neither a pure market economy nor a purely planned economy. It is an example of mixed capitalism in which government affects the operation of the economy in important ways.

7. Government in the American economy performs five economic functions. The first two of these functions are designed to enable the market system to operate more effectively; and the other three functions are designed to eliminate the major shortcomings of a purely market-type economy.

8. The first of these functions is to provide the legal and social framework that makes the effective operation of the market system possible.

9. The second function is the maintenance of competition and the regulation of monopoly.

10. Government performs its third function when it redistributes income to reduce income inequality.

11. When government reallocates resources it performs its fourth function:
  a. It reallocates resources to take account of spillover costs and benefits.
  b. It also reallocates resources to provide society with public (social) goods and services.
  c. It levies taxes and uses the tax revenues to purchase or produce the public goods.

12. Its fifth function is stabilization of the price level and the maintenance of full employment.

13. A circular flow diagram that includes the public sector as well as business firms and households in the private sector of the economy reveals that government purchases public goods from private businesses, collects taxes from and makes transfer payments to these firms, purchases labor services from households, and collects taxes from and makes transfer payments to these households; and government can alter the distribution of income, reallocate resources, and change the level of economic activity by affecting the real and monetary flows in the diagram.

14. Government's functions in the economy are felt most directly when it collects revenue by taxation and expends this revenue for goods and services; but there is an important difference between the voluntary transactions in the private and the compulsory transactions in the public sector of the economy.

15. In both absolute and relative terms, government tax collections and spending have increased during the past sixty or so years.
  a. The increased tax collections and spending are the result of hot and cold wars, population increases, urbanization and the greater demand for social goods, pollution of the environment, egalitarianism, and inflation.
  b. Government spending consists of purchases of goods and services and of transfer payments; but these two types of spending have different effects on domestic output.

16. At the Federal level of government about:
  a. 36% of the total expenditure is for income security, about 21% is for national defense, and some 14% is for interest on the national debt; and
  b. the major sources of revenue are personal income, payroll, and corporate income taxes.

17. At the other two levels of government:
  a. state governments depend largely on sales and excise taxes and personal income taxes, and use a large part of their revenues for education and public welfare;
  b. local governments rely heavily upon property taxes and spend the greatest part of their revenues for education.
  c. tax revenues are less than expenditures and the Federal government shares some of its revenues with these governments by making grants to them.

■ IMPORTANT TERMS

Private sectors
Functional distribution of income
Personal distribution of income
Personal consumption expenditures
Durable good
Nondurable good
Services
Personal taxes
Personal saving
Plant
Firm
Industry
Horizontal combination
Vertical combination
Conglomerate combination
Sole proprietorship
Partnership
Corporation
Unlimited liability
Limited liability
Double taxation
Separation of ownership and control

Mixed capitalism
Monopoly
Spillover (externality)
Spillover cost
Spillover benefit
Subsidy
Public (social) good
Private good
Exclusion principle
Quasi-public good
Free-rider problem
Government purchase
Government transfer payment
Personal income tax
Marginal tax rate
Average tax rate
Progressive tax
Payroll tax
Corporate income tax
Sales tax
Excise tax
Property tax
Fiscal federalism

■ HINTS AND TIPS

1. This chapter is a long one, so don't try to learn everything at once. Break the chapter into its three natural parts and work on each one separately. The first part describes features of the private sector. The second part explains the functions of government. The third part looks at government finance.

2. There are many descriptive statistics about the private and public sectors. Avoid memorizing these statistics. Instead, you should look for the trends and generalizations which these statistics illustrate about the private or public sector. For example, the discussion of government finance describes recent trends in government expenditures and taxes, and indicates the relative importance of taxes and expenditures at each level of government.

SELF-TEST

■ FILL-IN QUESTIONS

1. The approximately _____ million households in the United States play a dual role in the economy because they _____ and _____

_____

2. The largest single source of income in the United States is _____ and is equal to about _____% of total income.

3. In the United States the poorest 20% of all American families receive about _____% of total personal income and the richest 20% of these families receive about _____% of total personal income.

4. The total income of households is disposed of in three ways: _____, _____, and _____

5. Households use about _____% of their total income to pay personal taxes; and the greatest part of their personal taxes are the personal _____ taxes which they pay to the (Federal, state, local) _____ government.

6. Households save primarily in order to obtain _____ and for purposes of _____

7. Based on their durability, consumer spending is classified as spending for _____ , and _____

8. There are today about _____ business firms in the United States. The legal form of the great ma-

jority of these firms is the _____; but the legal form that produces 90 percent of the sales of the American economy is the _____

9. The liabilities of a sole proprietor and of partners are _____ but the liabilities of stockholders in a corporation are _____

10. All actual economies are "mixed" because they combine elements of a _____ economy and a role for _____

11. List the five economic functions of government.

a. _____

b. _____

c. _____

d. _____

e. _____

12. To control monopoly, United States government has:

a. created commissions to _____ the prices and the services of the _____ monopolies; and taken over at the local level the _____ of electric and water companies;

b. enacted _____ laws to maintain competition.

13. The market system, because it is an impersonal mechanism, results in an (equal, unequal) _____ distribution of income. To redistribute income from the upper- to the lower-income groups the government has:

a. provided _____ payments;

b. engaged in _____ intervention;

c. used the _____ tax to raise much of its revenues.

14. Government frequently reallocates resources when it finds instances of _____ failure; and the two major cases of such failure occur when the competitive market system either

a. _____

_____

b. or _____

_____

15. Competitive markets bring about an optimum allocation of resources only if there are no _____ costs or benefits in the consumption and production of the good or service.

16. There is a spillover whenever some of the costs of producing a product or some of the benefits from consuming it accrue to _____

17. What two things can government do to:
   a. Make the market reflect spillover costs?

   (1) _____

   (2) _____
   b. Make the market reflect spillover benefits?

   (1) _____

   (2) _____

18. Public (social) goods tend to be goods which are not subject to the _____ principle and which are (divisible, indivisible) _____. Quasi-public goods are goods which could be subjected to the exclusion principle but which are provided by government because they have large spillover _____

19. To reallocate resources from the production of private to the production of public goods government reduces the demand for private goods by _____ consumers and firms and then _____ _____ public goods.

20. To stabilize the economy, government:
   a. when there is less than full employment (increases, decreases) _____ aggregate demand by (increasing, decreasing) _____ its expenditures for public goods and services and by (increasing, decreasing) _____ taxes.
   b. where there are inflationary pressures _____ _____ aggregate demand by _____ its expenditures for public goods and services and by _____ taxes.

21. Throughout most of its history government in the United States has performed in some degree each of the five functions except that of _____ _____

22. The functions of government are most directly felt by the economy through the _____ it makes and the _____ it collects.

23. An examination of the public sector of the American economy reveals that:
   a. between 1929 and 1994 government **purchases** of goods and services as a percentage of domestic output have tended to (increase, decrease, remain constant) _____ and since the early 1950s have been about (10, 20, 30)_____% of the domestic output;
   b. but government **transfer payments** as a percentage of domestic output during the past 30 or so years have (increased, decreased, remained constant) _____;
   c. and the tax revenues required to finance both government expenditures and transfer payments are today about (11, 22, 33) _____% of domestic output.

24. Government transfer payments are defined as _____ _____ and are (exhaustive, nonexhaustive) _____

25. When government raises $20 billion by taxation and uses it to purchase goods it shifts resources from the production of (private, public) _____ goods to the production of _____ goods; but these expenditures are (exhaustive, nonexhaustive) _____ because they absorb resources and are part of current production.

26. The most important source of revenue for the Federal government is the _____ tax; next in importance are the _____ taxes. The three largest categories of Federal expenditures are for _____, for _____, and for interest on the _____

27. The Federal government uses the personal income tax to obtain most of the _____ it requires to finance its expenditures. In fact, the personal income tax accounts for _____% of Federal tax revenues. The Federal government also receives _____% from payroll taxes and _____% from corporate income taxes.

28. The state governments rely primarily upon _____ _____ and_____ taxes for their incomes which they spend mostly on _____ and _____

29. At local levels of government the single most important source of revenue is the _____ tax and the single most important expenditure is for _____

30. The amount by which the expenditures of state and local governments exceed their tax revenues is largely filled by grants from the _____ government; these grants account for _____% to _____% of all revenue received by state and local governments.

■ **TRUE-FALSE QUESTIONS**

Circle the T if the statement is true; the F if it is false.

1. The personal distribution of income describes the manner in which society's total personal income is divided among wages and salaries, corporate profits, proprietors' income, interest, and rents.   **T F**

2. Limited liability refers to the fact that all members of a partnership are liable for the debts incurred by one another.   **T F**

3. In both relative and absolute terms, personal taxes have exceeded personal saving in recent years.   **T F**

4. Most of the personal saving in the American economy is done by those households in the top 10% of its income receivers.   **T F**

5. *Dissaving* means that personal consumption expenditures exceed after-tax income.   **T F**

6. A "durable good" is defined as a good which has an expected life of one year or more.   **T F**

7. A plant is defined as a group of firms under a single management.   **T F**

8. An industry is a group of firms that produce the same or nearly the same products.   **T F**

9. The corporate form of organization is the least used by firms in the United States.   **T F**

10. The corporation in the United States today always has a tax advantage over other legal forms of business organization.   **T F**

11. Whether a business firm should incorporate or not depends chiefly upon the amount of money capital it must have to finance the enterprise.   **T F**

12. Corporations produce over one-half the total output produced by privately owned business firms in the United States.   **T F**

13. The American economy cannot be called "capitalistic" because its operation involves some "planning by government."   **T F**

14. When the Federal government provides for a monetary system, it is functioning to provide the economy with public goods and services.   **T F**

15. An economy in which strong and effective competition is maintained will find no need for programs designed to redistribute income.   **T F**

16. Competitive product markets ensure an optimal allocation of an economy's resources.   **T F**

17. In a competitive product market and in the absence of spillover costs, the supply curve or schedule reflects the costs of producing the product.   **T F**

18. If demand and supply reflected all the benefits and costs of a product, the equilibrium output of a competitive market would be identical with its optimal output.   **T F**

19. The inclusion of the spillover benefits would increase the demand for a product.   **T F**

20. When there are spillover costs involved in the production of a product, more resources are allocated to the production of that product and more of the product is produced than is optimal or most efficient.   **T F**

21. Governments have undertaken to provide lighthouse services because these services have social benefits and private producers of such services encounter the free-rider problem.   **T F**

22. In performing its stabilization function when there is widespread unemployment and no inflation in the economy, government should decrease its spending for public goods and services and increase taxes.   **T F**

23. Net taxes for businesses are taxes paid by business less a depreciation allowance.   **T F**

24. Flood control projects are usually undertaken by government because of the free-rider problem.   **T F**

25. When the Federal government takes actions to control unemployment or inflation it is performing the allocative function of government.   **T F**

26. Government purchases of goods and services are called *nonexhaustive* and government transfer payments are called *exhaustive* expenditures.   **T F**

27. When a government levies taxes and uses the tax revenue to make transfer payments it shifts resources from the production of private goods to the production of public goods.   **T F**

28. The chief source of revenue for the Federal government is the corporate income tax.   **T F**

29. If the marginal tax rate is higher than the average tax rate, the average tax rate will fall.   **T F**

30. Property taxes are the largest percentage of the total budget of local governments.   **T F**

■ **MULTIPLE-CHOICE QUESTIONS**

Circle the letter that corresponds to the best answer.

1. The functional distribution for the United States shows that the largest part of the personal income is:
   (a) wages and salaries
   (b) proprietors' income
   (c) corporate profits
   (d) interest and rents

2. The part of after-tax income which is not consumed is defined as:
   (a) saving
   (b) capital investment
   (c) wages and salaries
   (d) nondurable goods expenditure

3. If in an economy personal consumption expenditures were 80% of income and personal taxes were 8% of income, then personal savings would be:
   (a) 8% of income
   (b) 10% of income
   (c) 12% of income
   (d) 88% of income

4. Which of the following is a true statement?
   (a) the durable goods and service parts of personal consumption expenditures vary more over time than do the expenditures for nondurables
   (b) expenditures for nondurables vary more than do the expenditures for durable goods and services
   (c) expenditures for nondurables vary more than the expenditures for services and less than the expenditures for durables
   (d) expenditures for nondurables vary more than the expenditures for durables and less than the expenditures for services

5. A group of three plants which is owned and operated by a single firm and which consists of a farm growing wheat, a flour milling plant, and a plant which bakes and sells bakery products is an example of:
   (a) a horizontal combination
   (b) a vertical combination
   (c) a conglomerate combination
   (d) a corporation

6. Limited liability is associated with:
   (a) only proprietorships
   (b) only partnerships
   (c) both proprietorships and partnerships
   (d) only corporations

7. Which of the following forms of business organization can most effectively raise money capital?
   (a) corporation
   (b) partnership
   (c) proprietorship
   (d) vertical combination

8. Which of the following is *not* one of the methods utilized by government to control monopoly?
   (a) the imposition of special taxes on monopolists
   (b) government ownership of monopolies
   (c) government regulation of monopolies
   (d) antitrust laws

9. One of the following is *not* employed by government to redistribute income. Which one?
   (a) the negative income tax
   (b) direct market intervention
   (c) income taxes which take a larger part of the incomes of the rich than the poor
   (d) public assistance programs

10. Which of the following is the best example of a good or service providing the economy with spillover benefits?
   (a) an automobile
   (b) a drill press
   (c) a high school education
   (d) an operation for appendicitis

11. In the American economy the reallocation of resources needed to provide for the production of public goods is:
   (a) government subsidies to the producers of social goods
   (b) government purchases of social goods from producers
   (c) direct control of producers of both private and social goods
   (d) direct control of producers of social goods only

12. Which of the following is characteristic of public goods?
   (a) they are indivisible
   (b) they are sold in competitive markets
   (c) they are subject to the exclusion principle
   (d) they can be produced only if large spillover costs are incurred

13. Quasi-public goods are goods and services:
   (a) to which the exclusion principle could not be applied
   (b) which have large spillover benefits
   (c) which would not be produced by private producers through the market system
   (d) which are indivisible

14. To redistribute income from high-income to low-income households government might:
   (a) increase transfer payments to high-income and decrease transfer payments to low-income households
   (b) increase the taxes paid by high-income and increase the transfer payments to low-income households
   (c) increase the taxes paid by low-income and decrease the taxes paid by high-income households
   (d) decrease the taxes paid by high-income and decrease the transfer payments to low-income households

15. Which of the following is the best example of a good or service providing the economy with a spillover cost?
(a) a textbook
(b) an automobile
(c) a business suit
(d) an audit of a business firm's books

16. There is a "free-rider" problem when people:
(a) are willing to pay for what they want
(b) are not willing to pay for what they want
(c) benefit from a good without paying for its cost
(d) want to buy more than is available for purchase in the market

17. In the circular flow model, net taxes are:
(a) taxes minus depreciation
(b) taxes minus transfer payments
(c) subsidies minus transfer payments
(d) business receipts minus household expenditures

18. In the circular flow model, government provides goods and services and receives net taxes from:
(a) colleges and universities
(b) businesses and households
(c) resource and product markets
(d) foreign nations and corporations

19. Which of the following accounts for the largest percentage of all Federal expenditures?
(a) income security
(b) national defense
(c) interest on the public debt
(d) veterans' services

20. Which of the following is the largest source of the tax revenues of the Federal government?
(a) sales and excise taxes
(b) property taxes
(c) payroll taxes
(d) personal income taxes

21. A tax that would most likely alter consumer expenditures on a product would be:
(a) an excise tax
(b) a general sales tax
(c) a personal income tax
(d) a corporate income tax

22. Which of the following pairs represents the chief source of income and the most important type of expenditure of state governments?
(a) personal income tax and expenditures for education
(b) personal income tax and expenditures for highways
(c) sales and excise taxes and expenditures for highways
(d) sales and excise taxes and expenditures for public welfare

23. Which of the following pairs represents the chief source of income and the most important type of expenditure of *local* governments?
(a) property tax and expenditures for highways
(b) property tax and expenditures for education
(c) sales and excise taxes and expenditures for public welfare
(d) sales and excise taxes and expenditures for police, fire, and general government

*The next two questions (**24** and **25**) are based on the portion of the tax table given below:*

Taxable income	Total tax
$ 0	$ 0
30,000	5,000
70,000	15,000
150,000	42,000

24. The marginal tax rate at the $70,000 level of taxable income is:
(a) 16.6
(b) 21.4
(c) 25.0
(d) 28.0

25. The average tax rate at the $150,000 level of taxable income is:
(a) 21.4
(b) 28.0
(c) 31.5
(d) 33.8

■ **PROBLEMS**

1. The table below shows the functional distribution of total income in the United States in 1990.

	Billions of dollars
Wages and salaries	$2,905
Proprietors' income	325
Corporate profits	324
Interest	392
Rents	19
Total earnings	3,964

Of the total earnings about _____% were wages and salaries, and about _____% were corporate profits.

2. Indicate in the spaces to the right of each of the following whether these business characteristics are associated with the proprietorship (PRO), partnership (PART), corporation (CORP), two of these, or all three of these legal forms.

a. Much red tape and legal expense in beginning the

firm _____

b. Unlimited liability _____

c. No specialized management _____

d. Has a life independent of its owner(s) _____

e. Double taxation of income _____
f. Greatest ability to acquire funds for the expansion

of the firm _____
g. Permits some but not a great degree of specialized

management _____
h. Possibility of an unresolved disagreement among

owners over courses of action _____
i. The potential for the separation of ownership and

control of the business _____

3. Below is a list of various government activities. Indicate in the space to the right of each into which of the five classes of government functions the activity falls. If it falls under more than one of the functions, indicate this.

a. Maintaining an army _____
b. Providing for a system of unemployment compen-

sation _____

c. Establishment of the Federal Reserve Banks _____

_____
d. Insuring employees of business firms against in-

dustrial accidents _____
e. Establishment of an Antitrust Division in the De-

partment of Justice _____
f. Making it a crime to sell stocks and bonds under

false pretenses _____

g. Providing low-cost lunches to school children _____

_____

h. Taxation of whisky and other spirits _____

_____
i. Regulation of organized stock, bond, and commod-

ity markets _____
j. Setting tax *rates* higher for larger incomes than for

smaller ones _____

4. The circular flow diagram above includes business firms, households, and government (the public sector). Also shown are the product and resource markets.

a. Supply a label or an explanation for each of the twelve flows in the model:

(1) _____

(2) _____

(3) _____

(4) _____

(5) _____

(6) _____

(7) _____

(8) _____

(9) _____

(10) _____

(11) _____

(12) _____
b. If government wished to
(1) expand output and employment in the economy it

would increase expenditure flows _____ or

_____, decrease net tax flows

_____ or _____, or do both;
(2) increase the production of public (social) goods and decrease the production of private goods in the

economy it would increase flows _____

and _____ or _____;
(3) redistribute income from high-income to low-income households it would (increase, decrease)

_____ the net taxes (taxes minus transfers)

paid by the former and _____ the net taxes

paid by the latter in flow _____

5. In the table on the next page are several levels of taxable income and hypothetical marginal tax rates for each $1000 increase in income.

Taxable income	Marginal tax rate, %	Tax	Average tax rate, %
$1500		$300	20
2500	22	520	20.8
3500	25	____	____
4500	29	____	____
5500	34	____	____
6500	40	____	____

a. At the four income levels compute the tax and the average tax rate.

b. As the marginal tax rate:

(1) increases the average tax rate (increases, decreases, remains constant) _____

_____

(2) decreases the average tax rate _____

c. This tax is _____ because the average tax rate increases as income _____

■ **SHORT ANSWER AND ESSAY QUESTIONS**

1. Explain the difference between a functional and a personal distribution of income. Rank the five types of earned income in the order of their size.

2. Which would result in greater total saving and less consumption spending out of a national income of a given size: a more or less nearly equal distribution of income?

3. The purchase of what type of consumer goods is largely postponable? Why is this? How is it possible for a family's personal consumption expenditures to exceed its after-tax income?

4. What is the difference between a plant and a firm? Between a firm and an industry? Which of these three concepts is the most difficult to apply in practice? Why? Distinguish between a horizontal, a vertical, and a conglomerate combination.

5. What are the principal advantages and disadvantages of each type of the three legal forms of business organization? Which of the disadvantages of the proprietorship and partnership accounts for the employment of the corporate form among the big businesses of the American economy?

6. Explain what "separation of ownership and control" of the modern corporation means. What problems does this separation create for stockholders and the economy?

7. Is the American economy and manufacturing in the United States dominated by big business? What evidence do you use to reach this conclusion?

8. Why is it proper to refer to the United States economy as "mixed capitalism"?

9. What are the five economic functions of government in America's mixed capitalistic economy? Explain what the performance of each of these functions requires government to do.

10. Would you like to live in an economy in which government undertook only the first two functions listed in the text? What would be the advantages and disadvantages of living in such an economy?

11. Why does the market system provide some people with lower income than it provides others?

12. What is "market failure" and what are the two major kinds of such failures?

13. What is meant by a spillover in general and by spillover cost and spillover benefit in particular? How does the existence of such costs and benefits affect the allocation of resources and the prices of products? If a market could be required to take these costs and benefits into account, how would the allocation of resources and the price of the product bought and sold in that market be changed?

14. What methods does government employ to:

(a) redistribute income;

(b) reallocate resources to take account of spillover costs;

(c) reallocate resources to take account of spillover benefits?

15. Distinguish between a private and a public good. Include in your answer an explanation of the "exclusion principle" and the distinction between divisible and indivisible goods.

16. What basic method does government employ in the United States to reallocate resources away from the production of private goods and toward the production of social goods?

17. In a circular flow diagram that includes not only business firms and households but also government (or the public sector), what are the four flows of money into or out of the government sector of the economy? Using this diagram, explain how government redistributes income, reallocates resources from the private to the public sector, and stabilizes the economy.

18. What is the present size of government spending and taxation in the American economy?

19. Government expenditures fall into two broad classes: expenditures for goods and services, and transfer payments. Explain the difference between these and give examples of expenditures which fall into each of the two classes.

20. Explain the difference between exhaustive and nonexhaustive government spending.

21. When government collects taxes and spends the tax revenues it affects the composition of the total output of the economy. What is the effect on total output if government uses the tax revenues to purchase goods and services? What is the effect if it uses them to make transfer payments?

22. Explain precisely the difference between the marginal tax rate and the average tax rate.

23. Explain how the Federal personal income tax enables the Federal government to perform three (of the five) economic functions.

24. Explain in detail the differences that exist among Federal, state, and local governments in the taxes upon which they primarily rely for their revenues and the major purposes for which they use these revenues.

25. Why does the Federal government share its tax revenues with state and local governments? How has this fiscal federalism changed in recent years?

ANSWERS

Chapter 5 The Mixed Economy: Private and Public Sectors

FILL-IN QUESTIONS

1. 96, furnish resources, buy the bulk of the total output of the economy

2. wages and salaries, 75

3. 4, 47

4. personal consumption, personal saving, personal taxes

5. 13, income, federal

6. security, speculation

7. services, nondurable goods, durable goods (any order)

8. 20 million, sole proprietorship, corporation

9. unlimited, limited

10. market, government

11. *a.* provide legal foundation and social environment; *b.* maintain competition; *c.* redistribute income and wealth; *d.* reallocate resources; *e.* stabilize the economy

12. *a.* regulate, natural, ownership; *b.* antitrust (antimonopoly)

13. unequal; *a.* transfer; *b.* market; *c.* income

14. market; *a.* produces the "wrong" amounts of certain goods and services; *b.* fails to allocate any resources to the production of certain goods and services whose production is economically justified

15. spillover

16. people other than the buyers and sellers (third parties)

17. *a.* (1) enact legislation, (2) pass special taxes; *b.* (1) subsidize production, (2) finance or take over the production of the product

18. exclusion, indivisible, benefits

19. taxing, spends the revenue to buy

20. *a.* increases, increasing, decreasing; *b.* decreases, decreasing, increasing

21. stabilizing the economy

22. expenditures, taxes

23. *a.* increase, 20; *b.* increased; *c.* 33

24. expenditures for which government currently receives no good or service in return, nonexhaustive

25. private, public, exhaustive

26. personal income, payroll, income security, national defense, public debt

27. revenue, 44, 37, 10

28. sales and excise, personal income, public welfare, education

29. property, education

30. Federal, 15, 20

TRUE-FALSE QUESTIONS

1. F, p. 75	9. F, p. 78	17. T, p. 83	25. F, p. 85
2. F, p. 80	10. F, pp. 79-80	18. T, pp. 82-83	26. F, p. 87
3. T, pp. 75-76	11. T, p. 80	19. T, p. 83	27. F, pp. 87-88
4. T, p. 76	12. T, p. 80	20. T, p. 83	28. F, pp. 88, 90
5. T, p. 76	13. F, p. 81	21. T, p. 84	29. F, p. 90
6. T, p. 76	14. F, p. 81	22. F, p. 85	30. T, p. 91
7. F, p. 77	15. F, p. 82	23. F, p. 86	
8. T, p. 77	16. F, p. 82	24. T, p. 84	

MULTIPLE-CHOICE QUESTIONS

1. *a,* p. 75	8. *a,* pp. 81-82	15. *b,* pp. 82-83	22. *d,* p. 91
2. *a,* p. 76	9. *a,* p. 82	16. *c,* p. 84	23. *b,* p. 91
3. *c,* pp. 75-76	10. *c,* pp. 83-84	17. *b,* pp. 86-87	24. *c,* p. 89
4. *a,* p. 76	11. *b,* p. 85	18. *b,* p. 86	25. *b,* p. 89
5. *b,* p. 77	12. *a,* pp. 84-85	19. *a,* p. 88	
6. *d,* p. 78	13. *b,* p. 84	20. *d,* p. 88	
7. *a,* p. 79	14. *b,* p. 82	21. *a,* pp. 89-90	

PROBLEMS

1. 73, 8

2. *a.* CORP; *b.* PRO and PART; *c.* PRO; *d.* CORP; *e.* CORP; *f.* CORP; *g.* PART; *h.* PART; *i.* CORP

3. *a.* reallocates resources; *b.* redistributes income; *c.* provides a legal foundation and social environment *and* stabilizes the economy; *d.* reallocates resources; *e.* maintains competition; *f.* provides a legal foundation and social environment *and* maintains competition; *g.* redistributes income; *h.* reallocates resources; *i.* provides a legal foundation and social environment; *j.* redistributes income

4. *a.* (1) businesses pay costs for resources that become money income for households; (2) households provide resources to businesses; (3) household expenditures become receipts for businesses; (4) businesses provide goods and services to households; (5) government spends money in product market; (6) government receives goods and services from product market; (7) government spends money in resource market; (8) government receives re-

sources from resource market; (9) government provides goods and services to households; (10) government provides goods and services to businesses; (11) businesses pay net taxes to government; (12) households pay net taxes to government; *b.* (1) 5, 7 (either order), 11, 12 (either order); (2) 9, 10, 11 (either order); (3) increase, decrease, 12

5. *a.* tax; $770, 1,060, 1,400, 1,800; average tax rate: 22%, 23.6%, 25.5%, 27.7%; *b.* (1) increases, (2) decreases; *c.* progressive, increases

SHORT ANSWER AND ESSAY QUESTIONS

1. pp. 74-75	**8.** p. 81	**15.** p. 84	**22.** p. 90
2. p. 78	**9.** p. 81	**16.** p. 85	**23.** pp. 89-90
3. p. 76	**10.** pp. 81-85	**17.** pp. 85-88	**24.** pp. 89-91
4. p. 77	**11.** p. 82	**18.** pp. 87-89	**25.** p. 92
5. pp. 77-79	**12.** p. 82	**19.** pp. 87-88	
6. p. 80	**13.** pp. 82-84	**20.** p. 87	
7. p. 80	**14.** pp. 82-84	**21.** p. 87	

CHAPTER 6

The United States in the Global Economy

Chapter 6 introduces you to the global economy and its influence on the United States. International trade is important to the United States for many reasons, as you learn in the first section of the chapter. In **relative** terms, other nations have exports and imports which are a larger percentage of their GDPs—about 25 to 35%. Trade is a larger percentage of the economies of these nations because they often have a small domestic market and a limited resource base. By contrast, the United States exports and imports only about 11 to 13% of its GDP because it has a larger domestic market and a more abundant resource base. In **absolute** terms, however, the United States is the world's largest trading nation. Exports were $457 billion and imports were $590 billion in 1993, exceeding all other nations. Most of the trade is with other industrially advanced nations such as Canada, Japan, and Germany. This volume of trade has grown over the years with expansion of the global economy, the rise of multinational corporations, and with the emergence of new trading nations such as the "Asian tigers" (Hong Kong, Singapore, South Korea, and Taiwan).

The second section of the chapter briefly returns to the circular flow. Now the global economy ("rest of the world") can be added to the model by connecting it to the product market of that model to make it more complete. Four linkages are made to the model: export **flows** are paid for by foreign expenditure **flows**; import **flows** are paid for by U.S. expenditure **flows.**

In the third section, you learn about the principle of **comparative advantage.** This principle is the basis for all trade between individuals, regions, and nations. A nation, for example, will specialize in the production of a product at which it has a lower domestic opportunity cost and trade to obtain those products for which its domestic opportunity cost is higher. Thus, specialization and trade increases productivity within a nation and increases a nation's output and standard of living.

Trading in a global economy requires a **foreign exchange market** where national currencies are exchanged, as you discover in the fourth section of the chapter. This market is competitive, so the principles of supply and demand that you read about in Chapter 3 apply to it. Changes in supply and demand for currency will affect the price of a national currency. When the U.S. dollar price of another currency has increased, the value of the U.S. dollar has **depreciated** relative to the other currency. Conversely, when the U.S. dollar price of another currency increases, the value of the U.S. dollar has **appreciated** in value relative to the other currency.

Government actions and policies can affect international trade in many ways. Governments can impose protective tariffs, import quotas,and nontariff barriers, or they can foster exports through subsidies. The reasons for the interventions are difficult to explain given the strong economic rationale for free trade based on the principle of comparative advantage. Nevertheless, as you learn in the fifth section of the chapter, public misunderstanding of the gains from trade, or political considerations designed to protect domestic industries, often lead to government policies that create trade barriers and distort the free flow of products between the nations.

The sixth section discusses **multilateral** agreements among nations and the creation of free-trade zones that have been designed to reduce trade barriers and increase world trade. In the United States, the process of gradual tariff reduction began with the Reciprocal Trade Agreement Act of 1934. Since 1947, worldwide multilateral negotiations to reduce trade barriers have been conducted through the General Agreements on Tariffs and Trade (GATT). The Uruguay round of GATT negotiations were completed in 1993, and this new agreement included many provisions to improve trade among nations. The other major development has been the formation of free-trade zones. The European Union (originally the Common Market) is a trading bloc of sixteen European nations. In 1993, the North American Free Trade Agreement (NAFTA) created a free-trade zone covering the United States, Canada, and Mexico.

The final section of the chapter explores the issue of whether American businesses can compete in a global economy. Foreign competition has certainly changed production practices and employment in American industry since the 1960s. Some industries, such as textiles, now face a comparative **dis**advantage in world markets. Many American firms, however, have adapted to the changes in the global economy by increasing productivity to reducing costs, improving product quality, and expanding export markets.

■ CHECKLIST

When you have studied this chapter you should be able to:

☐ Explain the importance of international trade to the American economy in terms of volume, dependence, trade patterns, and financial linkages.

☐ Describe several factors that have facilitated the rapid growth of international trade since World War II.

☐ Identify the key participating nations in international trade.

☐ Add the international trade dimension to the circular flow model.

☐ Explain the basic principle of comparative advantage based on an individual example.

☐ Compute the comparative costs of production from production possibilities data when you are given an example with cost data for 2 units.

☐ Determine which of 2 economic units have a comparative advantage in the example.

☐ Indicate the range in which the terms of trade will be found in the example.

☐ Show the gains from specialization and trade in the example.

☐ Define the main characteristics of the foreign exchange market.

☐ Demonstrate how supply and demand analysis applies to the foreign exchange market.

☐ Distinguish between the appreciation and depreciation of a currency.

☐ Identify four types of trade impediments and subsidies.

☐ Discuss two reasons why governments intervene in international trade.

☐ Estimate the cost to consumers from trade restrictions.

☐ List the major features of the Reciprocal Trade and Agreements Act of 1934 and the General Agreements on Tariffs and Trade (GATT) of 1947.

☐ Identify the major provisions of the Uruguay round of GATT negotiations.

☐ Describe the history, goals, and results from the European Union.

☐ Explain the features and significance of the North American Free Trade Agreement.

☐ Discuss the capability of American business to compete in the global economy.

■ CHAPTER OUTLINE

1. Trade among nations is large and unique, and thus warrants special attention.

a. Although the relative importance of international trade to the United States is less than it is for other nations, it is still of considerable importance.

(1) Exports and imports are about 11–13% of GDP, and the United States is the largest trading nation in the world.

(2) The American economy depends on this trade for vital raw materials and a variety of finished products.

(3) There are some patterns in American trade: most is with industrially advanced nations, with Canada being the largest trade partner; overall imports exceed exports, but the deficits are greatest with Japan and OPEC.

(4) International trade must be financed, and in the case of the United States large trade deficits have required the selling of business ownership (securities) to companies in other nations.

b. Factors that have facilitated trade since World War II include improvements in transportation and communications technology, along with a general decline in tariffs and worldwide peace.

c. The major participants in international trade are the United States, Japan, and the nations of western Europe. Newer participants include the "Asian tigers" (Hong Kong, Singapore, South Korea, and Taiwan), and also China. The collapse of the former Soviet Union significantly changed trade patterns in Russia and the nations of eastern Europe.

2. The circular flow model of Chapter 5 can be expanded to include the international trade dimension by adding the "rest of the world" box to the model. This box would be connected to the U.S. product market through flows of imports and exports, and U.S. and foreign expenditures.

3. Specialization and trade among economic units (individuals, firms, states, regions, or nations) are based on the principle of *comparative advantage.* Specialization and trade increase productivity and the output of goods and services.

a. The basic principle can be illustrated with an example using two individuals.

(1) Suppose that an accountant wants to have her house painted, but the accountant can either do it herself or hire a professional painter to do the job. The law of comparative advantage suggests that the accountant will specialize in that work where the opportunity cost is lower relative to the work where the opportunity cost is higher.

(2) The same principle applies to the professional painter in deciding whether to prepare his own tax return, or specialize in painting and hire an accountant to prepare the tax return.

(3) Given the hypothetical labor time and wage data in the textbook example, both the accountant and the painter reduce their opportunity costs when they spe-

cialize in their respective jobs and exchange money for other services they desire.

b. The concept can also be illustrated with a hypothetical example of trade between two nations that produce two different products.

(1) Suppose that the production possibilities for each nation is a straight line (there is a constant cost ratio).

(2) Each nation will find it profitable to trade because there is a comparative (cost) advantage in the production of one of the two products; each nation can produce one of the products at a lower opportunity cost than the other.

c. The terms of trade between nations—the ratio at which one product is traded for another—lies between the cost ratios for the two nations.

d. Each nation gains from this trade because specialization allows for more total production from the same resources and permits a better allocation of resources; specialization and trade have the effect of easing the fixed constraints of the production possibilities curve for each nation.

4. National currencies are traded in a foreign exchange market. This market is competitive and establishes the exchange rate of a domestic currency for foreign currency. The price of a domestic currency, or its exchange rate, is the price paid in the domestic currency to buy 1 unit of another currency ($0.01 U.S. = 1 Japanese yen). Exchange rates are unusual prices because they link the prices of the currencies of nations.

a. The exchange rate for a nation's currency is determined by the supply of and demand for that currency. When the supply or demand changes, then the exchange rate of the currency changes (for example, change from $0.01 U.S. = 1 yen to $0.02 U.S. = 1 yen).

b. The exchange value of a currency can depreciate or appreciate.

(1) Increases in the exchange rate or price of a unit of foreign currency (the dollar price of a yen increases) means that there has been a *depreciation* in the value of one currency (the dollar) relative to the foreign currency; and

(2) decreases in the exchange rate for a foreign currency (a decrease in the dollar price of yen) means that there has been an *appreciation* in the value of one currency (the dollar) relative to the foreign currency (the yen).

5. Governments develop trade policies that can reduce trade between nations.

a. Government policies that restrict trade between nations include protective tariffs, import quotas, nontariff barriers, and export subsidies.

b. The reason for trade restrictions is that governments may not understand the gains from trade, or there are political concerns, such as the protection of businesses or groups in a nation against international competition.

c. But the costs of these restrictive trade policies outweigh the benefits, and as a consequence consumers pay higher prices and the nation makes less efficient use of its resources.

6. International trade policies have changed over the years with the development of multilateral agreements and free-trade zones.

a. United States trade policy has been significantly affected by the Reciprocal Trade Agreements Act of 1934 and by the General Agreements on Tariffs and Trade (GATT) begun in 1947.

(1) Until 1934, the United States steadily increased tariff rates to protect private-interest groups, but since the passage of the 1934 act, tariff rates have been substantially reduced. This act gave the President the authority to negotiate with foreign nations and included *most-favored-nation* clauses.

(2) GATT made trade negotiations multilateral and offered a continuing round of negotiations to settle trade differences.

(3) The Uruguay round of GATT began in 1986 and was completed in 1993. The major provisions, which will be phased in through 2005, will reduce tariffs, cover services, cut agricultural subsidies, protect intellectual property, reduce quotas on textiles and apparel, and establish a World Trade Organization.

b. The European Union is an example of a regional free-trade zone or trade bloc among fifteen nations. It has abolished tariffs among member nations, and developed common policies on various economic issues, such as the tariffs on goods and from nonmember nations. The EU has produced freer trade and increased economies of scale for production in its member nations, but such a trading bloc creates trade frictions with nonmember nations like the United States.

c. In 1993, the North American Free Trade Agreement (NAFTA) created a free-trade zone covering the United States, Mexico, and Canada. It was an extension of the type of free-trade agreement signed by the United States and Canada in 1989. Although concern has been expressed about job losses in the United States or the potential for abuse by other nations, the typical advantages from freer trade clearly outweigh any drawbacks.

7. Increased international trade has resulted in more competitive pressure on American businesses, which raises the question of whether America can compete in global markets. Most firms have been able to meet the competitive change by lowering production costs, improving products, or using new technology. Some firms and industries have had difficulty remaining competitive and continue to lose market share and employment. Overall, increased trade has produced substantial benefits for American consumers (lower prices and more products), and enabled the nation to make more efficient use of its scarce resources.

■ IMPORTANT TERMS

multinational corporations

"Asian tigers"

comparative advantage

cost ratio

terms of trade

foreign exchange market

depreciation

appreciation

protective tariffs

import quotas

nontariff barriers

export subsidies

Smoot-Hawley Tariff Act of 1930

Reciprocal Trade Agreements Act of 1934

most-favored-nation clauses

General Agreements on Tariffs and Trade (GATT)

European Union (EU)

trade bloc

North American Free Trade Agreement (NAFTA)

■ HINTS AND TIPS

1. Comparative advantage is directly related to the opportunity cost concept and production possibilities you learned about in Chapter 2.

a. A nation has a comparative advantage in the production of a product when it can produce the product at a lower domestic opportunity cost than can a trading partner. A nation will specialize in the production of a product for which it is the low (opportunity) cost producer.

b. When a production possibilities schedule for two nations and two products has a constant cost ratio, you can reduce the complicated production possibilities schedule to a 2 × 2 table. Put the two products in the two columns and the two nations in the two rows of the matrix. In each cell of the matrix put the *maximum* of each product that can be produced by a nation. Then for each nation, divide the maximum of one product into the maximum amount of the other product to get the domestic opportunity cost of one product in terms of the other.

c. This last point can be illustrated with an example from problem 2 in this study guide chapter. Lilliput can produce a *maximum* of 40 pounds of apples or 20 pounds of bananas. Brobdingnag can produce a *maximum* of 75 pounds of apples or 25 pounds of bananas. The 2 × 2 matrix would look like this:

	Apples	Bananas
Lilliput	40	20
Brobdingnag	75	25

For Lilliput, the domestic opportunity cost of producing 1 pound of apples is one-half pound of bananas. In Brobdingnag, the domestic opportunity cost of producing 1 pound of apples is one-third pound of bananas. Brobdingnag is the lower (opportunity) cost producer of apples and will specialize in the production of that product. Lilliput is the lower (opportunity) cost producer of bananas because producing 1 pound of bananas requires giving up 2 pounds of apples, whereas in Brobdingnag producing 1 pound of bananas requires giving up 3 pounds of apples.

2. Foreign exchange rates often confuse students because they can be expressed in two ways: the U.S. dollar price of a unit of foreign currency ($1.56 for one British pound), or the amount of foreign currency that can be purchased by one U.S. dollar ($1 can purchase .64 British pounds). If you know the exchange rate in one way, you can easily calculate it the other way. Using the information from the first way, dividing $1.56 into 1 British pound gives you the British pound price for one U.S. dollar (1/1.56 = .64 of a British pound). Using information from the second way, dividing .64 of a British pound into one U.S. dollar gives you the dollar price of a British pound (1/.64 = 1.56). Both ways may be used, although one way may be used more often than the other. Rates for British pounds or Canadian dollars are usually expressed the first way, in terms of U.S. dollars. Rates for the Swiss franc, Japanese yen, or German mark are expressed in the second way, per U.S. dollar.

SELF-TEST

■ FILL-IN QUESTIONS

1. The importance of international trade varies by nation. Nations where exports account for a relative high percentage of GDP tend to have a (limited, diversified)

_____ resource base and domestic market, whereas nations where exports account for a lower per-

centage of GDP tend to have a _____ resource base and domestic market. An example of a higher exporting nation would be the (United States, Netherlands)

_____ and lower exporting nation would be the

_____

2. The imports of the United States amount to about

_____ % of the economy's GDP, and exports

amount to about _____ %. In absolute terms the

United States is the world's _____ trading nation.

3. The United States is _____ on the world economy for many products. The bulk of its trade is with

(less developed, industrially advanced) _____

_____ nations. The largest trading partner for the United States is (Canada, Japan) _____. The United States has a large trade deficit with (Canada, Japan) _____

4. Factors that have helped increase the growth of world trade since World War II include improvement in _____ and _____ technology, a general decline in _____, and _____ relations between the major trading partners in the world economy.

5. The major "players" in international trade include the _____, _____, and the nations of western Europe. These nations serve as the headquarters for most _____ corporations and dominate world trade. The new industrializing economies of Hong Kong, Singapore, South Korea, and Taiwan, known as the "_____," have expanded their share of the world trade to almost 10%.

6. In the circular flow model that adds the "rest of the world," foreign expenditures pay for U.S. (imports, exports) _____ and U.S. expenditures pay for _____

7. Specialization and trade (increase, decrease) _____ the productivity of a nation's resources and _____ total output more than would be the case without it.

8. When one nation has a lower opportunity cost of producing a product relative to another state or nation it has a _____. The amount of one product that must be given up to obtain 1 unit of another product is the

_____

9. When the dollar price of foreign currency increases, there has been a(n) (appreciation, depreciation) _____ in value of the dollar. When the dollar price of foreign currency decreases, there has been a(n) _____ in the value of the dollar; for example, if the dollar price of a German mark (DM) decreases from $0.60 = 1 DM to $0.50 = 1 DM, then it means that there has been a(n) _____ in the value of the dollar; but if the dollar price of a German mark increases from $0.40 = 1 DM to $0.55 = 1 DM, then it means that there has been a(n) _____ in the value of the dollar.

10. In the market for Japanese yen, an increase in the (demand for, supply of) _____ yen will decrease the dollar price of yen, while an increase in the _____ yen will increase the dollar price of yen. If the dollar price of the yen increases, then Japanese goods imported into the United States will be (more, less) _____ expensive to American consumers, while American goods exported to Japan will be _____ expensive for Japanese consumers.

11. The major government policies that restrict trade include protective _____, import _____, _____ barriers, and _____ subsidies.

12. Governments may intervene in trade between nations because they **mistakenly** think of (exports, imports) _____ as helpful and _____ as harmful for a national economy. In fact, there are important gains from trade in the form of the extra output obtained from abroad. Trade makes it possible to obtain _____ at a lower cost than would be the case if they were produced using domestic resources, and the earnings from _____ help a nation pay for these lower cost _____

13. Another reason why governments interfere with free trade is based on _____ considerations. Groups and industries seek protection from foreign competition through _____ or import _____, or other kinds of trade restrictions. The costs of trade protectionism are (clear to, hidden from) _____ consumers in the protected product price. Removing trade barriers would reduce product prices an average of 3% in protected industries.

14. Tariffs and quotas (benefit, cost) _____ domestic firms in the protected industries but _____ domestic consumers in the form of (lower, higher) _____ prices than would be the case if there were free trade.

15. Until 1934, the trend of tariff rates in the United States was (upward, downward) _____. The trend has been _____ since the passage of the _____ Act of 1934. This act empowered the President to lower _____ rates by up to 50% in return for a reduction in foreign restrictions on American goods and incorporated _____ clauses in American trade agreements.

16. The three cardinal principles established in the General Agreements on Tariffs and Trade are:

a. _____

b. _____

c. _____

17. The major provisions of the Uruguay _____ of GATT negotiations include _____ reductions, coverage of _____ by GATT, cuts in subsidies to _____, protection of _____ property, phased reduction of _____ on textiles and apparel, and the formation of a _____ Organization.

18. An example of a free-trade zone or trade bloc is the _____ Union that was originally started in 1958 as the Common Market. The specific aims of the Common Market were the abolition of tariffs and _____ among member nations, the establishment of common tariffs on goods imported from _____ nations, the free movement of capital and _____ within the Common Market, and common policies on other matters.

19. A free-trade zone formed in 1993 covered three nations: _____, _____, and _____. This _____ Free Trade Agreement will eliminate _____ and other trade barriers between the three nations over a fifteen-year period.

20. Increased international trade has raised questions about whether American firms can _____ in the global economy. The evidence shows that many firms (can, cannot) _____ be successful in world markets. Some firms, however, that have benefitted from past trade protection may find it difficult to adjust to foreign _____ and may go out of business.

■ **TRUE-FALSE QUESTIONS**

1. For the United States, the volume of international trade has been increasing relatively, but not absolutely. **T F**

2. The American economy's share of world trade has decreased since 1947. **T F**

3. The United States exports and imports goods and services with a dollar value greater than any other nation in the world. **T F**

4. The United States is completely dependent on trade for certain commodities which cannot be obtained in domestic markets. **T F**

5. Canada is the most important trading partner for the United States in terms of the volume of exports and imports. **T F**

6. If a person, firm, or region has a comparative advantage in the production of a particular commodity, it should specialize in the production of that commodity. **T F**

7. If one nation has a better comparative advantage in the production of a commodity than another nation, then it has a higher opportunity cost of production than the other nation. **T F**

8. The economic effects of specialization and trade between nations are similar to increasing the quantity of resources or to achieving technological progress. **T F**

9. The interaction of the demand for, and supply of, Japanese yen will establish the dollar price of Japanese yen. **T F**

10. An increase in incomes in the United States would tend to cause the dollar price of the Japanese yen to fall. **T F**

11. When the dollar price of another nation's currency increases, there has been an appreciation in the value of the dollar. **T F**

12. When the dollar depreciates relative to the value of the currencies of the trading partners of the United States, then goods imported into the United States will tend to become more expensive. **T F**

13. Export subsidies are government payments to reduce the price of a product to buyers from other nations. **T F**

14. Nontariff barriers include excise taxes or duties placed on imported goods. **T F**

15. Through world trade an economy can reach a point beyond its domestic production possibilities curve. **T F**

16. One of the reasons that trade restrictions get public support is that the alleged benefits of the restrictions are often immediate and clear-cut, but the adverse affects are often obscure and dispersed over the economy. **T F**

17. Tariffs and quotas benefit domestic firms in the protected industries, and also help domestic consumers by lowering the prices for those products. **T F**

18. The Smoot-Hawley Tariff Act of 1930 reduced tariffs in the United States to the lowest level ever in an attempt to pull the nation out of the Great Depression. **T F**

19. If the United States concludes a tariff agreement which lowers the tariff rates on goods imported from another nation and that trade agreement contains a most-favored-nation clause, the lower tariff rates are then applied to those goods when they are imported from (most) other nations in the world. **T F**

20. The members of the European Union have experienced freer trade since it was formed. **T F**

21. The economic integration of nations creates larger markets for firms within the nations that integrate and makes it possible for these firms and their customers to benefit from the economies of large-scale (mass) production. **T F**

22. The formation of the European Union may make it more difficult for American firms to compete with firms located within the Union for customers there. **T F**

23. The United States—Canadian Free-Trade Agreement of 1989 is an example of the gains to be obtained from voluntary export restrictions. **T F**

24. The North American Free Trade Agreement also includes Central American nations. **T F**

25. The evidence is clear that major American firms are unable to compete in world markets without significant protection from foreign competition. **T F**

■ **MULTIPLE-CHOICE QUESTIONS**

Circle the letter that corresponds to the best answer.

1. In 1993, the imports and exports of the United States amounted to approximately what percentage of GDP?
(a) 3–4%
(b) 6–7%
(c) 11–13%
(d) 15–16%

2. Which nation is our most important trading partner in terms of the quantity of trade volume?
(a) Japan
(b) Canada
(c) Germany
(d) United Kingdom

3. Which of the following is true?
(a) exports as a percentage of GDP is greatest in the United States
(b) the United States is almost totally dependent on other nations for aircraft, machine tools, and coal
(c) most of the exports and imports trade of the United States is with industrially advanced nations
(d) the United States has a trade surplus with Japan

4. How is most of the trade deficit financed by a nation such as the United States?
(a) by buying securities or assets from other nations
(b) by selling securities or assets to other nations
(c) by borrowing from the Federal government
(d) by lending to the Federal government

5. Which factor has greatly facilitated international trade since World War II?
(a) expanded export subsidies
(b) greater import quotas
(c) increased nontariff barriers
(d) improved communications

6. "Asian tigers" refers to the:
(a) nations of Japan and China
(b) nations of Hong Kong, Singapore, South Korea, and Taiwan
(c) aggressive export strategies of the Philippines and Thailand
(d) multinational corporations located in Asian countries

7. In the circular flow model of the economy, U.S.:
(a) imports are paid for by foreign expenditures
(b) exports are paid for by U.S. expenditures
(c) imports are paid for by U.S. expenditures
(d) exports are paid for by U.S. multinational corporations

8. Why do nations specialize and engage in trade?
(a) to protect multinational corporations
(b) to increase output and income
(c) to improve communications
(d) to control other nations

*Answer the next four questions (**9, 10, 11, and 12**) on the basis of the data given for two regions. Slobovia and Utopia, which have the production possibilities tables below.*

SLOBOVIA PRODUCTION POSSIBILITIES TABLE

Product	Production alternatives					
	A	**B**	**C**	**D**	**E**	**F**
Cams	1,500	1,200	900	600	300	0
Widgets	0	100	200	300	400	500

UTOPIA PRODUCTION POSSIBILITIES TABLE

Product	Production alternatives				
	A	**B**	**C**	**D**	**E**
Cams	4,000	3,000	2,000	1,000	0
Widgets	0	200	400	600	800

9. In Slobovia, the comparative cost of:
(a) 1 cam is 3 widgets
(b) 1 widget is ⅓ cam
(c) 1 cam is ⅓ widget
(d) 3 widgets is 1 cam

10. Which of the following statements is *not* true?
(a) Slobovia should specialize in the production of widgets
(b) Slobovia has a comparative advantage in the production of widgets

(c) Utopia should specialize in the production of widgets

(d) Utopia has a comparative advantage in the production of cams

11. The terms of trade will be:

(a) greater than 7 cams for 1 widget

(b) between 7 cams for 1 widget and 5 cams for 1 widget

(c) between 5 cams for 1 widget and 3 cams for 1 widget

(d) less than 3 cams for 1 widget

12. Assume that if Slobovia did not specialize it would produce alternative C and that if Utopia did not specialize it would select alternative B. The gains from specialization are:

(a) 100 cams and 100 widgets

(b) 200 cams and 200 widgets

(c) 400 cams and 500 widgets

(d) 500 cams and 400 widgets

13. If the equilibrium exchange rate changes so that the dollar price of Japanese yen increases:

(a) the dollar has appreciated in value

(b) the dollar has depreciated in value

(c) Americans will be able to buy more Japanese goods

(d) Japanese will be able to buy fewer U.S. goods

14. A decrease in the United States demand for Japanese goods will:

(a) increase the demand for Japanese yen and increase the dollar price of yen

(b) increase the demand for Japanese yen but decrease the dollar price of yen

(c) decrease the demand for Japanese yen and decrease the dollar price of yen

(d) decrease the demand for Japanese yen but increase the dollar price of yen

15. If the exchange rate for one United States dollar changes from 1.4 German marks to 1.7 German marks, then there has been:

(a) an appreciation in the value of the mark

(b) a depreciation in the value of the dollar

(c) a depreciation in the value of the mark

(d) an increase in the price of the mark

16. Which of the following is designed to restrict trade?

(a) GATT

(b) NAFTA

(c) import quotas

(d) multinational corporations

17. Why do governments often intervene in international trade?

(a) to expand a nation's production possibilities

(b) to improve the position of multinational corporations

(c) to protect domestic industries from foreign competition

(d) to increase revenue from tariff duties and excise taxes

18. Which one of the following specifically empowered the President of the United States to reduce its tariff rates up to 50% if other nations would reduce their tariffs on American goods?

(a) the Underwood Act of 1913

(b) the Hawley-Smoot Act of 1930

(c) the Reciprocal Trade Agreements Act of 1934

(d) the General Agreement on Tariffs and Trade of 1947

19. Which of the following is characteristic of the General Agreement on Tariffs and Trade? Nations signing the agreement were committed to:

(a) the expansion of import quotas

(b) the reciprocal increase in tariffs by negotiation

(c) the nondiscriminatory treatment of all member nations

(d) the establishment of a world customs union

20. One important topic for discussion during the Uruguay round of GATT was:

(a) removing voluntary export restraints in manufacturing

(b) eliminating trade barriers and subsidies in agriculture

(c) abolishing the need for patent, copyright, and trademark protection

(d) increasing tariff barriers on services

21. The European Common Market:

(a) was designed to eliminate tariffs and import quotas among its members

(b) aimed to allow the eventual free movement of capital and labor within the member nations

(c) imposed common tariffs on goods imported into the member nations from outside the Common Market area

(d) did all of the above

22. One of the potential problems with the European Union is that:

(a) an unregulated free flow of labor and capital may reduce productivity

(b) economies of large-scale production may increase consumer prices

(c) tariffs may reduce trade with nonmember nations

(d) governments may have difficulty covering the shortfall from the elimination of duties and taxes

23. An example of the formation of a trade bloc would be the:

(a) Smoot-Hawley Tariff Act

(b) North American Free Trade Agreement

(c) Reciprocal Trade Agreements Act

(d) General Agreements on Tariffs and Trade

24. The defenders of the North American Free Trade Agreement argue that it will:

(a) reduce imports from Canada
(b) increase American exports to Mexico
(c) eliminate the trade deficit with Japan
(d) improve economic relations with the European Union

25. The Merosur is:
(a) the controlling body of the European Union
(b) one of the provisions of the North American Free Trade Agreement
(c) the name of the organization resulting from the latest GATT negotiations
(d) a free-trade zone covering Brazil, Argentina, Uruguay, and Paraguay

■ **PROBLEMS**

1. Here is a problem to help you understand the principle of comparative advantage and the benefits of specialization. A tailor named Hart has the production possibilities table for trousers and jackets given below. He chooses production alternative D.

HART'S PRODUCTION POSSIBILITIES TABLE

Product	Production alternatives					
	A	B	C	D	E	F
Trousers	75	60	45	30	15	0
Jackets	0	10	20	30	40	50

Another tailor, Schaffner, has the production possibilities table below and produces production alternative E.

SCHAFFNER'S PRODUCTION POSSIBILITIES TABLE

Product	Production alternatives						
	A	B	C	D	E	F	G
Trousers	60	50	40	30	20	10	0
Jackets	0	5	10	15	20	25	30

a. To Hart

(1) the cost of one pair of trousers is _____ jackets

(2) the cost of one jacket is ____ pairs of trousers
b. To Schaffner

(1) the cost of one pair of trousers is ____ jackets

(2) the cost of one jacket is ____ pairs of trousers
c. If Hart and Schaffner were to form a partnership to make suits

(1) _____ should specialize in the making of trousers because he can make a pair of trousers at the cost of ____ of a jacket while it costs his partner _____ of a jacket to make a pair of trousers.

(2) _____ should specialize in the making of jackets because he can make a jacket at the cost

of _____ pairs of trousers while it costs his partner _____ pairs of trousers to make a jacket.

d. Without specialization and between them Hart and Schaffner were able to make 50 pairs of trousers and 50 jackets. If each specializes completely in the item in the production of which he has a comparative advantage, their combined production will be _____ pairs of trousers and _____ jackets. Thus the gain from specialization is _____

_____

e. When Hart and Schaffner come to divide the income of the partnership between them, the manufacture of a pair of trousers should be treated as the equivalent of from _____ to _____ jackets (or a jacket should be treated as the equivalent of from _____ to _____ pairs of trousers).

2. The countries of Lilliput and Brobdingnag have the production possibilities tables for apples and bananas shown below.
Note that the costs of producing apples and bananas are constant in both countries.

LILLIPUT PRODUCTION POSSIBILITIES TABLE

Product (lbs.)	Production alternatives					
	A	B	C	D	E	F
Apples	40	32	24	16	8	0
Bananas	0	4	8	12	16	20

BROBDINGNAG PRODUCTION POSSIBILITIES TABLE

Product (lbs.)	Production alternatives					
	A	B	C	D	E	F
Apples	75	60	45	30	15	0
Bananas	0	5	10	15	20	25

a. In Lilliput the cost of producing:

(1) 8 apples is _____ bananas

(2) 1 apple is _____ bananas
b. In Brobdingnag the cost of producing:

(1) 15 apples is _____ bananas

(2) 1 apple is _____ bananas
c. In Lilliput the cost of producing:

(1) 4 bananas is _____ apples

(2) 1 banana is _____ apples
d. In Brobdingnag the cost of producing:

(1) 5 bananas is _____ apples

(2) 1 banana is _____ apples

e. The cost of producing 1 apple is lower in the country of _____ and the cost of producing 1 banana is lower in the country of _____

f. Lilliput has a comparative advantage in the production of _____ and Brobdingnag has a comparative advantage in the production of _____

g. The information in this problem is not sufficient to determine the exact terms of trade; but the terms of trade will be **greater** than _____ apples for 1 banana and **less** than _____ apples for 1 banana. Put another way, the terms of trade will be between _____ bananas for 1 apple and _____ bananas for 1 apple.

h. If neither nation could specialize, each would produce production alternative C. The combined production of apples in the two countries would be _____ apples and the combined production of bananas would be _____ bananas.

(1) If each nation specializes in producing the fruit for which it has a comparative advantage, their combined production will be _____ apples and _____ bananas.

(2) Their gain from specialization will be _____ apples and _____ bananas.

3. Use the table below that shows ten different currencies and how much of each currency can be purchased with a U.S. dollar.

a. In the far right column of the table, indicate whether the U.S. dollar has appreciated (A) or depreciated (D) from Year 1 to Year 2

Currency per U.S. $				
Country	**Currency**	**Year 1**	**Year 2**	**A or D**
Brazil	Real	0.85	0.91	_____
Britain	Pound	0.65	0.59	_____
Canada	Dollar	1.41	1.51	_____
France	Franc	5.44	5.22	_____
Germany	Mark	1.58	1.69	_____
India	Rupee	31.39	34.55	_____
Japan	Yen	100.15	110.23	_____
Mexico	Peso	4.65	5.09	_____
Norway	Krone	6.88	6.49	_____
Thailand	Bhat	25.12	23.22	_____

b. In Year 1, a U.S. dollar would purchase _____ French francs, but in Year 2, it would purchase _____ French francs. The U.S. dollar has (appreciated, de-

preciated) _____ against the French franc from Year 1 to Year 2.

c. In Year 1, a U.S. dollar would purchase _____ Japanese yen, but in Year 2, it would purchase _____ Japanese yen. The U.S. dollar has (appreciated, depreciated) _____ against the Japanese yen from Year 1 to Year 2.

■ **SHORT ANSWER AND ESSAY QUESTIONS**

1. In relative and absolute terms, how large is the volume of the international trade of the United States? What has happened to these figures over the past thirty or so years?

2. What are the principal exports and imports of the American economy? What commodities used in the economy come almost entirely from abroad and what American industries sell large percentages of their outputs abroad?

3. Which nations are the principal "trading partners" of the United States? How much of this trade is with the developed and how much of it is with the less developed nations of the world?

4. Are the American economy's exports of merchandise to greater or less than its imports of merchandise from:
   (a) Japan,
   (b) the OPEC nations, and
   (c) the rest of the world?

5. Give several international examples of specialization and efficiency.

6. How does a nation obtain more goods from other nations than it provides to them?

7. What are several factors that have facilitated trade since World War II?

8. Who are the major participants in international trade? Describe the relative influence of the key players.

9. Describe how the international trade component can be added to the circular flow model of the economy.

10. Explain what is meant by comparative cost and comparative advantage. What determines the terms of trade? What is the gain that results from specialization in the products in the production of which there is a comparative advantage?

11. Why might an appreciation of the value of the United States dollar relative to the Japanese yen depress the American economy and stimulate the Japanese economy? Why might a government intervene in the foreign exchange market and try to increase or decrease the value of its currency?

12. What are the major trade impediments and subsidies? How do they restrict international trade?

13. Why do governments intervene in international trade and develop restrictive trade policies?

14. What is the cost to society from trade protectionism? Who benefits and who is hurt by trade protectionism?

15. What was the Smoot-Hawley Tariff Act of 1930? What international trade problems are illustrated by this act?

16. What was the tariff policy of the United States between 1920 and 1930? What has been the policy since 1934? Explain the basic provisions of the Reciprocal Trade Agreements Act.

17. How has the United States cooperated with other nations since 1945 to reduce trade barriers? What were the three cardinal principles contained in the General Agreements on Tariffs and Trade? What were the basic objectives and what were the results of the "Uruguay Round" of GATT negotiations?

18. What is the European Union? What were its original goals under the Common Market? What has been its successes and what problems does it pose for world trade?

19. What is the North American Free Trade Agreement? What do its critics and defenders say about the agreement?

20. Can American firms compete in a global economy? Discuss the major issues.

ANSWERS

Chapter 6 The United States in the Global Economy

FILL-IN QUESTIONS

1. limited, diversified, Netherlands, United States

2. 11–13, 11–13, largest

3. dependent, industrially advanced, Canada, Japan

4. transportation, communications (any order), tariffs, peaceful

5. United States, Japan (any order), multinational, Asian tigers

6. exports, imports

7. increase, increase

8. comparative advantage, terms of trade

9. depreciation, appreciation, appreciation, depreciation

10. supply of, demand for, more, less

11. tariffs, quotas, nontariff, export

12. exports, imports, imports, exports, imports

13. political, tariffs, quotas, hidden from

14. benefit, cost, higher

15. upward, downward, Reciprocal Trade Agreements, tariff, most-favored-nation

16. *a.* equal, nondiscriminatory treatment of all member nations; *b.* reduction of tariffs by multilateral negotiations; *c.* elimination of import quotas

17. round, tariff, services, agriculture, intellectual, quotas, World Trade

18. European, quotas, nonmember, labor

19. United States, Canada, Mexico (any order), North American, tariffs

20. compete, can, competition

TRUE-FALSE QUESTIONS

1. F, p. 98	**8.** T, p. 106	**15.** T, p. 109	**22.** T, p. 112
2. T, p. 98	**9.** T, p. 107	**16.** T, pp. 109-110	**23.** F, pp. 112-113
3. T, p. 98	**10.** F, pp. 107-108	**17.** F, pp. 109-110	**24.** F, p. 112
4. T, p. 98	**11.** F, pp. 107-108	**18.** F, p. 110	**25.** F, pp. 113-114
5. T, p. 99	**12.** T, pp. 107-108	**19.** T, p. 110	
6. T, p. 105	**13.** T, p. 109	**20.** T, p. 112	
7. F, p. 104	**14.** F, p. 109	**21.** T, p. 112	

MULTIPLE-CHOICE QUESTIONS

1. *c*, p. 98	**8.** *b*, pp. 103-104	**15.** *c*, pp. 107-108	**22.** *c*, p. 112
2. *b*, p. 99	**9.** *c*, pp. 104-105	**16.** *c*, p. 109	**23.** *b*, p. 112
3. *c*, p. 99	**10.** *c*, pp. 104-105	**17.** *c*, p. 109	**24.** *b*, pp. 112-113
4. *b*, p. 99	**11.** *c*, pp. 104-105	**18.** *c*, p. 110	**25.** *d*, p. 113
5. *d*, p. 100	**12.** *a*, pp.104-105	**19.** *c*, pp. 110-112	
6. *b*, p. 100	**13.** *b*, p. 107	**20.** *b*, p. 111	
7. *c*, pp. 101-102	**14.** *c*, p. 107	**21.** *d*, p. 112	

PROBLEMS

1. *a.* (1) 2/3, (2) 1 1/2; *b.* (1) 1/2, (2) 2; *c.* (1) Schaffner, 1/2, 2/3; (2) Hart, 1 1/2, 2; *d.* 60, 50, 10 pairs of trousers; *e.* 1/2, 2/3, 1 1/2, 2

2. *a.* (1) 4, (2) 1/2; *b.* (1) 5, (2) 1/3; *c.* (1) 8, (2) 2; *d.* (1) 15, (2) 3; *e.* Brobdingnag, Lilliput; *f.* bananas, apples; *g.* 2, 3, 1/3, 1/2; *h.* 69, 18, (1) 75, 20, (2) 6, 2

3. *a.* A, D, A, D, A, A, A, A, D, D; *b.* 5.44, 5.22, depreciated; *c.* 100.15, 110.23, appreciated

SHORT ANSWER AND ESSAY QUESTIONS

1. p. 98	**6.** pp. 104-105	**11.** p. 107	**16.** p. 110
2. p. 99	**7.** p. 100	**12.** pp. 108-109	**17.** pp. 110-111
3. p. 99	**8.** p. 100	**13.** p. 109	**18.** p. 112
4. p. 99	**9.** pp. 101-102	**14.** pp. 109-110	**19.** pp. 112-113
5. pp. 103-104	**10.** pp 103-104	**15.** p. 110	**20.** pp. 113-114

CHAPTER 7

Measuring Domestic Output, National Income, and the Price Level

The subject of Chapter 7 is national income accounting. The first measure that you will learn about in the chapter is the gross domestic product (GDP). The GDP is an important economic statistic because it provides the best estimate of the total market value of all final goods and services produced by our economy in one year. As you will learn early in the chapter, GDP is very similar to another measure of the economy's output—gross national product (GNP). The two measures differ only in how the economy is defined, and GDP is the one used by most nations. You will then discover why GDP is a monetary measure that counts only the value of final goods and services and excludes from the calculation nonproductive transactions such as secondhand sales.

National income accounting involves estimating output or income for the nation's society as a whole, rather than for an individual business firm or family. Note that the terms "output" and "income" are interchangeable because the nation's domestic output and its income are identical. The value of the nation's output equals the total expenditures for this output, and these expenditures become the income of those who have produced this output. Consequently, there are two equally acceptable methods—expenditures or income—for determining GDP.

From an expenditure perspective, GDP is composed of four expenditure categories—personal consumption expenditures (C), gross private domestic investment (I_g), government purchases (G), and net exports (X_n). These expenditures become income for people when they are paid out in the form of employee compensation, rents, interest, proprietor's income, and corporate profits, with adjustments made for indirect business taxes, depreciation, and net foreign factor income earned in the United States. The chapter also explains the relationship of GDP to other social accounting measures: net domestic product (NDP), national income (NI), personal income (PI), and disposable income (DI).

By measuring the price level, economists are able to determine how much inflation (an increase in the price level) or deflation (a decrease in the price level) has occurred in the economy. This information is important because income-output measures are expressed in monetary units, so if accurate comparisons are to be made between years, these monetary measures must be adjusted to take account of changes in the price level. A simple example is presented to show how a GDP price index or deflator is constructed and then the index is used to adjust nominal GDP to determine real GDP for comparison purposes. But, as the last section of the chapter points out, it is especially dangerous to assume that GDP is a good measure of the welfare of the society.

Chapter 7 is the essential background for Parts 2 and 3, which explain the history of and the factors that determine the level of domestic output and income in the economy. This chapter is important because it explains the several methods used to measure the performance of the economy in a given year and make the adjustments necessary to ensure accurate measurements of performance over time.

■ CHECKLIST

When you have studied this chapter you should be able to:

☐ Give a definition of the gross domestic product (GDP) and the gross national product (GNP).

☐ Identify the major difference between the GDP and GNP.

☐ Explain why GDP is a monetary measure.

☐ Discuss how GDP avoids double counting.

☐ Give examples of nonproduction transactions that are excluded from GDP.

☐ Describe the four basic expenditure components of GDP.

☐ Explain: (1) the difference between gross and net investment; (2) why changes in inventories are investment; and (3) the relationship between net investment and economic growth.

☐ Compute GDP using the expenditures approach when you are given national income accounting data.

☐ Identify the major income and nonincome allocations of GDP in the income approach to GDP.

☐ Describe the effect of net foreign factor income earned in the United States on national income accounts.

☐ Compute GDP using the income approach when you are given national income accounting data.

☐ Define net domestic product (NDP), national income (NI), personal income (PI), and disposable income (DI).
☐ Compute NDP, NI, PI, and DI by two different methods when you are given the necessary data.
☐ Use Figure 7–3 in the text to describe the circular flow model as it relates to GDP.
☐ Explain how a price index or the GDP deflator is constructed.
☐ Calculate the GDP deflator or a price index when you are given the necessary price and quantity data.
☐ Find real GDP when you are given related data on nominal GDP and the price index.
☐ Present seven reasons why GDP may overstate or understate real output, and why it may not be a good measure of social welfare.

■ **CHAPTER OUTLINE**

1. National income accounting consists of concepts which enable those who use them to measure the economy's output, to compare it with past outputs, to explain its size and the reasons for changes in its size, and to formulate policies designed to increase it.

2. The market value of all final goods and services produced in the economy during the year is measured by the gross domestic product (GDP).
   a. A very similar measure to GDP is the gross national product (GNP).
   (1) The basic accounting difference between GDP and GNP is that GDP includes net foreign factor income earned in the United States. This net factor income is determined by subtracting the factor income received by Americans for resources supplied abroad from the factor income Americans made to the rest of the world.
   (2) GDP, rather than GNP, is used by most nations as the measure of an economy's output. The measurement of GDP in the United States is the central focus of Chapter 7.
   b. GDP is measured in dollar terms rather than in terms of physical units of output.
   c. To avoid double counting, GDP includes only **final** goods and services (goods and services that will not be processed further during the **current** year).
   d. Nonproduction transactions are not included in GDP; purely financial transactions and second-hand sales are, therefore, excluded.
   e. Measurement of GDP can be accomplished by either the expenditures or the income method but the same result is obtained by the two methods.

3. Computation of the GDP by the expenditures method requires the addition of the total amounts of the four types of spending for final goods and services.
   a. Personal consumption expenditures (**C**) are the expenditures of households for durable and nondurable goods and for services.

   b. Gross private domestic investment (I_g) is the sum of the spending by business firms for machinery, equipment, and tools; spending by firms and households for new buildings; and the changes in the inventories of business firms.
   (1) A change in inventories is included in investment because it is the part of output of the economy which was not sold during the year.
   (2) Investment does not include expenditures for stocks or bonds or for second-hand capital goods.
   (3) Gross investment exceeds net investment by the value of the capital goods worn out during the year.
   (4) An economy in which net investment is positive (zero, negative) is an expanding (a static, a declining) economy.
   c. Government purchases (**G**) are the expenditures made by all governments in the economy for products produced by business firms and for resource services from households.
   d. Net exports (X_n) in an economy equal the expenditures made by foreigners for goods and services produced in the economy less the expenditures made by the consumers, governments, and investors of the economy for goods and services produced in foreign nations.
   e. In symbols, $C + I_g + G + X_n = GDP$

4. Computation of GDP by the income method requires the addition of the nine uses to which the income derived from the production and sales of final goods and services are put. These nine items are:
   a. Compensation of employees (the sum of wages and salaries **and** wage and salary supplements).
   b. Rents.
   c. Interest (only the interest payments made by business firms are included and the interest payments made by government are excluded).
   d. Proprietors' income (the profits or net income of unincorporated firms).
   e. Corporate profits which are subdivided into:
   (1) Corporate income taxes
   (2) Dividends
   (3) Undistributed corporate profits
   f. Indirect business taxes.
   g. Depreciation (consumption of fixed capital).
   h. Adding these nine items together gives you GNP, not GDP. To obtain GDP, you must add to GNP the net foreign factor income earned in the United States.

5. In addition to GDP, four other national income measures are important in evaluating the performance of the economy. Each has a distinct definition and can be computed by making additions to or deductions from another measure.
   a. **NDP** is the annual output of final goods and services over and above the capital goods worn out during the year; and is equal to the GDP minus depreciation (consumption of fixed capital).

b. NI is the total income **earned** by American owners of land and capital and by the American suppliers of labor and entrepreneurial ability during the year; and equals NDP *minus* net foreign factor income earned in the United States and *minus* indirect business taxes.

c. PI is the total income **received**—whether it is earned or unearned—by the households of the economy before the payment of personal taxes; and is found by **adding** transfer payments to and **subtracting** social security contributions, corporate income taxes, and undistributed corporate profits from the NI.

d. DI is the total income available to households after the payment of personal taxes; and is equal to PI less personal taxes and also equal to personal consumption expenditures plus personal saving.

e. The relations among the five income-output measures are summarized for you in Table 7–4.

f. Figure 7–3 is a more realistic and complex circular flow diagram that shows the flows of expenditures and incomes among the households, business firms, and governments in the economy.

6. Because price levels change from year to year it is necessary to adjust the nominal GDP (or money GDP) computed for any year to obtain the real GDP before year-to-year comparison between the outputs of final goods and services can be made.

a. The price level is stated as an index number that measures the price ratio of a market basket of goods in a given year to a market basket of goods in a base year, and that ratio is multiplied by 100.

b. Although there are many price indexes, the GDP price index or deflator is used to adjust GDP measures for changes in the price level.

c. To adjust the GDP figures, divide the nominal GDP in any year by the price index for that year; the result is the adjusted or real GDP.

d. When the price index in a year is below (above) the 100 it was in the base year the nominal GDP figure for that year is inflated (deflated) by this adjustment.

7. The GDP is not, for the following reasons, a measure of social welfare in the economy.

a. It excludes the value of final goods and services not bought and sold in the markets of the economy.

b. It excludes the amount of leisure the citizens of the economy are able to have.

c. It does not record the improvements in the quality of products which occur over the years.

d. It does not measure changes in the composition and the distribution of the domestic output.

e. It is not a measure of per capita output because it does not take into account changes in the size of the economy's population.

f. It does not record the pollution costs to the environment of producing final goods and services.

g. It does not measure the market value of the final goods and services produced in the underground sector of the economy.

■ IMPORTANT TERMS

National income accounting
Gross national product
Gross domestic product
Final goods
Intermediate goods
Double counting
Value added
Nonproduction transaction
Nonmarket transaction
Expenditures approach
Income approach
Personal consumption expenditures
Government purchases
Gross private domestic investment
Noninvestment transaction
Net private domestic investment
Expanding economy
Static economy
Declining economy
Net exports

Nonincome charges
Consumption of fixed capital (depreciation)
Indirect business taxes
Compensation of employees
Wage and salary supplements
Net domestic product
National income
Personal income
Disposable income
Personal saving
Nominal GDP
Real GDP
Price index
Consumer price index
Base year
Given year
Inflating
Deflating
GDP deflator

■ HINTS AND TIPS

1. This chapter is fairly difficult and the only way to learn the material is to sit down and read through the chapter several times. A careful reading will enable you to avoid the necessity of memorizing. Begin by making sure you know precisely what GDP means, and what is included in and excluded from measurement of this most important statistic.

2. Accounting is essentially an adding-up process. This chapter explains in detail and lists the items which must be added to obtain GDP by the *expenditure* method or *income* method. It is up to you to learn what to add on the expenditure side, and what to add on the income side. Figure 7–1 is an important accounting reference for this task.

3. Changes in the price level have a significant effect on the measurement of GDP, and thus it is critical that you practice converting nominal GDP to real GDP using a price index. Problems 4 and 5 in this study guide should help you understand nominal and real GDP and the conversion process.

4. GDP is a good measure of the market value of the output of final goods and services that are produced in an economy in one year. The measure is not perfect, however, so you should be aware of its limitations, which are noted at the end of the chapter.

SELF-TEST

■ FILL-IN QUESTIONS

1. National income accounting is valuable because it provides a means of keeping track of the level of _____ in the economy and the course it has followed over the long run; and the information required to devise and put into effect the public _____ that will improve the performance of the economy.

2. Gross domestic product (GDP) and gross national product (GNP) measure the total _____ value of all _____ goods and services produced in the economy in _____ year.

3. GDP and GNP differ only in how the "_____" is defined. GDP is the value of (total, foreign) _____ output produced within the United States from American or _____ resources. GNP is the value of _____ output produced by American resources, whether the resources are located in the United States or _____ nations.

4. By definition, the difference between GDP and GNP is equal to net (American, foreign) _____ factor income earned in the United States. GDP equals GNP (plus, minus) _____ this net factor income.

5. In measuring GDP only final goods and services are included; if intermediate goods and services were included, the accountant would be _____

6. A firm buys materials for $2,000 from other firms in the economy and produces from them a product which sells for $3,015. The $1,015 is the _____ by the firm.

7. The total value added to a product at all stages of production equals the _____ value of the _____ product; and the total value added to all products produced in the economy during a year is the _____ product.

8. Personal consumption expenditures are the expenditures of households for _____ and _____ goods and for _____

9. Gross private domestic investment basically includes the final purchases of _____ goods (e.g., tools and equipment) by businesses, all _____ of new buildings and houses, and changes in _____

10. Net private domestic investment is less than gross private domestic investment by an amount equal to _____ , or the consumption of fixed capital.

11. If gross private domestic investment is less than depreciation, net private domestic investment is (positive, zero, negative) _____ and the economy is (static, declining, expanding) _____

12. An economy's *net* exports equal its _____ _____ less its _____

13. In symbols, the GDP by the expenditures approach = _____ + _____ + _____ + _____

14. The consumption of fixed capital and indirect business taxes, by the income approach, are referred to as _____ charges or allocations.

15. The compensation of employees in the system of social accounting consists of actual wages and salaries *and* wage and salary _____ The latter are the payments employers make to social _____ programs and to _____ pension, health, and welfare funds.

16. Corporate profits are disposed of in three ways: _____ _____ , _____ , and _____

17. Gross domestic product overstates the economy's net production because it fails to make allowance for that part of the output which replaces the _____ worn out or used up in producing the output. To compute the net domestic product it is, therefore, necessary to subtract the _____
_____

18. National income equals net domestic product minus _____ and minus _____

19. Personal income:
   a. equals national income plus _____ and minus the sum of _____ , _____ , and _____ ;
   b. also equals _____ plus _____ plus _____

20. Disposable income:

a. equals personal income minus _____

_____ ;

b. also equals _____

_____

21. To compare real gross domestic product in two different years, it is necessary to adjust nominal GDP for

changes in the _____ level.

22. A price index is the ratio of the price of a

_____ basket of goods and services in a

specific year to the price of the _____

basket in the base year, with the ratio being multiplied by

_____ .

23. The price index used to adjust nominal GDP for

changes in the price level is called the _____

24. Real GDP is calculated by dividing (the price index,

nominal GDP) _____ by _____

25. For several reasons the GDP is not a measure of social welfare in an economy.

a. It does not include the _____

transactions that result in the production of goods and

services or the amount of _____ enjoyed by
the citizens of the economy.

b. It fails to record improvements in the _____
of the products produced, changes in the composition

and distribution of the economy's total _____ ,
the undesirable effects of producing the GDP upon the

_____ of the economy, and the goods

and services produced in the _____
economy.

c. And because it is a measure of the *total* output of

the economy it does not measure the _____
output of the economy.

■ **TRUE-FALSE QUESTIONS**

Circle the T if the statement is true; the F if it is false.

1. Gross domestic product measures at their market values the total output of all goods and services produced in the economy during a year.　　**T　F**

2. The gross domestic product (GDP) is equal to the gross national product (GNP) when net foreign factor income earned in the United States is added to GNP.　**T　F**

3. GDP is simply a count of the quantity of output, and is not a monetary measure.　　**T　F**

4. The total market value of the wine produced in the United States during a year is equal to the number of bottles of wine produced in that year multiplied by the (average) price at which a bottle sold during that year.　**T　F**

5. GDP includes the sale of intermediate goods and excludes the sale of final goods.　　**T　F**

6. The total value added to a product and the value of the final product are equal.　　**T　F**

7. Social security payments and other public transfer payments are counted as part of GDP.　　**T　F**

8. The sale of stocks and bonds are excluded from GDP.
　　T　F

9. The two approaches to the measurement of the gross domestic product yield identical results because one approach measures the total amount spent on the products produced by business firms during a year while the second approach measures the total income of business firms during the year.　　**T　F**

10. In computing gross domestic product, net domestic product, and national income by the expenditures approach, transfer payments are excluded because they do not represent payments for currently produced goods and services.　　**T　F**

11. The expenditure made by a household to have a new home built for it is a personal consumption expenditure.
　　T　F

12. In national income accounting any increase in the inventories of business firms is included in gross private domestic investment.　　**T　F**

13. If gross private domestic investment is greater than depreciation during a given year, the economy has declined during that year.　　**T　F**

14. The net exports of an economy equals its exports of goods and services less its imports of goods and services.　　**T　F**

15. The income elements of GDP include compensation of employees, rents, interest income, proprietor's income, and corporate profits.　　**T　F**

*The data in the following table should be used to answer true-false questions **16** through **19**.*

	Billions of dollars
Net private domestic investment	$ 32
Personal taxes	39
Transfer payments	19
Indirect business taxes	8
Corporate income taxes	11
Personal consumption expenditures	217
Consumption of fixed capital	7
United States exports	15
Dividends	15
Government purchases	51
Net foreign factor income earned in the U.S.	0
Undistributed corporate profits	10
Social security contributions	4
United States imports	17

16. The stock of capital goods in the economy has expanded. **T F**

17. Gross private domestic investment is equal to $25 billion. **T F**

18. National income equals the net domestic product minus $8 billion. **T F**

19. Disposable income is equal to $245 billion. **T F**

20. Comparison of a gross domestic product with the gross domestic product of an earlier year when the price level has risen between the two years necessitates the "inflation" of the GDP figure in the later year. **T F**

21. To adjust nominal gross domestic product for a given year, it is necessary to divide nominal GDP by the price index—expressed in hundredths—for that year. **T F**

22. The consumer price index (CPI) is the price index used to adjust nominal GDP to measure real GDP. **T F**

23. The GDP is a good measure of the social welfare of society. **T F**

24. The productive services of a homemaker are included in GDP. **T F**

25. The spillover costs from pollution and other activities associated with the production of the GDP are deducted from total output. **T F**

■ **MULTIPLE-CHOICE QUESTIONS**

Circle the letter that corresponds to the best answer.

1. Which of the following is *not* an important use for national income accounting?
(a) it provides a basis for formulation and application of policies designed to improve the economy's performance
(b) it permits measurement of the economic efficiency of the economy
(c) it makes possible an estimate of the output of final goods and services in the economy
(d) it enables the economist to chart the growth or decline of the economy over a period of time

2. Gross domestic product (GDP) is defined as:
(a) personal consumption expenditures and gross private domestic investment
(b) the sum of wage and salary compensation of employees, corporate profits, and interest income
(c) the market value of final goods and services produced by the economy in one year
(d) the market value of all final and intermediate goods and services produced by the economy in one year

3. The difference between GDP and GNP consists of:
(a) the consumption of fixed capital
(b) indirect business taxes
(c) public and private transfer payments
(d) net foreign factor income earned in the U.S.

4. GDP provides an indication of society's evaluation of the relative worth of goods and services because it:
(a) provides an estimate of the value of second-hand sales
(b) gives increased weight to security transactions
(c) is an estimate of income received
(d) is a monetary measure

5. To include the value of the parts used in producing the automobiles turned out during a year in gross domestic product for that year would be an example of:
(a) including a nonmarket transaction
(b) including a nonproduction transaction
(c) including a noninvestment transaction
(d) double counting

6. Which of the following is a security transaction?
(a) the sale of a used (second-hand) ironing board at a garage sale
(b) the sale of shares of stock in the United States Steel Corporation
(c) the payment of social-security benefits to a retired worker
(d) the birthday gift of a check for $5 sent by a grandmother to her grandchild

7. The sale in 1996 of an automobile produced in 1995 would not be included in the gross domestic product for 1996; doing so would involve:
(a) including a nonmarket transaction
(b) including a nonproduction transaction
(c) including a noninvestment transaction
(d) double counting

8. The service a baby-sitter performs when she stays at home with her baby brother while her parents are out and for which she receives no payment is not included in the gross domestic product because:
(a) this is a nonmarket transaction
(b) this is a nonproduction transaction
(c) this is a noninvestment transaction
(d) double counting would be involved

9. According to national income accounting, money income derived from the production of this year's output is equal to:
(a) corporate profits and indirect business taxes
(b) the amount spent to purchase this year's total output
(c) the sum of interest income and the compensation of employees
(d) gross private domestic investment less the consumption of fixed capital

10. Which of the following does **not** represent investment?

(a) an increase in the quantity of shoes on the shelves of a shoe store

(b) the construction of a house which will be occupied by its owner

(c) the purchase of newly issued shares of stock in the General Motors Corporation

(d) the construction of a factory building using money borrowed from a bank

11. A refrigerator is produced by its manufacturer in 1995, sold during 1995 to a retailer, and sold by the retailer to a final consumer in 1996. The refrigerator was:

(a) counted as consumption in 1995

(b) counted as investment in 1996

(c) counted as investment in 1995

(d) not included in the gross domestic product of 1995

12. GDP in an economy is $3,452 billion. Consumer expenditures are $2,343 billion, government purchases are $865, and gross investment is $379 billion. Net exports are:

(a) + $93 billion

(b) + $123 billion

(c) – $45 billion

(d) – $135 billion

13. The annual charge which estimates the amount of capital equipment used up in each year's production is called:

(a) indirect business taxes

(b) inventory reduction

(c) depreciation

(d) investment

14. The income approach to GDP sums the total income earned by American resource suppliers, adds net foreign factor income earned in the United States, and then adds two nonincome charges:

(a) net investment and the consumption of fixed capital

(b) the consumption of fixed capital and indirect business taxes

(c) indirect business taxes and undistributed corporate profits

(d) undistributed corporate profits and financial transactions

15. What can happen to the allocation of corporate profits?

(a) it is paid to proprietors as income

(b) it is paid to to stockholders as dividends

(c) it is paid to government as interest income

(d) it is retained by the corporation as rents

*Questions **16** through **22** use the national income accounting data given in the table in the true-false section.*

16. The nonincome charges are equal to:

(a) $11 billion

(b) $15 billion

(c) $17 billion

(d) $19 billion

17. Corporate profits are equal to:

(a) $15 billion

(b) $25 billion

(c) $26 billion

(d) $36 billion

18. Net exports are equal to:

(a) – $2 billion

(b) $2 billion

(c) – $32 billion

(d) $32 billion

19. The gross domestic product is equal to:

(a) $298 billion

(b) $302 billion

(c) $317 billion

(d) $305 billion

20. The net domestic product is equal to:

(a) $298 billion

(b) $302 billion

(c) $317 billion

(d) $321 billion

21. National income exceeds personal income by:

(a) $6 billion

(b) $15 billion

(c) $21 billion

(d) $44 billion

22. Personal saving is equal to:

(a) – $28 billion

(b) – $8 billion

(c) $8 billion

(d) $28 billion

23. If both nominal gross domestic product and the level of prices are rising, it is evident that:

(a) real GDP is constant

(b) real GDP is rising but not so rapidly as prices

(c) real GDP is declining

(d) no conclusion can be drawn concerning the real GDP of the economy on the basis of this information

24. Suppose nominal GDP rose from $500 billion to $600 billion while the GDP deflator increased from 125 to 150. The real GDP

(a) remained constant

(b) increased

(c) decreased

(d) cannot be calculated from these figures

25. In an economy, the total expenditures for a market basket of goods in year 1 (the base year) was $4,000 billion. In year 2, the total expenditure for the same market basket of goods was $4,500 billion. What was the GDP price index for the economy in year 2?

(a) .88
(b) 1.13
(c) 188
(d) 113

26. Nominal GDP is less than real GDP in an economy in year 1. In year 2, nominal GDP is equal to real GDP. In year 3, nominal GDP is slightly greater than real GDP. In year 4, nominal GDP is significantly greater than real GDP. Which year is most likely to be the base year that is being used to calculate the price index for this economy?

(a) 1
(b) 2
(c) 3
(d) 4

27. Nominal GDP was $3,774 billion in year 1 and the GDP deflator was 108 and nominal GNP was $3,989 in year 2 and the GDP deflator that year was 112. What was real GDP in years 1 and 2, respectively?

(a) $3,494 billion and $3,562 billion
(b) $3,339 billion and $3,695 billion
(c) $3,595 billion and $3,725 billion
(d) $3,643 billion and $3,854 billion

28. A price index one year was 145, and the next year it was 167. What is the approximate percentage change in the price level from one year to the next as measured by that index?

(a) 12%
(b) 13%
(c) 14%
(d) 15%

29. The GDP includes:

(a) the goods and services produced in the underground economy
(b) expenditures for equipment to reduce the pollution of the environment
(c) the value of the leisure enjoyed by citizens
(d) the goods and services produced but not bought and sold in the markets of the economy

30. Changes in the real GDP from one year to the next do **not** reflect:

(a) changes in the quality of the goods and services
(b) changes in the size of the population of the economy
(c) changes in the average length of the workweek
(d) any of the above changes

■ **PROBLEMS**

1. At the top of the next column are national income accounting figures for the United States.

	Billions of dollars
Exports	$ 367
Dividends	60
Consumption of fixed capital	307
Wages and salaries	1442
Government purchases	577
Rents	33
Indirect business taxes	255
Wage and salary supplements	280
Gross private domestic investment	437
Corporate income taxes	88
Transfer payments	320
Interest	201
Proprietors' income	132
Personal consumption expenditures	1810
Imports	338
Social security contributions	148
Undistributed corporate profits	55
Personal taxes	372
Net foreign factor income earned in the U.S.	0

a. Compute each of the following.

(1) Compensation of employees: $_____

(2) Net exports: $_____

(3) Net private domestic investment: $_____

b. Use any of these figures and any of your computations in (a) above to prepare in the table below an Income Statement for the Economy similar to the one found in Table 7–3 (on page 127 of the text).

Receipts: Expenditures approach	Allocations: Income approach
$_____	$_____
$_____	$_____
$_____	$_____
$_____	$_____
	$_____
	$_____
	$_____
	$_____
	$_____
	$_____
Gross domestic product $_____	Gross domestic product $_____

c. In this economy:

(1) Net domestic product is $_____

(2) National income is $_____

(3) Personal income is $_____

(4) Disposable income is $_____

2. A farmer who owns a plot of ground sells the right to pump crude oil from his land to a crude-oil producer. The crude-oil producer agrees to pay the farmer $20 a barrel for every barrel pumped from the farmer's land.

   a. During one year 10,000 barrels are pumped.

   (1) The farmer receives a payment of $_____ from the crude-oil producer.

   (2) The value added by the farmer is $_____

   b. The crude-oil producer sells the 10,000 barrels pumped to a petroleum refiner at a price of $25 a barrel.

   (1) The crude-oil producer receives a payment of $_____ from the refiner.

   (2) The value added by the crude-oil producer is $_____

   c. The refiner employs a pipeline company to transport the crude oil from the farmer's land to the refinery and pays the pipeline company a fee of $1 a barrel for the oil transported.

   (1) The pipeline company receives a payment of $_____ from the refiner.

   (2) The value added by the company is $_____

   d. From the 10,000 barrels of crude oil the refiner produces 315,000 gallons of gasoline and various by-products which are sold to distributors and gasoline service stations at an average price of $1 per gallon.

   (1) The total payment received by the refiner from its customers is $_____

   (2) The value added by the refiner is $_____

   e. The distributors and service stations sell the 315,000 gallons of gasoline and by-products to consumers at an average price of $1.30 a gallon.

   (1) The total payment received by distributors and service stations is $_____

   (2) The value added by them is $_____

   f. The total value added by the farmer, crude-oil producer, pipeline company, refiner, and distributors and service stations is $_____ and the market value of the gasoline and by-products (the final good) is $_____

3. Below is a list of items which may or may not be included in the five income-output measures. Indicate in the space to the right of each which of the income-output measures includes this item; it is possible for the item to be included in none, one, two, three, four, or all of the measures. If the item is included in none of the measures, indicate why it is not included.

   a. Interest on the national debt _____

_____

   b. The sale of a used computer _____

   c. The production of shoes which are not sold by the manufacturer _____

   d. The income of a bootlegger in a "dry" state _____

   e. The purchase of a share of common stock on the New York Stock Exchange _____

   f. The interest paid on the bonds of the General Motors Corporation _____

   g. The labor performed by a homemaker _____

   h. The labor performed by a paid baby-sitter _____

   i. The monthly check received by an idler from his rich aunt _____

   j. The purchase of a new tractor by a farmer _____

   k. The labor performed by an assembly-line worker in repapering his own kitchen _____

   l. The services of a lawyer _____

   m. The purchase of shoes from the manufacturer by a shoe retailer _____

   n. The monthly check received from the Social Security Administration by a college student whose parents have died _____

   o. The rent a homeowner would receive if she did not live in her own home _____

4. Below is hypothetical data for a market basket of goods in year 1 and year 2 for an economy.

   a. Compute the expenditures for year 1.

MARKET BASKET FOR YEAR 1 (BASE YEAR)

Products	Quantity	Price	Expenditures
Toys	3	$10	$_____
Pencils	5	2	$_____
Books	7	5	$_____
Total			$_____

   b. Compute the expenditures for year 2.

MARKET BASKET FOR YEAR 2

Products	Quantity	Price	Expenditures
Toys	3	$11	$_____
Pencils	5	3	$_____
Books	7	6	$_____
Total			$_____

   c. In the space below, show how you computed the GDP price index for year 2.

_____.

5. In the table below are nominal GDP figures for three years and the price indices for each of the three years. (The GDP figures are in billions.)

Year	Nominal GDP	Price index	Real GDP
1929	$104	121	$_____
1933	56	91	$_____
1939	91	100	$_____

a. Which of the three years appears to be the base year? _____

b. Between:

(1) 1929 and 1933 the economy experienced (inflation, deflation) _____

(2) 1933 and 1939 it experienced _____

c. Use the price indices to compute the real GDP in each year. (You may round your answers to the nearest billion dollars.)

d. The nominal GDP figure:

(1) for 1929 was (deflated, inflated, neither) _____
_____

(2) for 1933 was _____

(3) for 1939 was _____

e. The price level:

(1) fell by _____ % from 1929 to 1933.

(2) rose by _____ % from 1933 to 1939.

■ SHORT ANSWER AND ESSAY QUESTIONS

1. Of what use is national income accounting to economists and to the policymakers in the economy?

2. How does GDP differ from GNP? Explain.

3. Why is GDP a monetary measure, and why is it necessary that it be a monetary measure?

4. Why does GDP exclude nonproduction transactions?

5. What are the two principal types of nonproduction transactions? List some examples of each.

6. Why are there two ways, both of which yield the same answers, of computing GDP, NDP, etc.?

7. Why are transfer payments excluded from GNP, NNP, and NI?

8. Is residential construction counted as investment or consumption? Why?

9. Why is a change in inventories an investment?

10. How do you define a static, an expanding, and a declining economy? What is the relationship between gross private domestic investment and the consumption of fixed capital in these three economies?

11. What are the five income components of GDP? Define and explain the characteristics of each.

12. What is meant by a nonincome charge or allocation? What are the two principal nonincome charges included in GDP? Why are they excluded from NI?

13. What are the basic differences between the GDP deflator and the consumer price index (CPI)? Why do economists use the GDP deflator to adjust GDP figures?

14. Why do economists find it necessary to inflate and deflate GDP when comparing GDP in different years? How do they do this?

15. Why is GDP not a measure of the social welfare of society?

ANSWERS

Chapter 7 Measuring Domestic Output, National Income, and the Price Level

FILL-IN QUESTIONS

1. production, policies

2. market, final, one

3. economy, total, foreign, total, foreign

4. foreign, plus

5. double counting

6. value added

7. market, final, gross domestic

8. durable, nondurable (either order), services

9. capital, construction, inventories

10. depreciation

11. negative, declining

12. exports, imports

13. C, I_g, G, X_n

14. nonincome

15. supplements, insurance, private

16. corporate income taxes, dividends, undistributed corporate profits

17. capital goods, consumption of fixed capital

18. net foreign factor income earned in the U.S., indirect business taxes

19. *a.* transfer payments, social security contributions, corporate income taxes, undistributed corporate profits; *b.* personal consumption expenditures, personal taxes, personal saving

20. *a.* personal taxes; *b.* personal consumption expenditures plus personal saving

21. price

22. market, market, 100

23. GDP deflator

24. nominal GDP, the price index

25. *a.* nonmarket, leisure; *b.* quality, output, environment, underground; *c.* per capita

TRUE-FALSE QUESTIONS

1. F, p. 120	**8.** T, p. 122	**15.** T, p. 128	**22.** F, p. 135
2. T, p. 120	**9.** F, pp. 122-123	**16.** T, pp. 124-125	**23.** F, pp. 137-138
3. F, pp. 120-121	**10.** T, pp. 124-125	**17.** F, pp. 124-125	**24.** F, p. 137
4. T, pp. 121-122	**11.** F, p. 124	**18.** T, p. 130	**25.** F, p. 138
5. F, pp. 121-122	**12.** T, p. 124	**19.** T, p. 131	
6. T, pp. 121-122	**13.** F, p. 125	**20.** F, pp. 133-134	
7. F, p. 122	**14.** T, pp. 125-127	**21.** T, p. 136	

MULTIPLE-CHOICE QUESTIONS

1. *b*, pp. 119-120	**9.** *b*, p. 122	**17.** *d*, p. 128	**25.** *d*, p. 135
2. *c*, p. 120	**10.** *c*, p. 124	**18.** *a*, pp. 126-127	**26.** *b*, p. 136
3. *d*, p. 120	**11.** *c*, p. 124	**19.** *d*, p. 129	**27.** *a*, p. 136
4. *d*, pp. 120-121	**12.** *d*, p. 127	**20.** *a*, p. 130	**28.** *d*, pp. 134-135
5. *d*, pp. 120-121	**13.** *c*, p. 129	**21.** *a*, p. 130	**29.** *b*, pp. 137-139
6. *b*, p. 122	**14.** *b*, pp. 128-129	**22.** *d*, p. 131	**30.** *d*, pp. 137-139
7. *b*, p. 122	**15.** *b*, p. 128	**23.** *d*, pp. 134-135	
8. *a*, pp.122; 137	**16.** *b*, p. 128	**24.** *a*, pp. 135-136	

PROBLEMS

1. *a.* (1) 1722, (2) 29, (3) 130; *b.* see table at top of next column; *c.* (1) 2546, (2) 2291, (3) 2320, (4) 1948

2. *a.* (1) 200,000, (2) 200,000; *b.* (1) 250,000, (2) 50,000; *c.* (1) 10,000, (2) 10,000; *d.* (1) 315,000, (2) 55,000; *e.* (1) 409,500, (2) 94,500; *f.* 409,500, 409,500

Receipts: Expenditures approach		Allocations: Income approach	
Personal consumption expenditures	$1810	Consumption of fixed capital	$ 307
Gross private domestic investment	437	Indirect business taxes	255
		Compensation of employees	1722
Government purchases	577	Rents	33
Net exports	29	Interest	201
		Proprietors' income	132
		Corporate income taxes	88
		Dividends	60
		Undistributed corporate profit	55
		Net American factor income earned abroad	0
Gross domestic product	2853	Gross domestic product	2853

3. *a.* personal income and disposable income, a public transfer payment; *b.* none; a second-hand sale; *c.* all, represents investment (additions to inventories); *d.* all, illegal production and incomes are included when known; *e.* none, a purely financial transaction; *f.* all; *g.* none, a nonmarket transaction; *h.* all; *i.* none, a private transfer payment; *j.* all; *k.* none, a nonmarket transaction; *l.* all; *m.* all, represents additions to the inventory of the retailer; *n.* personal income and disposable income, a public transfer payment; *o.* all; estimate of rental value of owner-occupied homes is included in rents as if it were income and in personal consumption expenditures as if it were payment for a service

4. *a.* 30, 10, 35, 75; *b.* 33, 15, 42, 90; *c.* ($90/$75) 100 = 120

5. *a.* 1939; *b.* (1) deflation, (2) inflation; *c.* 86, 62, 91; *d.* (1) deflated, (2) inflated, (3) neither; *e.* (1) 24.8 (2) 9.9

SHORT ANSWER AND ESSAY QUESTIONS

1. p. 120	**5.** p. 122	**9.** p. 124	**13.** p. 134
2. p. 120	**6.** pp. 122-123	**10.** p. 125	**14.** pp. 135-136
3. pp. 120-121	**7.** p. 122	**11.** p. 128	**15.** pp. 137-139
4. p. 122	**8.** p. 124	**12.** pp. 128-129	

CHAPTER 8

Macroeconomic Instability: Unemployment and Inflation

In the last chapter you learned how to define and how to compute the gross and net domestic product and domestic, personal, and disposable income in any year. This chapter begins the explanation of what determines how large each of these five income-output measures will tend to be. In the chapters that follow you will learn what causes the income and output of the economy to be what they are, what causes them to change, and how they might be controlled for the welfare of society.

Chapter 8 is concerned with the instability of the American economy or with what is commonly called the **business cycle:** the ups and downs in the employment of labor and the real output of the economy that occur over the years. That there have been expansions and contractions in economic (or business) activity since the end of the American Civil War is evident from even a casual look at American economic history. What is not immediately evident, however, is that these alternating and relatively short periods of prosperity and "hard times" have taken place over a longer period in which the trends in output, employment, and the standard of living have been upward. During this long history booms and busts have occurred quite irregularly; and their duration and intensity have been so varied that it is better to think of economic instability than of business cycles.

There are two principal problems that result from the instability of the economy—from the business cycle. After a brief look in the first major section of the chapter at the business cycle, its phases, and its impact on the production of different kinds of goods, Professors McConnell and Brue turn to the first of these two problems in the second major section. Here you will find an examination of the **unemployment** that accompanies a downturn in the level of economic activity in the economy. You will discover that there are three different kinds of unemployment, that full employment means about 5.5% to 6% of the labor force is unemployed, and that there are at least three problems encountered in measuring the percentage of the labor force actually unemployed at any time. That unemployment has an economic cost and that this cost is unequally distributed among different sectors of our society you will also learn; and you probably won't be too surprised to discover that widespread unemployment can be the cause of other social problems.

The second of the two problems that result from economic instability is **inflation** and it is examined in the remainder of the chapter. Inflation is an increase in the general (or average) level of prices in an economy. It does not have a unique cause: it may result from increases in demand; from increases in costs; or from both. But regardless of its cause, it works a real hardship on certain sectors within the economy. If it occurs at too rapid a rate it may bring about a severe breakdown in the economy.

One last word. The thing to keep your eye on when you consider economic fluctuations and unemployment and inflation in the American economy is the changes in aggregate expenditures which can occur because consumers, business firms, or the public sector decide to spend more or less for goods and services.

■ CHECKLIST

When you have finished this chapter you should be able to:

☐ Explain what is meant by the business cycle.
☐ Describe the four phases of an idealized business cycle.
☐ Identify the "immediate determinant" or cause of the levels of output and employment.
☐ Identify the two types of noncyclical fluctuations.
☐ Distinguish between the impact of cyclical fluctuations on industries producing capital and consumer durable goods and on those producing consumer nondurable goods; and on high- and low-concentration industries.
☐ Distinguish between frictional, structural, and cyclical unemployment, and explain the causes of these three kinds of unemployment.
☐ Define full employment and the full-employment unemployment rate (the natural rate of unemployment).
☐ Describe the process employed (by the Bureau of Labor Statistics) to measure the rate of unemployment; and list the three criticisms of the BLS data.
☐ Identify the economic cost of unemployment.
☐ Define the GDP gap and state Okun's law.
☐ Discuss the unequal burdens of unemployment.

☐ Define inflation and the rate of inflation.

☐ Make international comparisons of inflation rate and unemployment rate data.

☐ Define demand-pull inflation and explain its effects in ranges 1, 2, and 3 of a price level and real domestic output graph.

☐ Define cost-push inflation and its relation to per unit production costs.

☐ Identify two variants of cost-push or supply-side inflation.

☐ Distinguish between real and nominal income and calculate real income when given data on nominal income and the price level.

☐ List groups that are hurt by and groups that benefit from unanticipated inflation.

☐ Describe how the redistributive effects of inflation are changed when it is anticipated.

☐ Present three scenarios that describe the possible effects of inflation on real output and employment.

■ **CHAPTER OUTLINE**

1. The history of the American economy is a record of exceptional economic growth.

a. But this growth has been accompanied by periods of inflation, of depression, and of both.

b. The **business cycle** means alternating periods of prosperity and depression. These recurrent periods of ups and downs in employment, output, and prices are irregular in their duration and intensity; but the typical pattern is **peak, recession, trough,** and **recovery** to another peak.

c. Changes in the levels of output and employment are largely the result of changes in the level of aggregate spending or demand in the economy.

d. Not all changes in employment and output which occur in the economy are cyclical; some are due to seasonal and secular influences.

e. The business cycle affects almost the entire economy, but it does not affect all parts in the same way and to the same degree: the production of capital and durable consumer goods fluctuates more than the production of consumer nondurable goods during the cycle because

(1) the purchase of capital and durable consumer goods can be postponed, and

(2) the industries producing these goods are largely dominated by a few large firms that hold prices constant and let output decline when demand falls.

2. Full employment does not mean that all workers in the labor force are employed and that there is no unemployment; some unemployment is normal.

a. There are at least three kinds of unemployment.

(1) There is always some **frictional unemployment;** and this kind of unemployment is generally desirable.

(2) And in addition there is the **structural unemployment** that is the result of changes in technology and in the types of goods and services consumers wish to buy.

(3) **Cyclical unemployment** is the result of insufficient aggregate demand in the economy.

b. Because some frictional and structural unemployment is unavoidable, the full-employment unemployment rate (the **natural rate of unemployment**) is the sum of frictional and structural unemployment; is achieved when cyclical unemployment is zero (the real output of the economy is equal to its potential output); and is about 5.5% to 6% of the labor force.

c. Surveying some 60,000 households each month, the Bureau of Labor Statistics finds the unemployment rate by dividing the number of persons in the labor force who are unemployed by the number of persons in the labor force; but the figures collected in the survey have been criticized for at least three reasons.

d. Unemployment has an economic cost.

(1) The economic cost is the unproduced output (or the **GDP gap**), and **Okun's law** is that for every 1% the actual unemployment rate exceeds the natural rate of unemployment there is 2.5% GDP gap.

(2) This cost is unequally distributed among different groups of workers in the labor force.

e. Unemployment also leads to serious social problems.

3. Over its history the American economy has experienced not only periods of unemployment but periods of inflation.

a. **Inflation** is an increase in the general level of prices in the economy; and a decline in the level of prices is deflation.

b. The rate of inflation in any year is equal to the percentage change in the price index between that year and the preceding year; and the rule of 70 can be used to calculate the number of years it will take for the price level to double at any given rate of inflation.

c. There are at least two causes of inflation; and these two causes may operate separately or simultaneously to raise the price level.

(1) **Demand-pull inflation** is the result of excess aggregate demand in the economy; and while increases in aggregate demand do not increase the price level when the unemployment rate is high (in a depression) they do bring about inflation as the economy nears and reaches full employment.

(2) **Cost-push** or **supply-side inflation** is the result of factors that raise per unit production costs. This average cost is found by dividing the total cost of the resource inputs by the amount produced. There are two variants that explain this rise in costs: (*a*) excessive wage increases that push up unit costs; and (*b*) a supply shock from an increase in the prices of resource in-

puts. With cost-push inflation, output and employment are declining as the price level rises.

4. Even if the total output of the economy did not change, inflation would arbitrarily redistribute real income and wealth; and would benefit some groups and hurt other groups in the economy.

   a. Whether someone benefits or is hurt by inflation is measured by what happens to real income. Inflation injures those whose real income falls and benefits those whose real income rises.

   (1) **Real income** is determined by dividing nominal income by the price level expressed in hundredths; and (2) the percentage change in real income can be approximated by subtracting the percentage change in the price level from the percentage change in nominal income.

   b. It also injures savers because it decreases the real value of any savings the money value of which is fixed.

   c. And it benefits debtors and hurts creditors because it lowers the real value of debts.

   d. But when the inflation is anticipated and people can adjust their nominal incomes to reflect the expected rise in the price level the redistribution of income and wealth is lessened.

   e. Since World War II inflation in the United States has redistributed wealth from the household to the public sector of the economy.

   f. If short, inflation acts to tax some groups and to subsidize other groups.

5. Inflation may also affect the total output of the economy but economists disagree over whether it is likely to expand or contract total output.

   a. Mild demand-pull inflation seems likely to expand output and employment in the economy.

   b. Cost-push inflation is apt to contract output and employment.

   c. And hyperinflation may well lead to the breakdown of the economy.

■ IMPORTANT TERMS

Business cycle	Full-employment unemployment rate
Peak	
Recession	Natural rate of unemployment
Trough	
Recovery	Potential output
Seasonal variation	Unemployment rate
Secular trend	Labor force
Frictional unemployment	Discouraged workers
Structural unemployment	GDP gap
Cyclical unemployment	Okun's law
Full employment	Inflation

Deflation	Cost-of-living adjustment (COLA)
Rule of 70	
Demand-pull inflation	Anticipated inflation
Cost-push inflation	Unanticipated inflation
Per unit production cost	Nominal interest rate
Nominal income	Real interest rate
Real income	Hyperinflation

■ HINTS AND TIPS

1. Some students get confused by the seemingly contradictory term "full-employment unemployment rate" and related unemployment concepts. Full employment does not mean that everyone who wants to work has a job. It means that the economy is achieving its potential output and has a **natural** rate of unemployment. Remember that there are three types of unemployment—frictional, structural, and cyclical. There will always be some unemployment arising from frictional reasons (e.g., people searching for jobs) or structural reasons (e.g., changes in industry demand), and these two types of unemployment are "natural" for an economy. Cyclical reasons (e.g., a downturn in the business cycle) for unemployment, however, are not natural for an economy. Thus, full-employment unemployment rate means that there are no cyclical reasons causing unemployment, only frictional or structural reasons.

2. If you think you know how to calculate the unemployment rate, GDP gap, or inflation rate after reading the chapter, then check your understanding by doing problems 1, 2, and 3 in this study guide chapter.

3. Inflation is a rise in the general level of prices, not just a rise in the prices of a few products. An increase in product price is caused by supply or demand factors. You now learn why the prices for many products rise in an economy. The macroeconomic reasons given in Chapter 8 for the increase in general level prices are different from the microeconomic reasons for a price increase that you learned about in Chapter 3.

SELF-TEST

■ FILL-IN QUESTIONS

   1. The history of the American economy is one of (steady, unsteady) _____ economic growth; and at times its growth has been accompanied by price _____ , and at other times its expansion has been interrupted by low levels of _____ of goods and services and _____ of workers.

2. The business cycle is a term which means the recurrent _____ and _____ in the level of business activity in the economy

3. The four phases of a typical business cycle are peak, _____ , _____ , and _____

4. The basic determinant of the levels of employment and output in an economy is the level of total _____ or aggregate _____ in the economy.

5. In addition to the changes brought about by the operation of the business cycle, noncyclical fluctuations in output and employment may be due to _____ variations and to a _____ trend.

6. Production and employment in the (durable, nondurable) _____ and (capital, consumer) _____ goods industries are affected to a greater extent by the expansion and contraction of the economy than they are in the _____ goods industries; and prices vary to a greater extent in the (low-, high-) _____ concentration industries.

7. The three types of unemployment are:

a. _____

b. _____

c. _____

8. The full-employment unemployment rate is:

a. sometimes called the _____ rate of unemployment;

b. equal to the total of the _____ and _____ unemployment in the economy;

c. realized when the _____ unemployment in the economy is equal to zero and when the _____ output of the economy is equal to its _____ output; and

d. assumed in this chapter to be about _____%.

9. When the economy achieves its natural rate of unemployment the number of job seekers is (greater than, less than, equal to) _____ the number of job vacancies; and the price level is (rising, falling, constant) _____

10. The unemployment _rate_ is found by dividing _____ _____ by the _____

11. The GDP gap is equal to _____ GDP _minus_ _____ GDP; and for every percentage point the unemployment rate rises above the natural rate the GDP gap will, according to Okun's law, (increase, decrease) _____ by _____ %.

12. The burdens of unemployment are borne more heavily by (black, white) _____ , (adult, teenage) _____ , and (white-collar, blue-collar) _____ workers; and the percentage of the labor force unemployed for 15 or more weeks is (greater, less) _____ than the unemployment rate.

13. Inflation means a _____ in the general level of _____ in the economy; and the rate of inflation in year 1993 is equal to the price index for year _____ less the price index for year _____ all divided by the price index for year _____

14. To find the approximate number of years it takes the price level to double you divide the percentage annual increase in the rate of _____ into _____. This approximation is called the _____

15. Since the 1920s, the experience of the United States with inflation has varied.

a. The price level decreased during the early years of the Great Depression, which means there was _____ occurring in the economy.

b. The post-World War II period (1945–1948) was characterized by (high, low) _____ rates of inflation, the 1961–1965 period was a period of _____ inflation, and the mid-to-late 1970s was a period of _____ inflation for the United States.

c. Compared with other industrialized countries, the rate of inflation in the United States during the 1980s has neither been usually _____ nor _____

16. The basic cause of:

a. demand-pull inflation is (an increase, a decrease) _____ in aggregate demand;

b. cost-push inflation is explained in terms of factors that raise _____.
Two sources of cost-push inflation are increases in _____ and increases in _____

c. In practice, it is (easy, difficult) _____ to distinguish the two types of inflation.

17. The amount of goods and services one's nominal income can buy is called _____
    a. If one's nominal income rises by 10% and the price level rose by 7%, the percentage of increase in _____ _____ would be _____
    b. If nominal income was $30,000 and the price index, expressed in hundredths, was 1.06, then _____ _____ would be _____

18. Inflation:
    a. hurts those whose nominal incomes are relatively (fixed, flexible) _____
    b. penalizes savers when the inflation is (expected, unexpected) _____
    c. hurts (creditors, debtors) _____ and benefits _____
    d. has since World War II shifted wealth from (the public sector, households) _____ _____ to _____

19. The redistributive effects of inflation are less severe when it is (anticipated, unanticipated) _____
    a. Clauses in labor contracts that call for automatic adjustments of workers' income from the effects of inflation are called _____
    b. The percentage increase in purchasing power that the lender receives from the borrower is the (real rate of interest, nominal rate of interest) _____; the percentage increase in money that the lender receives is the _____

20. Despite considerable disagreement and uncertainty among economists it seems that:
    a. demand-pull inflation, unless there is full employment in the economy, will (increase, decrease) _____ _____ total output and employment;
    b. cost-push inflation will _____ output and employment in the economy;

    c. hyperinflation may bring about an economic _____ _____

■ **TRUE-FALSE QUESTIONS**

Circle the T if the statement is true; the F if it is false.

  1. The American economy has experienced a long period of substantial economic growth and shorter periods of inflation and of high employment.   **T F**

  2. The business cycle is best defined as alternating periods of increases and decreases in the rate of inflation in the economy.   **T F**

  3. Individual business cycles tend to be of roughly equal duration and intensity.   **T F**

  4. Not all changes which occur in output and employment in the economy are due to the business cycle. **T F**

  5. Industries which are highly concentrated show small relative decreases in output and large relative decreases in prices during a downswing of the business cycle. **T F**

  6. Frictional unemployment is not only inevitable but largely desirable.   **T F**

  7. The essential difference between frictionally and structurally unemployed workers is that the former **do not have** and the latter **do have** salable skills.   **T F**

  8. When the number of people seeking employment is less than the number of job vacancies in the economy the actual rate of unemployment is less than the natural rate of unemployment and the price level will tend to rise.   **T F**

  9. If unemployment in the economy is at its natural rate, the actual and potential outputs of the economy are equal.   **T F**

10. The natural rate of unemployment in the American economy is a constant 6% of the labor force.   **T F**

11. An economy cannot produce an actual real GDP that exceeds its potential real GDP.   **T F**

12. The unemployment rate is equal to the number of persons in the labor force divided by the number of people who are unemployed.   **T F**

13. The percentage of the labor force unemployed for fifteen or more weeks is always less than the unemployment rate and tends to rise during a recession.   **T F**

14. The economy's GDP gap is measured by deducting its actual GDP from its potential GDP.   **T F**

15. The economic cost of cyclical unemployment is the goods and services that are not produced.   **T F**

16. Inflation is defined as an increase in the total output of an economy. **T F**

17. From one year to the next the consumer price index rose from 311.1 to 322.2. The rate of inflation was, therefore, 5.6%. **T F**

18. If the price level increases by 10% each year the price level will double every ten years. **T F**

19. With a moderate amount of unemployment in the economy, an increase in aggregate spending will generally increase both the price level and the output of the economy. **T F**

20. The theory of cost-push inflation explains rising prices in terms of factors which increase per unit production cost. **T F**

21. A person's real income is the amount of goods and services which the person's nominal (or money) income will enable him or her to purchase. **T F**

22. Whether inflation is anticipated or unanticipated, the effects of inflation on the distribution of income are much the same. **T F**

23. Suppose a household has $10,000 on deposit in a savings and loan association upon which it earns 7% interest during a year and the rate of inflation is 9% in that year. By the end of the year the purchasing power of the $10,000 and the interest it has earned will have decreased to about $9,817. **T F**

24. Unemployment and inflation rates vary greatly among major industrialized nations. **T F**

25. Inflation in the United States has transferred wealth from the public sector to the households of the economy.

T F

■ **MULTIPLE-CHOICE QUESTIONS**

Circle the letter that corresponds to the best answer.

1. Which one of the following is one of the four phases of an idealized business cycle?
  (a) inflation
  (b) recession
  (c) unemployment
  (d) seasonal variation

2. Most economists believe that the immediate determinant of the levels of domestic output and employment is:
  (a) the price level
  (b) the size of the civilian labor force
  (c) the nation's stock of capital goods
  (d) the level of aggregate spending

3. Total employment in December of this year was greater than total employment in December of 1928. This is no doubt due to the effect of:
  (a) seasonal variations
  (b) secular trend
  (c) the business cycle
  (d) business fluctuations

4. If employment in the agricultural sector of the American economy during last August and September was 112% of what it normally is in those months, this is probably a consequence of:
  (a) seasonal variations
  (b) secular trend
  (c) the business cycle
  (d) both seasonal variations and the business cycle

5. Production and employment in which of the following industries would be least affected by a depression?
  (a) nondurable consumer goods
  (b) durable consumer goods
  (c) capital goods
  (d) iron and steel

6. A worker who loses a job at a petroleum refinery because consumers and business firms switch from the use of oil to the burning of coal is an example of:
  (a) frictional unemployment
  (b) structural unemployment
  (c) cyclical unemployment
  (d) disguised unemployment

7. A worker who has quit one job and is taking two weeks off before reporting to a new job is an example of:
  (a) frictional unemployment
  (b) structural unemployment
  (c) cyclical unemployment
  (d) disguised unemployment

8. Insufficient aggregate demand results in:
  (a) frictional unemployment
  (b) structural unemployment
  (c) cyclical unemployment
  (d) disguised unemployment

9. The full-employment unemployment rate in the economy has been achieved when:
  (a) frictional unemployment is zero
  (b) structural unemployment is zero
  (c) cyclical unemployment is zero
  (d) the natural rate of unemployment is zero

10. Which of the following has increased the natural rate of unemployment in the United States since the 1960s?
  (a) the increased size of unemployment benefits
  (b) more workers covered by unemployment programs
  (c) having more young workers in the labor force
  (d) all of the above

11. The labor force includes those who are:
(a) under sixteen years of age
(b) in mental institutions
(c) not seeking work
(d) employed

12. The unemployment rate in an economy is 8%. The total population of the economy is 250 million and the size of the civilian labor force is 150 million. The number of employed workers in this economy is:
(a) 12 million
(b) 20 million
(c) 138 million
(d) 140 million

13. The price has doubled in about fourteen years. The approximate annual percentage rate of increase in the price level over this period has been:
(a) 2%
(b) 3%
(c) 4%
(d) 5%

14. The unemployment data collected by the Bureau of Labor Statistics have been criticized because:
(a) part-time workers are not counted in the number of workers employed
(b) discouraged workers are treated as a part of the labor force
(c) some workers who are not working may claim they are looking for work and are included in the labor force
(d) the underground economy may understate unemployment

15. Okun's law predicts that when the actual unemployment rate exceeds the natural rate of unemployment by two percentage points the GDP gap will equal:
(a) 2% of the potential GDP
(b) 3% of the potential GDP
(c) 4% of the potential GDP
(d) 5% of the potential GDP

16. If the GDP gap were equal to 7.5% of the potential GDP the actual unemployment rate would exceed the natural rate of unemployment by:
(a) two percentage points
(b) three percentage points
(c) four percentage points
(d) five percentage points

17. The burden of unemployment is *least* felt by:
(a) white-collar workers
(b) teenagers
(c) blacks
(d) males

18. If the consumer price index was 110 in one year and 117 in the next year, then the rate of inflation from one year to the next was:

(a) 3.5%
(b) 4.7%
(c) 6.4%
(d) 7.1%

Use the graph below to answer question 19.

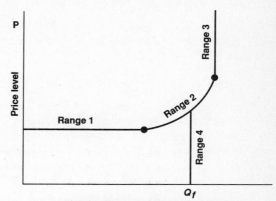

Real domestic output and employment

19. In which range does the price level begin to rise as the economy either approaches or surpasses the full employment level of output?
(a) range 1
(b) range 2
(c) range 3
(d) range 4

20. Only two resources, capital and labor, are used in an economy to produce an output of 300 million units. If the total cost of capital resources is $150 million and the total cost of labor resources is $50 million, then the per unit production costs in this economy are:
(a) $0.67 million
(b) $1.50 million
(c) $2.00 million
(d) $3.00 million

21. If the resources of the economy are fully employed, an increase in aggregate spending will cause:
(a) output and employment to increase
(b) output and prices to increase
(c) nominal income and prices to increase
(d) employment and nominal income to increase

22. If the economy is experiencing a depression with substantial unemployment, an increase in total spending will cause:
(a) a decrease in the *real* income of the economy
(b) little or no increase in the level of prices
(c) an increase in the *real* income and a decrease in the *nominal* income of the economy
(d) proportionate increases in the price level, output, and income in the economy

23. If a person's nominal income increases by 8% while the price level increases by 10% the person's real income will have:
(a) increased by 2%
(b) increased by 18%
(c) decreased by 18%
(d) decreased by 2%

24. The average level of nominal income is $21,000 and the price level index is 154. The average real income would be about:
(a) $12,546   (c) $15,299
(b) $13,636   (d) $17,823

25. With no inflation a bank would be willing to lend a business firm $10 million at an annual interest rate of 8%. But, if the rate of inflation was anticipated to be 6% the bank would charge the firm an annual interest rate of:
(a) 2%   (c) 8%
(b) 6%   (d) 14%

26. Which of the following would be hurt by unanticipated inflation?
(a) those living on incomes with cost-of-living adjustments
(b) those who find prices rising less rapidly than their nominal incomes
(c) those who lent money at a fixed interest rate
(d) those who became debtors when prices were lower

27. Many economists argue that mild demand-pull inflation at less than full employment results in:
(a) rising output
(b) rising real income
(c) falling unemployment
(d) all of the above

28. Which of the following contributes to cost-push inflation?
(a) an increase in employment and output
(b) an increase in per unit production costs
(c) a decrease in resource prices
(d) an increase in unemployment

29. Which of the following is *not* associated with hyperinflation?
(a) war or its aftermath
(b) rising output in the economy
(c) the hoarding of goods and speculation
(d) a halt to the use of money as both a medium of exchange and a standard of value

30. In recent years, Peru has experienced an inflation rate of over 3000% per year. This economic condition would best be described as:
(a) a wage-price inflationary spiral
(b) a cost-of-living adjustment
(c) cost-push inflation
(d) hyperinflation

■ **PROBLEMS**

1. In the table below are statistics showing the labor force and total employment during year 1 and year 5. Make the computations necessary to complete the table. (Numbers of persons are in thousands.)

	Year 1	Year 5
Labor force	84,889	95,453
Employed	80,796	87,524
Unemployed	_____	_____
Unemployment rate	_____	_____

a. How is it possible that *both* employment and unemployment increased? _____

_____

b. In relative terms, if unemployment increases, employment will decrease. Why? _____

_____

_____

c. Would you say that year 5 was a year of full employment? _____

_____

d. Why is the task of maintaining full employment over the years more than just a problem of finding jobs for those who happen to be employed at any given time?

_____

2. Suppose that in 1993 an economy is at full employment, has a potential and actual real GDP of $3,000 billion, and has an unemployment rate of 6%.
a. Compute the GDP gap in 1993 and enter it in the table below.

Year	Potential GDP	Actual GDP	GDP gap
1993	$3000	$3000.0	$_____
1994	3800	3705.0	_____
1995	4125	3712.5	_____

b. The potential and actual real GDPs in 1994 and 1995 are also shown in the table. Compute and enter into the table the GDP gaps in these two years.

c. In 1994, the actual real GDP is _____% of the potential real GDP. (*Hint:* divide the actual real GDP by the potential real GDP.)

(1) The actual real GDP is _____% *less* than the potential real GDP.

(2) Using Okun's law, the unemployment rate will rise from 6% in 1993 and be _____% in 1994.

d. In 1995 the actual real GDP is _____% of the potential real GDP.

(1) The actual real GDP is _____% *less* than the potential real GDP.
(2) The unemployment rate, according to Okun's law, will be _____%.

3. The table below shows the price index in the economy at the end of four different years.

Year	Price index	Rate of inflation
1	100.00	
2	112.00	_____%
3	123.20	_____
4	129.36	_____

a. Compute and enter in the table the rates of inflation in years 2, 3, and 4.
b. Employing the "rule of 70," how many years would it take for the price level to double at each of these three inflation rates? _____

_____

c. If nominal income increased by 15% from year 1 to year 2, what was the approximate percentage change in real income? _____
d. If nominal income increased by 7% from year 2 to year 3, what was the approximate percentage change in real income? _____
e. If nominal income was $25,000 in year 2, what was real income that year? _____
f. If nominal income was $25,000 in year 3, what was real income that year? _____
g. If the nominal interest rate was 14% to borrow money from year 1 to year 2, what was the approximate real rate of interest over that period? _____
h. If the nominal interest rate was 8% to borrow money from year 3 to year 4, what was the approximate real rate of interest over that period? _____

4. Indicate in the space to the right of each of the following the most likely effect—beneficial (B), detrimental (D), or indeterminate (I)—of unanticipated inflation on these persons:
a. A retired business executive who now lives each month by spending a part of the amount that was saved and deposited in a savings and loan association.

_____

b. A retired private-school teacher who lives on the dividends received from the shares of stock owned.

_____

c. A farmer who (by mortgaging a farm) borrowed at the local bank $500,000 that must be repaid during the next ten years. _____
d. A retired couple whose sole source of income is the pension they receive from a former employer.

_____

e. A widow whose income consists entirely of interest received from the corporate bonds she owns.

_____

f. A public school teacher. _____
g. A member of a union who works for a firm that produces computers. _____

5. In the space below, indicate for each of the following situations the effects of an increase in total spending on *real GDP, nominal GDP*, the *unemployment rate*, and the *price level*, respectively, using the following symbols: A, little, or no effect; B, increase; C, decrease; and D, sharp increase.
a. Depression and widespread unemployment

_____ _____ _____ _____

b. Prosperity, but moderate unemployment

_____ _____ _____ _____

c. Prosperity and full employment

_____ _____ _____ _____

6. On the graphs on the next page the price *level* is measured along the vertical axis and real *domestic* output is measured along the horizontal axis. The demand for and the supply of domestic output are shown by the curves labeled *D* and *S*.
a. Applying the principles of demand and supply which you learned in Chapter 3, the equilibrium price level is the price level at which the domestic output demanded and the domestic output supplied are _____ and the equilibrium domestic output is _____

_____

b. Draw on the first graph a new demand curve which represents an *increase* in the demand for domestic output.
(1) The effect of this increase in demand is a rise in the equilibrium price level and a(n) _____ in the equilibrium domestic output.
(2) This rise in the price level is an example of _____

_____ inflation.
c. On the second graph on the next page draw a new supply curve which represents a *decrease* in the supply of domestic output.

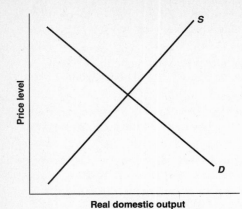

Real domestic output

(1) The effect of this decrease in supply is a _____ in the equilibrium price level and a _____ in the equilibrium domestic output.

(2) These effects are an example of _____

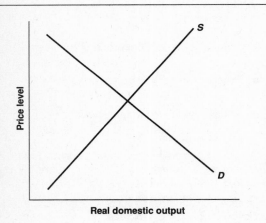

Real domestic output

■ SHORT ANSWER AND ESSAY QUESTIONS

1. What is the historical record of the American economy with respect to economic growth, full employment, and price-level stability?

2. Define the business cycle. Why do some economists prefer the term "business fluctuations" to "business cycle"?

3. Describe the four phases of an idealized business cycle.

4. What, in the opinion of most economists, is the immediate determinant or cause of the levels of output and employment in the economy?

5. The business cycle is only one of three general causes of changes in output and employment in the economy. What are the other influences which affect these variables?

6. Compare the manner in which the business cycle affects output and employment in the industries producing capital and durable goods with industries producing nondurable goods and services. What causes these differences?

7. Distinguish among frictional, structural, and cyclical unemployment.

8. When is there full employment in the American economy? (Answer in terms of the unemployment rate, the actual and potential output of the economy, and the markets for labor.)

9. What is the "natural" rate of unemployment? Will the economy always operate at the natural rate? Why is the natural rate subject to revision?

10. How is the unemployment rate measured in the United States? What criticisms have been made of the method used by the Bureau of Labor Statistics to determine the unemployment rate?

11. What is the economic cost of unemployment and how is this cost measured? What is the quantitative relationship (called Okun's law) between the unemployment rate and the cost of unemployment?

12. What groups in the economy tend to bear the burdens of unemployment? How are women affected by unemployment and how is the percentage of the labor force unemployed fifteen or more weeks related to the unemployment rate in the economy?

13. How does the unemployment rate in the United States compare with those for other industrialized nations in recent years?

14. What is inflation and how is the rate of inflation measured?

15. What has been the experience of the United States with inflation since the 1920s? How does the inflation rate in the United States compare with those for other industrialized nations in recent years?

16. Compare and contrast demand-pull and cost-push inflation.

17. What groups benefit from and what groups are hurt by inflation and how has the public sector of the economy been affected by it?

18. What is the difference between the effects of unanticipated and the effects of anticipated inflation on the redistribution of real incomes in the economy?

19. Explain what will tend to happen to employment, output, nominal and real income, and the price level if total spending increases and the resources of the economy are: (*a*) widely unemployed, (*b*) moderately unemployed, (*c*) fully employed. If total spending *decreased* would the effects on employment, output, income, and the price level be just the opposite?

20. Write three scenarios that describe the effects of inflation on the domestic output.

ANSWERS

Chapter 8 Macroeconomic Instability: Unemployment and Inflation

FILL-IN QUESTIONS

1. unsteady, inflation, output, employment

2. ups (increases), downs (decreases)

3. recession, trough, recovery

4. spending, demand

5. seasonal, secular

6. durable, capital, nondurable, low-

7. *a.* frictional unemployment; *b.* structural unemployment; *c.* cyclical unemployment (any order)

8. *a.* natural; *b.* frictional, structural (either order); *c.* cyclical, actual, potential (either order); *d.* 5.5 to 6

9. equal to, constant

10. the number of unemployed persons, labor force

11. the potential, the actual, increase, 2.5

12. black, teenage, blue-collar, less

13. rise (increase), prices, 1993, 1992, 1992

14. inflation, 70, rule of 70

15. *a.* deflation; *b.* high, low, high; *c.* high, low (either order)

16. *a.* increase; *b.* per unit production costs, wages, nonwage inputs; *c.* difficult

17. real income; *a.* real income, 3; *b.* real income, $28,301.88

18. *a.* fixed; *b.* unexpected; *c.* creditors, debtors; *d.* households, the public sector

19. anticipated; *a.* cost-of-living adjustments (COLA); *b.* real rate of interest, nominal rate of interest

20. *a.* increase; *b.* decrease; *c.* breakdown (collapse)

TRUE-FALSE QUESTIONS

1. T, p. 143	**8.** T, p. 148	**15.** T, p. 148	**22.** F, p. 158
2. F, pp. 143-144	**9.** T, p. 148	**16.** F, p. 154	**23.** T, p. 159
3. F, p. 144	**10.** F, p. 149	**17.** F, p. 154	**24.** T, p. 153
4. T, pp. 145-146	**11.** F, p. 152	**18.** F, p. 155	**25.** F, p. 159
5. F, p. 146	**12.** F, p. 150	**19.** T, p. 156	
6. T, p. 147	**13.** T, pp. 152-153	**20.** T, pp. 156-157	
7. F, pp. 147-148	**14.** T, p. 150	**21.** T, p. 158	

MULTIPLE-CHOICE QUESTIONS

1. *b*, p. 144	**9.** *c*, p. 148	**17.** *a*, p. 152	**25.** *d*, pp. 159-160
2. *d*, p. 145	**10.** *d*, p. 149	**18.** *c*, p. 154	**26.** *c*, p. 159
3. *b*, pp. 145-146	**11.** *d*, p. 149	**19.** *b*, p. 156	**27.** *d*, p. 161
4. *a*, pp. 145-146	**12.** *c*, p. 150	**20.** *a*, p. 157	**28.** *b*, pp. 156-157
5. *a*, p. 146	**13.** *d*, p. 154	**21.** *c*, p. 156	**29.** *b*, pp. 161-162
6. *b*, pp. 147-148	**14.** *c*, p. 150	**22.** *b*, pp. 155-156	**30.** *d*, pp. 161-162
7. *a*, p. 147	**15.** *d*, p. 150	**23.** *d*, p. 158	
8. *c*, p. 148	**16.** *b*, p. 151	**24.** *b*, p. 158	

PROBLEMS

1. year 1: 4,093, 4.8; year 5: 7,929, 8.3; *a.* the labor force increased more than employment increased; *b.* because unemployment and employment in relative terms are percentages of the labor force and **always** add to 100%, and if one increases the other must decrease; *c.* no economist would argue that the full-employment unemployment rate is as high as 8.3% and year 5 was not a year of full employment; *d.* the number of people looking for work expands

2. *a.* 0; *b.* 95, 412.5; *c.* 97.5, (1) 2.5, (2) 7; *d.* 90, (1) 10, (2) 10

3. *a.* 12, 10, 5; *b.* 5, 7, 14; *c.* 3; *d.* -3; *e.* $22,321; *f.* $20,292; *g.* 2; *h.* 3

4. *a.* D; *b.* I; *c.* B; *d.* D; *e.* D; *f.* I; *g.* B

5. *a.* B, B, C, A; *b.* B, B, C, B; *c.* A, D, A, D

6. *a.* equal, the domestic output demanded and supplied at the equilibrium price level; *b.* (1) increase, (2) demand-pull; *c.* (1) rise, fall, (2) cost-push inflation

SHORT ANSWER AND ESSAY QUESTIONS

1. pp. 143-144	**6.** p. 146	**11.** pp. 150-152	**16.** pp. 155-157
2. p. 144	**7.** pp. 147-148	**12.** p. 152	**17.** pp. 157-159
3. pp. 144-145	**8.** pp. 148-150	**13.** p. 153	**18.** pp. 159-160
4. p. 145	**9.** p. 148	**14.** p. 154	**19.** pp. 155-156
5. pp. 145-146	**10.** pp. 149-150	**15.** p. 155	**20.** pp. 160-161

CHAPTER 9

Building the Aggregate Expenditures Model

This chapter is the first of two chapters that develops the first macroeconomic model of the economy presented in the textbook—the aggregate expenditures model. In the chapter you will find out what determines the demand for real domestic output (real GDP) and how an economy achieves an equilibrium level of output (and employment).

The first section of Chapter 9 offers a brief historical perspective on the aggregate expenditures model. Here you will learn about classical economics and its conclusion that the economy will automatically function to produce the maximum output it is capable of producing and provide employment for all those who are willing and able to work. This conclusion is based on Say's law which held that production automatically provides the income necessary to purchase all output, or **supply creates its own demand.** The Great Depression and the work of John Maynard Keynes showed that there is no guarantee of maximum output and full employment, and that depression or inflation can prevail with no automatic tendency for it to be corrected by the economy. Keynesian analysis of the expenditure components of the economy became the basis for the aggregate expenditures model.

The second section of the chapter describes the largest component of aggregate expenditures—consumption. An examination of consumption, however, also entails a study of saving because saving is simply the part of disposable income that is not consumed. This section develops the consumption and saving schedules and describes their main characteristics. Other key concepts are also presented: average and marginal propensities to consume and save, and the nonincome determinants of consumption and saving.

Investment expenditures is the subject of the third section of the chapter. The purchase of capital goods depends upon the rate of net profits which business firms **expect** to earn from an investment and upon the real rate of interest they have to pay for the use of money. Because firms are anxious to make profitable investments and to avoid unprofitable ones, they undertake all investments which have an expected rate of net profit greater than (or equal to) the real rate of interest and do not undertake an investment when the expected rate of net profit is less than the real rate of interest. You should see that because

business firms behave this way the lower the real rate of interest the larger will be the dollar amount invested; and that this relationship between the real interest rate and the level of investment spending, called the investment-demand schedule, is an inverse one. But you should not confuse the investment-demand schedule (or curve) with the investment schedule (or curve) which relates investment spending to the GDP and which may show investment is either unrelated to or directly related to the GDP. Five noninterest determinants of investment spending influence the profit expectations of business firms; and these are analyzed. You should learn how changes in these determinants affect investment and why investment spending is unstable.

In the fourth and fifth sections of the chapter the equilibrium level of real GDP is explained with both tables and graphs, first by using the expenditures-output approach and then by employing the leakages-injections approach. These two approaches are complementary and are two different ways of analyzing the same process and of reaching the same conclusions. For each approach it is important for you to know, given the consumption (or saving) schedule and the level of gross investment expenditures, **what** real GDP will tend to be produced and **why** this will be the real GDP which will be produced.

The final section discusses the distinction between **planned** investment and **actual** investment. Saving and actual gross investment are always equal because they are defined in exactly the same way: the output of the economy minus its consumption. But saving and planned gross investment are not, however, equal by definition. They are equal only when real GDP is at its equilibrium level. When real GDP is **not** at its equilibrium level, saving and planned gross investment are **not** equal even though saving and actual investment are, as always, equal because the actual investment includes **un**planned investment or disinvestment. Remember: Equilibrium real GDP is achieved when saving and **planned** gross investment— **not** saving and **actual** gross investment—are equal.

In the next chapter the tools and ideas developed and explained in Chapter 9 are put together to form a complete and coherent picture of how aggregate expenditures determine the level of GDP.

■ CHECKLIST

When you have studied this chapter you should be able to:

☐ Describe Say's law and the main ideas of classical economics.

☐ Explain the major ideas of Keynesian economics and how it differs from classical economics.

☐ List four simplifying assumptions in this chapter for building the aggregate expenditures model and two implications of those assumptions.

☐ State what determines the amount of goods and services produced and the level of employment in the Keynesian theory.

☐ Explain how consumption and saving are related to disposable income.

☐ Compute, when you are given the necessary data, the four propensities.

☐ Explain what happens to the size of the two average propensities as income increases.

☐ Demonstrate that the MPC is the numerical value of the slope of the consumption schedule and that the MPS is the numerical value of the slope of the saving schedule.

☐ List four nonincome determinants of consumption and saving; and explain how a change in each of these determinants will affect the consumption and saving schedules.

☐ Explain the difference between a change in the amount consumed (or saved) and a change in the consumption (or saving) schedule.

☐ List the two basic determinants of investment; and explain when a firm will and will not invest.

☐ Compute, when given the appropriate data, the investment-demand schedule; and explain why the relationship between investment spending and the real rate of interest is inverse.

☐ List the five noninterest determinants of investment; and explain how a change in each of these determinants will affect the investment-demand curve.

☐ Explain the two variables found in an investment schedule; and the two kinds of relationships that might be found to exist between these two variables.

☐ List the four factors which explain why investment spending tends to be unstable.

☐ Find the equilibrium real GDP, when you are given the necessary tabular or graphical data, by employing either the aggregate-expenditures–national-output or the leakages-injections approach.

☐ Explain why the economy will tend to produce its equilibrium real GDP rather than some smaller or larger real GDP.

☐ State the difference between planned investment and actual investment.

☐ Explain how it is possible for saving and actual investment to be equal when saving and planned investment are not equal.

☐ Determine the economy's new equilibrium real GDP when there is a change in the consumption (or saving) schedule or in the investment schedule.

■ CHAPTER OUTLINE

1. The context for the development of the aggregate expenditures model developed in this chapter is historical debate between classical and Keynesian economics.

   a. Classical economics concluded that the economy would automatically tend to full employment of resources and maximum output, and that laissez faire is the best policy for the government to pursue. These employment and output conclusions are based on Say's law which states that supply creates its own demand. If there were an excess supply of goods or an excess supply of labor, price and wages would fall until the excesses were eliminated and full employment and maximum output were again achieved.

   b. The Great Depression and the ideas of J. M. Keynes, in *The General Theory of Employment, Interest and Money,* laid the foundation for a rejection of classical economics and the development of the aggregate expenditures model. Keynes challenged Say's law and showed that an economy can be inherently unstable and experience a long period of recession. Wages and prices are inflexible downward, and saving and investment decisions may not be coordinated, so there is no guarantee of full employment and maximum output. The economy is not self-regulating, so government policies are necessary to counteract economic instability.

2. To simplify the explanation of the aggregate expenditures model four assumptions are made: the economy is "closed"; government neither spends nor collects taxes; all saving is personal saving; and depreciation and net American income earned abroad are zero. These assumptions have two important implications: only consumption and investment are considered in the model, and output or income measures (GDP, NI, PI, DI) are treated as equal to each other.

3. Aggregate output and employment in the aggregate expenditures theory are directly related to the level of total or aggregate expenditures in the economy; and to understand what determines the level of total expenditures at any time it is necessary to explain the factors that determine the levels of consumption and investment expenditures.

4. Consumption is the largest component of aggregate expenditures; and saving is disposable income not spent for consumer goods.

   a. Disposable income is the most important determinant of both consumption and saving; the relationships between income and consumption and between income and saving are both direct (positive) ones.

b. The consumption schedule shows the amounts that households plan to spend for consumer goods at various levels of income, given a price level.

c. The saving schedule indicates the amounts households plan to save at different income levels, given a price level.

d. The average propensities to consume and to save and the marginal propensities to consume and to save can be computed from the consumption and saving schedules.

(1) The APC and the APS are, respectively, the percentages of income spent for consumption and saved, and their sum is equal to 1.

(2) The MPC and the MPS are, respectively, the percentages of *additional* income spent for consumption and saved; and their sum is equal to 1.

(3) The MPC is the slope of the consumption schedule and the MPS is the slope of the saving schedule when the two schedules are graphed.

e. In addition to income, there are several other important determinants of consumption and saving; and changes in these nonincome determinants will cause the consumption and saving *schedules* to change. The four nonincome determinants include wealth, expectations, consumer indebtedness, and taxation.

f. A change in the amount consumed (or saved) is not the same thing as a change in the consumption (or saving) schedule. If these schedules change they change in opposite directions; but the schedules are very stable.

5. The two important determinants of the level of gross investment spending in the economy are the expected rate of net profits from the purchase of additional capital goods and the real rate of interest.

a. The expected rate of net profits is directly related to the net profits (revenues less operating costs) that are expected to result from an investment and inversely related to the cost of making the investment (purchasing capital goods).

b. The rate of interest is the price paid for the use of money. When the expected real rate of net profits is greater (less) than the real rate of interest a business will (will not) invest because the investment will be profitable (unprofitable).

c. For this reason, the lower (higher) the real rate of interest, the greater (smaller) will be the level of investment spending in the economy; and the investment-demand curve (schedule) indicates this inverse relationship between the real rate of interest and the level of spending for capital goods.

d. There are at least five noninterest determinants of investment demand; and a change in any of these determinants will shift the investment-demand curve (schedule). These determinants include: acquisition, maintenance, and operating costs; business taxes; technological change; the stock of capital on hand; and expectations.

e. Investment spending in the economy may also be either independent or directly related to the real GDP; and the investment schedule may show that investment either remains constant or increases as real GDP increases.

f. Because the five noninterest determinants of investment are subject to sudden changes, investment spending tends to be unstable.

6. Employing the aggregate-expenditures–national-output approach, the equilibrium real GDP is the real GDP at which:

a. aggregate expenditures (consumption plus planned gross investment) equal the real GDP, or

b. in graphical terms, the aggregate-expenditures curve crosses the 45-degree line and its slope is equal to the marginal propensity to consume.

7. Using the leakages-injections approach, the equilibrium real GDP is the real GDP at which:

a. saving and planned gross investment are equal; or

b. in graphical terms, the saving curve crosses the planned gross investment curve.

8. The gross investment schedule indicates what investors *plan* to do; and when saving is greater (less) than planned gross investment,

a. *un*planned gross investment (disinvestment) in inventories will occur; and

b. producers will reduce (expand) their production and the real GDP will fall (rise) until there is no unplanned gross investment (disinvestment); but the *actual* gross investment and saving are always equal because the former includes unplanned investment or disinvestment.

■ IMPORTANT TERMS

Say's law

Keynesian economics

Consumption schedule

Saving schedule

Break-even income

Average propensity to consume

Average propensity to save

Marginal propensity to consume

Marginal propensity to save

Nonincome determinants of consumption and saving

Change in amount consumed (saved)

Change in the consumption (saving) schedule

Expected rate of net profits

Real rate of interest

Investment-demand schedule (curve)

Noninterest determinants of investment

Investment schedule (curve)

Aggregate-expenditures–output approach

Aggregate expenditures

Aggregate-expenditures schedule (curve)

Equilibrium (real) GDP

45-degree line

Leakages-injections approach

Leakage

Injection

Planned investment

Actual investment

Unplanned investment

■ HINTS AND TIPS

1. The most important graph in the chapter is the consumption schedule (see Key Graph 9–2). Know how to interpret it. There are two lines on the graph. The 45-degree reference line shows all points where disposable income equals consumption (there is no saving). The consumption schedule line shows the total amount of disposal income spent on consumption at each and every income level. Where the two lines *intersect,* all disposable income is spent (consumed). At all income levels to the right of the intersection, the consumption line lies below the 45-degree line, and not all disposable income is spent (there is saving). To the left of the intersection, the consumption line lies above the 45-degree line, and consumption exceeds disposable income (there is dissaving).

2. Always remember that marginal propensities equal 1 (MPC + MPS = 1). The same is true for average propensities (APC + APS = 1). Thus, if you know the value of one marginal propensity (e.g., MPC) you can always figure out the value of the other one (e.g., 1 − MPC = MPS).

3. The distinction between *actual* and *planned* investment is important for determining the equilibrium level of real GDP. *Actual* investment includes both *planned* and *unplanned* investment. At any level of real GDP, *saving* and *actual* investment will always be equal by definition, but *saving* and *planned* investment may not equal real GDP because there may be *unplanned* investment (unplanned changes in inventories). Only at the equilibrium level of real GDP will *saving* and *planned* investment be equal (this is not *unplanned* investment).

SELF-TEST

■ FILL-IN QUESTIONS

1. Classical economists believe a market (or capitalistic) economy will tend to produce an output at which its labor force is (fully, less than fully) _____ employed but Keynesian economists argue it will tend to produce an output at which its labor force is _____ employed.

2. According to the classical way of thinking, if total output exceeded the level of spending, prices in the output markets would tend to (rise, fall) _____ because of competition among business firms; this would make some production unprofitable and temporarily cause _____ in labor markets; but competition among workers would tend to drive wage rates (upward, downward) _____ and (increase, decrease) _____ their employment.

3. According to Say's law, the production of goods and services creates an equal _____ _____

4. J. M. Keynes (accepted, rejected) _____ Say's law and showed that an economy can be inherently (stable, unstable) _____ and experience long periods of (recession, economic growth) _____. According to Keynes, wages and prices are (flexible, inflexible) _____ downward, and thus costly unemployment can occur for long periods.

5. Four "simplifying assumptions" used throughout most of the chapter are that the economy is a(n) (open, closed) _____ economy; that all saving is (personal, business) _____ saving; that government does not collect _____, make _____ payments, or _____ for goods and services; and that depreciation and net American income earned abroad are _____. The implications of these assumptions are:

   a. GDP = _____ = _____ = _____

   b. total spending = _____ + _____

6. In modern capitalism, domestic output and employment depend (directly, indirectly) _____ on the level of _____ in the economy. The most important determinant of consumption and saving is the economy's disposable _____. Both consumption and saving are (directly, indirectly) _____ related to this determinant.

7. As disposable income falls, the average propensity to consume will (rise, fall) _____ and the average propensity to save will _____

8. The MPC is the change in (consumption, saving, income) _____ divided by the change in _____; it is the numerical value of the slope of the _____ schedule. The MPS is the change in _____ divided by the change in _____; it is the numerical value of the slope of the _____ schedule.

9. The most important determinants of consumption spending, other than the level of income, are:

  a. the wealthy or the sum of the _____ and the _____ asset households have accumulated

  b. _____

  c. _____

  d. _____

10. A change in the consumption (or saving) schedule means that _____
_____
but a change in the amount consumed (or saved) means that _____
_____

11. Investment is defined as spending for additional _____; and the total amount of investment spending in the economy depends upon:

  a. the _____ rate of net _____ , and the real rate of _____
  b. A business firm will invest in more capital if the expected rate of net profits on this investment is (greater, less) _____ than the real rate of interest it must pay for the use of money.

12. The relationship between the rate of interest and the total amount of investment in the economy is (direct, inverse) _____
This means that if the real rate of interest:

  a. rises, investment will_____

  b. falls, investment will _____

13. Five noninterest determinants of investment demand are:

  a. _____

  b. _____

  c. _____

  d. _____

  e. _____

14. The consumption schedule and the saving schedule tend to be (stable or unstable) _____ while investment demand tends to be _____

15. The demand for new capital goods tends to be unstable because of the _____ of capital goods, the _____ of innovation, and the _____ of actual and expected profits.

16. Two complementary approaches which are employed to explain the equilibrium level of real domestic output are the _____
approach and the _____ approach.

17. Assuming a private and closed economy, the equilibrium level of real GDP is the real GDP at which:

  a. aggregate _____ equal real domestic _____

  b. real GDP equals _____ plus _____
  c. the aggregate-expenditures schedule or curve intersects the _____ line.

18. When the leakages-injections approach is used:
  a. In this chapter the only leakage considered is _____ and the only injection considered is _____
  b. Later the two additional:

  (1) leakages considered are _____ and _____

  (2) injections considered are _____ and _____

19. If:
  a. Aggregate expenditures are greater than the real domestic output, saving is (greater, less) _____ than planned gross investment, there is unplanned (investment, disinvestment) _____ in inventories, and the real GDP will (rise, fall) _____
  b. Aggregate expenditures are less than the real domestic output, saving is _____ than

planned gross investment, there is unplanned _____

_____ in inventories, and the real GDP will _____

c. Aggregate expenditures are equal to the real domestic output, saving is _____ planned gross investment, unplanned investment in inventories is _____, and the real GDP will _____

20. At every level of real GDP saving is equal to (planned, actual) _____ gross investment.

a. But if planned gross investment is greater than saving by $10;

(1) there is $10 of unplanned (investment, disinvestment) _____

(2) the real GDP will (rise, fall) _____

b. And if planned gross investment is less than saving by $5:

(1) there is $5 of unplanned _____

(2) the real GDP will _____

■ **TRUE-FALSE QUESTIONS**

Circle the T if the statement is true; the F if it is false.

1. In the aggregate expenditures model of the economy the price level is constant.   T   F

2. According to the classical economists, full employment is normal in market economies.   T   F

3. The classical economists believed that government assistance was *not* required to bring about full employment and full production in the economy.   T   F

4. Say's law states that demand for goods and services creates an equal supply of goods and services.   T   F

5. Classical economists contend that prices and wages would be sufficiently flexible to assure full employment.   T   F

6. The level of saving in the economy, according to the Keynesians, depends primarily upon the level of its disposable income.   T   F

7. The consumption schedule which is employed as an analytical tool is also an historical record of the relationship of consumption to disposable income.   T   F

8. Empirical data suggest that households will tend to spend a similar proportion of a small disposable income than a larger disposable income.   T   F

9. An increase in taxation will increase the consumption schedule (shift the consumption curve upward).   T   F

10. An increase in the taxes paid by consumers will decrease both the amount they spend for consumption and the amount they save.   T   F

11. Both the consumption schedule and the saving schedule tend to be relatively stable over time.   T   F

12. The *real* interest rate is the nominal interest rate minus the rate of inflation.   T   F

13. A business firm will purchase additional capital goods if the real rate of interest it must pay exceeds the expected rate of net profits from the investment.   T   F

14. An increase in an economy's income may induce an increase in investment spending.   T   F

15. The relationship between the rate of interest and the level of investment spending is called the investment schedule.   T   F

16. The investment-demand schedule (or curve) tends to be relatively stable over time.   T   F

17. The irregularity of innovations and the variability of business profits contribute to the instability of investment expenditures.   T   F

18. The investment schedule is a schedule of planned investment rather than a schedule of actual investment.   T   F

19. Saving and actual gross investment are always equal.   T   F

20. Saving at any level of real GDP equals planned gross investment plus unplanned investment (or minus unplanned disinvestment).   T   F

■ **MULTIPLE-CHOICE QUESTIONS**

Circle the letter that corresponds to the best answer.

1. Classical economics suggests that in capitalist economies:
(a) unemployment may persist for extended periods
(b) the market system will ensure full employment
(c) a slump in output will increase prices, wages, and interest rates
(d) demand creates its own supply

2. From the perspective of classical economics, if total output was greater than total spending, competition would tend to force:
(a) product and resource prices down
(b) product prices up and resource prices down
(c) product prices up and resource prices up
(d) product prices down and resource prices up

3. Which would be considered part of Keynes' criticism of classical economics?

(a) investment spending will increase when the interest rate increases
(b) prices and wages are flexible downward in modern capitalist economies
(c) the act of producing goods generates an amount of income equal to the value of the goods produced
(d) a reduction in wage rates will lead only to a reduction in total spending, and not to an increase in employment

4. If the economy is closed, government neither taxes nor spends; all saving done in the economy is personal saving; and depreciation and net American income earned abroad are zero:
(a) gross domestic product equals personal consumption expenditures
(b) gross domestic product equals personal saving
(c) gross domestic product equals disposable income
(d) disposable income equals personal consumption expenditures

5. In the Keynesian theory, output and employment in the economy depend:
(a) directly on the level of total expenditures
(b) inversely on the quantity of resources available to it
(c) directly on the level of disposable income
(d) directly on the rate of interest

6. As disposable income decreases, ***ceteris paribus:***
(a) both consumption and saving increase
(b) consumption increases and saving decreases
(c) consumption decreases and saving increases
(d) both consumption and saving decrease

7. If consumption spending increases from $358 to $367 billion when disposable income increases from $412 to $427 billion, it can be concluded that the marginal propensity to consume is:
(a) 0.4
(b) 0.6
(c) 0.8
(d) 0.9

8. If disposable income is $375 billion when the average propensity to consume is 0.8, it can be concluded that:
(a) the marginal propensity to consume is also 0.8
(b) consumption is $325 billion
(c) saving is $75 billion
(d) the marginal propensity to save is 0.2

9. As the disposable income of the economy increases:
(a) both the APC and the APS rise
(b) the APC rises and the APS falls
(c) the APC falls and the APS rises
(d) both the APC and the APS fall

10. A decrease in the level of investment spending would be a consequence of:

(a) a decline in the rate of interest
(b) a decline in the level of wages paid
(c) a decline in business taxes
(d) a decline in stock market prices

11. Which of the following relationships is an inverse one?
(a) the relationship between consumption spending and disposable income
(b) the relationship between investment spending and the rate of interest
(c) the relationship between saving and the rate of interest
(d) the relationship between investment spending and net national product

12. The slope of the consumption schedule or line for a given economy is the:
(a) marginal propensity to consume
(b) average propensity to consume
(c) marginal propensity to save
(d) average propensity to save

13. According to the classical economists, aggregate demand will be reasonably stable if:
(a) aggregate supply is reasonably stable
(b) business investment does not fluctuate
(c) there is a constant supply of money
(d) interest rates are flexible

*Answer the next two questions (**14** and **15**) on the basis of the following diagram.*

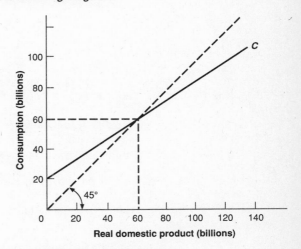

14. This diagram indicates that:
(a) consumption decreases after the $60 billion level of GDP
(b) the marginal propensity to consume decreases after the $60 billion level of GDP
(c) consumption decreases as a percentage of GDP as GDP increases
(d) consumption increases as GDP decreases

15. If the relevant saving schedule were constructed, one would find that:
(a) the marginal propensity to save is negative up to the $60 billion level of GDP
(b) the marginal propensity to save increases after the $60 billion level of GDP
(c) saving is zero at the $60 billion level of GDP
(d) saving is $20 billion at the $0 level of GDP

Answer the next three questions (16, 17, and 18) on the basis of the following disposable income (DI) and consumption (C) schedules for a private, closed economy. All figures are in billions of dollars.

DI	C
$ 0	$ 4
40	40
80	76
120	112
160	148
200	184

16. If plotted on a graph, the slope of the consumption schedule would be:
(a) .6
(b) .7
(c) .8
(d) .9

17. At the $160 billion level of disposable income, the average propensity to save is:
(a) .015
(b) .075
(c) .335
(d) .925

18. If consumption increases by $5 billion at each level of disposable income, then the marginal propensity to consume will:
(a) change, but the average propensity to consume will *not* change
(b) change, and the average propensity to consume will change
(c) *not* change, but the average propensity to consume will change
(d) *not* change, and the average propensity to consume will *not* change

19. If the slope of a linear saving schedule decreases in a private, closed economy, then it can be concluded that the:
(a) MPS has decreased
(b) MPC has decreased
(c) income has decreased
(d) income has increased

20. Which one of the following best explains the variability of investment?

(a) the predictable useful life of capital goods
(b) constancy or regularities in business innovations
(c) instabilities in the level of profits
(d) business pessimism about the future

21. When the economy's real GDP exceeds its equilibrium real GDP:
(a) there is unplanned gross investment in the economy
(b) planned gross investment exceeds saving
(c) the aggregate expenditures exceed the real domestic output
(d) there is an inflationary gap

22. If real GDP is $275 billion, consumption $250 billion, and planned gross investment $30 billion, real GDP:
(a) will tend to remain constant
(b) will tend to increase
(c) will tend to decrease
(d) equals aggregate expenditures

23. Which of the following is an injection?
(a) investment
(b) saving
(c) taxes
(d) imports

24. If saving is greater than planned gross investment:
(a) businesses will be motivated to increase their investments
(b) aggregate expenditures will be greater than the real domestic output
(c) real GDP will be greater than planned gross investment plus consumption
(d) saving will tend to increase

25. On a graph the equilibrium real GDP is found at the intersection of the 45-degree line and
(a) the consumption curve
(b) the investment-demand curve
(c) the saving curve
(d) the aggregate-expenditures curve

■ **PROBLEMS**

1. At the top of the next page is a consumption schedule. Assume taxes and transfer payments are zero and that all saving is personal saving.
a. Compute saving at each of the eight levels of GDP and the missing average propensities to consume and to save.

b. The break-even level of income (GDP) is $_____
c. As GDP rises the marginal propensity to consume remains constant. Between each two GDPs the MPC can be found by dividing $_____ by $_____; and is equal to _____%

GDP	C	S	APC,%	APS,%
$1500	$1540	$_____	1.027	–.027
1600	1620	_____	1.025	–.025
1700	1700	_____	_____	_____
1800	1780	_____	.989	.011
1900	1860	_____	.979	.021
2000	1940	_____	_____	_____
2100	2020	_____	.962	.038
2200	2100	_____	_____	_____

d. The marginal propensity to save also remains constant when the GDP rises. Between each two GDPs the MPS is equal to $_____ divided by $_____; or to _____%

e. Plot the consumption schedule, the saving schedule, and the 45° line on the graph below.

(1) The numerical value of the slope of the consumption schedule is _____ and the term that is used to describe it is the _____

(2) If the relevant saving schedule were constructed the numerical value of the slope of the saving schedule would be _____ and the term that is used to describe it is the _____

2. Indicate in the space to the right of each of the following events whether the event will tend to increase (+) or decrease (–) the *saving* schedule.

a. Development of consumer expectations that prices will be higher in the future _____

b. Gradual shrinkage in the quantity of real assets owned by consumers _____

c. Increase in the volume of consumer indebtedness _____

d. Growing belief that disposable income will be lower in the future _____

e. Rumors that a current shortage of consumer goods will soon disappear _____

f. Rise in the actual level of disposable income _____

g. A build-up in the dollar size of the financial assets owned by consumers _____

h. Development of a belief by consumers that the Federal government can and will prevent recessions in the future _____

3. The schedule (next page) has eight different rates of net profit and the dollar amounts of the investment projects expected to have each of these net profit rates.

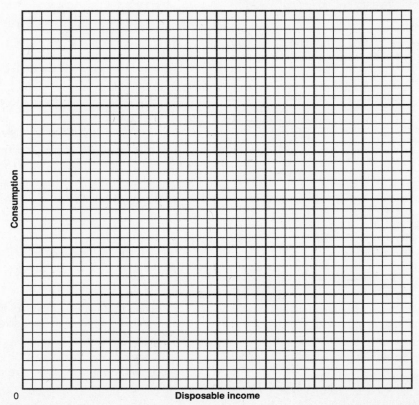

Consumption

0   Disposable income

Expected rate of net profit	Investment projects (billions)
18%	$ 0
16	10
14	20
12	30
10	40
8	50
6	60
4	70

a. If the real rate of interest in the economy were 18%, business firms would plan to spend $_____ billion for investment; but if the real interest rate were 16% they would plan to spend $_____ for investment.

b. Should the real interest rate be 14% they would still wish to make the investments they were willing to make at real interest rates of 18% and 16%; they would also plan to spend an additional $_____ billion for investment; and their total investment would be $_____ billion.

c. Were the real rate of interest 12% they would make all the investments they had planned to make at higher real interest rates plus an additional $_____ billion; and their total investment spending would be $_____ billion.

d. Complete the table below by computing the amount of planned investment at the four remaining real interest rates.

Real rate of interest	Amount of investment (billions)
18%	$ 0
16	10
14	30
12	60
10	_____
8	_____
6	_____
4	_____

e. Graph the schedule you completed on the graph in the next column. Plot the real rate of interest on the vertical axis and the amount of investment planned at each real rate of interest on the horizontal axis.

f. Both the graph and the table show that the relationship between the real rate of interest and the amount of investment spending in the economy is _____. This means that when the real rate of interest:

(1) increases, investment will (increase, decrease) _____

(2) decreases, investment will _____

g. It also means that should we wish to:

(1) increase investment, we would need to _____ the real rate of interest

(2) decrease investment, we would have to _____ the real rate of interest

h. This graph (or table) is the _____ _____ curve (or schedule).

0

4. Indicate in the space to the right of the following events whether the event would tend to increase (+) or decrease (−) investment expenditures.

a. Rising stock market prices _____
b. Development of expectations by businessmen that business taxes will be higher in the future _____
c. Step-up in the rates at which new products and new production processes are being introduced _____
d. Business belief that wage rates may be lower in the future _____
e. A mild recession _____
f. A belief that business is "too good" and the economy is due for a period of "slow" consumer demand _____
g. Rising costs in the construction industry _____
h. A rapid increase in the size of the economy's population _____
i. A period of a high level of investment spending which has resulted in productive capacity in excess of the current demand for goods and services _____

5. Below are two schedules showing several GDPs and the level of investment spending (*I*) at each GDP. (All figures are in billions of dollars.)

Schedule number 1		Schedule number 2	
GDP	I	GDP	I
$1850	$90	$1850	$ 75
1900	90	1900	80
1950	90	1950	85
2000	90	2000	90
2050	90	2050	95
2100	90	2100	100
2150	95	2150	105

a. Each of these schedules is an _____ schedule.

b. When such a schedule is drawn up it is assumed that the real rate of interest is _____

c. In schedule:
(1) number 1, GDP and *I* are (unrelated, directly related) _____

(2) number 2, GDP and *I* are _____

d. Should the real rate of interest rise, investment spending at each GDP would (increase, decrease) _____ and the curve relating GDP and investment spending would shift (upward, downward)

■ **SHORT ANSWER AND ESSAY QUESTIONS**

1. According to the classical economists, what level of employment would tend to prevail in the economy? Why?

2. In the classical analysis Say's law made it certain that whatever was produced would be sold. How did flexible prices, flexible wages, and competition drive the economy to full employment and maximum output?

3. On what grounds did J. M. Keynes argue that flexible interest rates would not assure the operation of Say's law? What were his reasons for asserting that flexible prices and wages would not assure full employment?

4. What are the three simplifying assumptions used in this chapter and what are the two implications of these assumptions?

5. Describe the relationship between consumption and disposable income called the consumption schedule and the one between saving the disposable income known as the saving schedule.

6. Define the two average propensities and the two marginal propensities.

7. Explain briefly how the average propensity to consume and the average propensity to save vary as disposable income varies. Why do APC and APS behave this way? What happens to consumption and saving as disposable income varies?

8. Why do the sum of the APC and the APS and the sum of the MPC and the MPS always equal exactly one?

9. Explain briefly and explicitly *how* changes in the four nonincome determinants will affect the consumption schedule and the saving schedule and *why* such changes will affect consumption and saving in the way you have indicated.

10. Explain:
(a) when a business firm will or will not purchase additional capital goods;
(b) how changes in the five noninterest determinants of investment spending will affect the investment-demand curve;
(c) why investment spending tends to rise when the rate of interest falls; and
(d) how changes in GDP might affect investment spending.

11. Why does the level of investment spending tend to be highly unstable?

12. Explain why the amount consumers spend and the amount investors spend matter all that much to the performance of the economy.

13. Why is the equilibrium level of real GDP that level of real GDP at which domestic output equals aggregate expenditures and at which saving equals planned gross investment? What will cause real GDP to rise if it is below this level and what will cause it to fall if it is above this level?

14. Explain what is meant by a leakage and by an injection. What are the three major leakages and the three major injections in the flow of income in the American economy? Which leakage and which injection are considered in this chapter? Why is the equilibrium real GDP the real GDP at which the leakages equal the injections?

15. What is meant by "the distinction between saving and investment plans and the actual amounts which households manage to save and businesses to invest"? Is the gross investment schedule planned or actual investment? What adjustment causes planned and actual gross investment to become equal?

ANSWERS

Chapter 9 Building the Aggregate Expenditures Model

FILL-IN QUESTIONS

1. fully, less than fully

2. fall, unemployment, downward, increase

3. demand for these goods and services

4. rejected, unstable, recession, inflexible

5. closed, personal, taxes, transfer, spend, zero; *a.* national income, personal income, disposable income; *b.* consumption, investment

6. directly, expenditures, income, directly

7. rise, fall

8. consumption, income, consumption, saving, income, saving

9. *a.* real, financial (either order); *b.* expectations; *c.* consumer indebtedness; *d.* taxation of consumer income

10. the amount that consumers plan to consume (save) will be different at every level of income, the level of income has changed and that consumers will change their planned consumption (saving) as a result

11. capital goods; *a.* expected, profits, interest; *b.* greater

12. inverse; *a.* decrease; *b.* increase

13. *a.* the cost of acquiring, maintaining, and operating the capital goods; *b.* business taxes; *c.* technological change; *d.* the stock of capital goods on hand; *e.* expectations

14. stable, unstable

15. durability, irregularity, variability

16. (aggregate)-expenditures-(domestic)-output, leakages-injections

17. *a.* expenditures, output; *b.* consumption, planned gross investment; *c.* 45-degree

18. *a.* saving, gross investment; *b.* (1) taxes, imports; (2) government purchases, exports

19. *a.* less, disinvestment, rise; *b.* greater, investment, fall; *c.* equal to, zero, neither rise nor fall

20. actual; *a.* (1) disinvestment, (2) rise; *b.* (1) investment, (2) fall

TRUE-FALSE QUESTIONS

1. T, p. 166	**6.** T, p. 168	**11.** T, p. 174	**16.** F, p. 179
2. T, pp. 166-167	**7.** F, pp. 169-170	**12.** T, pp. 175-176	**17.** T, pp. 179-180
3. T, p. 167	**8.** F, p. 170	**13.** F, pp. 176-177	**18.** T, p. 186
4. F, p. 168	**9.** F, p. 174	**14.** T, pp. 178-179	**19.** T, p. 188
5. T, p. 167	**10.** T, p. 174	**15.** F, p. 178	**20.** T, pp. 186-188

MULTIPLE-CHOICE QUESTIONS

1. *b*, pp. 166-167	**8.** *c*, pp. 170-172	**15.** *c*, p. 171	**22.** *b*, pp. 181-183
2. *a*, pp. 166-167	**9.** *c*, p. 171	**16.** *d*, p. 172	**23.** *a*, p. 184
3. *d*, p. 167	**10.** *d*, pp. 178-179	**17.** *b*, p. 171	**24.** *c*, p. 186-188
4. *c*, p. 168	**11.** *b*, p. 176	**18.** *c*, pp. 170-172	**25.** *d*, p. 183
5. *a*, p. 168	**12.** *a*, pp. 172-173	**19.** *a*, p. 172	
6. *d*, p. 170	**13.** *c*, p. 167	**20.** *c*, pp. 179-181	
7. *b*, p. 172	**14.** *c*, p. 171	**21.** *a*, pp. 181-183	

PROBLEMS

1. *a.* S: −40, −20, 0, 20, 40, 60, 80, 100; APC: 1.000, 0.970, 0.955; APS: 0.000, 0.030, 0.045; *b.* 1,700; *c.* 80, 100, 80; *d.* 20, 100, 20; *e.* (1) .8, MPC; (2) .2, MPS

2. *a.* −; *b.* −; *c.* +; *d.* +; *e.* +; *f.* none; *g.* −; *h.* −

3. *a.* 0, 10; *b.* 20, 30; *c.* 30, 60; *d.* 100, 150, 210, 280; *f.* inverse, (1) decrease, (2) increase; *g.* (1) lower, (2) raise; *h.* investment-demand

4. *a.* +; *b.* −; *c.* +; *d.* +; *e.* −; *f.* −; *g.* −; *h.* +; *i.* −

5. *a.* investment; *b.* constant (given); *c.* (1) unrelated, (2) directly related; *d.* decrease, downward

SHORT ANSWER AND ESSAY QUESTIONS

1. pp. 166-167	**5.** pp. 169-170	**9.** pp. 173-174	**13.** pp. 181-183
2. pp. 166-167	**6.** pp. 170-172	**10.** pp. 175-178	**14.** pp. 184-185
3. pp. 167-168	**7.** pp. 170-171	**11.** pp. 179-181	**15.** pp. 186-188
4. p. 168	**8.** pp. 170-172	**12.** pp. 174,179-181	

Aggregate Expenditures: The Multiplier, Net Exports, and Government

Chapter 10 extends the aggregate expenditures model of a private closed economy developed in the previous chapter. You now learn what causes real GDP to rise and fall. Changes in investment spending have an added effect on real GDP because of the multiplier. Including net exports in the aggregate expenditures model transforms the analysis from a closed economy to an open economy, and changes in net exports will change the equilibrium level of real GDP. Government spending and taxation make the economy "mixed" instead of private, and changes in public spending or taxes also shift the equilibrium real GDP.

The consumption (and the saving) schedule and the investment schedule—especially the latter—are subject to change, and when they change equilibrium real GDP will also change. The relationship between an initial change in the investment or consumption schedules and a change in equilibrium real GDP is called the multiplier. Three things to note here are: **how** the multiplier is defined, **why** there is a multiplier effect, and upon **what** the size of the multiplier depends.

The aggregate expenditures model of the economy can be extended by adding the **net exports** of an economy to the aggregate-expenditures schedule. Net exports are nothing more than the economy's exports less its imports of goods and services. Like investment, the exports of a nation are an injection into its circular flow of income; and they increase the flow. But imports are, like saving, a leakage from the circular flow, and decrease the flow.

The generalization used to find the equilibrium real GDP in an open economy (one that exports and imports) is the same one as for a closed economy: the economy will tend to produce a real GDP which is equal to aggregate expenditures. The only difference is that the aggregate expenditures include not only consumption and planned gross investment expenditures but the expenditures for net exports. So the equilibrium real GDP will equal $C + I_g + X_n$ (when X_n is the symbol used for net exports).

An increase in X_n, like an increase in I_g, will increase the equilibrium real GDP; and a decrease in X_n will decrease the equilibrium real GDP. And like a change in I_g, a change in X_n has a multiplier effect on real GDP.

The section entitled "Adding the Public Sector" introduces government taxing and spending into the analysis of equilibrium real GDP. Government purchases of goods and services add to aggregate expenditures and taxation reduces the disposable income of consumers, and thereby reduces both the amount of consumption and the amount of saving that will take place at any level of real GDP. Both "approaches" are again employed, and you are warned that you must know **what** real GDP will tend to be produced and **why.** Special attention should be directed to the exact effect taxes have upon the consumption and saving schedules and to the multiplier effects of changes in government purchases and taxes.

It is important to be aware that the equilibrium real GDP is not necessarily the real GDP at which full employment with inflationary pressures is achieved. Aggregate expenditures may be greater or less than the full-employment noninflationary real GDP; if they are greater there is an **inflationary gap,** and if they are less there exists a **recessionary gap.** Be sure that you know how to measure the size of each of these gaps: the amount by which the aggregate-expenditures schedule (or curve) must change to bring the economy to its full-employment real GDP without there being inflation in the economy. Several historical examples—the Great Depression and the Vietnam war inflation—are described to help you see the application of the recessionary and inflationary gaps concepts.

The aggregate expenditures model that you have learned about is a valuable tool for explaining such economic events as recession, inflation, prosperity, and economic growth. The model, however, has limitations. The last section of the chapter describes the major shortcomings and how later chapters address some of these deficiencies.

■ CHECKLIST

When you have studied this chapter you should be able to:

☐ Explain the multiplier effect in words and using an equation.
☐ Cite two facts on which the multiplier effect (a multiplier greater than one) is based.

☐ Discuss the relationship between the multiplier and the marginal propensities.

☐ Find the value of the multiplier when you are given the necessary information.

☐ Explain the difference between the simple and the complex multiplier.

☐ Use the concept of net exports to define aggregate expenditures in an open economy.

☐ Explain what the equilibrium real GDP in an open economy will be when net exports are positive and when net exports are negative.

☐ Find the equilibrium real GDP in an open economy when you are given the appropriate data.

☐ Give examples of how circumstances or policies abroad can affect domestic GDP.

☐ List five simplifying assumptions used to add the public sector to the aggregate expenditures model.

☐ Find the equilibrium real GDP in an economy in which government purchases goods and services and levies net taxes when you are given the necessary data.

☐ Determine the effect on the equilibrium real GDP of a change in government purchases of goods and services and in net taxes.

☐ Explain why the balanced-budget multiplier is equal to one.

☐ Distinguish between the equilibrium real GDP and the full-employment noninflationary level of real GDP.

☐ Find the recessionary and the inflationary gaps when you are provided the relevant data.

☐ Apply the concepts of recessionary and inflationary gaps to historical economic events.

☐ Explain four shortcomings of aggregate expenditures theory.

■ CHAPTER OUTLINE

1. Changes in planned gross investment (or in the consumption and saving schedules) will cause the equilibrium real GDP to change in the same direction by an amount greater than the initial change in investment (or consumption).

    a. This is called the **multiplier effect;** and the multiplier is equal to the ratio of the change in the real GDP to the initial change in spending.

    (1) The multiplier effect occurs because a change in the dollars spent by one person alters the income of another person in the same direction and because any change in the income of one person will change the person's consumption and saving in the same direction by a fraction of the change in income.

    (2) The value of the simple multiplier is equal to the reciprocal of the marginal propensity to save (1/MPS).

    (3) The significance of the multiplier is that relatively small changes in the spending plans of business firms or households bring about large changes in the equilibrium real GDP.

    (4) The simple multiplier has this value only in an economy in which the only leakage is saving; and the complex multiplier takes into account such other leakages as taxes and imports.

2. In an open economy the exports (X) of a nation increase and its imports (M) decrease aggregate expenditures in that economy; and aggregate expenditures are equal to the sum of consumption spending, planned gross investment spending, and net exports (X_n) when X_n is defined as X minus M.

    a. The equilibrium real GDP in an open economy is the real GDP equal to consumption plus planned gross investment plus net exports; and

    b. any increase (decrease) in its X_n will increase (decrease) its equilibrium real GDP with a multiplier effect.

    c. In an open economy model, circumstances and policies abroad, such as a change in the level of national incomes of trading partners, changes in tariffs or quotas, or changes in exchange rates can affect domestic GDP.

3. Changes in tax rates and government spending can offset cyclical fluctuations and increase economic growth.

    a. Five assumptions are made in order to simplify the explanation of the effects of government spending and taxes on the equilibrium real GDP.

    b. Government purchases of goods and services add to the aggregate-expenditures schedule and increase equilibrium real GDP; and an increase in these purchases has a multiplier effect on equilibrium real GDP.

    c. Taxes decrease consumption and the aggregate-expenditures schedule by the amount of the tax times the MPC (and decrease saving by the amount of the tax times the MPS); and an increase in taxes has a negative multiplier effect on the equilibrium real GDP. When government both taxes and purchases goods and services, the equilibrium GDP is the GDP at which (1) aggregate expenditures (consumption + planned gross investment + net exports + government purchases of goods and services) = the real domestic output (consumption + saving + taxes); or (2) using the leakages-injections approach, at which planned gross investment + exports + government purchases of goods and services = saving + imports + taxes.

    d. Equal increases (decreases) in taxes and in government purchases increase (decrease) equilibrium real GDP by the amount of the change in taxes (or in expenditures).

4. The equilibrium level of real GDP may turn out to be an equilibrium at less than full employment, at full employment, or at full employment with inflation.

    a. If the equilibrium real GDP is **less** than the real GDP consistent with full employment, there exists a **reces-**

sionary gap; the size of the recessionary gap equals the amount by which the aggregate-expenditures schedule must increase (shift upward) to increase the real GDP to its full-employment noninflationary level.
b. If equilibrium real GDP is **greater** than the real GDP consistent with stable prices there is an **inflationary gap**. The size of the inflationary gap equals the amount by which the aggregate-expenditures schedule must decrease (shift downward) if the economy is to achieve full employment without inflation.

5. The concepts of recessionary and inflationary gaps from the aggregate expenditures model can be applied to two events in American history.
a. The Great Depression is an example of a severe recessionary (or depressionary) gap as investment spending declined by 82%, thus reducing aggregate expenditures. Four reasons explain this decline in investment spending:
(1) overcapacity in production and increased business indebtedness during the 1920s;
(2) a decline in residential construction in the mid-to-late 1920s;
(3) the stock market crash of 1929 and its secondary effects; and
(4) a sharp decline in the money supply.
b. The economic expansion during the Vietnam war produced an inflationary gap in the American economy, as inflation went from 1.6% in 1965 to 5.7% in 1970. This inflationary gap occurred because of various factors that significantly increased aggregate expenditures. These factors included the tax cuts in 1962 and 1964 that increased investment and consumption spending, increased government expenditures from 1965–1968 to pay for the escalating Vietnam war, and a tightened labor market because of the military draft.

6. There are four shortcomings of the aggregate expenditures model: an inability to measure price level changes or the rate of inflation; no explanation for why demand-pull inflation can occur before the economy reaches its full-employment level of output; no insights into why the economy can expand beyond its full-employment level of real GDP; and no coverage of cost-push inflation. These shortcomings are overcome in the aggregate demand model and aggregate supply model of the next chapter.

■ IMPORTANT TERMS

Multiplier effect	**Net exports**
Multiplier	**Lump-sum tax**
Simple multiplier	**Balanced-budget multiplier**
Complex multiplier	
Open economy	**Recessionary gap**
Closed economy	**Inflationary gap**

■ HINTS AND TIPS

1. The multiplier effect is a key concept in this chapter and in the ones that follow, so make sure you understand how it works.
a. The multiplier is simply the ratio of the change in real GDP to the **initial** changes in spending. Multiplying the **initial** change in spending by the multiplier gives you the amount of change in real GDP.
b. The multiplier effect works in both positive and negative directions. An **initial** decrease in spending will result in a larger decrease in real GDP, or an **initial** increase in spending will create a larger increase in real GDP.
c. The multiplier is directly related to the marginal propensities. The multiplier equals 1/MPS. The multiplier also equals 1/ (1 - MPC).
d. The main reason for the multiplier effect is that the **initial** change in income (spending) induces additional rounds of income (spending) that add progressively less each round as some of the income (spending) gets saved because of the marginal propensity to save (see Table 10–1 of text).

2. There is an important difference between equilibrium and full-employment GDP in the aggregate expenditures model. Equilibrium means no tendency for the economy to change its output (or employment) level.Thus, an economy can experience a low level of output and high unemployment and still be at equilibrium. The recessionary gap shows how much aggregate expenditures need to increase, so that when this increase is multiplied by the multiplier, it will fit the economy to a higher equilibrium and to the full-employment level of real GDP. Remember that you multiply the needed increase in aggregate expenditures (the recessionary gap) by the multiplier to calculate the change in real GDP that moves the economy from below- to full-employment equilibrium.

SELF-TEST

■ FILL-IN QUESTIONS

1. In this chapter it is assumed that the price level is (variable, constant) _____ and the explanation is in terms of (real, nominal) _____ GDP.

2. The multiplier is the ratio of the change in _____ to an initial change in spending. When the initial change in spending is multiplied by the multiplier, the value equals the change in _____.

3. The multiplier has a value equal to 1 divided by the marginal propensity to (consume, save) _____ , which is the same thing as 1 divided by the quantity of 1 minus the marginal propensity to _____

4. The multiplier is based on two facts:

a. an initial increase in spending by business firms or consumers will increase the (debts, income) _____ of households in the economy; and

b. this increase in (debts, income) _____ will increase and expand the (consumption, investment) _____ spending of households by an amount equal to the incomes times the marginal propensity to (consume, save) _____

5. When planned gross investment spending increases the equilibrium real GDP (increases, decreases) _____ _____and when planned gross investment spending decreases the equilibrium real GDP _____

a. The changes in the equilibrium real GDP are (greater, less) _____ than the changes in planned gross investment spending.

b. The size of the multiplier varies (directly, inversely) _____ with the size of the marginal propensity to consume.

6. The (simple, complex) _____ multiplier is one divided by the marginal propensity to (consume, save) _____ because it reflects only the leakage of saving. The (simple, complex) _____ multiplier takes into account other leakages such as (exports, imports) _____ or (taxes, government spending) _____ along with saving.

7. In an open economy, a nation's net exports equal its _____ minus its _____. In the open economy, aggregate expenditures are equal to consumption plus planned gross investment plus _____

8. What would be the effect—increase (+) or decrease (−)—of each of the following upon an open economy's equilibrium real GDP?

a. An increase in its imports _____

b. An increase in its exports _____

c. A decrease in its imports _____

d. A decrease in its exports _____

e. An increasing level of national income among trading partners _____

f. An increase in trade barriers imposed by trading partners _____

g. A depreciation in the value of the economy's currency _____

9. Increases in public spending will (decrease, increase) _____ the aggregate-expenditures schedule and equilibrium real GDP; but decreases in public spending will _____ the aggregate-expenditures schedule and equilibrium real GDP.

10. Taxes tend to reduce consumption at each level of real GDP by an amount equal to the taxes multiplied by the marginal propensity to (consume, save) _____; saving will decrease by an amount equal to the taxes multiplied by the marginal propensity to _____

11. In an economy in which government both taxes and purchases goods and services, the equilibrium level of real GDP is the real GDP at which:

a. aggregate (output, expenditures) _____ equals domestic _____

b. Real GDP is equal to _____ , plus planned gross _____ , plus net _____ , plus purchases of goods and services by _____

12. When the public sector is added to the model, the equation for the leakages-injection approach shows planned gross _____ plus _____ , and purchases of goods and services by _____ equals _____ , _____ , and_____

13. Equal increases in taxes and government purchases will (increase, decrease) _____ real GDP by an amount equal to the _____ in taxes and government purchases. In this case, the _____ multiplier is 1.

14. A recessionary gap exits when equilibrium real GDP is (greater, less) _____ than the full-employment real GDP. To bring real GDP to the full-employment level, the aggregate-expenditures schedule must (increase, decrease) _____ by an amount equal to the difference between the equilibrium and the full-employment real GDP divided by the _____

15. The amount by which aggregate spending exceeds the full-employment level of real GDP is a(n) (recessionary, inflationary) _____ gap. To eliminate this gap, the aggregate-expenditures schedule must (increase, decrease) _____ by the amount by

which current GDP exceeds the full-employment noninflationary GDP divided by the multiplier.

16. The Great Depression is an historical example of a(n) (inflationary, recessionary) _____ gap, whereas the period of the escalation of the Vietnam war provides an historical example of a(n) _____

17. List the factors that caused the steep decline in investment spending during the Great Depression.

a. _____

b. _____

c. _____

d. _____

18. The inflation of the Vietnam war was caused by tax (increases, decreases) _____ during the early-to-mid-1960s, _____ in government spending from 1965–1968, and _____ in the demand for labor because of the military draft.

19. One problem with the aggregate expenditures model is that it can explain (cost-push, demand-pull) _____ but not _____ inflation. Another problem is that the model also has no way to measure the rate of _____ because there is no _____ axis.

20. Two other deficiencies of the aggregate expenditures model are its inability to explain _____ demand-pull inflation or how the economy can expand beyond the _____ level of output.

■ TRUE-FALSE QUESTIONS

Circle the T if the statement is true; the F if it is false.

Questions 1 and 2 are based on the data supplied in the following table.

Real GDP	C
$200	$200
240	228
280	256
320	284
360	312
400	340
440	368
480	396

1. If consumption spending at each level of real GDP increased by $10, the equilibrium level of the real GDP would tend to rise by $30. **T F**

2. If planned gross investment was $24, equilibrium real GDP would increase by $28. **T F**

3. If real GDP were to decline by $40, consumers would reduce their consumption expenditures by an amount less than $40. **T F**

4. A decrease in the rate of interest will, other things remaining the same, result in a decrease in the equilibrium real GDP. **T F**

5. The larger the marginal propensity to consume, the larger the size of the multiplier. **T F**

6. If the slope of a linear consumption schedule is steeper in economy A than economy B, then the MPC is less in economy A than economy B. **T F**

7. The multiplier is based on the idea that any change in income will cause both consumption and saving to vary in the same direction as a change in income and by a fraction of that change in income. **T F**

8. The value of the complex multiplier will usually be greater than the value of the simple multiplier because there will be more injections into the economy. **T F**

9. The net exports of an economy equal the sum of its exports and its imports of goods and services. **T F**

10. An increase in the volume of a nation's exports, other things being equal, will expand the nation's real GDP. **T F**

11. An increase in the imports of a nation will increase the exports of other nations. **T F**

12. An appreciation of the dollar will increase net exports. **T F**

13. If the MPS were 0.3 and taxes were levied by the government so that consumers paid $20 in taxes at each level of real GDP, consumption expenditures at each level of real GDP would be $14 less. **T F**

14. If taxes are reduced by only $10 at all levels of real GDP and the marginal propensity to save is 0.4, equilibrium real GDP will rise by $25. **T F**

15. Equal increases in government purchases and taxes expand GDP by an amount equal to the increase. **T F**

16. The equilibrium real GDP is the real GDP at which there is full employment in the economy. **T F**

17. The existence of a recessionary gap in the economy is characterized by the full employment of labor. **T F**

18. One of the major causes of the Great Depression was the decline in the level of government spending. **T F**

19. The main reasons for the inflationary gap that developed in the economy during the 1960s was the increases in investment spending resulting from tax cuts and added government purchases of goods and services for the Vietnam war. **T F**

20. The aggregate expenditures model provides a good explanation for cost-push inflation.   **T   F**

■ **MULTIPLE-CHOICE QUESTIONS**

Circle the letter that corresponds to the best answer.

Questions 1 and 2 below are based on the consumption schedule preceding true-false questions 1 and 2.

1. If planned gross investment is $60, the equilibrium level of real GDP will be:
(a) $320
(b) $360
(c) $400
(d) $440

2. If planned gross investment were to increase by $5, the equilibrium real GDP would increase by:
(a) $5
(b) $7.14
(c) $15
(d) $16.67

3. If the value of the marginal propensity to consume is 0.6 and real GDP falls by $25, this was caused by a decrease in the aggregate-expenditures schedule of:
(a) $10.00
(b) $15.00
(c) $16.67
(d) $20.00

4. If the marginal propensity to consume is 0.67 and if both planned gross investment and the saving schedule increase by $25, real GDP will:
(a) increase by $75
(b) not change
(c) decrease by $75
(d) increase by $25

5. If in an economy a $150 billion increase in investment spending creates $150 of new income in the first round of the multiplier process and $105 billion in the second round, the multiplier and the marginal propensity to consume will be, respectively:
(a) 5.00 and .80
(b) 4.00 and .75
(c) 3.33 and .70
(d) 2.50 and .40

Answer the following three questions (6, 7, and 8) on the basis of this table for a private, closed economy. All figures are in billions of dollars.

Expected rate of net profit	Investment	Consumption	GDP
10%	$ 0	$200	$200
8	50	250	300
6	100	300	400
4	150	350	500
2	200	400	600
0	250	450	700

6. If the real rate of interest is 4%, then the equilibrium level of GDP will be:
(a) $300 billion
(b) $400 billion
(c) $500 billion
(d) $600 billion

7. An increase in the interest rate by 4% will:
(a) increase the equilibrium level of GDP by $200 billion
(b) decrease the equilibrium level of GDP by $200 billion
(c) decrease the equilibrium level of GDP by $100 billion
(d) increase the equilibrium level of GDP by $100 billion

8. The multiplier for this economy is:
(a) 2.00
(b) 2.50
(c) 3.00
(d) 3.33

Use the data in the table below to answer questions 9, 10, and 11.

Real GDP	$C + I_g$	Net exports
$ 900	$ 913	$3
920	929	3
940	945	3
960	961	3
980	977	3
1,000	993	3
1,020	1,009	3

9. The equilibrium real GDP is:
(a) $960
(b) $980
(c) $1,000
(d) $1,020

10. If net exports are increased by $4 billion at each level of GDP, the equilibrium real GDP would be:
(a) $960
(b) $980
(c) $1,000
(d) $1,020

11. If the marginal propensity to save in this economy is 0.2, a $10 increase in its net exports would increase its equilibrium real GDP by:
(a) $40
(b) $50
(c) $100
(d) $200

12. Other things remaining constant, which of the following would increase an economy's real GDP and employment?
(a) the imposition of tariffs on goods imported from abroad

(b) a decrease in the level of national income among the trading partners for this economy
(c) a decrease in the exchange rates for foreign currencies
(d) an increase in the exchange rate for foreign currencies

13. An increase in the real GDP of an economy will, other things remaining constant:
(a) increase its imports and the real GDPs in other economies
(b) increase its imports and decrease the real GDPs in other economies
(c) decrease its imports and increase the real GDPs in other economies
(d) decrease its imports and the real GDPs in other economies

14. The economy is operating at the full-employment level of output. A depreciation of the dollar will most likely result in:
(a) a decrease in exports
(b) an increase in imports
(c) an increase in real GDP
(d) a decrease in real GDP

The next four questions (15, 16, 17, and 18) are based on the consumption schedule below. Investment figures are for planned investment.

Real GDP	C
$300	$290
310	298
320	306
330	314
340	322
350	330
360	338

15. If taxes were zero, government purchases of goods and services $10, and investment $6, and net exports are zero, equilibrium real GDP would be:
(a) $310
(b) $320
(c) $330
(d) $340

16. If taxes were $5, government purchases of goods and services $10, and investment $6, and net exports are zero, equilibrium real GDP would be:
(a) $300
(b) $310
(c) $320
(d) $330

17. Assume investment is $42, taxes are $40, net exports are zero, and government purchases of goods and services zero. If the full-employment level of real GDP is $340, the gap can be eliminated by reducing taxes by:

(a) $8
(b) $10
(c) $13
(d) $40

18. Assume that investment is zero, that taxes are zero, net exports are zero, and the government purchases of goods and services are $20. If the full-employment-without-inflation level of real GDP is $330, the gap can be eliminated by decreasing government expenditures by:
(a) $4
(b) $5
(c) $10
(d) $20

19. If the marginal propensity to consume is 0.67 and both taxes and government purchases of goods and services increase by $25, real GDP will:
(a) fall by $25
(b) rise by $25
(c) fall by $75
(d) rise by $75

20. Which of the following policies would do the *most* to reduce inflation?
(a) increase taxes by $5 billion
(b) reduce government purchases of goods and services by $5 billion
(c) increase taxes and government expenditures by $5 billion
(d) reduce both taxes and government purchases by $5 billion

21. If APS is .2 and MPS is .10, a simultaneous increase in both taxes and government spending of $30 billion will:
(a) reduce consumption by $27 billion, increase government spending by $27 billion, and increase GDP by $30 billion
(b) reduce consumption by $27 billion, increase government spending by $27 billion, and increase GDP by $27 billion
(c) reduce consumption by $24 billion, increase government spending by $30 billion, and increase GDP by $30 billion
(d) reduce consumption by $24 billion, increase government spending by $24 billion, and increase GDP by $24 billion

Answer the next three questions (22, 23, and 24) on the basis of the diagram on the following page.

22. The size of the multiplier associated with changes in government spending in this economy is approximately:
(a) .29
(b) 1.50
(c) 2.50
(d) 3.50

23. If this was an open economy without a government sector, the level of GDP would be:
- (a) $100
- (b) $170
- (c) $240
- (d) $310

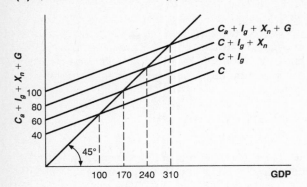

24. In this diagram it is assumed that investment, net exports, and government expenditures:
- (a) vary inversely with GDP
- (b) vary directly with GDP
- (c) are independent of GDP
- (d) are all negative

25. If the MPC in an economy is .75, government could eliminate a recessionary gap of $50 billion by decreasing taxes by:
- (a) $33.3 billion
- (b) $50 billion
- (c) $66.7 billion
- (d) $80 billion

26. In which of the following situations for an open mixed economy will the level of GDP contract?
- (a) when $C_a + S + M$ is less than $I_g + X + T$
- (b) when $I_g + M + T$ is less than $C + X + S$
- (c) when $S_a + M + T$ is less than $I_g + X + G$
- (d) when $I_g + X + G$ is less than $S_a + M + T$

27. If the economy's full-employment noninflationary real GDP is $1200 and its equilibrium real GDP is $1100 there is a recessionary gap of:
- (a) $100
- (b) $100 divided by the multiplier
- (c) $100 multiplied by the multiplier
- (d) $100 times the reciprocal of the marginal propensity to consume

28. To eliminate an inflationary gap of $50 in an economy in which the marginal propensity to save is 0.1, it will be necessary to:
- (a) decrease the aggregate-expenditures schedule by $50
- (b) decrease the aggregate-expenditures schedule by $5
- (c) increase the aggregate-expenditures schedule by $50
- (d) increase the aggregate-expenditures schedule by $5

29. Which of the following contributed to the decline in investment spending that led to the Great Depression?
- (a) a decrease in the business capacity during the 1920s
- (b) an increase in business indebtedness during the 1920s
- (c) a decrease in net exports during the 1930s
- (d) an increase in the money supply during the 1930s

30. One of the deficiencies of the aggregate expenditures model is that it:
- (a) fails to account for demand-pull inflation
- (b) gives more weight to cost-push then demand-pull inflation
- (c) explains recessionary gaps but not inflationary gaps
- (d) has no way of measuring the rate of inflation

■ **PROBLEMS**

1. Assume the marginal propensity to consume is 0.8 and the change in gross planned investment is $10. Complete the table below modeled after Table 10–1 in the textbook.

	Change in income	Change in consumption	Change in saving
Increase in gross investment of $10	$ + 10	$_____	$_____
Second round	_____	_____	_____
Third round	_____	_____	_____
Fourth round	_____	_____	_____
Fifth round	_____	_____	_____
All other rounds	16.38	13.10	3.28
Totals	_____	_____	_____

2. The table below shows consumption and saving at various levels of real GDP. Assume the price level is constant, the economy is closed and there are no government, no business savings, no depreciation, and no net American income earned abroad.

Real GDP	C	S	I_g	$C + I_g$	UI
$1300	$1290	$10	$ 22	$1312	− 12
1310	1298	12	22	1320	− 10
1320	1306	14	_____	_____	_____
1330	1314	16	_____	_____	_____
1340	1322	18	_____	_____	_____
1350	1330	20	_____	_____	_____
1360	1338	22	_____	_____	_____
1370	1346	24	_____	_____	_____
1380	1354	26	_____	_____	_____
1390	1362	28	22	1384	+6
1400	1370	30	22	1392	+8

a. The previous table is an investment-demand schedule which shows the net amounts investors plan to invest at different rates of interest. Assume the rate of interest is 6% and complete the gross investment, the consumption-plus-investment, and the unplanned investment (*UI*) columns—showing unplanned investment with a + and unplanned disinvestment with a −.

Interest rate	I_g
10%	$ 0
9	7
8	13
7	18
6	22
5	25
4	27
3	28

b. The equilibrium real GDP will be $ _____

c. The value of the marginal propensity to consume in this problem is _____ and the value of the marginal propensity to save is _____

d. The value of the simple multiplier is _____

e. If the rate of interest should fall from 6% to 5%, planned gross investment would (increase, decrease) _____ by $ _____; and the equilibrium real GDP would, as a result, (increase, decrease) _____ by $ _____

f. Suppose the rate of interest were to rise from 6% to 7%. Planned investment would _____ by $ _____; and the equilibrium real GDP would _____ by $ _____

g. Assume the rate of interest is 6%.

(1) On the graph below, plot *S* and I_g and indicate the equilibrium real GDP.

0   **Real GDP**

(2) On the graph (page 116), plot *C, C + I_g*, and the 45-degree line, and indicate the equilibrium real GDP.

3. Below are a saving schedule and an investment schedule (I_g) indicating that planned investment is constant.

Real GDP	S	I_g
$300	$ 5	$15
310	7	15
320	9	15
330	11	15
340	13	15
350	15	15
360	17	15
370	19	15
380	21	15
390	23	15
400	25	15

a. The equilibrium real GDP is $ _____ and saving and planned investment are both $ _____

b. The marginal propensity to save is _____ and the simple multiplier is _____

c. A $2 rise in the I_g **schedule** will cause real GDP to rise by $ _____

d. Use the investment schedule given in the table and assume a $2 increase in the saving schedule in the table—that is, saving at every real GDP increases by $2.

(1) Equilibrium real GDP will _____ to $ _____ and at this real GDP saving will be $ _____

(2) The effect of the increases in the saving schedule is to _____ equilibrium real GDP; this is called the _____

(3) The amount by which real GDP changes depends on the size of the change in the saving schedule and the size of _____

4. At the bottom of page 116 is a schedule showing what aggregate expenditures (consumption plus planned gross investment) would be at various levels of real net domestic product in a closed economy.

a. Were this economy to become an open economy the volume of exports would be a constant $90 billion; and the volume of imports would be a constant $86 billion. At each of the seven levels of real GDP, net exports would be $ _____ billion.

b. Compute aggregate expenditures in this open economy at the seven real GDP levels and enter them in the table.

c. The equilibrium real GDP in this open economy would be _____ billion.

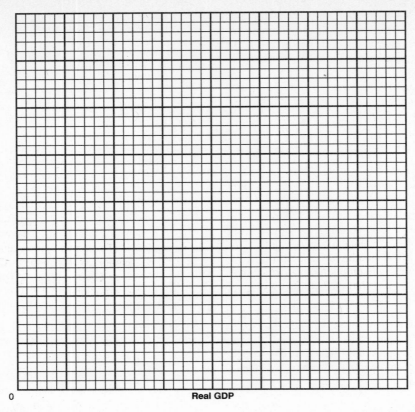

0   **Real GDP**

d. The value of the multiplier in this open economy is equal to _____

e. A $10 billion increase in:

(1) exports would (increase, decrease) _____ the equilibrium real GDP by $_____ billion.

(2) imports would (increase, decrease) _____ the equilibrium real GDP by $_____ billion.

5. Consumption and saving schedules are shown at the top of the next page.

a. Assume government levies a lump-sum tax of $100. Also assume that imports are $5.

(1) Because the marginal propensity to consume in this problem is _____ , the imposition of this tax will reduce consumption at all levels of real GDP by $_____. Complete the C_a column to show consumption at each real GDP after the levying of this tax.

(2) Because the marginal propensity to save in this problem is _____ , this tax will reduce saving at all levels of real GDP by $_____ _____. Complete the S_a column to show saving at each real GDP after this tax has been levied.

Possible levels of real GDP (billions)	Aggregate expenditures, closed economy (billions)	Exports (billions)	Imports (billions)	Net exports (billions)	Aggregate expenditures, open economy (billions)
$ 750	$ 776	$90	$86	$_____	$_____
800	816	90	86	_____	_____
850	856	90	86	_____	_____
900	896	90	86	_____	_____
950	936	90	86	_____	_____
1,000	976	90	86	_____	_____
1,050	1,016	90	86	_____	_____

Real GDP	C	S	C_a	S_a	$S_a + M + T$	$I_g + X + G$	$C_a + I_g + X_n + G$
$1500	$1250	$250	$_____	$_____	$_____	$_____	$_____
1600	1340	260	_____	_____	_____	_____	_____
1700	1430	270	_____	_____	_____	_____	_____
1800	1520	280	_____	_____	_____	_____	_____
1900	1610	290	_____	_____	_____	_____	_____
2000	1700	300	_____	_____	_____	_____	_____
2100	1790	310	_____	_____	_____	_____	_____

b. Compute the (after-tax) saving-plus-imports-plus-taxes at each real GDP and put them in the $S_a + M + T$ column.

c. Suppose that planned gross investment is $150, exports are $5, and government purchases of goods and services equal $200. Complete the investment-plus-exports-plus-government-purchases column ($I_g + X + G$) and the (after-tax) consumption-plus-investment-plus-net-exports-plus-government-purchases column ($C_a + I_g + X_n + G$).

d. The equilibrium real GDP is $ _____

e. On the graphs below and on page 118 plot:

(1) C_a, $I_g + X_n + G$, $C_a + I_g + X_n + G$, and the 45-degree line. Show the equilibrium real GDP.

(2) $S_a + M + T$ and $I_g + X + G$. Show the real equilibrium GDP. (To answer the questions that follow it is *not* necessary to recompute C, S, $S + M + T$, $I_g + X + G$, or $C + I_g + X_n + G$. They can be answered by using the multipliers.)

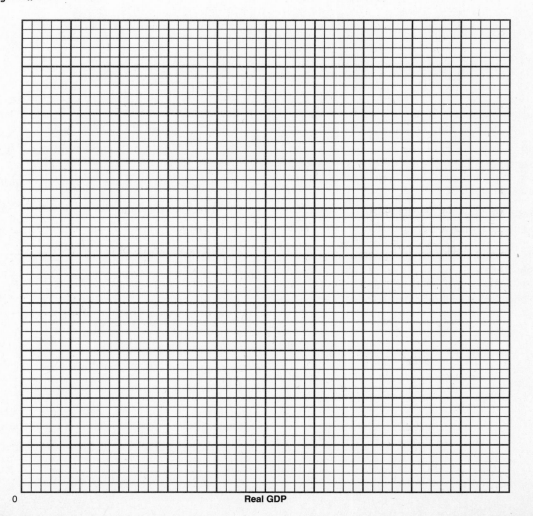

0   Real GDP

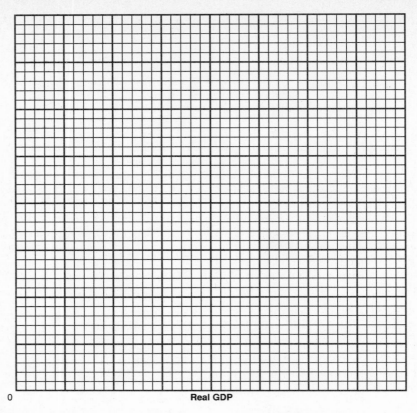

0   **Real GDP**

f. If taxes remained at $100 and government purchases rose by $10, the equilibrium real GDP would

(rise, fall) _____ by $ _____

g. If government purchases remained at $200 and the lump-sum tax increased by $10, the equilibrium real

GDP would _____ by $ _____

h. The combined effect of a $10 increase in government purchases **and** a $10 increase in taxes is to

_____ real GDP by $ _____

6. In the table below are consumption and saving schedules for a closed economy. Assume that the level of real GDP at which full employment without inflation is achieved is $590.

Real GDP	C	S
$550	$520	$30
560	526	34
570	532	38
580	538	42
590	544	46
600	550	50
610	556	54
620	562	58
630	568	62

a. The value of the multiplier is _____
b. If planned net investment is $58, the equilibrium

money GDP is $ _____ and exceeds the full-employment noninflationary real GDP by

$ _____. There is a(n) _____ gap

of $ _____
c. If planned investment is $38, the equilibrium real

GDP is $ _____ and is less than full-

employment real GDP by $ _____

There is a(n) _____

gap of $ _____

■ SHORT ANSWER AND ESSAY QUESTIONS

1. Why does the equilibrium level of real GDP change?

2. What is the multiplier effect?

3. Give a rationale for the multiplier effect.

4. How is the multiplier effect related to the marginal propensities? Explain in words and equations.

5. Explain the difference between the simple and complex multiplier.

6. How do exports and imports get included in the aggregate expenditures model?

7. What happens to the aggregate-expenditures schedule when net exports increase or decrease?

8. What are some examples of international economic linkages affecting the domestic level of GDP?

9. Explain the five simplifying assumptions that are used to include the public sector in the aggregate expenditures model.

10. Describe how government expenditures affect aggregate expenditures.

11. What is the effect that taxes will have on the consumption schedule? On the saving schedule?

12. Explain why, with government taxing and spending, the equilibrium real GDP is the real GDP at which real GDP equals consumption plus planned investment plus net exports plus government purchases of goods and services. Also explain why in this case saving plus imports plus taxes equals planned investment plus exports plus government purchases.

13. How will changes in the different components of aggregate expenditures cause GDP to move to its equilibrium level?

14. If both taxes and government purchases increase by equal amounts, real GDP will increase by that amount. Why does this happen?

15. Explain what is meant by a recessionary gap.

16. Describe the economic conditions that create an inflationary gap.

17. What factors influenced investment spending during the 1920s and early 1930s? How did these conditions contribute to the Great Depression? Explain using an aggregate expenditures graph.

18. What events led to the Vietnam war inflation of the 1960s? How can this event be characterized using the aggregate expenditures model?

19. What are the limitations of the aggregate expenditures model in terms of the measurement of the price level or demand-pull inflation?

20. Is it possible for the economy to expand beyond its full-employment level of real GDP? How does the aggregate expenditures model handle this situation?

ANSWERS

Chapter 10 Aggregate Expenditures: The Multiplier, Net Exports, and Government

FILL-IN QUESTIONS

1. constant, real

2. real GDP, real GDP

3. save, consume

4. *a.* income; *b.* income, consumption, consume

5. increases, decreases; *a.* greater; *b.* directly

6. simple, save, complex, imports, taxes

7. exports, imports, net exports

8. *a.* –; *b.* +; *c.* +; *d.* –; *e.* +; *f.* –; *g.* +

9. increase, decrease

10. consume, save

11. *a.* expenditures, output; *b.* consumption, investment, exports, government

12. investment, exports, government, saving, imports, net taxes

13. increase, increase, balanced-budget

14. less, increase, multiplier

15. inflationary, decrease

16. recessionary, inflationary

17. *a.* overcapacity and business indebtedness; *b.* decline in residential construction; *c.* the stock market crash; *d.* shrinking money supply (any order)

18. decreases, increases, increases

19. demand-pull, cost-push, inflation, price

20. premature, full-employment

TRUE-FALSE QUESTIONS

1. F, pp. 191-193   **6.** F, pp. 194-195   **11.** T, pp. 197-198   **16.** F, p. 205
2. F, pp. 191-193   **7.** T, p. 193   **12.** F, pp. 198-199   **17.** F, pp. 205-206
3. T, pp. 192-193   **8.** F, pp. 195-196   **13.** T, p. 202   **18.** F, p. 206
4. F, p. 192   **9.** F, p. 196   **14.** F, p. 202   **19.** T, p. 207
5. T, pp. 194-195   **10.** T, p. 198   **15.** T, p. 202   **20.** F, p. 209

MULTIPLE-CHOICE QUESTIONS

1. *c,* pp. 191-193   **9.** *b,* pp. 197-198   **17.** *b,* pp. 201-203   **25.** *c,* pp. 205-206
2. *d,* pp. 191-193   **10.** *c,* pp. 197-198   **18.** *a,* pp. 201-203   **26.** *d,* pp. 205-206
3. *a,* pp. 194-195   **11.** *b,* pp. 195, 197-198   **19.** *b,* pp. 204-205   **27.** *b,* pp. 205-206
4. *b,* pp. 186-188   **12.** *c,* pp. 198-199   **20.** *b,* p. 206   **28.** *a,* p. 206
5. *c,* pp. 194-196   **13.** *a,* p. 198   **21.** *a,* pp. 204-206   **29.** *b,* p. 206
6. *c,* pp. 191-193   **14.** *b,* pp. 198-199   **22.** *d,* p. 201-203   **30.** *d,* p. 208
7. *b,* pp. 191-193   **15.** *c,* p. 200   **23.** *c,* pp. 200-201
8. *a,* pp. 193-194   **16.** *b,* pp. 201-202   **24.** *c,* pp. 201-203

PROBLEMS

1. change in income: 8.00, 6.40, 5.12, 4.10, 50,000; change in consumption: 8.00, 6.40, 5.12, 4.10, 3.28, 40.00; change in saving: 2.00, 1.60, 1.28, 1.02, 0.82, 10.00

2. *a.* I_g 22, 22, 22, 22, 22, 22, 22; $C + I_g$: 1328, 1336, 1344, 1352, 1360, 1368, 1376; *UI:* −8, −6, −4, −2, 0, +2, +4; *b.* 1360; *c.* 0.8, 0.2; *d.* 5; *e.* increase, 3, increase, 15; *f.* decrease, 4, decrease, 20

3. *a.* 350, 15; *b.* 0.20, 5; *c.* 10; *d.* (1) decrease, 340, 15; (2) decrease, paradox of thrift; (3) the multiplier

4. *a.* $4; *b.* $780, 820, 860, 900, 940, 980, 1,020; *c.* $900; *d.* 5; *e.* (1) increase, $50, (2) decrease, $50

5. *a.* (1) 0.9, 90; C_a: 1160, 1250, 1340, 1430, 1520, 1610, 1700, (2) 0.1, 10, S_a: 240, 250, 260, 270, 280, 290, 300; *b.* $S_a + M + T$: 345, 355, 365, 375, 385, 395, 405; *c.* $I_g + X + G$: 355, 355, 355, 355, 355, 355, 355; $C_a + I_g + X_n + G$: 1510, 1600, 1690, 1780, 1870, 1960, 2050; *d.* 1600; *f.* rise, 100; *g.* fall, 90; *h.* raise, 10

6. *a.* 2 ½; *b.* 620, 30, inflationary, 12; *c.* 570, 20, recessionary, 8

SHORT ANSWER AND ESSAY QUESTIONS

1. pp. 191-193   **6.** pp. 196-197   **11.** pp. 201-202 **16.** p. 206
2. pp. 193-194   **7.** pp. 197-198   **12.** pp. 203-204 **17.** pp. 206-207
3. pp. 193-194   **8.** pp. 198-199   **13.** pp. 203-204 **18.** p. 207
4. pp. 194-195   **9.** p. 199   **14.** pp. 204-205 **19.** pp. 208-209
5. pp. 195-196 **10.** pp. 200-201 **15.** pp. 205-206 **20.** p. 209

CHAPTER 11

Aggregate Demand and Aggregate Supply

Chapter 11 introduces another macro model of the economy, one based on aggregate demand and aggregate supply. This model overcomes a limitation of the aggregate expenditures model because the price level is allowed to vary rather than be fixed. The aggregate demand–aggregate supply model allows you to determine the size of real domestic output or the level of prices at any time, and also understand what causes output and the price level to change.

The aggregate demand curve is **downsloping** because of the wealth, interest rate, and foreign-purchases effects on changes in the price level. With a downsloping aggregate demand curve, changes in the price level have an inverse effect on the level of spending by domestic consumers, businesses, government, and foreign buyers, and thus on real domestic output, assuming **other things equal.** This change would be equivalent to a movement along an existing aggregate demand curve: a lower price level increases the quantity of real domestic output, and a higher price level decreases the quantity of real domestic output.

Although the aggregate expenditures model is a fixed-price level model and the aggregate demand–aggregate supply is a variable-price level model, there is a close relationship between the two models. The important thing to understand is that prices can be fixed or constant at different levels. The price index in the economy, for example, might be constant at 100, 150, or 200. The AD curve can be derived from the aggregate expenditures model by letting price be **constant at different levels.** In this case, the lower (the higher) the level at which prices are constant in the aggregate expenditures model, the larger (the smaller) will be the equilibrium real GDP in that model of the economy. Various output-price level combinations can be traced to derive an AD curve that slopes downward.

The **aggregate demand curve can increase or decrease.** The reason for the shift in the curve is due to a change in the nonprice level determinants of aggregate demand. The determinants include changes in factors affecting consumer, investment, government, or net export spending. These determinants are similar to the components of the aggregate expenditures model. It is easy to show the relationship between the shifts in the two models.

A change in spending will cause a shift (upward or downward) in the aggregate expenditures schedule. The initial change in spending when multiplied times the multiplier would be equal to the size of the horizontal shift in AD, assuming a constant price level.

The **aggregate supply curve** differs from the shape of the aggregate demand curve because it reflects what happens to per unit production costs as real domestic output increases or decreases. For the purposes of this analysis, it has three ranges: (1) at low level of real domestic output, the price level is relatively constant, so the aggregate supply curve in this range is horizontal; (2) at high level of real domestic output, the aggregate supply curve is vertical; and (3) in the intermediate range, the level of real domestic output rises along with the price level, so the curve is upsloping.

You should remember that an assumption has also been made that other things are equal when one moves along an aggregate supply curve. When other things change, then the aggregate supply curve can shift. The determinants of aggregate supply include changes in input prices, changes in productivity, and changes in the legal and institutional environment for production.

The **intersection** of the aggregate demand and aggregate supply curves determines equilibrium output and the price level. Assuming that the determinants of aggregate demand and aggregate supply do not change, there are competitive pressures that will tend to keep the economy at equilibrium. If, however, a determinant changes, then aggregate demand, aggregate supply, or both, can shift.

When aggregate demand increases, this can lead to changes in real domestic output and the price level, depending on the range on the aggregate supply curve in which the economy is operating. In the intermediate and vertical ranges of AS, a change in AD demand will cause an increase in the price level. Thus, in these ranges the change in AD may not have its full multiplier effect on the real GDP of the economy, and will result in demand-pull inflation.

There can also be a decrease in aggregate demand, but it is less certain what the effects will be. Some economists think that there is a **ratchet effect** that occurs because prices are inflexible downward. This effect may arise for several reasons as you will learn from the chapter.

Aggregate supply may also increase or decrease. An increase in aggregate supply gives a double bonus for the economy because the price level falls and output (and employment) increase. Conversely, a decrease in aggregate supply doubly harms economy because the price level increases and output (and employment) falls, and thus the economy experiences cost-push inflation.

The aggregate demand–aggregate supply model is an important framework for determining the equilibrium level of real domestic output and prices in an economy. The model will be used extensively throughout the next eight chapters to analyze how different parts of the economy function.

■ CHECKLIST

When you have studied this chapter you should be able to:

☐ Contrast the aggregate expenditures and the aggregate demand–aggregate supply models by comparing the variability of the price level and real GDP.
☐ Define aggregate demand.
☐ Explain why the aggregate demand curve slopes downward.
☐ Derive the aggregate demand curve (or schedule) from the aggregate expenditures model.
☐ Identify the major determinants of aggregate demand and explain how they shift the aggregate demand curve.
☐ Explain the effect of a change in aggregate expenditures on the aggregate demand curve (or schedule).
☐ Define aggregate supply.
☐ Describe the shape of the aggregate supply curve and name the three ranges on it.
☐ List the major nonprice level determinants of aggregate supply and describe how they shift the aggregate supply curve.
☐ Explain what the real domestic output and price level will be in equilibrium and why the economy will tend to produce this output and price level (rather than another combination).
☐ State the effects on the real domestic output and on the price level of an increase in aggregate demand when the economy is in the horizontal, vertical, and intermediate ranges.
☐ Explain what determines how large the multiplier effect on the equilibrium real GDP will be in the aggregate demand–aggregate supply model.
☐ Explain why a decrease in aggregate demand will not reduce the price level so much as an equal increase in aggregate demand would have raised it.
☐ Predict the effects of a change in aggregate supply on the price level and the equilibrium real GDP.

■ CHAPTER OUTLINE

1. This chapter introduces the aggregate demand–aggregate supply model of the economy to explain why real domestic output **and** the price level fluctuate. This model has an advantage over the aggregate expenditures model because it allows the price level to vary (rise and fall) rather than be constant or fixed as in the aggregate expenditures model.

2. Aggregate demand is a curve which shows the total quantity of goods and services that will be purchased (demanded) at different price levels; and the curve slopes downward for three reasons.
   a. An increase in the price level also decreases the purchasing power of financial assets with a fixed money value, and because those who own such assets are now poorer they spend less for goods and services; and a decrease in the price level has the opposite effects.
   b. With the supply of money fixed, an increase in the price level increases the demand for money, increases interest rates, and as a result reduces those expenditures (by consumers and business firms) which are sensitive to increased interest rates; and a decrease in the price level has the opposite effects.
   c. In addition, an increase in the price level (relative to foreign price levels) will reduce American exports, expand American imports, and decrease the quantity of goods and services demanded in the American economy; and a decrease in the price level (relative to foreign price levels) will have opposite effects.
   d. The AD curve is derived from the intersections of the aggregate-expenditures curves and the 45-degree curve: as the price level falls (rises) the aggregate expenditures curve shifts upward (downward) and the equilibrium real GDP increases (decreases); and this inverse relationship between the price level and the equilibrium real GDP is the AD schedule (or curve).
   As the price level falls (rises):
   (1) the consumption curve shifts upward (downward) because of the *real balances* or *wealth* effect;
   (2) the investment curve shifts upward (downward) because of the *interest-rate* effect; and
   (3) the next export curve shifts upward (downward) because of the *foreign purchases* effect.

3. Spending by domestic consumers, businesses, government, and foreign buyers that is independent of changes in the price level shifts aggregate demand, as outlined in Table 11-1.
   a. For domestic consumers, increases in wealth, improved expectations, reductions in indebtedness, or lower taxes can increase consumer spending and aggregate demand; decreases in consumer wealth, less positive expectations, increases in indebtedness, and

higher taxes decrease consumer spending and aggregate demand.

b. For businesses, lower interest rates, improved profit expectations, lower taxes, improved technology, and less excess capacity may increase investment spending and aggregate demand; whereas higher interest rates, worse profit expectations, higher taxes, and more excess capacity may retard investment spending and aggregate demand.

c. More government spending tends to increase aggregate demand and less government spending will decrease it, assuming that tax collections and interest rates do not change as a result.

d. Net export spending and aggregate demand are increased by increases in the national incomes of other nations and by a dollar depreciation; declines in the incomes of foreign buyers and a dollar appreciation tend to reduce net exports and aggregate demand.

e. If the price level is constant, any change in the non-price level determinants of consumption and planned investment that shifts the aggregate expenditures curve upward (downward) will increase (decrease) the equilibrium real GDP and shift the AD curve to the right (left) by an amount equal to the initial increase (decrease) in aggregate expenditures times the multiplier.

4. Aggregate supply is a curve that shows the total quantity of goods and services that will be produced (supplied) at different price levels; and the curve has three ranges.

a. In the horizontal range (when the economy is in a severe recession or depression) the aggregate supply curve is horizontal; the price level need not rise to induce producers to supply larger quantities of goods and services.

b. In the vertical range (when the economy is at full employment) the aggregate supply curve is vertical: a rise in the price level cannot result in an increase in the quantity of goods and services supplied.

c. Between these two ranges is the intermediate range in which the supply curve slopes upward: the price level must rise to induce producers to supply larger quantities of goods and services.

5. Factors that shift the aggregate supply curve include changes in the prices of inputs for production, changes in productivity, and changes in the legal and institutional environment in the economy, as outlined in Table 11-2.

a. Lower prices for productive domestic resources (land, labor, capital, and entrepreneurial ability) and imported resources tend to reduce unit costs of production and increase aggregate supply, whereas higher input prices, which may be brought about by more market power on the part of resource suppliers, will tend to decrease aggregate supply.

b. As productivity improves, per unit production costs fall and aggregate supply increases; the converse occurs when productivity falls.

c. A decrease in the level of business taxation or reduced regulation of business may improve the business environment and increase aggregate supply; the opposite actions may reduce aggregate supply.

6. The equilibrium real domestic output and the equilibrium price level are at the intersection of the aggregate demand and the aggregate supply curves. Were the actual output greater (less) than the equilibrium output producers would find that their inventories were increasing (decreasing) and they would contract (expand) their output to the equilibrium output.

7. The aggregate demand and aggregate supply curves shift to change equilibrium.

a. An increase in aggregate demand in:
(1) the horizontal range would result in an increase in real output but the price level would remain unchanged;
(2) the vertical range would result in an increase in the price level but the real domestic output would remain unchanged;
(3) the intermediate range would result in an increase in both real domestic output and the price level.

b. If the economy is operating along the:
(1) horizontal range of the AS curve an increase in AD will have no effect on the price level and the increase in the equilibrium real GDP will equal the full multiplier effect of the increase in aggregate expenditures;
(2) intermediate range the increase in AD will increase the price level and the increase in the equilibrium real GDP will be less than the full multiplier effect of the increase in aggregate expenditures;
(3) vertical range the increase in AD will increase the price level and have no effect on the equilibrium real GDP.

c. But a decrease in aggregate demand may not have the opposite effect on the price level because prices (for five reasons) tend to be inflexible (sticky) downward.

d. A decrease in aggregate supply means there will be a decrease in real domestic output (economic growth) and employment, and at the same time a rise in the price level, or cost-push inflation.

e. An increase in aggregate supply, however, has the beneficial effects of improving real domestic output and employment, while simultaneously reducing the price level.

■ **IMPORTANT TERMS**

Aggregation	**Interest-rate effect**
Aggregates	**Foreign-purchases effect**
Aggregate demand curve	**Determinants of aggregate demand**
Wealth or real balances effect	
	Aggregate supply curve

Horizontal range

Vertical range

Intermediate range

Determinants of
aggregate supply

Productivity

Equilibrium price level

Equilibrium real
domestic output

Demand-pull inflation

Ratchet effect

Cost-push inflation

■ **HINTS AND TIPS**

1. Demand and supply are the tools employed to explain
what determines the economy's real output and price
level. These tools, however, are different from the demand
and supply used in Chapter 3 to explain what determines
the output and price of a *particular* product. Instead of
thinking about the quantity of a *particular* good or service
demanded or supplied, it is necessary to think about the
total or *aggregate* quantity of all final goods and services
demanded (purchased) and supplied (produced). You will
have no difficulty with the way demand and supply are
used in this chapter once you switch from thinking about
a *particular* good or service and its price to the *aggregate*
of all final goods and services and its average price.

2. The aggregate supply curve has a strange shape because there are three ranges—horizontal, upsloping (intermediate), and vertical. Make sure you understand the
rationale for each range. Also, the shape of the aggregate
supply curve means that graphically an *increase* in aggregate supply will move aggregate supply both *downward* (in the horizontal range) and *outward* (in the upsloping and vertical ranges). The opposite is the case for
an decrease in aggregate supply. Check your understanding of this point by referring to Figure 11-6 in the text.

3. Make sure you know the difference between a movement along an aggregate demand or supply curve and a
shift in an aggregate demand or supply curve. Tables 11-
1 and 11-2 in the text are extremely valuable summaries
of the determinants of aggregate demand and aggregate
supply that shift each curve.

SELF-TEST

■ **FILL-IN QUESTIONS**

1. In the aggregate demand–aggregate supply model,
the price level is (fixed, variable) _____ , but in
the aggregate expenditures model, the price level is

_____

2. Aggregate demand and aggregate supply together

determine the equilibrium real domestic _____

and the equilibrium price _____

3. The aggregate demand curve shows the quantity of

goods and services that will be _____

at various price _____

  a. It slopes (upward, downward) _____

  b. because of the _____ ,

the _____ ,

and the _____ effects.

4. For the aggregate demand curve:
  a. An increase in the price level leads to a(n) (in-

crease, decrease) _____ in the
quantity of real domestic output;
  b. whereas a decrease in the price level leads to a(n)

_____ in the quantity of real domestic
output,

  c. assuming _____

5. In the aggregate expenditures model:

  a. a lower price level would (raise, lower) _____

_____ the consumption, investment, and aggregate expenditures curves, and the equilibrium level

of real GDP would (rise, fall) _____

  b. a higher price level would (raise, lower) _____
the consumption, investment, and aggregate expenditures curves, and the equilibrium level of real GDP

would (rise, fall) _____

  c. This (direct, inverse) _____ relationship
between the price level and equilibrium real GDP in the
aggregate expenditures model can be used to derive

the aggregate (demand, supply) _____
curve (or schedule).

6. When the price level changes:

  a. there is a (movement along, change in) _____

_____ the aggregate demand curve;
  b. when the entire aggregate demand curve shifts,
there is a (change in the quantity of real output de-

manded, change in aggregate demand) _____

  c. and that change is caused by one or more of the

_____ of aggregate demand.

7. List the determinants of aggregate demand from
changes in consumer spending:

  a. _____

  b. _____

  c. _____

  d. _____

8. List the determinants of aggregate demand from changes in investment spending:

a. _____

b. _____

c. _____

d. _____

e. _____

9. Aggregate demand can also shift because of changes in _____ spending; it may also shift because of a change in net export spending resulting from a change in national _____ abroad or _____ rates.

10. If the price level were a constant, a(n)
a. increase in the aggregate expenditures curve would shift the aggregate demand curve to the (right, left) _____ by an amount equal to the upward shift in aggregate expenditures times the _____
b. decrease in the aggregate expenditures curve would shift the aggregate demand curve to the _____ by an amount equal to the _____

_____

11. The aggregate supply curve shows the quantity of goods and services that will be _____ at various price _____; and in the:
a. horizontal range is (vertical, horizontal, upsloping)

_____

b. the intermediate range is _____

c. the vertical range is _____

12. The basic cause of a decrease in aggregate supply is a(n) (increase, decrease) _____ in the per unit costs of producing goods and services; and the basic cause of an increase in aggregate supply is _____

_____,
all other things equal.

13. List the determinants of aggregate supply:
a. From a change in input prices due to a change in:

(1) _____

(2) _____

(3) _____

b. From a change in _____
c. From a change in the legal and institutional environment due to a change in:

(1) _____

(2) _____

14. The equilibrium real domestic output and price level are found at the _____ of the aggregate demand and the aggregate supply curves.
a. At this price level the aggregate quantity of goods and services _____ is equal to the aggregate quantity of goods and services _____
b. And at this real domestic output the prices producers are willing to (pay, accept) _____ are equal to the prices buyers are willing to _____

15. Were the actual real domestic output:
a. greater than the equilibrium domestic output producers would find that their inventories are (increasing, decreasing) _____ and they would (expand, reduce) _____ their production;
b. less than the equilibrium domestic output producers would find that their inventories are _____ and they would _____ their production.

16. When the economy is producing in:
a. the horizontal range of aggregate supply an increase in aggregate demand will (increase, decrease, have no effect on) _____ real domestic output and will _____ the price level;
b. the intermediate range an increase in aggregate demand will _____ real domestic output and will _____ the price level;
c. the vertical range an increase in aggregate demand will _____ real domestic output and will _____ the price level.

17. Were aggregate demand to increase,
a. the flatter the aggregate supply curve, the (greater, smaller) _____ is the multiplier effect on the real equilibrium GDP and the _____ is the effect on the equilibrium price level; and

b. the steeper the aggregate supply curve, the _____ _____ is the multiplier effect on the equilibrium real GDP and the _____ is the effect on the equilibrium price level.

18. Were the economy operating in the intermediate or vertical ranges and aggregate demand were to decrease, the price level would decline by (a larger, a smaller, the same) _____ amount as an equal increase in aggregate demand would have raised the price level; this is called the (interest-rate, real-balances, ratchet) _____ effect.

19. An increase in aggregate supply will not only (raise, lower) _____ real domestic output and (lead to, prevent) _____ inflation but will also (increase, decrease) _____ the full-employment level of domestic output; a decrease in aggregate supply will _____ real output and _____ the price level.

20. Demand-pull inflation is the result of a(n) (increase, decrease) _____ in aggregate demand and is accompanied by a (rise, fall) _____ in real output; but cost-push inflation is the result of a(n) _____ in aggregate supply and is accompanied by a _____

■ **TRUE-FALSE QUESTIONS**

Circle the T if the statement is true; the F if it is false.

1. Aggregation in macroeconomics is the process of combining all the prices of individual products and services into a price level and merging all the equilibrium quantities into real domestic output.　**T　F**

2. The aggregate demand curve slopes downward.　**T　F**

3. A fall in the price level increases the real value of financial assets with fixed money values and, as a result, increases spending by the holders of these assets.　**T　F**

4. A fall in the price level reduces the demand for money in the economy and drives interest rates upward.　**T　F**

5. A rise in the price level of an economy (relative to foreign price levels) tends to increase that economy's exports and to reduce its imports of goods and services.　**T　F**

6. The higher the price level, the smaller are the real balances of consumers, and the lower is the consumption schedule (curve).　**T　F**

7. An increase in the price level will shift the aggregate expenditures schedule upward.　**T　F**

8. A change in aggregate demand is caused by a change in the price level, ***other things equal.***　**T　F**

9. A fall in excess capacity, or unused existing capital goods, will retard the demand for new capital goods and therefore reduce aggregate demand.　**T　F**

10. The wealth or real-balances effect is one of the determinants of aggregate demand.　**T　F**

11. A high level of consumer indebtedness will tend to increase consumption spending and aggregate demand.　**T　F**

12. Appreciation of the dollar relative to foreign currencies will tend to increase net exports and aggregate demand.　**T　F**

13. The aggregate supply curve has a downsloping range.　**T　F**

14. When the determinants of aggregate supply change they alter the per unit production cost and thereby aggregate supply.　**T　F**

15. Productivity is a measure of real output per unit of input.　**T　F**

16. A change in the degree of market power or monopoly power held by sellers of resources can affect input prices and aggregate supply.　**T　F**

17. Per unit production cost is determined by dividing total input cost by units of output.　**T　F**

18. At the equilibrium price level the real domestic output purchased is equal to the real domestic output produced.　**T　F**

19. In the intermediate range on the aggregate supply curve an increase in aggregate demand will increase both the price level and the real domestic output.　**T　F**

20. In the horizontal range on the aggregate supply curve an increase in aggregate demand will have no effect on the real equilibrium GDP of the economy and will raise its price level.　**T　F**

21. The greater the increase in the price level that results from an increase in aggregate demand the greater will be the increase in the equilibrium real GDP.　**T　F**

22. Inflation has no effect on the strength of the multiplier.　**T　F**

23. A decrease in aggregate demand will lower the price level by the same amount as an equal increase in aggregate demand would have raised it because of the ratchet effect.　**T　F**

24. An increase in aggregate supply increases both the equilibrium real domestic output and the full-employment output of the economy.　**T　F**

25. A decrease in aggregate supply is "doubly good" because it increases the real domestic output and prevents inflation.　**T　F**

■ MULTIPLE-CHOICE QUESTIONS

Circle the letter that corresponds to the best answer.

1. The aggregate demand curve is the relationship between the:
 (a) price level and the real domestic output purchased
 (b) price level and the real domestic output produced
 (c) price level which producers are willing to pay
 (d) real domestic output purchased and the real domestic output produced

2. When the price level rises:
 (a) holders of financial assets with fixed money values increase their spending
 (b) the demand for money and interest rates rise
 (c) spending which is sensitive to interest-rate changes increases
 (d) holders of financial assets with fixed money values have more purchasing power

3. The slope of the aggregate demand curve is the result of:
 (a) the wealth effect
 (b) the interest-rate effect
 (c) the foreign-purchases effect
 (d) all of the above effects

4. If the price level in the aggregate expenditures model were lower the consumption and aggregate expenditures curves would be:
 (a) lower and the equilibrium real GDP would be smaller
 (b) lower and the equilibrium real GDP would be larger
 (c) higher and the equilibrium real GDP would be larger
 (d) higher and the equilibrium real GDP would be smaller

5. A decrease in the price level will shift the:
 (a) consumption, investment, and net exports curves downward
 (b) consumption, investment, and net exports curves upward
 (c) consumption and investment curves upward, but the net exports curve downward
 (d) consumption and net export curves upward, but the investment curve downward

6. The aggregate demand curve will tend to be increased by:
 (a) a decrease in the price level
 (b) an increase in the price level
 (c) an increase in the excess capacity of factories
 (d) a depreciation in the value of the United States dollar

7. A sharp decline in the real value of stock prices, which is independent of a change in the price level, would best be an example of:
 (a) the wealth effect
 (b) the real balance effect
 (c) a change in real wealth
 (d) a change in consumer indebtedness

8. An increase in aggregate expenditures shifts the aggregate demand curve to the:
 (a) right by the amount of the increase in aggregate expenditures
 (b) right by the amount of the increase in aggregate expenditures times the multiplier
 (c) left by the amount of the increase in aggregate expenditures
 (d) left by the amount of the increase in aggregate expenditures times the multiplier

9. The aggregate supply curve is the relationship between the:
 (a) price level and the real domestic output purchased
 (b) price level and the real domestic output produced
 (c) price level which producers are willing to accept and the price level purchasers are willing to pay
 (d) real domestic output purchased and the real domestic output produced

10. In the intermediate range the aggregate supply curve is:
 (a) upsloping
 (b) downsloping
 (c) vertical
 (d) horizontal

Suppose that real domestic output in an economy is 50 units, the quantity of inputs is 10, and the price of each input is $2. Answer the next four questions (11, 12, 13, and 14) on the basis of this information.

11. The level of productivity in this economy is:
 (a) 5
 (b) 4
 (c) 3
 (d) 2

12. The per unit cost of production is:
 (a) $0.40
 (b) $0.50
 (c) $2.50
 (d) $3.50

13. If real domestic output in the economy rose to 60 units, then per unit production costs would:
 (a) remain unchanged and aggregate supply would remain unchanged
 (b) increase and aggregate supply would decrease

(c) decrease and aggregate supply would increase

(d) decrease and aggregate supply would decrease

14. All else equal, if the price of each input increases from $2 to $4, productivity would:

(a) decrease from $4 to $2 and aggregate supply would decrease

(b) decrease from $5 to $3 and aggregate supply would decrease

(c) decrease from $4 to $2 and aggregate supply would increase

(d) remain unchanged and aggregate supply would decrease

15. If the prices of imported resources increase, then this event would most likely:

(a) decrease aggregate supply

(b) increase aggregate supply

(c) increase aggregate demand

(d) decrease aggregate demand

16. If Congress passed much stricter laws to control the air pollution from business, then this action would tend to:

(a) increase per unit production costs and shift the aggregate supply curve to the right

(b) increase per unit production costs and shift the aggregate supply curve to the left

(c) increase per unit production costs and shift the aggregate demand curve to the left

(d) decrease per unit production costs and shift the aggregate supply curve to the left

17. An increase in business taxes will tend to:

(a) decrease aggregate demand but not change aggregate supply

(b) decrease aggregate supply but not change aggregate demand

(c) decrease aggregate demand and decrease aggregate supply

(d) decrease aggregate supply and increase aggregate demand

18. If the real domestic output is less than the equilibrium real domestic output producers find:

(a) their inventories decreasing and expand their production

(b) their inventories increasing and expand their production

(c) their inventories decreasing and contract their production

(d) their inventories increasing and contract their production

Answer the next four questions (19, 20, 21, and 22) on the basis of the following aggregate demand and supply schedule for a hypothetical economy.

Real domestic output demanded (in billions)	Price level	Real domestic output supplied (in billions)
$1500	170	$4000
$2000	150	$4000
$2500	125	$3500
$3000	100	$3000
$3500	75	$2500
$4000	75	$2000

19. The equilibrium price level and quantity of real domestic output will be:

(a) 100 and $2500

(b) 100 and $3000

(c) 125 and $3500

(d) 150 and $4000

20. The horizontal range of the aggregate supply curve is associated with the quantity supplied of:

(a) $4000

(b) $4000 and $3500

(c) $3500 and $3000

(d) $2500 and $2000

21. If the quantity of real domestic output demanded increased by $2000 at each price level, the new equilibrium price level and quantity of real domestic output would be:

(a) 175 and $4000

(b) 150 and $4000

(c) 125 and $3500

(d) 100 and $3000

22. Using the original data from the table, if the quantity of real domestic output demanded *increased* by $500 and quantity of real domestic output supplied *decreased* by $500 at each price level, the new equilibrium price level and quantity of real domestic output would be:

(a) 175 and $4000

(b) 150 and $4000

(c) 125 and $3000

(d) 100 and $3500

23. When the economy is in the horizontal range an increase in aggregate demand will:

(a) increase the price level and have no effect on real domestic output

(b) increase the real domestic output and have no effect on the price level

(c) increase both real output and the price level

(d) increase the price level and decrease the real domestic output

24. An increase in aggregate demand will increase the equilibrium real GDP if the economy is operating in the:

(a) horizontal range only

(b) intermediate range only

(c) horizontal or intermediate ranges

(d) vertical range only

25. An increase in aggregate demand will increase both the equilibrium real GDP and the price level if the economy is operating in the:
  (a) horizontal range
  (b) intermediate range
  (c) intermediate or vertical ranges
  (d) vertical range

26. In the aggregate demand and aggregate supply model, an increase in the price level will:
  (a) increase the marginal propensity to consume
  (b) increase the strength of the multiplier
  (c) decrease the strength of the multiplier
  (d) have no effect on the strength of the multiplier

27. If aggregate demand decreases but the price level does not fall as much as would be expected if price were flexible, then this situation could be the result of:
  (a) an increase in aggregate supply
  (b) the foreign-purchases effect
  (c) lower interest rates
  (d) a ratchet effect

28. The ratchet effect is the result of:
  (a) a price level that is inflexible upward
  (b) a price level that is inflexible downward
  (c) a domestic output that cannot be increased
  (d) a domestic output that cannot be decreased

29. An increase in aggregate supply will:
  (a) reduce the price level and real domestic output
  (b) reduce the price level and increase the real domestic output
  (c) increase the price level and real domestic output
  (d) reduce the price level and decrease the real domestic output

30. If there were cost-push inflation in the economy that decreased aggregate supply:
  (a) both the real domestic output and the price level would decrease
  (b) the real domestic output would increase and rises in the price level would become smaller
  (c) the real domestic output would decrease and the price level would rise
  (d) both the real domestic output and rises in the price level would become greater

■ **PROBLEMS**

1. In the next table is an aggregate supply schedule.
  a. The economy is in the:
  (1) horizontal range when the real domestic output is

between _____ and _____

(2) vertical range when the real domestic output is

_____ and the price level is _____
or more
(3) intermediate range when the real domestic output

is between _____ and _____

Price level	Real domestic output supplied
250	2000
225	2000
200	1900
175	1700
150	1400
125	1000
125	500
125	0

b. Plot this aggregate supply schedule on the graph on the next page.
c. In the table below are three aggregate demand schedules.

Price level (1)	Real domestic output demanded		
	(2)	**(3)**	**(4)**
250	1400	1900	400
225	1500	2000	500
200	1600	2100	600
175	1700	2200	700
150	1800	2300	800
125	1900	2400	900
100	2000	2500	1000

(1) Plot the aggregate demand curve shown in columns (1) and (2) on the graph at the top of the next page; and label this curve **AD₁**. At this level of aggregate demand the equilibrium real domestic output is

_____

and the equilibrium price level is _____
(2) On the same graph plot the aggregate demand curve shown in columns (1) and (3); and label this curve

AD₂. The equilibrium real domestic output is _____

and the equilibrium price level is _____
(3) Now plot the aggregate demand curve in columns (1) and (4) and label it **AD₃**. The equilibrium real domestic output is _____ and the equilib-

rium price level is _____

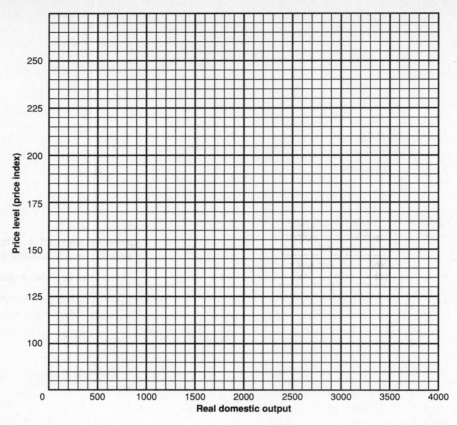

2. The real GDP an economy might produce is shown in column (1) below.

(1) Real GDP	(2) $AE_{1.20}$	(3) $AE_{1.00}$	(4) $AE_{0.80}$
$2100	$2110	$2130	$2150
2200	2200	2220	2240
2300	2290	2310	2330
2400	2380	2400	2420
2500	2470	2490	2510
2600	2560	2580	2600

a. If the price level in this economy were $1.20 the aggregate expenditures (AE) at each real GDP would be those shown in column (2) and the equilibrium real

GDP would be $_____

b. But if the price level were $1.00 the aggregate expenditures at each real GDP would be those shown in column (3) and the equilibrium real GDP would be

$_____

c. And if the price level were $0.80 the aggregate expenditures at each real GDP would be those shown in column (4) and the equilibrium real GDP would be

$_____

d. Show in the schedule below the equilibrium real GDP at each of the three price levels.

Price level	Equilibrium real GDP
$1.20	$_____
1.00	_____
.80	_____

(1) This schedule is the _____ schedule and

(2) in it the equilibrium real GDP is _____ related to the price level.

3. In the following list, what will most likely happen as a result of each event to: (1) aggregate demand (AD); (2) aggregate supply (AS); (3) the equilibrium price level; and (4) equilibrium real domestic output (**Q**)? Assume that all other things remain constant when the event occurs and that the economy is operating in the intermediate range of the aggregate supply curve. Use the following symbols to indicate the expected effects: **I** = increase; **D** = decrease; **S** = remains the same; and **U** = uncertain.

a. A decrease in labor productivity.

AD_____   AS_____   **P**_____   **Q**_____

b. A fall in the interest rate for business loans.

AD_____ AS_____ *P*_____ *Q*_____

c. Consumer incomes decline as the economy moves into a recession.

AD_____ AS_____ *P*_____ *Q*_____

d. The price of oil on the world market falls to a low level.

AD_____ AS_____ *P*_____ *Q*_____

e. There is an appreciation in the value of the United States dollar.

AD_____ AS_____ *P*_____ *Q*_____

4. Below are hypothetical data showing the relationships between the real domestic output and the quantity of input resources needed to produce each level of output.

Output	Input	Productivity		Per unit cost		
		(1)	(2)	(3)	(4)	(5)
2500	500	____	____	____	____	____
2000	400	____	____	____	____	____
1500	300	____	____	____	____	____

a. In column (1) compute the level of productivity at each level of real domestic output.
b. In column (2) compute the level of productivity if there is a doubling in the quantity of inputs required to produce each level of output.
c. In column (3) compute the per unit production cost at each level of output, if each unit of input costs $15, given the level of productivity in column (1).
d. In column (4) compute the new per unit production cost at each level of output given that input price is $15 per unit, given that there has been a doubling in the required quantity of inputs to produce each level of output as shown in column (2). What will happen to the aggregate supply curve if this situation occurs?

_____

e. In column (5), compute the new per unit production cost at each level of output, given that input price is now $10 instead of $15, but the level of productivity stays as it was originally, as shown in column (1). What will happen to the aggregate supply curve if this situation occurs?_____

5. Columns (1) and (2) in the table below are the aggregate supply schedule of an economy.
  a. The economy is in the

  (1) vertical range when its real GDP is $_____ and the price level is $_____ or higher;

  (2) horizontal range when its real GDP is $_____ or less and its price level is $_____
b. If the aggregate demand in the economy were columns (1) and (3) the equilibrium real GDP would be

$_____ and the equilibrium price level would be

$_____; and if aggregate demand should increase by $100 to that shown in columns (1) and (4)

the equilibrium real GDP would increase by $_____

and the price level would be _____
c. Should aggregate demand be that shown in columns (1) and (5) the equilibrium real GDP would be

$_____ and the equilibrium price would be

$_____; and if aggregate demand should increase by $100 to that shown in columns (1) and (6)

the equilibrium real GDP would increase by $_____

and the price level would rise to $_____
d. And if aggregate demand were that shown in columns (1) and (7) the equilibrium real GDP would be

$_____ and the equilibrium price level would

be $_____; but if aggregate demand increased by $100 to that shown in columns (1) and (8)

(1) Price level	(2) Real GDP	(3) AD₁	(4) AD₂	(5) AD₃	(6) AD₄	(7) AD₅	(8) AD₆
$2.60	$2390	$ 840	$ 940	$1900	$2000	$2190	$2290
2.40	2390	940	1040	2000	2100	2290	2390
2.20	2390	1040	1140	2100	2200	2390	2490
2.00	2390	1140	1240	2200	2300	2490	2590
1.90	2350	1190	1290	2250	2350	2540	2640
1.80	2300	1240	1340	2300	2400	2590	2690
1.60	2200	1340	1440	2400	2500	2690	2790
1.40	2090	1440	1540	2500	2600	2790	2890
1.20	1970	1540	1640	2600	2700	2890	2990
1.00	1840	1640	1740	2700	2800	2990	3090
1.00	1740	1640	1740	2700	2800	2990	3090
1.00	1640	1640	1740	2700	2800	2990	3090

the price level would rise to $_____ and the equilibrium real GDP would _____

6. In the diagram below are an aggregate supply curve and six aggregate demand curves.

  a. The movements of the aggregate demand curves from **AD₁** to **AD₂**, from **AD₃** to **AD₄**, and from **AD₅** to **AD₆** all portray (increases, decreases) _____ in aggregate demand.

  (1) The movement from **AD₁** to **AD₂** increases the (real domestic output, price level) _____ but does not change the _____

  (2) The movement from **AD₃** to **AD₄** will (raise, lower) _____ the price level and will (expand, contract) _____ the real domestic output.

  (3) The movement from **AD₅** to **AD₆** will _____ _____

  b. The movements of the aggregate demand curves to the left all portray (increases, decreases) _____ in aggregate demand.

  (1) If prices are flexible in a downward direction, what effects will these changes in aggregate demand have upon the real domestic output and the price level?____ _____

  (2) If prices are **not** flexible in a downward direction, what effects will these changes in aggregate demand have? _____ _____

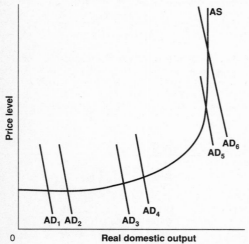

7. In the diagram in the next column there are two aggregate supply curves and three aggregate demand curves.

  a. The movement of the aggregate supply curve from **AS₁** to **AS₂** represents a(n) (increase, decrease) _____ in aggregate supply.

  (1) If the price level is flexible downward and upward, this change in aggregate supply in each of the three ranges along the aggregate supply curve will (raise, lower) _____ the price level and (expand, contract) _____ the real domestic output.

  (2) But if prices are inflexible in a downward direction, this change in aggregate supply will (increase, decrease) _____ real domestic output but (will, will not) _____ affect the price level.

  b. The movement of aggregate supply from **AS₂** to **AS₁** portrays a(n) _____ in aggregate supply and in each of the three ranges will _____ _____the price level and _____ the real domestic output.

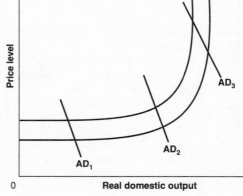

■ SHORT ANSWER AND ESSAY QUESTIONS

  1. What is the aggregate demand curve? Draw a graph of one and explain its features.

  2. Explain:
  (a) the interest-rate effect,
  (b) the wealth effect, and
  (c) the foreign-purchases effect of change in the price level on the quantity of goods and services demanded in an economy.

  3. What roles do the expectations of consumers and businesses play in influencing aggregate demand?

4. Explain the difference between the wealth effect and "a change in the real value of consumer wealth" for the interpretation of aggregate demand.

5. What is the effect of an increase in aggregate expenditures on the aggregate demand curve? Explain in words and with an equation.

6. The aggregate supply curve is divided into three distinct ranges. Describe the slope of this curve in each of the three ranges. What conditions prevail in the economy in each of the ranges?

7. Why does the aggregate supply curve slope upward in the intermediate range?

8. How does an increase or decrease in per unit production costs change aggregate supply? Give examples.

9. How does the legal and institutional environment affect the price level and real domestic output? Give examples.

10. Explain how a change in business taxes affects aggregate demand and aggregate supply.

11. Describe how changes in the international economy influence aggregate demand or aggregate supply.

12. What is the relationship between the production possibilities curve and aggregate supply?

13. What real domestic output is the equilibrium real domestic output? Why will business firms that produce the domestic output reduce or expand their production when they find themselves producing more or less than the equilibrium output?

14. What are the effects on the real domestic output and the price level when aggregate demand increases in each of the three ranges along the aggregate supply curve?

15. What is the effect of an increase in aggregate demand on: (a) real equilibrium GDP and the price level in the horizontal, intermediate, and vertical ranges of the aggregate supply curve; and (b) on the strength of the multiplier in each of these ranges? What is the relationship between the effect of an increase in aggregate demand on real GDP and the rise in the price level that accompanies it?

16. If prices were as flexible downward as they are upward, what would be the effects on real domestic output and the price level of a decrease in aggregate demand in each of the three ranges along the aggregate supply curve?

17. Prices in the economy tend to be "sticky" or inflexible in a downward direction. Why? How does this downward inflexibility alter your answers to question **7** (above)?

18. What are the effects on the real domestic output and the price level of a decrease in aggregate supply? What

are the effects of an increase in aggregate supply on the real domestic output, the price level, and the maximum real output the economy is able to produce?

19. Why is a decrease in aggregate supply "doubly bad" and an increase in aggregate supply "doubly good"?

20. Using the aggregate demand and aggregate supply concepts, explain the difference between demand-pull and cost-push inflation.

ANSWERS

Chapter 11 Aggregate Demand and Aggregate Supply

FILL-IN QUESTIONS

1. variable, fixed

2. output, level

3. demanded (purchased), levels *a.* downward; *b.* wealth (real balances), interest-rate, foreign-purchases (any order)

4. *a.* decrease; *b.* increase; *c.* other things equal

5. *a.* raise, rise; *b.* lower, fall; *c.* inverse, demand

6. *a.* movement along; *b.* change in aggregate demand; *c.* determinants

7. *a.* consumer wealth; *b.* consumer expectations; *c.* consumer indebtedness; *d.* personal taxes (any order)

8. *a.* interest rates; *b.* profit expectations; *c.* business taxes; *d.* technology; *e.* degree of excess capacity (any order)

9. government, income, exchange

10. *a.* right, multiplier; *b.* left, downward shift in aggregate expenditures times the multiplier

11. supplied (produced), levels; *a.* horizontal; *b.* upsloping; *c.* vertical

12. increase, a decrease in the per unit costs of production

13. *a.* (1) domestic resource availability, (2) prices of imported resources, (3) market power (any order); *b.* productivity; *c.* (1) business taxes and subsidies, (2) government regulation (either order)

14. intersection; *a.* purchased (demanded), produced (supplied) (either order); *b.* accept, pay

15. *a.* increasing, reduce; *b.* decreasing, expand

16. *a.* increase, have no effect on; *b.* increase, increase; *c.* have no effect on, increase

17. *a.* greater, smaller; *b.* smaller, greater

18. smaller, ratchet

19. raise, prevent, increase; lower, raise

20. increase, rise, decrease, fall in real output

TRUE-FALSE QUESTIONS

1. T, p. 213	**8.** F, p. 216	**15.** T, p. 223	**22.** F, p. 227
2. T, p. 214	**9.** F, p. 218	**16.** T, p. 223	**23.** F, pp. 227-228
3. T, p. 214	**10.** F, pp. 218-219	**17.** T, p. 224	**24.** T, p. 229
4. F, p. 214	**11.** F, p. 217	**18.** T, p. 225	**25.** F, p. 229
5. F, p. 214	**12.** F, pp. 218-219	**19.** T, p. 226	
6. T, p. 214	**13.** F, p. 220	**20.** F, p. 226	
7. F, p. 215	**14.** T, p. 222	**21.** F, p. 227	

MULTIPLE-CHOICE QUESTIONS

1. *a*, pp. 213-214	**9.** *b*, p. 220	**17.** *c*, p. 224	**25.** *b*, p. 226
2. *b*, p. 214	**10.** *a*, p. 220	**18.** *a*, p. 225	**26.** *c*, p. 227
3. *d*, pp. 214-215	**11.** *a*, p. 224	**19.** *b*, p. 225	**27.** *d*, p. 227
4. *c*, pp. 215-216	**12.** *a*, p. 224	**20.** *b*, p. 220	**28.** *b*, p. 227
5. *b*, p. 215	**13.** *c*, p. 224	**21.** *b*, p. 225	**29.** *b*, p. 229
6. *d*, pp. 218-219	**14.** *d*, p. 224	**22.** *c*, p. 225	**30.** *c*, p. 229
7. *c*, p. 217	**15.** *a*, p. 223	**23.** *b*, p. 226	
8. *b*, pp. 219-220	**16.** *b*, p. 224	**24.** *c*, p. 226	

PROBLEMS

1. *a.* (1) 0, 1000, (2) 2000, 225, (3) 1000, 2000; *c.* (1) 1700, 175, (2) 2000, 225, (3) 900, 125

2. *a.* 2200; *b.* 2400; *c.* 2600; *d.* 2200, 2400, 2600, (1) aggregate-demand, (2) inversely

3. *a.* S, D, I, D; *b.* I, S, I, I; *c.* D, S, D, D; *d.* I, I, U, I; *e.* D, I, D, U

4. *a.* 5, 5, 5; *b.* 2.5, 2.5, 2.5; *c.* $3, $3, $3; *d.* $6, $6, $6, it will decrease; *e.* $2, $2, $2, it will increase

5. *a.* (1) 2390, 2.00, (2) 1840, 1.00; *b.* 1640, 1.00, 100, remain constant; *c.* 2300, 1.80, 2350, 1.90; *d.* 2390, 2.20, 2.40, remain constant

6. *a.* increases, (1) real domestic output, price level, (2) raise, expand, (3) increase the price level but will not affect domestic output; *b.* decreases, (1) decrease the price level in the vertical and intermediate ranges and decrease domestic output in the intermediate and horizontal ranges, (2) decrease only output in the intermediate and horizontal ranges

7. *a.* increase, (1) lower, expand, (2) increase, will not; *b.* decrease, increase, decrease

SHORT ANSWER AND ESSAY QUESTIONS

1. pp. 213-214	**6.** pp. 220-221	**11.** pp. 218-219,223	**16.** p. 226
2. pp. 214-215	**7.** pp. 220-221	**12.** p. 229	**17.** pp. 226-227
3. p. 217	**8.** p. 224	**13.** pp. 225-226	**18.** p. 229
4. pp. 214, 217	**9.** p. 224	**14.** p. 226	**19.** p. 229
5. pp. 215-216	**10.** p. 224	**15.** p. 226	**20.** pp. 226-227, 229

CHAPTER 12

Fiscal Policy

Chapter 12 is really a continuation of the preceding chapter and is concerned with the chief practical application of the principles discussed in that chapter.

It is worth recalling that principles of economics are generalizations about the way the economy works; and that these principles are studied in order that policies may be devised to solve real problems. Over the past one hundred or so years the most serious problems encountered by the American economy have been those problems that resulted from the business cycle. Learning what determines the real output and price levels of an economy and what causes them to fluctuate will make it possible to discover ways to bring about full employment, maximum output, and stable prices. Economic principles, in short, suggest the policies that will lessen both recession and inflation.

Government spending and taxing have a strong influence on the economy's output and employment and its price level. Federal expenditure and taxation policies designed to expand total production and employment or reduce the rate of inflation are called fiscal policies. (The Federal Reserve Banks are also able to affect these variables by applying monetary policy; but the study of monetary policy must wait until the effect of banks on the operation of the economy is examined in Chapters 13, 14, and 15.)

The brief first section of the chapter makes it clear that Congress in the Employment Act of 1946 committed the Federal government to using fiscal (and monetary) policy to achieve a trio of economic goals—economic growth, stable prices, and full employment. This act also established the Council of Economic Advisers to advise the President and Joint Economic Committee to advise Congress on matters pertaining to national economic policy.

The second section of the chapter discusses *discretionary* fiscal policy, which can be either *expansionary* or *contractionary.* Here you will learn how these fiscal policies affect aggregate demand and the Federal budget. Expansionary fiscal policy is used to stimulate the economy and pull it out of a slump or recession. This type of policy can be achieved by increasing government spending, decreasing taxes, or some combination of the two. Contractionary fiscal policy is enacted to counter inflation-

ary pressure in the economy. The policy actions taken to dampen inflation include cutting government spending, raising taxes, or a combination of the two. As you will learn, each policy can have a significant effect on aggregate demand and the Federal budget. If the government has a budget deficit or surplus, the way the government finances it can affect the economy's operation as much as the size of the deficit or surplus.

Discretionary fiscal policy requires that Congress take action to change tax rates, transfer payment programs, or purchases of goods and services. *Non*discretionary fiscal policy does not require Congress to take any action; and is a *built-in stabilizer* of the economy. You should be sure that you understand *why* net taxes increase when the GDP rises and decrease when the GDP falls and *how* this tends to stabilize the economy.

Unfortunately, nondiscretionary fiscal policy by itself may not be able to eliminate any recessionary or inflationary gap that might develop; and discretionary fiscal policy may be necessary if the economy is to produce its full-employment GDP and avoid inflation. And the built-in stabilizers make it more difficult to use discretionary fiscal policy to achieve this goal because they create the illusion that the Federal government's policy is expansionary or contractionary when in fact its policy is just the opposite. Because of the illusions created by the built-in stabilizers, economists developed the *full-employment budget* and distinguished between a cyclical and structural deficit to enable them to discover whether Federal fiscal policy was actually expansionary or contractionary and to determine what policy should have been followed to move the economy toward full employment or slow the rate of inflation.

In addition to the problems of timing and the political problems encountered in using fiscal problems in the real world, you will discover in the last major section of the chapter that many economists and other people are concerned by three other important complications. They fear, first of all, that all expansionary fiscal policy which requires the Federal government to borrow in the money market will raise the level of interest rates in the economy and reduce (or *crowd out*) investment spending; this is called the crowding-out effect and if it is large it will reduce the effect of the expansionary fiscal policy on real GDP and unemployment. A second complication expressed by some economists is that the potential expansionary effects of a budget deficit (public dissaving) are offset by an equal increase in private saving, thereby reducing or eliminating the effects of fiscal policy on the economy. The third problem arises from the connection of the domestic economy to a world economy; aggregate demand shocks from abroad or a net export effect may increase or decrease the effectiveness of a given fiscal policy. The fourth concern is that an expansionary fiscal policy, if the economy is operating in the intermediate range along the aggregate supply curve, will drive up the price level and have only a small effect on real output and employment. But all is not gloom. The **supply-side** economists argue that a reduction in tax rates will not only increase aggregate demand but will also (for a number of reasons explained in the text) expand aggregate supply. In this way, they contend, the real equilibrium GDP of the economy can be increased with little or no rise in the price level. This viewpoint will be dealt with in more detail in Chapter 17.

■ CHECKLIST

When you have studied this chapter you should be able to:

☐ State the responsibility imposed on the Federal government by the Employment Act of 1946 and the roles of the CEA and JEC in fulfilling this responsibility.
☐ Distinguish between discretionary and nondiscretionary fiscal policy.
☐ Explain expansionary fiscal policy and the effect of different policy options on aggregate demand.
☐ Describe contractionary fiscal policy and the effect of different policy options on aggregate demand.
☐ Describe the best way to finance a government deficit and to dispose of a surplus.
☐ Indicate how the built-in stabilizers help to eliminate recession and inflationary pressures.
☐ Describe the relationship between progressive, proportional, and regressive tax systems and the built-in stability of the economy.
☐ Distinguish between the actual budget and the full-employment budget, and between cyclical deficits and structural deficits as indicators of the government's fiscal policy.
☐ Outline three timing problems that may arise with fiscal policy.
☐ Discuss four political problems with fiscal policy.
☐ Describe the crowding-out effect of an expansionary fiscal policy and how it may lessen the impact of an expansionary fiscal policy on real output and employment.
☐ Explain the criticism of fiscal policy that arises from the Ricardian equivalence theorem.
☐ Distinguish between the effects of an expansionary fiscal policy in the horizontal and intermediate ranges of the aggregate supply curve; and explain how the impact of such a policy is reduced when the economy is in the latter range.
☐ Explain two ways that interdependency with the world economy influences the effectiveness of domestic fiscal policy.
☐ Explain the effects of a reduction in tax rates on aggregate supply, real GDP, and the price level from a supply-side perspective.

■ CHAPTER OUTLINE

1. Fiscal policy is the manipulation by the Federal government of its expenditures and tax receipts in order to expand or contract the economy; and by doing so either increase its real output (and employment) or decrease its rate of inflation.

2. The Employment Act of 1946 set the goals of American fiscal policy and provided for a Council of Economic Advisers to the President and the Joint Economic Committee.

3. **Discretionary fiscal policy** involves changes in government spending or taxation by Congress which is designed to change the level of real GDP, employment, incomes, or the price level. Specific action needs to be taken by Congress to initiate this policy, in contrast to nondiscretionary fiscal policy that occurs automatically (see item 4 below).

    a. **Expansionary fiscal policy** is generally used to counteract the negative economic effects of a recession or cyclical downturn in the economy (a decline in real GDP and rising unemployment). The purpose of the policy is to stimulate the economy by increasing aggregate demand. Three policy options are used: an **increase in government spending; tax reductions** (which increases consumer spending); or a **combination** of an increase in government spending and a tax reduction. These policy actions will create a **budget deficit** if the budget was in balance before the policy actions were taken. The stimulative effect on the economy from the initial increase in spending from the policy change will be increased by the multiplier effect.

    b. **Contractionary fiscal policy** is a restrictive form of fiscal policy that is generally used to control demand-pull inflation. The purpose of this policy is to reduce aggregate demand pressures that increase the price level. Three policy options are used: a **decrease in government spending; increase taxes** (which reduces consumer spending); or a **combination** of a reduction in government spending and a tax increase. If the government budget is balanced before the policy actions are taken, it will create a **budget surplus.** The contractionary effect on the economy from the initial reduction in spending from the policy actions will be reinforced by the multiplier effect.

c. In addition to the size of the deficit or surplus, the manner in which government finances its deficit or disposes of its surplus affects the level of total spending in the economy. The government can either borrow money from the public or issue new money to creditors to finance a deficit. Budget surpluses may be used for debt reduction, or they may be impounded and the money taken out of circulation.

d. Whether government purchases or taxes should be altered to reduce recession and inflation depends to a large extent upon whether an expansion or a contraction of the public sector is desired.

4. In the United States economy net tax revenues (tax revenues minus government transfer payments) are not a fixed amount or lump sum; they increase as the GDP rises and decrease as the GDP falls.

a. This net tax system serves as a built-in stabilizer of the economy because it reduces purchasing power during periods of inflation and expands purchasing during periods of recession.

(1) As GDP increases, the average tax rates will increase in progressive systems, remain constant in proportional systems, and decrease in regressive systems; there is more built-in stability for the economy in progressive tax systems.

(2) Mainstream economists contend that built-in stabilizers can only reduce and cannot eliminate economic fluctuations.

b. The full-employment budget is a better index than the actual budget of the direction of government fiscal policy because it indicates what the Federal budget deficit or surplus would be if the economy were to operate at full employment. In the case of a budget deficit, the full employment budget:

(1) removes the cyclical portion that is produced by swings in the business cycle; and

(2) reveals the size of the structural deficit, indicating how expansionary fiscal policy was that year.

5. Certain problems and complications arise in enacting and applying fiscal policy.

a. There will be problems of timing because it requires time to recognize the need for fiscal policy; to take the appropriate steps in the Congress; and for the action taken there to affect output and employment, and the rate of inflation in the economy.

b. There will also be political problems because:

(1) the economy has goals other than full employment and stable prices;

(2) the fiscal policies of state and local government run counter to Federal fiscal policy;

(3) there is an expansionary bias (for budget deficits and against surpluses);

(4) there may be a political business cycle (if politicians lower taxes and increase expenditures before and then do the opposite after elections).

c. An expansionary fiscal policy may, by raising the level of interest rates in the economy, reduce (or crowd out) investment spending and weaken the effect of the policy on real GDP; but this crowding-out effect may be small and can be offset by an expansion in the nation's money supply.

d. The Ricardian equivalence theorem suggests that borrowing to finance a budget deficit (public dissaving) is offset by an increase in private saving as people save in anticipation of higher taxes in the future; thus, the effects of deficit spending (or an expansionary fiscal policy) are offset by the effects of an equal increase in private saving.

e. The effect of an expansionary fiscal policy on the real GDP will also be weakened to the extent that it results in a rise in the price level (inflation).

f. Aggregate demand and aggregate supply curves can be used to show how crowding out and inflation weaken the effects of an expansionary fiscal policy on real GDP.

g. The connection of the domestic economy to a world economy means that fiscal policy may be inappropriate or less effective because of aggregate demand shocks from the world economy or a net export effect that counteracts or reinforces domestic fiscal policy.

h. But an expansionary fiscal policy that includes a reduction in taxes (tax rates) may, by increasing aggregate supply in the economy, expand real GDP (and employment), and reduce inflation.

■ IMPORTANT TERMS

Fiscal policy	Built-in stabilizers
Employment Act of 1946	Progressive, proportional, and regressive tax systems
Council of Economic Advisers	
Joint Economic Committee	Actual budget
	Full-employment budget
Discretionary fiscal policy	Cyclical deficit
Expansionary fiscal policy	Structural deficit
Budget deficit	Political business cycle
Contractionary fiscal policy	Crowding-out effect
Budget surplus	Ricardian equivalence theorem
Nondiscretionary fiscal policy	Net export effect
Net taxes	Supply-side fiscal policy

■ HINTS AND TIPS

1. Fiscal policy is a broad concept that covers various taxation and spending policies of the Federal government; it is not limited to one policy. You will need to know the distinctions between the several kinds of fiscal policies. The main difference is between discretionary and nondiscretionary fiscal policy. **Discretionary** fiscal policy is **active** and means that Congress took specific actions to change taxes or government spending to influence. It can also be **expansionary** or **contractionary. Nondiscretionary** fiscal policy is **passive** or automatic because changes in taxes or government spending will occur without specific action by Congress.

2. An increase in government spending that is equal to a cut in taxes will not have an equal effect on real GDP. To understand this point, assume that the MPC is .75, the increase in government spending is $8 billion, and the decrease in taxes is $8 billion. The multiplier would be 4 because it equals $1/(1 - .75)$. The increase in government spending will increase real GDP by $32 billion ($8 billion $\times$ 4). Of the $8 billion decrease in taxes, however, one-quarter of it will be saved ($6 billion $\times$ .25 = $2 billion) and just three-quarters ($8 billion $\times$ .75 = $6 billion) will be spent. Thus, the tax cut results in an increase in **initial** spending in the economy of $6 billion, not $8 billion as was the case with the increase in government spending. The tax cut effect on real GDP is $24 billion ($6 $\times$ 4), not the $32 billion.

3. A large part of the chapter deals with seven problems (or criticisms and complications) of fiscal policy. Don't miss the big picture and get lost in the details of each problem when reading this section. The seven include: (a) timing; (b) politics; (c) crowding-out; (d) private savings offsetting fiscal policy; (e) inflation reducing the multiplier effect; (f) the net export effect offsetting fiscal policy; and (g) supply-side effect offsetting or reinforcing demand-side effects.

SELF-TEST

■ FILL-IN QUESTIONS

1. The use of monetary and fiscal policy to reduce inflation and recession became national economic policy

in the _____

This act also established the Council of _____

to the President and the _____
Committee of Congress.

2. Policy actions taken by Congress designed to change government spending or taxation are (discretionary, nondiscretionary) _____ fiscal policy, but when the policy takes effect automatically or independent of Congress then it is _____ fiscal policy.

3. Expansionary fiscal policy is generally designed to (increase, decrease) _____ aggregate de-

mand and thus _____ real GDP and employment in the economy. Contractionary fiscal policy is

generally used to _____ aggregate demand and

_____ the level of prices.

4. Expansionary fiscal policy can be achieved with an increase in (government spending, taxes) _____

_____, a decrease in _____ , or a combination of the two. Contractionary fiscal policy can be

achieved by a decrease in _____ , an

increase in _____ , or a combination of the two.

5. An increase of government spending of $5 billion from an expansionary fiscal policy for an economy ultimately produces an increase in real GDP of $20 billion.

This magnified effect occurs because of the _____

which has a size of _____ for this economy.

6. If the Federal budget is balanced and Congress passes legislation supporting an expansionary fiscal policy, then this action is likely to produce a budget (deficit,

surplus) _____. If, however, Congress passes legislation supporting a contractionary fiscal policy, then

the action will result in a budget _____

7. If fiscal policy is to have a countercyclical effect, it will probably be necessary for the Federal government to incur

a budget (surplus, deficit) _____

during a recession and a budget _____
during inflation.

8. The two principal means available to the Federal government for financing budget deficits are _____

and _____; and the (former,

latter) _____ is more expansionary.

9. Those economists who wish to expand the public sector of the economy during a period of **inflation** would most likely advocate a(n) (increase, decrease)

_____ in (government purchases, taxes)

_____; and those economists who wish to contract the public sector during a **recession** would

most likely advocate a(n) _____

in _____

10. Net taxes:

a. equal _____ minus _____
b. in the United States will (increase, decrease)

_____ as the GDP rises and

will _____ as the GDP falls.

11. When net tax receipts are directly related to the GDP the economy has some _____ stability because:

    a. when the GDP rises, leakages (increase, decrease) _____ and the budget surplus will (increase, decrease) _____ (or the budget deficit will _____);

    b. when the GDP falls, leakages _____ and the budget deficit will _____ (or the budget surplus will _____)

12. As GDP increases, the average tax rates will increase in (progressive, proportional, regressive) _____ systems, remain constant in _____ systems, and decrease in _____ systems; there is (more, less) _____ built-in stability for the economy in progressive tax systems.

13. The full-employment budget:

    a. indicates what the Federal _____ would have been if the economy had operated at _____ during the year;

    b. tells us whether the Federal budget was in fact _____ or _____

    c. A deficit produced by swings in the business cycle is (structural, cyclical) _____, whereas a deficit produced through government taxation and spending decision is _____. The full-employment budget indicates the size of the _____ deficit.

14. There is a problem of timing in the use of discretionary fiscal policy because of the _____ , _____ , and _____ lags.

15. Political problems arise in the application of discretionary fiscal policy to stabilize the economy because government has _____ goals; because state and local fiscal policies may (reinforce, counter) _____ Federal fiscal policy; because voters have a bias in favor of budget (surpluses, deficits) _____; and because politicians use fiscal policies in a way that creates a _____ business cycle.

16. When the Federal government employs an expansionary fiscal policy to increase real GDP and employment in the economy it usually has a budget (surplus, deficit) _____ and (lends, borrows) _____ in the money market.

    a. This will (raise, lower) _____ interest rates in the economy and (contract, expand) _____ investment spending.

    b. This change in investment spending is the _____ effect of the expansionary fiscal policy and it tends to (weaken, strengthen) _____ the impact of the expansionary fiscal policy on real GDP and employment.

17. The idea that public dissaving by borrowing to finance a budget deficit is offset by an increase in private saving to pay for expected taxes in the future is associated with the _____. This idea suggests that fiscal policy may be (less, more) _____ effective than originally thought.

18. An expansionary fiscal policy when the economy is operating in the intermediate range of the aggregate supply curve will increase the real GDP and employment in the economy and (raise, lower) _____ the price level. This change in the price level will (weaken, strengthen) _____ the impact of the expansionary fiscal policy on output and employment in the economy.

19. Fiscal policy is subject to further complications from _____ with the world economy.

    a. The economy can be influenced by _____ shocks that might reinforce or retard fiscal policy; or

    b. from a _____ effect that results from an expansionary or contractionary fiscal policy:
    (1) When fiscal policy is expansionary, it tends to (increase, decrease) _____ interest rates, which in turn tends to _____ the value of the dollar and _____ net exports.
    (2) When fiscal policy is contractionary, it tends to (increase, decrease) _____ interest rates, which in turn tends to _____ the value of the dollar, and _____ net exports.

20. If an expansionary fiscal policy is the result of reduction in taxes, the supply-side effects of the policy may be to (increase, decrease) _____ aggregate supply, to _____ productivity capacity of the economy, to _____

real GDP and employment, to _____
the rate of inflation, and to (weaken, strengthen)
_____ the impact of the fiscal policy on output and employment.

■ **TRUE-FALSE QUESTIONS**

Circle the T if the statement is true; the F if it is false.

1. The Council of Economic Advisers was established to give economic advice to Congress.   **T   F**

2. Discretionary fiscal policy is independent of Congress and is left to the discretion of state and local governments.   **T   F**

3. Expansionary fiscal policy during a recession or depression will create a budget deficit or add to an existing budget deficit.   **T   F**

4. A decrease in taxes is one of the options that can be used to pursue a contractionary fiscal policy.   **T   F**

5. To increase consumption by a specific amount, government must reduce taxes by more than that amount because some of the tax cut will be saved by households.   **T   F**

6. A full-employment budget deficit is contractionary.   **T   F**

7. A reduction in taxes and an increase in government spending during a recession would tend to contract the public sector of the economy.   **T   F**

8. Built-in stabilizers are not sufficiently strong to prevent recession or inflation, but they can reduce the severity of a recession or inflation.   **T   F**

9. The automatic (or built-in) stabilizers also increase the sizes of the government expenditures and investment multipliers.   **T   F**

10. The full-employment budget indicates how much government must spend and tax if there is to be full employment in the economy.   **T   F**

11. A cyclical deficit is the result of countercyclical actions by government to stimulate the economy.   **T   F**

12. If an economy had achieved a full-employment level of output, but tax revenues were less than government expenditures, then a structural deficit is created.   **T   F**

13. Recognition, administrative, and operational lags in the timing of Federal fiscal policy make fiscal policies more effective in reducing the rate of inflation and decreasing unemployment in the economy.   **T   F**

14. The fiscal policies of state and local governments have tended to assist and reinforce the efforts of the Federal government to counter recession and inflation.   **T   F**

15. The spending and taxing policies of the Federal government are designed solely to reduce unemployment and limit inflation in the economy.   **T   F**

16. It is generally easier to induce U.S. Senators and Representatives to vote for decreases in tax rates and for increases in government purchases than for increased taxes and decreased purchases.   **T   F**

17. Economists who see evidence of a political business cycle argue that members of Congress tend to increase taxes and reduce expenditures before and to reduce taxes and increase expenditures after elections.   **T   F**

18. For a domestic economy, there are gains for specialization and trade but also complications from the interdependency with the world economy.   **T   F**

19. A net export effect may partially offset an expansionary fiscal policy.   **T   F**

20. Supply-side economists maintain that reduction in tax rates decrease aggregate supply and are, therefore, inflationary.   **T   F**

■ **MULTIPLE-CHOICE QUESTIONS**

Circle the letter that corresponds to the best answer.

1. Which of the following was instrumental in assigning to the Federal government the basic responsibility for promoting economic stability in the American economy?
   (a) the Employment Act of 1946
   (b) the Tax Reform Act of 1986
   (c) the Ricardian equivalence theorem
   (d) the balanced-budget multiplier

2. If the government wishes to increase the level of real GDP, it might:
   (a) reduce taxes
   (b) reduce its purchases of goods and services
   (c) reduce transfer payments
   (d) reduce the size of the budget deficit

3. Which combination of fiscal policies would be the most contractionary?
   (a) an increase in government spending and taxes
   (b) a decrease in government spending and taxes
   (c) an increase in government spending and a decrease in taxes
   (d) a decrease in government spending and an increase in taxes

4. Which combination of policies would be the most expansionary?
   (a) an increase in government spending and taxes
   (b) a decrease in government spending and taxes
   (c) an increase in government spending and a decrease in taxes
   (d) a decrease in government spending and an increase in taxes

5. An economy is in a recession and the government decides to increase spending by $4 billion. The MPC is .8. What would be the full increase in real GDP from the change in government spending assuming the increase would be in the horizontal range of the aggregate supply curve?
 (a) $3.2 billion
 (b) $4 billion
 (c) $16 billion
 (d) $20 billion

6. Which of the following by itself is the most expansionary (least contractionary)?
 (a) redemption of government bonds held by the public
 (b) borrowing from the public to finance a budget deficit
 (c) a build-up in the size of the government's checking account in the central banks
 (d) issuing new money to finance a budget deficit

7. If the economy is to have built-in stability, when real GDP falls:
 (a) tax revenues and government transfer payments both should fall
 (b) tax revenues and government transfer payments both should rise
 (c) tax revenues should fall and government transfer payments should rise
 (d) tax revenues should rise and government transfer payments should fall

8. A direct relation between net tax revenues and real GDP:
 (a) automatically produces budget surpluses during a recession
 (b) makes it easier for discretionary fiscal policy to move the economy out of a recession and toward full employment
 (c) makes it easier to maintain full employment in a growing economy
 (d) reduces the effect of a change in planned investment spending upon the domestic output and employment

Answer the next three questions (9, 10, and 11) on the basis of the following diagram.

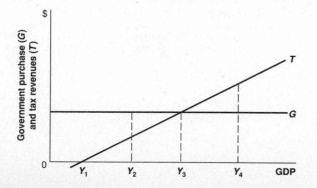

9. If the slope of the line *T* was steeper, there would be:
 (a) more built-in stability for the economy
 (b) less built-in stability for the economy
 (c) no change in the built-in stability for the economy
 (d) the need for more emphasis on discretionary fiscal policy

10. If the slope of the line *T* was flatter, there would be:
 (a) larger cyclical deficits produced as GDP moved from Y_3 to Y_2
 (b) smaller cyclical deficits produced as GDP moved from Y_3 to Y_2
 (c) larger structural deficits produced as GDP moved from Y_3 to Y_2
 (d) smaller structural deficits produced as GDP moved from Y_3 to Y_2

11. Actions by the Federal government to "index" personal income taxes and lower marginal tax rates would tend to:
 (a) flatten the slope of line *T* and increase built-in stability
 (b) flatten the slope of line *T* and decrease built-in stability
 (c) steepen the slope of line *T* and increase built-in stability
 (d) steepen the slope of line *T* and decrease built-in stability

12. With a proportional tax system, as the level of income increases in an economy, the average tax rate will:
 (a) increase
 (b) decrease
 (c) remain the same
 (d) either increase or decrease

13. If the full-employment budget shows a deficit of about $200 billion and the actual budget shows a deficit of about $230 billion over a several-year period, it can be concluded that fiscal policy is:
 (a) expansionary and that there is both a structural and a cyclical deficit
 (b) expansionary and that there is a structural but not a cyclical deficit
 (c) expansionary and that there is a cyclical but not a structural deficit
 (d) contractionary and that there is a cyclical but not a structural deficit

14. The length of time it takes for the fiscal action taken by Congress to affect output, employment, or the price level is referred to as the:
 (a) administrative lag
 (b) operational lag
 (c) recognition lag
 (d) fiscal lag

15. The crowding-out effect of an expansionary (deficit) fiscal policy is the result of government borrowing in the money market which:

(a) increases interest rates and net investment spending in the economy
(b) increases interest rates and decreases net investment spending
(c) decreases interest rates and increases net investment spending
(d) decreases interest rates and net investment spending

16. Which situation would best illustrate the ideas expressed in the Ricardian equivalence theorem as it is applied to the aggregate expenditures model? A rise in government spending or decline in tax that produces a budget deficit that is expected to increase in aggregate expenditures will actually be offset by:
(a) an upward shift in the consumption schedule and downward shift in the saving schedule
(b) a downward shift in the consumption schedule and an upward shift in the saving schedule
(c) an upward shift in the investment schedule and a downward shift in the net exports
(d) a downward shift in the investment schedule and an upward shift in net exports

17. Suppose that the economies of trading partners for the United States improved substantially and at the same time the United States had adopted an expansionary fiscal policy. What would most likely happen in the United States?
(a) there would be a rise in net exports, a rise in aggregate demand, and the potential for demand-pull inflation
(b) there would be a fall in interest rates, a rise in aggregate demand, and the potential for a recession
(c) there would be a rise in the incomes of trading partners, less demand for United States goods, and the potential for recession
(d) there would be a rise in the employment in other nations, a fall in net exports, and the potential for demand-pull inflation

18. If the United States pursued a contractionary fiscal policy, then what would be the likely effects?
(a) there would be a lower domestic interest rate and an increase in the demand for dollars that would partially offset the policy
(b) there would be a depreciation in the value of the dollar and a decrease in net exports that would partially reinforce the policy
(c) there would be an increase in net exports and an increase in aggregate demand that would partially offset the policy
(d) there would be a decrease in net exports and a decrease in aggregate demand that would partially reinforce the policy

19. The effect of an expansionary fiscal policy on the real GDP of an economy operating in the horizontal range on the aggregate supply curve is lessened by:
(a) increases in aggregate supply

(b) the crowding-out effect
(c) decreases in the price level
(d) both **b** and **c**

20. The effect of an expansionary fiscal policy on the real GDP of an economy operating in the intermediate range on the aggregate supply curve is lessened by:
(a) increases in aggregate supply
(b) the crowding-out effect
(c) increases in the price level
(d) both **b** and **c**

■ PROBLEMS

1. Columns (1) and (2) in the table below are the aggregate supply schedule and columns (1) and (3) are the aggregate demand schedule.

(1) Price level	(2) Real GDP$_1$	(3) AD$_1$	(4) AD$_2$	(5) Real GDP$_2$
220	2390	2100	2200	2490
200	2390	2200	2340	2490
190	2350	2250	2350	2450
180	2300	2300	2400	2400
160	2200	2400	2500	2300

a. The equilibrium real GDP is $_____
and the price level is _____
b. Suppose that an expansionary fiscal policy increases aggregate demand from that shown in columns (1) and (3) to that shown in columns (1) and (4).
(1) If the price level remained constant the equilibrium real GDP would increase to $_____
(2) But the increase in aggregate demand does raise the price level to _____; and this rise in the price level results in real GDP increasing to only $_____
c. If the expansionary fiscal policy that increased aggregate demand also has supply-side effects and increased aggregate supply from that shown in columns (1) and (2) to that shown in columns (1) and (5):
(1) The equilibrium real GDP would increase to $_____; and
(2) the price level would _____

2. In the table below are seven real GDPs and the net tax revenues of government at each real GDP.

Real GDP	Net tax revenues	Government purchases	Government deficit/surplus
$ 850	$170	$_____	$_____
900	180	_____	_____
950	190	_____	_____
1000	200	_____	_____
1050	210	_____	_____
1100	220	_____	_____
1150	230	_____	_____

a. Looking at the two columns on the left of the table, it can be seen that:

(1) when real GDP increases by $50, net tax revenues (increase, decrease) _____ by $_____

(2) when real GDP decreases by $100, net tax revenues _____ by $_____

(3) the relationship between real GDP and net tax revenues is (direct, inverse) _____

b. Assume the investment multiplier has a value of 10 and that investment spending in the economy decreases by $10.

(1) *If* net tax revenues remained constant, the equilibrium real GDP would decrease by $_____

(2) But when real GDP decreases, net tax revenues also decrease; and this decrease in net tax revenues will tend to (increase, decrease) _____ the equilibrium real GDP.

(3) And, therefore, the decrease in real GDP brought about by the $10 decrease in investment spending will be (more, less) _____ than $100.

(4) The direct relationship between net tax revenues and real GDP has (lessened, expanded) _____ the impact of the $10 decrease in investment spending on real GDP.

c. Suppose the government purchases multiplier is also 10 and government wishes to increase the equilibrium real GDP by $50.

(1) *If* net tax revenues remained constant, government would have to increase its purchases of goods and services by $_____

(2) But when real GDP rises, net tax revenues also rise; and this rise in net tax revenues will tend to (increase, decrease) _____ the equilibrium real GDP.

(3) The effect, therefore, of the $5 increase in government purchases will also be to increase the equilibrium real GDP by (more, less) _____ than $50.

(4) The direct relationship between net tax revenues and real GDP has (lessened, expanded) _____ the effect of the $5 increase in government purchases;

and to raise the equilibrium real GDP by $50 government will have to increase its purchases by (more, less) _____ than $5.

d. Imagine that the full-employment real GDP of the economy is $1150 and that government purchases of goods and services are $200.

(1) Complete the table on the previous page by entering the government purchases and by computing the budget deficit or surplus at each of the real GDPs. (Show a government deficit by placing a minus sign in front of the amount by which expenditures exceed net tax revenues.)

(2) The full-employment surplus equals $_____

(3) Were the economy in a recession and producing a real GDP of $900, the budget would show a (surplus, deficit) _____ of $_____

(4) This budget deficit or surplus makes it appear that government is pursuing a(n) (expansionary, contractionary) _____ fiscal policy; but this deficit or surplus is not the result of countercyclical fiscal policy but the result of the _____

(5) If government did not change its net tax **rates** it could increase the equilibrium real GDP from $900 to the full-employment real GDP of $1150 by increasing its purchases by (approximately) $70. At the full-employment real GDP the budget would show a (surplus, deficit) _____ of $_____

(6) If government did not change its purchases it would increase the equilibrium real GDP from $900 to the full-employment real GDP of $1150 by decreasing net tax revenues at all real GDPs by a lump sum of (approximately) $80. The full-employment budget would have a (surplus, deficit) _____ of $_____

3. a. Complete the table below by computing the average tax rates, given the net tax revenue data in columns (2), (4), and (6). Calculate the average tax rate in percentage to one decimal place (for example, 5.4%)

b. As real GDP increases in column (1), the average tax rate (increases, decreases, remains the same) _____ in column (3), _____, in column (5), and _____ in column (7). The tax system is (progressive, proportional, regressive) _____ in col-

(1) Real GDP	(2) Net tax revenue	(3) Average tax rate	(4) Net tax revenue	(5) Average tax rate	(6) Net tax revenue	(7) Average tax rate	(8) Government spending
$1000	$100	_____%	$100	_____%	$100	_____%	$120
$1100	$120	_____	$110	_____	$108	_____	$120
$1200	$145	_____	$120	_____	$115	_____	$120
$1300	$175	_____	$130	_____	$120	_____	$120
$1400	$210	_____	$140	_____	$123	_____	$120

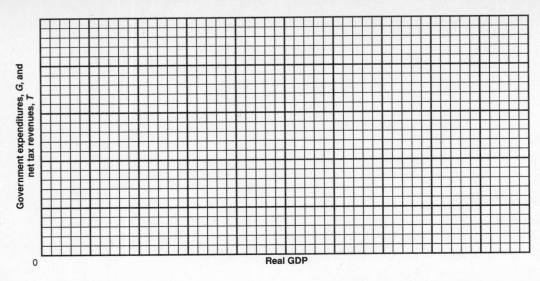

Government expenditures, G, and net tax revenues, T

0   Real GDP

umn (2), _____ in column (4), and _____ in column (6).

c. Now graph the real GDP, net tax revenue, and government spending data given in columns (1), (2), (4), (6), and (8) in the graph above. Tax revenue system with the steepest slope is found in column _____ and it is (progressive, proportional, regressive) _____ while the one with the flattest slope is found in column

_____ and it is _____

4. a. Complete the table below by stating whether the direction of discretionary fiscal policy was contractionary, expansionary, or had no effect, given the hypothetical budget data for an economy.

b. The best gauge of the direction of fiscal policy is the (actual, full-employment) _____ budget deficit or surplus because it removes the (cyclical, structural) _____ component from the discussion of the budget situation.

c. (1) In which years is there cyclical deficit and what was the size of the cyclical deficit in each of those years?_____

_____

(2) In what years were there structural deficits and what was the size of the structural deficits in each of those years?_____

■ **SHORT ANSWER AND ESSAY QUESTIONS**

1. In the Employment Act of 1946, (*a*) what responsibility was given to the Federal government; (*b*) what tasks were assigned to the Council of Economic Advisers and the Joint Economic Committee; and (*c*) what specific kinds of policy were to be used to achieve the goals established by the act?

2. What is the difference between discretionary fiscal policy and nondiscretionary fiscal policy?

3. What three options does the Federal government have to conduct expansionary or contractionary fiscal policy?

4. Under what economic conditions would expansionary or contractionary fiscal policy be used? What would be the effect on the Federal budget?

5. Compare and contrast the effect of expansionary and contractionary fiscal policy on aggregate demand. Draw a graph to illustrate the likely effects.

(1) Year	(2) Actual budget surplus (+) or deficit (−)	(3) Full-employment budget surplus (+) or deficit(−)	(4) Direction of fiscal policy
1	−$10 billion	+$10 billion	_____
2	+$10 billion	−$20 billion	_____
3	−$20 billion	+$0 billion	_____
4	−$120 billion	−$120 billion	_____
5	−$150 billion	−$130 billion	_____

6. What is the effect of the simple multiplier on the initial change in spending from fiscal policy? When the government wants to increase initial consumption by a specific amount, why must the government reduce taxes by more than that amount?

7. What three things might the Federal government do if its fiscal policy were to be (*a*) expansionary and if it were to be (*b*) contractionary? When would it invoke each of these two kinds of policy and what would be their effects on the Federal budget?

8. What are the alternative means of financing deficits and disposing of surpluses available to the Federal government? What is the difference between these methods insofar as their expansionary and contractionary effect is concerned?

9. Explain the fiscal policy that would be advocated during a recession and during a period of inflation (*a*) by those who wish to expand the public sector and (*b*) by those who wish to contract the public sector.

10. What is the difference between discretionary and nondiscretionary fiscal policy? How do the built-in stabilizers work to reduce rises and falls in the level of nominal GDP?

11. Explain why a tax system in which net tax revenues vary directly with the level of nominal GDP makes it difficult to achieve and sustain full employment.

12. Supply a definition of a progressive, proportional, and regressive tax system. What are the implications of the type of tax system for the built-in stability of the economy?

13. What is the full-employment budget? What was the problem which the use of the full-employment budget was designed to solve?

14. Explain the distinction between a cyclical deficit and structural deficit. Which type of deficit provides the best indication of the direction of fiscal policy? Why?

15. Explain the three kinds of time lags that make it difficult to use fiscal policy to stabilize the economy.

16. What are four political problems that complicate the use of fiscal policy to stabilize the economy?

17. How do (*a*) crowding out and (*b*) inflation reduce the effect of an expansionary (deficit) fiscal policy on real GDP and employment?

18. Explain how the Ricardian equivalence theorem can be applied to government budget deficits and fiscal policy. What conclusions would be drawn about fiscal policy based on this theorem? What criticisms have been leveled against this type of analysis?

19. What complications for fiscal policy arise from interdependency with the world economy? Explain how aggregate demand shocks from abroad and the net export effect influence fiscal policy.

20. What might be the supply-side effects of a reduction in tax rates on the capacity output of the economy, the equilibrium levels of real GDP and employment, and the price level?

ANSWERS

Chapter 12 Fiscal Policy

FILL-IN QUESTIONS

1. Employment Act of 1946, Economic Advisers, Joint Economic

2. discretionary, nondiscretionary

3. increase, increase, decrease, decrease

4. government spending, taxes, government spending, taxes

5. multiplier, 4

6. deficit, surplus

7. deficit, surplus

8. borrowing from the public, creating new money, latter

9. increase, taxes, decrease, taxes

10. *a.* taxes, transfer payments; *b.* increase, decrease

11. built-in; *a.* increase, increase, decrease; *b.* decrease, increase, decrease

12. progressive, proportional, regressive, more

13. *a.* budget surplus or deficit, full employment; *b.* expansionary, contractionary; *c.* cyclical, structural, structural

14. recognition, administrative, operational

15. other, counter, deficits, political

16. deficit, borrows; *a.* raise, contract; *b.* crowding-out, weaken

17. Ricardian equivalence theorem, less

18. raise, weaken

19. mutual interdependency; *a.* aggregate demand; *b.* net export, (1) increase, increase, decrease, (2) decrease, decrease, increase

20. increase, increase, increase, decrease, strengthen

TRUE-FALSE QUESTIONS

1. F, p. 235   **6.** F, p. 241   **11.** F, p. 241   **16.** T, p. 244
2. F, p. 235   **7.** F, p. 237   **12.** T, p. 241   **17.** F, p. 244
3. T, p. 236   **8.** T, p. 240   **13.** T, p. 243   **18.** T, p. 246
4. F, p. 238   **9.** F, p. 240   **14.** F, p. 243   **19.** T, p. 246
5. T, p. 238   **10.** F, p. 241   **15.** F, p. 243   **20.** F, pp. 247-248

MULTIPLE-CHOICE QUESTIONS

1. *a*, p. 235   **6.** *d*, p. 238   **11.** *b*, p. 240   **16.** *b*, p. 245
2. *a*, p. 236   **7.** *c*, p. 239   **12.** *c*, p. 240   **17.** *a*, pp. 246-247
3. *d*, p. 238   **8.** *d*, p. 240   **13.** *a*, p. 241   **18.** *c*, pp. 246-247
4. *c*, p. 237   **9.** *a*, p. 240   **14.** *b*, p. 243   **19.** *b*, pp. 244-245
5. *d*, p. 236   **10.** *b*, p. 240   **15.** *b*, p. 244   **20.** *d*, pp. 244-245

PROBLEMS

1. *a.* 2300, 180; *b.* (1) 2400, (2) 190, 2350; *c.* (1) 2400, (2) remain constant

2. *a.* (1) increase, $10, (2) decrease, $20, (3) direct; *b.* (1) $100, (2) increase, (3) less, (4) lessened; *c.* (1) $5, (2) decrease, (3) less, (4) lessened, more; *d.* (1) government expenditures are $200 at all GDPs, government surplus or deficit: 30, 20, 10, 0, 10, 20, 30, (2) $30, (3) deficit, $20, (4) expansionary, recession, (5) deficit, $40, (6) deficit, $50

3. *a.* column 3: 10.0, 10.9, 12.1, 13.5, 15.0; column 5: 10.0 at each GDP level; column 7: 10.0, 9.8, 9.6, 9.2, 8.8; *b.* increases, remains the same, decrease; progressive, proportional, regressive; *c.* 2, progressive, 6, regressive

4. *a.* contractionary, expansionary, no effect, expansionary, expansionary; *b.* full-employment, cyclical; *c.* (1) year 1 ($10 billion); year 3 ($20 billion); year 5 ($20 billion); (2) year 2 ($20 billion); year 4 ($120 billion); year 5 ($130 billion)

SHORT ANSWER AND ESSAY QUESTIONS

1. p. 235	**6.** pp. 236-237	**11.** p. 240	**16.** pp. 243-244
2. pp. 235, 239	**7.** pp. 235-238	**12.** p. 240	**17.** pp. 244-246
3. pp. 235-238	**8.** p. 238	**13.** p. 241	**18.** p. 245
4. pp. 235-237	**9.** pp. 238-239	**14.** p. 241	**19.** pp. 246-247
5. pp. 235-237	**10.** pp. 235, 239-240	**15.** p. 243	**20.** pp. 247-248

CHAPTER 13

Money and Banking

Chapter 13 explains how the financial system affects the operation of the economy. The chapter is largely descriptive and factual. You would do well to pay particular attention to the following: (1) what money is and the functions it performs, what types of money exist in the American economy and their relative importance, and how the three measures of the money supply (*M*1, *M*2, and *M*3) are defined; (2) what gives value to or "backs" American money; (3) why people want to have money in their possession and what determines how much money they want to have on hand at any time; (4) how the total demand for money and the money supply together determine the equilibrium rate of interest; and (5) the four principal institutions of the American financial system and their functions.

Several points are worth repeating here because so much depends upon their being fully understood. First, money is whatever performs the three functions of money, and in the United States money consists largely of the debts (promises to pay) of the Federal Reserve Banks and depository institutions. In the United States, this money is "backed" by the goods and services for which its owners can exchange it and not by gold.

Second, because money is used as a medium of exchange, consumers and business firms wish to have money on hand to use for transaction purposes; and the quantity of money they demand for this purpose is directly related to the size of the economy's nominal (or money) gross domestic product. This means that when either the price level or the real gross domestic product increases they will want to have more money on hand to use for transactions. But money is also used as a store of value: consumers and firms who own assets may choose to have some of their assets in the form of money (rather than in stocks, bonds, goods, or property). There is, therefore, also an asset demand for money. Holding money, however, imposes a cost on those who hold it. This cost is the interest they lose when they own money rather than (say) bonds. This means that people will demand less money for asset purposes when the rate of interest (the cost of holding money) is high and more when the rate of interest is low: the quantity of money demanded for this purpose is inversely related to the interest rate. The total demand for money is the sum of the transactions demand and the asset demand and, therefore, depends upon the nominal

GDP and the rate of interest. This total demand and the money supply determine interest rates in the economy.

Third, the central bank in the United States is the twelve Federal Reserve Banks and the Board of Governors of the Federal Reserve System which oversees their operation. These banks, while privately owned by the commercial banks, are operated more or less as an agency of the Federal government not for profit, but primarily to regulate the nation's money supply in the best interests of the economy as a whole and secondarily to perform other services for the banks, the government, and the economy. They are able to perform their primary function because they are bankers' banks where depository institutions (commercial banks and the "thrifts") can deposit and borrow money. They do not deal directly with the public.

Fourth, these depository institutions accept deposits and make loans, but they also are literally able to create money by lending checkable deposits. Because they are able to do this, they have a strong influence on the size of the money supply and the value of money. The Federal Reserve Banks exist primarily to regulate the money supply and its value by influencing and controlling the amount of money depository institutions create.

The final section of Chapter 13 discusses bank and thrift failures of the 1980s and early 1990s. These events are important because banks and thrifts are critical for the sound financial health of the economy and because there is a high long-term cost for taxpayers from bailing out financial institutions, especially the many insolvent savings and loan institutions. As you will learn, the reasons for the savings and loan collapse involve many factors, including deregulation of the banking industry, more competition among financial institutions, a higher level of deposit insurance, loan defaults, and fraud. The failure of many financial institutions led the government to institute new reforms in the banking industry that should be felt throughout the 1990s.

■ CHECKLIST

When you have studied this chapter you should be able to:

☐ List the three functions of money; and explain the meaning of each function.

147

☐ Define the money supply, *M*1.
☐ Identify the four kinds of checkable deposits; and the principal kinds of depository institutions.
☐ Explain the meaning of near-money and identify the principal near-monies; and then define *M*2 and *M*3.
☐ Present three reasons why near-monies are important.
☐ Distinguish between credit cards and money.
☐ Explain why money in the American economy is debt; and whose debts paper money and checkable deposits are.
☐ Present three reasons why currency and checkable deposits are money and have value.
☐ Indicate the precise relationship between the value of money and the price level.
☐ Explain what is meant by stabilizing the value of money.
☐ Enumerate the two devices government uses to stabilize the value of money.
☐ Identify the two demands for money and the determinant of each of these demands.
☐ Explain the relationship between each of the two demands from money.
☐ Describe what determines the equilibrium rate of interest.
☐ Explain how changes in nominal GDP and in the money supply affect the interest rate.
☐ Explain how disequilibrium in the money market is corrected through changes in bond prices.
☐ Describe the structure of the American financial system.
☐ Explain why the Federal Reserve Banks are central, quasi-public, bankers' banks.
☐ Enumerate the five functions of the Federal Reserve System; explain the meaning of each of these functions; and indicate which is the most important.
☐ State two reasons why the bank and thrift failures of the 1980s and early 1990s were important.
☐ State several reasons why many savings and loan institutions collapsed in recent years.
☐ Explain what actions were taken by government to solve the recent problems with financial institutions.

■ **CHAPTER OUTLINE**

1. Money is whatever performs the three basic functions of money: a medium of exchange, a measure of value, and a store of value.

2. In the American economy money is whatever is generally used as a medium of exchange; and consists of the debts of the Federal government and of commercial banks and other financial institutions.
  a. The narrowly defined money supply is called *M*1 and has two principal components.
  (1) The smaller component is currency: coins which are token money and paper money largely in the form of Federal Reserve Notes.

(2) The larger and more important component is checkable deposits in commercial banks and savings institutions.
(3) These checkable deposits include demand deposits (checking accounts), negotiable order of withdrawal (NOW) accounts, automatic transfer service (ATS) accounts, and share draft accounts, all of which give the depositor the ability to write checks.
(4) Currency and checkable deposits owned by the Federal government, commercial banks and savings institutions, and the Federal Reserve Banks are not, however, included in *M*1 or any of the more broadly defined money supplies.
  b. *M*2 and *M*3 are the more broadly defined money supplies; and include not only the currency and checkable deposits in *M*1 but such near-monies as noncheckable savings deposits and time deposits in commercial banks and savings institutions.
  (1) *M*2 includes *M*1 plus noncheckable savings deposits plus small time deposits (less than $100,000) plus money market deposit accounts (MMDA) plus money market mutual funds (MMMF).
  (2) *M*3 includes *M*2 plus large time deposits ($100,000 or more).
  (3) There are advantages to each of the different measures of money, but since *M*1 is included in all the definitions and the principles that apply to it are applicable to the other measures, that narrow definition is used for the textbook discussion unless noted otherwise.
  c. Near-monies held by the public are important because they affect spending habits, serve as a stabilizing force in economic activity, and provide different definitions of money for the conduct of monetary policy.
  d. Credit cards are not money but are a device by which the cardholders obtain a loan (credit) from the issuer of the card.

3. In the United States:
  a. Money is the promise of a commercial bank, a savings (thrift) institution, or a Federal Reserve Bank to pay; but these debts cannot be redeemed for anything tangible.
  b. Money has value only because people can exchange it for desirable goods and services.
  c. The value of money is inversely related to the price level.
  d. Money is "backed" by the confidence which the public has that the value of money will remain stable; and the Federal government can use monetary and fiscal policy to keep the value of money relatively stable.

4. Business firms and households wish to hold and, therefore, demand money for two reasons.
  a. Because they use money as a medium of exchange they have a transactions demand which is directly related to the nominal gross domestic product of the economy.

b. Because they also use money as a store of value they have an asset demand which is inversely related to the rate of interest.

c. Their total demand for money is the sum of the transactions and asset demands.

d. This total demand for money along with the supply of money determine the equilibrium interest rate in the money market of the economy.

e. Disequilibrium in the money market is corrected through changes in bond prices:

(1) lower bond prices increase interest rates; and

(2) higher bond prices decrease interest rates.

5. The financial sector of the American economy has changed dramatically in the past two decades; for example, the Depository Institutions Deregulation and Monetary Control Act of 1980 narrowed the earlier differences between a commercial bank and the various thrift institutions.

a. But, despite the trend toward deregulation, the financial system remains centralized and regulated by government because the absence of centralization in the past led to an inappropriate supply of money, a multitude of different kinds of money, and a mismanagement of the money supply.

b. In the Federal Reserve System:

(1) The Board of Governors exercises control over the supply of money and the banking system. Two important bodies help the Board of Governors in establishing and conducting policy—the Federal Open Market Committee (FOMC), which establishes policy over the buying and selling of government bonds, and the Federal Advisory Council, which provides advice on banking policy.

(2) The Federal Reserve Banks are central, quasi-public, bankers' banks.

(3) About 12,453 commercial banks exist in the American financial system; and some of them are state banks and some are national banks. But since 1980 the distinctions between state and national banks and between commercial banks and thrift institutions have all but been eliminated.

(4) The thrift institutions, like all commercial banks, are subject to the reserve requirements imposed by and may borrow from the Federal Reserve Banks; but they are also subject to the rules imposed upon them by other regulatory agencies. Both they and the commercial banks, by performing the two essential functions of holding deposits and making loans, expand the supply of money.

c. The Board of Governors and the Federal Reserve Banks perform five functions aimed at providing certain essential services, supervision of the member commercial banks, and the regulation of the supply of money.

d. The Federal Reserve is essentially an independent institution. Some argue that it should be put under the direct control of Congress or the executive branch, but proponents of independence believe it protects the Federal Reserve from undue political pressure on monetary matters.

6. Bank and thrift failures in the 1980s and early 1990s have been of concern because they affect the financial health of the economy and because of the high long-term cost of bailing out insolvent institutions, especially in the savings and loan industry.

a. Commercial bank problems resulted largely from economic problems in the agricultural and energy-producing regions of the economy in the 1980s, but the national recession that began in 1990 contributed to more bank failures.

b. The collapse of the savings and loan industry was due to many factors, such as deregulation, intense competition, a moral hazard problem caused by higher levels of deposit insurance, increased loan defaults, and fraud.

c. The cost of bailing out the thrifts may total $250 billion over a forty-year period. The savings and loan collapse and other bank problems have led to the passage of the Financial Institutions Reform, Recovery, and Enforcement Act (FIRREA), which may be only the first step in a major government reform of the banking industry.

d. Changes continue to affect the financial services industry, such as shifts in institutional holdings of financial assets, the globalization of financial markets, and regulatory reform.

■ IMPORTANT TERMS

Medium of exchange	Time deposit
Measure of value	MMDA (money market deposit account)
Store of value	
Money supply	MMMF (money market mutual fund)
*M*1 *M*2 *M*3	
Currency	Legal tender
Paper money	Fiat money
Token money	Transactions demand for money
Intrinsic value	
Federal Reserve Note	Asset demand for money
Checkable deposit	Total demand for money
Commercial bank	Money market
Thrift (savings) institution	Bonds
Savings and loan association	Depository Institutions Deregulation and Monetary Control Act
Mutual savings bank	
Credit union	Board of Governors
Near-monies	Federal Open Market Committee
Monies	
Noncheckable savings account	Advisory Councils
	Federal Reserve Bank

Central bank

Quasi-public bank

Bankers' bank

Commercial banks

State bank

National bank

Member bank

Federal Deposit Insurance Corporation

Moral hazard problem

Resolution Trust Corporation

Financial Institutions Reform, Recovery, and Enforcement Act

■ HINTS AND TIPS

1. Most students only think of currency as the major component of the money supply, but it is a very small component relative to checkable deposits. Actually, there are several definitions of the *money supply* that you must know about, from the narrow $M1$ to the broader $M2$ and $M3$.

2. Spend extra time understanding how the total demand for money is determined (see Figure 13-2 in the text). The total demand for money is composed of a transactions and an asset demand for money. The transactions demand is influenced by the level of nominal GDP and not affected by the interest rate, so it *is graphed as a vertical line.* The asset demand for money is affected by the interest rate, and so it *is graphed as a downsloping curve.* The total demand for money is also graphed as a *downsloping curve* because of the influence of asset demand, but the curve is shifted farther to the right than the asset demand curve because of the influence of transactions demand.

3. One of the most difficult concepts for students to understand is the inverse relationship between bond prices and interest rates. The simple explanation is that interest yield from a bond is the ratio of the *fixed* annual interest payment to the bond price. The numerator is fixed, but the denominator (bond price) is variable. If the bond price falls the interest yield on the bond rises because the fixed annual interest payment is being divided by a smaller denominator.

SELF-TEST

■ FILL-IN QUESTIONS

1. Three functions of money are:

a. _____

b. _____

c. _____

2. $M1$ is the sum of:

a. _____ which consists of _____ and paper _____;

b. and (time, checkable) _____ deposits in (commercial banks, thrift institutions, de-

pository institutions) _____

c. not owned by depository institutions, the _____ _____ Banks, or the _____ government.

3. $M2$ is equal to $M1$ plus (checkable, noncheckable) _____ savings deposits, (small, large) _____ time deposits, and money market (deposit, mutual funds) _____ accounts and money market _____

4. $M3$ is equal to $M2$ plus (small, large) _____ time deposits. Large time deposits are mainly _____ of deposits which have a face value of $_____ or more.

5. In addition to commercial banks, the principal depository institutions in the American economy are _____ associations, _____ banks, and _____ unions.

6. Checkable deposits include demand deposits, _____ and _____ accounts, and _____ drafts.

7. Near-money in the United States includes not only noncheckable savings and time deposits:

a. but such government securities as _____ bills and U.S. government savings _____

b. all of which can be easily converted into _____ _____ or _____ deposits without the risk of financial _____

8. List three reasons why the existence of near-money is important.

a. _____

_____

b. _____

_____

c. _____

_____

9. Money in the United States consists largely of the debts of _____ institutions and the _____ _____ Banks.

10. In the United States currency and checkable deposits:

a. (are, are not) _____ "backed" by gold and silver;

b. are money because they are used as a medium of

_____ , they are in some cases

_____ tender, and they are relatively

(abundant, scarce) _____

_____

11. Money has value because it can be exchanged for

_____ and its value varies

(directly, inversely) _____ with

changes in the _____
level.

12. The total demand for money is the sum of:
a. the transactions demand which depends (directly,

inversely) _____ on the _____

b. and the asset demand which depends _____

on the _____

13. The total demand for money and the _____

of money determine the equilibrium _____

rate in the _____ market.
a. When the quantity of money demanded exceeds
the quantity of money supplied, bond prices (increase,

decrease) _____ and interest

rates _____
b. When the quantity of money demanded is less than
the quantity of money supplied, bond prices (increase,

decrease) _____ and interest

rates _____

14. Many of the historical distinctions between commercial banks and the different thrift institutions were eliminated in the _____
of 1980. This act permitted all depository institutions to

offer (checkable, time) _____ deposit accounts. Despite this recent (regulation, deregulation) _____ ,
depository institutions continue to be subject to central

monetary control by the _____

15. Two groups which help the Board of Governors of the
Federal Reserve System to formulate its policies are the

_____

and _____

16. The three principle characteristics of the Federal Reserve Banks are:

a. _____

b. _____

c. _____

17. If a bank is a bankers' bank it means that it accepts

the _____ of and makes _____ to
(households, business firms, depository institutions, the

public sector) _____

18. Both commercial banks and thrift institutions perform
two essential functions for the economy: they hold the

_____ of and make _____
to the public; and in performing these functions they (in-

crease, decrease) _____ the money supply.

19. The five major functions of the Federal Reserve
Banks are:

a. _____

b. _____

c. _____

d. _____

e. _____

The most important of the functions which the Federal Re-

serve Banks perform is that of _____

_____

20. In the 1980s and early 1990s, the failure of institutions
in the banking and thrift industries were of special concern

because they created (more, less) _____ stability in
the monetary system, and because of the (high, low)

_____ cost of these events to taxpayers.
a. The reasons for failures in the savings and loans industry are related to: (regulation, deregulation)

_____ ; (more, less) _____ competition in

the industry; (an ethical, a moral hazard) _____

___ problem resulting from (lower, higher) _____

levels of deposit insurance and (risky, safe) _____

loans; and (legal, illegal) _____ activity.
b. To correct some of the problems, the Financial Institutions Reform, Recovery, and Enforcement Act

(FIRREA) established the _____

_____
to oversee the closing and sale of insolvent thrifts, and
place deposit insurance for banks and thrifts under the

control of the _____

■ **TRUE-FALSE QUESTIONS**

Circle the T if the statement is true; the F if it is false.

1. The money supply designated **M**1 is the sum of currency and noncheckable deposits.   **T F**

2. The currency component of **M**1 includes both coins and paper money. **T F**

3. If a coin is "token money," its face value is less than its intrinsic value. **T F**

4. Both commercial banks and thrift institutions accept checkable deposits. **T F**

5. The checkable deposits of the Federal government at the Federal Reserve Banks are a component of **M**1. **T F**

6. **M**2 exceeds **M**1 by the amount of noncheckable savings, small time deposits, and money market deposit accounts and money market mutual funds. **T F**

7. A **small** time deposit is one that is less than $100,000. **T F**

8. **M**2 is less than **M**3 by the amount of small time deposits in depository institutions. **T F**

9. Economists and public officials are in general agreement on how to define the money supply in the United States. **T F**

10. A near-money is a medium of exchange. **T F**

11. The larger the volume of near-monies owned by consumers, the larger will be their average propensity to save. **T F**

12. Currency and checkable deposits are money because they are acceptable to sellers in exchange for goods and services. **T F**

13. If money is to have a fairly stable value, its supply must be limited relative to the demand for it. **T F**

14. There is a transactions demand for money because households and business firms use money as a store of value. **T F**

15. An increase in the price level would, **ceteris paribus,** increase the transactions demand for money. **T F**

16. An increase in the nominal GDP, other things remaining the same, will increase both the total demand for money and the equilibrium rate of interest in the economy. **T F**

17. The Board of Governors of the Federal Reserve System is appointed by the President of the United States and confirmed by the Senate. **T F**

18. The Federal Reserve Banks are owned and operated by the United States government. **T F**

19. Federal Reserve Banks are bankers' banks because they make loans to and accept deposits from depository institutions. **T F**

20. The most important function of the Federal Reserve Banks is the control of the size of the economy's money supply. **T F**

■ **MULTIPLE-CHOICE QUESTIONS**

Circle the letter that corresponds to the best answer.

1. Which one is an economic function of money?
(a) a factor of production
(b) a medium of communications
(c) a store of bonds
(d) a measure of value

2. Checkable deposits are:
(a) all deposits in commercial banks
(b) demand deposits in commercial banks
(c) deposits in thrift institutions on which checks may be written
(d) the sum of **b** and **c** above

3. The largest element of the currency component of **M**1 is:
(a) coins
(b) United States Notes
(c) silver certificates
(d) Federal Reserve Notes

4. Which of the following constitutes the largest element in the **M**1 money supply?
(a) currency
(b) Federal Reserve Notes
(c) time deposits
(d) checkable deposits

5. Checkable deposits are money because they are:
(a) legal tender
(b) fiat money
(c) a medium of exchange
(d) token money

6. Which of the following is **not** called a thrift institution?
(a) a commercial bank
(b) a savings and loan association
(c) a credit union
(d) a mutual savings bank

7. Which of the following is **not** a checkable deposit?
(a) a NOW account
(b) a time deposit
(c) an ATS account
(d) a share draft

8. The supply of money **M**1 consists almost entirely of the debts of:
(a) the Federal government
(b) the Federal Reserve Banks
(c) depository institutions
(d) the Federal Reserve Banks and depository institutions

9. Which of the following is **not** a near-money?
(a) a noncheckable savings account
(b) a time deposit
(c) a credit card
(d) a money market mutual fund

Use the following table to answer the next three questions (10, 11, and 12) about the money supply, given the following hypothetical data for the economy.

Item	Billions of dollars
Checkable deposits	1,775
Small time deposits	345
Currency	56
Large time deposits	1,230
Noncheckable savings deposits	945
Money market deposit accounts	256
Money market mutual funds	587

10. The size of the *M*1 money supply is:
(a) $1,775
(b) $1,831
(c) $2,176
(d) $3,019

11. The size of the *M*2 money supply is:
(a) $2,176
(b) $3,146
(c) $3,964
(d) $4,532

12. The size of the *M*3 money supply is:
(a) $4,532
(b) $5,194
(c) $5,339
(d) $6,007

13. Which of the following **best** describes the "backing" of money in the United States?
(a) the gold bullion stored at Fort Knox, Kentucky
(b) the belief of holders of money that it can be exchanged for desirable goods and services
(c) the willingness of banks and the government to surrender something of value in exchange for money
(d) the faith and confidence of the public in the ability of government to pay its debts

14. If the price level increases 20%, the value of money decreases:
(a) 14.14%
(b) 16.67%
(c) 20%
(d) 25%

15. To keep the value of money fairly constant the Federal Reserve:
(a) uses price and wage controls
(b) employs fiscal policy
(c) controls the money supply
(d) buys stock

16. The total quantity of money demanded is:
(a) directly related to nominal GDP and the rate of interest
(b) directly related to nominal GDP and inversely related to the rate of interest

(c) inversely related to nominal GDP and directly related to the rate of interest
(d) inversely related to nominal GDP and the rate of interest

17. There is an asset demand for money because money is:
(a) a medium of exchange
(b) a measure of value
(c) a store of value
(d) a standard of deferred payment

18. If the dollars held for transactions purposes are, on the average, spent five times a year for final goods and services, then the quantity of money people will wish to hold for transactions is equal to:
(a) five times the nominal GDP
(b) 20% of the nominal GDP
(c) five divided by the nominal GDP
(d) 20% divided by the nominal GDP

19. An increase in the rate of interest would increase:
(a) the opportunity cost of holding money
(b) the transactions demand for money
(c) the asset demand for money
(d) the prices of bonds

Use the table below to answer questions 20 and 21.

Interest rate	Asset demand (billions)
14%	$100
13	150
12	200
11	250

20. Suppose the transactions demand for money is equal to 10% of the nominal GDP, the supply of money is $450 billion, and the asset demand for money is that shown in the table. If the nominal GDP is $3,000 billion, the equilibrium interest rate is:
(a) 14%
(b) 13%
(c) 12%
(d) 11%

21. If the nominal GDP remains constant an increase in the money supply from $450 billion to $500 billion would cause the equilibrium interest rate to:
(a) rise to 14%
(b) fall to 11%
(c) fall to 12%
(d) remain unchanged

22. The stock of money is determined by the Federal Reserve System and does not change when the interest rate changes, so therefore the:

(a) supply of money curve is downward sloping
(b) demand for money curve is downward sloping
(c) supply of money curve is upward sloping
(d) supply of money curve is vertical

23. If the legal ceiling on the interest rate was set below equilibrium, then the:
(a) quantity of money demanded would be greater than the quantity of money supplied
(b) quantity of money demanded would be less than the quantity of money supplied
(c) supply of money would increase and the demand for money would decrease
(d) demand for money would increase and the supply of money would decrease

24. Which one of the following points would be true?
(a) bond prices and the interest rate are directly related
(b) a lower interest rate raises the opportunity cost of holding money
(c) the supply of money is directly related to the interest rate
(d) the total demand for money is inversely related to the interest rate

Answer the next two questions (25 and 26) on the basis of the following information: Bond price = $10,000; bond fixed annual interest payment = $1,000; bond annual rate of interest = 10%.

25. If the price of this bond decreases by $2,500, the interest rate in effect will:
(a) decrease by 1.1 percentage points
(b) decrease by 1.9 percentage points
(c) increase by 2.6 percentage points
(d) increase by 3.3 percentage points

26. If the price of this bond increases by $2000, the interest rate in effect will:
(a) decrease by 1.7 percentage points
(b) decrease by 2.4 percentage points
(c) increase by 1.1 percentage points
(d) increase by 2.9 percentage points

27. Since the passage of the DIDMC Act in 1980:
(a) both nonmember commercial banks and thrift institutions have been subject to the reserve requirements set by the Federal Reserve Banks
(b) the thrift institutions have been allowed to accept checkable deposits
(c) nonmember commercial banks and the thrifts have been allowed to borrow at the Federal Reserve Banks
(d) all of the above

28. Both commercial banks and thrift institutions:
(a) accept the checkable deposits of the public
(b) make loans to the public

(c) expand the money supply
(d) do all of the above

29. A moral hazard problem is created in the banking industry when:
(a) there is more regulation of the industry by the government
(b) insurance is offered by the government to protect bank deposits
(c) the Federal Reserve System exercises less supervision of banking institutions
(d) the Resolution Trust Corporation sells off more failed thrifts

30. One of the major reasons for the failure of many savings and loan associations during the 1980s and early 1990s was:
(a) less intensive competition among depository institutions
(b) lower levels of deposit insurance for customers
(c) deregulation of the financial industry
(d) a reduction in loan losses as the economy moved out of recession

■ **PROBLEMS**

1. From the figures in the table below it can be concluded that:

Item	Billions of dollars
Small time deposits	630
Large time deposits	645
Money market deposit accounts	575
Money market mutual funds	425
Checkable deposits	448
Noncheckable savings deposits	300
Currency	170

a. *M*1 is equal to the sum of $_____

and $_____; and totals $_____ billion.

b. *M*2 is equal to *M*1 plus $_____ and $_____

and $_____ and $_____; and totals $_____ billion.

c. *M*3 is equal to *M*2 plus $_____; and

totals $_____ billion.

2. Complete the following table showing the relationship between a percentage change in the price level and the percentage change in the value of money. Calculate the percentage change in the value of money to one decimal place.

Change in price level	Change in value of money
a. *rise* by:	
5%	– _____._____%
10%	– _____._____
15%	– _____._____
20%	– _____._____
25%	– _____._____
b. *fall* by:	
5%	+ _____._____%
10%	+ _____._____
15%	+ _____._____

3. The total demand for money is equal to the transaction plus the asset demand for money.

a. Assume each dollar held for transaction purposes is spent (on the average) four times per year to buy final goods and services.

(1) This means that transaction demand for money will be equal to (what fraction or percent) _____ of the nominal GDP; and

(2) if the nominal GDP is $2000 billion, the transaction demand will be $_____ billion.

b. The table below shows the number of dollars demanded for asset purposes at each rate of interest.

(1) Given the transactions demand for money in (*a*), complete the table.

(2) On the graph on the bottom of the page plot the *total* demand for money (*D$_m$*) at each rate of interest.

c. Assume the money supply (*S$_m$*) is $580 billion.

(1) Plot this money supply on the graph which you drew.

Interest rate	Amount of money demanded (*billions*)	
	For asset purposes	Total
16%	$ 20	$_____
14	40	_____
12	60	_____
10	80	_____
8	100	_____
6	120	_____
4	140	_____

(2) Using either the graph or the table, the equilibrium rate of interest is _____ %.

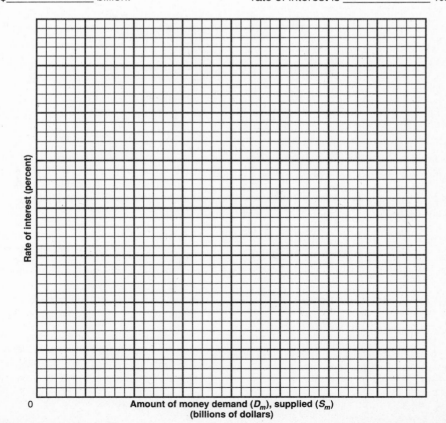

Rate of interest (percent)

0   Amount of money demand (*D$_m$*), supplied (*S$_m$*)
(billions of dollars)

d. Should the money supply:
(1) increase to $600 billion the equilibrium interest rate would (rise, fall) _____ to _____ %.
(2) decrease to $540 billion the equilibrium interest rate would _____ to _____ %.
e. If the nominal GDP:
(1) increased by $80 billion, the total demand for money would (increase, decrease) _____ by $_____ billion at each rate of interest and the equilibrium rate of interest would (rise, fall) _____ by _____ %.
(2) decreased by $120 billion, the total demand for money would _____ by $_____ billion at each rate of interest and the equilibrium interest rate would _____ by _____ %.

4. Suppose a bond with no expiration date pays a fixed $500 annually and sells for its face value of $5,000.
   a. Complete the table below, calculate the interest rate (to one decimal place) that would be obtained from the bond when the bond price is given, or calculate the bond price when the interest rate is given.

Bond price	Interest rate
$4,000	_____._____ %
$_____	11.0
$5,000	_____._____
$5,500	_____._____
$_____	8.0

   b. Based on the results of the table, as the price increases on a bond with a fixed annual payment, the interest yield on the bond (decreases, increases) _____ , but when the price of a bond decreases, the interest yield _____ . Given this situation in an economy, you can conclude that a higher price for bonds _____ interest rates and that a lower price for bonds _____ interest rates.

■ **SHORT ANSWER AND ESSAY QUESTIONS**

1. How would you define money?

2. What are the components of the *M*1 supply of money in the United States? Which of these components is the larger?

3. What is (*a*) a checkable deposit; (*b*) a noncheckable deposit; (*c*) a thrift (or savings) institution; (*d*) a depository institution?

4. What is a near-money? What are the more important near-monies in the American economy?

5. Define *M*2 and *M*3 and explain why the existence of near-monies is important.

6. For what reasons are checkable deposits included in the money supply?

7. What "backs" the money used in the United States? What determines the value of money?

8. Explain the relationship between the value of money and the price level.

9. What must government do if it is to stabilize the value of money?

10. What are the two reasons people wish to hold money? How are these two reasons related to the "functions" of money?

11. Explain the determinant of each of the two demands for money and how a change in the size of these determinants will affect the amount of money people wish to hold.

12. The rate of interest is a price. Of what good or service is it the price? Explain how demand and supply determine this price.

13. Describe how changes in bond prices correct disequilibrium in the money market. What is the relationship between bond prices and interest rates?

14. Outline the structure of the Federal Reserve System and explain the chief functions of each of the four parts of the system.

15. As briefly as possible outline the three characteristics of the Federal Reserve Banks and explain the meaning of these characteristics.

16. What are the chief functions which the Federal Reserve Banks perform? Explain briefly the meaning of each of these functions. Which of the chief functions is the most important?

17. What are the basic arguments for and against the independence of the Federal Reserve System?

18. Why did banks and savings and loan associations fail during the 1980s and early 1990s? What was the estimated cost to the taxpayers? What reforms have been instituted to correct the problems?

19. Explain why the provision of deposit insurance creates a "moral hazard" problem. How does this problem contribute to the potential for failure of financial institutions?

20. What are recent developments and reforms that will continue to change the financial system of the United States?

ANSWERS

Chapter 13 Money and Banking

FILL-IN QUESTIONS

1. *a.* medium of exchange; *b.* measure of value; *c.* store of value

2. *a.* currency, coins, money; *b.* checkable, depository institutions; *c.* Federal Reserve, Federal

3. noncheckable, small, deposit, mutual fund

4. large, certificates, 100,000

5. savings and loan, mutual savings, credit

6. NOW, ATS (either order), share

7. *a.* Treasury, bonds; *b.* currency, checkable, loss

8. *a.* their existence influences consuming-saving habits; *b.* conversion from near-money to money or from money to near-money may affect the stability of the economy; *c.* important when monetary policy is to be employed

9. depository, Federal Reserve

10. *a.* are not; *b.* exchange, legal, scarce

11. desirable goods and services, inversely, price

12. *a.* directly, nominal GDP; *b.* inversely, rate of interest

13. supply, interest, money; *a.* decrease, increase; *b.* increase, decrease

14. Depository Institutions Deregulation and Monetary Control (DIDMCA), checkable, deregulation, Federal Reserve System

15. Federal Open Market Committee, Advisory Councils

16. *a.* they are central banks, *b.* they are quasi-public banks; *c.* they are bankers' banks

17. deposits, loans, depository institutions

18. deposits, loans, increase

19. *a.* holding the deposits (reserves) of banks and thrifts; *b.* providing for the collection of checks; *c.* acting as fiscal agents for the Federal government; *d.* supervising member banks; *e.* regulating the money supply; regulating the money supply

20. less, high; *a.* deregulation, more, a moral hazard, higher, risky, illegal; *b.* Resolution Trust Corporation, Federal Deposit Insurance Corporation

TRUE-FALSE QUESTIONS

1. F, p. 255	6. T, p. 256	11. F, p. 257	16. T, p. 263
2. T, p. 255	7. T, p. 256	12. T, p. 258	17. T, p. 265
3. F, p. 255	8. F, p. 257	13. T, p. 259	18. F, p. 266
4. T, pp. 255-256	9. F, p. 257	14. F, p. 261	19. T, p. 267
5. F, p. 256	10. F, p. 257	15. T, p. 261	20. T, p. 268

MULTIPLE-CHOICE QUESTIONS

1. *d,* pp. 253-254	9. *c,* pp. 257-258	17. *c,* pp. 262-263	25. *d,* pp. 263-264
2. *d,* pp. 255-256	10. *b,* p. 255	18. *b,* p. 261	26. *a,* pp. 263-264
3. *d,* p. 255	11. *c,* p. 256	19. *a,* pp. 263-264	27. *d,* p. 265
4. *d,* p. 255	12. *b,* p. 257	20. *b,* pp. 262-263	28. *d,* pp. 264-265
5. *c,* p. 258	13. *b,* pp. 258-259	21. *c,* pp. 263-264	29. *b,* p. 270
6. *a,* p. 256	14. *b,* pp. 259-260	22. *d,* p. 263	30. *c,* p. 270
7. *b,* p. 255	15. *c,* pp. 260-261	23. *a,* pp. 263-264	
8. *d,* p. 258	16. *b,* p. 263	24. *d,* pp. 263-264	

PROBLEMS

1. *a.* 170, 448 (either order), 618; *b.* 300, 630, 575, 425 (either order), 2,548; *c.* 645, 3,193

2. *a.* 4.8, 9.1, 13, 16.7, 20; *b.* 5.3, 11.1, 17.6

3. *a.* (1) 1/4 (25%), (2) 500; *b.* (1) 520, 540, 560, 580, 600, 620, 640; *c.* (2) 10; *d.* (1) fall, 8, (2) rise, 14; *e.* (1) increase, 20, rise, 2, (2) decrease, 30, fall, 3

4. *a.* 12.5%, $4545, 10.0%, 9.1%, $6250; *b.* decreases, increases, decreases, increases

SHORT ANSWER AND ESSAY QUESTIONS

1. pp. 253-254	6. pp. 255-256	11. pp. 261-263	16. p. 268
2. p. 255	7. pp. 258-259	12. pp. 261-263	17. pp. 268-269
3. pp. 255-256	8. pp. 259-260	13. pp. 263-264	18. pp. 269-271
4. pp. 256-257	9. pp. 260-261	14. pp. 265-267	19. p. 270
5. pp. 256-257	10. pp. 261-263	15. pp. 266-267	20. pp. 271-272

CHAPTER 14

How Banks Create Money

Chapter 13 explained the institutional structure of banking in the United States today, the functions which banks and the other depository institutions and money perform, and the composition of the money supply. Chapter 14 explains how banks literally create money—checking account money—and the factors which determine and limit the money-creating ability of commercial banks. The other depository institutions also create checkable deposits, but this chapter focuses its attention on the commercial banks because they have created and will continue to create a very large part of the total amount of money created by all depository institutions in the United States. Note also that where the term **commercial bank** (or bank) appears it is legitimate to substitute depository **institution;** and it is permissible to substitute **checkable deposit** for **demand deposit** (or checking account).

The device (and a most convenient and simple device it is) employed to explain commercial banking operations and money creation is the **balance sheet.** All banking transactions affect this balance sheet, and the first step to understanding how money is created is to understand how various simple and typical transactions affect the commercial bank balance sheet.

In reading this chapter you must analyze for yourself the effect upon the balance sheet of each and every banking transaction discussed. The important items in the balance sheet are demand deposits and reserves, because **demand deposits are money,** and the ability of a bank to create new demand deposits is determined by the amount of reserves the bank has. Expansion of the money supply depends upon the possession by commercial banks of excess reserves. Excess reserves do not appear explicitly in the balance sheet but do appear there implicitly because excess reserves are the difference between the actual reserves and the required reserves of commercial banks.

Two cases—the single commercial bank and the banking system—are presented to help you build an understanding of banking and money creation. It is important to understand that the money-creating potential of a single commercial bank differs from the money-creating potential of the entire banking system; it is equally important to understand how the money-creating ability of many single commercial banks is **multiplied** and results in the money-creating ability of the banking system as a whole.

Certain assumptions are used throughout most of the chapter to analyze money-creating ability; in certain instances these assumptions may not be completely realistic and may need to be modified. The chapter concludes with a discussion of how the earlier analysis must be modified—but not changed in its essentials—to take account of these slightly unrealistic assumptions.

■ **CHECKLIST**

When you have studied this chapter you should be able to:

☐ Define the basic items in a bank's balance sheet.
☐ Recount the story of how goldsmiths came to issue paper money and became bankers who created money and held fractional reserves.
☐ Explain the effects of the deposit of currency in a checking account on the composition and size of the money supply.
☐ Compute a bank's required and excess reserves when you are given the needed balance-sheet figures.
☐ Explain why a commercial bank is required to maintain a reserve; and why this reserve is not sufficient to protect the depositors from losses.
☐ Indicate how the deposit of a check drawn on one commercial bank in a second commercial bank will affect the reserves and excess reserves of the two banks.
☐ Show what happens to the money supply when a commercial bank makes a loan (or buys securities).
☐ Show what happens to the money supply when a loan is repaid (or a bank sells securities).
☐ Explain what happens to a commercial bank's reserves and demand deposits after it has made a loan, a check has been written on the newly created demand deposit, deposited in another commercial bank and cleared; and what happens to the reserves and demand deposits of the commercial bank in which the check was deposited.
☐ Describe what would happen to a commercial bank's reserves if it made loans (or bought securities) in an amount that exceeded its excess reserves.

□ State the money-creating potential of a commercial bank (the amount of money a commercial bank can safely create by lending or buying securities).

□ Explain how the Federal funds market helps reconcile the goals of profits and liquidity for commercial banks.

□ State the money-creating potential of the banking system.

□ Explain how it is possible for the banking system to create an amount of money which is a multiple of its excess reserves when no individual commercial bank ever creates money in an amount greater than its excess reserve.

□ Compute the size of the monetary multiplier and the money-creating potential of the banking system when you are provided with the necessary data.

□ List the two leakages which reduce the money-creating potential of the banking system.

□ Explain why the size of the money supply needs to be controlled.

■ **CHAPTER OUTLINE**

1. The balance sheet of the commercial bank is a statement of the assets, liabilities, and net worth (capital stock) of the bank at a specific time; and in the balance sheet the bank's assets equal its liabilities plus its net worth.

2. The history of the early goldsmiths illustrates how paper money came into being, how they became bankers when they began to make loans and issue money in excess of their gold holdings, and how the presently used fractional reserve system with its two significant characteristics were developed.

3. By examining the ways in which the balance sheet of the commercial bank is affected by various transactions, it is possible to understand how a single commercial bank in a multibank system can create money.

  a. Once a commercial bank has been founded,

  (1) by selling shares of stock and obtaining cash in return;

  (2) and acquired the property and equipment needed to carry on the banking business;

  (3) the deposit of cash in the bank does not affect the total money supply; it only changes its composition by substituting demand deposits for currency in circulation;

  (4) three reserve concepts are vital to an understanding of the money-creating potential of a commercial bank.

  (a) The **legal reserve deposit** (required reserve) which a bank **must** maintain at its Federal Reserve Bank (or as vault cash—which can be ignored) equals the reserve ratio multiplied by the deposit liabilities of the commercial bank;

  (b) the **actual reserves** of a commercial bank are its deposits at the Federal Reserve Bank (plus the vault cash which is ignored);

  (c) the **excess reserves** equal to the actual reserves less the required reserve.

  (5) The writing of a check upon the bank and its deposit in a second bank results in a loss of reserves and deposits for the first and a gain in reserves and deposits for the second bank.

  b. When a single commercial bank lends or buys government securities it increases its own deposit liabilities and, therefore, the supply of money by the amount of the loan or security purchase. But the bank only lends or buys securities in an amount equal to its excess reserves because it fears the loss of reserves to other commercial banks in the economy.

  c. When a single commercial bank receives loan repayments or sells government securities, its deposit liabilities and, therefore, the supply of money are described by the amount of the loan repayments or securities sale.

  d. An individual commercial bank balances its desire for profits (which result from the making of loans and the purchase of securities) with its desire for liquidity or safety (which it achieves by having excess reserves or vault cash).

  e. The Federal funds market allows banks with excess reserves to lend funds overnight to banks which are short of reserves. The interest rate paid on the overnight loans is the Federal funds rate.

 4. The ability of a banking system composed of many individual commercial banks to lend and to create money is a multiple (greater than one) of its excess reserves; and is equal to the excess reserves of the banking system multiplied by the demand-deposit (or monetary) multiplier.

  a. The banking system as a whole can do this even though no single commercial bank ever lends an amount greater than its excess reserve because the banking system, unlike a single commercial bank, does not lose reserves.

  b. The monetary (or demand-deposit) multiplier is equal to the reciprocal of the required reserve ratio for demand deposits; and the maximum expansion of demand deposits is equal to the excess reserves in the banking system times the monetary multiplier.

  c. The potential lending ability of the banking system may not be fully achieved if there are leakages because borrowers choose to have additional currency or bankers choose to have excess reserves.

  d. If bankers lend as much as they are able during periods of prosperity and less than they are able during recessions, they add to the instability of the economy; and to reduce this instability the Federal Reserve Banks must control the size of the money supply.

■ IMPORTANT TERMS

Balance sheet

Assets

Liabilities

Net worth

Fractional reserve
system of banking

Vault cash (till money)

Legal (required)
reserve (deposit)

Reserve ratio

Fractional reserve

Actual reserve

Excess reserve

Federal Deposit Insurance
Corporation

The lending potential
of an individual
commercial bank

Federal funds rate

Commercial banking
system

Monetary (demand-
deposit) multiplier

The lending potential
of the banking system

Leakage

■ HINTS AND TIPS

1. A bank's balance sheet must balance. The bank's assets are either claimed by owners (net worth) or by nonowners (liabilities). Assets = liabilities + net worth.

2. Make a running balance sheet in writing for yourself as you read about each of the eight transactions in the text for the Wahoo bank. Then see if you understand the material, see if you can tell yourself (or a friend) the story for each transaction without using the text.

3. The maximum amount of demand-deposit expansion is determined by two factors: multiplying excess reserves by the monetary multiplier. Each factor, however, is affected by the required reserve ratio. The monetary multiplier is calculated by dividing one by the required reserve ratio. Excess reserves are determined by multiplying the required reserve ratio by the amount of new deposits. Thus, a change in the required reserve ratio will change the monetary multiplier **and** the amount of excess reserves. For example, a required reserve ratio of 25% gives a monetary multiplier a 4. For $100 in new money deposited, required reserves are $25 and excess reserves are $75. The maximum demand-deposit expansion is $300 (4 × $75). If the reserve ratio drops to 20%, the monetary multiplier is 5 and excess reserves are $80, so the maximum demand-deposit expansion is $400. Both factors have changed.

SELF-TEST

■ FILL-IN QUESTIONS

1. In this chapter, a "commercial bank" may also mean a "_____ institution" and "_____ deposit" may substitute for "demand deposit."

2. The balance sheet of a commercial bank is a statement of the bank's _____

_____

and _____
at some specific point in time.

3. The bank system that is used today is a (total, fractional) _____ reserve system, which means that (100%, less than 100%) _____ of the money deposited in a bank is kept on reserve.

4. There are two significant characteristics to the bank system of today.

    a. Banks in such a system can _____ money depending on the amount of _____ it holds.

    b. Banks under such a system are susceptible to "_____" or "runs," and to prevent this situation from happening, banks are _____ by government.

5. The coins and paper money which a bank has in its possession are called _____ cash or _____ money.

6. When a person deposits cash in a commercial bank and receives a demand deposit in return, the size of the money supply has (increased, decreased, not changed) _____

7. The legal reserve deposit of a commercial bank (ignoring vault cash) must be kept at the _____ _____ and must equal (at least) its _____ multiplied by the _____

8. The excess reserves of a commercial bank equal its _____ less its _____

9. If commercial banks are allowed to accept (or create) deposits in excess of their reserves, the banking system is operating under a system of _____ reserves.

10. When a check is drawn upon bank X, deposited in bank Y, and cleared, the reserves of bank X are (increased, decreased, not changed) _____ and the reserves of bank Y are _____;
deposits in bank X are _____
and deposits in bank Y are _____

11. A single commercial bank in a multibank system can safely make loans or buy government securities equal in amount to the _____ of that commercial bank.

12. When a commercial bank makes a new loan of $10,000, it (increases, decreases) _____ the supply of money by $_____; but when this loan is repaid, the supply of money _____ by $_____.

13. When a commercial bank sells a $2000 government bond to a securities dealer the supply of money (increases, decreases) _____ by $_____; but when a commercial bank buys a $2000 government bond from a securities dealer the supply of money _____ by $_____.

14. A bank ordinarily pursues two conflicting goals; they are _____ and _____.

15. When a bank lends temporary excess reserves held at the _____ banks to other commercial banks that are temporarily short of legally required reserves, it is participating in the _____ market. The interest rate paid on these overnight loans is the _____ rate.

16. The banking system can make loans (or buy government securities) and create money in an amount equal to its excess reserves multiplied by the _____ _____. Its lending potential per dollar of excess reserves is greater than the lending potential of a single commercial bank because it does not lose _____ to other banks.

17. The greater the reserve ratio is, the (larger, smaller) _____ is the monetary multiplier.

18. If the required reserve ratio is 16 2/3%, the banking system is $6 million short of reserves, and the banking system is unable to increase its reserves, the banking system must _____ the money supply by $_____.

19. The money-creating potential of the commercial banking system is lessened by the withdrawal of _____ from banks and by the decisions of bankers to keep _____ reserves.

20. Commercial banks in the past:
a. have kept considerable excess reserves during periods of (prosperity, recession) _____ and have kept few or no excess reserves during periods of _____.
b. and by behaving in this way have made the economy (more, less) _____ unstable.

■ **TRUE-FALSE QUESTIONS**

Circle the T if the statement is true; the F if it is false.

1. The balance sheet of a commercial bank shows the transactions in which the bank has engaged during a given period of time. **T F**

2. A commercial bank's assets plus its net worth equal the bank's liabilities. **T F**

3. Goldsmiths increased the money supply when they accepted deposits of gold and issued paper receipts to the depositors. **T F**

4. Mary Lynn, a music star, deposits a $30,000 check in a commercial bank and receives a demand deposit in return; an hour later the Manfred Iron and Coal Company borrows $30,000 from the same bank. The money supply has increased $30,000 as a result of the two transactions. **T F**

5. A commercial bank may maintain its legal reserve either as a deposit in its Federal Reserve Bank or as government bonds in its own vault. **T F**

6. The legal reserve which a commercial bank maintains must equal at least its own deposit liabilities multiplied by the required reserve ratio. **T F**

7. The actual reserves of a commercial bank equal excess reserves plus required reserves. **T F**

8. The reserve of a commercial bank in the Federal Reserve Bank is an asset of the Federal Reserve Bank. **T F**

9. A check for $1000 drawn on bank X by a depositor and deposited in bank Y will increase the excess reserves by bank Y by $1000. **T F**

10. A single commercial bank can safely lend an amount equal to its excess reserves multiplied by the required reserve ratio. **T F**

11. When a borrower repays a loan of $500, either in cash or by check, the supply of money is reduced by $500. **T F**

12. The granting of a $5000 loan and the purchase of a $5000 government bond from a securities dealer by a commercial bank have the same effect on the money supply.   **T   F**

13. A commercial bank seeks both profits and liquidity; but these are conflicting goals.   **T   F**

14. If the banking system has $10 million in excess reserves and if the reserve ratio is 25%, it can increase its loans by $40 million.   **T   F**

15. While a single commercial bank can increase its loans only by an amount equal to its excess reserves, the entire banking system can increase its loans by an amount equal to its excess reserves multiplied by the reciprocal of the reserve ratio.   **T   F**

16. When borrowers from a commercial bank wish to have cash rather than demand deposits, the money-creating potential of the banking system is increased. **T   F**

17. The Federal funds rate is the interest rate at which the Federal government lends funds to commercial banks.   **T   F**

18. Modern banking systems use gold as the basis for the fractional reserve system.   **T   F**

19. The selling of a government bond by a commercial bank will increase the money supply.   **T   F**

20. There is a need for the Federal Reserve System to control the money supply because profit-seeking banks tend to make changes in the money supply that are procyclical.   **T   F**

■ **MULTIPLE-CHOICE QUESTIONS**

Circle the letter that corresponds to the best answer.

1. The goldsmiths became bankers when they:
  (a) accepted deposits of gold for safe storage
  (b) issued receipts for the gold stored with them
  (c) used deposited gold to produce products for sale to others
  (d) issued paper money in excess of the amount of gold stored with them

2. When cash is deposited in a demand-deposit account in a commercial bank there is:
  (a) a decrease in the money supply
  (b) an increase in the money supply
  (c) no change in the composition of the money supply
  (d) a change in the composition of the money supply

3. A commercial bank has actual reserves of $9000 and deposit liabilities of $30,000; and the required reserve ratio is 20%. The excess reserves of the bank are:
  (a) $3000
  (b) $6000
  (c) $7500
  (d) $9000

4. A commercial bank is required to have a deposit at its Federal Reserve Bank in order:
  (a) to protect the deposits in the commercial bank against losses
  (b) to provide the means by which checks drawn on the commercial bank and deposited in other commercial banks can be collected
  (c) to add to the liquidity of the commercial bank and protect it against a "run" on the bank
  (d) to provide the Board of Governors of the Federal Reserve System with a means of controlling the lending ability of the commercial bank

5. A depositor places $750 in cash in a commercial bank, and the reserve ratio is 33 1/3%; the bank sends the $750 to the Federal Reserve Bank. As a result, the *reserves* and the *excess reserves* of the bank have been increased, respectively, by:
  (a) $750 and $250
  (b) $750 and $500
  (c) $750 and $750
  (d) $500 and $500

6. A commercial bank has no excess reserves, but then a depositor places $600 in cash in the bank, and the bank adds the $600 to its reserves by sending it to the Federal Reserve Bank. The commercial bank then lends $300 to a borrower. As a consequence of these transactions the size of the money supply has:
  (a) not been affected
  (b) increased by $300
  (c) increased by $600
  (d) increased by $900

7. A commercial bank has excess reserves of $500 and a required reserve ratio of 20%; it grants a loan of $1000 to a borrower. If the borrower writes a check for $1000 which is deposited in another commercial bank, the first bank will be short of reserves, after the check has been cleared, in the amount of:
  (a) $200
  (b) $500
  (c) $700
  (d) $1000

8. A commercial bank sells a $1000 government security to a securities dealer. The dealer pays for the bond in cash, which the bank adds to its vault cash. The money supply has:
  (a) not been affected
  (b) decreased by $1000
  (c) increased by $1000
  (d) increased by $1000 multiplied by the reciprocal of the required reserve ratio

9. A commercial bank has deposit liabilities of $100,000, reserves of $37,000, and a required reserve ratio of 25%. The amount by which a *single commercial bank* and the

amount by which the **banking system** can increase loans are, respectively:
- **(a)** $12,000 and $48,000
- **(b)** $17,000 and $68,000
- **(c)** $12,000 and $60,000
- **(d)** $17,000 and $85,000

10. If the required reserve ratio were 12 1/2% the value of the monetary multiplier would be:
- **(a)** 5
- **(b)** 6
- **(c)** 7
- **(d)** 8

11. The commercial banking system has excess reserves of $700 and makes new loans of $2100 and is just meeting its reserve requirements. The required reserve ratio is:
- **(a)** 20%
- **(b)** 25%
- **(c)** 30%
- **(d)** 33 1/3%

12. The commercial banking system, because of a recent change in the required reserve ratio from 20% to 30%, finds that it is $60 million short of reserves. If it is unable to obtain any additional reserves it must decrease the money supply by:
- **(a)** $60 million
- **(b)** $180 million
- **(c)** $200 million
- **(d)** $300 million

13. Only one commercial bank in the banking system has an excess reserve, and its excess reserve is $100,000. This bank makes a new loan of $80,000 and keeps an excess reserve of $20,000. If the required reserve ratio for all banks is 20%, the potential expansion of the money supply is:
- **(a)** $80,000
- **(b)** $100,000
- **(c)** $400,000
- **(d)** $500,000

14. The money-creating potential of the banking system is reduced when:
- **(a)** bankers choose to hold excess reserves
- **(b)** borrowers choose to hold none of the funds they have borrowed in currency
- **(c)** the Federal Reserve lowers the required reserve ratio
- **(d)** bankers borrow from the Federal Reserve

15. The excess reserves held by banks tend to:
- **(a)** rise during periods of prosperity
- **(b)** fall during periods of recession
- **(c)** rise during periods of recession
- **(d)** fall when interest rates in the economy fall

16. Unless controlled, the money supply will:
- **(a)** fall during periods of prosperity
- **(b)** rise during periods of recession

- **(c)** change in a procyclical fashion
- **(d)** change in an anticyclical fashion

*Use the following balance sheet for the First National Bank in answering the next five questions (**17, 18, 19, 20,** and **21**). Assume the required reserve ratio is 20%.*

Assets		Liabilities and Net Worth	
Reserves	$ 50,000	Demand Deposits	$150,000
Loans	70,000	Capital Stock	100,000
Securities	30,000		
Property	100,000		

17. This commercial bank has excess reserves of:
- **(a)** $10,000
- **(b)** $20,000
- **(c)** $30,000
- **(d)** $40,000

18. This bank can safely expand its loans by a maximum of:
- **(a)** $50,000
- **(b)** $40,000
- **(c)** $30,000
- **(d)** $20,000

19. Using the original bank balance sheet, assume that the bank makes a loan of $10,000 and has a check cleared against it for the amount of the loan, then its reserves and demand deposits will now be:
- **(a)** $40,000 and $140,000
- **(b)** $40,000 and $150,000
- **(c)** $30,000 and $150,000
- **(d)** $60,000 and $140,000

20. Using the original bank balance sheet, assume that the bank makes a loan of $15,000 and has a check cleared against it for the amount of the loan, then it will have excess reserves of:
- **(a)** $5,000
- **(b)** $10,000
- **(c)** $15,000
- **(d)** $20,000

21. If the original bank balance sheet was for the commercial banking **system,** rather than a single bank, loans and deposits could have been expanded by a maximum of:
- **(a)** $50,000
- **(b)** $100,000
- **(c)** $150,000
- **(d)** $200,000

22. The claims of the owners of the bank against the bank assets is the bank's:
- **(a)** net worth
- **(b)** liabilities
- **(c)** balance sheet
- **(d)** fractional reserves

23. The selling of government bonds by commercial banks is most similar to the:

(a) making of loans by banks because both actions increase the money supply
(b) making of loans by banks because both actions decrease the money supply
(c) repayment of loans to banks because both actions decrease the money supply
(d) repayment of loans to banks because both actions increase the money supply

Answer the next two questions (24 and 25) on the basis of the following consolidated balance sheet for the commercial banking system. All figures are in billions. Assume that the required reserve ratio is 12.5%.

Assets		Liabilities and Net Worth	
Reserves	$ 40	Demand Deposits	$200
Loans	80	Capital Stock	120
Securities	100		
Property	200		

24. The maximum amount by which this commercial banking system can expand the supply of money by lending is:
(a) $120 billion
(b) $240 billion
(c) $350 billion
(d) $440 billion

25. If there is a deposit of $20 billion of new currency into checking accounts in the banking system, excess reserves will increase by:
(a) $16.5 billion
(b) $17.0 billion
(c) $17.5 billion
(d) $18.5 billion

■ **PROBLEMS**

1. At the top of the next column is a table that shows the simplified balance sheet of a commercial bank. Assume that the figures given show the bank's assets and demand-deposit liabilities *prior to each of the following*

four transactions. Draw up the balance sheet as it would appear after each of these transactions is completed and place the balance-sheet figures in the appropriate column. *Do not* use the figures you place in columns **a, b,** and **c** when you work the next part of the problem; start all parts of the problem with the printed figures.

		(a)	(b)	(c)	(d)
Assets:					
Cash	$100	$___	$___	$___	$___
Reserves	200	___	___	___	___
Loans	500	___	___	___	___
Securities	200	___	___	___	___
Liabilities and net worth:					
Demand deposits	900	___	___	___	___
Capital stock	100	100	100	100	100

a. A check for $50 is drawn by one of the depositors of the bank, given to a person who deposits it in another bank, and cleared (column a).
b. A depositor withdraws $50 in cash from the bank, and the bank restores its vault cash by obtaining $50 in additional cash from its Federal Reserve Bank (column b).
c. A check for $60 drawn on another bank is deposited in this bank and cleared (column c).
d. The bank sells $100 in government bonds to the Federal Reserve Bank in its district (column d).

2. Below are five balance sheets for a single commercial bank (columns 1a–5a). The required reserve ratio is 20%.
a. Compute the required reserves (A); ignoring vault cash, the excess reserves (B) of the bank (if the bank is short of reserves and must reduce its loans or obtain additional reserves, show this by placing a minus sign in front of the amounts by which it is short of reserves); and the amount of new loans it can extend (C).
b. In the table at the top of the next page, draw up for the individual bank the five balance sheets as they appear after the bank has made the new *loans* that it is capable of making (columns 1b–5b).

	(1a)	(2a)	(3a)	(4a)	(5a)
Assets:					
Cash	$ 10	$ 20	$ 20	$ 20	$ 15
Reserves	40	40	25	40	45
Loans	100	100	100	100	150
Securities	50	60	30	70	60
Liabilities and net worth:					
Demand deposits	175	200	150	180	220
Capital stock	25	20	25	50	50
A. Required reserve	$___	$___	$___	$___	$___
B. Excess reserve	___	___	___	___	___
C. New loans	___	___	___	___	___

	(1b)	(2b)	(3b)	(4b)	(5b)
Assets:					
Cash	$_____	$_____	$_____	$_____	$_____
Reserves	_____	_____	_____	_____	_____
Loans	_____	_____	_____	_____	_____
Securities	_____	_____	_____	_____	_____
Liabilities and net worth:					
Demand deposits	_____	_____	_____	_____	_____
Capital stock	_____	_____	_____	_____	_____

3. In the table below are several reserve ratios. Compute the monetary multiplier for each of the reserve ratios and enter the figures in column 2. In column 3 show the maximum amount by which a single commercial bank can increase its loans for each dollar's worth of excess reserves it possesses. In column 4 indicate the maximum amount by which the banking system can increase its loans for each dollar's worth of excess reserves in the system.

(1)	(2)	(3)	(4)
12 ½%	$_____	$_____	$_____
16 ⅔%	_____	_____	_____
20%	_____	_____	_____
25%	_____	_____	_____
30%	_____	_____	_____
33 ⅓%	_____	_____	_____

4. Shown below is the simplified consolidated balance sheet for *all* commercial banks in the economy. Assume that the figures given show the banks' assets and liabilities *prior to each of the following three transactions* and that the reserve ratio is 20%. *Do not* use the figures you placed in columns 2 and 4 when you begin parts **b** and **c**

of the problem: start parts **a, b,** and **c** of the problem with the printed figures.

a. The public deposits $5 in cash in the banks and the banks send the $5 to the Federal Reserve, where it is added to their reserves. Fill in column 1. If the banking system extends the new loans it is capable of extending, show in column 2 the balance sheet as it would then appear.

b. The banking system sells $8 worth of securities to the Federal Reserve. Complete column 3. Assuming the system extends the maximum amount of credit of which it is capable, fill in column 4.

c. The Federal Reserve lends $10 to the commercial banks; complete column 5. Complete column 6 showing the condition of the banks after the maximum amount of new loans which the banks are capable of making is granted.

■ **SHORT ANSWER AND ESSAY QUESTIONS**

1. Why does a bank's balance sheet balance?

2. How did the early goldsmiths come to issue paper money and then become bankers?

3. Explain the difference between a 100% and fractional reserve system of banking.

4. What are two significant characteristics of a fractional reserve system of banking?

5. Explain what happens to the money supply when a bank accepts deposits of cash.

6. What are legal reserves? How are they determined? How are legal reserves related to the reserve ratio?

7. Define the meaning of "excess" reserves. How are they calculated?

8. Explain why bank reserves can be an asset to the depositing commercial bank but a liability to the Federal Reserve Bank receiving them.

		(1)	(2)	(3)	(4)	(5)	(6)
Assets:							
Cash	$ 50	$_____	$_____	$_____	$_____	$_____	$_____
Reserves	100	_____	_____	_____	_____	_____	_____
Loans	200	_____	_____	_____	_____	_____	_____
Securities	200	_____	_____	_____	_____	_____	_____
Liabilities and net worth:							
Demand deposits	500	_____	_____	_____	_____	_____	_____
Capital stock	50	50	50	50	50	50	50
Loans for Federal Reserve	0	_____	_____	_____	_____	_____	_____
Excess reserves		_____	_____	_____	_____	_____	_____
Maximum possible expansion of the money supply		_____	_____	_____	_____	_____	_____

9. Commercial banks seek both profits and safety. Explain how the balance sheet of the commercial banks reflects the desires of bankers for profits and for liquidity.

10. What is the Federal funds rate?

11. Discuss how the Federal funds market helps banks reconcile the two goals of profits and liquidity.

12. Do the reserves held by commercial banks satisfactorily protect the bank's depositors? Are the reserves of commercial banks needed? Explain your answers.

13. Explain why the granting of a loan by a commercial bank increases the supply of money. Why does the repayment of a loan decrease the supply of money?

14. How does the buying or selling of government securities by commercial banks influence the money supply?

15. The owner of a sporting goods store writes a check on his account in a Kent, Ohio, bank and sends it to one of his suppliers who deposits it in his bank in Cleveland, Ohio. How does the Cleveland bank obtain payment from the Kent bank? If the two banks were in Kent and New York City, how would one bank pay the other? How are the excess reserves of the two banks affected?

16. Why is a single commercial bank able to lend safely only an amount equal to its excess reserves?

17. No one commercial bank ever lends an amount greater than its excess reserve, but the banking system as a whole is able to extend loans and expand the money supply by an amount equal to the system's excess reserves multiplied by the reciprocal of the reserve ratio. Explain why this is possible and how the multiple expansion of deposits and money takes place.

18. What is the monetary multiplier? How does it work?

19. On the basis of a given amount of excess reserves and a given reserve ratio, a certain expansion of the money supply may be possible. What are two reasons why the potential expansion of the money supply may not be fully achieved?

20. Why is there a "need for monetary control" in the American economy?

ANSWERS

Chapter 14 How Banks Create Money

FILL-IN QUESTIONS

1. depository, checkable

2. assets, liabilities, net worth (capital)

3. fractional, less than 100%

4. *a.* create, reserves; *b.* panics, regulated

5. vault, till

6. not changed

7. Federal Reserve Bank in its district, deposit liabilities, reserve ratio

8. actual reserves, required reserves

9. fractional

10. decreased, increased, decreased, increased

11. excess reserves

12. increases, 10,000, decreases, 10,000

13. decreases, 2000, increases, 2000

14. profits, liquidity (safety)

15. Federal Reserve, Federal funds, Federal funds rate

16. monetary multiplier (reciprocal of the reserve ratio), reserves

17. smaller

18. decrease, 36 million

19. currency (cash), excess

20. *a.* recession, prosperity; *b.* more

TRUE-FALSE QUESTIONS

1. F, pp. 276-277	8. F, p. 280	15. T, p. 288
2. F, p. 277	9. F, pp. 281-282	16. F, p. 289
3. F, p. 277	10. F, p. 284	17. F, p. 285
4. T, p. 277	11. T, p. 284	18. F, p. 277
5. F, p. 279	12. T, p. 285	19. F, p. 285
6. T, p. 279	13. T, p. 285	20. T, p. 290
7. T, p. 280	14. T, p. 288	

MULTIPLE-CHOICE QUESTIONS

1. *d,* p. 277	10. *d,* p. 288	19. *b,* p. 282
2. *d,* pp. 278-279	11. *d,* p. 288	20. *a,* p. 282
3. *a,* p. 280	12. *c,* p. 289	21. *b,* p. 288
4. *d,* pp. 279-280	13. *c,* p. 288	22. *a,* p. 277
5. *b,* pp. 279-280	14. *a,* p. 289	23. *c,* pp. 284-285
6. *b,* p. 283	15. *c,* p. 290	24. *a,* p. 288
7. *b,* p. 284	16. *c,* pp. 290-291	25. *c,* p. 280
8. *b,* p. 285	17. *b,* p. 280	
9. *a,* p. 288	18. *d,* pp. 286-287	

PROBLEMS

1.

	(a)	(b)	(c)	(d)
Assets:				
Cash	$100	$100	$100	$100
Reserves	150	150	260	300
Loans	500	500	500	500
Securities	200	200	200	100
Liabilities and net worth:				
Demand deposits	850	850	960	900
Capital stock	100	100	100	100

2.

a.

	(1a)	(2a)	(3a)	(4a)	(5a)
A. Required reserve	$35	$40	$30	$36	$44
B. Excess reserve	5	0	−5	4	1
C. New loans	5	0	*	4	1

b.

	(1b)	(2b)	(3b)	(4b)	(5b)
Assets:					
Cash	$ 10	$ 20	$20	$ 20	$ 15
Reserves	40	40	25	40	45
Loans	105	100	*	104	151
Securities	50	60	30	70	60
Liabilities and net worth:					
Demand deposit	180	200	*	184	221
Capital stock	25	20	25	50	50

*If an individual bank is $5 short of reserves it must either obtain additional reserves of $5 by selling loans, securities, or its own IOUs to the reserve bank or contract its loans by $25.

3. column 2: 8, 6, 5, 4, 3 1/3, 3; column 3: 1, 1, 1, 1, 1, 1; column 4: 8, 6, 5, 4, 3 1/3, 3

4.

	(1)	(2)	(3)	(4)	(5)	(6)
Assets:						
Cash	$ 50	$ 50	$ 50	$ 50	$ 50	$ 50
Reserves	105	105	108	108	110	110
Loans	200	220	200	240	200	250
Securities	200	200	192	192	200	200
Liabilities and net worth:						
Demand deposit	505	525	500	540	500	550
Capital stock	50	50	50	50	50	50
Loans from Federal Reserve	0	0	0	0	10	10
Excess reserves	4	0	8	0	10	0
Maximum possible expansion of the money supply	20	0	40	0	50	0

SHORT ANSWER AND ESSAY QUESTIONS

1. pp. 276-277	**8.** pp. 280-281	**15.** pp. 281-282
2. p. 277	**9.** p. 285	**16.** pp. 279-280
3. p. 277	**10.** p. 285	**17.** pp. 286-287
4. p. 277	**11.** p. 285	**18.** pp. 288-289
5. p. 278	**12.** p. 280	**19.** p. 289
6. p. 279	**13.** pp. 282-285	**20.** p. 290
7. pp. 279-280	**14.** p. 285	

CHAPTER 15

The Federal Reserve Banks and Monetary Policy

Chapter 15 is the third chapter dealing with money and banking. It explains how the Board of Governors of the Federal Reserve System and the Federal Reserve Banks affect output, income, employment, and the price level of the economy. Central-bank policies designed to affect these variables are called monetary policies, the goal of which is full employment without inflation.

The first half of the chapter explains how the Federal Reserve achieves its basic goal. In this discussion, attention should be paid to the following: (1) the important items on the balance sheet of the Federal Reserve Banks; (2) the three major controls available to the Federal Reserve, and how the employment of these controls can affect the reserves, excess reserves, the actual money supply, and the money-creating potential of the banking system; (3) the actions the Federal Reserve would take if it were pursuing a tight money policy to curb inflation, and the actions it would take if it were pursuing an easy money policy to reduce unemployment: and (4) the relative importance of the three major controls which the Federal Reserve uses or has used to influence the economy.

Following the examination of "The Tools of Monetary Policy" Professors McConnell and Brue explain how the demand for and the supply of money determine the interest rate (in the "money market"); how the interest rate and the investment-demand schedule determine the level of equilibrium GDP. How an easy money policy and a tight money policy work through this cause-effect chain is illustrated with examples and summarized in Table 15-3.

This explanation of monetary policy makes it clear that the effect of a change in the money supply depends on just how steep or flat the money-demand and investment-demand curves are. There may also be feedback effects from an easy money policy because the increased economic activity may cause interest rates to rise and partially offset interest-rate decreases started by the easy money policy. Changes in monetary policy and aggregate demand also have different output and price-level outcomes depending on the range of the aggregate supply curve where the changes in aggregate demand occur.

A major section of the chapter discusses the **strengths and shortcomings** of monetary policy. Here you will learn about the target dilemma for the Federal Reserve: it can-

not simultaneously control both the money supply and the level of interest rates in the economy. In recent years, however, the Federal Reserve has targeted the interest rates and changed the money supply to achieve interest-rate targets. The effectiveness of monetary policy is further complicated by linkages with the international economy because of the effect of monetary policy on exchange rates and net exports.

The final section of the chapter is short, but extremely important. Figure 15-3 in that section gives you an overview of the economic factors and government policies that affect aggregate demand and supply. It summarizes much of the economic theory and policy that have been discussed in this chapter and the eight others that preceded it.

■ CHECKLIST

When you have studied this chapter you should be able to:

☐ State the goals of monetary policy.
☐ List the important assets and liabilities of the Federal Reserve Banks.
☐ Identify the three tools of monetary policy.
☐ Explain how the Federal Reserve expands or contracts the money supply by buying or selling government bonds.
☐ Describe how changes in reserve ratios or the discount rate by the Federal Reserve affect the money supply.
☐ Prescribe the three specific monetary policies the Federal Reserve should utilize to reduce unemployment; and the three specific policies it should employ to reduce inflationary pressures in the economy.
☐ Discuss the relative importance of monetary policy tools.
☐ Draw the demand-for-money and the supply-of-money curves and use them to show how a change in the supply of money will affect the interest rate.
☐ Draw an investment-demand curve to explain the effects of changes in the interest rate on investment spending.
☐ Construct an aggregate supply and demand graph to show how aggregate demand and the equilibrium level of

GDP are affected by changes in interest rates and investment spending.

☐ Use a cause-effect chain to explain the links between a change in the money supply and a change in the equilibrium level of GDP when there is an easy money policy and a tight money policy.

☐ State precisely how the steepness of the demand-for-money and of the investment-demand curves affects the impact of a change in the money supply on the equilibrium GDP.

☐ Explain the feedback effects from different monetary policies.

☐ Use the ranges of the aggregate supply curve to explain how a change in aggregate demand is divided between changes in real output and the price level.

☐ List three strengths of monetary policy.

☐ Discuss five shortcomings of monetary policy.

☐ State the target (or policy) dilemma confronted by the Fed; and explain why it faces this dilemma.

☐ Describe the relationship between the Federal funds rate, the prime interest rate, and monetary policy in recent years.

☐ Describe how the effectiveness of an easy money policy or a tight money policy is influenced by net exports and how these policies affect international trade deficits.

☐ Use Figure 15-3 to summarize the key factors and policies affecting aggregate supply and demand, and the level of output, employment, income, and prices in an economy.

■ CHAPTER OUTLINE

1. The fundamental objective of monetary policy is full employment without inflation. The Federal Reserve can accomplish this objective by exercising control over the amount of excess reserves held by commercial banks and thereby influencing the size of the money supply and the level of aggregate expenditures.

2. By examining the consolidated balance sheet and the principal assets and liabilities of the Federal Reserve Banks, an understanding of the ways in which the Federal Reserve can control and influence the reserves of commercial banks and the money supply can be obtained.

  a. The principal assets of the Federal Reserve Banks (in order of size) are U.S. government securities and loans to commercial banks.

  b. Their principal liabilities are Federal Reserve Notes, the reserve deposits of commercial banks, and U.S. Treasury deposits.

3. The Federal Reserve Banks employ three principal tools (techniques or instruments) to control the reserves of banks and the size of the money supply.

  a. The Federal Reserve can buy and sell government securities in the open market.

(1) Buying securities in the open market from either banks or the public increases the reserves of banks.

(2) Selling securities in the open market to either banks or the public decreases the reserves of banks.

  b. It can raise or lower the reserve ratio.

(1) Raising the reserve ratio decreases the excess reserves of banks and the size of the monetary (demand-deposit) multiplier.

(2) Lowering the reserve ratio increases the excess reserves of banks and the size of the monetary multiplier.

  c. It can also lower the discount rate to encourage banks to borrow reserves from the Fed and raise it to discourage them from borrowing reserves from the Fed.

  d. An easy money policy can be implemented by actions of the Federal Reserve to buy government bonds in the open market, decrease the discount rate, or decrease the reserve ratio.

  e. A tight money policy can be implemented by actions of the Federal Reserve to sell government bonds in the open market, increase the discount rate, or increase the reserve ratio.

4. To state the effects of monetary policy on the equilibrium GDP from the mainstream view:

  a. In the money market the demand-for- and the supply-of-money curves determine the real interest rate; the investment-demand curve and this rate of interest determine investment spending; and investment spending affects aggregate demand and the equilibrium levels of real output and prices.

  b. If unemployment and deflation is the problem, the Federal Reserve takes policy actions to increase the money supply, causing the interest rate to fall and investment spending to increase, thereby increasing aggregate demand, and increasing real GDP by a multiple of the increase in investment.

  c. But if inflation is the problem, the Federal Reserve uses its tools to decrease the money supply, causing the interest rate to rise and investment spending to decrease, and thereby reducing aggregate demand and inflation.

  d. There are refinements and feedback effects to monetary policy that must be considered:

(1) The steeper the demand-for-money curve and the flatter the investment-demand curve the greater will be the effect on the equilibrium GDP of a change in the money supply.

(2) Changes in the equilibrium GDP that result from a change in the money supply will alter the demand for money and dampen the effect of the change in the money supply on the GDP.

  e. The aggregate supply curve will influence how the change in investment spending and aggregate demand is divided between change in real output and changes in the price level.

(1) An easy money policy in the horizontal or recessionary range of the aggregate supply curve will increase aggregate demand, have a large effect on real output, but have little effect on the price level; such a policy, however, would be inappropriate if the economy was in the vertical range of aggregate supply and experiencing inflation because it would primarily increase the price level, not real output.

(2) A tight money policy in the vertical range of the aggregate supply curve will decrease aggregate demand, reduce the price level, but have little effect on real output; such a policy would not be appropriate if the economy was in the horizontal range of aggregate supply and experiencing a recession because it would reduce real output, but not the price level.

5. Whether monetary policy is effective in promoting full employment without inflation is a debatable question because monetary policy has both strengths and shortcomings in fighting recession and inflation.

a. Its strengths are that it can be more quickly changed than fiscal policy; it is more isolated from political pressure than fiscal policy; and it has been successful when it was used in recent situations.

b. Its five shortcomings or problems are that it:

(1) may be subject to less control by the Federal Reserve because of recent changes in banking practices;

(2) is more effective in fighting inflation than it is in curbing recession;

(3) can be offset by changes in the velocity of money;

(4) may not have a significant effect on investment spending; and

(5) may produce changes in interest income and expenses that have offsetting effects.

c. A most difficult problem for the Fed is its inability to control both the money supply and the level of interest rates at the same time.

(1) If the Fed's policy target is the stabilization of interest rates, an increase in the nominal GDP (and the resulting increase in the demand for money) will require it to increase the money supply; and if its policy target is the stabilization of the money supply, an increase in the nominal GDP (and the demand for money) will force interest rates upward.

d. The recent target of the monetary policy of the Federal Reserve has been interest rates rather than the money supply.

(1) The Federal Reserve can influence the *Federal funds rate* by buying or selling bonds. When the Federal Reserve buys bonds, it becomes cheaper for banks to borrow excess reserves overnight because the Federal funds rate falls; conversely, when the Federal Reserve sells bonds, the Federal funds rates rise and it becomes more expensive for banks to borrow funds.

(2) The *prime interest rate* is the rate that banks charge their most credit-worthy customers; it tends to rise and fall with the Federal funds rate.

6. There are international linkages to monetary policy:

a. An easy money policy to bring the economy out of recession or slow growth will tend to lower domestic interest rates and cause the dollar to depreciate. In this situation, net exports will increase, thus increasing aggregate demand and reinforcing the effect of the easy money policy.

b. A tight money policy to reduce inflation will tend to raise domestic interest rates and cause the dollar to appreciate. These events will decrease net exports and reduce aggregate demand, thereby strengthening the tight money policy.

c. An easy policy is compatible with the goal of correcting a balance of trade deficit, but a tight money policy conflicts with this economic goal.

7. The equilibrium levels of output, employment, income, and prices are determined by the interaction of aggregate supply and demand.

a. There are four expenditure components of aggregate demand: consumption, investment, net export spending, and government spending.

b. There are three major components of aggregate supply: the prices of inputs or resources, factors affecting the productivity with which resources are used, and the legal and institutional environment.

c. Fiscal, monetary, or other government policies may have an effect on the components of aggregate demand or supply, which in turn affect the level of output, employment, income, and prices.

■ IMPORTANT TERMS

Monetary policy	Tight money policy
Open-market operations	Velocity of money
Discount rate	Target dilemma
Reserve ratio	Federal funds rate
Money market	Prime interest rate
Easy money policy	Net export effect

■ HINTS AND TIPS

1. To acquire a thorough knowledge of how the Federal Reserve transactions affect reserves, excess reserves, the actual money supply, and the potential money supply, you must carefully study each of the sets of balance sheets which are used to explain these transactions. The items to watch are the reserves and demand deposits. Be sure that you know why a change is made in each of the balance sheets, and be able to make the appropriate balance-sheet entries as you trace through the effects of each transaction. Problem 2 in this study guide will give you additional practice.

2. You will need to understand and remember the cause-effect chain of monetary policy. The best way to learn them is to draw your own chain (diagram or table) that shows the links for an easy money policy and a tight money policy. Then check your work against Table 15-3 in the text. Draw another chain for describing monetary policy and the net export effect. Check your cause-effect chain against Table 15-4 in the text.

3. The single most important figure for the macroeconomics part of the textbook is probably Figure 15-3. It gives an excellent overview and summary of the determinants of aggregate supply and demand and identifies the key policy variables that have been discussed in this chapter and the eight that preceded it.

SELF-TEST

■ FILL-IN QUESTIONS

1. The objective of monetary policy in the United States is a _____ level of total output. Responsibility for these monetary policies rests with the _____ of the Federal Reserve System; and they are put into effect by the twelve Federal Reserve _____

2. The two important assets of the Federal Reserve Banks are _____ and _____ _____. Their three major liabilities are _____, _____, and _____

3. The three tools (or instruments) employed by the monetary authority to control the money supply are _____, changing _____ _____, and changing _____

4. The Federal Reserve Banks buy and sell government securities in the open market in order to change the amount of new _____ commercial banks are able to create and the rate of _____ in the economy.

5. If the Federal Reserve Banks were to sell $10 million in government bonds to the **public** and the reserve ratio were 25%, the supply of money would immediately be reduced by $_____, the reserves of commercial banks would be reduced by $_____, and the excess reserves of the banks would be reduced by $_____. But if these bonds were sold to the commercial banks, the supply of money would immediately be reduced by $_____, the reserves of

the banks would be reduced by $_____, and the excess reserves of the banks would be reduced by $_____

6. Changes in the reserve ratio affect the ability of commercial banks to create money in two ways: they affect the amount of _____ held by the commercial banks and the size of the monetary _____

7. If the Federal Reserve Banks were to lower the discount rate commercial banks would tend to borrow (more, less) _____ from them; and this would (increase, decrease) _____ their excess reserves.

8. To increase the supply of money, the Federal Reserve Banks should (raise, lower) _____ the reserve ratio, (buy, sell) _____ securities in the open market, and/or (increase, decrease) _____ the discount rate.

9. An easy money policy would be characterized by actions of the Federal Reserve to (increase, decrease) _____ the discount rate, _____ reserve ratios, and (buy, sell) _____ government bonds; whereas a tight money policy would include actions taken to (increase, decrease) _____ the discount rate, to _____ reserve ratios, and (buy, sell) _____ government bonds.

10. The most effective and most often used tool of monetary policy is _____ operations. A change in the _____ may have an important "announcement effect" about the direction of monetary policy, but it is relatively weak because it does not affect much borrowing of bank reserve; conversely, the _____ are rarely changed because the impact on bank reserves is so powerful, blunt, and immediate.

11. Graphically, in an economy in which government neither purchases goods and services nor collects net taxes and which neither exports nor imports goods and services:

  a. the equilibrium real interest rate is determined by the demand-for- and the supply-of-_____ curves;

  b. this equilibrium interest rate and the_____ _____ curve determine the level of investment spending;

  c. and investment spending affects aggregate (supply, demand) _____, and the intersection of aggregate supply and demand determine the equilibrium

level of real _____ and _____

d. but when the supply-of-money curve increases (shifts to the right), the real interest rate will (increase, decrease) _____ , investment spending will

_____ , aggregate demand will _____ ,

and real GDP will _____

12. To eliminate inflationary pressures in the economy the traditional view holds that the monetary authority

should seek to (increase, decrease) _____ the reserves of commercial banks; this would tend to

_____ the money supply and to

_____ the rate of interest; and this in turn would cause investment spending, aggregate demand,

and GDP to _____. This action by

monetary authorities would be considered a(n) _____

_____ policy.

13. If there was a serious problem with unemployment in the economy, the traditional view would be that the

Federal Reserve should pursue a(n) _____ policy, in which case the Federal Reserve would (buy, sell)

_____ government bonds as a way of (increas-

ing, decreasing) _____ the money supply, and

thereby _____ interest rates; these events would

have the effect of _____ investment spending

and thus _____ real GDP.

14. The effect of a $1 billion increase or decrease in the money supply upon the equilibrium GDP is greater the

(flatter, steeper) _____ the demand-for-

money curve and the _____ the invest-ment-demand curve.

15. An increase in the money supply will shift the aggre-

gate (supply, demand) _____ curve to the

(right, left) _____
  a. In the horizontal (or recession) range along the ag-gregate-supply curve this increase in the money sup-

ply will have a (small, large) _____

effect on real domestic output and a _____
effect on the price level.
  b. In the vertical range along the aggregate-supply curve this increase in the money supply will have a

_____ effect on real domestic output

and a _____ effect on the price level.
  c. In the intermediate range along the aggregate-sup-ply curve the effect of an increase in the money supply on the real domestic output is greater the (steeper, flat-

ter) _____ the aggregate-supply curve, and the effect on the price level is greater the

_____ the aggregate-supply curve.

16. Monetary policy has strengths and shortcomings.
  a. Compared to fiscal policy, monetary policy is

speedier and (more, less) _____ flexible;

_____ isolated from political pressure, and

_____ successfully used to counter inflation and recession in recent years.
  b. The shortcomings or problems with monetary policy are that it:

  (1) may be subject to (more, less) _____ control by the Federal Reserve because of recent changes in banking practices that affect control of the money supply;
  (2) may be more effective in curbing (recession, infla-

tion) _____ than _____ ;
  (3) can be successful if the _____ of money

changes in the (same, opposite) _____ direction;
  (4) will not be effective if changes in the interest rate

have little or no effect on _____ spending; and

  (5) will cause changes in _____ rates that have offsetting effects.

17. The target dilemma faced by the Fed is that it is (able,

unable) _____ to control both the money supply and the level of interest rates simultane-ously.
  a. If it is to stabilize the interest rate it must (increase,

decrease) _____ the money sup-ply when the nominal GDP rises.
  b. And if it stabilizes the money supply it must allow

the interest rate to _____ when the nominal GDP rises.

18. The interest rate that banks charge one another for overnight loans is the (prime interest, Federal funds)

_____ rate, but the rate banks charge

their most credit-worthy customers is the _____

_____ rate. The _____ rate has been the recent focus of the monetary policy of the Fed-eral Reserve.

19. An easy money policy (increases, decreases) _____ net exports; a tight money policy _____ net exports. The net export effect from an easy money policy thus (strengthens, weakens) _____ domestic monetary policy and the net export effect from a tight money policy _____ it. Also, an easy money policy is (compatible, incompatible) _____ with the economic goal of reducing a balance of trade deficit, but a tight money policy is _____ with this economic goal.

20. In the macroeconomic theory developed in the chapters of the text, the interaction of aggregate demand and supply determine the level of _____ , _____ , _____ , and _____ in the economy.
  a. Aggregate demand depends on the amounts of _____ , _____ , _____ , and _____ spending in the economy.
  b. Aggregate supply is influenced by input _____ , _____ , and the legal-institutional _____

■ TRUE-FALSE QUESTIONS

Circle the T if the statement is true; the F if it is false.

1. The fundamental goal of monetary policy is to stabilize interest rates.　**T　F**

2. The securities owned by the Federal Reserve Banks are almost entirely U.S. government bonds.　**T　F**

3. If the Federal Reserve Banks buy $15 in government securities from the public in the open market, the effect will be to increase the excess reserves of commercial banks by $15.　**T　F**

4. When the Federal Reserve sells bonds in the open market, the price of these bonds falls.　**T　F**

5. A change in the reserve ratio will affect the multiple by which the banking system can create money, but it will not affect the actual or excess reserves of member banks.　**T　F**

6. If the reserve ratio is lowered, some required reserves are turned into excess reserves.　**T　F**

7. When commercial banks borrow from the Federal Reserve Banks they increase their excess reserves and their money-creating potential.　**T　F**

8. If the monetary authority wished to follow a tight money policy, it would sell government bonds in the open market.　**T　F**

9. An increase in the required reserve ratio tends to reduce the profits of banks.　**T　F**

10. The least effective and used tool of monetary policy is the open-market operation where government securities are bought and sold.　**T　F**

11. The equilibrium rate of interest is found at the intersection of the demand-for-money and the supply-of-money curves.　**T　F**

12. An increase in the equilibrium GDP will shift the demand-for-money curve to the left and increase the equilibrium interest rate.　**T　F**

13. Consumer spending is more sensitive to changes in the rate of interest than is investment demand.　**T　F**

14. There can be a feedback effect from an easy money policy because an increase in GDP resulting from the policy will also cause an increase in the demand for money, partially offsetting the interest-reducing effect of the policy.　**T　F**

15. When the economy is at or near full employment an increase in the money supply tends to be inflationary.　**T　F**

16. It is generally agreed that fiscal policy is more effective than monetary policy in controlling the business cycle because fiscal policy is more flexible.　**T　F**

17. Monetary policy is subject to more political pressure than fiscal policy.　**T　F**

18. A tight money policy suffers from a "You can lead a horse to water, but you can't make him drink" problem.　**T　F**

19. When interest rates increase, the reduction in spending by purchases of capital goods, homes, and autos is partially offset by the increase in spending by those who receive interest income.　**T　F**

20. Monetary policy is more effective in fighting depression than it is in curbing inflation.　**T　F**

21. In an economy in which the GDP is either rising or falling the Fed is unable to control both the money supply and interest rates.　**T　F**

22. The prime interest rate is the rate that banks charge other banks for overnight loans of excess reserves at Federal Reserve banks.　**T　F**

23. An easy money policy decreases net exports.　**T　F**

24. A tight money policy will tend to cause the dollar to appreciate.　**T　F**

25. A tight money policy is compatible with the goal of correcting a trade deficit.　**T　F**

■ **MULTIPLE-CHOICE QUESTIONS**

Circle the letter that corresponds to the best answer.

1. The agency directly responsible for monetary policy in the United States is:
(a) the twelve Federal Reserve Banks
(b) the Board of Governors of the Federal Reserve System
(c) the Congress of the United States
(d) the U.S. Treasury

2. The largest single asset in the Federal Reserve Banks' consolidated balance sheet is:
(a) securities
(b) the reserves of commercial banks
(c) Federal Reserve Notes
(d) loans to commercial banks

3. The largest single liability of the Federal Reserve Banks is:
(a) securities
(b) the reserves of commercial banks
(c) Federal Reserve Notes
(d) loans to commercial banks

4. Assuming that the Federal Reserve Banks sell $20 million in government securities to commercial banks and the reserve ratio is 20%, then the effect will be:
(a) to reduce the actual supply of money by $20 million
(b) to reduce the actual supply of money by $4 million
(c) to reduce the potential money supply by $20 million
(d) to reduce the potential money supply by $100 million

5. Which of the following acts would *not* have the same general effect upon the economy as the other three?
(a) the Federal Reserve Banks sell bonds in the open market
(b) the Federal Reserve increases the discount rate
(c) the Federal Reserve eases credit for the purchase of consumer durables
(d) the Federal Reserve raises the reserve ratio

6. Which of the following is the most important control used by the Federal Reserve Banks to regulate the money supply?
(a) changing the reserve ratio
(b) open-market operations
(c) changing the discount rate
(d) changing the Federal funds rate

7. Assume that there is a 20% reserve ratio and that the Federal Reserve buys $100 million worth of government securities. If the securities are purchased from the public, then this action has the potential to increase bank lending by a maximum of:
(a) $500 million, but only by $400 million if the securities are purchased directly from commercial banks

(b) $400 million, but by $500 million if the securities are purchased directly from commercial banks
(c) $500 million, and also by $500 million if the securities are purchased directly from commercial banks
(d) $400 million, and also by $400 million if the securities are purchased directly from commercial banks

8. In the traditional or Keynesian chain of cause and effect between changes in the excess reserves of commercial banks and the resulting changes in output and employment in the economy:
(a) an increase in excess reserves will decrease the money supply
(b) a decrease in the money supply will increase the rate of interest
(c) an increase in the rate of interest will increase aggregate demand
(d) an increase in aggregate demand will decrease output and employment

9. Which of the following is more likely to be affected by changes in the rate of interest?
(a) consumer spending
(b) investment spending
(c) the spending of the Federal government
(d) the exports of the economy

10. The economy is experiencing inflation and the Federal Reserve decides to pursue a tight money policy. Which set of actions by the Fed would be most consistent with this policy?
(a) buying government securities and lowering the discount rate
(b) buying government securities and lowering the reserve ratio
(c) selling government securities and raising the discount rate
(d) selling government securities and lowering the discount rate

11. A newspaper headline reads: "Fed Cuts Discount Rate for Third Time This Year." This headline indicates that the Federal Reserve is most likely trying to:
(a) reduce inflationary pressures in the economy
(b) increase the Federal funds rate
(c) reduce the cost of credit and stimulate the economy
(d) increase the value of the dollar

12. A change in the money supply has the *least* effect on the equilibrium GDP when:
(a) both the demand-for-money and the investment-demand curves are steep
(b) both the demand-for-money and the investment-demand curves are flat
(c) the demand-for-money curve is flat and the investment-demand curve is steep
(d) the demand-for-money curve is steep and the investment-demand curve is flat

13. Which explanation best describes the feedback effects of an easy money policy? The increase in GDP resulting from the policy will:
   (a) decrease the demand for money, and partially offset the interest-reducing effect of the policy
   (b) increase the demand for money, and partially offset the increasing effect of the policy
   (c) increase the demand for money, and partially offset the interest-reducing effect of the policy
   (d) decrease the demand for money, and partially offset the increasing effect of the policy

14. An increase in the money supply will have little or no effect on the price level in:
   (a) the horizontal range of the aggregate-supply curve
   (b) the intermediate range of the aggregate-supply curve
   (c) the vertical range of the aggregate-supply curve
   (d) any of the three ranges of the aggregate-supply curve

15. An increase in the money supply will have little or no effect on the real domestic output and employment in:
   (a) the horizontal range of the aggregate-supply curve
   (b) the intermediate range along the aggregate-supply curve
   (c) the vertical range on the aggregate-supply curve
   (d) any of the three ranges on the aggregate supply curve

Use the graph below to answer the next three questions (16, 17, and 18).

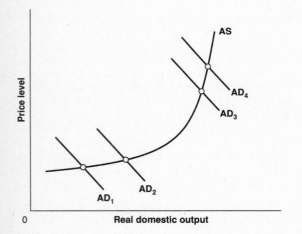

16. A shift from AD₁ to AD₂ would be most consistent with:
   (a) an increase in the prime interest rate
   (b) an increase in the discount rate by the Federal Reserve
   (c) the buying of securities by the Federal Reserve
   (d) the selling of securities by the Federal Reserve

17. Which shift would be most consistent with the potential effects of tight money policy in an inflationary period in an economy where prices are flexible?
   (a) AD₁ to AD₂
   (b) AD₃ to AD₄
   (c) AD₄ to AD₃
   (d) AD₂ to AD₁

18. If the Federal Reserve adopted an easy money policy in a period of high unemployment, the situation can best be characterized by a shift from:
   (a) AD₁ to AD₂
   (b) AD₃ to AD₄
   (c) AD₄ to AD₃
   (d) AD₂ to AD₁

19. Which one is considered a **strength** of monetary policy compared to fiscal policy?
   (a) feedback effects
   (b) cyclical asymmetry
   (c) isolation from political pressure
   (d) effect on changes in the velocity of money

20. An increase in the money supply is **least** effective in stimulating aggregate expenditures when the velocity of money:
   (a) falls as the money supply increases
   (b) remains constant
   (c) rises as the money supply increases
   (d) is equal to 5

21. A shortcoming of monetary policy is that actions taken to increase the interest rate:
   (a) decrease investment spending and decrease interest income, thus doubling the effect
   (b) increase investment spending and increase interest income, thus doubling the effect
   (c) decrease investment spending, but increase interest income, thus offsetting the effect
   (d) increase investment spending, but decrease interest income, thus offsetting the effect

22. The target dilemma refers to a decision the Federal Reserve must make about whether to:
   (a) change the discount rate or reserve ratios
   (b) buy or sell government securities
   (c) pursue an easy or tight money policy
   (d) stabilize the interest rate or the money supply

23. Suppose nominal GDP is decreasing. If the Federal Reserve wants to keep the interest rate constant, it would most likely:
   (a) increase the money supply
   (b) decrease the money supply
   (c) decrease the Federal funds rate
   (d) decrease the discount rate

24. The Federal funds rate is the rate that:
   (a) banks charge for overnight use of excess reserves held at the Federal Reserve banks

(b) banks charge for loans to the most credit-worthy customers

(c) the Federal Reserve charges for short-term loans to commercial banks

(d) government bonds are sold at in the open-market operations of the Federal Reserve

25. When the Federal Reserve uses open-market operations to reduce the Federal funds rate it is pursuing a(n):

(a) easy money policy and targeting interest rates

(b) easy money policy and targeting the money supply

(c) tight money policy and targeting interest rates

(d) tight money policy and targeting the money supply

26. When the Federal Reserve Banks decide to buy government bonds, the demand for government bonds will:

(a) decrease, bond prices will decrease, and the interest rate will decrease

(b) increase, bond prices will increase, and the interest rate will decrease

(c) increase, bond prices will increase, and the interest rate will increase

(d) decrease, bond prices will increase, and the interest rate will decrease

27. A tight money policy in the United States is most likely to:

(a) increase domestic interest rates and cause the value of the dollar to depreciate

(b) decrease domestic interest rates and cause the value of the dollar to appreciate

(c) increase domestic interest rates and cause the value of the dollar to appreciate

(d) decrease domestic interest rates and cause the value of the dollar to depreciate

28. Which policy combination would tend to reduce net exports?

(a) tight money policy and expansionary fiscal policy

(b) easy money policy and expansionary fiscal policy

(c) tight money policy and contractionary fiscal policy

(d) easy money policy and contractionary fiscal policy

29. A tight money policy that is used to reduce inflation in the domestic economy:

(a) is best conducted by reducing the required reserve ratios at commercial banks

(b) increases net exports and the effectiveness of the policy

(c) conflicts with the economic goal of correcting a trade deficit

(d) causes the dollar to depreciate

30. Which of the following are coordinated policies?

(a) an increase in government expenditures and in the money supply

(b) a decrease in personal tax rates and in the money supply

(c) an increase in transfer payments and a decrease in the money supply

(d) an increase in corporate tax rates and in the money supply

■ PROBLEMS

1. Assume that the consolidated balance sheet below is for all commercial banks. Assume also that the required reserve ratio is 25% and that cash is **not** a part of the commercial banks' legal reserve.

Assets		Liabilities	
Cash	$ 50	Demand deposits	$400
Reserves	100	Loans from Federal	
Loans	150	Reserve	25
Securities	200	Net worth	75
	$500		$500

a. To **increase** the supply of money by $100, the Federal Reserve Banks could **either:**

(1) (increase, decrease) _____ the reserve ratio to _____%, **or**

(2) (buy, sell) _____ securities worth

$_____ in the open market.

b. To **reduce** the supply of money by $50, the Federal Reserve Banks could **either:**

(1) _____ the reserve ratio to _____%, **or**

(2) _____ securities worth

$_____ in the open market.

2. On the next page are the consolidated balance sheets of the Federal Reserve and of the commercial banks. Assume that the reserve ratio for commercial banks is 25%, that cash is **not** a part of a bank's legal reserve, and that the figures in column 1 show the balance sheets of the Federal Reserve and the commercial banks **prior to each of the following five transactions.** Place the new balance-sheet figures in the appropriate columns and complete A, B, C, D, and E in these columns. **Do not** use the figures you place in columns (2) through (5) when you work the next part of the problem; start all parts of the problem with the printed figures in column (1).

a. The Federal Reserve Banks sell $3 in securities to the public, which pays by check (column 2).

b. The Federal Reserve Banks buy $4 in securities from the commercial banks (column 3).

c. The Federal Reserve Banks lower the required reserve ratio for commercial banks to 20% (column 4).

d. The U.S. Treasury buys $5 worth of goods from American manufacturers and pays the manufacturers

	(1)	(2)	(3)	(4)	(5)	(6)
Federal Reserve Banks						
Assets:						
Gold certificates	$ 25	$_____	$_____	$_____	$_____	$_____
Securities	30	_____	_____	_____	_____	_____
Loans to commercial banks	10	_____	_____	_____	_____	_____
Liabilities						
Reserves of commercial banks	50	_____	_____	_____	_____	_____
Treasury deposits	5	_____	_____	_____	_____	_____
Federal Reserve Notes	10	_____	_____	_____	_____	_____
Commercial Banks						
Assets:						
Reserves	$ 50	$_____	$_____	$_____	$_____	$_____
Securities	70	_____	_____	_____	_____	_____
Loans	90	_____	_____	_____	_____	_____
Liabilities						
Demand deposits	200	_____	_____	_____	_____	_____
Loans from Federal Reserve	10	_____	_____	_____	_____	_____
A. Required reserves		_____	_____	_____	_____	_____
B. Excess reserves		_____	_____	_____	_____	_____
C. How much has the money supply changed?		_____	_____	_____	_____	_____
D. How much *more* can the money supply change?		_____	_____	_____	_____	_____
E. What is the total of C and D?		_____	_____	_____	_____	_____

by checks drawn on its accounts at the Federal Reserve Banks (column 5).

e. Because the Federal Reserve Banks have raised the discount rate, commercial banks repay $6 which they owe to the Federal Reserve (column 6).

3. On the graph below, is the demand-for-money curve which shows the amounts of money consumers and firms wish to hold at various rates of interest (when the nominal GDP in the economy is given).

a. Suppose the supply of money is equal to $300 billion.

(1) Draw on this graph the supply-of-money curve.

(2) The equilibrium rate of interest in the economy is

_____%.

b. On the graph at the top of the left column on the next page is an investment-demand curve which shows the amounts of planned investment at various rates of interest. Given your answer to (2) above, how much will investors plan to spend for capital goods?

$_____ billion.

c. On the following graph is the aggregate supply (AS) curve in this economy. On the graph, draw an aggregate demand curve (AD$_1$) so that it crosses the AS curve in the horizontal range of aggregate supply. Label the price level (P_1) and output level (Q_1) associated with the intersection of AD$_1$ and AS.

d. Now assume that monetary authorities increase the money supply to $400.

(1) On the *first* graph plot the new money supply curve. The new equilibrium interest rate is _____%.

(2) On the *second* graph determine the level of investment spending that is associated with this new interest rate: $_____ billion. By how much has investment spending increased as a result of the

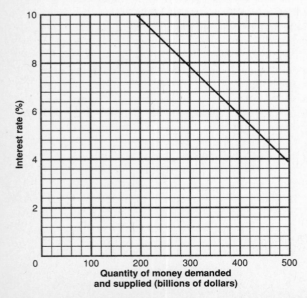

Interest rate (%)

Quantity of money demanded
and supplied (billions of dollars)

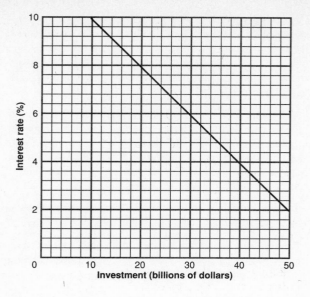

Investment (billions of dollars)

(1) Price level	(2) Real output	(3) AD$_1$	(4) AD$_2$	(5) AD$_3$	(6) AD$_4$	(7) AD$_5$	(8) AD$_6$
.30	$1500	$1600	$1700	$2070	$2400	$2920	$3020
.30	1600	1600	1700	2070	2400	2920	3020
.30	1700	1600	1700	2070	2400	2920	3020
.40	1790	1500	1600	1970	2300	2820	2920
.50	1870	1400	1500	1870	2200	2720	2820
.60	1940	1300	1400	1770	2100	2620	2720
.70	2000	1200	1300	1670	2000	2520	2620
.80	2050	1100	1200	1570	1900	2420	2520
.90	2090	1000	1100	1470	1800	2320	2420
1.00	2120	900	1000	1370	1700	2220	2320
1.10	2120	800	900	1270	1600	2120	2220
1.20	2120	700	800	1170	1500	2020	2120

a. The horizontal range on this aggregate-supply schedule is from a real domestic output of zero to $_____ billion.

b. The vertical range on this aggregate-supply curve is at the real domestic output of $_____ billion.

c. If the aggregate-demand schedule were that shown in columns (1) and (3) the equilibrium real domestic output would be $_____ billion and the price level would be _____

d. If the aggregate-demand schedule increased from that shown in columns (1) and (3) to the one shown in columns (1) and (4) the equilibrium real domestic output would _____ and the price level would _____

e. If the aggregate-demand schedule increased from that shown in columns (1) and (5) to the one shown in columns (1) and (6) the equilibrium real domestic output would _____ and the price level would _____

f. And if the aggregate-demand schedule increased from that shown in columns (1) and (7) to the one shown in columns (1) and (8) the equilibrium real domestic output would _____ and the price level would _____

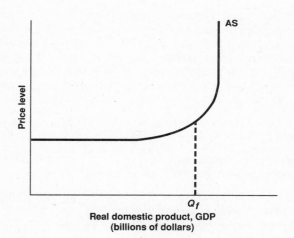

Real domestic product, GDP (billions of dollars)

change in the interest rate? $_____ billion.

(3) Assume that the marginal propensity to consume is .75. What is the multiplier? _____ By how much will the new investment spending increase aggregate demand? $_____ billion.

(4) On the *third* graph, indicate how the change in investment spending affects aggregate demand. Draw a new aggregate demand curve (AD$_2$) so that it crosses the AS curve in the intermediate range of aggregate supply at the output level (Q$_f$). Also label the new price level (P$_2$) associated with the intersection of AD$_2$ and AS.

4. Columns (1) and (2) of the next table show the aggregate-supply schedule. (The price level is a price index and real domestic output is measured in billions of dollars.)

5. Columns (1) and (2) in the following table show the money supply and column (3) shows the demand for money. (Dollar figures are in billions and the interest rate is a percentage.)

a. The equilibrium interest rate is _____ %.

b. Suppose the Fed wishes to stabilize the interest rate at this level; but the nominal GDP produced by the economy increases, and as a result the demand for money in the economy increases from that shown in column (3) to that shown in column (4). The Fed will have to (increase, decrease) _____ the supply of money to $_____ billion.

(1) Supply of money	(2) Interest rate	(3) Demand for money	(4) Demand for money
$400	.08	$100	$200
400	.07	200	300
400	.06	300	400
400	.05	400	500
400	.04	500	600
400	.03	600	700
400	.02	700	800

c. But if the Fed stabilizes the supply of money at $400 billion and the nominal GDP increases to increase the demand for money from that shown in column (3) to that shown in column (4) the interest rate will (rise, fall)

_____ to _____ %.

d. If the Fed stabilizes the interest rate it must (increase, decrease) _____ the supply of

money when the nominal GDP rises and _____ it when the nominal GDP falls; and if it holds the supply of money constant the interest rate will (rise, fall)

_____ when the nominal GDP increases and _____ when the nominal GDP decreases.

■ **SHORT ANSWER AND ESSAY QUESTIONS**

1. What is the basic goal of monetary policy? What actions are taken to achieve this goal during recession or during a period of high inflation?

2. What are the important assets and liabilities of the Federal Reserve Banks?

3. Explain how the monetary-policy tools of the Federal Reserve Banks would be used to contract the supply of money. How would they be used to expand the supply of money?

4. What is the difference between the effects of the Federal Reserve's buying (selling) government securities in the open market from (to) commercial banks and from (to) the public?

5. Which of the monetary-policy tools available to the Federal Reserve is most effective? Why is it more effective than other tools?

6. Using mainstream theory and three graphs, explain what determines (a) the equilibrium interest rate; (b) investment spending; and (c) the equilibrium GDP. Now employ these three graphs to show the effects of a decrease in the money supply upon the equilibrium GDP.

7. Utilizing your answers to the question above, (a) what determines how large the effect of the decrease in the money supply on the equilibrium GDP will be; and (b) how would the change in the equilibrium GDP affect the demand-for-money curve, the interest rate, investment spending, and the GDP itself?

8. Explain from a traditional viewpoint how the Board of Governors and the Federal Reserve Banks can influence income, output, employment, and the price level. In your explanation, employ the following concepts: reserves, excess reserves, the supply of money, the availability of bank credit, and the rate of interest.

9. Why are changes in the rate of interest more likely to affect investment spending than consumption and saving?

10. What are the characteristics of an easy money policy or a tight money policy? How does the Federal Reserve implement such policies?

11. What are two factors or situations that may limit the effectiveness of monetary policy?

12. How does a change in the money supply affect the aggregate-demand curve? How will a change in the money supply and the resulting shift in the aggregate-demand curve affect the real domestic output and the price level in (a) the horizontal range, (b) the vertical range, and (c) the intermediate range along the aggregate-supply curve?

13. What are the strengths and shortcomings of monetary policy?

14. Why is monetary policy more effective in controlling inflation than in reducing unemployment?

15. What is the target or policy dilemma of the Federal Reserve? What approach has the Fed taken in recent years to resolve this dilemma?

16. What is the prime interest rate and how is it related to the Federal funds rate? What happens to the Federal funds rate when the Federal Reserve expands or contracts the money supply through open-market operations?

17. Suppose the nominal GDP in the American economy is increasing or decreasing. Why is the Federal Reserve unable to keep both interest rates and the size of the money supply from changing?

18. Explain how the net export effect influences the effectiveness of a tight or an easy money policy.

19. What type of monetary policy would you recommend to correct a balance of trade deficit? Why?

20. Explain as briefly as possible what mainstream economists believe determines the level of real output, employment, income, and prices in the American economy.

ANSWERS

Chapter 15 The Federal Reserve and Monetary Policy

FILL-IN QUESTIONS

1. full-employment noninflationary, Board of Governors, Banks

2. securities, loans to commercial banks (either order), reserves of commercial banks, Treasury deposits, Federal Reserve Notes (any order)

3. open-market operations, reserve ratio, the discount rate (any order)

4. money, interest

5. 10 million, 10 million, 7.5 million, 0, 10 million, 10 million

6. excess reserves, multiplier

7. more, increase

8. lower, buy, decrease

9. decrease, decrease, buy, increase, increase, sell

10. open-market, discount rate, reserve ratios

11. *a.* money; *b.* investment-demand; *c.* demand, output, prices; *d.* decrease, increase, increase, increase

12. decrease, decrease, increase, decrease, tight money

13. easy money, buy, increasing, decreasing, increasing, increasing

14. steeper, flatter

15. demand, right; *a.* large, small; *b.* small, large; *c.* flatter, steeper

16. *a.* more, more, more; *b.* (1) less, (2) inflation, recession, (3) velocity, opposite, (4) investment, (5) interest

17. unable; *a.* increase; *b.* increase

18. Federal funds, prime interest, Federal funds

19. increases, decreases, strengthens, weakens, compatible, incompatible

20. output, employment, income, prices (any order); *a.* consumption, investment, net export, government (any order); *b.* prices, productivity, environment

TRUE-FALSE QUESTIONS

1. F, p. 294	**10.** F, p. 301	**19.** T, p. 308
2. T, p. 294	**11.** T, p. 302	**20.** F, p. 307
3. F, p. 296	**12.** F, p. 302	**21.** T, p. 307
4. T, pp. 297-298	**13.** F, p. 302	**22.** F, p. 309
5. F, pp. 299-300	**14.** T, p. 304	**23.** F, pp. 309-310
6. T, p. 299	**15.** T, p. 306	**24.** T, pp. 309-310
7. T, p. 300	**16.** F, pp. 306-307	**25.** F, pp. 311-312
8. T, pp. 300-301	**17.** F, p. 306	
9. T, p. 301	**18.** F, p. 307	

MULTIPLE-CHOICE QUESTIONS

1. *b*, pp. 293-294	**11.** *c*, p. 304	**21.** *c*, p. 307
2. *a*, p. 294	**12.** *c*, p. 305	**22.** *d*, p. 308
3. *c*, pp. 294-295	**13.** *c*, p. 305	**23.** *b*, p. 305
4. *d*, pp. 297-298	**14.** *a*, p. 306	**24.** *a*, p. 309
5. *c*, p. 301	**15.** *c*, p. 306	**25.** *a*, p. 308
6. *b*, p. 301	**16.** *c*, p. 306	**26.** *b*, pp. 309-310
7. *b*, pp. 296-297	**17.** *c*, p. 306	**27.** *c*, pp. 309-310
8. *b*, p. 302	**18.** *a*, p. 306	**28.** *a*, pp. 309-310
9. *b*, pp. 305-306	**19.** *c*, p. 306	**29.** *c*, pp. 311-312
10. *c*, p. 305	**20.** *a*, p. 307	**30.** *a*, pp. 312-313

PROBLEMS

1. *a.* (1) decrease, 20, (2) buy, 25; *b.* (1) increase, 28 4/7, (2) sell, 12 1/2

2.

	(2)	(3)	(4)	(5)	(6)
			Federal Reserve Banks		
Assets:					
Gold certificates	$ 25	$ 25	$ 25	$ 25	$ 25
Securities	27	34	30	30	30
Loans to commercial banks	10	10	10	10	4
Liabilities:					
Reserves of commercial banks	47	54	50	55	44
Treasury deposits	5	5	5	0	5
Federal Reserve Notes	10	10	10	10	10
			Commercial Banks		
Assets:					
Reserves	$ 47	$ 54	$ 50	$ 55	$ 44
Securities	70	66	70	70	70
Loans	90	90	90	90	90
Liabilities:					
Demand deposits	197	200	200	205	200
Loans from Federal Reserve	10	10	10	10	4
A. Required reserves	49.25	50	40	51.25	50
B. Excess reserves	−2.25	4	10	3.75	−6
C. How much has the money supply changed?	−3	0	0	+5	0
D. How much **more** can the money supply change?	−9	+16	+50	+15	−24
E. What is the total of C and D?	−12	+16	+50	+20	−24

3. *a.* (2) 8; *b.* 20; *c.* see Figure 15-2 in text; *d.* (1) 6, (2) 30, 10, (3) 4, 80, (4) see Figure 15-2 in text

4. *a.* 1700; *b.* 2120; *c.* 1600, .30; *d.* rise to $1700 billion, remain constant; *e.* rise from $1870 billion to $2000 billion, rise from .50 to .70; *f.* remain constant at $2120 billion, rise from 1.10 to 1.20

5. *a.* 5; *b.* increase, 500; *c.* rise, 6; *d.* increase, decrease, rise, fall

SHORT ANSWER AND ESSAY QUESTIONS

1. p. 294	**8.** pp. 302-304	**15.** pp. 308-309
2. pp. 294-295	**9.** pp. 302-303	**16.** p. 309
3. pp. 295-298	**10.** pp. 304-305	**17.** p. 308
4. pp. 295-298	**11.** p. 305	**18.** pp. 309-311
5. p. 301	**12.** pp. 305-306	**19.** pp. 311-314
6. pp. 302-304	**13.** pp. 306-308	**20.** pp. 312-314
7. pp. 302-304	**14.** p. 307	

CHAPTER 16

Alternative Views on Macro Theory and Policy

Now that you understand the basic ideas behind fiscal and monetary policy you are ready to learn about different theories of how the economy functions and you are prepared to explore controversial issues to expand your knowledge of macroeconomics. Chapter 16 begins the first of a four-chapter section of the text that examines **Problems and Controversies in Macroeconomics.** This chapter focuses on alternative views to the basic Keynesian positions on monetary and fiscal policy for the economy. Chapter 17 explores reasons for the simultaneous occurrence of inflation and unemployment in the economy and explains the principal features of supply-side economics. In Chapter 18, the problems with the Federal budget and the public debt are examined. Finally, Chapter 19 deals with economic growth and the long-term performance of the economy.

Economics has always been an arena in which conflicting theories and policies opposed each other. This field of intellectual combat, in major engagements, has seen Adam Smith do battle with the defenders of a regulated economy. It witnessed the opposition of Karl Marx to the orthodox economics of his day. In more recent times it saw Keynes in conflict with the classical economists. Around the major engagements have been countless minor skirmishes between opposing viewpoints. Out of these major and minor confrontations have emerged not winners and losers but the advancement of economic theory and the improvement of economic policy.

Chapter 16 begins by comparing **classical** and **Keynesian** views of macroeconomic theory and stabilization policy using the now familiar aggregate demand and aggregate supply framework. After establishing this foundation, the chapter introduces the modern forms of classical economics—**monetarism** and **rational expectations**—and then compares those theories to Keynesian economics. Monetarism and rational expectations theory are newer challengers to enter the intellectual arena of macroeconomic debate. The opponent is the reigning champion, Keynesianism, which bested classical economics in the same arena during the 1940s. Monetarists and rational-expectations theorists wish to free the economy from what they see as the destabilizing effects of discretionary fiscal and monetary policies. They view the Keynesians as the

proponents of government intervention and see themselves as the defenders of **laissez-faire.**

Chapter 16 examines both monetarism and rational-expectations theory; but it directs most of its attention toward monetarism. But this chapter is more than a comparison of the attitudes of Keynesians and monetarists toward the role of government in the economy. And it is more than a comparison of the basic equations of the two schools of thought. The basic equation of the Keynesians and the equation of exchange of the monetarists say pretty much the same thing. The equation of exchange (**MV = PQ**) is another way of saying that the economy will produce the GDP which is equal to the aggregate quantity of goods and services demanded.

The issue is whether the velocity of money—the **V** in the equation of exchange—is stable or unstable. If it is stable, as the monetarists contend, then the only kind of policy that can be used to control (to increase or decrease) nominal GDP is monetary policy; and fiscal policy cannot expand or contract nominal GDP. But if **V** is unstable, as the Keynesians argue, then fiscal policy is the only effective means and monetary policy is an ineffective means of controlling nominal GDP. The issue of whether **V** is stable or unstable becomes an issue of whether the size of the money supply matters very much or very little. Monetarists argue that the **M** in the equation of exchange is the only thing that matters and their Keynesian rivals contend that it doesn't matter very much.

The emphasis in Chapter 16 is on monetarism because earlier chapters have emphasized Keynesianism. You are not expected, however, to determine which of the two groups is correct. But you should see that monetarism is an alternative to Keynesianism; that the economic issue is the stability of **V;** that the political issue is whether monetary or fiscal policy is more effective; and that the policy issue is whether rules or discretion should be used to conduct monetary policy.

Rational-expectations theorists take a more extreme position in the debate over the relative effectiveness of monetary and fiscal policies. Their position is that the economy tends to produce its full-employment output and that neither of the two types of policy can expand real output and employment in either the short run or the long run:

the only effect on the economy of an expansionary monetary or fiscal policy is inflation. They are modern-day (or the new) classical economists who argue that neither the size of the money supply nor the fiscal policies of government has any effect on real output and employment. While this extreme position will be strange to those who have come to believe government can bring about full employment without inflation in the economy, advocates of the rational-expectations theory are careful to explain how they reach these conclusions; and you should be sure you understand the assumptions they make in order to reach their unusual conclusions before you dismiss their extreme position.

Economic theory has been changed by the debate among Keynesians, monetarists, and rational expectationists, as has been the case with similar debates over macroeconomics in the past. In particular, there is now recognition that "money matters" and that both the money supply and monetary policy have a significant effect on the economy. More attention is also being given to the coordination of fiscal and monetary policy, and to the influence of expectations on markets and the economy. These debates have caused economists to reconsider the basic aspects of macroeconomics and have resulted in the incorporation of new ideas into mainstream thinking about macroeconomics.

■ CHECKLIST

When you have studied this chapter you should be able to:

☐ Compare and contrast the classical and Keynesian views of the aggregate-demand curve and the aggregate-supply curve.
☐ Compare the positions of Keynesian and monetarist economists on the competitiveness of a capitalistic economy and its inherent stability and on the role government should play in stabilizing it.
☐ Write the equation of exchange and define each of the four terms in the equation.
☐ Show how the basic Keynesian equation is "translated" into the equation of exchange.
☐ Compare the monetarist and Keynesian views on the functions of money; on why households and firms demand money; and on what determines the quantity of money demanded.
☐ Explain why the monetarists believe nominal GDP is directly and predictably linked to *M.*
☐ Write a brief scenario which explains what monetarists believe will happen to change the nominal GDP and to *V* when *M* is increased.
☐ Construct a scenario which explains why Keynesians believe what will happen to the interest rate and to *V* and nominal GDP if *M* is increased.
☐ Discuss empirical evidence about velocity from a monetarist or Keynesian perspective.

☐ Explain why Keynesians favor and monetarists reject the use of fiscal policy to stabilize the economy.
☐ State the monetary rule of the monetarists, and the two reasons why they propose a rule instead of discretionary monetary policy.
☐ Use the aggregate demand-aggregate supply models of the Keynesians and the monetarists to compare and contrast the effects of an expansionary monetary or fiscal policy on the real domestic output and the price level.
☐ Clarify the debate over the monetarist call for a monetary rule using the aggregate demand-aggregate supply model.
☐ State the two basic assumptions of the rational-expectations theory (RET).
☐ Explain how RET advocates believe firms, workers, and consumers react to the announcement of an expansionary monetary or fiscal policy to frustrate the achievement of the goal of the policy.
☐ Use aggregate demand and aggregate supply to show the effects of an expansionary monetary or fiscal policy on real output and the price level in the RET.
☐ Write a brief scenario to explain why rational-expectations theorists believe discretionary monetary and fiscal policies are ineffective.
☐ State what type of government policy is advocated by RET theorists.
☐ Present three criticisms of the RET.
☐ Cite three examples of how ideas from monetarism and rational expectations have been absorbed into mainstream thinking about macroeconomics.

■ CHAPTER OUTLINE

1. Classical and Keynesian economics can be compared by examining their aggregate-demand–aggregate-supply models of the economy.
   a. In the classical model the aggregate-supply curve is vertical at the economy's full-employment output; and a decrease in aggregate demand will lower the equilibrium price level and have no effect on the real output of (or employment in) the economy because of Say's law, flexible interest rates, and responsive prices and wages.
   b. In the Keynesian model the aggregate-supply curve is horizontal at the current price level; and a decrease in aggregate demand will lower the real output of (and employment in) the economy and have no effect on the equilibrium price level because of the downward inflexibility of prices and wages.
   c. In both the classical and Keynesian models the aggregate-demand curve slopes downward.
   (1) In the classical model it slopes downward because (with a fixed money supply in the economy) a fall in the price level increases the purchasing power of money and enables consumers and business firms to pur-

chase a larger real output; aggregate demand will be reasonably stable if the nation's monetary authorities maintain a constant supply of money.

(2) Keynesians view aggregate demand as being unstable over time, even if the supply of money is held constant, in part because of fluctuations in investment spending; and a decline in aggregate demand decreases real domestic output, but has no effect on the price level, thereby causing output to stay permanently below the full-employment level.

2. Monetarism is a modern form of classical economics that offers an alternative to Keynesian macroeconomic theory and policy recommendation. Keynesians and monetarists differ over the inherent stability of capitalistic economies and ideologically over the role government should play in the economy.

    a. Keynesians believe that, because many markets in a capitalistic economy are noncompetitive, it is unstable, that government should intervene to stabilize the economy, and that fiscal policy is a more effective stabilizer than monetary policy.

    b. Monetarists believe that because markets in a capitalistic economy are competitive the economy would be stable if it were not for government interference, that government intervention destabilizes the economy, and that government should not use either discretionary fiscal or monetary policy to try to stabilize it.

3. In the Keynesian model the equilibrium output of the economy is the output at which

$$C_a + I_g + X_n + G = GDP$$

    a. In the monetarist model the basic equation is the equation of exchange

$$MV = PQ$$

but because **MV** (total spending) = $C_a + I_g + X_n + G$ and **PQ** = **GDP** the equations are different ways of stating the same relationship.

    b. While Keynesians assign a secondary role to money because they believe the links in the cause-effect chain are loose ones, monetarists, believing **V** in the equation of exchange is stable, find that while a change in **M** may affect **Q** in the short run it will in the long run affect only **P**. These competing views of the monetary transmission mechanism are illustrated for you in Figure 16-1 of the textbook.

4. Whether **V** in the equation of exchange is stable or unstable is a critical question because if it is stable **PQ** is closely linked to **M;** and if it is unstable the link between **PQ** and **M** is loose and uncertain.

    a. Reasoning that people have a stable desire to hold money relative to holding other assets or to making purchases, monetarists conclude that the quantity of money demanded is a stable percentage of GDP (that GDP/**M** is constant); that an increase (a decrease) in

M will leave firms and households with more (less) money than they wish to have; that they will, therefore, increase (decrease) spending for consumer and capital goods; and that this will cause the GDP and the amount of money they wish to hold for transactions purposes to rise (fall) until their demand for money is equal to **M** and GDP/**M** = **V**.

    b. But Keynesians argue that consumers and business firms also have an asset demand for money as well as a transactions demand for money; that this asset demand for money is inversely related to the rate of interest; and that an increase (a decrease) in **M** will decrease (increase) the interest rate, increase (decrease) the amount of money people wish to hold as an asset, lower (raise) **V,** and leave the effect on GDP uncertain.

    c. Empirical evidence confirms neither the contention of the monetarists that **V** is stable nor the contention of the Keynesians that it is variable (or unstable).

5. Because their theories (their views on the stability of **V**) differ, Keynesians and monetarists disagree over the effectiveness of fiscal and monetary policies in stabilizing the economy.

    a. Keynesians favor the use of fiscal policy to stabilize the economy because they believe it is a more powerful stabilizer; but the monetarists argue that the use of fiscal policy is both harmful and ineffective because of the crowding-out effect it has on investment expenditures in the economy.

    b. Arguing that discretionary changes in **M** have produced monetary mismanagement and macroeconomic instability, the monetarists have proposed the monetary rule that **M** be increased at the same annual rate as the potential annual rate of increase in the real GDP.

    c. In the aggregate demand-aggregate supply model the monetarists see an aggregate-supply curve that is very steep (or vertical) and in which an increase in aggregate demand has little (or no) effect on real domestic output and increases the price level by a relatively large amount; but the Keynesians see an aggregate-supply curve that is nearly flat (or horizontal) and in which an increase in aggregate demand has little (or no) effect on the price level and increases the real domestic output by a relatively large amount. At the full employment level of output, where the aggregate-supply curve is vertical, both Keynesians and monetarists would agree that expansionary policies would lead to demand-pull inflation.

    d. The debate over the call for a monetary rule by the monetarists is also illustrated in the aggregate demand-aggregate supply model.

(1) From the monetarist perspective, a monetary rule would shift aggregate demand rightward to match a shift in the aggregate-supply curve because of economic growth, thus keeping the price level stable.

(2) From the Keynesian view, the loose link between changes in money and aggregate demand mean that

a monetary rule might produce too great a shift in aggregate demand (and demand-pull inflation) or too small a shift (and deflation) to match the shift in aggregate supply, and therefore such a rule would contribute to price instability.

6. The RET, developed since the mid-1970s and called the new classical economics, is an alternative to Keynesian economics and to monetarism.

    a. Economists who advocate the RET make two basic assumptions:

    (1) business firms, consumers, and workers understand how the economy works so that they can anticipate the effect on the economy of an economic event or a change in economic policy, and use all available information to make decisions in a way to further their own self-interests; and

    (2) all markets in the economy are so competitive that equilibrium prices and quantities quickly adjust to these events and changes in public policy.

    b. From these assumptions the proponents of the RET conclude that the response of the public to the expected inflationary effect of an expansionary monetary (or fiscal) policy will cancel the intended effect on output and employment in the economy.

    c. In an aggregate demand-aggregate supply model of the RET the aggregate supply curve is vertical; and any monetary or fiscal policy that increases or decreases aggregate demand affects only the price level, and has no effect on real output or employment, real wages, or real interest rates in either the short or the long run.

    d. Rational-expectations theorists argue that discretionary monetary and fiscal policies are ineffective, and would (like the monetarist) replace discretionary monetary policies with rules; however, rational expectationists argue for monetary rules because the actions and knowledge of the public will counteract the intent of the policies, but monetarists argue for rules because monetary authorities do not have sufficient information to correct for time lags and other problems.

    e. The appeal of the RET comes from the inability of Keynesian economics to explain and to develop policies to correct simultaneous inflation and unemployment, and from the long-sought connection between micro- and macroeconomics; but RET has been subjected to three basic criticisms.

    (1) One criticism is that people are not so well informed on the workings of the economy and the effect of economic policy on it as the rational-expectations theorists assume.

    (2) A second criticism is that many markets in the economy are not so competitive as assumed in the RET and do not, therefore, adjust their prices as rapidly as assumed.

    (3) And the third criticism is that monetary and fiscal policies have worked in the past to expand real output and employment in the economy.

7. The controversies in macroeconomics in the past two decades have led to the incorporation of several ideas from monetarism and rational expectations into mainstream thinking about macroeconomics. Three examples illustrate this point: first, changes in the money supply and monetary policy are given more importance than in the past; second, there is recognition of the need to coordinate fiscal and monetary policy and to prevent crowding-out of economic activity; and third, more attention is given to the effects of expectations on markets and the economy. As in the past, debates in macroeconomics have changed the views about macroeconomic theory and policy.

■ IMPORTANT TERMS

Classical economics	Crowding-out effect
Keynesianism	Monetary rule
Monetarism	Rational-expectations
Equation of exchange	theory
Velocity of money	

■ HINTS AND TIPS

1. Review Chapter 9's discussion of aggregate demand and supply as preparation for the comparison of classical and Keynesian views in this chapter.

2. Monetarist and Keynesian theories are two approaches of looking at the same thing. The similarities can best be seen in equations in nominal form. The monetarist equation of exchange is $MV = PQ$. The Keynesian equation is $C_a + I_g + X_n + G = GDP$. The MV term is the monetarist expression for the Keynesian equilibrium $C_a + I_g + X_n + G$. The PQ term is the monetarist expression for GDP. Monetarists give more emphasis to the role of money and assume that velocity is relatively stable. Keynesians give more emphasis to consumption, investment, or government factors affecting GDP.

3. Review Figure 15-2 in the text before you read about the fiscal policy debates. The effectiveness of fiscal policy depends on whether you assume that the demand for money curve is relatively flat **and** the investment-demand curve is relatively steep (the extreme Keynesian view), or whether you assume that the demand for money curve is relatively steep **and** the investment-demand curve is relatively flat (monetarist view). It is recommended that you draw graphs of money demand and investment-demand curves with each set of assumptions to check your understanding.

SELF-TEST

■ **FILL-IN QUESTIONS**

1. The aggregate-supply curve of the classical economists is (horizontal, vertical) _____ and the aggregate-supply curve of the Keynesian economists is

_____ up to the full-employment level of output. Therefore, a decrease in aggregate demand will have no effect on the price level and will decrease output and

employment in the (classical, Keynesian) _____ model; but a decrease in aggregate demand will decrease the price level and have no effect on output and employ-

ment in the _____ model.

2. The views of classical and Keynesian economists also differ on the nature of the aggregate-demand curve.
   a. In the classical way of thinking, the money supply sets the basis for aggregate demand: if the price level falls and the money supply is constant, the purchasing

   power of money will (rise, fall) _____ and consumers and business firms will (expand, contract)

   _____ their expenditures for goods and services; aggregate demand will be reasonably stable

   if the nation's monetary authorities maintain a _____

   _____
   b. From the Keynesian perspective, aggregate demand is (stable, unstable) _____ , even if there are no changes in the supply of money, in part

   because business investment tends to be _____

3. Keynesians believe that capitalism is inherently (stable, unstable) _____ because many of its markets are (competitive, noncompetitive)

_____ , advocate (government intervention,

laissez-faire) _____ , and favor

(monetary, fiscal) _____ over _____ policy.

4. Monetarists argue that capitalism is inherently

_____ because most of its markets are

_____ , advocate _____ and favor the use of (discretionary, nondiscretionary)

_____ (monetary, fiscal) _____ policy.

5. The basic equation of the monetarists is _____

= _____

   a. This equation is called the _____

   _____
   b. Indicate below what each of the four letters in this equation represents.
   (1) **M:** _____
   (2) **V:** _____
   (3) **P:** _____
   (4) **Q:** _____

6. The basic equation of the Keynesians is $C_a + I_g + X_n + G =$ GDP.
   a. $C_a + I_g + X_n + G$ is _____ and in the equation of exchange is equal to _____
   b. Nominal GDP is equal to _____ in the equation of exchange.

7. Monetarists argue that:
   a. any increase in **M** will (increase, decrease) _____ **PQ;**
   b. in the **short run** any increase in **M** will (increase, decrease) _____ both **P** and **Q;** but
   c. in the **long run** any increase in **M** will (increase, decrease) _____ only (**P, Q**) _____

8. In the debate on the stability of **V:**
   a. monetarists argue that people have a (stable, unstable) _____ desire to hold money relative to holding other assets or to making purchases, that the amount of money people will want to hold will de-

   pend on the level of _____ and

   that **V** is, therefore, _____
   b. Keynesians contend that, in addition to a transactions demand for money, there is also a(n) _____ demand for money, that this demand is inversely re-

   lated to the _____ , and that **V** is, there-

   fore, _____

9. An increase in **M:**
   a. to the monetarist's way of thinking will

   (1) leave the public with (more, less) _____ money than it wishes to have,
   (2) induce the public to (increase, decrease)

   _____ its spending for consumer and capital goods,

   (3) which will result in a(n) _____ in nominal GDP

   (4) until the nominal GDP (or **MV**) is equal to _____

   times _____

b. to the Keynesian's way of thinking will

(1) result in a(n) _____ in the rate of interest,

(2) which will _____ the demand for money

(3) and _____ *V*

(4) and the effect on nominal GDP will be

_____

10. In short, it is the view of the:

a. monetarists that *V* (in the equation of exchange) is stable and that there is a direct relationship between

_____ and _____

b. Keynesians that *V* is (directly, inversely) _____ related to the interest rate; that the interest rate (increases, decreases) _____ when *M* increases; and that, therefore, *M* and *V* are (directly, inversely)

_____ related to each other.

11. The empirical evidence about velocity (*V*) is mixed and can support two positions:

a. The fact that there is a (strong, weak) _____ correlation between the money supply (*M*) and nominal domestic output (*PQ*) suggest that velocity (*V*) is (stable, unstable) _____. This evidence tends to support the (Keynesian, monetarist) _____ position.

b. In contrast, (Keynesians, monetarists) _____ calculate *V* by dividing *M* by _____ and find that *V* is (stable, unstable) _____. A plot of *V* with the interest rate also shows a (strong, weak) _____ correlation, which suggests that *V* is (stable, unstable)

_____. Another criticism is that the (Keynesians, monetarists) _____ were forced to change to an (*M*1, *M*2) _____ definition of velocity to correct past problems with velocity.

12. In the debate on the use of fiscal policy:

a. the Keynesians contend that the more effective tool for stabilizing the economy is (fiscal, monetary)

_____ policy; but

b. the monetarists reply that government borrowing to finance a budget deficit will (raise, lower) _____ the rate of interest and have a _____ effect on investment spending.

13. Monetarists would have the supply of money increase at the same annual rate as the potential rate of growth of

_____ and this is a rate of from _____ to _____ %.

14. Monetarists proposed the adoption of the "Monetary Rule" because they believe that discretionary monetary policy tends to (stabilize, destabilize) _____ the economy. Two important sources of the problem are irregular _____ for monetary policy to take effect and a focus on the wrong policy target of _____

15. In the

a. Keynesian model of the economy the aggregate supply curve is relatively (steep, flat) _____ and an increase in aggregate demand will have a relatively (large, small) _____ effect on the price level and a relatively _____ effect on the real domestic output.

b. monetarist model the aggregate-supply curve is relatively _____ and an increase in aggregate demand will have a relatively _____ effect on price level and a relatively _____ effect on real domestic output.

c. From the monetarist perspective, a monetary rule would keep the price level (stable, unstable) _____ because a rightward shift in the aggregate supply from economic growth would be (greater than, less than, or equal to) _____ the rightward shift of aggregate demand, but Keynesians would argue that the shift in aggregate demand with a monetary rule might be _____ or _____ the shift in aggregate supply, therefore, making the price level (stable, unstable) _____

_____

16. In the rational-expectations theory:

a. Individuals correctly anticipate the effects of any economic event or a change in public policy on the economy and make decisions based on their anticipations to maximize their own _____;

b. the markets in the economy are (noncompetitive, purely competitive) _____ and prices in these markets are perfectly (inflexible, flexible) _____; and as a result,

c. an expansionary monetary or fiscal policy will lead the public to expect (inflation, a recession) _____

_____ and they will react in a way that results in (an increase, a decrease, no change) _____ in the real output of the economy and _____ in the price level.

17. The aggregate supply curve in the RET is (vertical, horizontal) _____ and a change in aggregate demand brings about a change in (the price level, the real output) _____ and no change in _____ of the economy.

18. Proponents of the RET:
a. contend that discretionary monetary and fiscal policies are (effective, ineffective) _____; and
b. like the monetarists, favor (policy rules, discretionary policy) _____
c. however, the problems of time lags and information that reduce the ability of monetary authorities to conduct monetary policy are the reasons (monetarists, rational expectationists) _____ favor rules, whereas _____ favor them because the reaction of the public can counteract or change the intended effects of monetary policy.

19. The critics of the RET maintain that people are (less well, better) _____ informed than assumed in the theory; markets are (more, less) _____ competitive than assumed in the theory and prices are, therefore, (sticky, flexible) _____; and monetary and fiscal policies have been employed in the past to (stabilize, destabilize) _____ the economy and to expand its (real, nominal) _____ output.

20. Many ideas from monetarism and rational expectations have been absorbed into mainstream thinking about macroeconomics. For example, there is more recognition that the money supply and monetary policy are (important, unimportant) _____ , that there needs to be (less, more) _____ coordination between monetary and fiscal policy, and that _____ on the reactions of the public affect economic policies that are established for the economy.

■ **TRUE-FALSE QUESTIONS**

Circle the T if the statement is true; the F if it is false.

1. The classical view is that the aggregate supply curve is horizontal (to full-employment output).   **T F**

2. Classical economists consider the aggregate demand curve to be stable.   **T F**

3. Keynesians think that there is perfect wage flexibility, and that a change in the price level will not cause the economy to deviate from full employment.   **T F**

4. Keynesians consider investment spending to be one of the more volatile components of aggregate demand.   **T F**

5. The classical economists' view of aggregate demand is that if the money supply is constant a decrease in the price level will decrease the purchasing power of money and increase the quantities of goods and services demanded by consumers and business firms.   **T F**

6. The chief proponent of the monetarist position is Milton Friedman.   **T F**

7. The basic equations of the Keynesians and the monetarists are no more than two different ways of stating the same relationship.   **T F**

8. Most monetarists believe that an increase in the money supply will have no effect on real output and employment in either the short run or the long run.   **T F**

9. Keynesians contend that changes in the money supply will have little or no effect on the rate of interest. **T   F**

10. Keynesians also maintain that relatively small changes in the interest rate have relatively large effects on investment spending.   **T F**

11. Monetarists argue that *V* in the equation of exchange is stable and that a change in *M* will bring about a direct and proportional change in *P*.   **T F**

12. In the monetarists' analysis the demand for money is directly related to nominal GDP.   **T F**

13. From the monetarist viewpoint, the economy is in equilibrium when the amount of money firms and households want to hold is equal to the money supply.   **T F**

14. Keynesians contend that the velocity of money is unstable.   **T F**

15. In the Keynesians' analysis the demand for money is directly related to the rate of interest.   **T F**

16. Keynesians argue that a decrease in the rate of interest will decrease the velocity of money.   **T F**

17. Statistical evidence reveals that the velocity of money has remained almost constant from one year to the next.   **T F**

18. An expansionary fiscal policy will, the Keynesians contend, decrease the velocity of money.   **T F**

19. Monetarists conclude that discretionary monetary policy has resulted in macroeconomic instability.   **T F**

20. Monetarists and Keynesians would agree that expansionary stabilization policies will produce demand-pull inflation in the vertical range of the aggregate supply curve. **T F**

21. According to Keynesians, a monetary rule would help promote price stability in the economy. **T F**

22. Rational-expectations theory assumes that both product and resource markets are uncompetitive and that wages and prices are "sticky." **T F**

23. Economists who have advanced the rational-expectations theory argue that discretionary fiscal and monetary policies have helped to stabilize the economy. **T F**

24. Most economists are proponents of the rational-expectations theory. **T F**

25. A legacy of rational expectations is that economists and policy makers are more sensitive about how expectations might affect the outcome of a policy change. **T F**

■ **MULTIPLE-CHOICE QUESTIONS**

Circle the letter that corresponds to the best answer.

1. The Keynesian aggregate-supply curve:
(a) is horizontal (to full-employment output)
(b) slopes upward
(c) is vertical
(d) slopes downward

2. The aggregate-supply curve of classical economists:
(a) is horizontal (to full-employment output)
(b) slopes upward
(c) is vertical
(d) slopes downward

3. In the classical theory of employment a decrease in aggregate demand results in:
(a) a decrease in both the price level and domestic output
(b) a decrease in the price level and no change in domestic output
(c) no change in the price level and a decrease in domestic output
(d) no change in either the price level or domestic output

4. A decrease in aggregate demand, in the Keynesian theory of employment, results in:
(a) a decrease in both the price level and domestic output
(b) a decrease in the price level and no change in domestic output
(c) no change in the price level and a decrease in domestic output
(d) no change in either the price level or domestic output

5. Classical theory concludes that the production behavior of firms will not change when the price level:
(a) decreases because input costs would rise along with product prices to leave real profits and output unchanged
(b) decreases because input costs would fall but product price would rise, offsetting any change in real profits or output
(c) increases because input costs would fall along with product prices to leave real profits and output unchanged
(d) increases because input costs would rise along with product prices to leave real profits and output unchanged

6. Keynesians:
(a) believe capitalism is inherently stable
(b) believe the markets in a capitalistic economy are highly competitive
(c) argue against the use of discretionary monetary policy
(d) contend that government intervention in the economy is desirable

7. Monetarists
(a) argue for the use of discretionary monetary policy
(b) contend that government policies have reduced the stability of the economy
(c) believe a capitalistic economy is inherently unstable
(d) believe the markets in a capitalistic economy are largely noncompetitive

8. Which of the following is *not* true?
(a) MV is total spending
(b) PQ is the real GDP
(c) PQ is nominal GDP
(d) $MV = C_a + I_g + X_n + G$

9. If V in the equation of exchange is constant, an increase in M will necessarily increase:
(a) P
(b) Q
(c) both P and Q
(d) P times Q

10. When nominal gross domestic product (GDP) is divided by the money supply (M), then you will obtain the:
(a) income velocity of money
(b) monetary multiplier
(c) equation of exchange
(d) monetary rule

11. Monetarists argue that velocity is stable and that the amount of money the public will want to hold depends primarily on the level of:
(a) nominal GDP
(b) investment

(c) consumption
(d) prices

12. From the monetarist viewpoint, an increase in the supply of money will:
(a) raise the rate of interest
(b) increase spending for consumer and capital goods
(c) increase the asset demand for money
(d) increase the demand for government securities

13. Keynesians argue that:
(a) the only demand for money is the asset demand
(b) the only demand for money is the transactions demand
(c) there is no transactions demand
(d) there is both a transactions and an asset demand for money

14. From the Keynesian viewpoint, an increase in supply of money will:
(a) raise the rate of interest
(b) decrease spending for consumer and capital goods
(c) increase the asset demand for money
(d) decrease the demand for government securities

15. Which of the following would be considered as evidence for the monetarist position that velocity is stable?
(a) a strong correlation between the velocity of money and the interest rate
(b) a strong correlation between the money supply and nominal domestic output
(c) the use of *M*2 to define velocity rather than *M*1
(d) cyclical and secular changes in velocity as the economy changes

16. The crowding-out effect is the effect of borrowing funds to finance a government deficit on:
(a) imports into the economy
(b) the money supply
(c) investment spending
(d) consumer expenditures

17. Keynesians contend that borrowing to finance a government deficit incurred in order to increase employment and output in the economy will:
(a) have little or no effect on the rate of interest
(b) have little or no effect on investment spending
(c) have a significant effect on *Q* in the equation of exchange
(d) have all of the above effects

18. From a monetarist perspective, two important sources of monetary mismanagement are:
(a) cyclical variations and secular trends in the economy
(b) monetary rules and a constant velocity
(c) irregular time lags and interest rates as the wrong policy target

(d) a flat demand for money curve and a steep investment demand curve

19. The rule suggested by the monetarists is that the money supply should be increased at the same rate as:
(a) the price level
(b) the interest rate
(c) the velocity of money
(d) the potential growth in real GDP

20. In the monetarist model:
(a) the aggregate-supply curve is very steep and an increase in aggregate demand will have little or no effect on the price level
(b) the aggregate-supply curve is nearly flat and an increase in aggregate demand will have little or no effect on the price level
(c) the aggregate-supply curve is very steep and an increase in aggregate demand will have a large effect on the price level
(d) the aggregate-supply curve is nearly flat and an increase in aggregate demand will have a large effect on the price level

21. In the Keynesian model:
(a) the aggregate-supply curve is very steep and an increase in aggregate demand will have a large effect on real domestic output
(b) the aggregate-supply curve is nearly flat and an increase in aggregate demand will have a large effect on real domestic output
(c) the aggregate-supply curve is very steep and an increase in aggregate demand will have little or no effect on real domestic output
(d) the aggregate-supply curve is nearly flat and an increase in aggregate demand will have little or no effect on real domestic output

22. Which perspective would be most closely associated with the view that discretionary monetary policy is ineffective because of policy errors and timing problems?
(a) monetarism
(b) Keynesianism
(c) rational expectations
(d) new classical economics

23. In the rational-expectations theory:
(a) individuals understand how the economy works and can correctly anticipate the effects of an event or a change in public policy on the economy
(b) the markets in the economy are purely competitive
(c) individuals, to maximize their own self-interests, respond to any expansionary fiscal or monetary policy in a way that prevents an increase in real output and fosters an increase in the price level
(d) all of the above are true

24. In the rational-expectations model, an increase in aggregate demand will:

(a) increase the price level and have no effect on real domestic output
(b) increase real domestic output and have no effect on the price level
(c) increase both the price level and the real domestic output
(d) have none of the above effects

25. To stabilize the economy rational-expectations theorists favor the use of:
(a) price controls
(b) discretionary fiscal policy
(c) discretionary monetary policy
(d) policy rules

26. The contention that changes in the money supply cause direct and predictable changes in aggregate demand and therefore changes in nominal GDP would be most closely associated with the view of:
(a) Keynesians
(b) monetarists
(c) new classical economists
(d) rational-expectations economists

27. Proponents of rational expectations argue that people:
(a) are not as rational as they are assumed to be by monetarists
(b) tend to make perfect forecasts, which frustrates policy makers
(c) have considerable knowledge about policy decisions and their impacts, which limits the effects of policies
(d) do not respond quickly to changes in wages and prices, causing a misallocation of resources in the economy

28. The idea that the Federal Reserve should follow a monetary rule would find the most support from which combination?
(a) Keynesians and monetarists
(b) RET economists and Keynesians
(c) RET economists and monetarists
(d) classical economists and Keynesians

29. A distinguishing feature of the rational expectations in the aggregate demand–aggregate supply model would be an aggregate:
(a) demand curve that is downward sloping
(b) demand curve that is vertical
(c) supply curve that is vertical
(d) supply curve that is horizontal

30. Which of the following would be an example of an idea from monetarism or rational expectations which has been absorbed into mainstream macroeconomics?
(a) the importance of government spending, taxation, and fiscal policy

(b) the importance of the money supply and monetary policy
(c) the building of macro foundations for microeconomics
(d) the emphasis on discretion rather than rules for guiding economic policy

■ PROBLEMS

1. You must imagine that you are a monetarist in this problem and assume that **V** is stable and equal to 4. In the table below is the aggregate supply schedule: the real output **Q** which producers will offer for sale at seven different price levels **P**.

P	Q	PQ	MV
$1.00	100	$_____	$_____
2.00	110	_____	_____
3.00	120	_____	_____
4.00	130	_____	_____
5.00	140	_____	_____
6.00	150	_____	_____
7.00	160	_____	_____

a. Compute and enter in the table above the seven values of **PQ**.
b. Assume **M** is $90. Enter the values of **MV** on each of the seven lines in the table. The equilibrium

(1) nominal domestic output (**PQ** or **MV**) is $_____

(2) price level is $_____

(3) real domestic output (**Q**) is $_____
c. When **M** increases to $175, **MV** at each price level

is $_____; and the equilibrium

(1) nominal domestic output is $_____

(2) price level is $_____

(3) real domestic output is $_____

2. In this problem you are a Keynesian. The left side of the table on the next page shows the amounts of money firms and households wish to have for transactions at different levels of nominal GDP. The right side of the table shows the amounts of money they want to have as assets at different rates of interest.
a. Suppose the nominal GDP is $500, the interest is 7%, and the supply of money is $125.

Nominal GDP	Transactions demand	Interest rate	Asset demand
$ 500	$ 50	7.0%	$ 75
600	60	6.8	80
700	70	6.6	85
800	80	6.4	90
900	90	6.2	95
1000	100	6.0	100

(1) The amount of money demanded for transactions

is $_____

(2) The amount of money demanded as an asset is

$_____

(3) The total amount of money demanded for both pur-

poses is $_____

(4) The amount of money firms and households wish to have is (greater than, less than, equal to)

_____ the amount of money they ac-

tually have.

(5) The velocity of money (equal to nominal GDP di-

vided by the supply of money) is _____

b. Assume the Federal Reserve Banks expand the supply of money to $160 by purchasing securities in the open market; and that as a result the rate of interest falls to 6% and the nominal GDP rises to $600.

(1) The amount of money demanded for transactions

is now $_____ and the amount demanded

as an asset is now $_____

(2) The total amount of money demanded is

$_____ and the amount of money the

public wishes to have is _____ the amount of money they actually have.

(3) The velocity of money is _____

c. Suppose the Federal government pursues an expansionary fiscal policy which raises the nominal GDP from $600 to $800 and the interest rate from 6% to 6.8%, and the money supply remains at $160.

(1) The transactions demand for money is

$_____ , the asset demand

is $_____ , and the total de-

mand is $_____

(2) The velocity of money is _____

d. The effect of the easy money policy was to (in-

crease, decrease) _____ the velocity of money and the effect of the expansionary fiscal pol-

icy was to _____ it.

3. On the graph that follows are three aggregate-supply curves: S_1, S_2, and S_3.

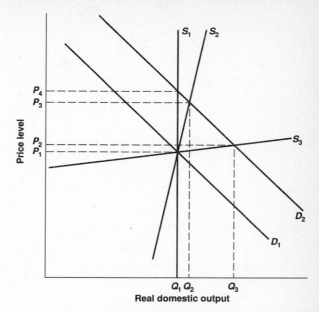

a. S_1 is the (Keynesian, monetarist, rational-expecta-

tions) _____ supply curve, S_2 is

the _____ supply curve, and S_3 is

the _____ supply curve.

b. Regardless of which is the economy's supply curve, if the aggregate-demand curve is D_1, the equilibrium

real domestic output is _____ and

the equilibrium price level is _____

c. Should aggregate demand increase from D_1 to D_2 in the

(1) monetarist model the equilibrium real domestic output would (increase, decrease, remain constant)

_____ to (at) _____ and the equilibrium price level would (increase, de-

crease, remain constant) _____

to (at) _____;

(2) Keynesian model the equilibrium real domestic out-

put would _____ to (at)

_____ and the equilibrium price level

would _____ to (at)

_____;

(3) rational-expectations model the equilibrium real do-

mestic output would _____ to

(at) _____ and the equilibrium price

level would _____ to (at)

_____

■ SHORT ANSWER AND ESSAY QUESTIONS

1. What is the difference between the classical and Keynesian aggregate supply curve? Draw a graph showing the difference. What is the justification for each viewpoint?

2. What is the effect of a decrease in aggregate demand on the price level and real domestic output in the classical and Keynesian model? Show the change in a graph.

3. Why did classical economists consider the aggregate demand curve to be stable? What is the response of Keynesians to this position?

4. Why does the classical aggregate demand curve have a native (downward) slope?

5. How do the views of Keynesians and monetarists on the competitiveness of capitalistic economies, their stability, and the need for government intervention in the economy differ?

6. What is the basic equation of the Keynesians and the basic equation of the monetarists? Define all terms in both equations and explain how the Keynesian equation can be converted to the monetarist equation.

7. Why do Keynesians believe that monetary policy is an "uncertain, unreliable, and weak stabilization tool as compared to fiscal policy"?

8. Explain how a change in *M* in the equation of exchange will, to the monetarist way of thinking, affect
  (a) *P* times *Q*,
  (b) *P* and *Q* in the short run, and
  (c) *P* and *Q* in the long run.

9. Explain the differences between the monetarist and Keynesian views on why firms and households demand money (or liquid balances); on what determines the demand for money; and the stability, therefore, of the velocity of money.

10. Suppose firms and households, because of an increase in the money supply, find themselves with more money than they wish to have. What do the monetarists believe they will do with this excess money? What effect will this have on the velocity of money and nominal GDP?

11. Suppose the supply of money increases. What do Keynesians believe will happen to the rate of interest, the amount of money firms and households will wish to hold, planned investment spending, and to the nominal GDP?

12. What empirical evidence is there to support the Keynesian contention that *V* is unstable or the monetarist contention that it is relatively stable?

13. Why do the Keynesians advocate and the monetarists reject the use of fiscal policy to stabilize the economy?

14. What is the monetary rule? Why do monetarists suggest this rule to replace discretionary monetary policy?

15. How do the aggregate demand-aggregate supply models of the Keynesians and monetarists differ? What effect will an expansionary monetary or fiscal policy have upon real domestic output and the price level in each of these models?

16. Use the aggregate demand-aggregate supply model to explain monetarist and Keynesian views of the use of a monetary rule for an expanding economy.

17. In as few words as possible, explain how and why rational-expectations theorists believe firms, workers, and consumers will respond to an expansionary monetary or fiscal policy; and how these responses make the policy ineffective and promote economic instability.

18. How will an expansionary monetary or fiscal policy affect real domestic output and the price level in the rational-expectations theorists' aggregate demand-aggregate supply model? Why does it have these effects?

19. What criticisms have been made of the RET by its opponents?

20. What influence has monetarism and rational expectations had on mainstream macroeconomic theory and policy? Give three examples of ideas that have changed mainstream thinking.

ANSWERS

Chapter 16 Alternative Views on Macro Theory and Policy

FILL-IN QUESTIONS

1. vertical, horizontal, Keynesian, classical

2. *a.* rise, expand, constant supply of money; *b.* unstable, unstable

3. unstable, noncompetitive, government intervention, fiscal, monetary

4. stable, competitive, laissez faire, nondiscretionary, monetary

5. *MV = PQ; a.* equation of exchange; *b.* (1) the money supply, (2) the (income or circuit) velocity of money, (3) the average price of each unit of physical output, (4) the physical volume of goods and services produced

6. *a.* total spending (aggregate demand), *MV; b. PQ*

7. *a.* increase; *b.* increase; *c.* increase, *P*

8. *a.* stable, nominal GDP, stable; *b.* asset, interest rate, unstable

9. *a.* (1) more, (2) increase, (3) increase, (4) *P, Q; b.* (1) decrease, (2) increase, (3) decrease, (4) uncertain

10. *a.* **M, PQ;** *b.* directly, decreases, inversely

11. *a.* strong, stable, monetarists; *b.* Keynesians, GDP, unstable, strong, unstable, monetarists, **M**2

12. *a.* fiscal; *b.* raise, crowding-out

13. real GDP, 3, 5

14. destabilize, time lags, interest rates

15. *a.* flat, small, large; *b.* steep, large, small; *c.* stable, equal to, less than, greater than (either order), unstable

16. *a.* self-interests; *b.* purely competitive, flexible; *c.* inflation, no change, an increase

17. vertical, the price level, the real output

18. *a.* ineffective; *b.* policy rules; *c.* monetarists, rational expectationists

19. less well, less, sticky, stabilize, real

20. important, more, expectations

TRUE-FALSE QUESTIONS

1. F, p. 318   **8.** F, p. 322   **15.** F, p. 323 **22.** F, pp. 330-331
2. T, p. 318   **9.** T, pp. 321-322 **16.** T, p. 323 **23.** F, p. 331
3. F, p. 319   **10.** F, p. 322   **17.** F, p. 325 **24.** F, p. 333
4. T, p. 319   **11.** F, pp. 322-323 **18.** F, p. 327 **25.** T, p. 334
5. F, p. 318   **12.** T, p. 323   **19.** T, p. 327
6. T, p. 317   **13.** T, p. 323   **20.** T, p. 329
7. T, p. 321   **14.** T, p. 323   **21.** F, p. 330

MULTIPLE-CHOICE QUESTIONS

1. *a*, p. 319   **9.** *d*, p. 320   **17.** *d*, p. 327   **25.** *d*, p. 332
2. *c*, p. 318   **10.** *a*, p. 323   **18.** *c*, pp. 327-328 **26.** *b*, p. 323
3. *b*, p. 318   **11.** *a*, p. 323   **19.** *d*, p. 328   **27.** *c*, p. 331
4. *c*, p. 319   **12.** *b*, p. 323   **20.** *c*, p. 328   **28.** *c*, pp. 331-332
5. *d*, p. 318   **13.** *d*, p. 323   **21.** *b*, p. 328   **29.** *c*, pp. 331-332
6. *d*, p. 319   **14.** *c*, p. 323   **22.** *a*, pp. 327-328 **30.** *b*, pp. 333-334
7. *b*, p. 318   **15.** *b*, p. 325   **23.** *d*, pp. 330-331
8. *b*, p. 320   **16.** *c*, p. 326   **24.** *a*, pp. 331-332

PROBLEMS

1. *a.* 100, 220, 360, 520, 700, 900, 1120; *b.* 360, 360, 360, 360, 360, 360, 360, (1) 360, (2) 3.00, (3) 120; *c.* 700, (1) 700, (2) 5.00, (3) 140

2. *a.* (1) 50, (2) 75, (3) 125, (4) equal to, (5) 4; *b.* (1) 60, 100, (2) 160, equal to, (3) 3.75; *c.* (1) 80, 80, 160, (2) 5; *d.* decrease, increase

3. *a.* rational-expectations, monetarist, Keynesian; *b.* Q_1, P_1; *c.* (1) increase, Q_2, increase, P_3, (2) increase, Q_3, increase, P_2, (3) remain constant, Q_1, increase, P_4

SHORT ANSWER AND ESSAY QUESTIONS

1. pp. 318-319 **6.** pp. 320-321 **11.** p. 323   **16.** pp. 329-330
2. pp. 318-319 **7.** pp. 321-322 **12.** pp. 324-326 **17.** pp. 330-331
3. pp. 318-319 **8.** p. 323   **13.** pp. 326-327 **18.** pp. 331-332
4. pp. 318-319 **9.** pp. 323-325 **14.** p. 328   **19.** pp. 332-333
5. p. 320   **10.** p. 323   **15.** pp. 328-329 **20.** pp. 333-334

CHAPTER 17

The Inflation-Unemployment Relationship

This chapter continues the discussion of alternative perspectives of macroeconomic theory and policy by examining the explanations for the simultaneous presence of unemployment and inflation in the United States economy. The mainstream or Keynesian views of the relationship between unemployment and inflation during the past three decades as embodied in the **Phillips Curve** are contrasted with new classical economics, with its natural rate hypothesis and the distinction made between the short-run and long-run aggregate-supply curve. The chapter also presents other policy options for dealing with inflation and unemployment and introduces the perspective of supply-side economics.

In the early 1960s most economists believed that it was possible for the American economy to have both full employment and stable prices. This belief was based on the assumption that the price level would not rise until the labor force was fully employed. All that was necessary for full employment without inflation was just the right level of aggregate expenditures. Fiscal and monetary policy, thought Keynesian economists, could be used to assume the aggregate demand was adequate but not excessive.

But the assumption underlying this simplest Keynesian model was not realistic. The price level can rise before full employment is achieved; and the closer the economy moves to full employment the greater the rate at which prices rise. This observation became the basis for the concept of an unemployment-inflation rate tradeoff and its menu of policy choices as described in the supposedly stable Phillips Curve. According to Keynesians, the reason for inflation before full employment and for the Phillips Curve is that some types of labor become fully employed before other types of labor, and possibly also the market power of businesses and unions to raise prices and wages.

While this apparent unemployment-inflation rate tradeoff created a policy dilemma for economists of the 1960s, the situation and the problem became much more complicated in the 1970s and early 1980s. The problem was **stagflation,** with rising prices and rising unemployment rates. Keynesians explained stagflation of the period by citing events that produced aggregate-supply shocks, decreasing the aggregate-supply curve and driving up the

price level and reducing real output and employment. The leftward shift in the aggregate-supply curve caused the Phillips Curve to move to the right; hence the occurrence of both rising prices and unemployment. The events of the 1982–1989 period shifted the aggregate-supply curve rightward again and the Phillips Curve to the left, or so the Keynesian view went.

An alternative explanation of the events of the 1970s and 1980s came from the **natural rate hypothesis** of new classical economics. The two variants of this hypothesis were those of **adaptive-expectations** and **rational-expectations** theorists. Both adaptive- and rational-expectations theorists contend that the downsloping Phillips Curve is a figment of Keynesian imagination; that it is actually a vertical line; and that government attempts to reduce the unemployment rate below the rate at which the vertical Phillips Curve meets the horizontal axis produce a higher rate of inflation. The major difference between the adaptive expectationists and rational expectationists is that the former believe that expansionary monetary or fiscal policies can bring about a temporary decline in the unemployment rate; the latter argue that such policies do not even reduce unemployment temporarily, and any short-term instability in the macro economy is a product of price-level surprises.

New classical economists also distinguish between **a short-run and a long-run aggregate-supply curve.** In the short run, nominal wages are fixed so an increase in the price level increases business profits and real output. In the long run, nominal wages are flexible so business profits and employment return to their original level, making the long-run aggregate supply curve vertical at the potential level of real output. Keynesians question the speed of these adjustments because of the downward inflexibility of wages and prices and hold that there are opportunities for the use of stabilization policies to reduce the high cost of unemployment or inflation.

The distinction between the short-run and long-run aggregate-supply curve requires a reinterpretation of **demand-pull and cost-push inflation.** Although demand-pull inflation will increase the price level and real output in the short run, once nominal wages increase, the temporary increase in output will be gone, but the price level will be higher at the potential level of output for the economy.

Cost-push inflation will increase the price level and decrease real output in the short run, but again, once nominal wages fall, output and the price level will return to the original level. If policy makers try to counter cost-push inflation by increasing aggregate demand, they may make matters worse by increasing the price level and causing the short-run aggregate-supply curve to decrease again.

Other solutions for stagflation have been sought by the United States and other mixed market economies. Discussed in the chapter are employment and training policy and **wage-price policies** that have been used to correct aspects of the unemployment and inflation problem. Of more recent appeal, however, was **supply-side economics,** which gained visibility during the Reagan administration (1981–1989). Supply-side economists pointed to the role of the Federal government in causing the slump in productivity and economic growth in the economy during the 1970s. The solutions, which became the program of Reaganomics, were to come from massive reduction in personal and corporate income taxes, reduced government regulation, cuts in social and welfare spending by government, and control over the rate of growth of the money supply. Despite its successes, this program and supply-side economics have been criticized, especially for the failure of the large cuts in the tax rates to increase significantly the aggregate-supply curve beyond its historical level.

The chapter concludes with a recap of the alternative macroeconomic theories and policies presented in this and the previous chapter.

■ CHECKLIST

When you have studied this chapter you should be able to:

☐ Explain how early Keynesian analysis was able to conclude that the economy could achieve both full employment and stable prices; and what was needed to reach these two goals simultaneously.

☐ Draw a traditional Phillips Curve (after properly labeling the two axes); and explain how to derive this curve by using the aggregate demand–aggregate supply model.

☐ State the two basic causes of the inflation shown on the Phillips Curve.

☐ Explain and use the Phillips Curve to illustrate the stabilization policy dilemma.

☐ Define stagflation; and contrast stagflation with the relationship shown by a Phillips Curve.

☐ Enumerate the supply-side shocks experienced by the American economy in the 1970s and early 1980s; and use the aggregate demand–aggregate supply model to explain why these shocks led to stagflation.

☐ List the events that contributed to stagflation's demise during the 1982–1989 period.

☐ Describe the Keynesians view of the Phillips Curve from 1960 to 1989.

☐ Explain the natural rate hypothesis and the two variants of this hypothesis—adaptive expectations and rational expectations.

☐ Use the adaptive expectations model to explain the process of inflation and disinflation in the economy.

☐ Compare and contrast how adaptive expectations and rational expectations theorists view the Phillips Curve.

☐ Distinguish the short-run aggregate-supply curve from the long-run aggregate-supply curve.

☐ Compare and contrast Keynesian and new classical perspectives of stabilization policy.

☐ Apply the distinction between the short-run and long-run aggregate-supply curve to explain demand-pull and cost-push inflation.

☐ Describe how employment and training policy works to combat cost-push inflation.

☐ Distinguish between wage-price guideposts and wage-price controls; and explain why they are called income policies.

☐ Explain what the advocates of supply-side economics saw as the three tax-transfer disincentives in the American economy.

☐ Explain the hypothesized relationship between tax rates and tax revenues as suggested by the Laffer Curve.

☐ State three criticisms of the Laffer Curve.

☐ Describe two other tenets of supply-side economics.

☐ Explain the four economic policies of the Reagan administration to deal with stagflation.

☐ Evaluate the program of the Reagan administration (Reaganomics) and the effectiveness of that program.

☐ Summarize the alternative macroeconomic theories and policies of various issues.

■ CHAPTER OUTLINE

1. In the simple Keynesian model of aggregate demand and aggregate supply, an assumption is made that the aggregate-supply curve is shaped as a reverse "L" with a horizontal (Keynesian) range and a vertical (classical) range.

  a. With this basic model, the economy may realize either unemployment or inflation, but not both problems simultaneously. The stagflation episodes of the 1970s showed this conclusion to be incorrect.

  b. The model can be revised to account for the events of the 1970s by including an upsloping portion in the intermediate range of the aggregate-supply curve and by allowing the aggregate-supply curve to shift left.

2. If aggregate supply is constant and the economy is operating in the intermediate range on the aggregate-supply curve, the greater the rate of increase in aggregate demand the greater is the rate of increase in the price level and in real output, and the lower is the rate of unemployment (and **vice versa**); and there is, therefore, an inverse relationship (or tradeoff) called the Phillips Curve between the inflation rate and the unemployment rate.

a. There are at least two reasons why inflation occurs before the economy reaches full employment.

(1) Scarcities of some kinds of labor develop before the economy's entire labor force is fully employed; and these scarcities increase wage rates, production costs, and prices.

(2) Labor unions and business firms have market power and they raise wage rates and prices as the economy approaches full employment.

b. While fiscal and monetary policy can be employed to manage aggregate demand and to affect unemployment and the rate of inflation, the nation faces a serious policy dilemma; full employment without inflation and price stability without unemployment are impossible and the nation must choose one of the combinations of inflation and unemployment that lies on the Phillips Curve.

c. Events in the 1960s seemed to confirm the inverse relationship between the unemployment and inflation rates.

3. Events of the 1970s and 1980s, however, called into question the stability of the Phillips Curve:

a. In the 1970s and early 1980s the American economy experienced both higher rates of inflation and greater unemployment rates; and this stagflation suggests either that there is no dependable relationship between the inflation and unemployment rates or that the Phillips Curve had shifted to the right.

(1) During these years six cost- or supply-side shocks decreased aggregate supply (moved the aggregate-supply curve left) to increase both prices and unemployment in the United States; and the experiences of the American economy suggest that the Phillips Curve is not a stable relationship and cannot be used as the basis for economic policy.

(2) The demise of stagflation came in the 1982–1989 period because of a variety of factors; but unemployment and inflation moved in the same direction at times, not in the opposite direction implied by the Phillips Curve of the 1960s.

b. The Keynesian view is that a tradeoff between unemployment and inflation does exist; the explanation for the data problems were the supply shocks that produced a rightward shift in the Phillips Curve during the 1971–1982 period, and changes in the economy that produced a leftward shift during the 1982–1989 period.

4. The natural rate hypothesis questions the existence of a downsloping Phillips Curve and views the economy as stable in the long run at the natural rate of unemployment. There are two variants to this hypothesis:

a. The theory of adaptive expectations suggests that an increase in aggregate demand sponsored by government may temporarily reduce unemployment as the

price level increases and profits expand, but the actions also set into motion other events:

(1) The increase in the price level reduces the real wages of workers who demand and obtain higher nominal wages; these actions return unemployment to its original level.

(2) Back at the original level, there is now a higher actual and expected rate of inflation for the economy, so the short-run Phillips Curve has shifted upward.

(3) The process is repeated when government tries again to reduce unemployment and the rise in the price level accelerates as the short-run Phillips Curve shifts upward.

(4) In the long run, the Phillips Curve is stable only as a vertical line at the natural rate of unemployment; there is no tradeoff between unemployment and inflation.

b. Rational expectations theory assumes that workers fully anticipate that government policies to reduce unemployment will also be inflationary, and they increase their nominal wage demands to offset the expected inflation; thus there will not even be a temporary decline in unemployment, or even a short-run Phillips Curve.

5. The aggregate-supply curve has short- and long-run characteristics, and implications for policy:

a. In the short run, where nominal wages are fixed, the aggregate-supply curve is upward sloping: an increase in the price level will increase profits and cause a rise in real output; in contrast, when the price level decreases, profits are reduced and so is real output.

b. In the long run, where nominal wages are variable, the aggregate-supply curve is vertical at the potential level of output: increases in the price level will increase nominal wages and cause a shift to the left in the short-run aggregate-supply curve; or declines in the price level reduce nominal wages and shift the short-run aggregate-supply curve to the right; but in either case, although the price level changes, output returns to its potential level, so the long-run aggregate supply curve is vertical.

c. Proponents of new classical economics subscribe to the view that with flexible nominal wages the economy is basically stable at the full-employment level of output in the long run, and thus there is no need for policy actions; modern Keynesians contend that nominal wages may be slow to adjust to price level changes and support the use of stabilization policies to reduce unemployment or inflation costs to the economy.

6. Knowledge of the short- and long-run features of aggregate supply provide insights into these types of inflation:

a. Demand-pull inflation will shift the aggregate-demand curve, which increases the price level and causes a temporary increase in real output; but in the long run, nominal wages will increase and the short-run aggregate supply will shift to the left, resulting in an even higher price level with real output returning to its previous level.

b. Cost-push inflation will shift the short-run aggregate supply curve left:

(1) this action increases the price level and temporarily decreases real output;

(2) the resulting recession will reduce nominal wages, shifting the short-run aggregate supply to its original position;

(3) but if government takes actions to counter the cost-push inflation and recession by shifting aggregate demand, the price level will move to an even higher level.

c. The aggregate supply curve is vertical in the long run.

7. Because of the ineffectiveness of demand-management policies in coping with stagflation, the American economy has sought other kinds of policies to prevent decreases in or to increase aggregate supply (to shift the Phillips Curve to the left).

a. Employment and training policy has been used to reduce the scarcities of particular kinds of labor that occur before the labor force is fully employed.

b. Wage-price (or incomes) policies restrict increases in wages and prices by utilizing either guideposts or controls.

(1) Wage-price guideposts are voluntary restraints.

(2) Wage-price controls are mandatory (or legal) restraints.

(3) Whether to employ wage-price policies has been a vigorously debated issue; and the proponents and opponents have based their arguments on the questions of workability and compliance and allocative efficiency.

8. Supply-side economists argue that mainstream economics has overemphasized aggregate demand and neglected aggregate supply in explaining changes in the price level and unemployment.

a. They argue that high marginal tax rates and a widespread system for public transfer payments reduce incentives to work, and that high taxes also reduce incentives to save and to invest; these policies lead to a misallocation of resources, less productivity, and a decrease in aggregate supply.

b. To increase aggregate supply, and thus decrease inflation and increase employment, supply-side economists call for a cut in marginal tax rates.

(1) The Laffer Curve suggests in theory that it is possible to lower tax rates and increase tax revenues, thus avoiding a budget deficit because the policies will result in less tax evasion and reduced transfer payments.

(2) Critics of supply-side economics and the Laffer Curve suggest that the policy of cutting tax rates will not work because:

(a) It has only a small or uncertain effect on incentives to work (on aggregate supply);

(b) it would increase aggregate demand relative to aggregate supply and thus reinforce inflation when there is full-employment and also add to an existing budget deficit;

(c) the expected tax revenues from tax rate cuts depend on assumptions about the position on the Laffer Curve; if tax cuts reduce tax revenues, it only contributes to problems with an existing budget deficit.

c. There are two other tenets of supply-side economics:

(1) Taxes are a "wedge" between the cost of resources and the price of a product. This cost ultimately gets passed on to consumers in the form of higher prices, and shifts the aggregate-supply curve to the left.

(2) Overregulation of the economy by government has decreased productivity and led to higher costs.

d. The economic program of the Reagan administration (1981–1989) or "Reaganomics" was based on supply-side ideas:

(1) The program called for a reduction in almost all government spending (except defense expenditures), less government regulation of private businesses, restricting the growth in the money supply to prevent inflation, and cuts in personal and corporate income tax rates.

(2) The record shows that by the late 1980s there was a reduction in inflation and interest rates, an economic expansion, and the achievement of full employment, but most economists do not attribute this success to supply-side economics but to other factors and they point to other problems with the program.

(a) The reduction in inflation came not from tax cuts and other supply-side policies but from a tight monetary policy of the Federal Reserve in the 1980s that produced a severe recession in the 1980–1982 period (reducing aggregate demand), and from a drop in oil prices in the mid-1980s.

(b) The tax cuts of the 1980s increased the budget deficit and stimulated economic expansion from the demand side; they also crowded-out investment and caused problems in exporting and importing industries.

(c) Little evidence is found that the tax cuts increased saving or investment, or provided strong incentives to work, and thus did not shift aggregate supply.

9. Table 17-1 contains a recap of the differences among Keynesianism, monetarism, rational expectations, and supply-side economics on various issues discussed in this chapter and previous chapters.

■ **IMPORTANT TERMS**

Phillips Curve

Stagflation

Aggregate-supply shocks

Inflationary expectations

Natural-rate hypothesis

Adaptive expectations theory

Rational expectations theory

Short-run aggregate-
supply curve

Long-run aggregate-
supply curve

Disinflation

New classical economics

Price-level surprises

Demand-pull inflation

Cost-push inflation

Employment and training
policy

Wage-price guideposts

Wage-price controls

Incomes policies

Supply-side economics

Laffer Curve

Tax "wedge"

Reaganomics

■ **HINTS AND TIPS**

1. Chapter 17 is a longer and more difficult chapter because several new economic theories and graphs are
presented. Spend extra time mastering the material, but
don't try to read everything at once. The best way to
achieve that objective is to break your studying into four
parts and master each section. Also, practice drawing
each new figure in the chapter and explain to yourself
what each graph means.

a. First, learn about the ***Phillips Curve*** and its recent
history. Identify the tradeoffs in the curve. Explain what
happens when the curve shifts.

b. Second, use Figure 17-5 to understand the ***natural
rate hypothesis*** and its two variants—adaptive expectations and rational expectations.

c. Third, learn the distinction between the ***short-run***
and ***long-run aggregate supply*** curves (see Figure
17-6), then use the ideas to explain demand-pull or
cost-push inflation (see Figure 17-7).

d. Fourth, try to learn how the three types of economic
policies—employment and training policy, wage-price
(incomes) policies, and supply-side economies—might
be helpful for reducing stagflation in the economy.

2. Table 17-1 is an excellent table for you to use for reviewing your understanding of the four different economic
theories and the associated views on seven issues.

SELF-TEST

■ **FILL-IN QUESTIONS**

1. In the simplest Keynesian view, the price level of the
economy would not increase until the economy reached

_____ and inflation was the result of
(excess, insufficient) _____ aggregate
demand; and the economy can have (either, both)
_____ unemployment and/or inflation.

2. In the aggregate demand–aggregate supply model,
when the economy is producing in the intermediate range
along the aggregate-supply curve:

a. An increase in aggregate demand will (increase, decrease) _____ real output and employ-
ment.

b. A decrease in aggregate supply will _____
real output and employment.

3. If aggregate supply remains constant, along the intermediate range of aggregate supply:

a. the greater the increase in aggregate demand, the
(greater, smaller) _____ will be the increase
in the price level, the _____ will be the increase in real output, and the _____ will
be the unemployment rate;

b. there will be a(n) (direct, inverse) _____
relationship between the rate of inflation and the unemployment rate.

4. When prices rise before _____

_____ ,
this is the result of the market power of _____
and _____ and of imbalances or bottlenecks in
_____ markets.

5. The Phillips Curve:

a. is the relationship between the annual rate of increase in the _____ and the
_____ rate;

b. has a (positive, negative) _____
slope.

6. The stabilization policy dilemma faced by the American economy is that:

a. to have full employment it must also have
_____ and to have stable prices it must
tolerate _____

b. to reduce the unemployment rate, the rate of inflation must (increase, decrease) _____
and to reduce the rate of inflation the unemployment
rate must _____

7. Policies to manage aggregate demand can be used
to (shift the, select a point on the) _____
Phillips Curve, but such policies do not improve the "unemployment rate-inflation rate" _____

8. List the six factors (supply-side shocks) that shifted the Phillips Curve to the right after 1972 according to Keynesian economists.

a. _____

b. _____

c. _____

d. _____

e. _____

f. _____

9. In the equation that relates unit labor costs to nominal wage rates and the productivity of labor:

a. If the rate at which nominal wages increases is greater than the rate at which productivity increases, unit labor costs will (increase, decrease) _____

b. If the productivity of labor decreases and nominal wage rates are constant, unit labor costs will

_____

10. The expectation of inflation by workers and employers leads to (higher, lower) _____ wage rates and in turn to a (rise, fall) _____ in production costs, to a(n) (increase, decrease) _____ in aggregate supply, to a (higher, lower) _____ price level, and to a _____ rate of unemployment in the economy.

11. The rising unemployment rates and the sharp inflation following the supply-side shocks can be understood by using the aggregate demand–aggregate supply model.

a. The shocks (increased, decreased) _____ aggregate supply.

b. Which in turn increased both the _____ level and the _____ rate.

c. And these two events when they occur simultaneously are called _____

12. List four factors that contributed to stagflation's demise during the 1982–1989 period:

a. _____

b. _____

c. _____

d. _____

13. During the 1960s, the empirical data indicate that unemployment and inflation moved in the (same, opposite) _____ direction; in 1973–1974,

1978–1980, and in some years during the 1982–1989 period, unemployment and inflation moved in the _____ direction.

14. There is much debate among economists about the Phillips Curve:

a. Keynesian economists contend that during the stagflation of the 1970s, the Phillips Curve shifted (right, left) _____; during the demise of stagflation from 1982–1989, the Phillips Curve shifted _____

b. Other economists associated with new classical thinking conclude that the downsloping Phillips Curve does not _____ in the long run and subscribe to the _____ hypothesis, for which there are two variants— _____ and _____ expectations.

15. The theory of adaptive expectations suggests that people form their expectations of _____ based on experience and (immediately, gradually) _____ change expectations over time. With this theory:

a. the (short-run, long-run) _____ Phillips Curve may be downsloping, but the _____ Phillips Curve is vertical at the _____ _____

b. attempts by government to reduce the unemployment rate bring about a rate of inflation that (increases, decreases) _____

16. Rational expectations theory suggests that:

a. attempts by government to reduce the unemployment rate lead workers to anticipate the amount of _____ this will cause and to keep their (real, nominal) _____ wages constant they obtain a(n) (increase, decrease) _____ in their _____ wages; and

b. this brings about (a rise, a fall, no change) _____ in the price level and _____ in the unemployment rate.

17. With the aggregate-supply curve:

a. In the short run, the curve is (upsloping, vertical) _____ and in the long run the curve is _____;

b. In the short run, nominal wages are (fixed, variable)

_____ , and in the long run, nominal

wages are _____ .

c. Proponents of new classical economics think that wages and prices are (flexible, inflexible)

_____ and that the economy is (stable,

unstable) _____ in the long run at the full-employment level of real output; policy changes by

government (will, will not) _____ be antici-

pated in advance and _____ influence the

economy in the short run, only _____ sur-prises produce temporary changes in real output.

d. Modern Keynesians accept the distinction be-tween short- and long-run aggregate supply, but con-tend that wages and prices are (flexible, inflexible)

_____ downward, and therefore they

advocate a(n) (active, hands-off) _____ policy by government in the short run to reduce the

(low, high) _____ cost of inflation and unemployment.

18. Demand-pull inflation will shift the aggregate-demand

curve (right, left) _____ , which will (decrease, in-

crease) _____ the price level and tempo-

rarily _____ real output. As a conse-

quence, the (short-run, long-run) _____ aggregate-supply curve will shift left because of a rise in

(real, nominal) _____ wages, producing a

(lower, higher) _____ price level at the original level of real output.

19. Cost-push inflation will shift the short-run aggregate-

supply curve (right, left) _____ , thus the price

level will (increase, decrease) _____ and

real output will temporarily _____ ; if govern-ment takes no actions to counter the cost-push infla-

tion, the resulting recession will _____ nominal wages, and shift the short-run aggregate-supply curve back to its original position; yet, if the government tries to counter the cost-push inflation and recession with a(n)

_____ in aggregate demand, the price level will move even higher.

20. Two economic policies might be used to deal with cost-push inflation.

a. A policy designed to improve the efficiency of labor

markets is the _____ and

policy. This policy would provide programs to improve

_____ training, increase information about

_____ , and reduce bias or _____ in labor markets.

b. Wage-price policies are sometimes called

_____ policies. These policies involve either

wage-price (controls, guideposts) _____ that rely on the voluntary cooperation of labor unions and

business firms, or wage-price _____ that are mandated by government and have the force of law to make them effective.

21. It is the view of supply-side economists that:

a. high marginal tax rates reduce _____ to work, save, invest, and take risks;

b. the remedy for stagflation is a substantial (increase,

decrease) _____ in marginal tax rates; and

c. a cut in tax rates would significantly shift the (ag-

gregate-demand, aggregate-supply) _____

_____ curve (leftward, rightward) _____ and make the economy grow at a pace greater than historical experience.

22. The Laffer Curve depicts the relationship between tax rates and tax revenues.

a. In theory, as the tax rates increase from 0%, tax rev-

enues will (increase, decrease) _____ to some maximum level, after which tax revenues will

_____ as the tax rates increase; or, as tax rates are reduced from 100%, tax revenues will

_____ to some maximum level, after which

tax revenues will _____ as tax rates decrease.

b. The criticisms of the Laffer Curve are that the effects of a cut in tax rates on incentives to work, save, and in-

vest are (large, small) _____ ; that the tax cuts generate an increase in aggregate (demand, supply)

_____ that outweigh any increase in aggregate

_____ and in a full-employment situation will lead to

_____ ; and that tax cuts can produce (gain, loss)

_____ in tax revenues that only adds to or creates a budget deficit.

23. Two other supply-side tenets are that business costs and product prices have increased because govern-ment has raised taxes and these taxes are a business

_____ and a tax "_____" between the

price of a product and the cost of resources; and that the productivity of business has been decreased by

_____ of industry by government.

24. The four principal elements of Reaganomics were:

a. _____

b. _____

c. _____

d. _____

25. The evidence suggests that supply-side economics ideas (did, did not) _____ work as proposed in Reaganomics.

a. Although inflation fell in the 1980s, it was primarily because of a (tight, easy) _____ money policy of the Federal Reserve, the effects of a severe _____ in 1980–1982, and because of a (rise, fall) _____ in oil prices in the mid-1980s.

b. The cut in tax rate primarily (increased, decreased) _____ aggregate demand and sparked an economic expansion in the 1980s, but the tax cuts also _____ tax revenues contributing to increasing budget _____.

c. The effect of tax cuts on saving, investment, and productivity was (minimal, substantial) _____

■ **TRUE-FALSE QUESTIONS**

Circle the T if the statement is true; the F if it is false.

1. In the simplest Keynesian model the aggregate-supply curve has no intermediate range. **T F**

2. The simple Keynesian model provides a reasonably satisfactory explanation of the macroeconomic behavior of the American economy between 1930 and 1970, but does not explain the stagflation of the 1970s and early 1980s. **T F**

3. When aggregate supply is constant, higher rates of inflation are accompanied by higher rates of unemployment. **T F**

4. According to the conventional Phillips Curve the rate of inflation increases as the level of unemployment decreases. **T F**

5. Labor market imbalances and market power are explanations offered by Keynesians to explain the intermediate range of the aggregate supply curve. **T F**

6. According to Keynesian economists, as the economy approaches full employment, some types of labor become

fully employed before all the labor force is fully employed. **T F**

7. Policies to manage aggregate supply can be used to choose a point on the Phillips Curve, but these policies do not improve the "unemployment rate-inflation rate" trade-off reflected in the Phillips Curve. **T F**

8. Stagflation refers to a situation in which both the price level and the unemployment rate are rising. **T F**

9. Keynesian economists contend that the Phillips Curve shifted left during the 1973–1982 period and shifted right during the 1982–1989 period. **T F**

10. Expectations of inflation induce workers to demand a higher nominal wage and their employers to pay them higher wages. **T F**

11. When the nominal wage rate increases at a rate greater than the rate at which the productivity of labor increases, unit labor cost will rise. **T F**

12. The demise of stagflation and a decline in unit labor costs will tend to shift the aggregate-supply curve rightward and the Phillips Curve leftward. **T F**

13. The natural rate hypothesis suggests that there is a natural rate of inflation for the economy. **T F**

14. The theory of adaptive expectations indicates that there may be a short-run tradeoff between inflation and unemployment, but no long-run tradeoff. **T F**

15. From the adaptive expectations perspective, when the actual rate of inflation is higher than expected, the unemployment rate will rise. **T F**

16. Adaptive expectation theorists believe that they are able to explain disinflation in the economy. **T F**

17. The theory of rational expectations maintains that if workers believe expansionary monetary and fiscal policies will be inflationary and therefore lower their real wages, then the reaction of the workers to these expectations results in higher nominal wages, higher labor costs, and no change in employment in the economy. **T F**

18. Natural rate theorists conclude that demand-management policies cannot influence real output and employment in the long run, but only the price level. **T F**

19. The long-run aggregate supply curve is upsloping at the potential level of real domestic output. **T F**

20. New classical economists hold that price level surprises produce short-run fluctuations in the economy, but in the long run the economy is stable at the full-employment level of output. **T F**

21. Keynesian economists contend that nominal wages are inflexible upward and therefore they advocate a hands-off approach to stabilization policy. **T F**

22. Demand-pull inflation will increase the price level and real output in the short run, but in the long run, only the price level will increase.   **T F**

23. An inflationary spiral is likely to result from the use of stabilization policies to maintain full employment when the economy is experiencing cost-push inflation.   **T F**

24. Incomes policies to reduce stagflation would include programs for vocational training, the improvement of job information, and the elimination of discrimination in labor markets.   **T F**

25. Of the policies that might be employed to deal with stagflation, wage-price policies were designed to move the Phillips Curve to the right.   **T F**

26. Voluntary restraint by business and labor leaders is not apt to be effective in preventing price and wage increases because such restraint requires them to abandon their major goals.   **T F**

27. Supply-side economists contend that Keynesian economics is unable to explain stagflation because costs and aggregate supply play an "active" role in the Keynesian model.   **T F**

28. The tax "wedge" to which supply-side economists refer is the difference between the price of a product and the cost of economic resources required to produce it.   **T F**

29. If the economy were at point **A** on the Laffer Curve shown below, a decrease in tax rates would increase tax revenues.   **T F**

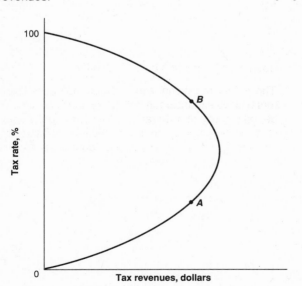

30. The supply-side economists believe that the economy is at a point such as point **B** on the Laffer Curve above, and that a substantial reduction in tax rates would both increase tax revenues and increase incentives to work, invest, innovate, and take risks.   **T F**

■ **MULTIPLE-CHOICE QUESTIONS**

Circle the letter that corresponds to the best answer.

1. In the Keynesian expenditures-output model it is impossible for the economy to experience:
(a) full employment
(b) inflation
(c) unemployment and inflation
(d) full employment and stable prices

2. As long as aggregate supply remains constant and the economy operates along the intermediate range of the aggregate-supply curve, the greater the increase in aggregate demand:
(a) the greater is the increase in the price level
(b) the greater is the increase in the unemployment rate
(c) the smaller is the increase in real output
(d) the smaller is the increase in employment

3. The conventional Phillips Curve:
(a) shows the inverse relationship between the rate of increase in the price level and the unemployment rate
(b) makes it possible for the economy to achieve full employment and stable prices
(c) indicates that prices do not rise until full employment has been achieved
(d) slopes upward from left to right

4. Labor-market adjustments do not eliminate bottleneck problems when there is less than full employment in the economy. Which of the following is *not* one of the reasons for these labor-market imbalances?
(a) unemployed workers often lack the skills or training needed for a new occupation
(b) the demand for workers in the markets in which there are labor shortages is inadequate
(c) there are artificial restrictions which prevent unemployed workers from filling the job openings
(d) unemployed workers do not know of the shortages of workers in other labor markets in the economy

5. If inflation during periods of less than full employment is to be explained by market power, it must be assumed that:
(a) only unions possess considerable market power
(b) only employers possess considerable market power
(c) both unions and employers possess considerable market power
(d) neither unions nor employers possess considerable market power

6. The stabilization policy dilemma illustrated by a Phillips Curve is the mutual inconsistency of:
(a) more employment and price stability
(b) a higher unemployment rate and price stability
(c) inflation and more employment
(d) inflation and a lower unemployment rate

7. Demand-management (monetary and fiscal) policies can be employed to:
- **(a)** shift the Phillips Curve to the right
- **(b)** shift the Phillips Curve to the left
- **(c)** achieve full employment without inflation
- **(d)** reduce the unemployment rate

8. Which of the following was one of the supply-side shocks to the American economy during the 1970s and early 1980s?
- **(a)** the removal of wage and price controls
- **(b)** the appreciation of the dollar
- **(c)** the fall in the price charged by OPEC nations for oil
- **(d)** worldwide agricultural surpluses

9. If the percentage change in the productivity of labor is 2% and the percentage change in nominal-wage rates is 5%, the percentage change in unit labor costs is:
- **(a)** 1%
- **(b)** 3%
- **(c)** 7%
- **(d)** 10%

10. Supply shocks which cause a leftward shift in the aggregate-supply curve, aggregate demand remaining constant, will:
- **(a)** decrease the price level
- **(b)** decrease the unemployment rate
- **(c)** increase real output
- **(d)** increase both the price level and the unemployment rate

11. Which one of the following would be a factor contributing to the demise of stagflation during the 1982–1989 period?
- **(a)** a lessening of foreign competition
- **(b)** a strengthening of the monopoly power of OPEC
- **(c)** a recession brought on largely by a tight monetary policy
- **(d)** an increase in regulation of airline and trucking industries

12. According to the Keynesian view, the collapse of the traditional unemployment rate-inflation rate tradeoff and the likely shift in the Phillips Curve during the 1980s were the consequence of a:
- **(a)** rightward shift in aggregate demand
- **(b)** rightward shift in aggregate supply
- **(c)** leftward shift in aggregate demand
- **(d)** leftward shift in aggregate supply

13. The natural rate hypothesis suggests that the economy is stable only in the:
- **(a)** short run at the natural rate of unemployment
- **(b)** short run at the natural rate of inflation
- **(c)** long run at the natural rate of unemployment
- **(d)** long run at the natural rate of inflation

14. The theory of adaptive expectations suggests that if increases in nominal wage rates lag behind increases in the price level, and government attempts to reduce unemployment by using fiscal and monetary policies, then employment:
- **(a)** and the price level increase in the long run
- **(b)** remains constant and the price level increases in the short run
- **(c)** increases and the price level remains constant in the short run
- **(d)** remains constant and the price level increases in the long run

15. The rational expectations theorists contend that when government attempts to reduce unemployment by using monetary and fiscal policies, unemployment decreases:
- **(a)** temporarily and the price level rises
- **(b)** permanently and the price level rises
- **(c)** both temporarily and permanently and the price level rises
- **(d)** neither temporarily nor permanently and the price level rises

16. In the view of natural rate theorists, the long-run Phillips Curve is:
- **(a)** horizontal
- **(b)** vertical
- **(c)** upsloping
- **(d)** downsloping

17. Disinflation, or reductions in the rate of inflation, can be explained based on the natural rate conclusion that when the:
- **(a)** actual rate of inflation is lower than the expected rate, the unemployment rate will rise to bring the expected and actual rates into balance
- **(b)** expected rate of inflation is lower than the actual rate, the unemployment rate will rise to bring the expected and actual rates into balance
- **(c)** actual rate of inflation is higher than the expected rate, the unemployment rate will fall to bring the expected and actual rates into balance
- **(d)** expected rate of inflation is higher than the actual rate, the unemployment rate will fall to bring the expected and actual rates into balance

18. The natural rate theory suggests that the aggregate-supply curve:
- **(a)** is stable in the short run so long as nominal wages do not increase in the short run in response to the increase in the price level
- **(b)** unstable in the long run because real wages are continually changing
- **(c)** will shift to the right when the price of capital increases
- **(d)** will shift to the right when nominal wages increase

19. According to new classical thinking, fully anticipated changes in the price level do *not* change the:
  (a) level of real output
  (b) level of prices
  (c) inflexibility of wages and prices
  (d) effectiveness of stabilization policy

20. In the short run, demand-pull inflation:
  (a) is caused by a rightward shift in the Phillips Curve
  (b) is the result of a decrease in aggregate demand
  (c) produces an increase in real output
  (d) creates price level surprises

21. In the long run, demand-pull inflation will:
  (a) decrease the unemployment rate
  (b) decrease the level of nominal wages
  (c) increase the level of prices
  (d) increase real national output

22. A likely result of treating unemployment associated with cost-push inflation by stimulating aggregate demand with monetary and fiscal policies is:
  (a) an inflationary spiral
  (b) a price level surprise
  (c) disinflation
  (d) a recession

23. Which of the following is *not* an employment and training policy program that might relieve the problem of stagflation?
  (a) application of antimonopoly laws to labor unions
  (b) removal of discrimination as an obstacle to employment
  (c) improvement of the flow of job information between workers without jobs and employers with unfilled positions
  (d) expansion of programs that provide job training

24. The two targets of wage-price guideposts or controls are:
  (a) workability and compliance
  (b) allocative efficiency and rationing
  (c) the size of nominal income and the prices of products
  (d) increasing aggregate demand and decreasing aggregate supply

25. From the viewpoint of supply-side economists, stagflation is the result of:
  (a) excessive taxation
  (b) government deregulation
  (c) a shifting Phillips Curve
  (d) unanticipated inflation

26. Supply-side economists of the 1980s thought that the American system of taxes reduced:
  (a) unemployment, but increased inflation
  (b) incentives to work, save, and invest

  (c) transfer payments to the poor and homeless
  (d) the effectiveness of wage-price guideposts for the economy

For multiple-choice question 27 refer to the graph used for true-false question 29.

27. A cut in the tax rate from 100% to point **B** on the Laffer Curve would tend to:
  (a) decrease tax revenues and support the view of supply-side economists
  (b) increase tax revenues and support the views of supply-side economists
  (c) increase tax revenues and support the views of Keynesian economists
  (d) decrease tax revenues and support the views of Keynesian economists

28. In the case of cuts in the tax rates, most mainstream economists take the position that:
  (a) the demand-side effects outweigh the supply-side effects
  (b) the supply-side effects outweigh the demand-side effects
  (c) the demand-side and supply-side effects offset each other
  (d) there are only supply-side effects

29. Which one of the following was an element in the Reaganomics program for reducing stagflation in the American economy?
  (a) a reduction in defense expenditures
  (b) a reduction in personal income tax rates
  (c) an increase in rate of growth of the money supply
  (d) an increase in the regulation of private business firms

30. One general criticism of supply-side economics during the 1980–1988 period was that:
  (a) the growth of the money supply was not slowed to a more moderate rate
  (b) all sectors of the economy failed to achieve optimal efficiency from increased regulation by government
  (c) the productive capacity of the economy did not expand significantly
  (d) there was a significant increase in the inflation rate over the period

■ **PROBLEMS**

1. On the next page is a traditional Phillips Curve.
  a. At full employment (a 4% unemployment rate) the price level would rise by _____% each year.
  b. If the price level were stable (increasing by 0% a year) the unemployment rate would be _____%.

c. Which of the combinations along the Phillips Curve would you choose for the economy? _____

Why would you select this combination? _____

_____

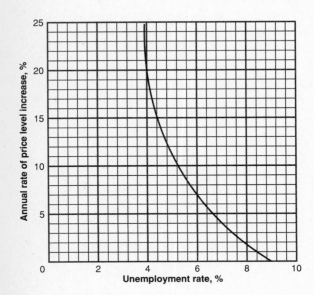

2. In columns (1) and (2) of the table below is a portion of an aggregate-supply schedule. Column (3) shows the number of full-time workers (in millions) that would have to be employed to produce each of the seven real domestic outputs (in billions) in the aggregate-supply schedule.

The labor force is 80 million workers and the full-employment output of the economy is $_____
  a. If the aggregate-demand schedule were that shown by columns (1) and (4):

(1) The price level would be _____ and

the real output would be $_____
(2) the number of workers employed would be

_____ , the number of workers unemployed would be _____ , and the unemployment **rate** would be _____%.

b. If aggregate demand were to increase to that shown in columns (1) and (5) and aggregate supply remained constant:

(1) the price level would rise to _____

and the real output would rise to $ _____

(2) employment would increase by _____

_____ workers and the unemployment

rate would fall to _____%.
(3) the price level has increased by and the rate of

inflation has been _____%.
c. If aggregate demand were to decrease to that shown in columns (1) and (6) and aggregate supply remained constant:

(1) the price level would fall to _____

and the real output would fall to $_____

(2) employment would decrease by _____ compared with situation a, and workers and the un-

employment rate would rise to _____ %
(3) the price level has decreased and the rate of inflation has been (positive, negative) _____

3. Below is an adaptive expectations model of the short- and long-run Phillips Curve.

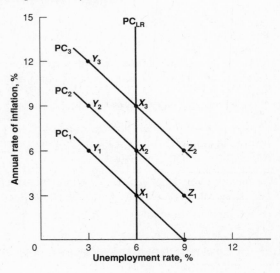

(1) Price level	(2) Real output supplied	(3) Employment (in millions)	(4) Real output demanded	(5) Real output demanded	(6) Real output demanded
130	$ 800	69	$2300	$2600	$1900
140	1300	70	2200	2500	1800
150	1700	72	2100	2400	1700
160	2000	75	2000	2300	1600
170	2200	78	1900	2200	1500
180	2300	80	1800	2100	1400
190	2300	80	1700	2000	1300

a. Suppose you begin at point X_1; then an assumption is made that nominal wages are set on the original expectation that a 3% rate of inflation will continue in the economy.
(1) If government invokes expansionary monetary and fiscal policy to reduce the unemployment rate from 6% to 3%, then the actual rate of inflation will move to

_____%. The higher product prices will lift profits of firms and they will hire more workers; thus in the short run the economy will temporarily move to point

_____

(2) If workers then demand and receive higher wages to compensate for the loss of purchasing power from higher than expected inflation, then business profits will fall from previous levels and firms will reduce employment. Therefore, employment will move from point

_____ to point _____ on the graph.

The short-run Phillips Curve has shifted from _____

to _____ on the graph.
(3) If government again tries to stimulate aggregate demand with monetary and fiscal policy to reduce the unemployment rate from 6% to 3%, then prices will rise before nominal wages, and output and employment will increase, so that there will be a move from point

_____ to point _____ on the graph.
(4) But when workers get nominal wage increases, profits fall, and employment moves from point

_____ at _____% to point

_____ at _____%. The short-run

Phillips Curve has now shifted from _____

to _____ on the graph.

(5) The long-run Phillips Curve is the line _____

_____

b. Suppose you begin at point X_3, where the expected and actual rate of inflation is 9% and the unemployment rate is 6%.
(1) If there should be a decline in aggregate demand because of a recession and if the actual rate of inflation should fall to 6%, well below the expected rate of 9%, then business profits will fall and the unemployment rate will decrease to 9% as shown by the movement

from point X_3 to point _____
(2) If firms and workers adjust their expectation to the 6% rate of inflation, the nominal wages will fall, profits will rise, and the economy will move from point

_____ to point _____. The short-run

Phillips Curve has shifted from _____ to

_____

(3) If this process is repeated, the long-run Phillips Curve will be traced as line _____
4. Below is an aggregate-demand and aggregate-supply model. Assume that the economy is initially in equilibrium at AD_1 and AS_1. The price level will be _____ and the real domestic output will be _____

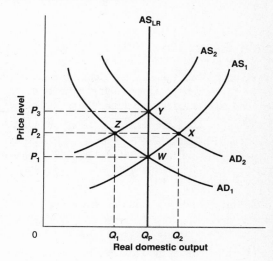

a. If there is demand-pull inflation, then:
(1) in the short run, the new equilibrium is at point

_____ , with the price level at _____

and real output at _____ ;
(2) in the long run, nominal wages will rise so the aggregate-supply curve will shift from _____ to

_____ . The equilibrium will be at point

_____ with the price level at _____

and real output at _____ ; and so the increase in aggregate demand has only moved the economy

along its _____ curve.
b. Now assume that the economy is initially in equilibrium at point **W**, where AD_1 and AS_1 intersect. If there is cost-push inflation, then:
(1) In the short run, the new equilibrium is at point

_____ , with the price level at _____

and real output at _____
(2) If the government tries to counter the cost-push inflation with expansionary monetary and fiscal policy,

then aggregate demand will shift from _____

to _____ , with the price level becoming

_____ and real output _____ ; but this policy has a trap because the price level has shifted from _____ to _____ and the new

level of inflation might shift _____ leftward.
(3) If government does not counter the cost-push infla-

tion, the price level will eventually move to _____

and real output to _____ as the recession re-

duces nominal wages and shifts the aggregate-supply

curve from _____ to _____

■ SHORT ANSWER AND ESSAY QUESTIONS

1. Why does the simplest Keynesian model imply that the economy may have either unemployment or inflation but will not experience unemployment and inflation simultaneously?

2. What is a Phillips Curve? Explain how a Phillips Curve with a negative slope may be derived by holding aggregate supply constant and mentally increasing aggregate demand.

3. What factors do Keynesian economists point to that underline the Phillips Curve? How are those factors related to the intermediate range of the aggregate-supply curve?

4. What is the stabilization policy dilemma illustrated by the traditional Phillips Curve? Does the manipulation of aggregate demand through monetary and fiscal policy move the Phillips Curve or cause a movement along the Phillips Curve?

5. Were the rates of inflation and of unemployment consistent with the Phillips Curve in the 1950s and 1960s? What do these two rates suggest about the curve in the 1970s and early 1980s?

6. What were the supply-side shocks to the American economy during the 1970s and early 1980s? How did these shocks affect aggregate supply and the Phillips Curve in the United States?

7. How do expectations of inflation and declines in the productivity of labor affect aggregate supply and the Phillips Curve?

8. When do increases in nominal-wage rates increase unit labor costs, decrease aggregate supply, and increase the price level in the economy?

9. Describe the factors that contributed to stagflation's demise during the 1982–1989 period. What do mainstream economists contend happened to the Phillips Curve during this period compared to the 1970s and early 1980s?

10. Explain the natural rate hypothesis and briefly describe the two variants of the interpretation of the unemployment-inflation rate data of 1960–1991.

11. What does "adaptive" refer to in the theory of adaptive expectations? Illustrate how this theory is used to explain both inflation and disinflation in the economy.

12. What are the views of the adaptive expectationists on:
(a) the effects of expansionary monetary and fiscal policy on employment in the short run and on the short-run Phillips Curve; and,
(b) the long-run Phillips Curve? How do they reach these conclusions?

13. How do rational expectationists believe expansionary monetary and fiscal policy affects the price level and employment in the short run and the long run? What assumptions do they make to reach this conclusion?

14. Compare and contrast the theories of rational expectations and adaptive expectations in terms of views on inflationary expectations, the interpretation of the Phillips Curve, and the effectiveness of demand-management policies.

15. Identify the basic difference between a short-run and a long-run aggregate-supply curve. Explain what happens to aggregate supply when an increase in the price level results in an increase in nominal wages.

16. How do Keynesian economists and new classical economists view wage and price flexibility in the economy? What implications does each group draw about economic policy for the economy?

17. Describe the process of demand-pull inflation in the short run and in the long run. How does demand-pull inflation influence the aggregate-supply curve?

18. What are two generalizations that emerge from the analysis of cost-push inflation? Describe the two scenarios that provide the basis for the generalizations.

19. What types of programs would be included in employment and training policy? How does this policy help alleviate inflationary pressure?

20. Explain why wage-price policies are often called incomes policies. State the cases for and against the use of wage-price (incomes) policies to limit inflation. Build each case on the two points on which the wage-price debates have been centered.

21. Why do supply-side economists criticize mainstream or Keynesian economics? Discuss three ways that supply-side economists contend there are tax and transfer payment disincentives in the economy.

22. Draw a Laffer Curve showing the relationship between tax rates and tax revenues. Explain the position of supply-side economists and Keynesian economists using the curve. Outline the three criticisms of the ideas expressed in the Laffer Curve.

23. What were the four major steps the Reagan administration proposed to increase employment and reduce inflation in the American economy?

24. Criticize and defend the contention that Reaganomics worked well to reduce stagflation in the United States. Did supply-side economics accomplish its goals under Reaganomics?

25. Compare and contrast the competing macroeconomic theories and policy perspectives.

ANSWERS

Chapter 17 The Inflation-Unemployment Relationship

FILL-IN QUESTIONS

1. full employment, excess, either

2. *a.* increase; *b.* decrease

3. *a.* greater, greater, smaller; *b.* inverse

4. full employment is reached, business firms, labor unions, labor

5. *a.* price level, unemployment; *b.* negative

6. *a.* inflation, unemployment; *b.* increase, increase

7. select a point on the; tradeoff

8. *a.* the dramatic rise in the oil prices of OPEC; *b.* agricultural shortfalls throughout the world (higher agricultural prices); *c.* the devaluation of the dollar; *d.* the abandonment of wage-price controls; *e.* the fall in the rate of growth of labor productivity; *f.* inflationary expectations

9. *a.* increase; *b.* increase

10. higher, rise, decrease, higher, higher

11. *a.* decreased; *b.* price, unemployment; *c.* stagflation

12. (any order) *a.* recession of 1981–1982 with tight monetary policy; *b.* intensive foreign competition suppressed some wages and prices; *c.* deregulation in some industries depressed wages; *d.* a decline in the monopoly power of OPEC

13. opposite, same

14. *a.* right, left; *b.* exist, natural rate, adaptive, rational (either order for last two)

15. inflation, gradually; *a.* short-run, long-run, natural rate of unemployment; *b.* increases

16. *a.* inflation, real, increase, nominal; *b.* a rise, no change

17. *a.* upsloping, vertical; *b.* fixed, variable; *c.* flexible, stable, will, will not, price level; *d.* inflexible, active, high

18. right, increase, increase, short-run, nominal, higher

19. left, increase, decrease, decrease, increase

20. *a.* employment, training, vocational, jobs, discrimination; *b.* incomes, guideposts, controls

21. *a.* incentives; *b.* decrease, aggregate supply, rightward

22. *a.* increase, decrease, increase, decrease; *b.* small, demand, supply, inflation, loss

23. cost, wedge, overregulation

24. *a.* substantial reduction in Federal expenditures except those for defense; *b.* reduction in government regulation of private business; *c.* limitation of the rate of growth in the money supply; *d.* sharp reduction in personal and corporate income tax rates

25. *a.* did not, tight, recession, fall; *b.* increased, decreased, deficits; *c.* minimal

TRUE-FALSE QUESTIONS

1. T, p. 338	**9.** F, p. 341	**17.** T, p. 346	**25.** F, p. 352
2. T, p. 339	**10.** T, p. 343	**18.** T, p. 346	**26.** T, pp. 353-354
3. F, p. 339	**11.** T, p. 343	**19.** F, pp. 348-349	**27.** F, p. 354
4. T, p. 339	**12.** T, p. 343	**20.** T, p. 349	**28.** F, p. 356
5. T, p. 340	**13.** F, p. 344	**21.** F, p. 349	**29.** F, p. 355
6. T, p. 340	**14.** T, p. 344	**22.** T, p. 350	**30.** T, p. 355
7. F, pp. 340-341	**15.** F, p. 345	**23.** T, p. 351	
8. T, p. 341	**16.** T, p. 346	**24.** F, p. 352	

MULTIPLE-CHOICE QUESTIONS

1. *c*, p. 338	**9.** *b*, p. 342	**17.** *a*, p. 346	**25.** *a*, p. 354
2. *a*, p. 339	**10.** *d*, pp. 341-342	**18.** *a*, p. 347	**26.** *b*, p. 354
3. *a*, p. 339	**11.** *c*, p. 343	**19.** *a*, p. 349	**27.** *b*, p. 355
4. *b*, p. 340	**12.** *b*, p. 343	**20.** *c*, pp. 349-350	**28.** *a*, p. 355
5. *c*, pp. 340-341	**13.** *c*, p. 344	**21.** *c*, p. 350	**29.** *b*, p. 356
6. *a*, pp. 340-341	**14.** *d*, p. 345	**22.** *a*, pp. 350-351	**30.** *c*, p. 357
7. *d*, pp. 340-341	**15.** *d*, p. 346	**23.** *a*, p. 352	
8. *a*, pp. 342-343	**16.** *b*, p. 345	**24.** *c*, pp. 352-353	

PROBLEMS

1. *a.* 20; *b.* 9; *c.* (it's your choice)

2. 2300; *a.* (1) 160, 2000, (2) 75, 5, 6.25; *b.* (1) 170, 2200, (2) 3, 2.5, (3) 6.25; *c.* (1) 150, 1700, (2) 3, 10, (3) negative

3. *a.* (1) 6, Y_1; (2) Y_1, X_2, PC_1, PC_2, (3) X_2, Y_2, (4) Y_2, 3, X_3, 6, PC_2, PC_3, (5) PC_{LR}; *b.* (1) Z_2, (2) Z_2, X_2, PC_3, PC_2, (3) PC_{LR}

4. P_1, Q_p; *a.* (1) X, P_2, Q_2, (2) AS_1, AS_2, Y, P_3, Q_p, AS_{LR}; *b.* (1) Z, P_2 Q_1, (2) AD_1, AD_2, P_3, Q_p, P_2, P_3, AS_2, (3) P_1, Q_p, AS_2, AS_1

SHORT ANSWER AND ESSAY QUESTIONS

1. pp. 338-339	**8.** p. 342	**15.** pp. 347-348	**22.** pp. 355-356
2. pp. 339-340	**9.** p. 343	**16.** p. 349	**23.** p. 356
3. p. 340	**10.** pp. 344-346	**17.** pp. 349-350	**24.** pp. 356-357
4. pp. 340-341	**11.** pp. 344-345	**18.** p. 351	**25.** pp. 357-358
5. pp. 339-340	**12.** pp. 344-345	**19.** p. 352	
6. pp. 342-343	**13.** p. 346	**20.** pp. 352-353	
7. pp. 342-343	**14.** pp. 344-346	**21.** pp. 354-355	

Budget Deficits and the Public Debt

Over the past thirty-five years, the Federal government has had budget deficits in all but one year. In the past decade these budget deficits have grown quite large and have caused problems for the American Economy. Chapter 18, therefore, looks at data and the issues surrounding budget deficits and the related public debt.

The Federal government can operate with a budget deficit, a budget surplus, or with a balanced budget during a year. Any budget surplus or deficit affects the size of the public (sometimes called national) debt; surpluses decrease it and deficits increase it. After defining a budget deficit and the public debt, three budget philosophies are discussed. You should be aware that the philosophies adopted by the Federal government have a significant impact on output and employment in the economy **and** on the public debt.

The chapter then discusses how four major factors—wars, recessions, tax cuts, and lack of political will—have contributed to increases in the public debt since 1929. The increased public debt resulting from these factors is placed into perspective for you with a quantitative description of the size of the public debt (and interest payments for it) relative to the size of the economy (GDP), and how the public debt in the United States compares with that found in other industrial nations, who owns the debt, and measurement problems caused by accounting and inflation.

The two middle sections of the chapter examine the economic implications or consequences of the public debt and deficits. These economic problems do not include bankrupting the Federal government because the government has three ways that it can meet its obligations. Nor does the public debt simply shift the economic burden to future generations because the public debt is a public credit for the many people who hold that debt in the form of government bonds. Rather, the public debt and payment of interest on the debt contribute to five important problems: increased inequality in income; reduced incentives for work and production; decreased standard of living when part of the debt is paid to foreigners; curbs on fiscal policy; and less capital investment.

The crowding-out of investment in plant and equipment in the United States is probably the most serious of these five problems. You should understand how crowding out

works and how it may impose a burden on future generations by reducing the growth of the nation's capital stock. Whether it does impose a burden on a future generation depends on how the increased government spending is financed. Raising taxes to pay for increased spending imposes a burden on the current taxpayers, whereas government borrowing to finance increased spending tends to reduce private investment and future capital stock.

The final section of the chapter is an extensive discussion of the macroeconomic problems with the Federal deficits of the past decade. The recent deficits are of great concern because of their relatively large size, high interest cost, and the problems they pose for domestic macroeconomic and trade policy. Be sure that you study each link in the chain of events that lead to the contractions of output and employment in the United States economy as a result of large deficits. There is not any new economic theory in this discussion, just an application of theory you have learned in previous chapters. The chapter then concludes with an explanation of four different policy responses to eliminate or reduce our persistent Federal budget deficits.

■ **CHECKLIST**

When you have studied this chapter you should be able to:

☐ Define a budget deficit (and surplus) and the public debt; and explain how the latter is related to the former.

☐ Explain each of the three budget philosophies.

☐ Identify the four principal causes of the public debt.

☐ Describe the absolute and relative sizes of the public debt and interest payments on it since 1929.

☐ Compare the relative size of the public debt of the United States to public debts in other industrial nations.

☐ Explain how adjusting the size of the nominal public debt for inflation affects the real size of the debt and the real size of a budget deficit; and why the accounting procedures employed by the Federal government do not accurately reflect its financial condition.

☐ Give three reasons why a large public debt will not bankrupt the government.

☐ Discuss whether the public debt imposes a burden on future generations; and why the public debt is for the most part also a public credit.

☐ Enumerate the five real issues related to the public debt.

☐ Compare the effects of an internal debt with the effects of an external debt on the economy.

☐ Describe the crowding-out effect of borrowing to finance an increase in government expenditures and the burden this method of financing expenditures places on future generations.

☐ Compare the burden imposed on future generations by borrowing to finance expenditures with the burden placed on them if the increased expenditures are financed by increased taxation; and qualify in two ways this comparison.

☐ Discuss five concerns with the deficits and the public debt in the past decade.

☐ Trace the effects of borrowing to finance an increase in government expenditures on interest rates, the attractiveness of American securities to foreigners, the international debts of the United States, the international value of the dollar, American exports and imports, and output and employment in the United States.

☐ Contrast the mainstream analysis of recent budget deficits with the analysis by economists who adhere to the Ricardian equivalence theorem.

☐ List four policy responses to the budget deficits of the Federal government and to the public debt of the United States.

☐ Describe the features and history of legislative actions in Congress since 1985 to reduce budget deficits.

☐ Identify two examples of other proposals that have been suggested for use in reducing budget deficits.

☐ Explain why increasing debt is necessary in a growing economy if the economy is to remain at full employment and when it is necessary for the public debt to expand.

■ **CHAPTER OUTLINE**

1. The budget deficit of the Federal government is the amount by which its expenditures exceed its revenues in any year; and the public debt at any time is the sum of the Federal government's previous annual deficits (less any annual surpluses).

2. If the Federal government utilizes fiscal policy to combat recession and inflation its budget is not likely to be balanced in any particular year. Three budgetary philosophies may be adopted by the government; and the adoption of any of these philosophies will affect employment, real output, and the price level of the economy.

　a. Proponents of an annually balanced budget would have government expenditures and tax revenues equal in every year; such a budget is pro- rather than counter-cyclical: but conservative economists favor it to prevent the expansion of the public sector (and the contraction of the private sector) of the economy without the increased payment of taxes by the public.

　b. Those who advocate a cyclically balanced budget propose matching surpluses (in years of prosperity) with deficits (in depression years) to stabilize the economy: but there is no assurance that the surpluses will equal the deficits over the years.

　c. Advocates of functional finance contend that deficits, surpluses, and the size of the debt are of minor importance; that the goal of full employment without inflation should be achieved regardless of the effects of the necessary fiscal policies upon the budget and the size of the public debt.

3. Any government deficit increases the size of the public debt; and the public debt has grown substantially since 1929.

　a. There are four basic causes of the debt:

　(1) *wars* require increased Federal borrowing to finance the war effort;

　(2) *recessions* result in budget deficits because of the built-in stability of the economy (tax revenues fall and domestic spending rises);

　(3) *cuts in tax rates* without offsetting reductions in expenditures contribute to budget deficits, as occurred during the early 1980s; and

　(4) *a lack of political will* to control expenditures for popular entitlement programs or raise taxes to pay for them adds to budget deficits.

　b. The public debt in 1994 was $4.6 trillion.

　(1) The size of the debt as a percentage of the economy's GDP did not grow so rapidly as the absolute size of the debt between 1940 and 1994; but relative to the GDP it has increased significantly since the early 1980s.

　(2) Other industrial nations have relative public debts similar to or greater than the United States.

　(3) Since the 1970s the interest payments on the debt (because of increases in the size of the debt and higher interest rates in the economy) have also increased significantly; and interest payments as a percentage of the economy's GDP have grown dramatically.

　(4) About one-third of the public debt is owed to government agencies and the Federal Reserve Banks and two-thirds to others; but, more importantly, about 14% of it is owed to foreign citizens, firms, and governments.

　(5) Because the accounting system used by the Federal government records its debts but not its assets the public debt is not a true picture of its financial position; and when adjusted for inflation, the decrease in the real value of its debt can exceed its nominal deficit and result in a real budget surplus.

4. The contentions that a large debt will eventually bankrupt the government and that borrowing to finance expenditures passes the cost on to future generations are false.

a. The debt cannot bankrupt the government
(1) because the government need not retire (reduce) the debt and can refund (or refinance) it;
(2) because the government has the constitutional authority to levy and collect taxes; and
(3) because the government can always print (or create) money to pay both the principal and the interest on it.
b. The debt cannot shift the burdens of the debt to future generations because the debt is largely internally held, and repayment of any portion of the principal and the payment of interest on it does not reduce the wealth or purchasing power of Americans.

5. But the debt does create real and potential problems in the economy.
a. The payment of interest on the debt probably increases the extent of income inequality.
b. The payment of taxes to finance these interest payments may also reduce the incentives to bear risks, to innovate, to invest, and to save, and so slow economic growth in the economy.
c. The portion of the debt that is externally held (by foreign citizens and institutions) requires the repayment of principal and the payment of interest to foreign citizens and institutions and transfers a part of the real output of the American economy to them.
d. It creates political problems for the use of fiscal policy as an antirecessionary measure because increasing government expenditures or cutting taxes during a recession adds to the public debt.
e. An increase in government spending may or may not impose a burden on future generations.
(1) If the increase in government spending is financed by increased personal taxes, the burden of the increased spending is on the present generation whose consumption is reduced; but if it is financed by an increased public debt, the increased borrowing of the Federal government will raise interest rates, crowd-out investment spending, and future generations will inherit a smaller stock of capital goods.
(2) The burden imposed on future generations is lessened if the increase in government expenditures is for real or human capital or if the economy were initially operating at less than full employment (and it stimulates an increase in investment demand).

6. In the 1980s the Federal government incurred large deficits and the public debt rose substantially. In addition:
a. recent budget deficits may be understated because surpluses from social security are being used to offset current government spending;
b. interest costs of the debt have risen;
c. the deficits have taken place in an economy operating close to full employment, which means there is great potential for the "crowding out" of real private investment and for demand-pull inflation; and

d. large budget deficits make it difficult for a nation to achieve a balance in its international trade.

7. These large deficits have produced a cause-and-effect chain of events with balance of trade deficits.
a. They have increased interest rates; higher interest rates have crowded-out real private investment and made financial investment by foreigners in the United States more attractive; the latter increased the external debt of the United States and raised the international value of the dollar; and the latter reduced U.S. exports, expanded U.S. imports, and had a contractionary effect on employment and output in the American economy, which softened the overall expansionary impact of a deficit.
b. There are three loose ends to the complex chain of events as described in **a** above:
(1) The inflow of foreign funds helped keep interest rates lower than would otherwise be the case and diminished the size of the crowding-out effect.
(2) High interest rates in the United States resulting from large deficits placed an increased burden on less developed countries, thereby contributing to the world debt problem and banking problems in the United States.
(3) The unfavorable trade balance meant that the United States had to borrow heavily from other nations and to sell assets to foreign investors, thereby affecting the course of economic growth in the future.
c. The mainstream analysis is contested by some economists who use the Ricardian equivalence theorem to study the effects of budget deficits. They conclude that interest rates will not increase as a result of large Federal deficits because people will increase private saving in anticipation of higher future taxes. The increased saving offsets the increased government borrowing in the money market, and thus the interest rate does not change.

8. A number of policy responses have been suggested to lessen the budget deficits and the increases in the public debt.
a. The ***Budget Reconciliation Act of 1990*** was a package of tax increases and spending cuts for reducing the budget deficits from 1991 to 1996 by $500 billion. In addition, the Budget Enforcement Act of 1990 required that new legislation that increased spending or decreased taxes must be "paid for" by legislative actions to decrease other government spending or increase other taxes.
b. The ***Deficit Reduction Act of 1993*** increased tax revenues by $250 billion and cut government expenditures by about the same amount over a five-year period.
c. Several other proposals have been considered: (a) an amendment to the U.S. Constitution that would require Congress to balance the Federal budget each

year; and (b) a measure giving the President line-item veto power over appropriation bills.

d. Despite the problems associated with deficits and the public debt, private and public debt has an important role to play: it absorbs the saving from a growing economy at full employment and sustains the aggregate expenditures of consumers, businesses, and governments at the full-employment level; and if consumers and firms do not borrow sufficient amounts, the public debt must be increased to maintain full employment and economic growth in the economy.

■ **IMPORTANT TERMS**

Budget deficit	Budget Reconciliation Act of 1990
Public debt	
Annually balanced budget	Budget Enforcement Act of 1990
Cyclically balanced budget	Deficit Reduction Act of 1993
Functional finance	Balanced Budget Amendment
External debt	
Crowding-out effect	Line-item veto

■ **HINTS AND TIPS**

1. Make sure you know the difference between the public debt and the budget deficit. Students often confuse the two.

2. The best way to gauge the public debt and the budget deficit is to calculate each one as a percentage of real GDP to put each in proper context. The absolute size of the public debt or the deficit is not a good indicator of whether it causes problems for the economy.

3. Try to understand the real rather than the imagined problems caused by the public debt. The debt will not cause the country to go bankrupt, nor will it be the burden on future generations that people often state that it is. Carefully read the section on the "false issues" and the "real issues."

SELF-TEST

■ **FILL-IN QUESTIONS**

1. The budget deficit of the Federal government in any year is equal to its (expenditures, revenues) _____ less its _____ in that year; and the public debt is equal to the sum of the Federal government's past budget _____ less its budget _____

2. An annually balanced budget is (pro-, counter-) _____ cyclical because governments tend to (raise, lower) _____ taxes and to _____ their purchases of goods and services during a recession (and to do just the opposite during an inflation).

3. A cyclically balanced budget suggests that to ensure full employment without inflation, the government incur deficits during periods of _____ and surpluses during periods of _____ with the deficits and surpluses equaling each other over the business cycle.

4. Functional finance has as its main goal the achievement of _____ ; _____ and would regard budget _____ and increases in the _____ as of secondary importance.

5. The principal causes of the public debt are the expense of paying for (wars, inflation) _____, changes in the economy such as (a recession, an expansion) _____, cuts in _____ rates without offsetting reductions in government expenditures, and the lack of _____ will to control entitlement spending or increase taxes to balance the budget.

6. There are several quantitative aspects to the public debt:

a. In 1994, it was equal to about $ _____ trillion and to about _____ % of GDP, and the annual interest charges on this debt were about $ _____ billion and equal to about _____ % of GDP.

b. The public debt as a percentage of GDP was (higher, lower) _____ in Japan and Canada, and _____ in Germany and Britain.

c. Federal government agencies and our central banks hold about (one-third, two-thirds) _____ of the debt, and commercial banks, financial institutions, and private individuals hold about _____ of the debt.

d. The majority of the public debt is (internal, external) _____ because foreigners hold only about _____ % of the public debt.

e. The public debt and budget deficits are subject to measurement problems because the accounting procedures used by the Federal government reflect (assets, debts) _____ but do not reflect its

_____.

f. If the Federal government used a capital budget which included depreciation costs, then the Federal budget deficit would be (increased, decreased) _____; and, if the Federal budget was adjusted for the effects of inflation, the budget deficit would be _____.

7. The possibility that the Federal government will go bankrupt is a false issue. It need not (reduce, refinance) _____ its debt; and it can retire maturing securities by _____ them or by creating _____. The government can also levy and collect _____ to pay its debts.

8. As long as the government expenditures which lead to the increase in the public debt are not financed by borrowing from foreigners, the public debt of the United States is also an _____ of the American people who own government securities; and the cost of a government program financed by borrowing from the American public is equal to their decreased _____ of goods and services and is a burden on (the present, a future) _____ generation.

9. The public debt is a burden on an economy if it is (internally, externally) _____ held. It and the payment of interest on it may, however (increase, decrease) _____ income inequality in the economy, dampen the _____ to work, take risks, save, and invest in the economy, and have a _____ effect on investment.

10. A public debt which is internally held imposes a burden on future generations if the borrowing done to finance an increase in government expenditures (increases, decreases) _____ interest rates, _____ investment spending, and leaves future generations with a smaller stock of _____ goods.
  a. But if the increased government expenditures are financed by an increase in the taxes on personal income, the present generation will have fewer _____ goods and the burden of the increased government expenditures will be on the _____ generation.
  b. These generalizations are subject to two qualifications: The size of the burden of increased government expenditures financed by borrowing on future genera-

tions is weakened if the government expenditures finance increases in physical or human _____ or if the economy had been operating at (full, less than full) _____ employment.

11. The increased concern of the public with Federal deficits and the expanding public debt in the 1980s is the result of the large _____ of these deficits, the use of _____ surpluses that offset and understate the deficit, the rising interest _____ of the public debt, inappropriate macroeconomic _____ for dealing with the deficit, and the difficulty of achieving a _____ in international trade.

12. Large deficits during times of full employment raise two problems. First, there is great potential for the _____ of real private investment. Second, the stimulus to the economy from the deficits may create the conditions for _____.

13. Large budget deficits tend to increase _____ _____ and decrease _____ to create an unfavorable trade balance. This trade imbalance has contributed to making the United States a (creditor, debtor) _____ nation and (increased, decreased) _____ the selling of domestic assets to foreign investors.

14. The deficits of the Federal government tend to (increase, decrease) _____ interest rates in the money markets.
  a. This change in interest rates (expands, contracts) _____ private investment spending and makes financial investments by foreigners in the U.S. (more, less) _____ attractive.
  b. This change in the financial investments of foreigners in the U.S. (increases, decreases) _____ the external debts of the U.S. and (raises, lowers) _____ the international value of the dollar.
  c. This change in the international value of the dollar (expands, contracts) _____ American exports, _____ American imports, and _____ *net* exports.
  d. This change in American net exports has a(n) (expansionary, contractionary) _____ effect on real output and employment in the United States.
  e. The overall expansionary effect of a budget deficit may be reduced somewhat by the _____ effect and the _____ effect.

15. There are other points to be considered in the chain of events from the budget deficits of the 1980s. First, the inflow of funds from abroad (raised, lowered)

_____ domestic interest rates than would otherwise be the case and therefore (strengthened, weak-

ened) _____ the crowding-out effect. Second, the high interest rates in the United States placed greater

burden on (developed, underdeveloped) _____

countries and created debt problems for the _____ system. Third, the value of imports became (greater than,

less than) _____ , so the United States had to borrow from foreigners and sold more assets.

16. A few economists disagree with mainstream analysis of the problems caused by budget deficits. From their per-spective:

a. financing a deficit by borrowing is the same as fi-nancing a deficit through tax increases because of their

use of the _____ theorem;

b. and they think that with a budget deficit the interest

rate (will, will not) _____ increase and private saving will increase in anticipation of higher future taxes, and this saving increase will (increase, offset)

_____ the borrowing demands of government in credit markets.

17. In 1990, Congress sought to trim $500 billion from the 1991–1996 deficits with the passage of the

_____ Act. This legislation was sup-

plemented by the _____ Act that established a "pay-as-you-go" test for financing increased government spending or reducing taxes.

18. In 1993, the Congress passed the _____

_____. This legislation increased _____ revenues by $250 billion over a five-year period and cut

_____ by a similar amount.

19. Two other policy responses to the problems of large budget deficits of the Federal government are a

_____ amendment to balance the budget, and

to grant the President the power to use a _____ on the spending proposals of Congress.

20. Public and private debts play a positive role if they

absorb a sufficient amount of _____ to enable an economy that is (stationary, growing)

_____ to remain at _____

■ **TRUE-FALSE QUESTIONS**

Circle the T if the statement is true; the F if it is false.

1. The budget deficit of the Federal government in any year is equal to its revenues less its expenditures. **T F**

2. There is no assurance that a nation can both use fis-cal policy to promote full employment and balance its budget cyclically. **T F**

3. Proponents of functional finance argue that a bal-anced budget, whether it is balanced annually or over the business cycle, is of minor importance when compared with the objective of full employment without inflation.
T F

4. The primary reason for the increase in the public debt since 1929 has been because of government spending associated with recessions. **T F**

5. One of the reasons for the growth in the public debt is the difficulty of getting political support for specific pro-posals to cut government spending or raise taxes to pay for government programs. **T F**

6. The defense spending for new weapons programs by the U.S. government are examples of entitlement programs. **T F**

7. The public debt was about $1800 billion in 1994.
T F

8. Between 1940 and the present both the public debt and the interest charges on this debt as percentages of GDP have decreased. **T F**

9. About one-tenth of the public debt is currently held by foreigners and about three-fourths of it is held by agencies of the Federal government and the American central banks. **T F**

10. Inflation increases the *real* value of the *nominal* pub-lic debt. **T F**

11. A large public debt will bankrupt the Federal government. **T F**

12. The public debt is a public credit. **T F**

13. The payment of interest on the public debt probably increases income inequality. **T F**

14. Selling government securities to foreigners to finance increased expenditures by the Federal government im-poses a burden on future generations. **T F**

15. A large and growing public debt makes it politically dif-ficult to use fiscal policy during a recession. **T F**

16. The crowding-out effect is caused by a rise in inter-est rates resulting from an increase in government bor-rowing in the money market to finance government expenditures. **T F**

17. Financing increased government expenditures by increasing personal taxes imposes a burden on future generations. **T F**

18. Crowding-out shifts the investment-demand curve to the left. **T F**

19. Higher interest rates in the United States not only crowd-out real investment but make financial investment by foreigners in the United States less attractive. **T F**

20. Increases in the international value of the dollar tend to have an expansionary effect on output and employment in the United States. **T F**

21. New classical economists who use the Ricardian equivalence theorem in their analysis believe that large Federal deficits have significant stimulative effects on the economy. **T F**

22. The Budget Reconciliation Act of 1990 is a constitutional amendment that requires a balanced Federal budget by 1996. **T F**

23. The Deficit Reduction Act of 1993 increased the top marginal tax rate of the personal income tax from 50% to 60%. **T F**

24. The amount of saving done at full employment increases in a growing economy. **T F**

25. To maintain full employment in a growing economy it is necessary for the total of public and private debt to increase. **T F**

■ **MULTIPLE-CHOICE QUESTIONS**

Circle the letter that corresponds to the correct answer.

1. The public debt is the sum of all previous:
(a) expenditures of the Federal government
(b) budget deficits of the Federal government
(c) budget deficits less the budget surpluses of the Federal government
(d) budget surpluses less the current budget deficit of the Federal government

2. Which of the following would involve reducing government expenditures and increasing tax rates during a recession?
(a) an annually balanced budget policy
(b) functional finance
(c) a cyclically balanced budget policy
(d) a policy employing built-in stability

3. What three factors largely explain why the public debt has increased since 1929?
(a) interest payments on the public debt, spending for social security, and depreciation of the dollar

(b) deficit spending to finance a war, effects of automatic stabilizers on the budget during recessions, and tax cuts not offset by spending cuts
(c) deficit spending caused by depressions, borrowing funds from other nations, and increased government spending to cover economic problems such as the saving and loan bailout
(d) interest payments on the public debt, government spending for welfare programs, and the crowding-out of investment spending

4. Since the 1980s, the public debt relative to GDP has:
(a) increased and interest payments relative to GDP have increased
(b) decreased and interest payments relative to GDP have decreased
(c) decreased, but interest payments relative to GDP have decreased
(d) increased, but interest payments relative to GDP have decreased

5. As a percentage of the gross domestic product, the public debt and interest on the debt were in 1994, respectively, about:
(a) 49% and 1%
(b) 49% and 2%
(c) 53% and 2%
(d) 69% and 3%

6. Which nation has the larger public debt relative to its domestic output in 1990?
(a) United States
(b) Germany
(c) United Kingdom
(d) Japan

7. The annual interest payments on the public debt in 1994 were about:
(a) $192 billion
(b) $119 billion
(c) $100 billion
(d) $89 billion

8. The accounting procedures used by the Federal government record:
(a) only its assets
(b) only its debts
(c) both its assets and debts
(d) its net worth

9. Inflation is a tax on:
(a) the holders of the public debt, and it reduces the real size of the public debt
(b) the holders of the public debt, and expands the real size of the public debt
(c) the Federal government, and reduces the real size of the public debt
(d) the Federal government, and expands the real size of the public debt

10. The public debt cannot bankrupt the Federal government because the Federal government:
(a) has the power to levy taxes
(b) is able to refinance the debt
(c) can create money to repay the debt and pay the interest on it
(d) all of the above

11. Incurring an internal debt to finance a war does not pass the cost of the war on to future generations because:
(a) the opportunity cost of the war is borne by the generation that fights it
(b) the government need not pay interest on internally held debts
(c) there is never a need for government to refinance the debt
(d) wartime inflation reduces the relative size of the debt

12. Which of the following would be a consequence of the retirement of the internally held portion of the public debt?
(a) a reduction in the nation's productive capacity
(b) a reduction in the nation's standard of living
(c) a redistribution of the nation's wealth among its citizens
(d) an increase in aggregate expenditures in the economy

13. Which of the following is an important consequence of the public debt of the United States?
(a) it increases incentives to work and invest
(b) it transfers a portion of the American output of goods and services to foreign nations
(c) it reduces income inequality in the United States
(d) it leads to greater saving at every level of disposable income

14. A large and growing public debt creates political problems for the Congress and President to adopt:
(a) an easy money policy
(b) a tight money policy
(c) an antirecessionary fiscal policy
(d) a trade policy calling for increased U.S. exports and decreased U.S. imports

15. The crowding-out effect of borrowing in the money market to finance an increase in government expenditures:
(a) reduces current private investment expenditures
(b) decreases the rate at which the privately owned stock of real capital increases
(c) imposes a burden on future generations
(d) does all of the above

16. The crowding-out effect from government borrowing is reduced:
(a) when the economy is operating at less than full employment

(b) when the expenditures expand human capital in the economy
(c) when the government's deficit financing improves the profit expectations of business firms
(d) when any one or more of the above are true

17. Which one of the following is *not* one of the sources of the concern with the deficits of the Federal government and the growth of the public debt during the 1980s?
(a) the large increases in the size of the deficits and in the public debt
(b) the operation of the economy substantially below full employment throughout the decade
(c) the rising interest costs of the debt
(d) problems with the balance of trade

18. Deficits in the early 1990s were primarily increased by:
(a) an increase in spending for social security
(b) a recession and a bailout of the savings and loan industry
(c) an increased demand by foreigners for government securities
(d) an easy money policy of the Federal Reserve

19. The increased foreign demand for American securities that results from higher interest rates in the United States during the 1980s:
(a) increases the external debts of the United States and the international value of the dollar
(b) increases the external debts of the United States and decreases the international value of the dollar
(c) decreases the external debts of the United States and increases the international value of the dollar
(d) decreases the external debts of the United States and the international value of the dollar

20. When the international value of the dollar rises:
(a) American exports tend to increase
(b) American imports tend to decrease
(c) American net exports tend to decrease
(d) all of the above tend to occur

21. High interest rates in the United States which were related to Federal budget deficits of the 1980s tended to:
(a) contribute to the debt burden of underdeveloped nations that traded with the United States
(b) reduce the flow of funds from foreign nations to the United States
(c) increase the long-term economic growth and domestic investment of foreign nations that transferred funds to the United States
(d) enable the United States to become a major creditor nation for the first time in many decades

22. Some economists use the Ricardian equivalence theorem to argue that recent Federal deficits have:
(a) had desirable effects on the economy because of the fiscal policy stimulus

(b) had little effect on the economy because households respond to budget deficits by increasing their present saving in anticipation of higher future taxes

(c) created a sizable trade imbalance with other nations and contributed to the selling of United States assets to foreigners

(d) caused interest rates to rise and crowded-out private investment

23. The Budget Reconciliation Act of 1990 was:

(a) a failed attempt by Congress to balance the 1990 budget

(b) a package of tax increases and spending cuts designed to reduce budget deficits by $500 billion between 1991 and 1996

(c) a cut in marginal tax rate from 50% to 28% that was enacted to stimulate work, investment, and saving

(d) an accord between Congress and the Federal Reserve to finance the borrowing needs of the Federal government

24. The Deficit Reduction Act of 1993 was legislation passed by Congress and signed by the President that was designed to:

(a) decrease marginal tax rates on personal income, but increase corporate income taxes and the Federal tax on gasoline

(b) increase taxes on personal income and corporations and hold all discretionary government spending to 1993 nominal levels

(c) use fiscal policy to stimulate the sluggish U.S. economy during 1993

(d) coordinate fiscal policy with the monetary policy of the Federal Reserve to achieve a budget balance by the year 2003

25. Two serious proposals that have been suggested to help reduce the Federal budget deficit are:

(a) balanced budget amendment and the line-item veto

(b) changes in accounting practices and use of social security surpluses

(c) a moratorium on interest payments on the public debt and a reduction in interest rates

(d) using countercyclical fiscal policy and increasing the supply of money

■ **PROBLEMS**

1. The table below gives data on the public debt and the GDP for selected five-year periods from 1961–1994. Data for the public debt and the GDP are in billions of dollars.

a. Calculate the ratio of the public debt to GDP expressed as a percentage of GDP. Enter the numbers into the column of the table below.

Year	Debt	GDP	Debt/GDP
1961	$ 292.6	$ 531.8	_____ %
1966	328.5	769.8	_____
1971	408.2	1097.2	_____
1976	629.0	1768.4	_____
1981	994.3	3030.6	_____
1986	2120.1	4268.6	_____
1991	3599.0	5671.8	_____
1994	4643.7	6736.9	_____

b. On the graph below, plot the year on the horizontal axis and plot the public debt as a percentage of GDP on the vertical axis.

c. Explain what happened to the public debt as a percentage of GDP over the thirty-year period.

_____

_____

_____

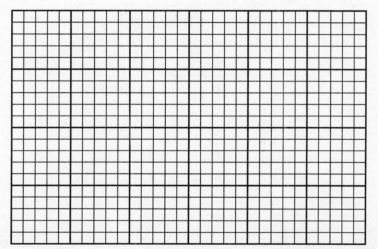

2. The table below gives data on interest rates and investment demand in a hypothetical economy.

Interest rate	I_{d1}	I_{d2}
10%	$250	$300
8	300	350
6	350	400
4	400	450
2	450	500

a. Use the I_{d1} schedule. Assume that the government needs to finance a budget deficit and this public borrowing increases the interest rate from 4% to 6%. How much crowding-out of private investment will occur?

_____

b. Now assume that the deficit is used to improve the performance of the economy, and that as a consequence, the investment-demand schedule changes from I_{d1} to I_{d2}. At the same time, the interest rate rises from 4% to 6% as the government borrows money to finance the deficit. How much crowding out of private

investment will occur in this case? _____

c. Graph the two investment-demand schedules on the graph below and show the difference between the two events. Put the interest rate on the vertical axis and the quantity of investment demanded on the horizontal axis.

3. Columns (1) and (2) in the table top right are the investment-demand schedules and show planned investment (*I*) at different rates of interest (*i*). Assume the marginal propensity to consume in the economy is 0.8.

(1) *i*	(2) *I*	(3) *I'*
.08	$115	$125
.07	140	150
.06	165	175
.05	190	200
.04	215	225

a. If the Federal government were to spend an additional $20 for goods and services the equilibrium real

GDP would (increase, decrease) _____ by

$ _____

b. If the Federal government had obtained the additional $20 by

(1) increasing taxes by $20 the equilibrium real GDP

would have (increased, decreased) _____

a total of $ _____ ;

(2) borrowing $20 in the money market and this borrowing had increased the interest rate from 5% to 6%,

(a) planned investment spending would have (increased, decreased) _____ by $ _____ ,

(b) the equilibrium real GDP would have _____

by $ _____ , and

(c) the net effect of the increased government spending of the $20 borrowed in the money market would

have been to _____ the equilibrium real

GDP by $ _____

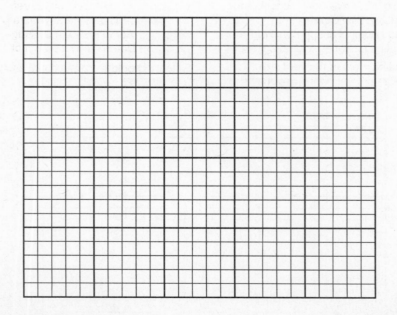

c. But if the government deficit-spending had improved business profit expectations and shifted the investment-demand schedule to the one shown in columns (1) and (3) in the table above the total effect of the increased government spending of the $20 borrowed in the money market would have been to

_____ the equilibrium real GDP by $ _____

■ **SHORT ANSWER AND ESSAY QUESTIONS**

1. What is the difference between the (Federal) budget deficit and the public debt?

2. Explain why an annually balanced budget is not "neutral" and how it can intensify, rather than reduce, the tendencies for GDP to rise and fall.

3. How does a cyclically balanced budget philosophy differ from the philosophy of functional finance? Why do advocates of functional finance argue that budget deficits and a mounting national debt are of secondary importance?

4. What are the four basic causes of the public debt over the past fifty-five years?

5. How does the lack of political will and entitlement programs affect the public debt and Federal budget deficits?

6. How big is the public debt of the United States absolutely and relative to the GDP? How large are the interest payments on this debt absolutely and relative to the GDP? What has happened to the size of the debt and the interest payments on it absolutely and relatively since 1930 and since 1980? Why have these changes occurred?

7. In what way do the accounting procedures of the Federal government misstate its actual financial position (its net worth)? How does inflation effect the *real* size of the public debt and the real size of the Federal government's budget deficits?

8. Why can't the public debt result in the bankruptcy of the Federal government?

9. Explain the difference between an internally held and an externally held public debt. If the debt is internally held government borrowing to finance a war does not pass the cost of the war on to future generations. Why?

10. How does the public debt and the payment of interest on this debt affect:
(a) the distribution of income and
(b) incentives?

11. Who owns the public debt? What percentage is held by the two major groups? What percentage of the public debt is held by foreigners? What are the economic implications of the portion of the public debt held by foreigners?

12. How can a large and growing public debt put curbs on the use of fiscal policy?

13. How can deficit financing impose a burden on future generations? Why don't increases in government expenditures financed by increased personal taxes impose the same burden on future generations? What will lessen the burden of deficit financing on future generations?

14. What heightened the concern of the public over recent budget deficits and the increase in the public debt?

15. How do budget deficits (and the increase in the public debt) affect:
(a) interest rates;
(b) planned domestic investment in real capital and the financial investment of foreigners in American securities;
(c) the external debts of the United States and the international value of the dollar;
(d) American exports and imports of goods and services; and
(e) employment and real output in the American economy?

16. Discuss other deficit-related effects on interest rates and crowding out, interest rates and the international debt crisis, and the trade imbalance and the borrowing needs of the United States.

17. Explain how an economist would use the Ricardian equivalence theorem to explain the effects of large budget deficits on the economy.

18. Explain the policy responses that have been suggested for the Federal budget deficits and the increasing public debt. Explain the key features of the Budget Reconciliation Act of 1990, the Budget Enforcement Act of 1990, and Deficit Reduction Act of 1993.

19. How would a constitutional amendment or a line-item veto help reduce budget deficits?

20. What tends to happen to the amount of saving done at full employment as the full-employment real GDP grows? Why, in a growing economy, must debt increase in order to maintain full employment and economic growth?

ANSWERS

Chapter 18 Budget Deficits and the Public Debt

FILL-IN QUESTIONS

1. expenditures, revenues, deficits, surpluses

2. pro-, raise, lower

3. recession, inflation

4. full employment without inflation, deficits, public debt

5. wars, a recession, tax, political

6. *a.* $4–6, 69, 192, 189, 3.3; *b.* higher, lower; one-third, two-thirds; *d.* internal, 14; *e.* debts, assets; *f.* decreased, decreased

7. reduce, refinancing, money, taxes

8. asset, consumption, the present

9. externally, increase, incentives, crowding-out

10. increases, decreases, capital; *a.* consumer, present; *b.* capital, less than full

11. size, social security, cost, policies, balance

12. crowding-out, demand-pull inflation

13. imports, exports, debtor, increased

14. increase; *a.* contracts, more; *b.* increases, raises; *c.* contracts, expands, contracts; *d.* contractionary; *e.* crowding-out, net export (either order)

15. lowered, weakened, underdeveloped, banking, greater than

16. Ricardian equivalence, will not, offset

17. Budget Reconciliation, Budget Enforcement

18. Deficit Reduction Act, tax, spending

19. constitutional, line-item veto

20. saving, growing, full employment

TRUE-FALSE QUESTIONS

1. F, p. 362	**8.** F, p. 364	**15.** T, p. 369	**22.** F, p. 374
2. T, pp. 363-364	**9.** F, p. 367	**16.** T, p. 369	**23.** F, p. 375
3. T, p. 364	**10.** F, p. 367	**17.** F, p. 370	**24.** T, p. 375
4. T, p. 365	**11.** F, p. 367	**18.** F, p. 370	**25.** T, p. 376
5. T, pp. 365-366	**12.** T, p. 368	**19.** F, p. 373	
6. F, p. 365	**13.** T, p. 368	**20.** F, p. 373	
7. F, p. 366	**14.** T, p. 369	**21.** F, p. 374	

MULTIPLE-CHOICE QUESTIONS

1. *c*, p. 363	**10.** *d*, pp. 367-368	**19.** *a*, pp. 372-373
2. *a*, p. 363	**11.** *a*, p. 368	**20.** *c*, pp. 372-373
3. *b*, p. 365	**12.** *c*, p. 369	**21.** *a*, p. 374
4. *a*, p. 364	**13.** *b*, p. 369	**22.** *b*, p. 374
5. *d*, p. 364	**14.** *c*, p. 369	**23.** *b*, p. 375
6. *d*, p. 366	**15.** *d*, pp. 369-370	**24.** *b*, p. 375
7. *a*, p. 364	**16.** *d*, pp. 370-371	**25.** *a*, pp. 375-376
8. *b*, p. 367	**17.** *b*, pp. 371-372	
9. *a*, p. 367	**18.** *b*, p. 371	

PROBLEMS

1. *a.* 55, 43, 37, 36, 33, 50, 63, 69; *c.* The debt as a percent of GDP fell from 1961 to 1981 and then rose substantially from 1981 to 1994.

2. *a.* $50 billion; *b.* none

3. *a.* increase, 100; *b.* (1) increased, 20 (2) (a) decreased, 25, (b) decreased, 125 (c) decrease, 25; *c.* increase, 25

SHORT ANSWER AND ESSAY QUESTIONS

1. pp. 362-363	**6.** pp. 364,365-366	**11.** pp. 367-369	**16.** p. 374
2. p. 363	**7.** p. 367	**12.** p. 369	**17.** p. 374
3. pp. 363-364	**8.** pp. 367-368	**13.** p. 370	**18.** p. 374-375
4. pp. 365-366	**9.** pp. 368-369	**14.** pp. 371-372	**19.** pp. 375-976
5. pp. 365-366	**10.** p. 369	**15.** p. 372-374	**20.** p. 376

CHAPTER 19

Economic Growth

Chapter 19 is the last of four chapters that discuss macroeconomic issues and problems. While the previous chapters focused primarily on short-term instability in output and the price level, this chapter looks at the longer-term problem of economic growth.

After briefly defining and explaining the significance of growth, the text analyzes the six factors that make growth possible. The four *supply* factors increase the output potential of the economy. Whether the economy actually produces its full potential—that is, whether the economy has both full employment and full production—depends upon two other factors: the level of aggregate demand (the *demand* factor) and the efficiency with which the economy allocates resources (the *efficiency* factor).

The next section of the chapter places the factors contributing to economic growth in graphical perspective with the use of two familiar models. The production possibilities model was originally presented in Chapter 2 and is now used to discuss how the two major supply factors—labor input and labor productivity—shift the production possibilities curve outward. The second model is the aggregate-demand and aggregate-supply framework that was first explained in Chapter 11 and was discussed in more detail in Chapter 17. Here you learn how both the short-run and the long-run shifts in aggregate supply combined with shifts in aggregate demand (and the supply and demand factors underlying those shifts) affect the output and the price level.

The growth record of the United States has been impressive both in terms of increases in real GDP and in real GDP per capita. What accounts for this long-term economic growth of the United States? First, the American population and the size of its labor force have grown. Second and more important, the productivity of the labor force in the United States has increased. The increase in the productivity of labor is the result of technological advances: the expansion of the stock of capital goods in the American economy; the improved education and training of its labor force; economies of scale; the reallocation of resources; the generous quantities of natural resources with which the American economy was endowed; and its social, cultural, and political environment. (Note, however, that the regulations of government tend to slow the rates

at which the productivity of labor and the output of the economy grow.) In addition to the supply and allocative factors, aggregate demand has expanded sufficiently (though unsteadily) to bring about most of the growth made possible by the increases in the quantity and the productivity of labor.

The rate of increase in labor productivity was less in the 1970s and 1980s compared with previous decades, and also less when compared with some of our major trading partners. This slowdown in labor productivity is significant for several reasons related to our standard of living, inflation, and the competitiveness of the United States in world markets. As you will learn, the decline stems from at least five major problems experienced by the economy in the past two decades. Although productivity growth has increased modestly in recent years, the resurgence may be transitory and low productivity may continue to limit the long-term potential for economic growth in the American economy.

The latter part of Chapter 19 asks an important question—whether economic growth in the industrially advanced nations can continue over the coming decades. This controversy has two sides to it. The results from the *doomsday models* indicate that the world economy is using resources at unsustainable rates and producing wastes in such quantities that they cannot be absorbed by the planet. The critics respond that the doomsday perspective is exaggerated on several counts. It assumes absolute limits on resources and technology while economic growth continues at current rates, and fails to account for the incentives effects of market prices. Finally, if you think that economic growth is desirable, the last section of the chapter outlines demand-side, supply-side, and industrial policies for sustaining economic growth.

■ CHECKLIST

When you have studied this chapter you should be able to:

☐ Define economic growth in two different ways.
☐ Explain why economic growth is important to any economy.

☐ Use the "rule of 70" to demonstrate how different growth rates affect real domestic output over time.

☐ Identify four supply factors in economic growth.

☐ Explain demand and efficiency factors in economic growth.

☐ Show graphically how economic growth shifts the production possibilities curve.

☐ Illustrate graphically how economic growth affects supply and demand curves.

☐ Describe the growth record of the American economy since 1940 and its rates of economic growth since World War II.

☐ Compare the relative importance of the two major means of increasing the real GDP in the United States since 1929.

☐ Enumerate the several sources of the growth of the productivity of labor in the United Sates since 1929; and state their relative importance in the growth of its real national income.

☐ Identify the chief detriment to the increase in labor productivity; and state by how much it and other factors have slowed the growth of real national income in the United States since 1929.

☐ Explain why the actual rate of growth in the United States has been less than its potential rate of growth and why it has been unstable.

☐ Give three reasons why the slowdown in productivity is significant.

☐ Enumerate the five principal causes of the slowdown in the rate of labor productivity in the United States.

☐ Discuss whether there has been a resurgence of productivity.

☐ Describe the predictions and recommendations from doomsday models of the world economy.

☐ State three criticisms of doomsday models.

☐ Outline three economic policies that might be used to sustain economic growth in the United States.

■ CHAPTER OUTLINE

1. Growth economics deals with the long run and changes in productive capacity over time.

   a. Economic growth means an increase in either the total or the per capita real output of an economy; and is measured in terms of the annual percentage rate of growth of either total or per capita real output.

   b. Economic growth is important because it lessens the burden of scarcity; it provides the means of satisfying existing wants more fully and fulfilling new wants.

   c. One or two percentage point differences in the rate of growth result in substantial differences in annual increases in the economy's output.

2. Whether economic growth *can* occur depends on supply, demand, and efficiency factors:

   a. supply factors include the quantity and quality of resources (natural, human, and capital), and technology;

   b. demand factors influence the level of aggregate demand in the economy that is important for sustaining full employment of resources; and

   c. efficiency factors affect the efficient use of resources to obtain maximum production of goods and services (production efficiency) and allocates them to their highest and best use by society (allocative efficiency).

3. Two familiar economic models can be used for the analysis of economic growth.

   a. In the production possibilities model, economic growth shifts the production possibilities curve outward because of improvement in supply factors that:

   (1) increase real output by increasing the labor inputs and by increasing the productivity of labor (in equation terms: total output = worker-hours × labor productivity);

   (2) however, whether the economy operates on the frontier of the curve depends on demand factors affecting the full employment of resources efficiency factors affecting full production.

   b. In the aggregate-demand and aggregate-supply model, economic growth is also affected by these supply, demand, and efficiency factors.

   (1) Supply factors that contribute to economic growth shift the vertical long-run aggregate supply to the right in the model.

   (2) But since the price level has increased over time, this suggests that the increase in potential output has been accompanied by an even greater shift in aggregate demand (and its underlying demand and allocative factors).

4. Over the last sixty years, the growth record of the American economy has been impressive; but economic growth in America has been less impressive than the record of many advanced industrialized nations in recent decades.

   a. Economic well-being may be understated by economic growth figures because the figures do not take into account improvements in product quality or increase in leisure time.

   b. But growth may have adverse effects on the environment or the quality of life that are not reflected in growth figures, thus the figures may overstate the benefits of growth.

5. Many factors account for the economic growth of the United States. Economist Edward Denison estimates that between 1929 and 1982 the real national income in the United States grew at an average annual rate of 2.9%.

   a. Two-thirds of this growth was the result of the increased productivity of labor, and one-third of it was the result of the increased quantity of labor employed in the economy.

b. During this period the American population and its labor force expanded; and despite decreases in the length of the workweek and birthrates, the increased participation of women in the labor force and the growth of its population continue to expand the size of the labor force by two million workers a year.

c. Technological advance is combining given amounts of resources in new ways that result in a larger output; and during the 1929–1982 period it accounted for 28% of the increase in real national income.

d. Saving and investment have expanded the American economy's stock of capital; increased the quantity of tools, equipment, and machinery with which each worker has to work; and accounted for 19% of the increase in real national income between 1929 and 1982.

e. Increased investment in human capital (in the training and education of workers) expands the productivity of workers; and accounted for 14% of the 1929–1982 increase in real national income.

f. Economies of scale and the improved allocation of resources also expand the productivity of workers; and in the American economy 9% and 8%, respectively, of the increase in real national income between 1929 and 1982 can be attributed to them.

g. But such detriments (or deterrents) to the growth of productivity as the government regulation of industry, of pollution, and of worker health and safety divert investment away from productivity-increasing additions to capital; and they accounted for a negative 9% of the increased real national income in the 1929–1982 period.

h. Such difficult-to-quantify factors as its general abundance of natural resources and social-cultural-political environment have also contributed to economic growth in the United States.

i. While actual growth in real national income during the 1929–1982 period averaged 2.9% a year, it would have been higher if aggregate demand had not at times fallen below its full-employment levels.

j. Increases in the productivity of labor have been more important than increases in the quantity of labor employed in expanding real national income in the American economy; but these increases in productivity cannot be taken for granted, are not automatic, and are the results of the changes in the economy described above.

6. The annual rates of growth in labor productivity in the United States declined substantially during the 1970s, and rose only modestly during the 1980s and early 1990s. Productivity rates achieved in the United States are also less than those found in other major industrial nations such as Japan or Germany.

a. The **slowdown in the growth of labor productivity** is significant because it affects the standard of living, inflation, and the prices of American goods in world markets.

b. The suggested causes of the productivity slowdown have included:

(1) *labor quality*—a decline in the quality (education, training, and experience) of the American labor force;

(2) *less technological progress*—a decline in research and development expenditures as a percentage of GDP;

(3) *low investment*—reduced investment in capital goods as a percentage of GDP than in previous periods stemming from low saving rates, import competition, regulation, and less spending for infrastructure;

(4) *high energy prices*—higher prices in 1973–1975 and 1978–1980 increased production costs and had inflationary and adverse macro policy effects on the economy;

(5) *adversarial labor relations*—worker and management relations can be adversarial rather than cooperative, especially when compared with the Japanese.

c. Productivity improved in the 1981–1990 period and in recent years, when compared with the 1973–1981 period, but it is not known if this modest "resurgence" is permanent or transitory.

7. *Doomsday models* indicate that future economic growth in the world economy may be unsustainable because of the rates at which natural resources are being depleted and the harm from the growing quantity of wastes being dumped into the environment.

a. Recommendations for changes include slowing exponential pollution and economic growth, reducing the use of renewable and nonrenewable resources to reasonable rates, and limiting pollution to the capacity of the environment to absorb waste.

b. Doomsday models, however, can be criticized for three reasons:

(1) The assumptions of continuing exponential economic and pollution growth or of absolute limits on resources or technology are not realistic.

(2) Technological improvements and the expansion of the resource base have permitted the rate of economic growth to be sustained over time despite increases in population.

(3) Changes in market prices provide incentives to allocate scarce resources efficiently to sustain economic growth.

8. Three economic policies have been discussed for achieving more economic growth in the United States.

a. *Demand-side policies* focus on the use of monetary and fiscal policies to influence aggregate demand and maintain full employment and full production of resources.

b. *Supply-side policies* call for expansion of the economy's output potential and often involve changes in tax policy to increase investment, saving, and work effort.

c. Some economists advocate an *industrial policy* that would shape the structure and composition of industry by targeting those industries or technologies with the best possibility for contributing to the nation's economic growth.

■ IMPORTANT TERMS

Economic growth	Labor productivity
Supply factor	Infrastructure
Demand factor	Doomsday models
Efficiency factor	Industrial policy
Labor force participation rate	

■ HINTS AND TIPS

1. Chapter 19 contains very little economics that should be new to you. You learned about real GDP and how to measure its growth in Chapter 7. Chapter 2 introduced you to the production possibilities model that is now discussed in more detail. In Chapter 11 you learned about the aggregate demand and aggregate supply models that are now used to discuss economic growth. You might review these concepts and models from previous chapters before reading Chapter 19.

2. Table 19–2 is important if you want to understand the factors that influence economic growth in the United States. The figures in the table indicate the relative importance of each factor. About two-thirds of American economic growth comes from eight factors that affect labor productivity. One-third comes from the increase in the quantity of labor.

3. Make sure you remember the distinction between positive and normative economics when you read the section on doomsday models and whether economic growth in the world economy is desirable or sustainable.

SELF-TEST

■ FILL-IN QUESTIONS

1. Growth economics is concerned with an economy whose productive capacity (increases, remains constant) _____ over time.

2. Economic growth can mean an increase in either the _____ or the _____ _____ of an economy.

3. A rise in output per capita (increases, decreases) _____ the standard of living and _____ the burden of scarcity in the economy.

4. Assume an economy has a GDP of $3600 billion. If the growth rate is 5%, GDP will increase by $ _____ billion a year; but if the rate of growth is only 3%, the annual increase in GDP will be $ _____ billion. A two percentage point difference in the growth rate results in a $ _____ billion difference in the annual increase in GDP.

5. The four supply factors in economic growth are _____ , _____ , _____ , and _____ . The other two growth factors are the _____ _____ factor and the _____ factor.

6. In the production possibilities model, economic growth increases primarily because of (demand, supply) _____ factors that shift the production possibilities curve to the (left, right) _____ ; but the economy may not realize its potential because there may be less than full _____ and full _____

7. The real GDP of any economy in any year is equal to the _____ of labor employed *multiplied* by the _____ of labor.

a. The former is measured by the number of (workers, hours of labor) _____ employed.

b. The latter is equal to the real GDP per _____ per _____

8. The quantity of labor employed in the economy in any year depends on the size of the employed _____ force and the _____ of the average workweek. The size element depends upon the size of the working-age _____ and the labor-force _____ _____ rate.

9. In the aggregate-demand and aggregate-supply framework, economic growth is illustrated by an (increase, decrease) _____ in the long-run aggregate-supply curve; and when the price level also increases, it indicates that the aggregate-demand curve has increased (more, less) _____ rapidly than the long-run aggregate supply.

10. Since 1948, the average rate of growth in real GDP has been _____ %.

11. Economist Edward Denison studied economic growth in the United States from 1929–1982 and found that the increase in the quantity of labor accounted for (one-third, two-thirds) _____ of economic growth and increases in labor productivity accounted for _____ of economic growth. Factors contributing to labor productivity include:

   a. technological _____ ;

   b. increases in the quantity of _____ employed and in the quantity employed per _____ ;

   c. the improved _____ and _____ of workers;

   d. economies of _____ ; and

   e. the improved _____ of resources.

12. An increase in the stock of capital of a nation is the result of saving and _____ . In the United States the stock of capital has historically grown (more, less) _____ rapidly than the quantity of labor employed.

13. Technological progress means that we learn how to employ given quantities of resources to obtain greater _____ ; and, more often than not, this progress requires _____ in new machinery and equipment.

14. The principal detriment to growth of real national income in the 1929–1982 period seems to have been government _____ which diverted (consumption, investment) _____ spending away from uses that would have increased the _____ of labor.

15. Two other factors that have led to economic growth in the United States are its abundant _____ resources and its social-cultural-political _____

16. Denison's analysis is designed to explain (actual, potential) _____ real national income. When there is a deficiency of aggregate demand the _____ rate of economic growth falls short of the _____ .

17. The annual rates of increase in the productivity of labor, between the middle 1960s and 1981, (rose, fell, remained constant) _____

_____

This resulted in a (rise, fall) _____ in the rates at which the standard of _____ and the (nominal, real) _____ wages of labor increased, in a (rise, fall) _____ in unit labor costs and (inflation, deflation) _____ in the United States, and the loss of international markets to (American, foreign) _____ producers of goods and services.

18. The slowdown in productivity growth is a result of problems with _____ quality, less _____ progress, relatively low levels of _____ spending as a percent of GDP, high _____ prices in certain years, adversarial _____ relations. Some of these problems have lessened in the past decade, and as a consequence, there has been a resurgence in _____ , but it is not known whether the change is permanent or _____

19. Computer models that indicate future economic growth in the world economy may be unsustainable because of resources depletion and environmental waste and destruction are called _____ models. The results from these models are criticized because _____ of exponential rates of economic and pollution growth but absolute limits to the resource base are unrealistic. The models do not take into account advances in _____ that expand the supply of resources, or the offsetting effects of changes in market _____

20. Three types of growth policies have been suggested for stimulating economic growth in the United States. (Supply, Demand) _____ - side policies involve the use of monetary and fiscal policies to sustain and expand the full employment of resources in the economy, whereas _____ - side policies focus primarily on tax changes to stimulate saving, investment, and entrepreneurship, and thereby expand capacity output. Shaping the structure and composition of American industry is the target of _____ policies for economic growth.

■ TRUE-FALSE QUESTIONS

Circle the T if the statement is true; the F if it is false.

1. Growth economics concerns an economy in which productive capacity is not fixed.   **T   F**

2. The better of the two definitions of economic growth is an increase in the per capita real output of the economy.   **T   F**

3. Suppose two economies both have GDPs of $500 billion. If the GDPs grow at annual rates of 3% in the first and 5% in the second economy, the difference in their amounts of growth in one year is $10 billion.   **T   F**

4. If the rate of growth in real GDP averages 2.5% a year, it will take about 28 years for real GDP to double.   **T   F**

5. The potential of an enhanced productive capacity in an economy will not be completely realized unless there is full employment of resources and full production in the economy.   **T   F**

6. An increase in economic growth will increase the long-run aggregate supply curve and the short-run aggregate supply curve, but decreases the aggregate demand curve.   **T   F**

7. The demand factor in economic growth refers to the ability of the economy to expand its production as the demand for products grows.   **T   F**

8. The allocative factor in economic growth refers to the ability of the economy to move resources from one use to another as the productive capacity of the economy grows.   **T   F**

9. The real GDP of an economy in any year is equal to its input of labor divided by the productivity of labor.   **T   F**

10. Real GDP has tended to increase more rapidly than real per capita GDP in the United States.   **T   F**

11. Growth and rates-of-growth estimates generally attempt to take account of changes in the quality of goods produced and in the amount of leisure members of the economy enjoy.   **T   F**

12. Increased labor productivity has been more important than increased labor inputs in the growth of the American economy since 1929.   **T   F**

13. Since 1929 improved technology has accounted for about 28% of the increase in labor productivity in the United States.   **T   F**

14. More often than not technological progress requires the economy to invest in new machinery and equipment.   **T   F**

15. The single most important source of the growth of labor productivity in the United States since 1929 has been the increase in the size of the American labor force.   **T   F**

16. The regulation of industry, the pollution of the environment, and increased regulation of the health and safety of workers by government tend to reduce the rate at which labor productivity grows.   **T   F**

17. The availability of natural resources in the United States has been a significant factor in the growth of the American economy.   **T   F**

18. Over the past sixty years, the American social, cultural, and political environment has slowed the economic growth of the United States.   **T   F**

19. Increases in labor productivity can, at least in the American economy, be taken pretty much for granted because the rate of increase has been nearly constant for well over half a century.   **T   F**

20. Between the mid-1960s and 1981 the productivity of labor in the United States fell.   **T   F**

21. Productivity growth is a major factor contributing to increases in real wage rates and the standard of living in a nation.   **T   F**

22. There was a significant improvement in the education, employment training, and work experience of workers in the 1970s and 1980s that contributed to increased labor productivity in those decades.   **T   F**

23. During the 1970s and 1980s the United States invested a larger percentage of its GDP in capital goods.   **T   F**

24. Adversarial industrial relations between managers and their employees in the United States can slow the rate at which the productivity of labor increases.   **T   F**

25. Supply-side economists favor increasing taxes to stimulate saving, investment, and economic growth in the economy.   **T   F**

■ MULTIPLE-CHOICE QUESTIONS

Circle the letter that corresponds to the best answer.

1. Which of the following is a benefit of real economic growth to a society?
   (a) everyone enjoys a greater nominal income
   (b) the standard of living increases
   (c) the burden of scarcity increases
   (d) the society is less able to satisfy new wants

2. If the real output of an economy were to increase from $2000 billion to $2100 billion in one year the rate of growth of real output during that year would be:

(a) 0.5%
(b) 5%
(c) 10%
(d) 50%

3. Suppose an economy has a real GDP of $700 billion and an annual growth rate of 5%. Over a *two*-year period real GDP will increase by:
(a) $14 billion
(b) $35 billion
(c) $70 billion
(d) $71 3/4 billion

4. If a nation's real GDP is growing by 2% per year, then approximately how many years will it take for real GDP to double?
(a) 25 years
(b) 30 years
(c) 35 years
(d) 40 years

Use the following graph to answer the next two questions (5 and 6).

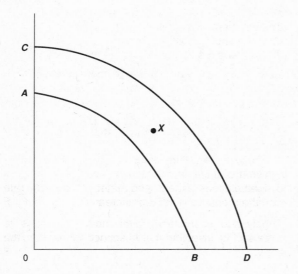

5. If the production possibilities curve of an economy shifts from **AB** to **CD**, it is most likely caused by:
(a) supply factors
(b) demand factors
(c) efficiency factors
(d) industrial policy

6. If the production possibilities curve for an economy is at **CD** but the economy is operating at point **X**, the reasons are most likely to be because of:
(a) supply and environmental factors
(b) demand and efficiency factors
(c) labor inputs and labor productivity
(d) technological progress

7. Which of the following is *not* a supply factor in economic growth?
(a) an expansion in purchasing power
(b) an increase in the economy's stock of capital goods
(c) more natural resources
(d) technological progress

Use the graph below to answer the next two questions (8 and 9).

8. A shift from Q_1 to Q_2 is caused by a shift in the:
(a) level of prices
(b) aggregate demand curve
(c) short-run aggregate supply curve
(d) long-run aggregate supply curve

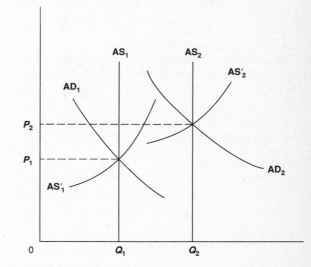

9. Which combination would best explain a shift in the price level from P_1 to P_2 and an increase in real domestic output from Q_1 to Q_2?
(a) an increase in the long-run aggregate supply (AS_1 to AS_2) and in short-run aggregate supply (AD_1 to AD_2).
(b) an increase in aggregate demand (AD_1 to AD_2) and an increase in aggregate supply (AD_1 to AD_2).
(c) an increase in the long-run aggregate supply (AS_1 to AS_2), an increase in aggregate demand (AD_1 to AD_2), and an increase in short-run aggregate supply (AS_1 to AS_2).
(d) a decrease in the long-run aggregate supply (AS_2 to AS_1), a decrease in aggregate demand (AD_2 to AD_1), and a decrease in short-run aggregate supply (AS_2 to AS_1)

10. Since 1940 real GDP in the United States has increased about:
(a) twofold
(b) threefold
(c) fourfold
(d) fivefold

11. The real GDP of the American economy since 1948 increased at an average *annual* rate of about:
(a) .5%
(b) 2.1%
(c) 3.3%
(d) 5.4%

12. Real GDP per capita in the United States since 1948 increased at an average annual rate of about:
(a) 1%
(b) 2%
(c) 3%
(d) 4%

13. Data on real GDP, real GDP per capita, and the respective growth rates of those measured in the United States take into account:
(a) improvement in product quality
(b) increases in available leisure time
(c) environmental problems
(d) changes in domestic output

14. About what fraction of the growth in the real national income of the United States since 1929 has been due to increases in the quantity of labor employed?
(a) one-fourth
(b) one-third
(c) one-half
(d) two-thirds

15. The factor accounting for the greatest increase in the productivity of labor in the United States between 1929 and 1982 was:
(a) economies of scale
(b) technological advance
(c) the improved education and training of the labor force
(d) the expanded quantity of capital

16. Approximately what percentages of the labor force have completed high school and four years of college?
(a) 45% and 8%
(b) 44% and 13%
(c) 60% and 8%
(d) 80% and 20%

17. The average rate of growth in labor productivity in the United States:
(a) fell from 1966 to 1981, and rose from 1981 to 1994
(b) rose from 1966 to 1981, and fell from 1981 to 1994
(c) fell from 1966 to 1981, and has continued to fall
(d) rose from 1966 to 1981, and rose again from 1981 to 1994

18. The decline in the rate of productivity of labor from 1966–1981 in the United States led to:
(a) a fall in the relative prices of American goods in world markets
(b) a rise in the standard of living in the United States

(c) a rise in unit labor costs and inflation in the United States
(d) a fall in energy prices

19. Which factor has contributed to the slowdown in the growth of productivity in recent decades?
(a) more cooperative rather than competitive relationships between workers and management
(b) an increase in the rate of technological progress
(c) an increase in the amount of investment in capital goods
(d) a work force that was less experienced and less prepared for employment

20. Which of the following best explains why there has been a lower level of capital investment in the United States in the past two decades?
(a) less regulation of business practices
(b) less competition from imported goods
(c) higher level of spending for infrastructure
(d) a lower rate of saving

21. What factor has contributed to the resurgence of productivity growth in recent years?
(a) increased inflation
(b) higher energy prices
(c) more experienced workers
(d) greater expenditures by government

22. One of the basic conclusions of doomsday models is that:
(a) the population rate will decline and lead to human extinction
(b) the industrial sector will grow at the expense of the agricultural sector
(c) the world economy is using resources and dumping waste at unsustainable rates
(d) warfare will reduce productivity and economic growth and cause a rapid decline in the standards of living

23. Which of the following is a criticism of doomsday modeling?
(a) it idealistically sets the growth of the natural resource base at too high of a rate
(b) it unrealistically assumes that population and economic growth will continue at exponential rates
(c) it includes incentives effects from changes in the market prices of goods and services
(d) it gives too much weight to technological improvement

24. The active use of monetary and fiscal policy to eliminate or reduce the severity of recession would be an example of:
(a) industrial policy
(b) demand-side policy
(c) supply-side policy
(d) investment policy

25. What type of policy is being suggested by the person who makes this statement: "What this nation needs is a comprehensive plan developed by government and business to direct economic activity to those opportunities that have the best chance of creating more economic growth for the nation"?

(a) a demand-side policy
(b) a supply-side policy
(c) an industrial policy
(d) an investment policy

■ PROBLEMS

1. The table below shows the quantity of labor (measured in hours) and the productivity of labor (measured in real GDP per hour) in a hypothetical economy in three different years.

Year	Quantity of labor	Productivity of labor	Real GDP
1	1000	$100	$ ___
2	1000	105	___
3	1100	105	___

a. Compute the economy's real GDP in each of the three years and enter them in the table.

b. Between years 1 and 2, the quantity of labor remained constant, but

(1) the productivity of labor increased by _____ %; and

(2) as a consequence, real GDP increased by _____ %.

c. Between years 2 and 3, the productivity of labor remained constant; but

(1) the quantity of labor increased by _____ %; and

(2) as a consequence, real GDP increased by _____ %.

d. Between years 1 and 3

(1) real GDP increased by _____ %; and

(2) this rate of increase is approximately equal to the sum of the rates of increase in the _____ and the _____ of labor.

2. Suppose the real GDP and the population of an economy in seven different years were those shown in the next table.

a. How large would the real per capita GDP of the economy be in each of the other six years? Put your figures in the table.

Year	Population, million	Real GDP, billions of dollars	Per capital real GDP
1	30	$ 9	$ 300
2	60	24	___
3	90	45	___
4	120	66	___
5	150	90	___
6	180	99	___
7	210	105	___

b. What would have been the size of the optimum population of this economy? _____

c. What was the *amount* of growth in real GDP between year 1 and year 2? $ _____

d. What was the *rate* of growth in real GDP between year 3 and year 4? _____ %

3. Given the hypothetical data in the table below, calculate the average annual rates of growth in real GDP and real per capita GDP over the period given. (**Note:** Remember to adjust rate of growth for the number of years in the period so you get average annual rates. Real GDP is in billions.)

Year	Real GDP	Annual growth in %	Real GDP per capita	Annual growth in %
1970	$2,416		$11,785	
1975	2,695	___	12,593	___
1980	3,187	___	13,978	___
1985	3,618	___	15,139	___
1988	3,995	___	16,240	___
1991	4,545	___	17,110	___

■ SHORT ANSWERS AND ESSAY QUESTIONS

1. What is meant by economic growth? Why should the citizens of the United States be concerned with economic growth?

2. What are the six basic ingredients of economic growth? What is the essential difference between the supply factors and the other two factors? Is there any relationship between the strength of the supply factors and the strength of the demand factor?

3. What is the relationship between the real GDP produced in any year and the quantity of labor employed and labor productivity?

4. In what units are the quantity of labor and the productivity of labor measured? What:
  (a) are the two principal determinants of the quantity of the labor input;
  (b) determines the size of the labor force?

5. How does economic growth affect production possibilities? What demand and efficiency assumptions are necessary to achieve maximum productive potential?

6. Describe how economic growth can be illustrated in an aggregate-demand and aggregate-supply framework. What has happened to aggregate demand compared to long-run aggregate supply when the price level and real domestic output both increase?

7. What has been the growth record of the American economy? Compare recent American growth rates with those in other nations.

8. What have been the sources of the growth of the real national income in the United States since 1929? What has tended to slow the increase in labor productivity and in real national income?

9. What changes have occurred in the size of the American population and labor force since 1929? What factor has slowed the rate of growth of the former and what factor has speeded the growth of the latter?

10. What is the relationship between investment and the stock of capital? By how much has capital per worker expanded since 1889? What is the connection between increases in the capital stock and the rate of economic growth?

11. What is technological advance and why are technological advance and capital formation closely related processes?

12. What is meant by and, therefore, tends to increase the "quality" of labor? How is this quality usually measured?

13. What are the economic consequences if aggregate demand increases less than productive capacity increases? What are the long-term consequences of this macroeconomic instability?

14. By how much did the annual increases in the productivity of labor decline in the United States between the mid-1960s and 1981? What are three significant features of this decline in this productivity growth?

15. What are five causes of the slowdown in the growth of labor productivity since the mid-1960s? Explain how each cause affects productivity.

16. How might changes in labor quality dampen productivity growth? What factors in the United States have contributed to this situation?

17. What is the relationship between the capital investment and productivity growth? What four conditions in the United States have affected the relative level of investment?

18. Has economic growth resurged since 1981? What long-term problems does productivity growth pose for the economy of the United States?

19. What arguments can be presented to support the doomsday models of economic growth and what criticisms can be made of those models? Is economic growth desirable and sustainable?

20. What are the basic differences between demand-side, supply-side, and industrial policies that are designed to stimulate economic growth?

ANSWERS

Chapter 19 Economic Growth

FILL-IN QUESTIONS

1. increases

2. real output (GDP), real output (GDP) per capita

3. increases, decreases

4. 180, 108, 72

5. quantity and quality of natural resources, quantity and quality of human resources, the supply or stock of capital goods, technology, demand, allocative

6. supply, right, employment, production (either order for last two)

7. quantity, productivity; *a.* hours of labor; *b.* worker, hour (either order)

8. labor, length, population, participation

9. increase, more

10. 3.3

11. one-third, two-thirds; *a.* progress (advance); *b.* capital, worker; *c.* education, training; *d.* scale; *e.* allocation

12. investment, more

13. output (production), investment

14. regulations, investment, productivity

15. natural, environment

16. actual, potential

17. fell, fall, living, real, rise, inflation, foreign

18. labor, technological, investment, energy, industrial, productivity, transitory

19. doomsday, assumptions, technology, prices (or signals)

20. Demand, supply, industrial

TRUE-FALSE QUESTIONS

1. T, p. 379	**10.** T, p. 383	**19.** F, pp. 388-389
2. F, p. 379	**11.** F, pp. 383-384	**20.** F, p. 388
3. T, p. 380	**12.** T, p. 384	**21.** T, p. 388
4. T, p. 380	**13.** F, p. 385	**22.** F, pp. 389-390
5. T, pp. 380-381	**14.** T, p. 385	**23.** F, p. 390
6. F, p. 382	**15.** F, p. 385	**24.** T, pp. 390-391
7. F, p. 380	**16.** T, p. 387	**25.** F, p. 394
8. T, p. 380	**17.** T, p. 387	
9. F, p. 381	**18.** F, p. 387	

PROBLEMS

1. *a.* 100,000, 105,000, 115,500; *b.* (1) 5, (2), 5; *c.* (1) 10, (2) 10; *d.* (1) 15.5, (2) quantity, productivity

2. *a.* 400, 500, 550, 600, 550, 500; *b.* 150 million; *c.* $15 billion; *d.* 46.7%

3. *real GDP:* 1970-75 (2.3%); 1975-80 (3.7%); 1980-85 (2.7%); 1985-88 (3.5%); 1988-91 (4.6%); *real GDP per capita:* 1970-75 (1.4%); 1975-80 (2.2%); 1980-85 (1.7%); 1985-88 (2.4%); 1988-91 (1.8%)

MULTIPLE-CHOICE QUESTIONS

1. *b*, p. 380	**10.** *d*, p. 383	**19.** *d*, pp. 389-390
2. *b*, p. 380	**11.** *c*, p. 383	**20.** *d*, p. 390
3. *d*, p. 380	**12.** *b*, p. 383	**21.** *c*, p. 391
4. *c*, p. 380	**13.** *d*, pp. 383-384	**22.** *c*, pp. 391-393
5. *a*, p. 381	**14.** *b*, p. 385	**23.** *b*, pp. 393-394
6. *b*, p. 381	**15.** *b*, p. 385	**24.** *b*, p. 394
7. *a*, p. 380	**16.** *d*, p. 386	**25.** *c*, pp. 394-395
8. *d*, pp. 382-383	**17.** *a*, p. 388	
9. *c*, pp. 382-383	**18.** *c*, pp. 388-389	

SHORT ANSWER AND ESSAY QUESTIONS

1. pp. 379-380	**8.** pp. 384-387	**15.** pp. 388-391
2. p. 380	**9.** pp. 384-385	**16.** pp. 389-390
3. p. 381	**10.** pp. 385-386	**17.** p. 390
4. pp. 381-382	**11.** p. 385	**18.** p. 391
5. pp. 381-382	**12.** p. 386	**19.** pp. 391-394
6. pp. 382-383	**13.** p. 388	**20.** pp. 394-395
7. pp. 383-384	**14.** pp. 388-389	

CHAPTER 20

International Trade

In Chapter 6 you learned about the role of the United States in the global economy and the basic principles of international trade. Chapter 20 extends that analysis in several ways. It gives you a more advanced understanding of comparative advantage. It uses the tools of supply and demand to explain the equilibrium prices and quantities of imports and exports, and the economic effects of tariffs and quotas. It examines the fallacious arguments for trade protectionism and the cost of this protection on American society.

After a brief review of the facts of international trade that were presented in Chapter 6, the text uses graphical analysis to explain the reason that nations trade: to take advantage of the benefits of specialization. Nations specialize in and export those goods and services in the production of which they have a comparative advantage. A comparative advantage means that the opportunity cost of producing a particular good or service is lower in that nation than in another nation. These nations will avoid the production of and import the goods and services in the production of which other nations have a comparative advantage. In this way all nations are able to obtain products which are produced as inexpensively as possible. Put another way, when nations specialize in those products in which they have a comparative advantage, the world as a whole can obtain more goods and services from its resources; and each of the nations of the world can enjoy a standard of living higher than it would have if it did not specialize and export and import.

The principle of comparative advantage tells us why nations trade, but what determines the equilibrium prices and quantities of the imports and exports resulting from trade? To answer this question, the text uses the supply and demand analysis, originally presented in Chapter 3, to explain equilibrium in the world market for product. A simplified two-nation and one product model of trade is used to construct export supply curves and import demand curves for each nation. Equilibrium occurs where one nation's export supply curve intersects another nation's import demand curve.

Regardless of the advantages of specialization and trade among nations, people in the United States and throughout the world have for well over 200 years debated whether free trade or protection was the better policy for their nation. Economists took part in this debate and, with few exceptions, argued for free trade and against protection. Those who favor free trade contend that free trade benefits both the nation and the world as a whole. "Free traders" argue that tariffs, import quotas, and other barriers to international trade prevent or reduce specialization and decrease both a nation's and the world's production and standard of living.

But nations have and continue to erect barriers to trade with other nations. The questions upon which the latter part of this chapter focuses attention are (1) what motivates nations to impose tariffs and to limit the quantities of goods imported from abroad; (2) what are the economic effects of protection on a nation's own prosperity and on the prosperity of the world economy; (3) what kinds of arguments do those who favor protection employ to support their position—on what grounds do they base their contention that their nation will benefit from the erection of barriers which reduce imports from foreign nations; and (4) what are the costs of protectionism for the United States.

The chapter's final section is a brief review of the international trade policy of the United States. Three general approaches to trade policy are identified in the discussion. First, the United States has participated in a generalized liberalization of trade as a result of General Agreements on Tariffs and Trade (GATT) negotiations, or regional accords such as the North American Free Trade Agreement (NAFTA). Second, the United States has pursued an aggressive policy of promoting exports. The United States government has subsidized exports, supported export-oriented industries, and lobbied other nations to purchase American exports, all in an effort to increase American exports. Third, bilateral negotiations have been conducted between the United States and other nations. In recent years, the United States has held bilateral negotiations with China and also with Japan to resolve major trade disputes.

Whether the direction of the international trade policy in the United States will be toward freer trade or more protectionism is a question that gets debated as each new trade issue is presented to the American public. The decision on each issue may well depend on your understanding of the advantages of free trade and the costs of trade protection for the nation and the world economy.

■ **CHECKLIST**

When you have studied this chapter you should be able to:

☐ Cite some key facts about international trade.

☐ State the two economic circumstances which make it desirable for nations to specialize and trade.

☐ Compute the costs of producing two commodities when you are given the necessary data in a two-nation example.

☐ Determine which nation has the comparative advantage in the production of each commodity using the cost data you computed for the two-nation example.

☐ Calculate the range in which the terms of trade will occur in the two-nation example.

☐ Explain how nations benefit from trade and specialization based on the two-nation example.

☐ Restate the case for free trade.

☐ Construct domestic supply and demand curves for two nations that trade a product.

☐ Construct export supply and import demand curves for two nations that trade a product.

☐ Use supply and demand analysis to explain how the equilibrium prices and quantities of exports and imports are determined for two nations that trade a product.

☐ Identify the four principal types of artificial barriers to international trade and the motive for erecting these barriers.

☐ Explain the economic effects of a protective tariff on resource allocation, the price of the commodity, the total production of the commodity, and the outputs of foreign and domestic producers of the commodity.

☐ Analyze the economic effects of an import quota and compare them with the economic effects of a tariff.

☐ Enumerate six arguments used to support the case for protection and find the weakness in each of these arguments.

☐ Discuss the costs of trade protectionism for society.

☐ Explain how trade protectionism affects income distribution.

☐ Describe actions taken to promote trade liberalization.

☐ Cite examples of export promotion undertaken by the United States.

☐ Discuss the issues involved in the bilateral trade negotiations of the United States.

■ **CHAPTER OUTLINE**

1. Some of the facts about international trade presented in Chapter 6 are worth reviewing.

    a. About 10 to 11% of the GDP of the United States is accounted for by exports and imports of goods and

services, a percentage which has more than doubled since 1965. The percentage of exports and imports is much higher (25 to 30%) in other industrially advanced nations (e.g., Germany, the Netherlands), but the size of the United States economy means that it has the largest volume of imports and exports in the world.

    b. The United States has a trade deficit in goods, a trade surplus in services, and a trade deficit in goods and services.

    c. The principal exports of the United States are chemicals, computers, consumer durables, and aircraft, while its major imports are petroleum, automobiles, and clothing. Most of the trade occurs with other industrially advanced nations. Canada is the largest trading partner for the United States.

    d. Factors that have facilitated trade since World War II include improvements in transportation and communications technology, along with a general decline in tariffs and worldwide conflict. The major participants in international trade are the United States, Japan, and the nations of western Europe. Newer participants include the "Asian tigers" (Hong Kong, Singapore, South Korea, and Taiwan) and China. The collapse of the former Soviet Union has changed trade patterns for Russia and the nations of eastern Europe.

    e. International trade policy has been a subject of recent concern as evidenced by the North American Free Trade Agreement (NAFTA), the conclusion of negotiations on the General Agreements on Tariffs and Trade (GATT), and bilateral negotiations between the United States and Japan.

2. Specialization and trade among nations is advantageous because the world's resources are not evenly distributed and the efficient production of different commodities necessitates different methods and combinations of resources.

3. The principle of **comparative advantage,** originally presented in Chapter 6 to explain the gains from trade, can now be reexamined with the aid of graphical analysis.

    a. Suppose the world is composed of only two nations, each of which is capable of producing two different commodities and in which the production possibilities curves are different straight lines (whose opportunity cost ratios are constant but different).

    (1) With different opportunity cost ratios, each nation will have a comparative (cost) advantage in the production of one of the two commodities; and if the world is to use its resources economically each nation must specialize in the commodity in the production of which it has a comparative advantage.

    (2) The ratio at which one product is traded for another—the terms of trade—lies between the opportunity cost ratios of the two nations.

    b. Each nation gains from this trade because specialization permits a greater total output from the same resources and a better allocation of the world's resources.

c. If opportunity cost ratios in the two nations are not constant, specialization may not be complete.

d. the basic argument for free trade among nations is that it leads to a better allocation of resources and a higher standard of living in the world; but it also increases competition and deters monopoly in these nations.

4. Supply and demand analysis can be used to explain how the equilibrium price and quantity of exports and imports for a product (e.g., aluminum) are determined when there is trade between two nations (e.g., the United States and Canada).

a. For the United States, there will be domestic supply and demand, and export supply and import demand for aluminum.

(1) The price and quantity of aluminum are determined by the intersection of the **domestic** demand and supply curves in a world without trade.

(2) In a world with trade, the **export supply** curve for the United States shows the amount of aluminum that American producers will export at each world price above the domestic equilibrium price. American exports will increase when the world price rises relative to the domestic price.

(3) The **import demand** curve for the United States shows the amount of aluminum that Americans will import at each world price below the domestic equilibrium price. American imports will increase when world prices fall relative to the domestic price.

b. For Canada, there will be domestic supply and demand, and export supply and import demand for aluminum. The description of these supply and demand curves is similar for those of the United States described in point **a** above.

c. The equilibrium world price and equilibrium world levels of exports and imports can be determined with further supply and demand analysis. The export supply curves of the two nations can be plotted on one graph. The import demand curves of both nations can be plotted on the same graph. In this two-nation model, equilibrium will be achieved when one nation's import demand curve intersects another nation's export supply curve.

5. Nations, however, limit international trade by erecting artificial barriers; and tariffs, import quotas, a variety of nontariff barriers, and voluntary export restrictions are the principal barriers to trade.

a. Special interest groups with nations benefit from protection and persuade their nations to erect trade barriers; but the costs to consumers of this protection exceed the benefits to the economy.

b. The imposition of a tariff on a good imported from abroad has both direct and indirect effects on an economy.

(1) The tariff increases the domestic price of the good, reduces its domestic consumption, expands its domestic production, decreases foreign production, and transfers income from domestic consumers to government.

(2) It also reduces the income of foreign producers and the ability of foreign nations to purchase goods and services in the nation imposing the tariff, causes the contraction of relatively efficient industries in that nation, decreases world trade, and lowers the real output of goods and services.

c. The imposition of a quota on an imported product has the same direct and indirect effects as that of a tariff on that product, with the exception that a tariff generates revenue for government use whereas an import quota transfers that revenue to foreign producers.

6. The arguments for protectionism are many but they often are of questionable validity.

a. The military self-sufficiency argument can be challenged because it is difficult to determine which industry is "vital" to national defense and must be protected; it would be more efficient economically to provide a direct subsidy to military producers rather than impose a tariff.

b. Trade barriers do not necessarily increase domestic employment because:

(1) imports may eliminate some jobs, but create others; therefore, imports may only change the composition of employment, not the overall level of employment;

(2) the exports of one nation become the imports of another; tariffs barriers can be viewed as "beggar thy neighbor" policies;

(3) there is likely to be retaliation from other nations from the imposition of trade barriers that will reduce domestic output and employment; and,

(4) they create a less efficient allocation of resources by shielding protected domestic industries from the rigors of competition.

c. Using tariff barriers to permit diversification for stability in economy is not necessary for advanced economies such as the United States and there may be economic costs to diversification in less developed nations.

d. It is alleged that infant-industries need protection until they are sufficiently large to compete. But the argument may not apply to developed economies; it is difficult to select which industries will prosper; protectionism tends to persist long after it is needed; and direct subsidies may be more economically efficient. A variant of this argument for advanced nations is "strategic trade policy" to justify barriers that protect the investment in high risk, growth industries for a nation, but these policies often lead to retaliation and smaller policies from other trading nations.

e. Sometimes protection is sought against the "dumping" of excess foreign goods on American markets. Dumping is a legitimate concern and is restricted under United States trade law, but to use dumping as an excuse for widespread tariff protection is unjustified and the number of documented cases is few. If foreign companies are more efficient (low cost) producers, what may appear to be dumping may actually be comparative advantage at work.

f. Protection is sometimes sought because of the cheap foreign labor argument; it should be realized that nations gain from trade based on comparative advantage and without trade living standards will be lower.

g. In summary, most of the protectionist arguments are fallacious or based on half-truths. The only points that have some validity, under certain conditions, are the infant-industry and military-sufficiency arguments, but both are subject to abuse. The historical evidence suggests that free trade promotes and protectionism defers prosperity and economic growth in the world.

7. There are costs to trade protectionism for the United States.

a. There is a significant cost to society:

(1) It raises product prices by raising the imported price of the product, causes some consumers to switch to higher-priced domestic products, and increases the price of domestic products.

(2) The benefits for businesses and workers from trade protection are outweighed by the costs to American society. The net cost to Americans was more than $20 billion annually in the early 1990s.

b. There is an effect on income distribution because import restrictions are more costly for low-income families than for high-income families.

8. The trade policies of the United States in recent years can be categorized in three ways.

a. The United States has participated in regional and global agreements to liberalize trade. Two examples are the North American Free Trade Agreement (NAFTA) and the completion of the Uruguay round of the General Agreements on Tariffs and Trade (GATT).

b. Export promotion policies have included governmental lobbying for contracts, relaxation of export controls, advantageous loans through America's Export-Import Bank, and increased support for an industrial policy.

c. Bilateral trade negotiations to resolve trade differences with trading partners, such as with China over most-favored-nation status and Japan over persistent trade deficits, have been utilized.

■ **IMPORTANT TERMS**

Labor- (land-, capital-) intensive commodity

Cost ratio

Principle of comparative advantage

Terms of trade

Trading possibilities line

Gains from trade

World price

Domestic price

Export supply curve

Import demand curve

Revenue tariff

Protective tariff

Import quota

Nontariff barriers

Voluntary export restrictions

Smoot-Hawley Tariff Act of 1930

Strategic trade policy

Dumping

North American Free Trade Agreement (NAFTA)

General Agreements on Tariffs and Trade (GATT)

World Trade Organization

Export controls

Export-Import Bank

Industrial policy

Most-favored nation (MFN)

■ **HINTS AND TIPS**

1. In the discussion of comparative advantage, the assumption of a constant cost ratio means the production possibilities "curves" for each nation can be drawn as straight lines. The slope of the line in each nation is the opportunity cost of one product (wheat) in terms of the other product (coffee). The reciprocal of the slope of each line is the opportunity cost of the other product (coffee) in terms of the first product (wheat).

2. The export supply and import demand curves in Figures 20-3 and 20-4 in the text look different from the typical supply and demand curves that you've seen so far, so you should understand how they are constructed. The export supply and import demand curves for a nation do not intersect. Each curve meets at the price point on the Y-axis showing the equilibrium price for domestic supply and demand. At this point there are no exports or imports.

a. The *export supply* curve is upsloping from that point because as world prices rise above the domestic equilibrium price there will be increasing domestic surpluses produced by a nation that can be exported. The export supply curve reflects the positive relationship between rising world prices (above the domestic equilibrium price) and the increasing quantity of exports.

b. The *import demand* curve is downsloping from the domestic equilibrium price because as world prices fall below the domestic equilibrium price, there will be increasing domestic shortages that need to be covered by increasing imports. The import demand curve reflects the inverse relationship between falling world prices (below the domestic price) and the increasing quantity of imports.

SELF-TEST

■ **FILL-IN QUESTIONS**

1. Exports and imports of goods and services account for about _____% of GDP in the United States, and have more than (doubled, quadrupled)

_____ since 1965.

2. Other industrially advanced nations such as Germany, the Netherlands, Canada, and New Zealand have a (larger, smaller) _____ percentage of imports and exports than the United States, but the United States' volume makes it the world's _____ importing and exporting nation.

3. The four major exports of the United States are _____ , _____ , _____ , and consumer durables. The three major imports are _____ , _____ , and _____

4. World trade is dominated by the _____ , _____ , and the nations of western Europe. Recent "new players" include the four "Asian tigers"— _____ , _____ , _____ , and _____ . The share of world trade accounted for by these four nations is almost _____%.

5. Nations tend to trade among themselves because the distribution of economic resources among them is (even, uneven) _____ and because the efficient production of various goods and services necessitates (the same, different) _____ technologies or combinations of resources.

6. The nations of the world tend to specialize in those goods in the production of which they have a _____ , to export those goods, and to import those goods in the production of which they do not have a _____

7. If the cost ratio in country X is 4 Panama hats equal 1 pound of bananas, while in country Y, 3 Panama hats equal 1 pound of bananas:

a. In country X hats are relatively (expensive, inexpensive) _____ and bananas relatively _____

b. In country Y hats are relatively _____ and bananas relatively _____

c. X has a comparative advantage and should specialize in the production of _____ and Y has a comparative advantage and should specialize in the production of _____

d. When X and Y specialize and trade, the terms of trade will be somewhere between _____ and _____ hats for each pound of bananas; and will depend upon _____

_____

e. When the actual terms of trade turn out to be 3½ hats for 1 pound of bananas, the cost of obtaining:

(1) 1 Panama hat has been decreased from _____ to _____ pounds of bananas in Y.

(2) 1 pound of bananas has been decreased from _____ to _____ Panama hats in X.

f. This international specialization will not be complete if the cost of producing either good (increases, decreases, remains constant) _____ as a nation produces more of it.

8. The basic argument for free trade is that it results in a better _____ of resources and a higher _____ of living.

9. The world equilibrium price is determined by the interaction of world _____ and _____ . The domestic equilibrium price is determined by domestic _____ and _____

10. When world prices fall relative to domestic prices in a nation, then the nation will (increase, decrease) _____ its imports. When world prices rise relative to domestic prices, then the nation will _____ its exports.

11. In a two-nation model for a product, the equilibrium price and quantity of imports and exports occurs where one nation's import demand curve intersects another nation's _____ curve.

12. The barriers to international trade include _____ , _____ quotas, the non _____ barriers, and _____ restrictions.

13. Nations erect barriers to international trade to benefit the economic positions of _____ groups even though these barriers (increase, decrease) _____ economic efficiency and trade among nations, and the benefits to a nation are (greater, less) _____ than the costs to it.

14. When the United States imposes a tariff on a good which is imported from abroad:

a. the price of that good in the United States will (increase, decrease) _____

b. the total purchases of the good in the United States will _____

c. the output of:

(1) American producers of the good will _____

(2) foreign producers will _____

d. the ability of foreigners to buy goods and services in the United States will _____ and, as a result, output and employment in American industries that sell goods and services abroad will _____

15. When comparing the effects of a tariff with the effects of a quota to restrict the U.S. imports of a product, the basic difference is that with a (tariff, quota) _____ the U.S. government will receive revenue, but with a _____ foreign producers will receive the revenue that would have gone to the U.S. government.

16. List the six arguments which protectionists employ to justify trade barriers.

a. _____

b. _____

c. _____

d. _____

e. _____

f. _____

17. The only two protectionism arguments containing any reasonable justification for protection are the _____ argument and the _____ argument.

18. Protectionism will raise the price of a product by (increasing, decreasing) _____ the imported price of the product, _____ consumer purchases of the domestically produced product, and thus _____ the demand and the price of the domestically produced product.

19. The (gains, losses) _____ American trade barriers create for protected industries and their workers come at the expense of much greater _____ for the American economy.

20. The international trade policy of the United States has been a mixture of generalized trade _____, aggressive _____, and _____ negotiations on specific trade issues. Export promotion strategies have included a relaxation of _____, subsidized loans through the _____ Bank, and

more emphasis given to _____ policy that supports export-oriented industries.

■ **TRUE-FALSE QUESTIONS**

Circle the T if the statement is true; the F if it is false.

1. American exports and imports have increased in volume and more than doubled as a percentage of GDP since 1965.   **T   F**

2. Exports and imports as a percentage of GDP is greater in the United States than in Germany or the Netherlands.   **T   F**

3. The principal imports of the United States are chemicals and computers and the principal exports are automobiles and clothing.   **T   F**

4. Since World War II, international trade has been restricted by increases in the level of tariffs and major international conflicts.   **T   F**

5. The "Asian tigers" and China now dominate international trade.   **T   F**

Use the following production possibilities to answer the next five questions (6, 7, 8, 9, and 10).

NEPAL PRODUCTION POSSIBILITIES TABLE

	Production alternatives					
Product	A	B	C	D	E	F
Yak fat	0	4	8	12	16	20
Camel hides	40	32	24	16	8	0

KASHMIR PRODUCTION POSSIBILITIES TABLE

	Production alternatives					
Product	A	B	C	D	E	F
Yak fat	0	3	6	9	12	15
Camel hides	60	48	36	24	12	0

6. In Kashmir the cost of 1 camel hide is 3 units of yak fat.   **T   F**

7. Nepal has a comparative advantage in producing camel hides.   **T   F**

8. The best terms of trade for Nepal and Kashmir are 5 camel hides for 1 yak fat.   **T   F**

9. With specialization and trade, the trading possibilities curves of both nations would move to the right of their production possibilities curve.   **T   F**

10. Assume that prior to specialization and trade, Nepal and Kashmir produced combination B. If these two nations now specialized by comparative advantage, the total gains from specialization and trade would be 60 camel hides.

T F

11. Increasing production costs tend to prevent specialization among trading nations from being complete. **T F**

12. Trade among nations tends to bring about a more efficient use of the world's resources and a greater world output of goods and services. **T F**

13. Free trade among nations tends to increase monopoly and lessen competition in these nations. **T F**

14. A tariff on coffee in the United States is an example of a protective tariff. **T F**

15. The imposition of a tariff on a good imported from abroad will raise the price of the good and lower the quantity of it bought and sold. **T F**

16. The major difference between a tariff and a quota on an imported product is that a quota produces revenue for the government. **T F**

17. To advocate tariffs which would protect domestic producers of goods and materials essential to national defense is to substitute a political-military objective for the economic objectives of efficiently allocating resources.

T F

18. An increase in a nation's imports will, other things remaining constant, expand aggregate demand, real output, and employment in that nation. **T F**

19. One crop economies may be able to make themselves more stable and diversified by imposing tariffs on goods imported from abroad; but these tariffs are apt also to lower the standard of living in these economies. **T F**

20. Protection against the "dumping" of foreign goods at low prices on the American market is one good reason for widespread, permanent tariffs. **T F**

21. The only argument for tariffs that has, in the appropriate circumstances, any economic justification is the increase-domestic-employment argument. **T F**

22. The cost of protecting American firms and employees from foreign competition is the rise in the prices of products produced in the United States, and this cost almost always exceeds its benefits. **T F**

23. Trade protectionism has no effect on income distribution. **T F**

24. An example of generalized trade liberalization is most-favored nation status. **T F**

25. The Export-Import Bank is a GATT organization.

T F

■ **MULTIPLE-CHOICE QUESTIONS**

Circle the letter that corresponds to the best answer.

1. Which nation leads the world in the volume of exports and imports?
(a) Japan
(b) Germany
(c) United States
(d) United Kingdom

2. Which group of nations dominates world trade?
(a) Saudi Arabia and other OPEC nations
(b) Hong Kong, Singapore, South Korea, and Taiwan
(c) United States, Japan, and the nations of western Europe
(d) China, Russia, and the nations of eastern Europe

3. Nations need to engage in trade because:
(a) world resources are evenly distributed among nations
(b) world resources are unevenly distributed among nations
(c) all products are produced from the same technology
(d) all products are produced from the same combinations of resources

*Use the tables preceding true-false question **6** to answer the following four questions (**4, 5, 6,** and **7**).*

4. The data in the table show that production in:
(a) both Nepal and Kashmir are subject to increasing opportunity costs
(b) both Nepal and Kashmir are subject to constant opportunity costs
(c) Nepal is subject to increasing opportunity costs and Kashmir to constant opportunity costs
(d) Kashmir is subject to increasing opportunity costs and Nepal to constant opportunity costs

5. If Nepal and Kashmir engage in trade, the terms of trade will be:
(a) between 2 and 4 camel hides for 1 unit of yak fat
(b) between 1/3 and 1/2 units of yak fat for 1 camel hide
(c) between 3 and 4 units of yak fat for 1 camel hide
(d) between 2 and 4 units of yak fat for 1 camel hide

6. Assume that prior to specialization and trade Nepal and Kashmir both choose production possibility "C." Now if each specializes according to its comparative advantage, the resulting gains from specialization and trade will be:
(a) 6 units of yak fat
(b) 8 units of yak fat
(c) 6 units of yak fat and 8 camel hides
(d) 8 units of yak fat and 6 camel hides

7. Each nation produced only one product in accordance with its comparative advantage and the terms of trade were set at 3 camel hides for 1 yak fat. In this case, Nepal could obtain a maximum combination of 8 yak fat and:
  (a) 12 camel hides
  (b) 24 camel hides
  (c) 36 camel hides
  (d) 48 camel hides

8. What happens to a nation's imports or exports of a product when world prices rise relative to domestic prices?
  (a) imports of the product increase
  (b) imports of the product stay the same
  (c) exports of the product increase
  (d) exports of the product decrease

9. What happens to a nation's imports or exports of a product when world prices fall relative to domestic prices?
  (a) imports of the product increase
  (b) imports of the product decrease
  (c) exports of the product increase
  (d) exports of the product stay the same

10. Which one of the following is characteristic of tariffs?
  (a) they prevent the importation of goods from abroad
  (b) they specify the maximum amounts of specific commodities which may be imported during a given period of time
  (c) they often protect domestic producers from foreign competition
  (d) they enable nations to reduce their exports and increase their imports during periods of depression

11. The motive for barriers to the importation of goods and services from abroad is to:
  (a) improve economic efficiency in that nation
  (b) protect and benefit special interest groups in that nation
  (c) reduce the prices of the goods and services produced in that nation
  (d) expand the export of goods and services to foreign nations

12. When a tariff is imposed on a good imported from abroad:
  (a) the demand for the good increases
  (b) the demand for the good decreases
  (c) the supply of the good increases
  (d) the supply of the good decreases

Answer the next five questions (13, 14, 15, 16, and 17) on the basis of the following diagram, where S_d and D_d are the domestic supply and demand for a product and P_w is the world price of that product.

13. In a closed economy (without international trade), the equilibrium price would be:
  (a) P_d but in an open economy, the equilibrium price will be P_t

(b) P_d but in an open economy, the equilibrium price will be P_w
(c) P_w but in an open economy, the equilibrium price will be P_d
(d) P_w but in an open economy, the equilibrium price will be P_t

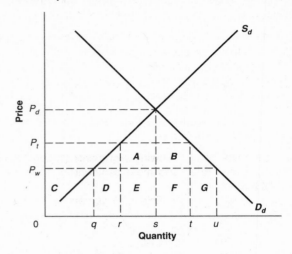

14. If there is free trade in this economy and no tariffs, the total revenue going to the foreign producers is represented by:
  (a) area C
  (b) areas A and B combined
  (c) areas A, B, E, and F combined
  (d) areas D, E, F, and G combined

15. If a per unit tariff was imposed in the amount of P_wP_t, then domestic producers would supply:
  (a) q units and foreign producers would supply qu units
  (b) s units and foreign producers would supply su units
  (c) r units and foreign producers would supply rt units
  (d) t units and foreign producers would supply tu units

16. Given a per unit tariff in the amount of P_wP_t, the amount of the tariff revenue paid by consumers of this product is represented by:
  (a) area A
  (b) area B
  (c) areas A and B combined
  (d) areas D, E, F, and G combined

17. Assume an import quota of rt units is imposed on the foreign nation producing this product. The amount of *total* revenue going to foreign producers is represented by areas:
  (a) $A + B$
  (b) $E + F$
  (c) $A + B + E + F$
  (d) $D + E + F + G$

18. Tariffs lead to:
(a) the contraction of relatively efficient industries
(b) an overallocation of resources to relatively efficient industries
(c) an increase in the foreign demand for domestically produced goods
(d) an underallocation of resources to relatively inefficient industries

19. "The nation needs to protect itself from foreign countries that sell their products in our domestic markets at less than the cost of production." This quotation would be most closely associated with which protectionist argument?
(a) diversification for stability
(b) increase domestic employment
(c) protection against dumping
(d) cheap foreign labor

20. Which one of the following arguments for protection is the least fallacious and most pertinent in the United States today?
(a) the military self-sufficiency argument
(b) the increase-domestic-employment argument
(c) the cheap foreign labor argument
(d) the infant-industry argument

21. Which of the following is the likely result of the United States employing tariffs to protect its high wages and standard of living from cheap foreign labor?
(a) an increase in U.S. exports
(b) a rise in the American real GDP
(c) a decrease in the average productivity of American workers
(d) a decrease in the quantity of labor employed by industries producing the goods on which tariffs have been levied

22. Which of the following is a likely result of imposing tariffs to increase domestic employment?
(a) a short-run increase in domestic employment
(b) retaliatory increase in the tariff rates of foreign nations
(c) a long-run decline in exports
(d) all of the above

23. The infant-industry argument for tariffs:
(a) is especially pertinent for the European Economic Community
(b) generally results in tariffs that are removed after the infant industry has matured
(c) makes it rather easy to determine which infant industries will become mature industries with comparative advantages in producing their goods
(d) might better be replaced by an argument for outright subsidies for infant industries

24. Which factor would contribute to the increase in the price of a product from protectionism?
(a) the price of the imported good rises
(b) the supply of the imported good increases

(c) import competition increases for domestically produced goods
(d) consumers shift purchases away from domestically produced goods

25. What international trade policy has the United States pursued in recent years?
(a) increasing the level of tariffs
(b) increasing import quotas
(c) export promotion
(d) import subsidies

■ **PROBLEMS**

1. Shown on the next page are the production possibilities curves for two nations: the United States and Chile. Suppose these two nations do not currently engage in international trade or specialization, and suppose that points **A** and **a** show the combinations of wheat and copper they now produce and consume.
a. The straightness of the two curves indicates that the cost ratios in the two nations are (changing, constant)

_____

b. Examination of the two curves reveals that the cost ratio in:

(1) The United States is _____ million tons of wheat for _____ thousand pounds of copper.

(2) Chile is _____ million tons of wheat for _____ thousand pounds of copper.
c. If these two nations were to specialize and trade wheat for copper,
(1) The United States would specialize in the production of wheat because _____

_____
(2) Chile would specialize in the production of copper because _____
d. The terms of trade, if specialization and trade occur, will be greater than 2 and less than 4 million tons of wheat for 1 thousand pounds of copper because _____

_____
e. Assume the terms of trade turn out to be 3 million tons of wheat for 1 thousand pounds of copper. Draw in the trading possibilities curve for the United States and Chile.
f. With these trading possibilities curves, suppose the United States decides to consume 5 million tons of wheat and 1 thousand pounds of copper while Chile decides to consume 3 million tons of wheat and 1 thousand pounds copper. The gains from trade to:

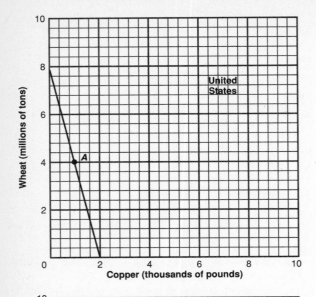

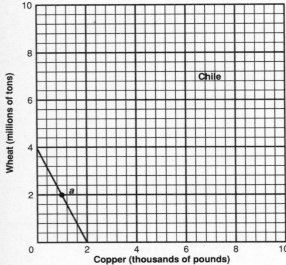

(1) The United States are _____ million

tons of wheat and _____ thousand
pounds of copper.

(2) Chile are _____ million tons of

wheat and _____ thousand pounds of
copper.

2. In the next column are tables showing the domestic
supply and demand schedule and the export supply and
import demand schedule for two nations (A and B).

    a. For nation A, the first column of the table is the price
of a product. The second column is the quantity
demanded domestically (Q_{dd}). The third column is
the quantity supplied domestically (Q_{sd}). The fourth column is the quantity demanded for imports (Q_{di}). The
fifth column is the quantity of exports supplied (Q_{se}).

NATION A

Price	Q_{dd}	Q_{sd}	Q_{di}	Q_{se}
3.00	100	300	0	200
2.50	150	250	0	100
2.00	200	200	0	0
1.50	250	150	100	0
1.00	300	100	200	0

(1) At a price of $2.00, there (will, will not)

_____ be a surplus or shortage, and there

_____ be exports or imports.

(2) At a price of $3.00, there will be a domestic (short-

age, surplus) _____ of _____

units. This domestic _____ will be eliminated by

(exports, imports) _____ of _____ units.

(3) At a price of $1.00, there will be a domestic (short-

age, surplus) _____ of _____

units. This domestic _____ will be eliminated

by (exports, imports) _____ of _____ units.

    b. For nation B, the first column is the price of a prod-
uct. The second column is the quantity demanded domestically (Q_{dd}). The third column is the quantity supplied domestically (Q_{sd}). The fourth column is the
quantity demanded for imports (Q_{di}). The fifth column
is the quantity of exports supplied (Q_{se}).

NATION B

Price	Q_{dd}	Q_{sd}	Q_{di}	Q_{se}
2.50	100	300	0	200
2.00	150	250	0	100
1.50	200	200	0	0
1.00	150	250	100	0

(1) At a price of $1.50, there (will, will not) _____

be a surplus or shortage, and there _____ be

exports or imports.

(2) At a price of $2.50, there will be a domestic (short-

age, surplus) _____ of _____ units.

This domestic _____ will be eliminated

by (exports, imports) _____ of _____ units.

(3) At a price of $1.00, there will be a domestic (short-

age, surplus) _____ of _____

units. This domestic _____ will be eliminated

by (exports, imports) _____ of _____ units.

    c. The table below shows a schedule of the import de-
mand in Nation A and the export supply in Nation B at
various prices. The first column is the price of the product. The second column is the quantity demanded for

imports (Q_{diA}) in Nation A. The third column is the quantity of exports supplied (Q_{seB}) in Nation B.

Price	(Q_{diA})	(Q_{seB})
2.00	0	100
1.75	50	50
1.50	100	0

(1) If the world price is $2.00, then Nation (A, B)

_____ will want to import _____ units and Nation

_____ will want to export _____ units of the product.
(2) If the world price is $1.75, then Nation (A, B)

_____ will want to import _____ units and Nation

_____ will want to export _____ units of the product.
(3) If the world price is $1.50, then Nation (A, B)

_____ will want to import _____ units and Nation

_____ will want to export _____ units of the product

3. The following table shows the quantities of woolen gloves demanded (**D**) in the United States at several different prices (**P**). Also shown in the table are the quantities of woolen gloves that would be supplied by American producers (S_a) and the quantities that would be supplied by foreign producers (S_f) at the nine different prices.

P	D	S_a	S_f	S_t	S'_f	S'_t
$2.60	450	275	475	_____	_____	_____
2.40	500	250	450	_____	_____	_____
2.20	550	225	425	_____	_____	_____
2.00	600	200	400	_____	_____	_____
1.80	650	175	375	_____	_____	_____
1.60	700	150	350	_____	_____	_____
1.40	750	125	325	_____	_____	_____
1.20	800	0	300	_____	_____	_____
1.00	850	0	0	_____	_____	_____

a. Compute and enter in the table the total quantities that would be supplied (S_t) by American and foreign producers at each of the prices.
b. If the market for woolen gloves in the United States is a competitive one the equilibrium price for woolen

gloves is $_____ and the equilibrium quantity is

_____
c. Suppose now that the United States government imposes an 80 cent ($0.80) per pair of gloves tariff on all gloves imported into the United States from abroad. Compute and enter into the table the quantities that would be supplied (S'_f) by foreign producers at the nine different prices. (**Hint:** If foreign producers were willing to supply 300 pairs at a price of $1.20 when there was

no tariff they are now willing to supply 300 pairs at $2.00, the $0.80 per pair tariff plus the $1.20 they will receive for themselves. The quantities supplied at each of the other prices may be found in a similar fashion.)
d. Compute and enter into the table the total quantities that would be supplied (S'_t) by American and foreign producers at each of the nine prices.
e. As a result of the imposition of the tariff the equilib-

rium price has risen to $_____ and the equi-

librium quantity has fallen to _____
f. The number of pairs sold by:
(1) American producers has (increased, decreased)

_____ by _____
(2) foreign producers has (increased, decreased)

_____ by _____
g. The total revenues (after the payment of the tariff) of:
(1) American producers—who **do not** pay the tariff—

have (increased, decreased) _____

by $_____
(2) foreign producers—who **do** pay the tariff—have

(increased, decreased) _____ by $_____
h. The total amount spent by American buyers of

woolen gloves has _____ by $_____
i. The total number of dollars earned by foreigners

has _____ by $_____; and, as a result, the total foreign demand for goods and services produced in the

United States will _____ by $_____
j. The tariff revenue of the United States government

has _____ by $_____
k. If an import quota was imposed that had the same effect as the tariff on price and output, the amount of

the tariff revenue, $_____ , would now be re-

ceived as revenue by _____ producers.

■ **SHORT ANSWER AND ESSAY QUESTIONS**

1. Describe the quantity of imports and exports for the United States in absolute and relative terms. How has the quantity of imports and exports changed over time?

2. What are the major imports and exports of the United States? With which nations does the United States trade?

3. What role does the United States play in international trade? What are the other major players in international trade?

4. What two facts—one dealing with the distribution of the world's resources and the other related to the technology of producing different products—are the basis for the trade among nations?

5. Explain:
(a) the theory or principle of comparative advantage;
(b) what is meant by and what determines the terms of trade; and
(c) the gains from trade.

6. What is the "case for free trade"?

7. Explain how the equilibrium prices and quantities of exports and imports are determined.

8. Why will exports in a nation increase when world prices rise relative to domestic prices?

9. What motivates nations to erect barriers to the importation of goods from abroad and what types of barriers do they erect?

10. Suppose the United States were to increase the tariff on automobiles imported from Germany (and other foreign countries). What would be the effect of this tariff-rate increase on:
(a) the price of automobiles in the United States;
(b) the total number of cars sold in the United States during a year;
(c) the number of cars produced by and employment in the German automobile industry;
(d) production by and employment in the American automobile industry;
(e) German income obtained by selling cars in the United States;
(f) the German demand for goods produced in the U.S.;
(g) the production of and employment in those American industries which now export goods to Germany;
(h) the standards of living in the U.S. and in Germany;
(i) the allocation of resources in the American economy; and
(j) the allocation of the world's resources?

11. Compare and contrast the economic effects of a tariff with the economic effects of an import quota on a product. Give an example of a recent import quota and explain how it affected foreign producers.

12. Critically evaluate the military self-sufficiency and infant-industry arguments (including strategic trade policy) as a basis for protectionism.

13. Is there a "strong case" for protectionism that can be made on the basis of one of the following reasons: increasing domestic employment, diversifying for stability, defending against the "dumping" of products, or shielding domestic workers from competition from "cheap" foreign labor? Summarize the case for and the case against protectionism.

14. How costly have trade barriers been for the United States? What have been the costs to society? What are the effects on income distribution?

15. Describe the mixture of approaches used in American trade policy in recent years.

ANSWERS

Chapter 20 International Trade

FILL-IN QUESTIONS

1. 10–11, doubled

2. larger, largest (or leading)

3. chemical, computers, aircraft (any order for first three), petroleum, automobiles, clothing (any order for last three)

4. United States, Japan, Hong Kong, Singapore, South Korea, Taiwan (any order for last four), 10

5. uneven, different

6. comparative advantage, comparative advantage

7. *a.* inexpensive, expensive; *b.* expensive, inexpensive; *c.* hats, bananas; *d.* 3, 4, world demand and supply for hats and bananas; *e.* (1) 1/3, 2/7, (2) 4, 3 1/2; *f.* increases

8. allocation, standard

9. supply, demand (any order for first two), supply, demand (any order for last two)

10. increase, increase

11. export supply

12. tariffs, import, tariff, voluntary export

13. special interest, decrease, less

14. *a.* increase; *b.* decrease; *c.* (1) increase, (2) decrease; *d.* decrease, decrease

15. tariff, quota

16. *a.* military self-sufficiency; *b.* infant industry; *c.* increase domestic employment; *d.* diversification for stability; *e.* protection against dumping; *f.* cheap foreign labor

17. military self-sufficiency, infant-industry

18. increasing, increasing, increasing

19. gains, losses

20. liberalization, export promotion, bilateral, export controls, Export-Import, industrial

TRUE-FALSE QUESTIONS

1. T, p. 399	**8.** F, p. 403	**15.** T, p. 410	**22.** T, p. 416
2. F, p. 399	**9.** T, p. 403	**16.** F, pp. 410-411	**23.** F, p. 417
3. F, p. 400	**10.** F, p. 403	**17.** T, p. 410	**24.** F, p. 418
4. F, p. 400	**11.** T, p. 405	**18.** F, p. 412	**25.** F, p. 418
5. F, p. 400	**12.** T, p. 405	**19.** T, p. 413	
6. F, p. 402	**13.** F, p. 405	**20.** F, p. 413	
7. F, p. 402	**14.** F, p. 409	**21.** F, p. 413	

MULTIPLE-CHOICE QUESTIONS

1. *c,* p. 399	**8.** *c,* p. 408	**15.** *c,* p. 410	**22.** *d,* p. 412
2. *c,* p. 400	**9.** *a,* p. 408	**16.** *c,* p. 410	**23.** *d,* p. 413
3. *b,* p. 400	**10.** *c,* p. 410	**17.** *c,* p. 411	**24.** *a,* p. 417
4. *b,* p. 402	**11.** *b,* p. 409	**18.** *a,* p. 411	**25.** *c,* p. 417
5. *a,* p. 403	**12.** *d,* p. 410	**19.** *c,* p. 414	
6. *a,* p. 403	**13.** *b,* p. 407	**20.** *a,* p. 411	
7. *c,* p. 403	**14.** *d,* p. 407	**21.** *c,* p. 414	

PROBLEMS

1. *a.* constant; *b.* (1) 8, 2, (2) 4, 2; *c.* (1) it has a comparative advantage in producing wheat (its cost of producing wheat is less than Chile's), (2) it has a comparative advantage in producing copper (its cost of producing copper is less than the United States), *d.* one of the two nations would be unwilling to trade if the terms of trade are outside this range; *f.* (1) 1, 0, (2) 1, 0

2. *a.* (1) will not, will not, (2) surplus, 200, surplus, exports, 200, (3) shortage, 200, shortage, imports, 200; *b.* (1) will not, will not, (2) surplus, 200, surplus, exports, 200, (3) shortage, 100, shortage, imports, 100; *c.* (1) A, 0, B, 100, (2) A, 50, B, 50, (3) A, 100, B, 0

3. *a.* 750, 700, 650, 600, 550, 500, 450, 300, 0; *b.* $2.00, 600; *c.* 375, 350, 325, 300, 0, 0, 0, 0, 0; *d.* 650, 600, 550, 500, 175, 150, 125, 0, 0; *e.* $2.20, 550; *f.* (1) increased, 25, (2) decreased, 75; *g.* (1) increased, $95, (2) decreased, $345; *h.* increased, $10; *i.* decreased, $345, decrease, $345; *j.* increased, $260; *k.* $260, foreign

SHORT ANSWER AND ESSAY QUESTIONS

1. pp. 399-400	**5.** pp. 401-403	**9.** pp. 409-410	**13.** pp. 411-415
2. pp. 399-400	**6.** p. 405	**10.** pp. 410-411	**14.** pp. 416-417
3. pp. 399-400	**7.** pp. 406-407	**11.** pp. 410-411	**15.** pp. 417-419
4. p. 400	**8.** pp. 408-409	**12.** pp. 411-412	

CHAPTER 21

Exchange Rates, the Balance of Payments, and Trade Deficits

In the last chapter you learned *why* nations engage in international trade and *why* they erect barriers to trade with other nations. In Chapter 21 you will learn *how* nations using different monies (or currencies) are able to trade with each other.

The means nations employ to overcome the difficulties that result from the use of different monies is fairly simple. When the residents of a nation (its consumers, business firms, or governments) wish to buy goods or services or real or financial assets from, make loans or gifts to, or pay interest and dividends to the residents of other nations they *buy* some of the money used in that nation. They pay for the foreign money with some of their own money. In other words, they *exchange* their own money for foreign money.

When the residents of a nation sell goods or services or real or financial assets to, receive loans or gifts from, or are paid dividends or interest by the residents of foreign nations and obtain foreign money they *sell* this foreign money—often called foreign exchange—in return for some of their own money. That is, they *exchange* foreign money for their own money.

The markets in which one money is sold and is paid for with another money are called foreign exchange markets. The price that is paid (in one money) for a unit of another money is called the foreign exchange rate (or the rate of exchange). And like most prices, the foreign exchange rate for any foreign currency is determined by the demand for and the supply of that foreign currency.

As you know from Chapter 20, nations buy and sell large quantities of goods and services across national boundaries. But the residents of these nations also buy and sell such financial assets as stocks and bonds and such real assets as land and capital goods in other nations; and the governments and individuals in one nation make gifts (remittances) in other nations. At the end of a year, nations summarize their foreign transactions with the rest of the world. This summary is called the nation's international balance of payments: a record of how it obtained foreign money during the year and what it did with this foreign money.

Of course, all foreign money obtained was used for some purpose—it did not evaporate—and consequently the balance of payments *always* balances. The international balance of payments is an extremely important and useful device for understanding the amounts and kinds of international transactions in which the residents of a nation engage. But it also enables us to understand the meaning of a balance of payments imbalance (a deficit or a surplus), the causes of these imbalances, and how to deal with them.

Probably the most difficult section of this chapter is concerned with balance of payments deficits and surpluses. A balance of payments deficit (surplus) is found when the receipts of foreign money are less (greater) than the payments of foreign money and the nation must reduce (expand) its official reserves to make the balance of payments balance. You should pay particular attention to the way in which a system of *flexible* exchange rates and the way in which a system of *fixed* exchange rates will correct balance of payments deficits and surpluses; and the advantages and disadvantages of these two alternative methods of eliminating imbalances.

As examples of these two types of exchange rate systems you will find in the third section of the chapter an examination of the gold standard, of the Bretton Woods system, and of the managed floating exchange rate system. In the first two systems exchange rates are fixed; and in the third system exchange rates are fixed in the short run (to obtain the advantages of fixed exchange rates) and flexible in the long run (to enable nations to correct balance of payments deficits and surpluses).

The final section of the chapter examines trade deficits of the United States of the 1980s and early 1990s. The problem is that during the early 1980s the United States imported goods and services with a dollar-and-cents value greater than the value of the goods and services it exported; and it incurred very large current-account deficits in those years. It was able to do this only by increasing its debts to (by borrowing from) the rest of the world; and by 1985 it owed more to foreigners than they owed to people in the United States. The primary (though not the only) cause of the trade deficit was the high international value of (exchange rate for) the American dollar during the mid-1980s. The high exchange rate for the dollar meant that the exchange rates for foreign currencies were low. The low exchange rates for other currencies and the high exchange rate for the dollar expanded American imports, contracted American exports, and produced the foreign-trade problem in the United States.

The relatively high exchange rate for the dollar in the mid-1980s was the result of real interest rates which were higher in the United States than in the rest of the world. Real interest rates were higher in the American economy than in the rest of the world because the large budget deficits of the Federal government forced it to borrow in the American money market; and these high real interest rates in the United States increased the attractiveness to foreigners of financial investment (buying bonds or lending) in the U.S., increased the foreign demand for dollars in the foreign exchange markets, and drove the price of the dollar upward in these markets. Although the value of the dollar fell over the 1985–1987 period, the trade deficit persisted for several reasons, and only in mid-1988 did the deficit begin to fall. Even today, however, the trade deficit remains large.

The undesirable effects of the trade deficit have led to a search for policy options. Two are worthy of note while five others are more limited remedies. First, it is thought by many economists that a reduction in the budget deficit of the Federal government would help reduce real interest rates in the United States relative to other nations, increase foreign investment in the United States and the demand for dollars, and cause the value of the dollar to fall. Putting the nation's "fiscal house" in order would help reduce the value of the dollar and move exports and imports to balance in a way that would be more acceptable to the major trading partners of the United States. Second, it is thought that if nations with large trade surpluses with the United States, such as Japan and Germany, would take actions to increase their rate of economic growth, this condition would help increase exports from the United States to those nations.

■ **CHECKLIST**

When you have studied this chapter you should be able to:

☐ Explain how American exports create a demand for dollars and generate a supply of foreign exchange; and how American imports create a demand for foreign exchange and generate a supply of dollars.

☐ Define each of the five balances found in a nation's international balance of payments; and distinguish between a deficit and a surplus in each of these five balances.

☐ Explain the relationship between the current and capital account balances; and between the balance of payments and changes in the official reserves of a nation.

☐ Using a supply and demand graph, illustrate how a foreign exchange market works to establish the price and quantity of a currency.

☐ Identify the five principal determinants of the demand for and supply of a particular foreign money.

☐ Explain how a change in each of these determinants would affect the rate of exchange for that foreign money.

☐ Provide an explanation of how flexible (floating) exchange rates function to eliminate payments deficits and surpluses; and enumerate the three disadvantages of this method of correcting imbalances.

☐ Enumerate the four means by which a nation may fix (or "peg") foreign exchange rates.

☐ Explain how a nation with a payments deficit might employ its international reserves to prevent a rise in foreign exchange rates.

☐ Describe how a nation with a payments deficit might use trade policies, fiscal and monetary policies, and exchange controls to eliminate the deficit.

☐ List the three conditions which a nation had to fulfill if it was to be on the gold standard.

☐ Explain how gold flows operated to reduce payments deficits and surpluses; and identify its basic advantages and its disadvantages.

☐ Explain how the Bretton Woods system stabilized exchange rates and attempted to provide for orderly changes in exchange rates to eliminate payments imbalances.

☐ Define the international monetary reserves of nations in the Bretton Woods system.

☐ Explain why the United States had to incur balance of payments deficits to expand these reserves, and describe the dilemma this created for the United States.

☐ Describe how the United States severed the link between gold and the international value of the dollar in 1971 that led to the floating of the dollar and brought to an end the old Bretton Woods system.

☐ Explain what is meant by a system of managed floating exchange rates.

☐ Enumerate the two alleged virtues and three alleged shortcomings of a system of managed floating exchange rates.

☐ Contrast the adjustments necessary to correct payments deficits and surpluses when exchange rates are flexible and when they are fixed.

☐ Describe the causes of the large trade deficits of the 1980s and 1990s.

☐ Analyze the effects of the trade deficit on domestic consumption in the United States and on the indebtedness of Americans to foreigners.

☐ Explain two major policies proposed for reducing the foreign-trade deficit of the United States.

☐ Discuss five other "remedies" for large trade deficits.

■ **CHAPTER OUTLINE**

1. Trade between two nations differs from domestic trade because the nations use different monies; but this problem is resolved by the existence of foreign-exchange markets in which the money used by one nation can be purchased and paid for with the money of the other nation.

a. American exports create a demand for dollars and generate a supply of foreign money in the foreign-exchange markets; increase the money supply in the United States and decrease foreign money supplies; and earn monies that can be used to pay for American imports.

b. American imports create a supply of dollars and generate a demand for foreign money in foreign-exchange markets; decrease the money supply in the United States and increase foreign money supplies; and use monies obtained by exporting.

2. The international balance of payments for a nation is an annual record of all its transactions with the other nations in the world; and it records all the payments received from and made to the rest of the world.

a. The current-account section of a nation's international balance of payments records its trade in currently produced goods and services; and within this section:
(1) the trade balance of the nation is equal to its exports of goods (merchandise) less its imports of goods (merchandise), and the nation has a trade surplus (deficit) if the exports are greater (less) than the imports;
(2) the balance on goods and services is equal to its exports of goods and services less its imports of goods and services; and
(3) the balance on the current account is equal to its balance on goods and services plus its net investment income (dividends and interest) from other nations and its net private and public transfers to other nations, and this balance may be either a surplus or a deficit.

b. The capital-account section of a nation's international balance of payments records its sales of real and financial assets (which earn it foreign money) and its purchases of real and financial assets (which use up foreign money), and the nation has a capital-account surplus (deficit) if its sales are greater (less) than its purchases of real and financial assets.

c. The current and capital accounts in a nation's international balance of payments are interrelated: a nation with a current-account deficit can finance the deficit by borrowing or selling assets abroad (with a capital-account surplus) and a nation with a current-account surplus can lend or buy assets abroad (incur a capital-account deficit).

d. The official reserves of a nation are the foreign currencies (monies) owned by its central bank; these reserves a nation uses to finance a net deficit on its current and capital accounts, and these reserves increase when a nation has a net surplus on its current and capital accounts; and in this way the nation's total outpayments and inpayments are made to equal each other (to balance).

e. A nation is said to have a balance-of-payments surplus (deficit) when the current and capital account balance is positive (negative) and its official reserves increase (decrease).

f. The merchandise or trade deficit of a nation implies its producers are losing their competitiveness in foreign markets, but is beneficial to consumers in that nation who receive more goods (imports) from abroad than they must pay for (export); and a balance-of-payments deficit is undesirable to the extent that the nation's official reserves are limited and require the nation to take painful macroeconomic adjustments to correct it.

3. The kinds of adjustments a nation with a balance-of-payments deficit or surplus must make to correct the imbalance depends upon whether exchange rates are flexible (floating) or fixed.

a. If foreign exchange rates *float freely* the demand for and the supply of foreign exchange determine foreign exchange rates; and the exchange rate for any foreign money is the rate at which the quantity of that money demanded is equal to the quantity of it supplied.
(1) A change in the demand for or supply of a foreign money will cause the exchange rate for that money to rise or fall; and
(2) When there is a rise (fall) in the price paid in dollars for a foreign money it is said that the dollar has depreciated (appreciated) and that the foreign money has appreciated (depreciated).

b. Changes in the demand for or supply of a foreign currency are largely the result of changes in tastes, relative income changes, relative price changes, changes in relative real interest rates, and speculation.

c. When a nation has a payments deficit (surplus), foreign exchange rates will rise (fall); this will make foreign goods and services more (less) expensive, decrease (increase) imports, make a nation's goods and services less (more) expensive for foreigners to buy, increase (decrease) its exports; and these adjustments in foreign exchange rates and in imports and exports correct the nation's payments deficit (surplus).

d. But flexible exchange rates increase the uncertainties faced by exporters, importers, and investors (and reduce international trade); change the terms of trade; and destabilize economies (by creating inflation or unemployment).

4. When nations *fix* (or "peg") foreign exchange rates, the governments of these nations must intervene in the foreign exchange markets to prevent shortages and surpluses of foreign monies.

a. One way for a nation to stabilize foreign exchange rates is for its government to sell (buy) a foreign money in exchange for its own money (or gold) when there is a shortage (surplus) of the foreign money.

b. A nation with a payments deficit might also discourage imports by imposing tariffs, import quotas, and special taxes; and encourage exports by subsidizing them.

c. To eliminate a payments deficit a nation might require exporters who earn foreign exchange to sell it to the government; and the government would then ration the available foreign exchange among importers and make the value of imports equal to the value of exports.

d. Another way for a nation to stabilize foreign exchange rates is to employ fiscal and monetary policies to reduce its national income and price level and to raise interest rates relative to those in other nations; and, thereby, reduce the demand for and increase the supply of the different foreign monies.

5. The nations of the world in their recent history have employed three different exchange rate systems.

a. Between 1879 and 1934 (with the exception of the World War I years) the operation of the **gold standard** kept foreign exchange rates relatively stable.

(1) A nation was on the gold standard when it:

(a) defined its monetary unit in terms of a certain quantity of gold;

(b) maintained a fixed relationship between its stock of gold and its money supply; and

(c) allowed gold to be exported and imported without restrictions.

(2) Foreign exchange rates between nations on the gold standard would fluctuate only within a narrow range (determined by the cost of packing, insuring, and shipping gold from country to country); and if a foreign exchange rate rose (fell) to the upper (lower) limit of the range gold would flow out of (into) a nation.

(3) But if a nation has a balance-of-payments deficit (surplus) and gold flowed out of (into) the country, its money supply would decrease (increase); this would raise (lower) interest rates and reduce (expand) aggregate demand, national output, employment, and prices in that country; and the balance-of-payments deficit (surplus) would be eliminated.

(4) The gold standard resulted in nearly stable foreign-exchange rates (which by reducing uncertainty stimulated international trade), and automatically corrected balance-of-payments deficits and surpluses; but it required that nations accept such unpleasant adjustments as recession and inflation to eliminate their balance-of-payments deficits and surpluses.

(5) During the worldwide Great Depression of the 1930s nations felt that remaining on the gold standard threatened their recoveries from the Depression, and the devaluations of their currencies (to expand exports and reduce imports) led to the breakdown and abandonment of the gold standard.

b. From the end of World War II until 1971 the **Bretton Woods system,** committed to the adjustable-peg system of exchange rates and managed by the **International Monetary Fund** (IMF), kept foreign-exchange rates relatively stable.

(1) The adjustable-peg system required the United States to sell gold to other member nations at a fixed price and the other members of the IMF to define their monetary units in terms of either gold or dollars (which established fixed exchange rates among the currencies of all member nations); and for the other member nations to keep the exchange rates for their currencies from rising by selling foreign currencies, selling gold, or borrowing on a short-term basis from the IMF.

(2) The system also provided for orderly changes in exchange rates to correct a fundamental imbalance (persistent and sizable balance-of-payments deficits) by allowing a nation to devalue its currency (increase its defined gold or dollar equivalent).

(3) The other nations of the world used gold and dollars as their international monetary reserves in the Bretton Woods system: for these reserves to grow the United States had to continue to have balance-of-payments deficits, but to continue the convertibility of dollars into gold it had to reduce the deficits; and, faced with this dilemma, the United States in 1971 suspended the convertibility of the dollar, brought an end to the Bretton Woods system of fixed exchange rates, and allowed the exchange rates for the dollar and the other currencies to float.

c. Exchange rates today are managed by individual nations to avoid short-term fluctuations and allowed to float in the long term to correct balance-of-payments deficits and surpluses; and this new system of **managed floating exchange rates** is favored by some and criticized by others.

(1) Its proponents contend that this system has not led to any decrease in world trade and it has enabled the world to adjust to severe economic shocks.

(2) Its critics argue that it has resulted in volatile exchange rates and has not reduced balance-of-payments deficits and surpluses; and that it is a "nonsystem" that a nation may employ to achieve its own domestic economic goals.

6. During the 1980s and into the 1990s, the United States ran large trade deficits because its exports grew slowly but its imports grew rapidly. There are now large merchandise and current-account deficits.

a. These deficits have had two major causes.

(1) The international value of the dollar rose from 1980–1985 because of large Federal budget deficits, a tighter monetary policy during the early 1980s, and lower rates of inflation in the United States and higher real interest rates than in the rest of the world. The value of the dollar declined from 1985–1987 because of intervention by G-7 nations to supply dollars to the foreign exchange market and the increasing demand for foreign currency to purchase imports. The dollar's fall helped increase American exports, but imports continued to rise until mid-1988 in part because foreign producers kept price increases low by accepting low per unit profits. The recession of 1990–1991 helped reduce the trade deficit, but it remains large.

(2) The more rapid recovery of the American economy from the 1980–1982 recession increased its imports by large amounts; and the less rapid recovery of the rest of the world increased American exports by only small amounts. A similar disparity in growth rates occurred in the 1992–1994 period, thus keeping the American trade deficit at a relatively high level.

b. The trade deficits of the United States have had two principal effects: they increased current domestic consumption and allowed the nation to operate outside its production possibility frontier, and they increased the indebtedness of Americans to foreigners. To reverse these trends will require increased exports, but this policy may reduce future domestic consumption. There are other harmful effects of trade deficits on specific industries (autos and steel), politics (protectionist pressure), and on relations with major trading partners (Japan).

c. Several policies have been considered to deal with the trade deficits:

(1) Reductions in Federal budget deficits lower government borrowing needs and reduce upward pressure on real interest rates. These actions help keep the value of the dollar lower, and thus help increase exports and reduce imports.

(2) The adoption of expansionary monetary and fiscal policies by the major trading partners of the United States would tend to increase economic growth in those nations and thereby increase exports from the United States to those nations.

(3) Other "remedies"—easy money, protective tariffs, recession, increasing competitiveness, and direct foreign investment—are possible but some have limitations and drawbacks.

■ IMPORTANT TERMS

International balance of payments	Capital outflow
Current account	Balance on the capital account
Credits	Current account deficit
Debits	Current account surplus
Trade balance	Capital account deficit
Trade surplus	Capital account surplus
Trade deficit	Official reserves
Balance on goods and services	Balance of payments deficit
Balance on current account	Balance of payments surplus
Net investment income	Fixed exchange rate
Net transfers	Flexible (floating) exchange rate
Capital account	Exchange rate (currency) depreciation
Capital inflow	

Exchange rate (currency) appreciation	Devaluation
Purchasing power parity	Bretton Woods system
Exchange control	International Monetary Fund
Gold standard	Managed floating exchange rate
Gold flow	G-7 nations
Gold export point	
Gold import point	

■ HINTS AND TIPS

1. The chapter is filled with many new terms. Some of these are just special words used in international economics to mean things with which you are already familiar. Others will be new to you and you must spend time learning them if you are to understand the chapter.

2. The terms *depreciate* and *appreciate* often confuse students when applied to foreign exchange markets.

a. First, know the related terms. Depreciate means decrease or fall, whereas appreciate means increase or rise.

b. Second, think of depreciation or appreciation in terms of quantities:

(1) what *decreases* when the currency of Country A *depreciates* is the *quantity* of Country B's currency that can be purchased for *1 unit* of Country A's currency;

(2) what increases when the currency of Country A *appreciates* is the *quantity* of Country B's currency that can be purchased for *1 unit* of Country A's currency.

c. Third, consider the effect of changes in exchange rates:

(1) when the exchange rate for Country B's currency *rises,* this means that Country A's currency has *depreciated* in value because 1 unit of Country A's currency will now purchase a smaller quantity of Country B's currency;

(2) when the exchange rate for Country B's currency *falls,* this means that Country A's currency has appreciated in value because 1 unit of Country A's currency will now purchase a larger quantity of Country B's currency.

3. The meaning of the balance of payments can be confusing also because of the number of accounts in the balance sheet. Remember that the balance of payments must always balance and sum to zero. That's because one account in the balance of payments can be in surplus, but it will be offset by a deficit in another account. However, when people talk about a *balance of payments surplus or deficit,* they are referring to the sum of the current and capital account balances. If the total is positive, there is a balance of payments surplus, but if it is negative, there is a balance of payments deficit.

SELF-TEST

■ **FILL-IN QUESTIONS**

1. The rate of exchange for the French franc is the number of (francs, dollars) _____ which an American must pay to obtain one (franc, dollar) _____

2. When the rate of exchange for the Saudi Arabian riyal is 30 American cents, the rate of exchange for the American dollar is _____ riyals.

3. American:

    a. exports create a (demand for, supply of) _____ _____ foreign money, generate a _____ dollars, (increase, decrease) _____ the money supply in the United States, and _____ money supplies abroad;

    b. imports create a _____ foreign money, generate a _____ dollars, _____ the money supply in the United States, and _____ money supplies abroad.

4. In addition to the demand for foreign currency by American firms that wish to import goods from foreign countries, Americans also demand foreign money to purchase _____ and _____ services abroad and to pay _____ and _____ on foreign investments in the United States.

5. The balance of payments of a nation records all payments its residents make to and receive from residents in

_____

    a. Any transaction that *earns* foreign exchange for that nation is a (debit, credit) _____ and is shown with a (+, −) _____ sign.

    b. A transaction that *uses up* foreign exchange is a _____ and is shown with a _____ sign.

6. When a nation has a:

    a. balance of trade deficit its exports are (greater, less) _____ than its imports of _____;

    b. balance-on-goods-and-services surplus its exports are _____ than its imports of goods and services;

    c. current-account deficit its balance on goods and services plus its net _____ income and net _____ is (positive, negative) _____

7. The capital account records the capital inflows and capital outflows of a nation.

    a. The capital inflows are the expenditures made (in that nation, abroad) _____ by residents of (that nation, other nations) _____; and the capital outflows are the expenditures made _____ by residents of _____ for _____ and _____ assets.

    b. A nation has a capital-account surplus when its capital-account inflows are (greater, less) _____ than its outflows.

8. A nation:

    a. may finance a current-account deficit by (buying, selling) _____ assets or by (borrowing, lending) _____ abroad; and

    b. may use a capital-account surplus to (buy, sell) _____ assets or to (borrow, lend) _____ abroad.

9. The official reserves of a nation are the quantities of (foreign monies, its own money) _____ owned by its _____ bank. If that nation has

    a. a deficit on the current and capital accounts its official reserves (increase, decrease) _____;

    b. a surplus on the current and capital accounts its official reserves _____;

    c. either a current and capital account deficit or surplus, the sum of the current and capital balances and the increases or decreases in its official reserves total

_____

10. A country has a balance-of-payments deficit if the sum of its current and capital accounts balance is (positive, negative) _____ and its official reserves (increase, decrease) _____; and a payments surplus when the sum of its current and capital accounts balance is _____ and its official reserves _____

11. If foreign exchange rates float freely and a nation has a balance of payments *deficit:*

    a. that nation's money in the foreign exchange markets will (appreciate, depreciate) _____ and foreign monies will _____

    b. as a result of these changes in foreign exchange rates, the nation's imports will (increase, decrease) _____ , its exports will _____ , and the size of its deficit will _____

12. What effect would each of the following have on the appreciation (**A**) or depreciation (**D**) of the French franc in the foreign exchange market (***ceteris paribus***)?

    a. The increased preference in the United States for domestic wines over wines produced in France:_____

    b. A rise in the national income of the United States:

    _____

    c. An increase in the price level in France: _____

    _____

    d. A rise in real interest rates in the United States:

    _____

    e. The belief of speculators in France that the dollar will appreciate in the foreign exchange market: _____

13. There are three disadvantages of freely floating foreign exchange rates: The risks and uncertainties associated with flexible rates tend to (expand, diminish) _____ trade between nations; when a nation's currency depreciates, its terms of trade with other nations are (worsened, bettered) _____; and fluctuating exports and imports can destabilize an economy and result in _____ or in _____ in that economy.

14. To fix or "peg" the rate of exchange for the German mark when:

    a. the exchange rate for the mark is rising, the United States would (buy, sell) _____ marks in exchange for dollars;

    b. the exchange rate for the mark is falling, the United States would _____ marks in exchange for dollars.

15. Under a fixed exchange rate system, a nation with a balance of payments deficit:

    a. might attempt to eliminate the deficit by (taxing, subsidizing) _____ imports or by _____ exports;

    b. might employ exchange controls and ration foreign exchange among those who wish to (export, import) _____ goods and services and require all those who _____ goods and services to sell the foreign exchange they earn to the _____

16. If the United States has a payments deficit with Japan and the exchange rate for the Japanese yen is rising, then under a fixed exchange rate system the United States might employ (expansionary, contractionary) _____ fiscal and monetary policies to re-duce the demand for the yen; but this would bring about (inflation, recession) _____ in the United States.

17. A nation is on the gold standard when it defines its money in terms of _____ , maintains a fixed relationship between its _____ supply and gold _____ , and allows gold to be freely _____ from and _____ into the nation.

18. When the nations of the world were on the gold standard

    a. exchange rates were relatively (stable, unstable) _____ ,

    b. but when a nation had a payments deficit:

    (1) gold flowed (into, out of) _____ the nation;

    (2) its money supply and price level (increased, decreased) _____ and its interest rates _____ ;

    (3) its payments deficit (rose, fell) _____ and it experienced (inflation, recession) _____

    _____

19. The Bretton Woods system was established to bring about (flexible, fixed) _____ exchange rates; and, to accomplish this, it employed the _____ system of exchange rates. Under the Bretton Woods system;

    a. a member nation defined its monetary unit in terms of _____ or _____ ;

    b. each member nation stabilized the exchange rate for its currency and prevented it from rising by (buying, selling) _____ foreign currency which it obtained from its _____ fund, by (buying, selling) _____ gold, or by (borrowing from, lending to) _____ the International Monetary Fund;

    c. a nation with a deeply rooted payments deficit could (devalue, revalue) _____ its currency;

    d. international monetary reserves included both _____ and _____ ;

    e. it was hoped that exchange rates in the short run would be (stable, flexible) _____ enough to promote international trade and in the long run would be _____ enough to correct balance of payments imbalances.

20. The role of the dollar as a component of international monetary reserves produced a dilemma:

   a. For these reserves to grow the United States had to incur balance of payments (surpluses, deficits) _____

   b. This resulted in an increase in the foreign holding of American dollars and in a decrease in the American reserves (stock) of _____

   c. The ability of the United States to convert dollars into gold and the willingness of foreigners to hold dollars (because they were "as good as gold") therefore (increased, decreased) _____

   d. For the dollar to remain an acceptable international monetary reserve the U.S. payments deficits had to be (eliminated, continued) _____ ; but for international monetary reserves to grow the U.S. payments deficits had to be _____

21. The United States completed the destruction of the Bretton Woods system in 1971 when it suspended the convertibility of dollars into _____ and allowed the value of the dollar to be determined by _____ . Since then the international monetary system has moved from exchange rates which (for all practical purposes) were (fixed, floating) _____ to exchange rates which are _____

22. The system of exchange rates which has developed since 1971 has been labeled a system of _____ exchange rates. This means that individual nations will:

   a. in the short term buy and sell foreign exchange to keep exchange rates _____

   b. in the long term allow exchange rates to rise or fall to correct payments _____

23. The advantages of the current system of exchange rates are that it did not reduce the _____ of trade over the years and it has survived much economic _____ , but its disadvantages are the _____ of the system, and the lack of clear rules and guidelines for nations that make it a " _____ "

24. The major problem with foreign trade in the United States concerns the American merchandise and current-account (surpluses, deficits) _____ which were brought about by the sharp increases in its (exports, imports) _____ and the small increases in its _____

25. One major cause of the large trade deficits during the early and mid-1980s was the rapid (appreciation, depreciation) _____ of the U.S. dollar.

   a. From 1980–1985, the rise in the value of the dollar made American goods (more, less) _____ expensive and foreign goods _____ expensive, (increased, decreased) _____ American exports, and _____ American imports and

   b. was the result of relatively (high, low) _____ real interest rates in the United States caused by large Federal-budget (surpluses, deficits) _____ , a (light, easy) _____ monetary policy, and relatively (high, low) _____ rates of inflation in the United States.

   c. From 1985–1987, the value of the dollar (rose, fell) _____ but imports continued to rise because foreign producers accepted lower per unit _____ and in 1987 _____ nations agreed to halt the decline of the dollar.

   d. Finally, from 1987 the trade deficit began to (increase, decrease) _____ but not by the same rate as the dollar fell, resulting in continuing large trade deficits.

26. A more recent cause has been (stronger, weaker) _____ economic growth in the United States relative to _____ economic growth in Europe and Japan. This difference in rate of economic growth tends to (increase, decrease) _____ U.S. imports more than exports.

27. One effect of the trade deficits of the United States has been (decreased, increased) _____ current domestic consumption that allows the nation to operate outside its production possibility frontier. To reverse this trend will require _____ U.S. exports, but this policy may cause _____ future domestic consumption.

28. Another effect of the trade deficit is a (rise, fall) _____ in the indebtedness of Americans to foreigners. When U.S. exports are (less, greater) _____ than the imports, then the nation finances the difference by borrowing from foreigners and going into debt. The United States has changed from a net (creditor, debtor) _____ nation in 1985 to a net _____ nation today.

29. Two policies to correct the trade deficit include a(n) (expansion, contraction) _____ in the budget deficit of the Federal government to help lower real interest rates in the United States relative to other nations, and a(n) _____ in the economies of major trading partners, such as Japan and Germany, to help increase demand for exports for the United States.

30. Other "remedies" for large trade deficits include: _____ money, protective _____ , forced _____ , increased _____ of American products, and direct foreign _____

■ TRUE-FALSE QUESTIONS

Circle the T if the statement is true; the F if it is false.

1. The importation of goods and services by Americans from abroad creates a supply of dollars in the foreign exchange market. **T F**

2. American exports expand foreign money supplies and reduce the supply of money in the United States. **T F**

3. The international balance of payments of the United States records all the payments its residents receive from and make to the residents of foreign nations. **T F**

4. Exports are a debit item and are shown with a plus sign (+) and imports are a credit item and are shown with a minus sign (−) in the international balance of payments of a nation. **T F**

5. The United States had a balance of trade deficit in 1993. **T F**

6. The United States would have a balance of payments surplus if the balance on its current and capital accounts were positive. **T F**

7. Any nation with a balance of payments deficit must reduce its official reserves. **T F**

8. The sum of a nation's current-account balance, its capital-account balance, and the change in its official reserves in any year is always equal to zero. **T F**

9. A large trade deficit in Brazil is harmful to consumers in Brazil. **T F**

10. If a nation has a balance of payments deficit and exchange rates are flexible, the price of that nation's money in the foreign exchange markets will fall and this will reduce its imports and increase its exports. **T F**

11. The purchasing power parity theory basically explains why there is an inverse relationship between the price of dollars and the quantity demanded. **T F**

12. The expectations of speculators in the United States that the exchange rate for the Japanese yen will fall in the future will increase the supply of yen in the foreign exchange market and decrease the exchange rate for the yen. **T F**

13. Were the United States' terms of trade with Nigeria to worsen, Nigeria would obtain a greater quantity of American goods and services for every barrel of oil it exported to the United States. **T F**

14. If a nation wishes to fix (or "peg") the foreign exchange rate for the Swiss franc, it must buy Swiss francs with its own currency when the rate of exchange for the Swiss franc rises. **T F**

15. If exchange rates are stable or fixed and a nation has a payments surplus, prices and money incomes in that nation will tend to rise. **T F**

16. A nation using exchange controls to eliminate a balance of payments surplus might depreciate its currency. **T F**

17. If country A defined its money as worth 100 grains of gold and country B defined its money as worth 20 grains of gold, then, ignoring packing, insuring, and shipping charges, 5 units of country A's money would be worth 1 unit of country B's money. **T F**

18. When nations were on the gold standard, foreign exchange rates fluctuated only within limits determined by the cost of moving gold from one nation to another. **T F**

19. If a nation maintains an exchange stabilization fund it would purchase its own money with gold or foreign monies when the value of its money falls in foreign exchange markets. **T F**

20. In the Bretton Woods system a nation could not devalue its currency by more than 10% without the permission of the International Fund. **T F**

21. In the Bretton Woods system a nation with persistent balance of payments surpluses had an undervalued currency and should have increased the pegged value of its currency. **T F**

22. Because the world's stock of gold did not grow very rapidly it became necessary for the United States to have payments deficits if international monetary reserves were to increase. **T F**

23. One of the basic shortcomings of the Bretton Woods system was its inability to bring about the changes in exchange rates needed to correct persistent payments deficits and surpluses. **T F**

24. Another basic shortcoming of the Bretton Woods system was its failure to maintain stable foreign exchange rates. **T F**

25. The United States shattered the Bretton Woods system in August 1971 by raising tariff rates on nearly all the goods it imported by an average of 40%. **T F**

26. Using the managed floating system of exchange rates, a nation with a persistent balance of payments surplus should allow the value of its currency in foreign exchange markets to decrease. **T F**

27. Two criticisms of the current managed floating exchange rate system are its potential for volatility and its lack of clear policy rules or guidelines for nations to manage exchange rates. **T F**

28. The foreign-trade deficits experienced by the American economy in the 1980s were caused by sharp increases in American exports and slight increases in American imports. **T F**

29. The principal reason for the strong dollar in the early 1980s was the high real interest rates in the United States. **T F**

30. High real interest rates in the United States would tend to increase the attractiveness of financial investment in the United States to foreigners and the foreign demand for American dollars. **T F**

31. The negative net exports of the United States have increased the indebtedness of Americans to foreigners. **T F**

32. In 1985 the status of the United States was changed from net-debtor to net-creditor nation. **T F**

33. The major trading partners in the United States contend that it must work to reduce the Federal budget deficit if it is to achieve a better balance of international trade. **T F**

34. Improved economic growth in the major economies of the major trading partners of the United States would tend to worsen the trade deficit. **T F**

35. Under the right circumstances, an easy money policy can help reduce a trade deficit. **T F**

■ MULTIPLE-CHOICE QUESTIONS

Circle the letter that corresponds to the best answer.

1. If an American could buy £25,000 for $100,000, the rate of exchange for the pound would be:
   (a) $40
   (b) $25

   (c) $4
   (d) $.25

2. American residents demand foreign currencies in order:
   (a) to pay for goods and services imported from foreign countries
   (b) to receive interest payments and dividends on their investments outside the United States
   (c) to make real and financial investments in foreign nations
   (d) to do all of the above

3. A nation's balance of trade is equal to its:
   (a) exports less its imports of merchandise (goods)
   (b) exports less its imports of goods and services
   (c) exports less its imports of goods and services plus its net investment income and net transfers
   (d) exports less its imports of goods, services, and capital

4. A nation's balance on the current account is equal to its:
   (a) exports less its imports of merchandise (goods)
   (b) exports less its imports of goods and services
   (c) exports less its imports of goods and services plus its net investment income and net transfers
   (d) exports less its imports of goods, services, and capital

5. The net investment income of the United States in its international balance of payment is:
   (a) the interest income it receives from foreign residents
   (b) the dividends it receives from foreign residents
   (c) the interest payments and dividends it receives from foreign residents
   (d) the interest payments, dividends, and transfers it receives from foreign residents

6. Capital flows into the United States include the purchase by foreign residents of:
   (a) a factory building owned by Americans
   (b) shares of stock owned by Americans
   (c) bonds owned by Americans
   (d) all of the above

7. An American current account deficit may be financed by:
   (a) borrowing abroad
   (b) selling real assets to foreigners
   (c) selling financial assets to foreigners
   (d) doing any of the above

8. The official reserves of the United States are:
   (a) the stock of gold owned by the Federal government
   (b) the foreign currencies owned by the Federal Reserve Banks
   (c) the money supply of the United States
   (d) all of the above

9. A nation may be able to correct or eliminate a persistent (long-term) balance of payments deficit by:
  (a) lowering the barriers on imported goods
  (b) reducing the international value of its currency
  (c) expanding its national income
  (d) reducing its official reserves

10. If exchange rates float freely the exchange rate for any currency is determined by:
  (a) the demand for it
  (b) the supply of it
  (c) the demand for and the supply of it
  (d) the official reserves that "back" it

11. If a nation had a balance of payments surplus and exchange rates floated freely:
  (a) the foreign exchange rate for its currency would rise, its exports would increase, and its imports would decrease
  (b) the foreign exchange rate for its currency would rise, its exports would decrease, and its imports would increase
  (c) the foreign exchange rate for its currency would fall, its exports would increase, and its imports would decrease
  (d) the foreign exchange rate for its currency would fall, its exports would decrease, and its imports would increase

12. Assuming exchange rates are flexible, which of the following should increase the dollar price of the Swedish krona?
  (a) a rate of inflation greater in Sweden than in the United States
  (b) real interest-rate increases greater in Sweden than in the United States
  (c) national-income increases greater in Sweden than in the United States
  (d) the increased preference of Swedes for American over Swedish automobiles

13. Which of the following would be one of the results associated with the use of freely floating foreign exchange rates to correct a nation's balance of payments surplus?
  (a) the nation's terms of trade with other nations would be worsened
  (b) importers in the nation who had made contracts for the future delivery of goods would find that they had to pay a higher price than expected for the goods
  (c) if the nation were at full employment the decrease in exports and the increase in imports would be inflationary
  (d) exporters in the nation would find their sales abroad had decreased

14. When exchange rates are fixed and a nation at full employment has a balance of payments surplus, the result in that nation will be:
  (a) a declining price level
  (b) falling money income

(c) inflation
  (d) rising real income

15. The use of exchange controls to eliminate a nation's balance of payments deficit results in:
  (a) decreasing the nation's imports
  (b) decreasing the nation's exports
  (c) decreasing the nation's price level
  (d) decreasing the nation's income

16. A nation with a balance of payments surplus might attempt to eliminate this surplus by employing:
  (a) import quotas
  (b) higher tariffs
  (c) subsidies on items which the nation exports
  (d) none of the above

17. Which one of the following conditions did a nation **not** have to fulfill if it was to be one under the gold standard?
  (a) use only gold as a medium of exchange
  (b) maintain a fixed relationship between its gold stock and its money supply
  (c) allow gold to be freely exported from and imported into the nation
  (d) define its monetary unit in terms of a fixed quantity of gold

18. If the nations of the world were on the gold standard and one nation has a balance of payments surplus:
  (a) foreign exchange rates in that nation would rise toward the gold import point
  (b) gold would tend to be imported into that country
  (c) the level of prices in that country would tend to fall
  (d) employment and output in that country would tend to fall

19. Under the gold standard a nation with a balance of payments deficit would experience all but one of the following. Which one?
  (a) gold would flow out of the nation
  (b) the nation's money supply would contract
  (c) interest rates in the nation would fall
  (d) real national output, employment, and prices in the nation would decline

20. Which of the following was the principal disadvantage of the gold standard?
  (a) unstable foreign exchange rates
  (b) persistent payments imbalances
  (c) the uncertainties and decreased trade that resulted from the depreciation of gold
  (d) the domestic macroeconomic adjustments experienced by a nation with a payments deficit or surplus

21. All but one of the following were elements in the adjustable-peg system of foreign exchange rates. Which one?
  (a) each nation defined its monetary unit in terms of gold or dollars

(b) nations bought and sold their own currencies to stabilize exchange rates

(c) nations were allowed to devalue their currencies freely within a range when faced with persistent payments deficits

(d) the gold deposits of all member nations were held by the IMF

22. Which one of the following was *not* characteristic of the International Monetary Fund in the Bretton Woods system?

(a) made short-term loans to member nations with balance of payments deficits

(b) tried to maintain relatively stable exchange rates

(c) required member nations to maintain exchange stabilization funds

(d) extended long-term loans to less developed nations for the purpose of increasing their productive capacities

23. The objective of the adjustable-peg system was exchange rates which were:

(a) adjustable in the short run and fixed in the long run

(b) adjustable in both the short and long run

(c) fixed in both the short and long run

(d) fixed in the short run; adjustable in the long run

24. Which of the following is the best definition of international monetary reserves in the Bretton Woods system?

(a) gold

(b) dollars

(c) gold and dollars

(d) gold, dollars, and British pounds

25. The dilemma created by the U.S. payments deficits was that:

(a) to maintain the status of the dollar as an acceptable international monetary reserve the deficit had to be reduced and to increase these reserves the deficits had to be continued

(b) to maintain the status of the dollar the deficit had to be continued and to increase reserves the deficit had to be eliminated

(c) to maintain the status of the dollar the deficit had to be increased and to expand reserves the deficit had to be reduced

(d) to maintain the status of the dollar the deficit had to be reduced and to expand reserves the deficit had to be reduced

26. "Floating" the dollar means:

(a) the value of the dollar is determined by the demand for and the supply of the dollar

(b) the dollar price of gold has been increased

(c) the price of the dollar has been allowed to crawl upward at the rate of one-fourth of 1% a month

(d) the IMF decreased the value of the dollar by 10%

27. A system of managed floating exchange rates:

(a) allows nations to stabilize exchange rates in the short term

(b) requires nations to stabilize exchange rates in the long term

(c) entails stable exchange rates in both the short and long term

(d) fixes exchange rates at market levels

28. Floating exchange rates:

(a) tend to correct balance of payments imbalances

(b) reduce the uncertainties and risks associated with international trade

(c) increase the world's need for international monetary reserves

(d) tend to expand the volume of world trade

29. The foreign-trade problem facing the United States is:

(a) its merchandise and current-account surpluses

(b) its merchandise deficit and current-account surplus

(c) its merchandise and current-account deficit

(d) its merchandise surplus and current-account deficit

30. Which is one of the causes of the growth of American trade deficits during the 1980s?

(a) protective tariffs imposed by the U.S.

(b) slower economic growth in the U.S.

(c) direct foreign investment in the U.S.

(d) appreciation of the U.S. dollar

31. High real interest rates in the United States during the mid-1980s were primarily the result of:

(a) increasing U.S. exports

(b) decreasing Federal budget deficits

(c) the low demand of foreign investors for the dollar

(d) the tight money policy of the Federal Reserve

32. What would be the effect on U.S. imports and exports when the U.S. experiences strong economic growth but its major trading partners experience sluggish economic growth?

(a) U.S. imports will increase more than U.S. exports

(b) U.S. exports will increase more than U.S. imports

(c) U.S. imports will decrease but U.S. exports will increase

(d) there will be no effect on U.S. imports and exports

33. Two major outcomes from the trade deficits of the 1980s and early 1990s were:

(a) decreased domestic consumption and American indebtedness

(b) increased domestic consumption and American indebtedness

(c) increased domestic consumption but decreased American indebtedness

(d) decreased domestic consumption but increased American indebtedness

34. One policy solution for large trade deficits is a reduction in the Federal budget deficit because this change would tend to:

(a) increase real interest rates and increase the demand for dollars in the United States

(b) decrease real interest rates and increase the demand for dollars in the United States

(c) decrease real interest rates and decrease the demand for dollars in the United States

(d) increase real interest rates and decrease the demand for dollars in the United States

35. Economists suggest that the large trade deficits of the United States can best be reduced with:

(a) an easy money policy in the United States

(b) an expansionary fiscal policy in the United States

(c) economic policies that increase the rate of growth in the G-7 nations with trade surpluses

(d) an appreciation in the value of the currencies of less developed nations

■ **PROBLEMS**

1. Assume an American exporter sells $3 million worth of wheat to an importer in Colombia. If the rate of exchange for the Colombian peso is $0.02 (two cents), the wheat has a total value of 150 million pesos.

a. There are two ways the importer in Colombia may pay for the wheat. It might write a check for 150 million pesos drawn on its bank in Botogá and send it to the American exporter.

(1) The American exporter would then sell the check to its bank in New Orleans and its demand deposit there would increase by $_____ million.

(2) This New Orleans bank now sells the check for 150 million pesos to a correspondent bank (an American commercial bank that keeps an account in the Botogá bank).

(a) The New Orleans bank's account in the correspondent bank increases by _____ million (dollars, pesos) _____; and

(b) the correspondent bank's account in the Botogá bank increases by _____ million (pesos, dollars) _____

b. The second way for the importer to pay for the wheat is to buy from its bank in Botogá a draft on an American bank for $3 million, pay for this draft by writing a check for 150 million pesos drawn on the Botogá bank, and send the draft to the American exporter.

(1) The American exporter would then deposit the draft in its account in the New Orleans bank and its demand

deposit account there would increase by $_____ million.

(2) The New Orleans bank collects the amount of the draft from the American bank on which it is drawn through the Federal Reserve Banks.

(a) Its account at the Fed increases by $_____ million; and

(b) the account of the bank on which the draft was drawn decreases by $_____ million.

c. Regardless of the way employed by the Colombian importer to pay for the wheat:

(1) The export of the wheat created a (demand for, supply of) _____ dollars and a _____ pesos

(2) The number of dollars owned by the American exporter has (increased, decreased) _____ and the number of pesos owned by the Colombian importer has _____

2. The table below contains hypothetical international balance of payments data for the United States. All figures are in billions.

Current account		
(1) U.S. merchandise exports	$+150	
(2) U.S. merchandise imports	−200	
(3) Balance of trade		_____
(4) U.S. exports of services	+75	
(5) U.S. imports of services	−60	
(6) Balance on goods and services		_____
(7) Net investment income	+12	
(8) Net transfers	−7	
(9) Balance on current account		_____
Capital account		
(10) Capital inflows to the U.S.	+80	
(11) Capital outflows from the U.S.	−55	
(12) Balance on capital account		_____
(13) Current and capital account balance		_____
(14) Official reserves		_____
		$ 0

a. Compute with the appropriate sign (+ or −) and enter in the table the six missing items.

b. The United States had a payments (deficit, surplus) _____ of $_____

3. In the table on the next page are the supply and demand schedules for the British pound.

Quantity of pounds supplied	Price	Quantity of pounds demanded
400	$5.00	100
360	4.50	200
300	4.00	300
286	3.50	400
267	3.00	500
240	2.50	620
200	2.00	788

a. If the exchange rates are flexible:

(1) What will be the rate of exchange for the pound?

$_____

(2) What will be the rate of exchange for the dollar?

£_____

(3) How many pounds will be purchased in the market?

_____

(4) How many dollars will be purchased in the market?

_____

b. If the government of the United States wished to fix or "peg" the price of the pound at $5.00 it would have

to (buy, sell) _____ (how many) _____

pounds for $_____

c. And if the British government wishes to fix the price of the dollar at £⅗ it would have to (buy, sell)

_____ (how many) _____

pounds for $_____

■ **SHORT ANSWER AND ESSAY QUESTIONS**

1. What is foreign exchange and the foreign exchange rate? Who are the demanders and suppliers of a particular foreign exchange, say, the French franc? Why is a buyer (demander) in the foreign exchange markets always a seller (supplier) also?

2. What is meant when it is said that "a nation's exports pay for its imports"? Do nations pay for all their imports with exports?

3. What is an international balance of payments? What are the principal sections in a nation's international balance of payments and what are the principal "balances" to be found in it?

4. How can a nation finance a current account deficit and what can it do with a current account surplus?

5. How does a nation finance a balance of payments deficit and what does it do with a balance of payments surplus?

6. Is it good or bad for a nation to have a balance of payments deficit or surplus?

7. What types of events cause the exchange rate for a foreign currency to appreciate or to depreciate? How will each of these events affect the exchange rate for a foreign money and for a nation's own money?

8. How can freely floating foreign exchange rates eliminate balance of payments deficits and surpluses? What are the problems associated with this method of correcting payments imbalances?

9. How may a nation employ its international monetary reserves to fix or "peg" foreign exchange rates? Be precise. How does a nation obtain or acquire these monetary reserves?

10. What kinds of trade controls may nations with payments deficits employ to eliminate their deficits?

11. How can foreign exchange controls be used to restore international equilibrium? Why do such exchange controls necessarily involve the rationing of foreign exchange? What effect do these controls have upon prices, output, and employment in nations that use them?

12. If foreign exchange rates are fixed, what kind of domestic macroeconomic adjustments are required to eliminate a payments deficit? To eliminate a payments surplus?

13. When was a nation on the gold standard? How did the international gold standard correct payments imbalances?

14. What were the disadvantages of the gold standard for eliminating payments deficits and surpluses?

15. Why does the operation of the international gold standard ensure relatively stable foreign exchange rates, that is, rates which fluctuate only within very narrow limits? What are limits and what are the advantages of stable exchange rates?

16. What is the "critical difference" between the adjustments necessary to correct payments deficits and surpluses under the gold standard and those necessary when exchange rates are flexible? How did this difference lead to the demise of the gold standard during the 1930s?

17. Explain:
(a) why the International Monetary Fund was established and what the objectives of the adjustable-peg (or Bretton Woods) system were
(b) what the adjustable-peg system was and the basic means it employed to stabilize exchange rates in the short run; and
(c) when and how the system was to adjust exchange rates in the long run.

18. What did nations use as international monetary reserves under the Bretton Woods system? Why was the dollar used by nations as an international money and how could they acquire additional dollars?

19. Explain the dilemma created by the need for expanding international monetary reserves and for maintaining the status of the dollar.

20. Why and how did the United States shatter the Bretton Woods system in 1971? If the international value of the dollar is no longer determined by the amount of gold for which it can be exchanged, what does determine its value?

21. Explain what is meant by a managed floating system of foreign exchange rates. When are exchange rates managed and when are they allowed to float?

22. Explain the arguments of the proponents and the critics of the managed floating system.

23. What were the causes of the trade deficits of the United States during the 1980s and early 1990s?

24. What were the effects of the trade deficits on the American economy?

25. What two major policies are suggested for reducing the large trade deficits in the United States? What other five remedies have also been discussed?

ANSWERS

Chapter 21 Exchange Rates, the Balance of Payments, and Trade Deficits

FILL-IN QUESTIONS

1. francs, dollar

2. 3 1/3

3. *a.* supply of, demand for, increase, decrease; *b.* demand for, supply of, decrease, increase

4. transportation, insurance (either order), interest, dividends (either order)

5. the other nations of the world: *a.* credit, +; *b.* debit, −

6. *a.* less, merchandise; *b.* greater; *c.* investment, transfers, negative

7. *a.* in that nation, other nations, in other nations, that nation, real, financial (either order); *b.* greater

8. *a.* selling, borrowing; *b.* buy, lend

9. foreign monies, central; *a.* decrease; *b.* increase; *c.* zero

10. negative, decrease, positive, increase

11. *a.* depreciate, appreciate; *b.* decrease, increase, decrease

12. *a.* depreciate; *b.* appreciate; *c.* depreciate; *d.* depreciate; *e.* depreciate

13. diminish, worsened, recession, inflation (either order)

14. *a.* sell; *b.* buy

15. *a.* taxing, subsidizing; *b.* import, export, government

16. contractionary, recession

17. gold, money, stock, exported, imported

18. *a.* stable; *b.* (1) out of, (2) decreased, rose, (3) fell, recession

19. fixed, adjustable-peg; *a.* gold, dollars (either order); *b.* buying, exchange-stabilization, selling, borrowing from; *c.* devalue; *d.* gold, dollars (either order); *e.* stable, flexible

20. *a.* deficits; *b.* gold; *c.* decreased; *d.* eliminated, continued

21. gold, market forces (demand and supply), fixed, floating

22. managed floating; *a.* stable; *b.* imbalances

23. growth, turbulence, volatility, nonsystem

24. deficits, imports, exports

25. appreciation; *a.* more, less, decreased, increased; *b.* high, deficits, tight, low; *c.* fell, profits, G-7; *d.* decrease

26. stronger, weaker, increase

27. increased, increased, decreased

28. rise, less, creditor, debtor

29. contraction, expansion

30. easy, tariffs, recession, competitiveness, investment

TRUE-FALSE QUESTIONS

1. T, p. 424	**10.** T, p. 432	**19.** T, p. 436	**28.** F, pp. 441-442
2. F, p. 424	**11.** F, p. 431	**20.** T, p. 437	**29.** T, p. 442
3. T, p. 425	**12.** T, p. 431	**21.** T, p. 437	**30.** T, p. 442
4. F, p. 426	**13.** T, p. 433	**22.** T, p. 439	**31.** T, pp. 443-444
5. T, p. 427	**14.** F, pp. 433-434	**23.** T, p. 439	**32.** F, p. 444
6. T, pp. 427-428	**15.** T, p. 434	**24.** F, p. 439	**33.** T, p. 444
7. T, pp. 427-428	**16.** F, p. 434	**25.** F, p. 439	**34.** F, p. 444
8. T, pp. 427-428	**17.** F, pp. 435-536	**26.** F, p. 439	**35.** T, p. 445
9. F, p. 429	**18.** T, p. 436	**27.** T, p. 441	

MULTIPLE-CHOICE QUESTIONS

1. *c*, pp. 423-424	**10.** *c*, p. 429	**19.** *c*, p. 436	**28.** *a*, p. 441
2. *d*, pp. 423-424	**11.** *b*, p. 432	**20.** *d*, p. 437	**29.** *c*, p. 441
3. *a*, p. 426	**12.** *b*, p. 431	**21.** *d*, p. 438	**30.** *d*, pp. 442-443
4. *c*, p. 427	**13.** *d*, p. 432	**22.** *d*, pp. 437-438	**31.** *d*, p. 442
5. *c*, p. 427	**14.** *c*, p. 435	**23.** *d*, p. 438	**32.** *a*, p. 443
6. *d*, p. 427	**15.** *a*, p. 434	**24.** *c*, p. 439	**33.** *b*, p. 443
7. *d*, pp. 427-428	**16.** *d*, pp. 434-435	**25.** *a*, p. 439	**34.** *c*, p. 445
8. *b*, p. 428	**17.** *a*, p. 435	**26.** *a*, pp. 439-440	**35.** *c*, p. 444
9. *b*, p. 428	**18.** *b*, p. 436	**27.** *a*, p. 439	

PROBLEMS

1. *a.* (1) 3, (2) (a) 3, dollars, (b) 150, pesos; *b.* (1) 3, (2) (a) 3, (b) 3; *c.* (1) demand for, supply of, (2) increased, decreased

2. *a.* −50, −35, −30, +25, −5, +5; *b.* deficit, 5

3. *a.* (1) 4.00, (2) 1/4, (3) 300, (4) 1200; *b.* buy, 300, 1500; *c.* sell, 380, 950

SHORT ANSWER AND ESSAY QUESTIONS

1. pp. 423-425	**8.** pp. 432-433	**15.** p. 436	**22.** pp. 440-441
2. p. 425	**9.** pp. 433-434	**16.** pp. 436-437	**23.** pp. 441-443
3. pp. 425-427	**10.** pp. 434-435	**17.** pp. 437-438	**24.** pp. 443-444
4. pp. 426-427	**11.** pp. 434-435	**18.** pp. 437-438	**25.** pp. 444-445
5. pp. 426-427	**12.** p. 435	**19.** pp. 438-439	
6. pp. 428-429	**13.** pp. 435-436	**20.** p. 439	
7. pp. 429-431	**14.** p. 437	**21.** p. 439	

CHAPTER 22

Growth and the Less Developed Countries

This chapter looks at the problem of raising the standard of living faced by the less developed countries of the world. Economic growth both in these less developed countries and in the developed or the industrially advanced countries requires that the country's resources and technological knowledge be expanded. Application of this principle in the less developed countries, however, faces a set of obstacles quite different from those that limit economic growth in the United States.

These obstacles do not mean that increases in the living standards of the less developed countries are impossible. What they do mean is that the less developed countries must do things to encourage growth that did not need to be done in the United States, or in the other industrial countries. Governments of the less developed countries will have to take an active role in promoting growth and limit public sector problems for economic development. Large population increases are going to have to be reduced. Dramatic changes in social practices and institutions will be required. If these actions are not taken it will not be possible to reduce the obstacles to growth.

No matter how successful the less developed countries are in reducing these obstacles they probably will still not be able to grow very rapidly without the help of the developed countries. There are at least two reasons why the developed countries will offer the less developed ones some assistance. The citizens of the more advanced countries feel some moral obligation to aid the less fortunate peoples of the world; and they may feel it is in their own self-interest to aid the poor of the world.

The debts of less developed countries rose thirteenfold in the past two decades. The causes of this debt problem were due in part to the events of the 1970s and early 1980s. During this period, less developed countries paid more for imported oil, incurred high borrowing costs because of higher interest rates, made unproductive investments, and faced lower net export earnings because of the appreciation of the dollar. To reduce the debt burdens, these nations were forced to enact restrictive domestic programs that often had adverse effects on net export earnings and economic growth. Steps have been taken to reduce the debt load of LDCs and encourage economic reforms, but debt problems still persist in many LDCs.

Less developed countries have grown during the past thirty years, but the rate at which they grew was about the same as that at which the developed countries grew. Because the per capita incomes in the less developed countries were initially so much smaller, equal rates of growth increased the gap between the two groups over this period of time. For this and other reasons, less developed countries have become increasingly dissatisfied with their relationships with the advanced industrial nations. They have argued for a New Global Compact to address the problem. Here you should look at these relationships from the viewpoint of the less developed countries. To understand the proposals they have made, you must understand why they feel their relationships with the developed countries mostly benefit the developed and largely hurt the less developed countries.

■ CHECKLIST

When you have studied this chapter you should be able to:

□ Describe income disparity among nations.
□ Compare industrially advanced countries and less developed countries in terms of economic growth and population.
□ Discuss the human implications of poverty in less developed countries.
□ Identify two basic avenues for economic growth in industrially advanced and less developed countries.
□ Describe natural resource problems in less developed countries.
□ Identify the three specific problems related to human resources that plague the less developed countries.
□ Explain the difficulties for economic growth that are created by population growth in less developed countries.
□ Compare the traditional and the demographic transition view of population and economic growth in less developed countries.
□ Describe the conditions of unemployment and underemployment in less developed countries.
□ State reasons for low labor productivity in less developed countries.

☐ Present three reasons for the emphasis on capital formation in the less developed countries.

☐ Identify two obstacles to domestic capital formation through saving.

☐ List two obstacles to domestic capital formation through investment.

☐ Explain why transferring the technologies used in the industrially advanced countries to the less developed ones may not be a realistic method of improving the technology of the latter nations.

☐ Identify three potential sociocultural factors that can inhibit economic growth.

☐ Describe the institutional obstacles to growth.

☐ Explain why poverty in the poor nations is a vicious circle.

☐ List five reasons why governments in the less developed countries will have to play a crucial role if the vicious circle of poverty is to be broken.

☐ Describe the problems with the public sector in fostering economic development.

☐ Identify the three ways in which the industrially advanced countries may help the less developed countries to grow economically.

☐ Explain the importance of a reduction in international trade barriers to economic growth in less developed countries.

☐ Describe the two sources of foreign aid for less developed countries.

☐ Give three criticisms of foreign aid to less developed countries.

☐ Discuss the importance of private capital flows for economic development in less developed countries.

☐ Describe the debt problem in less developed countries and identify five potential causes.

☐ Explain the economic consequences of the debt problem in less developed countries.

☐ Discuss the steps that have been taken to alleviate the debt crisis.

☐ List and describe six parts of an agenda proposed by less developed countries to improve economic conditions and reduce income disparity.

■ **CHAPTER OUTLINE**

1. There is considerable inequality in income among nations.

  a. Nations can be classified into three major groups.

  (1) *Industrially advanced countries* (IACs) are characterized by high per capita incomes, large stocks of capital goods, advanced technology for production, and a highly educated work force. These nations include the United States, Canada, Japan, Australia, New Zealand, and most of the nations in Western Europe.

  (2) Most of the remaining 109 nations are considered *less developed countries* (LDCs). LDCs are poor, not industrialized, are heavily dependent on agriculture, have high population growth, and have low rates of literacy. These countries comprise about three-fourths of the world's population. Of this group, there are 67 middle-income LDCs with average annual per capita income of $2,490 and 42 low-income LDCs with per capita income averaging $390.

  b. The newly industrialized countries such as Hong Kong, South Korea, Taiwan, and Singapore have experienced high rates of economic growth over the past thirty years, while many other LDCs have experienced a decrease in GDP per capita; if the growth rates were the same for high and low income countries, the gap in per capita income would widen because the income base is higher.

  c. The human implications of extreme poverty are important. Compared with the developed countries, LDCs have not only lower per capita incomes but also lower life expectancies, higher infant mortality, lower literacy rates, less food per person, and fewer nonhuman sources of energy.

2. Economic growth requires that the quantity and quality of economic resources be increased, that economic resources be used efficiently, and that technological knowledge be expanded. There are many obstacles to such factors in LDCs.

  a. Many (but not all) LDCs possess inadequate natural resources and the farm products which LDCs typically export are subject to significant price variation.

  b. Many LDCs are overpopulated, there is substantial unemployment and underemployment of labor, and labor productivity is low.

  c. LDCs are short of capital goods and these countries find it difficult to accumulate capital because of low savings potential, the flight of capital to IACs, and the absence of investors or incentives to invest.

  d. Technological knowledge is primitive in LDCs; although they might adopt the technologies of the advanced nations, those technologies are not always appropriate to the resource endowments of the LDCs and they must therefore develop their own technologies.

  e. In addition, it is difficult for LDCs to alter the social, cultural, and institutional environment in the process of promoting economic growth.

3. In summary, LDCs save little and, therefore, invest little in real and human capital because they are poor; and because they do not invest, their outputs per capita remain low and they remain poor. Even if the vicious circle were to be broken, a rapid increase in population would leave the standard of living unchanged.

4. There are differing views about the role that government plays in fostering economic growth in LDCs.

  a. The positive view holds that in the initial stages of economic development government action is needed to help overcome such obstacles as the lack of law and order, entrepreneurship, and infrastructure. Government policies may also assist capital formation, and in resolving social and institutional problems.

b. There are also problems and disadvantages with government involvement in promoting growth from such factors as bureaucratic impediments, corruption, maladministration, and the importance of political objectives over economic goals. Central planning does not work because it restricts competition and individual incentives, which are important ingredients in the growth process.

5. Industrially advanced nations of the world can help the poor countries develop in a number of ways.

a. They can lower the trade barriers which prevent the LDCs from selling their products in the developed countries.

b. Loans and grants from governments and from international organizations such as the World Bank also enable the LDCs to accumulate capital. This foreign aid has been criticized because it increases dependency, bureaucracy, and corruption.

c. The flow of private capital from industrially advanced countries helps the LDCs increase their productive capacities and per capita outputs.

6. The large external debts of LDCs are a continuing problem.

a. The debt that LDCs owe to foreign governments and foreign financial institutions increased significantly over the last two decades.

b. The causes of the debt crisis rest with world events during the 1970s and early 1980s.

(1) Higher prices for imported oil during the 1970s and early 1980s forced LDCs to borrow to cover current account deficits.

(2) The United States and other industrially advanced nations imposed tight monetary policies in the early 1980s to restrain inflation but this policy raised interest rates and costs for LDC borrowing and brought on recession to industrially advanced countries, which reduced imports from LDCs.

(3) The appreciation in the international value of the dollar during the 1981–1985 period forced LDCs to pay more for imported manufactured goods from the United States and to receive less in return for exports to the United States.

(4) Loans went into unproductive investments or were mismanaged.

(5) And, severe debt problems in Mexico in 1982 signaled problems with LDC loans in the financial community and resulted in reduced loans from private sources; increasing Federal budget deficits in the United States during most of the 1980s absorbed more private capital that might otherwise be lent to LDCs.

c. In recent years, the International Monetary Fund worked with countries on an individual basis to resolve debt problems. In return for debt rescheduling, LDCs often must impose austerity measures and use net export earning to pay for debt retirement, but these conditions have reduced economic development funds, retarded economic growth, and lowered capital income.

d. The debt problem in some countries has been resolved by restructuring the debt, forgiving loans, increasing loans to finance the debt, or through debt-equity swaps. Economic reforms and revived interest in investing in LDCs has helped alleviate some of the problems, but the developments are uneven and vary by country.

7. LDCs would like to see more progress in reducing the disparity between rich and poor nations. The following actions have been recommended to achieve this objective: sharing the IAC peace dividend with LDCs, increasing foreign aid, more debt relief for LDCs, improving global demand for LDC products, increased immigration from LDCs to IACs, eliminating economic neocolonialism.

■ **IMPORTANT TERMS**

Less developed countries (LDCs)	**Capital-saving technological advance**
Industrially advanced countries (IACs)	**Capital-using technological advance**
Demographic transition	**The will to develop**
Unemployment	**Capricious universe view**
Underemployment	
Investment in human capital	**Land reform**
Brain drain	**Vicious circle of poverty**
Domestic capital formation	**World Bank**
	Debt-equity swaps
Capital flight	**New Global Compact**
Infrastructure	**Neocolonialism**
Nonfinancial (in-kind) investment	**Terms of trade**

■ **HINTS AND TIPS**

1. This chapter offers a comprehensive look at the various factors affecting growth and economic development. There is no one factor that explains why some nations prosper and others remain poor, and you should not look for one. The chapter should give you insights into how natural, human, and capital resources together with government policies may influence a nation's economic development.

2. Several economic and demographic statistics for comparing rich and poor nations appear in the tables of the chapter. You don't need to memorize the numbers, but you should try to get a sense of the magnitude of the differences between industrially advanced and less developed countries on several key indicators. To do this, ask yourself questions calling for relative comparisons. For example, how many times larger is per capita income in IACs than in low-income LDCs? Answer: 57 times greater ($22,160/$390 = 56.8).

SELF-TEST

■ FILL-IN QUESTIONS

1. There is considerable income inequality among nations. The richest 20% of the world's population receive about _____% of world income while the poorest 20% of the world's population receive about _____% of world income.

2. Nations can be classified as _____ (IACs) or as _____ (LDCs). The GNP per capitain 1992 dollars was $_____ for 23 IACs, $_____ for 67 middle-income LDCs, and $_____ for 42 low-income LDCs.

3. IACs have a (higher, lower) _____ starting base for per capita income than LDCs, so the same percentage growth rate for both IACs and LDCs mean an increase in the _____ income gap.

4. Low per capita income in LDCs means that life _____, adult _____, daily _____ supply, and _____ consumption are (higher, lower) _____ and infant mortality is _____

5. The process for economic growth is the same for IACs and LDCs. It involves more _____ use of existing resources and also increasing supplies of productive _____

6. The distribution of natural resources among LDCs is (even, uneven) _____; many LDCs lack vital natural resources. Although _____ nations have been able to use oil resources for economic growth, much of the natural resources in LDCs are owned or controlled by companies in _____; exports of products from LDCs are subject to _____ fluctuations.

7. In terms of human resources:

a. Many LDCs are _____ and have population growth rates of about _____% compared to _____% for IACs; given the growth rate for LDCs, "rule of 70" would suggest that the population of LDCs will double in about _____ years. Rapid population growth can cause per capita GDP to (increase, decrease) _____

b. There is both _____ and _____ among workers in LDCs.

c. Labor _____ is also very low in most LDCs in part because these countries have not been able to invest in _____; and the so-called _____ contributes to the decline in skill level and productivity as the best-trained workers leave LDCs to work in IACs.

8. Capital accumulation is critical to the development of LDCs. If there were more capital goods, this would improve _____ and help boost per capita GDP; an increase in capital goods is necessary because the _____ of arable land is limited; the process of capital formation is "cumulative," investment increases the (population, output, natural resources) _____ of the economy and this in turn makes it possible for the economy to save more and invest more in capital goods.

9. The formation of domestic capital requires that a nation save and invest.
a. The former is difficult in LDCs because of a low _____ and the latter is difficult because of a lack of _____ and of _____ to invest; there is also the problem of _____ where savings are transferred to IACs.
b. Many LDCs do not have much public capital goods, or _____, that are necessary for productive _____ investment.
c. Nonfinancial (or in-kind) investment involves the transfer of surplus labor from (agriculture, industry) _____ to the improvement of agricultural facilities or the _____

10. The technologies used in the advanced industrial countries might be borrowed by and used in the less developed countries; but

a. the technologies used in the advanced countries are based upon a labor force that is (skilled, unskilled)

_____ , labor that is relatively (abundant, scarce) _____ , and capital that is relatively _____ , and their technologies tend to be (labor, capital)-_____ using; while

b. the technologies required in the underdeveloped countries must be based on a labor force that is

_____ , labor that is relatively

_____ , and capital that is relatively _____ , and their technologies need to be _____-using.

c. If technological advances make it possible to replace a worn-out plow, costing $10 when new, with a new $5 plow, the technological advance is capital (saving, using) _____

11. The "will to develop" in less developed countries involves a willingness to change the _____ and _____ arrangements of the country.

12. In most less developed countries, there is a vicious circle of poverty. Saving is small because the _____ per capita is small. Because saving is small, _____ in real and human capital is also small. And for this reason the _____ of labor and _____ per capita remain small.

13. List five reasons why the role of government in fostering economic development will need to be large in the less developed countries, especially during the early stages of development:

a. _____

b. _____

c. _____

d. _____

e. _____

14. There can also be _____ with government's role in the economy of LDCs because government _____ can impede social and economic change, central planners give too much emphasis to _____ objectives rather than economic objectives, and there can be _____

-administration and _____ in government. Central planning models also restrict _____ and individual _____ which are factors in economic development.

15. Three major ways that IACs can assist in the economic development in LDCs is by lowering international _____ barriers, extending _____ aid, and increasing the flow of private _____ investment.

16. Foreign aid in the form of public loans and grants can come from an individual _____. It can also come from the World _____, which is supported by 180 member nations. This organization is a "_____" resort lending agency for LDCs, and provides _____ assistance for LDCs.

17. Foreign aid has been criticized in recent years because: it may generate _____ in a nation instead of creating self-sustained growth; it may increase government _____ and control over a nation's economy; and the funds are subject to misuse or _____

18. The causes of the LDC debt problem were due to world events during the 1970s and early 1980s.

a. Oil prices (increased, decreased) _____ during the 1970s and this event _____ the borrowing needs of LDCs to pay for imported oil.

b. In the early 1980s, the United States had a (tight, easy) _____ monetary policy that (increased, decreased) _____ real interest rates and _____ the cost to LDCs of servicing debts; the recession of the early 1980s in the United States also _____ the exports of farm products from LDCs to the United States.

c. Over the 1981–1984 period, the international value of the dollar (appreciated, depreciated) _____ which meant that LDCs had to pay (more, less) _____ for imports and receive _____ in return for exports.

d. Some LDCs borrowed funds and used them for investments that were not _____

e. The debt crisis in _____ in 1982 shook confidence in LDCs and reduced private _____ by banks and financial institutions; the increasing Federal budget _____ during the early 1980s also absorbed more private capital.

19. There have been a number of developments in the LDC debt crisis:

a. Creditor nations and the International _____ Fund restructured or rescheduled debts to reduce the annual burden of interest and principal payment.

b. Government and business have also used _____ - _____ swaps, which means that debts are paid off by giving shares of stock to foreign creditors.

c. In return for debt concessions, LDCs had to implement domestic _____ reform programs to reduce budget _____, control a high level of _____, and encourage economic activity through _____ rather than through government.

d. Actions taken to resolve the debt crisis have lead to a modest (increase, decrease) _____ in foreign private investment in LDCs.

20. LDCs have offered an agenda for economic reform to reduce the income gap between LDCs and IACs that include six items:

a. There should be a reduction in IAC military expenditures and sharing the _____ dividend with LDCs in the form of more aid.

b. There should be more _____ aid. It should become more _____ so that wealthier nations make a larger contribution, and should be allocated for _____, not political or military reasons.

c. There needs to be relief from the burden of _____

d. Global markets can be improved by improving the _____ of trade for LDC commodities and by reducing trade _____ for LDC products.

e. IACs should permit more _____ from LDCs to IACs so that surplus labor can find other employment opportunities.

f. Actions should be taken to reduce the economic _____ that persists even with political independence and makes LDCs dependent on governments and businesses in IACs.

■ TRUE-FALSE QUESTIONS

Circle the T if the statement is true; the F if it is false.

1. The richest 20% of the world's population receive about 50% of the world's income while the poorest 20% receive only about 20% of the world's income.   **T F**

2. Less developed countries generally have high unemployment, low literacy rates, rapid population growth, and a labor force committed to agricultural production.   **T F**

3. The United States has about 5% of the world's population and produces about one-fourth of the world's output.   **T F**

4. The absolute income gap between less developed countries and industrially advanced countries has decreased over the past thirty years.   **T F**

5. Economic growth in both industrially advanced and less developed countries requires using economic resources more efficiently and increasing the supplies of some of these resources.   **T F**

6. It is impossible to achieve a high standard of living with a small supply of natural resources.   **T F**

7. Countries with large populations are less developed.   **T F**

8. The demographic transition view of population growth is that rising incomes must first be achieved and only then will slower population growth follow.   **T F**

9. The chief factor preventing the elimination of unemployment in the less developed countries is the small number of job openings available in the cities.   **T F**

10. Saving in LDCs is a smaller percentage of domestic output than in IACs, and this is the chief reason total saving in LDCs is small.   **T F**

11. Before private investment can be increased in less developed countries it is necessary to reduce the amount of investment in infrastructure.   **T F**

12. Technological advances in LDCs will be made rapidly because they do not require pushing forward the frontiers of technological knowledge and the technologies used in IACs can be easily transferred to the less developed ones.   **T F**

13. When technological advances are capital-saving it is possible for an economy to increase its productivity without any **net** investment in capital goods.   **T F**

14. Emancipation from custom and tradition is often the fundamental prerequisite of economic development.   **T F**

15. The capricious universe view is that there is a strong correlation between individual effort and results.   **T F**

16. The policies of the governments of less developed countries have often tended to reduce the incentives of foreigners to invest in the less developed countries. **T F**

17. Governments always play a positive role in the economic development of LDCs. **T F**

18. LDCs will not need foreign aid if the developed countries will reduce tariffs and import quotas on the goods which the less developed countries export. **T F**

19. An increase in the output and employment of the United States works to the advantage of the less developed countries because it provides the less developed countries with larger markets for their exports. **T F**

20. Foreign aid from the United States to the less developed countries has consistently exceeded 1% of its GDP. **T F**

21. Many in LDCs believe that the public and private aid extended by the IACs to the LDCs is designed to increase profits in the former and to exploit the latter countries. **T F**

22. One reason that foreign aid is viewed as harmful is that it tends to promote dependency and reduces the effectiveness of market incentives. **T F**

23. The simplest solution to the lingering LDC debt problem and the one with fewest repercussions would be to have the creditors in IACs forgive the debts of LDCs. **T F**

24. LDCs argue that the terms of trade have shifted against them because the prices of their exports tend to increase while the prices of their imports tend to decrease. **T F**

25. One of the items in the LDC agenda for a new global compact calls for reform of foreign aid to increase the quantity, make it progressive for IAC nations, and allocate it for economic rather than political or military reasons. **T F**

■ **MULTIPLE-CHOICE QUESTIONS**

Circle the letter that corresponds to the best answer.

1. Which of the following would be considered a LDC?
  (a) China
  (b) Kuwait
  (c) Taiwan
  (d) New Zealand

2. If per capita income is $600 a year in an LDC and per capita income is $12,000 in an IAC, then a 2% growth rate increases the absolute income gap by:
  (a) $120
  (b) $228

  (c) $240
  (d) $252

3. When the average annual rate of growth in per capita GDP in a LDC is 1%, approximately how many years will it take for the standard of living to double?
  (a) 27 years
  (b) 35 years
  (c) 57 years
  (d) 70 years

4. Which of the following is high in the less developed countries?
  (a) life expectancy
  (b) infant mortality
  (c) literacy
  (d) per capita energy consumption

5. Which of the following is an obstacle to economic growth in most less developed countries?
  (a) the supply of national resources
  (b) the size and quality of the labor force
  (c) the supply of capital equipment
  (d) all of the above

6. An increase in the total output of consumer goods in a less developed country may not increase the average standard of living because:
  (a) of capital flight
  (b) it may lead to an increase in the population
  (c) of disguised unemployment
  (d) the quality of the labor force is so poor

7. Which of the following best describes the unemployment found in the less developed countries?
  (a) the result of cyclical fluctuations in aggregate demand
  (b) the agricultural workers who have migrated from rural to urban areas and failed to find employment in the cities
  (c) the workers in excess of the optimum population
  (d) workers whose productivity is subject to diminishing returns

8. Which of the following is a reason for placing special emphasis on capital accumulation in less developed countries?
  (a) the flexible supply of arable land
  (b) the high productivity of workers
  (c) the high marginal contribution of capital equipment
  (d) the possibility of capital flight

9. Which of the following is a factor limiting saving in less developed countries?
  (a) the output of the economy is too low to permit a large volume of saving
  (b) those who do save make their saving available to their own economies

(c) the equal distribution of income

(d) the high marginal contribution of capital equipment to production

10. When citizens of LDCs transfer savings or invest savings in IACs, it is referred to as:

(a) brain drain

(b) capital flight

(c) savings potential

(d) in-kind investment

11. Which of the following is *not* an obstacle to capital formation (investment) in less developed countries?

(a) the absence of strong incentives to invest

(b) the lack of basic social capital

(c) the absence of a large entrepreneurial class

(d) the lack of capital-saving changes in technology

12. Which of the following is an example of infrastructure?

(a) a steel plant

(b) an electric power plant

(c) a farm

(d) a deposit in a financial institution

13. Which of the following seems to be the most acute *institutional* problem that needs to be resolved in many less developed countries?

(a) adoption of birth control

(b) development of strong labor unions

(c) increase in the nation's public capital

(d) land reform

14. Assume the total real output of an LDC increases from $100 billion to $115.5 billion while its population expands from 200 million to 210 million people. Real income per capita has, as a result, increased by:

(a) $50

(b) $100

(c) $150

(d) $200

15. The role of government in the early stages of economic development will probably be a major one for several reasons. Which one of the following is *not* one of these reasons?

(a) only government can provide a larger amount of the needed infrastructure

(b) the absence of private entrepreneurs to accumulate capital and take risks

(c) the necessity of creating *new* money to finance capital accumulation

(d) the slowness and uncertainty of the market system in fostering development

16. In recent years, many LDCs have come to recognize that:

(a) competition and economic incentives for individuals are necessary for economic development

(b) there are few disadvantages from government involvement in the development process

(c) private capital is not required for economic development

(d) the World Bank serves as an institutional barrier to economic growth

17. An event that occurred during the 1970s or early 1980s that contributed to the LDC debt crisis was:

(a) a sharp decline in price of oil charged by OPEC countries

(b) a depreciation in the international value of the dollar

(c) a tight monetary policy and recession in the United States

(d) a rise in net export earnings of the LDCs

18. To raise funds to pay interest and principal on external debt, LDCs had to adopt domestic economic policies that tended to:

(a) decrease imports, increase exports, and lower the standard of living

(b) increase imports, decrease exports, and lower the standard of living

(c) decrease imports, decrease exports, and lower the standard of living

(d) increase imports, decrease exports, and raise the standard of living

19. The terms of trade for a nation exporting copper worsen whenever:

(a) the price of copper rises

(b) the price of copper falls

(c) the price of copper rises and the prices of imported goods decline

(d) the price of copper falls and the prices of imported goods rise

20. Which of the following is one of the agenda items in the new global compact of the LDCs?

(a) the elimination of OPEC

(b) the elimination of the World Bank

(c) increased debt relief for LDCs

(d) increased trade barriers

■ **PROBLEMS**

1. Suppose that the real per capita income in the average industrially advanced country is $8000 per year and in the average less developed country is $500 per year.

a. The gap between their standards of living is

$_____ per year.

b. If GDP per capita were to grow at a rate of 5% during a year in both the industrially advanced and the less developed countries:

(1) the standard of living in the industrially advanced countries would rise to $_____ a year;

(2) the standard of living in the less developed countries would rise to $_____ a year; and

(3) the gap between their standards of living would

(narrow, widen) _____ to

$_____ a year.

2. While economic conditions are not identical in all less developed countries, there are certain conditions common to or typical of most of them. In the spaces after each of the following characteristics, indicate briefly the nature of this characteristic in most less developed countries.

   a. Standard of living (per capita income). _____

   b. Average life expectancy. _____

   c. Extent of unemployment. _____

   d. Literacy. _____

   e. Technology. _____
   f. Percentage of the population engaged in agricul-

ture. _____

   g. Size of the population relative to the land and capital

available. _____

   h. The birth and death rates. _____

   i. Quality of the labor force. _____
   j. Amount of capital equipment relative to the labor

force. _____

   k. Level of saving. _____

   l. Incentive to invest. _____

   m. Amount of basic social capital. _____

   n. Extent of industrialization. _____
   o. Size and quality of the entrepreneurial class and the

supervisory class. _____
   p. Per capita public expenditures for education and

per capita energy consumption. _____

   q. Per capita consumption of food. _____

   r. Disease and malnutrition. _____

3. Suppose that it takes a minimum of 5 units of food to keep a person alive for a year, that the population can double itself every 10 years, and that the food supply can increase every 10 years by an amount equal to what it was in the beginning (year 0).

   a. Assume that both the population and the food supply grow at these rates. Complete the following table by computing the size of the population and the food supply in years 10 through 60.

Year	Food supply	Population
0	200	20
10	____	____
20	____	____
30	____	____
40	____	____
50	____	____
60	____	____

   b. What happens to the relationship between the food supply and the population in the 30th year?

_____

_____

   c. What would actually prevent the population from growing at this rate following the 30th year?

_____

_____

   d. Assuming that the actual population growth in the years following the 30th does not outrun the food supply, what would be the size of the population in:

   (1) Year 40:_____

   (2) Year 50:_____

   (3) Year 60:_____
   e. Explain why the standard of living failed to increase in the years following the 30th even though the food supply increased by 75% between years 30 and 60.

_____

■ **SHORT ANSWER AND ESSAY QUESTIONS**

   1. What is the degree of income inequality among nations of the world?

   2. How do the overall level of economic growth per capita and the rates of economic growth compare among rich nations and poor countries? Why does the income gap widen?

   3. What are the "human implications" of poverty found in LDCs? (Use the socioeconomic indicators found in Table 39-3 of the text to contrast the quality of life in IACs and LDCs).

   4. Describe the basic avenues of economic growth. Do these avenues differ for IACs and LDCs?

   5. How would you describe the natural resource situation for LDCs? In what ways do price fluctuations affect LDC exports? Is a weak natural resource base an obstacle to economic growth?

   6. Describe the implications of the high rate of growth in population and its effects on the standard of living. Can the standard of living be raised by merely increasing the output of consumer goods in LDCs? What is the meaning of the cliché, "the rich get richer and the poor get children," and how does it apply to LDCs?

7. Compare and contrast the traditional view of population and economic growth with the demographic transition view.

8. What is the distinction between unemployment and underemployment? How do these concepts apply to LDCs?

9. What are the reasons for the low level of labor productivity in LDCs?

10. How does the "brain drain" affect LDCs?

11. What reasons exist for placing special emphasis on capital accumulation as a means of promoting economic growth in LDCs?

12. Why is domestic capital accumulation difficult in LDCs? Answer both in terms of the saving side and the investment side of capital accumulation. Is there "capital flight" from LDCs?

13. In addition to the obstacles which limit domestic investment, what other obstacles tend to limit the flow of foreign capital into LDCs? What role does infrastructure play in capital formation?

14. How might the LDCs improve their technology without engaging in slow and expensive research? Why might this be an inappropriate method of improving the technology used in the LDCs?

15. What is meant by the "will to develop"? How is it related to social and institutional change in LDCs?

16. Explain the "vicious circle" of poverty found in the LDCs. How does population growth make an escape from this vicious circle difficult?

17. Why is the role of government expected to be a positive one in the early phases of development in LDCs? What have been the problems with the involvement of government in economic development?

18. What are three ways that advanced nations help LDCs?

19. How is it possible for the United States to assist LDCs without spending a penny on "foreign aid"? Is this type of aid sufficient to ensure rapid and substantial development in LDCs?

20. Discuss the World Bank in terms of its purposes, characteristics, sources of funds, promotion of private capital flows, and success. What are its affiliates and their purposes?

21. Discuss three criticisms of foreign aid to LDCs.

22. Describe the dimension and basic causes of the lingering LDC debt crisis.

23. What have been the economic consequences of the LDC debt crisis?

24. What are the prospects for reform and revival from the LDC debt crisis?

25. Explain the six major parts of the LDC agenda for a new global compact.

ANSWERS

Chapter 22 Growth and the Less Developed Countries

FILL-IN QUESTIONS

1. 83, 1

2. Industrially advanced countries, less developed countries, $22,160, $2,490, $390

3. higher, absolute

4. expectancies, literacy, calorie, energy, lower, higher

5. efficient, resources

6. uneven, OPEC, IACs, price

7. *a.* overpopulated, 2, .7, 35, decrease; *b.* unemployment, underemployment; *c.* productivity, human capital, brain drain

8. *a.* labor productivity, supply, output

9. *a.* saving potential, investors, incentives, capital flight; *b.* infrastructure, private; *c.* agriculture, infrastructure

10. *a.* skilled, scarce, abundant, capital; *b.* unskilled, abundant, scarce, labor; *c.* saving

11. institutions, social

12. income, investment, productivity, output (income)

13. *a.* the existence of widespread banditry and intertribal warfare in the poorest less developed nations; *b.* the absence of a sizable and vigorous entrepreneurial class; *c.* the great need for public goods and services; *d.* government action may be the only means of promoting saving and investment; *e.* government can more effectively deal with the social-institutional obstacles to growth

14. public sector problems, bureaucracy, political, mal, corruption, competition, incentives

15. trade, foreign, capital

16. nation, Bank, last, technical

17. dependency, bureaucracy, corruption

18. *a.* increased, increased; *b.* tight, increased, increased, decreased; *c.* appreciated, more, less; *d.* productive; *e.* Mexico, lending, deficits

19. *a.* Monetary; *b.* debt-equity; *c.* economic, deficits, inflation, markets; *d.* increase

20. *a.* peace; *b.* foreign, progressive, economic; *c.* debt; *d.* terms, barriers; *e.* immigration; *f.* neocolonialism

TRUE-FALSE QUESTIONS

1. F, p. 450	**8.** T, p. 454	**15.** F, p. 459	**22.** T, p. 464
2. T, pp. 450-451	**9.** T, pp. 455-456	**16.** T, pp. 457-458	**23.** F, p. 467
3. T, p. 451	**10.** F, p. 457	**17.** F, p. 462	**24.** F, p. 468
4. F, p. 451	**11.** F, pp. 457-458	**18.** F, pp. 463-464	**25.** T, p. 467
5. T, pp. 452-453	**12.** F, p. 458	**19.** T, p. 463	
6. F, p. 453	**13.** T, p. 458	**20.** F, p. 463	
7. F, pp. 453-454	**14.** T, p. 459	**21.** T, p. 464	

MULTIPLE-CHOICE QUESTIONS

1. *a*, p. 451	**6.** *b*, pp. 453-454	**11.** *d*, pp. 457-458	**16.** *a*, p. 462
2. *b*, pp. 451-452	**7.** *b*, pp. 455-456	**12.** *b*, p. 458	**17.** *c*, p. 465
3. *d*, p. 453	**8.** *c*, pp. 456-457	**13.** *d*, p. 460	**18.** *a*, p. 466
4. *b*, p. 452	**9.** *a*, p. 457	**14.** *a*, p. 461	**19.** *d*, pp. 467-468
5. *d*, pp. 452-453	**10.** *b*, p. 457	**15.** *c*, pp. 461-462	**20.** *c*, p. 467

PROBLEMS

1. *a.* 7500, *b.* (1) 8400, (2) 525, (3) widen, 7875

2. *a.* low; *b.* short; *c.* widespread; *d.* low; *e.* primitive; *f.* large; *g.* large; *h.* high; *i.* poor; *j.* small; *k.* low; *l.* absent; *m.* small; *n.* small, *o.* small and poor; *p.* small; *q.* low; *r.* common

3. *a.* food supply; 400, 600, 800, 1000, 1200, 1400; population; 40, 80, 160, 320, 640, 1280; *b.* the food supply is just able to support the population; *c.* the inability of the food supply to support a population growing at this rate; *d.* (1) 200, (2) 240, (3) 280; *e.* the population increased as rapidly as the food supply

SHORT ANSWER AND ESSAY QUESTIONS

1. pp. 450-451	**8.** pp. 455-456	**15.** p. 459	**22.** pp. 465-466
2. p. 451	**9.** p. 456	**16.** pp. 460-461	**23.** p. 466
3. p. 452	**10.** p. 456	**17.** pp. 461-462	**24.** pp. 466-467
4. pp. 452-453	**11.** pp. 456-457	**18.** p. 463	**25.** pp. 466-467
5. p. 453	**12.** p. 457	**19.** p. 463	
6. pp. 453-454	**13.** pp. 457-458	**20.** pp. 463-464	
7. p. 455	**14.** pp. 458-459	**21.** pp. 464-465	

CHAPTER 23

Russia: An Economy in Transition

In the years following the Russian Revolution of 1917, many people in the United States were convinced that the economic system of the Soviet Union was unworkable and that it would break down sooner or later—proof that Marx and Lenin were unrealistic dreamers—and that the reconversion of the Soviet economy to a market system would follow. Now, almost eighty years after the revolution, the economy of the former Soviet Union is being transformed into a market economy. Chapter 23 provides insights into this profound turn of events by examining the reasons why the Soviet economic system failed, and by discussing reforms and obstacles in the path to a market economy for Russia and other successor republics from the former Soviet Union.

The first two sections of the chapter explain the basic ideas behind Marxian ideology and discuss the two institutional features that were most characteristic of the economy of the former Soviet Union. For over seven decades, the Soviet economy operated under a system of state ownership of property resources and direct control. Central planning was used to set prices, to restrict consumption, and to direct investment to heavy industry and to the military. Although central planning served as a powerful form of economic decision-making, it had serious problems and flaws as a coordinating mechanism because it resulted in production bottlenecks, missed production targets, and reduced the economic freedom and decision-making for producers, workers, and consumers.

As you will learn in the third and fourth sections of the chapter, the slowing of economic growth in the Soviet economy in 1970s and 1980s set the stage for the failure of communism and for the final attempts to reform the faltering economic system of the former Soviet Union. What contributed to the deterioration of Soviet economy were many factors, among them being the economic burden of supporting a large military, inefficiencies in the agricultural sector that hurt other sectors of the economy, and the reliance on more inputs rather than increasing the productivity and efficiency of available inputs to fuel economic growth. By 1986, then-Soviet President Mikhail Gorbachev proposed a series of economic changes designed to restructure the economy (**perestroika**) and to give peo-

ple more freedom in the conduct of economic and business affairs (**glasnost**). Although the Gorbachev reforms attempted to correct the deficiencies of central control and modernize the economy, the proposal did not eliminate central planning.

The fifth, and major, section of the chapter explains the eight elements for the transformation of the Russian economy and the economies of other republics created from the breakup of the former Soviet Union. The transition will require the privatization of property resources, the promotion of competition, a reduced and altered role for government, major price reforms, and stronger connections to the international economy. These transition policies will result in high rates of inflation that must be controlled by the government. There will be a negative attitude among workers and bureaucrats toward the market economy that must be overcome. Finally, none of the reforms can be achieved alone; they must be worked on simultaneously if there is to be a successful transition.

The final section discusses the actions that can be taken by the major capitalist nations to help transform a centrally planned economy into one based on markets and prices. The most obvious assistance is foreign aid, but as you will learn, it is not without much criticism. Private investment is the most important avenue for long-term change, yet the amount of investment and its effectiveness will depend on the progress in economic restructuring. The economy of Russia will also benefit from the steps it takes to join international organizations that promote world trade and economic development.

The transformation of the Russian economy into a market economy is one of the most important economic events of this decade. Whether the sweeping economic reforms will work, or what the final outcomes will be, is still unknown and uncertain. Nevertheless, this examination of the sweeping change of an economic system from one based on central planning to one based on markets and prices should deepen your understanding of the principles of economics. This dramatic development is a fitting topic for the conclusion to your study of economics.

■ CHECKLIST

When you have studied this chapter you should be able to:

☐ Outline the key elements of Marxian ideology.

☐ Identify two outstanding institutions of the economy of the former Soviet Union.

☐ Make seven generalizations about the functioning of central economic planning in the former Soviet Union.

☐ Compare the coordination mechanism in a market economy with that in a centrally planned economy.

☐ Describe the deteriorating economic performance of the Soviet economy after the 1960s.

☐ Identify six factors that contributed to the collapse of the Soviet economic system.

☐ Discuss the elements of the Gorbachev reforms.

☐ List eight factors that are important in the transition to a market economy for the Russian economy.

☐ Explain the effects of privatization and competition in the transition.

☐ Describe the changed role for government in the transition.

☐ Use a supply and demand graph to discuss the difficulties posed by price reforms in the transition.

☐ Explain the importance of opening the economy to international trade and finance in the transition.

☐ Describe how inflation can threaten macroeconomic stability.

☐ Explain two difficulties in achieving public support for the transition to a market economy.

☐ Discuss the simultaneity problem in the transition.

☐ List three actions by the capitalist industrial nations of the world to assist Russia to build a market economy.

☐ Evaluate the importance of foreign aid and private investment in the transformation of the Russian economy.

☐ Identify the key international organizations and actions that would help with the transition to a market economy for Russia.

☐ Describe two accomplishments with economic reforms in Russia.

☐ Identify three problems with economic reforms in Russia.

☐ State an optimistic and a pessimistic view of the future prospects for economic reforms in Russia.

■ CHAPTER OUTLINE

1. The Soviet economy was based on ideology and institutions.

a. The Soviet government was viewed as a dictatorship of the proletariat (or working class), and the economy was based on *Marxian* ideology.

(1) The Marxian concept of a *labor theory of value* held that only labor creates value in production, and that profits are a *surplus value* expropriated from workers by capitalists, who because of the institution of

private property, were able to control the means of production (capital goods).

(2) The communist system of the former Soviet Union sought to end this exploitation of workers by eliminating private property and by creating a classless society.

b. The two major institutional features of the Soviet economy were state ownership of property resources and central economic planning.

2. Central planning was used throughout much of the history of the Soviet Union.

a. Historically, the operation of central planning in the Soviet Union exhibited seven features:

(1) the attachment of great importance to military strength and to industrialization;

(2) the overcommitment of available resources and the missing of planning targets;

(3) a stress on increasing the quantity of resources rather than using given resources more productively;

(4) the use of directives to allocate inputs for production rather than markets and prices;

(5) price fixing and price controls by government;

(6) an emphasis on the self-sufficiency of the nation; and

(7) passive use of monetary and fiscal policies.

b. The basic problem encountered in a centrally planned economy such as that of the former Soviet Union was the difficulty of coordinating the many interdependent segments of the economy and the avoidance of the chain reaction that would result from a bottleneck in any one of the segments.

3. Communism failed in many ways in the former Soviet Union.

a. Economic growth declined in the 1970s and 1980s. Real output also fell sharply before the country's breakup.

b. Technology lagged by western standards and manufacturing goods were of poor quality.

c. Consumers received few material benefits from years of sacrifice for the rapid industrialization and sizable public expenditures to support a large military.

d. Six interrelated factors contributed to the collapse of the economy of the former Soviet Union.

(1) The large financial burden for military expenditures diverted resources from the production of consumer and capital goods.

(2) Inefficiencies in agriculture acted as a drag on economic growth and hurt productivity in other sectors of the economy.

(3) Economic growth was achieved throughout much of the Soviet history by increasing the quantity of economic resources (especially labor) rather than by using the more difficult route of increasing the productivity of existing resources; however, growing labor shortages limited growth by the historical route and the lack of incentives and technology needs made the second route more difficult.

(4) The increased complexity of production processes in a modern industrial society compounded the difficulties of central planning.

(5) There were inadequate measures of economic performance to determine the degree of success or failure of enterprises or to give clear signals to the economy.

(6) Economic incentives were ineffective for encouraging initiative and work or for coordination of productive activities.

4. In 1986, President Mikhail Gorbachev offered a series of proposals for economic reform (**perestroika**) and also called for more openness (**glasnost**) in discussions about economic affairs, both designed to improve the economic performance of the centrally planned system. The Gorbachev reforms called for: the modernization of industry; the decentralization of decision-making; the encouragement of some private production of products; the increased use of economic incentives to motivate workers and fire incompetent managers; the institution of price reforms and a more rational price system; and a greater involvement in the world economy. The reforms did not work in large part because they only modified the major deficiencies of the centrally planned system.

5. There are eight components to the transition from a command economy to a market economy for Russia.

a. Private property rights must be established and government property must be transferred to private ownership. Several options are possible to achieve the privatization objective: selling enterprises directly, employee stock ownership, or conversion of large government enterprises into corporations or publicly owned businesses.

b. Competition must be promoted by splitting up or restructuring large state-owned enterprises to reduce the potential for monopoly power by having only one privatized business in an industry.

c. The government must reduce its extensive involvement in the economy to the more limited and traditional role of providing a legal system, maintaining competition, redistributing income, reallocating resources to necessary public goods, addressing the problems of spillovers, and stabilizing the economy.

d. The government will need to eliminate price fixing and price controls so that prices for goods and services are free to change and reflect relative scarcities.

e. Action must be taken to open the economy to international trade and finance by making the ruble a convertible currency. Eventually, this action will promote more competition and efficiency in production.

f. Inflation needs to be controlled. Inflation increases when prices are decontrolled. In the extreme, there can be hyperinflation and a loss of confidence in the ruble as a functioning currency. Hoarding and speculation cause additional price instability and makes business decisions more difficult.

g. There may be public resistance to the reforms because they threaten job status and require workers and managers to change old methods and procedures of work.

h. The reforms must be pursued simultaneously; a failure to achieve one reform will affect the success of all the reforms.

6. The major capitalist economies of the world will facilitate the transition of the Russian economy to a market economy.

a. Foreign aid is being provided by capitalist nations.

(1) This aid is needed for Russia to reform its economy, sustain democracy, and join the international economy.

(2) Critics contend that foreign aid is wasteful under present conditions, it delays needed cuts in military spending, and is of little benefit to the average citizen. The aid would be better spent on social and economic problems in donor nations.

(3) Foreign aid was $23 billion in 1992–1993. It came from world financial institutions ($3 billion) and bilateral aid ($20 billion). The latter was mostly export credits to subsidize loans for Russia to buy exports.

b. Private investment will be very important, but there are many obstacles for private businesses that desire to invest: unclear ownership and control of enterprises; inadequacies in the distribution system and public infrastructure; high business taxes; racketeering; and inflation.

c. Membership in international organizations, such as the International Monetary Fund, the World Bank, and the General Agreement on Tariffs and Trade, will help integrate Russia into the world's market economy.

7. A progress report on economic reforms in Russia shows both accomplishments and problems.

a. Three reform accomplishments are worthy of note.

(1) Most of the economy—about 70% at the end of 1994—has been privatized. This privatization was achieved through government distribution of vouchers that could be used to purchase businesses, or through the direct sale of state enterprises. Market reforms in agriculture, however, have been slow.

(2) Most prices—about 90%—have been decontrolled and the value of the ruble is being set by supply and demand.

(3) Unemployment is relatively low, although wages were cut and living standards fell as a consequence.

b. The problems with the transition are several.

(1) Inflation continues to hinder the economy. Contributing factors include price decontrols, the ruble overhang (excess currency saved when there were few consumer goods to purchase), large government budget deficits, and the printing of money to finance the deficits.

(2) Real output and living standards fell during the reforms, although the decline may have bottomed out. In-

flation, reduced international trade, market uncertainty, the need to reallocate resources, and the fall in the value of the ruble precipitated the decline in output.
(3) Growing inequality in income and social problems plague the economy. Market reforms enrich some groups and hurt others. Economic insecurity raises tensions, reduces the quality of life, and means less investment in public goods.

8. The prospects for Russia's transition to a market economy are still uncertain. On the one hand, the pessimistic view is that the government will remain weak, with a mounting public debt, minimal control of inflation, and an inability to provide basic public services. These destabilizing conditions will lead to hyperinflation and a collapse of the economy. On the other hand, the more optimistic view is that the fall in real output has ended and the rate of inflation will fall. Market reforms are now taking hold and the economy will prosper. Although the transition will continue for at least another decade, an economic collapse and return to socialism is unlikely given the progress that has been made.

■ **IMPORTANT TERMS**

Labor theory of value	Gorbachev reforms
Surplus value	*Perestroika*
State ownership	*Glasnost*
Central economic planning	Ruble overhang

■ **HINTS AND TIPS**

1. This chapter applies your knowledge of economics to explain the transformation of Russia from a socialist to a capitalist economy. You will be familiar with most of the economic terminology, but a few terms that are unique to Russia may be new to you: surplus value, labor theory of value, ruble overhang, or *perestroika.*

2. View the chapter as a culminating exercise in your study of economics that gives you a chance to *review, apply,* and *integrate* many of the economic concepts and ideas you've learned from the text.

3. Supply and demand analysis is used to explain price controls in Figure 23-1 in the text. The figure differs from those you've seen in previous chapters (Chapter 3) because there are two supply curves. One is vertical (perfectly inelastic) because it assumes fixed government control of production and no effect on quantity supplied as price controls are lifted. The upsloping supply curve shows an increase in quantity supplied as price controls are lifted—a situation more likely to occur as Russia becomes a market economy.

SELF-TEST

■ **FILL-IN QUESTIONS**

1. The ideology of the economy of the former Soviet Union was that:
  a. the value of any commodity is determined by the amount of _____ required to produce it;
  b. in capitalist economies, capital is (privately, publicly) _____ owned, and capitalists exploit workers by paying them a wage that is equal to the _____ wage and obtain _____ value at the expense of workers; and
  c. in a communist economy, capital and other property resources will be _____ , society will be _____-less, and it will be governed by the Communist Party as a dictatorship of the _____

2. The two major institutions of the former Soviet Union are the ownership of property resources by the _____ and _____ economic planning.

3. Economic planning in the former Soviet Union functioned in several ways.
  a. The Soviet five-year plans sought to achieve rapid _____ and _____ strength, but these policies created an (over, under) _____-commitment of resources and resulted in an _____-production of goods for consumers.
  b. Early economic growth was achieved by _____ resources and reallocating surplus labor from _____ to industry.
  c. The government allocated inputs among industries by planning _____ and the government fixed _____ for goods and services and inputs.
  d. The Soviet Union considered itself to be a (capitalist, socialist) _____ nation surrounded by _____ nations, and central plans were designed to achieve economic _____-sufficiency.
  e. Monetary and fiscal policies in the Soviet Union were (active, passive) _____. Prices were _____ by government and ambitious planning targets essentially eliminated the _____ of workers. The _____ issued credit or working

capital to state enterprises and accepted deposits, but it did not manipulate the supply of _____

4. Decision-making in a market economy is (centralized, decentralized) _____ , but in the Soviet economy it was _____. The market system tends to produce a reasonably (efficient, inefficient) _____ allocation of resources, but central planning in the Soviet economy was _____ and resulted in production bottlenecks and failures to meet many production targets.

5. There are a number of reasons for the collapse of communism and the failure of the Soviet economy.

   a. There was a large _____ burden on the economy that diverted resources from the production of investment and _____ goods.

   b. Agriculture was (efficient, inefficient) _____ and (helped, hurt) _____ economic growth and productivity in other sectors of the economy.

   c. Traditionally, economic growth was achieved by increasing the (quality, quantity) _____ of economic resources rather than by increasing the _____ , or productivity, of existing resources, but shortages of labor and capital have limited economic growth in the traditional path, and improving the productivity of existing resources was difficult because of lagging _____ progress.

   d. Central planning became (more, less) _____ complex and difficult as the Soviet economy grew and changed over time.

   e. Measures of economic performance were (adequate, inadequate) _____ for determining the success or failure of economic activities.

   f. Economic incentives were (effective, ineffective) _____ for encouraging work or for giving signals for efficient allocation of resources in the economy.

6. In 1986, reform of the Soviet economy was proposed by Mikhail _____. His economic program for reform and restructuring was referred to as _____; it was accompanied by _____ , which means that there was to be more openness in the discussion of economic issues among participants in the economy.

7. List the six elements of the 1986 reforms.

   a. _____

   b. _____

   c. _____

   d. _____

   e. _____

   f. _____

8. The transition to a market economy for Russia will require success in achieving more sweeping changes. One of the most important changes is the establishment of _____ rights and the transfer of government property to _____ ownership. This objective may be achieved by the _____ of state enterprises, by employee _____ ownership, and in the case of large state enterprise, conversion into _____ or into businesses owned by the _____

9. The economy must also promote _____ by splitting up the large state-owned enterprises so that there is more than one business producing a good or service and to reduce the potential for _____ power.

10. In the transition, the role of government will need to be _____ and refocused on the traditional functions of providing a _____ system, maintaining _____ , redistributing _____ , reallocating resources to essential _____ goods, addressing the problems of _____ costs and benefits, and macroeconomic _____ of the economy.

11. In the past, prices of goods and services were kept at low levels through price _____ , but the movement to a market economy will require them to be lifted.

12. Russia needs to join the international economy by making the ruble a stable _____ or exchangeable currency on international markets, and by opening the economy to more international _____ with other nations.

13. The move to a market economy will be accompanied by macroeconomic instability in the form of high rates of _____ because of the decontrol of _____. In the worst case scenario, there could be _____ which would mean that the ruble would cease to function as a medium of _____

14. Another factor critical to the success is widespread public _____ for the reforms. Resistance has come from party and government _____ because they are threatened by the loss of power and jobs. There must also be a change in work _____ and incentives so worker productivity improves and entrepreneurship is encouraged.

15. The components of the reforms are interlinked, so there is a _____ problem. Progress must be made on the reforms (separately, together) _____ if the transition is to be successful.

16. Advanced capitalist nations can ease the transformation of the Russian economy by providing _____ aid. This aid will help the Russian government control (prices, inflation) _____ and sustain economic reforms and domestic peace. Critics, however, charge that this aid is (efficient, wasteful) _____ given current economic conditions, that it (fosters, delays) _____ cuts in military spending and could be better spent in donor nations.

17. Foreign aid to Russia was about $_____ billion in 1992–1993. About $_____ billion came from world financial institutions and about $_____ billion came from bilateral, or nation-to-nation, aid. The bilateral aid was mostly in the form of _____ credits designed to subsidize loans for Russians to purchase exports from the donor nation.

18. Other assistance from advanced capitalist nations has included _____ investment and _____ in international institutions.

   a. This _____ investment is subject to problems because of uncertainty about (government, international) _____ authority in negotiations, unreliable sources for (outputs, inputs) _____ , a poor (private, public) _____ infrastructure, business taxes that are too (low, high) _____ , and (unemployment, inflation) _____.

   b. Russia was admitted to the _____ Bank and the International _____ Fund in 1992. It would also help if Russia became a member of the General _____.

19. The major accomplishments since the transition began include _____ of the economy, the decontrol of _____ , and a low rate of _____

20. Major problems remain for Russia. The rate of _____ has been high because of price _____ , a _____ overhang, and government budget _____. Also, there has been declining real _____ and a fall in the _____ of living. The transition has increased income _____ and caused greater economic _____

■ TRUE-FALSE QUESTIONS

Circle the T if the statement is true; the F if it is false.

1. The labor theory of value is the Marxian idea that the exchange value of a product is determined by the supply and demand of labor resources.   **T F**

2. Surplus value in Marxian ideology is the value or price of a commodity at equilibrium in a competitive market.   **T F**

3. The Soviet economy was characterized by both state ownership of resources and decentralized economic decision-making.   **T F**

4. The Soviet government set the economic objectives of the economy, directed the resources of the economy toward the achievement of those objectives, and used the market system as one means of achieving those objectives.   **T F**

5. Historically, the Soviet Union placed strong emphasis on rapid industrialization and economic self-sufficiency.   **T F**

6. Economic resources tended to be undercommitted in the Soviet economy.   **T F**

7. The Soviet Union actively used monetary and fiscal policies to manipulate aggregate levels of employment, output, and prices.   **T F**

8. In the few years before the breakup of the Soviet Union real output increased.   **T F**

9. Greater productivity and technological progress in the civilian sector were often sacrificed or limited by the demands to support a large military in the Soviet Union. **T   F**

10. Agriculture was one of the most productive sectors of the Soviet economy.   **T F**

11. Soviet economic growth slowed in the years after the 1970s because of a surplus of labor and extensive unemployment.   **T F**

12. The problems of central planning became easier and less complex as the Soviet economy grew over time, but the economy was undermined by calls for democratic reform.   **T F**

13. *Glasnost* refers to the economic restructuring proposed in 1986 by Mikhail Gorbachev.　　　**T　F ·**

14. The Gorbachev reforms called for the development of a limited private enterprise sector and more use of economic incentives.　　　**T　F**

15. The transition to a market economy in Russia requires the breakup of large industries and actions to promote competition.　　　**T　F**

16. Government is more likely to expand rather than contract its role in the transition to a market economy in Russia.　　　**T　F**

17. Price decontrol will be a minor problem in the conversion of the Russian economy to capitalism because the prices established by the Soviet government over the years were very similar to the economic value established in a competitive market.　　　**T　F**

18. Old work habits and bureaucratic resistance will be obstacles in the movement to capitalism in Russia. **T　F**

19. The "simultaneity" problem refers to the need to achieve a simultaneous decrease in inflation and unemployment in Russia.　　　**T　F**

20. Foreign aid to Russia has come mainly in the form of cash grants from other nations.　　　**T　F**

21. A critic of foreign aid to Russia would argue that the aid is wasteful and ineffective until the transition to capitalism has been achieved.　　　**T　F**

22. Private investment from capitalist nations will be an important source of real capital and business skills in management, marketing, and entrepreneurship for Russia.
　　　T　F

23. Russia has been admitted to membership in the World Bank and the International Monetary Fund. **T　F**

24. One of the major accomplishments of Russian economic reform has been limited inflation because of the reduction in the ruble overhang and tight control of the money supply.　　　**T　F**

25. One of the major problems still facing Russia is the elimination of price controls that cover over 90% of all prices.　　　**T　F**

■ MULTIPLE-CHOICE QUESTIONS

Circle the letter that corresponds to the best answer.

1. Which of the following was an element in the ideology of the Soviet Union?
　(a) dictatorship over the business class
　(b) the creation of surplus value by government
　(c) the labor theory of value
　(d) the private ownership of property

2. Marxian (or communist) ideology in the Soviet Union was highly critical of capitalist societies because in those societies:
　(a) capitalists own the machinery and equipment necessary for production
　(b) capitalists pay workers a wage that is less than the value of their production
　(c) capitalists expropriate the surplus value of workers
　(d) all of the above are true

3. The institution that was most characteristic of the Soviet Union was:
　(a) private ownership of property
　(b) authoritarian central planning
　(c) a system of markets and prices
　(d) consumer sovereignty

4. Industrialization and rapid economic growth in the Soviet Union were initially achieved by:
　(a) the mobilization of economic resources
　(b) the overcommitment of economic resources
　(c) price controls and price fixing
　(d) active use of fiscal policy by the government

5. The Soviet Union viewed itself historically as a single socialist nation surrounded by hostile capitalist nations, and as a consequence central planning stressed the need for:
　(a) consumer sovereignty
　(b) economic self-sufficiency
　(c) allocation by directive
　(d) manipulation of the money supply by the *Gosbank*

6. In the system of central planning in the Soviet Union, the outputs of some industries became the inputs for other industries, but a failure of one industry to meet its target would cause:
　(a) inflation in wholesale and retail prices
　(b) the decay of the infrastructure
　(c) a chain reaction of production problems and bottlenecks
　(d) widespread unemployment and underemployment among workers

Use the table below to answer the next question (7).

	Growth in real domestic output (percent)			
Years	**A**	**B**	**C**	**D**
1950s	3	4	5	6
1960s	4	3	3	5
1970s	5	6	1	3
1980s (mid)	6	2	1	2

7. The column that best portrays the record of Soviet economic growth from the 1950s through the mid-1980s is:
　(a) A
　(b) B
　(c) C
　(d) D

8. In the last year or two before the Soviet Union break up, real economic growth:
  (a) increased slightly
  (b) decreased significantly
  (c) remained the same in both years
  (d) increased in 1990, but decreased significantly in 1991

9. Which of the following is evidence of economic failure of communism in the Soviet Union?
  (a) lagging technology compared to Western standards
  (b) the inability to supply consumer goods that people wanted
  (c) the poor quality of consumer goods
  (d) all of the above

10. What was the size of expenditures for the military as a percentage of domestic output in the Soviet Union versus the United States?
  (a) 15–20% in Soviet Union versus 15–20% in the United States
  (b) 5–10% in Soviet Union versus 10–15% in the United States
  (c) 15–20% in Soviet Union versus 6% in the United States
  (d) 10% in Soviet Union versus 6% in the United States

11. Which of the following was a cause of low productivity in agriculture in the Soviet Union?
  (a) inability to make productive use of the abundance of good farmland in the country
  (b) the failure to construct an effective incentive system for agriculture
  (c) an increase in the length of the growing season
  (d) the overuse of certain chemical fertilizers on crops

12. Which factor contributed to the slowing of Soviet economic growth in the 1980s?
  (a) labor shortages
  (b) unemployment
  (c) idle plant capacity
  (d) decreased consumption

13. What was the major success indicator for Soviet enterprises?
  (a) profits
  (b) the level of prices
  (c) production targets
  (d) the turnover tax

14. The restructuring of the Soviet economy under Mikhail Gorbachev is referred to as:
  (a) *Gosbank*
  (b) *glasnost*
  (c) *perestroika*
  (d) the "second economy"

15. The modernization proposal of Gorbachev's economic program basically involved:
  (a) increased production of consumer goods and decreased production of investment goods
  (b) reallocation of investment to research and development and to high-tech industries
  (c) the building of new housing facilities to address the pressing problems of overcrowding and the deterioration in dwellings
  (d) increasing the productivity of agriculture by improving the quality of equipment available to agricultural workers

16. Which of the following is *not* one of the components of the most recent and sweeping reform effort in Russia?
  (a) privatization
  (b) promotion of competition
  (c) an increased role for government
  (d) more participation in the world economy

17. The effect of price controls on most consumer goods in the Soviet Union was that:
  (a) shortages developed because quantity demanded was greater than the quantity supplied by the competitive market at the controlled price set by government
  (b) prices rose because the quantity demanded by consumers was greater than the quantity supplied by government
  (c) prices fell because the quantity supplied by the competitive market was greater than the quantity demanded by consumers
  (d) shortages developed because the quantity demanded by consumers was greater than the quantity supplied by the government at the price set by government

18. An important avenue that has been suggested for industrialized capitalist nations to assist in the development of a market economy in the former Soviet Union is for those nations to:
  (a) eliminate the ruble overhang
  (b) increase private investment
  (c) forgive past debt
  (d) reduce foreign aid

19. Which would be considered a major accomplishment of economic reforms in Russia in the 1990–1994 period?
  (a) greater income equality
  (b) an increase in price controls
  (c) extensive privatization of the economy
  (d) rising output and rising living standards

20. Which set of factors contributed to the recent inflationary pressure in the former Soviet Union?
  (a) the breakup of state monopolies, the extension of credit to enterprises by the *Gosbank,* the increase in the turnover tax

(b) central planning, production targets, and production bottlenecks

(c) increasing the money supply to finance government deficits, the ruble overhang, and the decontrol of prices

(d) increased military spending, investment in new technology, and making the ruble a convertible currency

■ PROBLEMS

1. In the table below are several of the major institutions and characteristics of either the American economy or the economy of the former Soviet Union. In the appropriate space, name the corresponding institution or characteristic of the other economy.

American institution or characteristic	Soviet institution or characteristic
a. _____	labor theory of value
b. _____	surplus value
c. Private ownership of economic resources	_____
d. a market economy	_____
e. _____	state industrial enterprises
f. privately owned farms	_____
g. entrepreneurial freedom	_____
h. consumer sovereignty	_____
i. _____	price controls
j. _____	turnover tax
k. democracy	_____

2. Answer the next set of questions based on the table below. In the table are the columns for the price, quantity demanded (Q_d) by consumers, and a fixed quantity supplied by government (Q_{s1}) for a product in the former Soviet Union. The column for Q_{s2} shows the supply curve for the product *after* privatization in the industry producing the product.

Price (in rubles)	Q_d	Q_{s1}	Q_{s2}
90	25	25	55
80	30	25	50
70	35	25	45
60	40	25	40
50	45	25	35
40	50	25	30
30	55	25	25

a. When only the government supplies the product as shown in the Q_{s1} schedule, the equilibrium price will be

_____ rubles and the equilibrium quantity will be _____ units.

b. If the government tries to make the product more accessible to lower-income consumers by setting the price at 30 rubles, then the quantity demanded will be

_____ units and the quantity supplied will be

_____ units, producing a shortage of _____ units.

c. If the government decontrolled prices but did not privatize industry, then prices would rise to _____ rubles and the government would still produce

_____ units.

d. With privatization, there will be a new quantity supplied schedule (Q_{s2}). The equilibrium price will be

_____ rubles and the equilibrium quantity will be

_____ units. The equilibrium price has risen by

_____ rubles and the equilibrium quantity by

_____ units.

■ SHORT ANSWER AND ESSAY QUESTIONS

1. What are the essential features of Marxian ideology on which the command economy of the Soviet Union was based?

2. What were the two principal economic institutions of the Soviet Union? How do these institutions compare with those of the United States?

3. Describe how Soviet planning functioned historically. What are some generalizations you can make about resource use, directives, prices, self-sufficiency, and macroeconomic policies?

4. Why does central planning result in a "coordination" problem? Compare the operation of central planning with the use of markets and prices for economic decision-making.

5. What economic evidence can you present on the failure of communism in the Soviet Union in the 1980s and early 1990s?

6. Discuss the six factors that contributed to the collapse of the Soviet economy. In particular, explain the difference between achieving economic growth by increasing the quantity of resources and increasing economic growth by increasing the productivity and efficiency with which existing resources are used.

7. What were the six elements of Gorbachev's economic reform program? How do these reforms compare with past economic reforms?

8. What problems are posed by privatization for Russia as it moves to a market economy?

9. Discuss what must be done in Russia to promote competition. To what extent are "state monopolies" a problem?

10. What is the traditional role for government in a market economy? Describe the anticipated changes in the role of government in Russia as it adopts capitalism.

11. Why was there a need for price reform in Russia in its transition to a market economy? What has been the **general** effect of this change? Use a supply and demand graph to explain the effect of the price decontrol on a specific product.

12. What is the major problem confronting Russia as it seeks to join the world economy?

13. How will high rates of inflation affect the transition to a market economy in Russia?

14. What role do public attitudes and values play in the economic transformation of Russia?

15. Why must economic reforms be achieved simultaneously?

16. What are the contributions of foreign aid in the transition to capitalism in Russia? How much foreign aid has been given and what type is it? What are the criticisms of foreign aid?

17. How can private investment help the Russian economy? What conditions must be overcome to increase private investment?

18. Describe the major accomplishments of economic reform in Russia.

19. What are the major problems that Russia continues to face as it makes its transition to a market economy?

20. Evaluate the prospects for the transformation of Russia into a market economy.

ANSWERS

Chapter 23 Russia: An Economy in Transition

FILL-IN QUESTIONS

1. *a.* labor; *b.* privately, subsistence, surplus; *c.* publicly owned, class, proletariat

2. state, central

3. *a.* industrialization, military, over, under; *b.* mobilizing, agriculture; *c.* targets, prices; *d.* socialist, capitalist, self; *e.* passive, controlled, unemployment, **Gosbank,** money

4. decentralized, centralized, efficient, inefficient

5. *a.* military, consumer; *b.* inefficient, hurt; *c.* quantity, quality, technological; *d.* more; *e.* inadequate; *f.* ineffective

Gorbachev, **perestroika, glasnost**

a. modernization of industry; *b.* greater decentralization of making; *c.* creation of a limited private enterprise sector;

d. improved worker discipline and incentive; *e.* a more rational price system; *f.* increased role in the international economy

8. property, private, sale, stock, corporations, government

9. competition, monopoly

10. limited, legal, competition, income, public, spillover, stabilization

11. controls

12. convertible, trade

13. inflation, prices, hyperinflation, exchange

14. support, bureaucrats, habits

15. simultaneity, together

16. foreign, inflation, wasteful, delays

17. 23, 3, 20, export

18. private, membership, *a.* private, government, inputs, public, high, inflation; *b.* World, Monetary, Agreements on Tariffs and Trade

19. privatization, prices, unemployment

20. inflation, decontrols, ruble, deficits, output, standard, inequality, insecurity

TRUE-FALSE QUESTIONS

1. F, p. 474	**8.** F, p. 476	**15.** T, p. 479	**22.** T, pp. 482-483
2. F, p. 474	**9.** T, p. 476	**16.** F, pp. 479-480	**23.** T, p. 483
3. F, p. 474	**10.** F, p. 476	**17.** F, p. 480	**24.** F, p. 484
4. F, pp. 474-475	**11.** F, p. 477	**18.** T, p. 481	**25.** F, p. 484
5. T, p. 474	**12.** F, p. 477	**19.** F, p. 482	
6. F, pp. 474-475	**13.** F, p. 478	**20.** F, p. 482	
7. F, p. 475	**14.** T, pp. 478-479	**21.** T, p. 482	

MULTIPLE-CHOICE QUESTIONS

1. *c*, pp. 473-474	**6.** *c*, p. 475	**11.** *b*, pp. 476-477	**16.** *c*, p. 479
2. *d*, pp. 473-474	**7.** *d*, p. 476	**12.** *a*, p. 477	**17.** *d*, p. 480
3. *b*, p. 474	**8.** *b*, p. 476	**13.** *c*, pp. 477-478	**18.** *b*, pp. 482-483
4. *a*, p. 475	**9.** *d*, p. 476	**14.** *c*, p. 478	**19.** *c*, p. 483
5. *b*, p. 475	**10.** *c*, p. 476	**15.** *b*, p. 479	**20.** *c*, p. 484

PROBLEMS

1. *a.* supply and demand; *b.* profit; *c.* state ownership of resources; *d.* command or centrally planned economy; *e.* corporations; *f.* agricultural cooperatives or collective farms; *g.* central economic planning (or production targets); *h.* central economic planning; *i.* free markets and flexible prices; *j.* excise tax; *k.* dictatorship by the party

2. *a.* 90, 25; *b.* 55, 25, 30; *c.* 90, 25; *d.* 60, 40, 30, 15

SHORT ANSWER AND ESSAY QUESTIONS

1. pp. 473-474	**6.** pp. 476-478	**11.** pp. 480-481	**16.** p. 482
2. p. 474	**7.** pp. 478-479	**12.** p. 481	**17.** pp. 482-483
3. pp. 474-475	**8.** pp. 479-482	**13.** p. 481	**18.** p. 483
4. pp. 475-476	**9.** p. 479	**14.** pp. 481-482	**19.** p. 484
5. pp. 476-477	**10.** pp. 479-480	**15.** p. 482	**20.** p. 485

Glossary

Ability-to-pay principle   The belief that those who have greater income (or wealth) should be taxed absolutely and relatively more than those who have less.

Abstraction   Elimination of irrelevant and noneconomic facts to obtain an economic principle.

Actual budget   The amount spent by the Federal government (to purchase goods and services and for transfer payments) less the amount of tax revenue collected by it in any (fiscal) year; and which can **not** reliably be used to determine whether it is pursuing an expansionary or contractionary fiscal policy. Compare (*see*) the Full-employment budget.

Actual deficit   The size of the Federal government's Budget deficit (*see*) actually measured or recorded in any given year.

Actual investment   The amount which business Firms do invest; equal to Planned investment plus Unplanned investment.

Actual reserves   The funds which a Member bank has on deposit at the Federal Reserve Bank of its district (plus its Vault cash).

Adaptive expectations theory   The idea that people determine their expectations about future events (for example, inflation) on the basis of past and present events (rates of inflation) and only change their expectations as events unfold.

Adjustable pegs   The device used in the Bretton Woods system (*see*) to change Exchange rates in an orderly way to eliminate persistent payments deficits and surpluses: each nation defined its monetary unit in terms of (pegged it to) gold or the dollar, kept the Rate of exchange for its money stable in the short run, and changed (adjusted) it in the long run when faced with international disequilibrium.

AFDC   (*See* Aid to families with dependent children.)

Aggregate demand   A schedule or curve which shows the total quantity of goods and services demanded (purchased) at different price levels.

Aggregate demand–aggregate supply model   The macroeconomic model which uses Aggregate demand and Aggregate supply (*see* both) to determine and explain the Price level and the real Domestic output.

Aggregate expenditures   The total amount spent for final goods and services in the economy.

Aggregate expenditures–domestic output approach   Determination of the Equilibrium gross domestic product (*see*) by finding the real GDP at which aggregate expenditures are equal to the Domestic output.

Aggregate expenditures schedule   A schedule or curve showing the total amount spent for final goods and services at different levels of GDP.

Aggregate supply   A schedule or curve showing the total quantity of goods and services supplied (produced) at different Price levels.

Aggregation   Combining individual units or data into one unit or number. For example, all prices of individual goods and services are combined into a Price level, or all units of output are aggregated into Real gross domestic product.

Annually balanced budget   The equality of government expenditures and tax collections during a year.

Anticipated inflation   Inflation (*see*) at a rate equal to the rate expected in that period of time.

Applied economics   (*See* Policy economics.)

Appreciation of the dollar   An increase in the value of the dollar relative to the currency of another nation; a dollar now buys a larger amount of the foreign currency. For example, if the dollar price of a British pound changes from $3 to $2, the dollar has appreciated.

"Asian tigers"   The newly industrialized and rapidly growing nations of Hong Kong, Singapore, South Korea, and Taiwan.

Asset   Anything of monetary value owned by a firm or individual.

Asset demand for money   The amount of money people want to hold as a Store of value (the amount of their financial assets they wish to have in the form of Money); and which varies inversely with the Rate of interest.

Authoritarian capitalism   An economic system in which property resources are privately owned and government extensively directs and controls the economy.

Average product   The total output produced per unit of a resource employed (total product divided by the quantity of a resource employed).

Average propensity to consume   Fraction of Disposable income which households spend for consumer goods and services; consumption divided by Disposable income.

Average propensity to save   Fraction of Disposable income which households save; Saving divided by Disposable income.

Average tax rate   Total tax paid divided by total (taxable) income; the tax rate on total (taxable) income.

Balanced-budget amendment   Proposed constitutional amendment which would require Congress to balance the Federal budget annually.

Balanced budget multiplier   The effect of equal increases (decreases) in government spending for goods and services and in taxes is to increase (decrease) the Equilibrium gross domestic product by the amount of the equal increases (decreases).

Balance of payments deficit The sum of the Balance on current account (*see*) and the Balance on the capital account (*see*) is negative.

Balance of payments surplus The sum of the Balance on current account (*see*) and the Balance on the capital account (*see*) is positive.

Balance on current account The exports of goods (merchandise) and services of a nation less its imports of goods (merchandise) and services plus its Net investment income and Net transfers.

Balance on goods and services The exports of goods (merchandise) and services of a nation less its imports of goods (merchandise) and services.

Balance on the capital account The Capital inflows (*see*) of a nation less its Capital outflows (*see*).

Balance sheet A statement of the Assets (*see*), Liabilities (*see*), and Net worth (*see*) of a firm or individual at some given time.

Bank deposits The deposits which banks have at the Federal Reserve Banks (*see*).

Bankers' bank A bank which accepts the deposits of and makes loans to Depository institutions; a Federal Reserve Bank.

Bank reserves Bank reserves held at the Federal Reserve Banks (*see*) plus bank Vault cash (*see*).

Barrier to entry Anything that artificially prevents the entry of Firms into an industry.

Barter The exchange of one good or service for another good or service.

Base year The year with which prices in other years are compared when a Price index (*see*) is constructed.

Benefit-cost analysis Deciding whether to employ resources and the quantity of resources to employ for a project or program (for the production of a good or service) by comparing the marginal benefits with the marginal costs.

Big business A business Firm which either produces a large percentage of the total output of an industry, is large (in terms of number of employees or stockholders, sales, assets, or profits) compared with other Firms in the economy, or both.

Board of Governors The seven-member group that supervises and controls the money and banking system of the United States; formally, the Board of Governors of the Federal Reserve System; the Federal Reserve Board.

Brain drain The emigration of highly educated, highly skilled workers from a country.

Break-even income The level of Disposable income at which Households plan to consume (spend) all of their income and to save none of it; also denotes that level of earned income at which subsidy payments become zero in an income maintenance program.

Bretton Woods system The international monetary system developed after World War II in which Adjustable pegs (*see*) were employed, the International Monetary Fund (*see*) helped to stabilize Foreign exchange rates, and gold and the dollar (*see*) were used as International monetary reserves (*see*).

Budget deficit The amount by which the expenditures of the Federal government exceed its revenues in any year.

Budget surplus The amount by which the revenues of the Federal government exceeds its expenditures in any year.

Built-in stability The effect of Nondiscretionary fiscal policy (*see*) on the economy; when Net taxes vary directly with the Gross domestic product, the fall (rise) in Net taxes during a recession (inflation) lessens unemployment (inflationary pressures).

Business cycle Recurrent ups and downs over a period of years in the level of economic activity.

Capital Human-made resources (machinery and equipment) used to produce goods and services; goods which do not directly satisfy human wants; capital goods.

Capital account The section in a nation's International balance of payments (*see*) in which are recorded the Capital inflows (*see*) and the Capital outflows (*see*) of that nation.

Capital account deficit A negative Balance on the capital account (*see*).

Capital account surplus A positive Balance on the capital account (*see*).

Capital flight The transfer of savings from less developed to industrially advanced countries to avoid government expropriation, taxation, and high rates of inflation or to realize better investment opportunities.

Capital gain The gain realized when securities or properties are sold for a price greater than the price paid for them.

Capital goods (*See* Capital.)

Capital inflow The expenditures made by the residents of foreign nations to purchase real and financial capital from the residents of a nation.

Capital-intensive commodity A product which requires a relatively large amount of Capital to produce.

Capital outflow The expenditures made by the residents of a nation to purchase real and financial capital from the residents of foreign nations.

Capital-saving technological advance An improvement in technology that permits a greater quantity of a product to be produced with a specific amount of Capital (or the same amount of the product to be produced with a smaller amount of Capital).

Capital-using technological advance An improvement in technology that requires the use of a greater amount of Capital to produce a specific quantity of a product.

Causation A cause-and-effect relationship; one or several events bring about or result in another event.

CEA (*See* Council of Economic Advisers.)

Central bank A bank whose chief function is the control of the nation's money supply.

Central economic planning Government determination of the objectives of the economy and the direction of its resources to the attainment of these objectives.

***Ceteris paribus* assumption** (*See* "Other things equal" assumption.)

Change in amount consumed Increase or decrease in consumption spending that results from an increase or decrease in Disposable income, the Consumption schedule (curve) remaining unchanged; movement from one row (point) to another on the same Consumption schedule (curve).

Change in amount saved Increase or decrease in Saving that results from an increase or decrease in Disposable income, the Saving schedule (curve) remaining unchanged; movement from one row (point) to another on the same Saving schedule (curve).

Change in the consumption schedule An increase or decrease in consumption at each level of Disposable income caused by changes in the Nonincome determinants of consumption and saving (*see*); an upward or downward movement of the Consumption schedule.

Change in the saving schedule An increase or decrease in Saving at each level of Disposable income caused by changes in the Nonincome determinants of consumption and saving (*see*); an upward or downward movement of the Saving schedule.

Checkable deposit Any deposit in a Commercial bank or Thrift institution against which a check may be written; includes Demand deposits and NOW, ATS, and share draft accounts.

Checking account A Checkable deposit (*see*) in a Commercial bank or Thrift institution.

Circular flow of income The flow of resources from Households to Firms and of products from Firms to Households accompanied in an economy using money by flows of money from Households to Firms and from Firms to Households.

Classical economics The Macroeconomic generalizations accepted by most economists before the 1930s which led to the conclusion that a capitalistic economy would employ its resources fully.

Closed economy An economy which neither exports nor imports goods and services.

Coincidence of wants The item (good or service) which one trader wishes to obtain is the same as another trader desires to give up and the item which the second trader wishes to acquire is the same as the first trader desires to surrender.

COLA (*See* Cost-of-living adjustment.)

Collection of checks The process by which funds are transferred from the checking accounts of the writers of checks to the checking accounts of the recipients of the checks; also called the "clearing" of checks.

Command economy An economic system (method of organization) in which property resources are publicly owned and Central economic planning (*see*) is used to direct and coordinate economic activities.

Commercial bank Firm which has a charter from either a state government or the Federal government to engage in the business of banking.

Commercial banking system All Commercial banks and Thrift institutions as a group.

Communism (*See* Command economy.)

Comparative advantage A lower relative or Comparative cost (*see*) than another producer.

Comparative cost The amount by which one product must be reduced to increase the production of another product; Opportunity cost (*see*).

Compensation to employees Wages and salaries paid by employers to workers plus Wage and salary supplements (*see*).

Competing goods (*See* Substitute goods.)

Competition The presence in a market of a large number of independent buyers and sellers and the freedom of buyers and sellers to enter and leave the market.

Complementary goods Goods and services for which there is an inverse relationship between the price of one and the demand for the other; when the price of one falls (rises) the demand for the other increases (decreases).

Complex multiplier The Multiplier (*see*) when changes in the Gross domestic product change Net taxes and Imports, as well as Saving.

Conglomerate combination A group of Plants (*see*) owned by a single Firm and engaged at one or more stages in the production of different products (of products which do not compete with each other).

Consumer goods Goods and services which satisfy human wants directly.

Consumer price index (CPI) An index which measures the prices of a fixed "market basket" of some 300 consumer goods bought by a "typical" consumer.

Consumer sovereignty Determination by consumers of the types and quantities of goods and services produced from the scarce resources of the economy.

Consumption of fixed capital Estimate of the amount of Capital worn out or used up (consumed) in producing the Gross domestic product; depreciation.

Consumption schedule A schedule showing the amounts Households plan to spend for Consumer goods at different levels of Disposable income.

Contractionary fiscal policy A decrease in Aggregate demand brought about by a decrease in Government expenditures for goods and services, an increase in Net taxes, or some combination of the two.

Corporate income tax A tax levied on the net income (profit) of Corporations.

Corporation A legal entity ("person") chartered by a state or the Federal government which is distinct and separate from the individuals who own it.

Correlation Systematic and dependable association between two sets of data (two kinds of events); does not necessarily indicate causation.

Cost-of-living adjustment An increase in the incomes (wages) of workers which is automatically received by them when there is inflation and guaranteed by a clause in their labor contracts with their employer.

Cost-push inflation Inflation resulting from a decrease in Aggregate supply (from higher wage rates and raw material prices) and accompanied by decreases in real output and employment (and by increases in the Unemployment rate).

Cost ratio The ratio of the decrease in the production of the product to the increase in the production of another product when resources are shifted from the production of the first to the second; the amount the production of one product decreases when the production of a second increases by one unit.

Council of Economic Advisers A group of three persons which advises and assists the President of the United States on economic matters (including the preparation of the economic report of the President to Congress).

Credit An accounting notation that the value of an asset (such as the foreign money owned by the residents of a nation) has increased.

Credit union An association of persons who have a common tie (such as being employees of the same Firm or members of the same Labor union) which sells shares to (accepts deposits from) its members and makes loans to them.

Crowding-out effect The rise in interest rates and the resulting decrease in planned investment spending in the economy caused by increased borrowing in the money market by the Federal government.

Currency Coins and Paper money.

Currency appreciation (*See* Exchange rate appreciation.)

Currency depreciation (*See* Exchange rate depreciation.)

Current account The section in a nation's International balance of payments (*see*) which records its exports and imports of goods (merchandise) and services, its net investment income, and its net transfers.

Current account deficit A negative Balance on current account (*see*).

Current account surplus   A positive Balance on current account (*see*).

Customary economy   (*See* Traditional economy.)

Cyclical deficit   A Federal Budget deficit which is caused by a recession and the consequent decline in tax revenues.

Cyclical unemployment   Unemployment caused by insufficient Aggregate expenditures (or by insufficient Aggregate demand).

Cyclically balanced budget   The equality of Government expenditures and Net tax collections over the course of a Business cycle; deficits incurred during periods of recession are offset by surpluses obtained during periods of prosperity (inflation).

Debit   An accounting notation that the value of an asset (such as the foreign money owned by the residents of a nation) has decreased.

Debt-equity swaps   The transfer of stock in private or government-owned enterprises of Less developed countries (*see*) to foreign creditors.

Declining economy   An economy in which Net private domestic investment (*see*) is less than zero (Gross private domestic investment is less than Depreciation).

Declining industry   An industry in which Economic profits are negative (losses are incurred) and which will, therefore, decrease its output as Firms leave the industry.

Decrease in demand   A decrease in the Quantity demanded of a good or service at every price; a shift of the Demand curve to the left.

Decrease in supply   A decrease in the quantity supplied of a good or service at every price; a shift of the Supply curve to the left.

Deduction   Reasoning from assumptions to conclusions; a method of reasoning that first develops a hypothesis (an assumption) and then compares the conclusions to which it leads with economic facts.

Deficit Reduction Act of 1993   Federal legislation intended to reduce the budget deficit by about $500 billion over five years by increasing taxes and cutting expenditures.

Deflating   Finding the Real gross domestic product (*see*) by decreasing the dollar value of the Gross domestic product produced in a year in which prices were higher than in the Base year (*see*).

Deflation   A fall in the general (average) level of prices in the economy.

Demand   A Demand schedule or a Demand curve (*see* both).

Demand curve   A curve showing the amounts of a good or service buyers wish to purchase at various prices during some period of time.

Demand deposit   A deposit in a Commercial bank or Thrift against which checks may be written; a Checking account or checking-account money.

Demand-deposit multiplier   (*See* Monetary multiplier.)

Demand factor   The increase in the level of Aggregate demand which brings about the Economic growth made possible by an increase in the productive potential of the economy.

Demand management   The use of Fiscal policy (*see*) and Monetary policy (*see*) to increase or decrease Aggregate demand.

Demand-pull inflation   Inflation resulting from an increase in Aggregate demand.

Demand schedule   A schedule showing the amounts of a good or service buyers will purchase at various prices during some period of time.

Dependent variable   A variable which changes as a consequence of a change in some other (independent) variable; the "effect" or outcome.

Depository institution   A Firm that accepts the deposits of Money of the public (businesses and persons); Commercial banks, Savings and loan associations, Mutual savings banks, and Credit unions.

Depository Institutions Deregulation and Monetary Control Act   Federal legislation of 1980 which, among other things, allowed Thrift institutions to accept Checkable deposits and to use the check-clearing facilities of the Federal Reserve and to borrow from the Federal Reserve Banks; subjected the Thrifts to the reserve requirements of the Fed; and provided for the gradual elimination of the maximum interest rates that could be paid by Depository institutions on Savings and Time deposits.

Depreciation   (*See* Consumption of fixed capital.)

Depreciation of the dollar   A decrease in the value of the dollar relative to another currency; a dollar now buys a smaller amount of the foreign currency. For example, if the dollar price of a British pound changes from $2 to $3, the dollar has depreciated.

Derived demand   The demand for a good or service which is dependent on or related to the demand for some other good or service; the demand for a resource which depends on the demand for the products it can be used to produce.

Descriptive economics   The gathering or collection of relevant economic facts (data).

Determinants of aggregate demand   Factors such as consumption, investment, government, and net export spending which, if they change, will shift the aggregate demand curve.

Determinants of aggregate supply   Factors such as input prices, productivity, and the legal-institutional environment which, if they change, will shift the aggregate supply curve.

Determinants of demand   Factors other than its price which determine the quantities demanded of a good or service.

Determinants of supply   Factors other than its price which determine the quantities supplied of a good or service.

Devaluation   A decrease in the governmentally defined value of a currency.

DI   (*See* Disposable income.)

Diagnosis-related-group system (DRG)   A program by which hospitals are paid a fixed amount for Medicare patients based on one of 468 diagnostic categories.

DIDMCA   (*See* Depository Institutions Deregulation and Monetary Control Act.)

Directing function of prices   (*See* Guiding function of prices.)

Directly related   Two sets of economic data that change in the same direction; when one variable increases (decreases) the other increases (decreases).

Direct relationship   The relationship between two variables which change in the same direction, for example, product price and quantity supplied.

Discount rate   The interest rate which the Federal Reserve Banks charge on the loans they make to Depository institutions.

Discouraged workers   Workers who have left the Labor force (*see*) because they have not been able to find employment.

Discretionary fiscal policy   Deliberate changes in taxes (tax rates) and government spending (spending for goods and services and transfer payment programs) by Congress to achieve a full-employment noninflationary Gross domestic product and economic growth.

Disinflation   A reduction in the rate of Inflation (*see*).

Disposable income   Personal income (*see*) less personal taxes; income available for Personal consumption expenditures (*see*) and Personal saving (*see*).

Dissaving   Spending for consumer goods and services in excess of Disposable income; the amount by which Personal consumption expenditures (*see*) exceed Disposable income.

Division of labor   Dividing the work required to produce a product into a number of different tasks which are performed by different workers; Specialization (*see*) of workers.

Dollar votes   The "votes" which consumers and entrepreneurs in effect cast for the production of the different kinds of consumer and capital goods, respectively, when they purchase them in the markets of the economy.

Domestic capital formation   Adding to a nation's stock of Capital by saving and investing part of its own domestic output.

Domestic output   Gross (or net) domestic product; the total output of final goods and services produced in the economy.

Domestic price   The price of a good or service within a country, determined by domestic demand and supply.

Doomsday models   Computer-based models which predict that continued growth of population and production will exhaust available resources and the environment, causing an economic collapse.

Double counting   Including the value of Intermediate goods (*see*) in the Gross domestic product; counting the same good or service more than once.

Double taxation   Taxation of both corporate net income (profits) and the dividends paid from this net income when they become the Personal income of households.

Dumping   The sale of products below cost in a foreign country.

Durable good   A consumer good with an expected life (use) of three years or more.

Dynamic progress   The development over time of more efficient (less costly) techniques of producing existing products and of improved products; technological progress.

Earnings   The money income received by a worker; equal to the Wage (rate) multiplied by the quantity of labor supplied (the amount of time worked) by the worker.

Easy money policy   Expanding the Money supply.

EC   European Economic Community. (*See* European Union.)

Economic analysis   Deriving Economic principles (*see*) from relevant economic facts.

Economic cost   A payment that must be made to obtain and retain the services of a resource; the income a Firm must provide to a resource supplier to attract the resource away from an alternative use; equal to the quantity of other products that cannot be produced when resources are employed to produce a particular product.

Economic efficiency   The relationship between the input of scarce resources and the resulting output of a good or service; production of an output with a specific dollar-and-cents value with the smallest total expenditure for resources; obtaining the largest total production of a good or service with resources of a specific dollar-and-cents value.

Economic growth   (1) An increase in the Production possibilities schedule or curve that results from an increase in resource supplies or an improvement in Technology; (2) an increase either in real output (Gross domestic product) or in real output per capita.

Economic integration   Cooperation among and the complete or partial unification of the economies of different nations; the elimination of the barriers to trade among these nations; the bringing together of the markets in each of the separate economies to form one large (a common) market.

Economic law   (*See* Economic principle.)

Economic model   A simplified picture of reality; an abstract generalization.

Economic perspective   A viewpoint which envisions individuals and institutions making rational or purposeful decisions based on a consideration of the marginal benefits and marginal costs associated with their actions.

Economic policy   Course of action intended to correct or avoid a problem.

Economic principle   Generalization of the economic behavior of individuals and institutions.

Economic profit   The Total revenue of a firm less all its Economic costs; also called "pure profit" and "above normal profit."

Economic rent   The price paid for the use of land and other natural resources, the supply of which is fixed (perfectly inelastic).

Economic resources   Land, labor, capital, and entrepreneurial ability which are used in the production of goods and services.

Economics   Social science concerned with using scarce resources to obtain the maximum satisfaction of the unlimited material wants of society.

Economic theory   Deriving economic principles (*see*) from relevant economic facts; an Economic principle (*see*).

Economies of scale   The forces which reduce the Average total cost of producing a product as the Firm expands the size of its Plant (its output) in the Long run (*see*); the economies of mass production.

Economizing problem   Society's material wants are unlimited but the resources available to produce the goods and services that satisfy wants are limited (scarce); the inability to produce unlimited quantities of goods and services.

Efficiency factors in growth   The capacity of an economy to combine resources effectively to achieve the growth of real output which the Supply factors (*see*) make possible.

Efficient allocation of resources   That allocation of the resources of an economy among the production of different products which leads to the maximum satisfaction of the wants of consumers; producing the optimal mix of output.

Employment Act of 1946   Federal legislation which committed the Federal government to the maintenance of economic stability (a high level of employment, stable prices, and Economic growth); established the Council of Economic Advisors (*see*) and the Joint Economic Committee (*see*) and provided for the annual economic report of the President to Congress.

Employment and training policy   Policies and programs involving vocational training, job information, and antidiscrimination which are designed to improve labor-market efficiency and lower unemployment at any level of aggregate demand.

Employment rate   The percentage of the Labor force (*see*) employed at any time.

Entrepreneurial ability   The human resource which combines the other resources to produce a product, makes nonroutine decisions, innovates, and bears risks.

Equation of exchange $MV = PQ$, in which M is the Money supply (*see*), V is the Velocity of money (*see*), P is the Price level, and Q is the physical volume of final goods and services produced.

Equilibrium gross domestic product The Gross domestic product at which the total quantity of final goods and services produced (the Domestic output) is equal to the total quantity of final goods and services purchased (Aggregate expenditures); the real Domestic output at which the Aggregate demand curve intersects the Aggregate supply curve.

Equilibrium price The price in a competitive market where the Quantity demanded (*see*) and the Quantity supplied (*see*) are equal; where there is neither a shortage nor a surplus; and where there is no tendency for price to rise or fall.

Equilibrium price level The price level at which the Aggregate demand curve intersects the Aggregate supply curve.

Equilibrium quantity The Quantity demanded (*see*) and Quantity supplied (*see*) at the Equilibrium price (*see*) in a competitive market.

European Common Market (*See* European Union.)

European Union (EU) The association of European nations initiated in 1958 to abolish gradually the Tariffs and Import quotas that exist among them, to establish common Tariffs for goods imported from outside the member nations, to allow the eventual free movement of labor and capital among them, and to create other common economic policies. (Earlier known as "European Economic Community" and the "Common Market.")

Excess reserves The amount by which a bank or thrift's Actual reserves (*see*) exceed its Required reserves (*see*); Actual reserves minus Required reserves.

Exchange control (*See* Foreign exchange control.)

Exchange rate The Rate of exchange (*see*).

Exchange rate appreciation An increase in the value of a nation's money in Foreign exchange markets; an increase in the Rate of exchange for foreign monies.

Exchange rate depreciation A decrease in the value of a nation's money in Foreign exchange markets; a decrease in the Rate of exchange for foreign monies.

Exchange rate determinant Any factor other than the Rate of exchange (*see*) that determines a currency's demand and supply in the Foreign exchange market (*see*).

Excise tax A tax levied on the expenditure for a specific product or on the quantity of the product purchased.

Exclusion principle The exclusion of those who do not pay for a product from the benefits of the product.

Exhaustive expenditure An expenditure by government resulting directly in the employment of economic resources and in the absorption by government of the goods and services these resources produce; a Government purchase (*see*).

Expanding economy An economy in which Net private domestic investment (*see*) is greater than zero (Gross private domestic investment is greater than Depreciation).

Expanding industry An industry in which economic profits are obtained by the firms in the industry and which will, therefore, increase its output as new firms enter the industry.

Expansionary fiscal policy An increase in Aggregate demand brought about by an increase in Government expenditures for goods and services, a decrease in Net taxes, or some combination of the two.

Expectations What consumers, business Firms, and others believe will happen or what conditions will be in the future.

Expected rate of net profit Annual profit a firm anticipates it will obtain by purchasing Capital (by investing) expressed as a percentage of the price (cost) of the Capital.

Expenditures approach The method which adds all the expenditures made for Final goods and services to measure the Gross domestic product.

Expenditures-output approach (*See* Aggregate expenditures–domestic output approach.)

Export controls The limitation or prohibition of the export of certain high-technology products on the basis of foreign policy or national security objectives.

Export-Import Bank A Federal institution which provides interest-rate subsidies to foreign borrowers who buy American exports on credit.

Exports Goods and services produced in a nation and sold to customers in other nations.

Export subsidies Government payments which reduce the price of a product to foreign buyers.

Export supply curve An upsloping curve showing the amount of a product domestic firms will export at each World price (*see*) above the Domestic price (*see*).

Export transactions A sale of a good or service which increases the amount of foreign money held by the citizens, firms, and governments of a nation.

External benefits (*See* Spillover benefit.)

External cost (*See* Spillover cost.)

External debt Private or public debt (*see*) owed to foreign citizens, firms, and institutions.

Externality (*See* Spillover.)

Face value The dollar or cents value stamped on a coin.

Factors of production Economic resources: Land, Capital, Labor, and Entrepreneurial ability.

Fallacy of composition Incorrectly reasoning that what is true for the individual (or part) is therefore necessarily true for the group (or whole).

FDIC (*See* Federal Deposit Insurance Corporation.)

Federal Advisory Committee The group of twelve commercial bankers which advises the Board of Governors (*see*) on banking policy.

Federal Deposit Insurance Corporation (FDIC) The Federally chartered corporation which insures the deposit liabilities of Commercial banks and Thrift institutions.

Federal funds rate The interest rate banks and other depository institutions charge one another on overnight loans made out of their excess reserves.

Federal Open Market Committee (*See* Open Market Committee.)

Federal Reserve Bank Any one of the twelve banks chartered by the United States government to control the Money supply and perform other functions. (*See* Central bank, Quasi-public bank, *and* Banker's bank.)

Federal Reserve Note Paper money issued by the Federal Reserve Banks.

Feedback effects The effects which a change in the money supply will have (because it affects the interest rate, planned investment, and the equilibrium GDP) on the demand for money which is itself directly related to the GDP.

Fiat money Anything that is Money because government has decreed it to be Money.

Final goods Goods which have been purchased for final use and not for resale or further processing or manufacturing (during the year).

Financial capital (*See* Money capital.)

Financing exports and imports The use of Foreign exchange markets by exporters and importers to receive and make payments for goods and services they sell and buy in foreign nations.

Firm An organization that employs resources to produce a good or service for profit and owns and operates one or more Plants (*see*).

Fiscal federalism The system of transfers (grants) by which the Federal government shares its revenues with state and local governments.

Fiscal policy Changes in government spending and tax collections designed to achieve a full-employment and noninflationary domestic output.

Five fundamental economic questions The five questions which every economy must answer: what to produce, how to produce, how to divide the total output, how to maintain Full employment, and how to assure economic flexibility.

Fixed exchange rate A Rate of exchange which is prevented from rising or falling.

Flexible exchange rate A rate of exchange determined by the international demand for and supply of a nation's money; a rate free to rise or fall.

Floating exchange rate (*See* Flexible exchange rate.)

Foreign exchange control The control a government may exercise over the quantity of foreign money demanded by its citizens and business firms and over the Rates of exchange in order to limit its outpayments to its inpayments (to eliminate a Payments deficit, *see*).

Foreign exchange market A market in which the money (currency) used by one nation is used to purchase (is exchanged for) the money used by another nation.

Foreign exchange rate (*See* Rate of exchange.)

Foreign purchases effect The inverse relationship between the Net exports (*see*) of an economy and its Price level (*see*) relative to foreign Price levels.

45-degree line A line along which the value of the GDP (measured horizontally) is equal to the value of Aggregate expenditures (measured vertically).

Fractional reserve A Reserve ratio (*see*) which is less than 100 percent of the deposit liabilities of a Commercial bank.

Freedom of choice Freedom of owners of property resources and money to employ or dispose of these resources as they see fit, of workers to enter any line of work for which they are qualified, and of consumers to spend their incomes in a manner which they deem appropriate (best for them).

Freedom of enterprise Freedom of business Firms to employ economic resources, to use these resources to produce products of the firm's own choosing, and to sell these products in markets of their choice.

Freely floating exchange rates Rates of exchange (*see*) which are not controlled and which may, therefore, rise and fall; and which are determined by the demand for and the supply of foreign monies.

Free-rider problem The inability of potential providers of an economically desirable but indivisible good or service to obtain payment from those who benefit, because the Exclusion principle (*see*) is not applicable.

Free Trade The absence of artificial (government imposed) barriers to trade among individuals and firms in different nations.

Frictional unemployment Unemployment caused by workers voluntarily changing jobs and by temporary layoffs; unemployed workers between jobs.

Full employment (1) Using all available resources to produce goods and services; (2) when the Unemployment rate is equal to the Full-employment unemployment rate and there is Frictional and Structural but no Cyclical unemployment (and the Real output of the economy is equal to its Potential real output).

Full-employment budget What government expenditures and revenues and its surplus or deficit would be if the economy were to operate at Full employment throughout the year.

Full-employment unemployment rate The Unemployment rate (*see*) at which there is no Cyclical unemployment (*see*) of the Labor force (*see*); and because some Frictional and Structural unemployment is unavoidable, equal to about 5.5 to 6 percent.

Full production The maximum amount of goods and services which can be produced from the employed resources of an economy; occurs when both Allocative efficiency and Productive efficiency are realized.

Functional distribution of income The manner in which national income is divided among those who perform different functions (provide the economy with different kinds of resources); the division of National income (*see*) into wages and salaries, proprietors' income, corporate profits, interest, and rent.

Functional finance Use of Fiscal policy to achieve a full-employment noninflationary Gross domestic product without regard to the effect on the Public debt (*see*).

G-7 Nations A group of seven major industrial powers (the United States, Japan, Germany, United Kingdom, France, Italy, and Canada) whose leaders meet regularly to discuss common economic problems and try to coordinate economic policies.

GATT (*See* General Agreement on Tariffs and Trade.)

GDP (*See* Gross domestic product.)

GDP deflator The Price index (*see*) for all final goods and services used to adjust the money (or nominal) GDP to measure the real GDP.

GDP gap Potential Real gross domestic product less actual Real gross domestic product.

General Agreement on Tariffs and Trade The international agreement reached in 1947 in which twenty-three nations agreed to give equal and nondiscriminatory treatment to the other nations, to reduce tariff rates by multinational negotiations, and to eliminate Import quotas. Now includes 124 nations.

Generalization Statistical or probability statement; statement of the nature of the relation between two or more sets of facts.

Glasnost A Soviet campaign of the mid-1980s for greater "openness" and democratization in political and economic activities.

GNP (*See* Gross national product.)

Gold export point The rate of exchange for a foreign money above which—when nations participate in the International gold standard (*see*)—the foreign money will not be purchased and gold will be sent (exported) to the foreign country to make payments there.

Gold flow The movement of gold into or out of a nation.

Gold import point The Rate of exchange for a foreign money below which—when nations participate in the International gold standard (*see*)—a nation's own money will not be purchased and gold will be sent (imported) into that country by foreigners to make payments there.

Gorbachev's reforms A mid-1980s series of reforms designed to revitalize the Soviet economy. The reforms stressed the modernization of productive facilities, less centralized control, improved worker discipline and productivity, more emphasis on market prices, and an expansion of private economic activity.

Government purchases Disbursements of money by government for which government receives a currently produced good or service in return; the expenditures of all governments in the economy for Final goods (*see*) and services.

Government transfer payment The disbursement of money (or goods and services) by government for which government receives no currently produced good or service in return.

Gross domestic product (GDP) The total market value of all Final goods (*see*) and services produced annually within the boundaries of the United States, whether by American or foreign-supplied resources.

Gross national product (GNP) The total market value of all Final goods (*see*) and services produced annually by land, labor, and capital, and entrepreneurial talent supplied by American residents, whether these resources are located in the United States or abroad.

Gross private domestic investment Expenditures for newly produced Capital goods (*see*)—machinery, equipment, tools, and buildings—and for additions to inventories.

Guiding function of prices The ability of price changes to bring about changes in the quantities of products and resources demanded and supplied. (*See* Incentive function of price.)

Horizontal axis The "left-right" or "west-east" axis on a graph or grid.

Horizontal combination A group of Plants (*see*) in the same stage of production which are owned by a single Firm (*see*).

Horizontal range Horizontal segment of the Aggregate-supply curve along which the price level is constant as real domestic output changes.

Household An economic unit (of one or more persons) which provides the economy with resources and uses the money paid to it for these resources to purchase goods and services which satisfy material wants.

Hyperinflation A very rapid rise in the price level.

IMF (*See* International Monetary Fund.)

Import competition Competition which domestic firms encounter from the products and services of foreign suppliers.

Import demand curve A downsloping curve showing the amount of a product which an economy will import at each World price (*see*) below the Domestic price (*see*).

Import quota A limit imposed by a nation on the quantity of a good which may be imported during some period of time.

Imports Spending by individuals, Firms, and governments for goods and services produced in foreign nations.

Import transaction The purchase of a good or service which decreases the amount of foreign money held by citizens, firms, and governments of a nation.

Income approach The method which adds all the incomes generated by the production of Final goods and services to measure the Gross domestic product.

Income effect The effect of a change in price of a product on a consumer's Real income (purchasing power) and thus on the quantity of the product purchased, after the Substitution effect (*see*) has been determined and eliminated.

Income inequality The unequal distribution of an economy's total income among persons or families.

Incomes policy Government policy which affects the Nominal incomes of individuals (the wages workers receive) and the prices they pay for goods and services and alters their Real incomes. (*See* Wage-price policy.)

Income velocity of money (*See* Velocity of money.)

Increase in demand An increase in the Quantity demanded of a good or service at every price; a shift in the Demand curve to the right.

Increase in supply An increase in the Quantity supplied of a good or service at every price; a shift in the Supply curve to the right.

Independent goods Goods or services for which there is no relationship between the price of one and the demand for the other; when the price of one rises or falls the demand for the other remains constant.

Independent variable The variable causing a change in some other (dependent) variable.

Indirect business taxes Such taxes as Sales, Excise, and business Property taxes (*see all*), license fees, and Tariffs (*see*) which Firms treat as costs of producing a product and pass on (in whole or in part) to buyers of the product by charging them higher prices.

Individual demand The Demand schedule (*see*) or Demand curve (*see*) of a single buyer.

Individual supply The Supply schedule (*see*) or Supply curve (*see*) of a single seller.

Induction A method of reasoning which proceeds from facts to Generalization (*see*).

Industrially advanced countries (IACs) Countries such as the United States, Canada, Japan, and the nations of western Europe which have developed Market economies based on large stocks of technologically advanced capital goods and skilled labor forces.

Industrial policy Any policy in which government takes a direct and active role in promoting specific firms or industries to expand output and achieve economic growth.

Industry A group of (one or more) Firms which produce identical or similar products.

Inferior good A good or service of which consumers purchase less (more) at every price when their incomes increase (decrease).

Inflating Finding the Real gross domestic product (*see*) by increasing the dollar value of the Gross domestic product produced in a year in which prices are lower than in the Base year (*see*).

Inflation A rise in the general (average) level of prices in the economy.

Inflation premium The component of the nominal interest rate which reflects anticipated inflation.

Inflationary expectations The belief of workers, business Firms, and consumers that there will be substantial inflation in the future.

Inflationary gap   The amount by which the Aggregate-expenditures schedule (curve) must decrease (shift downward) to decrease the nominal GDP to the full-employment noninflationary level.

Inflationary recession   (*See* Stagflation.)

Infrastructure   The capital goods usually provided by the Public sector for the use of its citizens and Firms (e.g., highways, bridges, transit systems, waste water treatment facilities, municipal water systems, and airports).

Injection   An addition of spending to the income-expenditure stream: Investment, Government purchases, and Exports.

In-kind investment   Nonfinancial investment (*see*).

Innovation   The introduction of a new product, the use of a new method of production, or the creation of a new form of business organization.

Inpayments   The receipts of (its own or foreign) money which the individuals, Firms, and governments of one nation obtain from the sale of goods and services, investment income, Remittances, and Capital inflows from abroad.

Interest   The payment made for the use of money (of borrowed funds).

Interest income   Income of those who supply the economy with Capital (*see*).

Interest rate   The Rate of interest (*see*).

Interest-rate effect   The tendency for increases (decreases) in the Price level to increase (decrease) the demand for money; raise (lower) interest rates; and, as a result, to reduce (expand) total spending in the economy.

Intermediate goods   Goods which are purchased for resale or further processing or manufacturing during the year.

Intermediate range   The upsloping segment of the Aggregate supply curve lying between the Horizontal range and the Vertical range (*see both*).

Internally held public debt   Public debt (*see*) owed to (United States government securities owned by) American citizens, Firms, and institutions.

International balance of payments   Summary statement of the transactions which took place between the individuals, Firms, and governments of one nation and those in all other nations during the year.

International balance of payments deficit   (*See* Balance of payments deficit.)

International balance of payments surplus   (*See* Balance of payments surplus.)

International Bank for Reconstruction and Development   (*See* World Bank.)

International economic goal   Assumed to be a current-account balance of zero.

International gold standard   An international monetary system employed in the nineteenth and early twentieth centuries in which each nation defined its money in terms of a quantity of gold, maintained a fixed relationship between its gold stock and money supply, and allowed the free importation and exportation of gold.

International Monetary Fund   The international association of nations which was formed after World War II to make loans of foreign monies to nations with temporary Payments deficits (*see*) and to administer the Adjustable pegs (*see*).

International monetary reserves   The foreign monies and such assets as gold a nation may use to settle a Payments deficit (*see*).

International value of the dollar   The price that must be paid in foreign currency (money) to obtain one American dollar.

Intrinsic value   The market value of the metal in a coin.

Inverse relationship   The relationship between two variables which change in opposite directions, for example, product price and quantity demanded.

Investment   Spending for (the production and accumulation of) Capital goods (*see*) and additions to inventories.

Investment curve (schedule)   A curve (schedule) which shows the amounts firms plan to invest (along the vertical axis) at different income (Gross domestic product) levels (along the horizontal axis).

Investment-demand curve (schedule)   A curve (schedule) which shows Rates of interest (along the vertical axis) and the amount of Investment (along the horizontal axis) at each Rate of interest.

Invisible hand   The tendency of Firms and resource suppliers seeking to further their self-interests in competitive markets to further the best interest of society as a whole (the maximum satisfaction of wants).

JEC   (*See* Joint Economic Committee.)

Joint Economic Committee   Committee of Senators and members of Congress which investigates economic problems of national interest.

Keynesian economics   The macroeconomic generalizations which lead to the conclusion that a capitalistic economy does not always employ its resources fully and that Fiscal policy (*see*) and Monetary policy (*see*) can be used to promote Full employment (*see*).

Keynesianism   The philosophical, ideological, and analytical views pertaining to Keynesian economics (*see*).

Labor   The physical and mental talents (efforts) of people which can be used to produce goods and services.

Labor force   Persons sixteen years of age and older who are not in institutions and who are employed or are unemployed and seeking work.

Labor force participation rate   The percentage of the working-age population which is actually in the labor force.

Labor-intensive commodity   A product which requires much Labor to produce.

Labor productivity   Total output divided by the quantity of labor employed to produce the output; the Average product (*see*) of labor or output per worker per hour.

Labor theory of value   The Marxian notion that the economic value of any commodity is determined solely by the amount of labor required to produce it.

Laffer curve   A curve showing the relationship between tax rates and the tax revenues of government and on which there is a tax rate (between zero and 100 percent) where tax revenues are a maximum.

Laissez faire capitalism   (*See* Pure capitalism.)

Land   Natural resources ("free gifts of nature") used to produce goods and services.

Land-intensive commodity   A product requiring a relatively large amount of Land to produce.

Law of demand   The inverse relationship between the price and the Quantity demanded (*see*) of a good or service during some period of time.

Law of increasing opportunity cost   As the amount of a product produced is increased, the Opportunity cost (*see*)—Marginal cost (*see*)—of producing an additional unit of the product increases.

Law of supply   The direct relationship between the price and the Quantity supplied (*see*) of a good or service during some period.

Leakage   (1) A withdrawal of potential spending from the income-expenditures stream; Saving (*see*), tax payments, and Imports (*see*); (2) a withdrawal which reduces the lending potential of the Commercial banking system.

Leakages-injections approach   Determination of the Equilibrium gross domestic product (*see*) by finding the GDP at which Leakages (*see*) are equal to Injections (*see*).

Least-cost combination rule (of resources)   The quantity of each resource a Firm must employ if it is to produce an output at the lowest total cost; the combination at which the ratio of the Marginal product (*see*) of a resource to its Marginal resource cost (*see*) (to its price if the resource is employed in a competitive market) is the same for all resources employed.

Legal reserves (deposit)   The minimum amount a Depository institution (*see*) must keep on deposit with the Federal Reserve Bank in its district, or in Vault cash (*see*).

Legal tender   Anything that government has decreed must be accepted in payment of a debt.

Lending potential of an individual commercial bank   The amount a single Commercial bank can safely increase the Money supply by making new loans to (or buying securities from) the public; equal to the Commercial bank's Excess reserves (*see*).

Lending potential of the banking system   The amount the Commercial banking system (*see*) can increase the Money supply by making new loans to (or buying securities from) the public; equal to the Excess reserves (*see*) of the Commercial banking system multiplied by the Monetary multiplier (*see*).

Less developed countries (LDCs)   Most countries of Africa, Asia, and Latin America which are characterized by a lack of capital goods, primitive production technologies, low literacy rates, high unemployment, rapid population growth, and labor forces heavily committed to agriculture.

Liability   A debt with a monetary value; an amount owed by a Firm or an individual.

Limited liability   Restriction of the maximum loss to a predetermined amount; for the owners (stockholders) of a Corporation, the maximum loss is the amount they paid for their shares of stock.

Limited-liability company   An unincorporated business whose owners are protected by Limited liability (*see*).

Line-item veto   A proposal to give the President the power to delete specific expenditure items from spending legislation passed by Congress.

Liquidity   Money or things which can be quickly and easily converted into Money with little or no loss of purchasing power.

Loaded terminology   Terms which arouse emotions and elicit approval or disapproval.

Long-run aggregate supply curve   The aggregate supply curve associated with a time period in which input prices (especially nominal wages) are fully responsive to changes in the price level.

Lotteries   Games of chance where people buy numbered tickets and winners are drawn by lot; a source of state and local government revenue.

Lump-sum tax   A tax which is a constant amount (the tax revenue of government is the same) at all levels of GDP.

M1   The narrowly defined Money supply; the Currency and Checkable deposits (*see*) not owned by the Federal government, Federal Reserve Banks, or Depository institutions.

M2   A more broadly defined Money supply; equal to M1 (*see*) plus Noncheckable savings deposits, Money market deposit accounts, small Time deposits (deposits of less than $100,000), and individual Money market mutual fund balances.

M3   Very broadly defined Money supply; equal to M2 (*see*) plus large Time deposits (deposits of $100,000 or more).

Macroeconomics   The part of economics concerned with the economy as a whole; with such major aggregates as the household, business, and governmental sectors and with totals for the economy.

Managed floating exchange rate   An Exchange rate allowed to change (float) to eliminate Payments deficits and surpluses and is controlled (managed) to reduce day-to-day fluctuations.

Marginal analysis   Decision making which involves a comparison of marginal ("extra" or "additional") benefits and marginal costs.

Marginal propensity to consume   Fraction of any change in Disposable income spent for Consumer goods; equal to the change in consumption divided by the change in Disposable income.

Marginal propensity to save   Fraction of any change in Disposable income which households save; equal to change in Saving (*see*) divided by the change in Disposable income.

Marginal tax rate   The fraction of additional (taxable) income which must be paid in taxes.

Market   Any institution or mechanism which brings together the buyers (demanders) and sellers (suppliers) of a particular good or service.

Market demand   (*See* Total demand.)

Market economy   An economy in which only the private decisions of consumers, resource suppliers, and business Firms determine how resources are allocated; the Market system.

Market failure   The failure of a market to bring about the allocation of resources which best satisfies the wants of society (that maximizes the satisfaction of wants). In particular, the over- or underallocation of resources to the production of a particular good or service (because of Spillovers or informational problems) and no allocation of resources to the production of Public goods (*see*).

Market policies   Government policies designed to reduce the market power of labor unions and large business firms and to reduce or eliminate imbalances and bottlenecks in labor markets.

Market socialism   An economic system (method of organization) in which property resources are publicly owned and markets and prices are used to direct and coordinate economic activities.

Market system   All the product and resource markets of the economy and the relationships among them; a method which allows the prices determined in these markets to allocate the economy's scarce resources and to communicate and coordinate the decisions made by consumers, business firms, and resource suppliers.

Medium of exchange   Money (*see*); a convenient means of exchanging goods and services without engaging in Barter (*see*); what sellers generally accept and buyers generally use to pay for a good or service.

Microeconomics   The part of economics concerned with such individual units within the economy as Industries, Firms, and Households; and with individual markets, particular prices, and specific goods and services.

Mixed capitalism   An economy in which both government and private decisions determine how resources are allocated.

Monetarism   An alternative to Keynesianism (*see*); the macroeconomic view that the main cause of changes in aggregate output and the price level are fluctuations in the money supply; advocates a Monetary rule (*see*).

Monetary multiplier   The multiple of its Excess reserves (*see*) by which the Commercial banking system (*see*) can expand the Money supply and Demand deposits by making new loans (or buying securities); and equal to one divided by the Required reserve ratio (*see*).

Monetary policy   Changing the Money supply (*see*) to assist the economy to achieve a full-employment, noninflationary level of total output.

Monetary rule   The rule suggested by Monetarism (*see*); the Money supply should be expanded each year at the same annual rate as the potential rate of growth of the Real gross domestic product; the supply of money should be increased steadily at from 3 to 5 percent per year.

Money   Any item which is generally acceptable to sellers in exchange for goods and services.

Money capital   Money available to purchase Capital goods (*see*).

Money income   (*See* Nominal income.)

Money interest rate   The Nominal interest rate (*see*).

Money market   The market in which the demand for and the supply of money determine the Interest rate (or the level of interest rates) in the economy.

Money market deposit account (MMDA)   Interest-earning accounts at banks and thrift institutions which pool the funds of depositors to buy various short-term securities.

Money market mutual funds (MMMF)   Interest-bearing accounts offered by brokers which pool depositors' funds for the purchase of short-term securities; depositors may write checks in minimum amounts or more against their accounts.

Money supply   Narrowly defined (*see*) *M*1, more broadly defined (*see*) *M*2 and *M*3.

Money wage   The amount of money received by a worker per unit of time (hour, day, etc.); nominal wage.

Money wage rate   (*See* Money wage.)

Monopoly   A market in which the number of sellers is so small that each seller is able to influence the total supply and the price of the good or service. (Also *see* Pure monopoly.)

Monopsony   A market in which there is only one buyer of a good, service, or resource.

Most-favored-nation (MFN) clause   A clause in a trade agreement between the United States and another nation which provides that the other nation's Imports into the United States will be subjected to the lowest tariff levied then or later on any other nation's Imports into the United States.

Multinational corporations   A firm which owns production facilities in other countries and produces and sells its products abroad.

Multiplier   The ratio of the change in the Equilibrium GDP to the change in Investment (*see*), or to the change in any other component of Aggregate expenditures or Aggregate demand; the number by which a change in any component of Aggregate expenditures or Aggregate demand must be multiplied to find the resulting change in the Equilibrium GDP.

Multiplier effect   The effect on Equilibrium gross domestic product of a change in Aggregate expenditures or Aggregate demand (caused by a change in the Consumption schedule, Investment, Government expenditures, or Net exports).

Mutually exclusive goals   Goals which conflict and cannot be achieved simultaneously.

Mutual savings bank   A Firm without stockholders which accepts deposits primarily from small individual savers and which lends primarily to individuals to finance the purchases of residences.

National bank   A Commercial bank (*see*) chartered by the United States government.

National income   Total income earned by resource suppliers for their contributions to the production of the Gross domestic product (*see*); equal to the Gross domestic product minus the Nonincome charges (*see*) minus Net foreign factor income earned in the United States (*see*).

National income accounting   The techniques employed to measure the overall production of the economy and other related totals for the nation as a whole.

Natural monopoly   An industry in which Economies of scale (*see*) are so great the product can be produced by one Firm at a lower average total cost than if the product were produced by more than one Firm.

Natural rate hypothesis   The idea that the economy is stable in the long run at the natural rate of unemployment; views the long-run Phillips Curve (*see*) as vertical at the natural rate of unemployment.

Natural rate of unemployment   (*See* Full-employment unemployment rate.)

NDP   (*See* Net domestic product.)

Near-money   Financial assets, the most important of which are Noncheckable savings accounts, Time deposits, and U.S. short-term securities and savings bonds, which are not a medium of exchange but can be readily converted into Money.

Negative relationship   (*See* Inverse relationship.)

Net capital movement   The difference between the real and financial investments and loans made by individuals and Firms of one nation in the other nations of the world and the investments and loans made by individuals and Firms from other nations in a nation; Capital inflows less Capital outflows.

Net domestic product   Gross domestic product (*see*) less that part of the output needed to replace the Capital goods worn out in producing the output (Consumption of fixed capital, *see*).

Net export effect   The notion that the impact of a change in Monetary policy (Fiscal policy) will be strengthened (weakened) by the consequent change in Net exports (*see*). For example, a tight (easy) money policy will increase (decrease) domestic interest rates, increasing (decreasing) the foreign demand for dollars. The dollar appreciates (depreciates) and causes American net exports to decrease (increase).

Net exports   Exports (*see*) minus Imports (*see*).

Net foreign factor income earned in the United States Payments of resource income to the rest of the world minus receipts of resource income from the rest of the world; the difference between GDP (*see*) and GNP (*see*).

Net investment income The interest and dividend income received by the residents of a nation from residents of other nations less the interest and dividend payments made by the residents of that nation to the residents of other nations.

Net private domestic investment Gross private domestic investment (*see*) less Consumption of fixed capital (*see*); the addition to the nation's stock of Capital during a year.

Net taxes The taxes collected by government less Government transfer payments (*see*).

Net transfers The personal and government transfer payments made to residents of foreign nations less the personal and government transfer payments received from residents of foreign nations.

Net worth The total Assets (*see*) less the total Liabilities (*see*) of a Firm or an individual; the claims of the owners of a firm against its total Assets.

New classical economics The theory that, although unanticipated price level changes may create macroeconomic instability in the short run, the economy is stable at the full-employment level of domestic output in the long run because of price and wage flexibility.

New Global Compact A reform agenda by which Less developed countries (*see*) seek more foreign aid, debt relief, greater access to world markets, freer immigration, and an end to neo-colonialism.

Nominal gross domestic output (GDP) The GDP (*see*) measured in terms of the price level at the time of measurement (unadjusted for changes on the price level).

Nominal income The number of dollars received by an individual or group during some period of time.

Nominal interest rate The rate of interest expressed in dollars of current value (not adjusted for inflation).

Nominal wage The Money wage (*see*).

Noncheckable savings account A Savings account (*see*) against which a check can not be written.

Nondiscretionary fiscal policy The increases (decreases) in Net taxes (*see*) which occur without Congressional action when the gross domestic product rises (falls) and which tend to stabilize the economy; also called Built-in stability.

Nondurable good A Consumer good (*see*) with an expected life (use) of less than three years.

Nonexhaustive expenditure An expenditure by government which does not result directly in the employment of economic resources or the production of goods and services; *see* Government transfer payment.

Nonfinancial investment An investment which does not require households to save a part of their money incomes; but which uses surplus (unproductive) labor to build Capital goods.

Nonincome charges Consumption of fixed capital (*see*) and Indirect business taxes (*see*).

Nonincome determinants of consumption and saving All influences on consumption spending and saving other than the level of **GDP**.

Noninterest determinants of investment All influences on the level of investment spending other than the rate of interest.

Noninvestment transaction An expenditure for stocks, bonds, or second-hand Capital goods.

Nonmarket transactions The production of goods and services not included in the measurement of the Gross domestic product because the goods and services are not bought and sold.

Nonproduction transaction The purchase and sale of any item which is not a currently produced good or service.

Nontariff barriers All barriers other than Tariffs (*see*) which nations erect to impede international trade: Import quotas (*see*), licensing requirements, unreasonable product-quality standards, unnecessary red tape in customs procedures, etc.

Normal good A good or service whose consumption increases (decreases) when income increases (decreases); price remaining constant.

Normal profit Payment that must be made by a Firm to obtain and retain Entrepreneurial ability (*see*); the minimum payment (income) Entrepreneurial ability must (expect to) receive to induce it to perform the entrepreneurial functions for a Firm; an Implicit cost (*see*).

Normative economics That part of economics pertaining to value judgments about what the economy should be like; concerned with economic goals and policies.

North American Free Trade Agreement (NAFTA) A 1993 agreement establishing a trade bloc (*see*) comprising Canada, Mexico, and the United States. The goal is to establish free trade between the three nations. In late 1994 Chile was invited to apply for membership.

NTBs (*See* Nontariff barriers.)

Official reserves The foreign monies (currencies) owned by the central bank of a nation.

Okun's law The generalization that any one percentage point rise in the Unemployment rate above the Full-employment unemployment rate will increase the GDP gap by 2.5 percent of the Potential output (GDP) of the economy.

OPEC An acronym for the Organization of Petroleum Exporting Countries (*see*).

Open economy An economy which both exports and imports goods and services.

Open Market Committee The twelve-member group which determines the purchase-and-sale policies of the Federal Reserve Banks in the market for United States government securities.

Open-market operations The buying and selling of United States government securities by the Federal Reserve Banks.

Opportunity cost The amount of other products which must be forgone or sacrificed to produce a unit of a product.

Organization of Petroleum Exporting Countries The cartel formed in 1970 by thirteen oil-producing countries to control the price and quantity of crude oil exported by its members, and which accounts for a large proportion of the world's export of oil.

"Other things equal" assumption Assuming that factors other than those being considered are constant.

Outpayments The expenditures of (its own or foreign) money which the individuals, Firms, and governments of one nation make to purchase goods and services, for Remittances, as investment income, and Capital outflows abroad.

Output effect The change in labor input resulting from the effect of a change in the wage rate on a Firm's cost of production and the subsequent change in the desired level of output, after the Substitution effect (*see*) has been determined and eliminated.

Paper money Pieces of paper used as a Medium of exchange (*see*); in the United States, Federal Reserve Notes (*see*).

Partnership An unincorporated business Firm owned and operated by two or more persons.

Payments deficits (*See* Balance of payments deficit.)

Payments surplus (*See* Balance of payments surplus.)

Payroll tax A tax levied on employers of Labor equal to a percentage of all or part of the wages and salaries paid by them; and on employees equal to a percentage of all or part of the wages and salaries received by them.

Perestroika The essential feature of Mikhail Gorbachev's mid-1980s reform program to "restructure" the Soviet economy; included modernization, decentralization, some privatization, and improved worker incentives.

Personal consumption expenditures The expenditures of Households for Durable and Nondurable consumer goods and services.

Personal distribution of income The manner in which the economy's Personal or Disposable income is divided among different income classes or different households.

Personal income The earned and unearned income available to resource suppliers and others before the payment of Personal taxes (*see*).

Personal income tax A tax levied on the taxable income of individuals (households and unincorporated firms).

Personal saving The Personal income of households less Personal taxes (*see*) and Personal consumption expenditures (*see*); Disposable income not spent for Consumer goods (*see*).

Phillips Curve A curve showing the relationship between the Unemployment rate (*see*) (on the horizontal axis) and the annual rate of increase in the Price level (on the vertical axis).

Planned economy An economy in which government determines how resources are allocated.

Planned investment The amount which business firms plan or intend to invest.

Plant A physical establishment (Land and Capital) which performs one or more of the functions in the production (fabrication and distribution) of goods and services.

Policy economics The formulation of courses of action to bring about desired results or to prevent undesired occurrences (to control economic events).

Political business cycle The tendency of Congress to destabilize the economy by reducing taxes and increasing government expenditures before elections and to raise taxes and lower expenditures after elections.

Positive economics The analysis of facts or data to establish scientific generalizations about economic behavior; compare Normative economics.

Positive relationship The relationship between two variables which change in the same direction, for example, product price and quantity supplied.

***Post hoc, ergo propter hoc* fallacy** Incorrectly reasoning that when one event precedes another the first event is the cause of the second.

Potential output The real output (GDP) an economy is able to produce when it fully employs its available resources.

Premature inflation Inflation (*see*) which occurs before the economy has reached Full employment (*see*).

Price The quantity of money (or of other goods or services) paid and received for a unit of a good or service.

Price-decreasing effect The effect in a competitive market of a decrease in Demand or an increase in Supply upon the Equilibrium price (*see*).

Price guidepost A government exhortation that the price charged by an industry for its product should increase by no more than the increase in the Unit labor cost (*see*) of producing the product.

Price-increasing effect The effect in a competitive market of an increase in Demand or a decrease in Supply on the equilibrium price.

Price index An index number which shows how the average price of a "market basket" of goods changes through time. A price index is used to change nominal output (income) into real output (income).

Price level The weighted average of the Prices paid for the final goods and services produced in the economy.

Price level surprises Unanticipated changes in the price level.

Price-wage flexibility Changes in the prices of products and in the Wages paid to workers; the ability of prices and Wages to rise or to fall.

Prime interest rate The interest rate banks charge their most credit worthy borrowers, for example, large corporations with impeccable financing credentials.

Private good A good or service subject to the Exclusion principle (*see*) and which is provided by privately owned firms to those who are willing to pay for it.

Private property The right of private persons and Firms to obtain, own, control, employ, dispose of, and bequeath Land, Capital, and other Assets.

Private sector The Households and business firms of the economy.

Production possibilities curve (table) A curve (table) showing the different combinations of two goods or services that can be produced in a Full-employment (*see*), Full-production (*see*) economy where the available supplies of resources and technology are constant.

Productive efficiency The production of a good in the least costly way; occurs when production takes place at the output where Average total cost is at a minimum and where Marginal product per dollar's worth of each input is the same.

Productivity A measure of average output or real output per unit of input. For example, the productivity of labor may be determined by dividing hours of work into real output.

Productivity slowdown The recent decline in the rate at which Labor productivity (*see*) in the United States has increased.

Product market A market in which Households buy and Firms sell the products they have produced.

Profit (*see*) Economic profit and Normal profit; without an adjective preceding it, the income of those who supply the economy with Entrepreneurial ability (*see*) or Normal profit.

Progressive tax A tax such that the Average tax rate increases as the taxpayer's income increases and decreases as income decreases.

Property tax A tax on the value of property (Capital, Land, stocks and bonds, and other Assets) owned by Firms and Households.

Proprietors' income The net income of the owners of unincorporated Firms (proprietorships and partnerships).

Prosperous industry (*See* Expanding industry.)

Protective tariff A Tariff (*see*) designed to protect domestic producers of a good from the competition of foreign producers.

Public debt The total amount owed by the Federal government (to the owners of government securities) and equal to the sum of its past Budget deficits (less its budget surpluses).

Public finance The branch of economics which analyzes government revenues and expenditures.

Public good A good or service to which the Exclusion principle (*see*) is not applicable; and which is provided by government if it yields substantial benefits to society.

Public sector The part of the economy that contains all its governments; government.

Purchasing power parity The idea that exchange rates between nations equate the purchasing power of various currencies; exchange rates between any two nations adjust to reflect the price level differences between the countries.

Pure capitalism An economic system in which property resources are privately owned and markets and prices are used to direct and coordinate economic activities.

Pure competition (1) A market in which a very large number of Firms sells a Standardized product (*see*), into which entry is very easy, in which the individual seller has no control over the price at which the product sells, and in which there is no Nonprice competition (*see*); (2) a market in which there is a very large number of buyers.

Pure profit (*See* Economic profit.)

Pure rate of interest (*See The* rate of interest.)

Quantity-decreasing effect The effect in a competitive market of a decrease in Demand or a decrease in Supply on the Equilibrium quantity (*see*).

Quantity demanded The amount of a good or service buyers wish (or a buyer wishes) to purchase at a particular price during some period.

Quantity-increasing effect The effect in a competitive market of an increase in Demand or an increase in Supply on the Equilibrium quantity (*see*).

Quantity supplied The amount of a good or service sellers offer (or a seller offers) to sell at a particular price during some period.

Quasi-public bank A bank which is privately owned but governmentally (publicly) controlled; each of the Federal Reserve Banks.

Quasi-public good A good or service to which the Exclusion principle (*see*) could be applied, but which has such a large Spillover benefit (*see*) that government sponsors its production to prevent an underallocation of resources.

R & D Research and development; activities undertaken to bring about Technological progress.

Ratchet effect The tendency for the Price level to rise when Aggregate demand increases, but not fall when Aggregate demand declines.

Rate of exchange The price paid in one's own money to acquire one unit of a foreign money; the rate at which the money of one nation is exchanged for the money of another nation.

Rate of interest Price paid for the use of Money or for the use of Capital; interest rate.

Rational An adjective which describes the behavior of any individual who consistently does those things enabling him or her to achieve the declared objective of the individual; and which describes the behavior of a consumer who uses money income to buy the collection of goods and services yielding the maximum amount of Utility (*see*).

Rational expectations theory The hypothesis that business firms and households expect monetary and fiscal policies to have certain effects on the economy and take, in pursuit of their own self-interests, actions which make these policies ineffective.

Rationing function of price The ability of a price in a competitive market to equalize Quantity demanded and Quantity supplied and to eliminate shortages and surpluses by rising or falling.

Reaganomics The policies of the Reagan administration based on Supply-side economics (*see*) and intended to reduce inflation and the Unemployment rate (Stagflation).

Real-balances effect The tendency for increases (decreases) in the price level to lower (raise) the real value (or purchasing power) of financial assets with fixed money values; and, as a result, to reduce (expand) total spending in the economy.

Real capital (*See* Capital.)

Real gross domestic product Gross domestic product (*see*) adjusted for changes in the price level; Gross domestic product in a year divided by the GDP deflator (*see*) for that year expressed as a decimal.

Real income The amount of goods and services an individual or group can purchase with his, her, or its Nominal income during some period of time. Nominal income adjusted for changes in the Price level.

Real interest rate The rate of interest expressed in dollars of constant value (adjusted for inflation); and equal to the Nominal interest rate (*see*) less the expected rate of inflation.

Real rate of interest The Real interest rate (*see*).

Real wage The amount of goods and services a worker can purchase with his or her Nominal wage (*see*); the purchasing power of the Nominal wage; the Nominal wage adjusted for changes in the Price level.

Real wage rate (*See* Real wage.)

Recessionary gap The amount by which the Aggregate expenditures schedule (curve) must increase (shift upward) to increase the real GDP to the full-employment noninflationary level.

Reciprocal Trade Agreements Act of 1934 The Federal act which gave the President the authority to negotiate agreements with foreign nations and lower American tariff rates by up to 50 percent if the foreign nations would reduce tariff rates on American goods and which incorporated Most-favored-nation clauses (*see*) in the agreements reached with these nations.

Refinancing the public debt Paying owners of maturing United States government securities with money obtained by selling new securities or with new securities.

Remittance A gift or grant; a payment for which no good or service is received in return; the funds sent by workers who have legally or illegally entered a foreign nation to their families in the nations from which they have migrated.

Rental income Income received by those who supply the economy with Land (*see*).

Required reserve ratio (*See* Reserve ratio.)

Required reserves (*See* Legal reserves.)

Reserve ratio The specified minimum percentage of its deposit liabilities which a Member bank (*see*) must keep on deposit at the Federal Reserve Bank in its district, or in Vault cash (*see*).

Resolution Trust Corporation (RTC) A Federal institution created in 1989 to oversee the closing and sale of failed Savings and loan institutions.

Resource market   A market in which Households sell and Firms buy the services of resources.

Retiring the public debt   Reducing the size of the Public debt by paying money to owners of maturing United States government securities.

Revaluation   An increase in the governmentally defined value of a currency.

Revenue tariff   A Tariff (**see**) designed to produce income for the (Federal) government.

Ricardian equivalence theorem   The idea that an increase in the public debt will have little or no effect on real output and employment because taxpayers will save more in anticipation of future higher taxes to pay the higher interest expense on the debt.

Roundabout production   The construction and use of Capital (**see**) to aid in the production of Consumer goods (**see**).

Ruble overhang   The large amount of forced savings formerly held by Russian households due to the scarcity of consumer goods; these savings fueled inflation when Russian prices were decontrolled.

Rule of 70   A method for determining the number of years it will take for the Price level to double; divide 70 by the annual rate of inflation.

Sales tax   A tax levied on expenditures for a broad group of products.

Saving   Disposable income not spent for Consumer goods (**see**); equal to Disposable income minus Personal consumption expenditures (**see**).

Savings account   A deposit in a Depository institution (**see**) which is interest-earning and which can normally be withdrawn by the depositor at any time.

Savings and Loan association (S&L)   A Firm which accepts deposits primarily from small individual savers, and lends primarily to individuals to finance purchases of residences.

Saving schedule   Schedule which shows the amounts Households plan to save (plan not to spend for Consumer goods, **see**) at different levels of Disposable income.

Savings institution   A Thrift institution (**see**).

Say's law   The (discredited) macroeconomic generalization that the production of goods and services (supply) creates an equal Aggregate demand for these goods and services.

Scarce resources   The fixed (limited) quantities of Land, Capital, Labor, and Entrepreneurial ability (**see all**) which are never sufficient to satisfy the virtually unlimited material wants of humans.

Seasonal variation   An increase or decrease during a single year in the level of economic activity caused by a change in the season.

Secular trend   The expansion or contraction in the level of economic activity over a long period of years.

Self-interest   What each Firm, property owner, worker, and consumer believes is best for itself and seeks to obtain.

Separation of ownership and control   Difference between the group that owns the Corporation (the stockholders) and the group that manages it (the directors and officers) and between the interests (goals) of the two groups.

Service   That which is intangible (invisible) and for which a consumer, firm, or government is willing to exchange something of value.

Shortage   The amount by which the Quantity demanded of a product exceeds the Quantity supplied at a particular (below-equilibrium) price.

Short-run aggregate supply curve   The aggregate supply curve relevant to a time period in which input prices (particularly nominal wages) remain constant when the price level changes.

Simple multiplier   The Multiplier (**see**) in an economy in which government collects no Net taxes (**see**), there are no Imports (**see**), and Investment (**see**) is independent of the level of income (Gross domestic product); equal to one divided by the Marginal propensity to save (**see**).

Slope of a line   The ratio of the vertical change (the rise or fall) to the horizontal change (the run) in moving between two points on a line. The slope of an upward sloping line is positive, reflecting a direct relationship between two variables; the slope of a downward sloping line is negative, reflecting an inverse relationship between two variables.

Smoot-Hawley Tariff Act   Passed in 1930, this legislation established some of the highest tariffs in United States history. Its objective was to reduce imports and stimulate the domestic economy.

Social accounting   (See National income accounting.)

Sole proprietorship   An unincorporated business firm owned and operated by a single person.

Specialization   The use of the resources of an individual, a Firm, a region, or a nation to produce one or a few goods and services for which there is a Comparative advantage.

Speculation   The activity of buying or selling with the motive of then reselling or rebuying to make a profit.

Spillover   A benefit or cost from production or consumption, accruing without compensation to nonbuyers and nonsellers of the product (**see** Spillover benefit and Spillover cost).

Spillover benefit   A benefit obtained without compensation by third parties from the production or consumption of other parties. Example: A bee keeper benefits when the neighboring farmer plants clover.

Spillover costs   A cost imposed without compensation on third parties by the production or consumption of other parties. Example: A manufacturer dumps toxic chemicals into a river, killing the fish sought by sport fishers.

Stabilization policy dilemma   The use of monetary and fiscal policy to decrease the Unemployment rate increases the rate of inflation, and the use of monetary and fiscal policy to decrease the rate of inflation increases the Unemployment rate.

Stagflation   Inflation accompanied by stagnation in the rate of growth of output and a high unemployment rate in the economy; simultaneous increases in both the Price level and the Unemployment rate.

State bank   A Commercial bank chartered to engage in the business of banking by a state government.

State ownership   The ownership of property (Land and Capital) by government (the state); in the former Soviet Union by the central government (the nation).

Static economy   (1) An economy in which Net private domestic investment (**see**) is zero—Gross private domestic investment (**see**) is equal to the Consumption of fixed capital (**see**); (2) an economy in which the supplies of resources, technology, and the tastes of consumers do not change and in which, therefore, the economic future is perfectly predictable and there is no uncertainty.

Store of value   Any asset (**see**) or wealth set aside for future use; a function of Money.

Strategic trade policy   The use of trade barriers to reduce the risk of product development by domestic firms, particularly products involving advanced technology.

Structural deficit   The difference between Federal tax revenues and expenditures when the economy is at full employment.

Structural unemployment Unemployment caused by changes in the structure of demand for Consumer goods and in technology; workers who are unemployed because their skills are not demanded by employers, they lack sufficient skills to obtain employment, or they cannot easily move to locations where jobs are available.

Subsidy A payment of funds (or goods and services) by a government, business firm, or household for which it receives no good or service in return. When made by a government, it is a Government transfer payment (*see*).

Substitute goods Goods or services for which there is a direct relationship between the price of one and the Demand for the other; when the price of one falls (rises) the Demand for the other decreases (increases).

Substitution effect (1) The effect which a change in the price of a Consumer good would have on the relative expensiveness of that good and the resulting effect on the quantity of the good a consumer would purchase if the consumer's Real income (*see*) remained constant; (2) the effect which a change in the price of a resource would have on the quantity of the resource employed by a firm if the firm did not change its output.

Superior good (*See* Normal good.)

Supply A Supply schedule or a Supply curve (*see both*).

Supply curve A curve showing the amounts of a good or service sellers (a seller) will offer to sell at various prices during some period.

Supply factor An increase in the availability quantity of a resource, an improvement in its quality, or an expansion of technological knowledge which makes it possible for an economy to produce a greater output of goods and services.

Supply schedule A schedule showing the amounts of a good or service sellers (or seller) will offer at various prices during some period.

Supply shock One of several events of the 1970s and early 1980s which increased production costs, decreased Aggregate supply, and generated Stagflation in the United States.

Supply-side economics A view of macroeconomics which emphasizes the role of costs and Aggregate supply in explaining Inflation, unemployed labor, and Economic growth.

Supply-side view The view of fiscal policy held by the advocates of Supply-side economics which emphasizes increasing Aggregate supply (*see*) as a means of reducing the Unemployment rate and Inflation and encouraging Economic growth.

Surplus The amount by which the Quantity supplied of a product exceeds the Quantity demanded at a specific (above-equilibrium) price.

Surplus value A Marxian term; the amount by which the value of a worker's daily output exceeds his daily wage; the output of workers appropriated by capitalists as profit.

Tangent The point where a line touches, but does not intersect, a curve.

Target dilemma A problem arising because monetary authorities cannot simultaneously stabilize both the money supply and the level of interest rates.

Tariff A tax imposed by a nation on an imported good.

Tax A nonvoluntary payment of money (or goods and services) to a government by a Household or Firm for which the Household or Firm receives no good or service directly in return.

Tax incidence The income or purchasing power different persons and groups lose as a result of a tax after Tax shifting (*see*) has occurred.

Tax "wedge" Such taxes as Indirect business taxes (*see*) and Payroll taxes (*see*) which are treated as a cost by business firms and reflected in the prices of their products; equal to the price of the product less the cost of the resources required to produce it.

Technology The body of knowledge which can be used to produce goods and services from Economic resources.

Terms of trade The rate at which units of one product can be exchanged for units of another product; the Price (*see*) of a good or service; the amount of one good or service given up to obtain one unit of another good or service.

***The* rate of interest** The Rate of interest (*see*) which is paid solely for the use of money over an extended period of time and which excludes the charges made for the riskiness of the loan and its administrative costs; and which is approximately equal to the rate of interest paid on the long-term and virtually riskless bonds of the United States government.

Thrift institution A Savings and loan association, Mutual savings bank, or Credit union (*see all*).

Tight money policy Contracting, or restricting the growth of, the nation's Money supply (*see*).

Till money (*See* Vault cash.)

Time deposit An interest-earning deposit in a Depository institution (*see*) which the depositor can withdraw without a loss of interest after the end of a specific period.

Token money Coins having a Face value (*see*) greater than their Intrinsic value (*see*).

Total demand The Demand schedule (*see*) or the Demand curve (*see*) of all buyers of a good or service.

Total demand for money The sum of the Transactions demand for money (*see*) and Asset demand for money (*see*); the relationship between the total amount of money demanded, nominal GDP, and the Rate of Interest.

Total product The total output of a particular good or service produced by a firm (a group of firms or the entire economy).

Total revenue The total number of dollars received by a Firm (or Firms) from the sale of a product; equal to the total expenditures for the product produced by the Firm (or firms); equal to the quantity sold (demanded) multiplied by the price at which it is sold—by the Average revenue (*see*) from its sale.

Total spending The total amount buyers of goods and services spend or plan to spend. Also called Aggregate expenditures.

Total supply The Supply schedule (*see*) or the Supply curve (*see*) of all sellers of a good or service.

Trade balance The export of merchandise (goods) of a nation less its imports of merchandise (goods).

Trade bloc A group of nations which lower or abolish trade barriers among members. Examples include the European Union (*see*) and the North American Free Trade Agreement (*see*).

Trade controls Tariffs (*see*), Export subsidies, Import quotas (*see*), and other means a nation may employ to reduce Imports (*see*) and expand Exports (*see*).

Trade deficit The amount a nation's imports of merchandise (goods) exceed its exports of merchandise (goods).

Tradeoffs The notion that one economic goal or objective must be sacrificed to achieve some other goal.

Trade surplus The amount a nation's exports of merchandise (goods) exceed its imports of merchandise (goods).

Trading possibilities line A line which shows the different combinations of two products an economy is able to obtain (consume) when it specializes in the production of one product and trades (exports) this product to obtain the other product.

Traditional economy An economic system in which traditions and customs determine how the economy will use its scarce resources.

Transactions demand for money The amount of money people want to hold to use as a Medium of exchange (to make payments); and which varies directly with the nominal GDP.

Transfer payment A payment of money (or goods and services) by a government or a Firm to a Household or Firm for which the payer receives no good or service directly in return.

Unanticipated inflation Inflation (*see*) at a rate which was greater than the rate expected for that period of time.

Underemployment Failure to produce the maximum amount of goods and services that can be produced from the resources employed; failure to achieve Full production (*see*).

Undistributed corporate profits After-tax corporate profits not distributed as dividends to stockholders; corporate or business saving.

Unemployment Failure to use all available Economic resources to produce goods and services; failure of the economy to employ fully its Labor force (*see*).

Unemployment compensation (*See* Unemployment insurance).

Unemployment rate The percentage of the Labor force (*see*) unemployed at any time.

Unit labor cost Labor costs per unit of output; equal to the Nominal wage rate (*see*) divided by the Average product (*see*) of labor.

Unlimited liability Absence of any limit on the maximum amount which may be lost by an individual and which the individual may become legally required to pay; the amount which may be lost and which a sole proprietor or partner may be required to pay.

Unlimited wants The insatiable desire of consumers (people) for goods and services which will give them satisfaction or utility.

Unplanned investment Actual investment less Planned investment; increases or decreases in the inventories of business firms resulting from production greater than sales.

Unprosperous industry (*See* Declining industry.)

Uruguay Round The eighth and most recent round of trade negotiations under GATT (*see*).

Utility The want-satisfying power of a good or service; the satisfaction or pleasure a consumer obtains from the consumption of a good or service (or from the consumption of a collection of goods and services).

Value added The value of the product sold by a Firm less the value of the goods (materials) purchased and used by the Firm to produce the product; and equal to the revenue which can be used for Wages, rent, interest, and profits.

Value judgment Opinion of what is desirable or undesirable; belief regarding what ought or ought not to be (regarding what is right or just and wrong or unjust).

Value of money The quantity of goods and services for which a unit of money (a dollar) can be exchanged; the purchasing power of a unit of money; the reciprocal of the Price level.

Variable resource Any resource employed by a firm which can be increased or decreased (varied) in quantity.

Vault cash The Currency (*see*) a bank has in its safe (vault) and cash drawers.

Velocity of money The number of times per year the average dollar in the Money supply (*see*) is spent for Final goods and services (*see*).

VERs (*See* Voluntary export restrictions.)

Vertical axis The "up-down" or "north-south" axis on a graph or grid.

Vertical combination A group of Plants (*see*) engaged in different stages of the production of a final product and owned by a single Firm (*see*).

Vertical intercept The point at which a line meets the vertical axis of a graph.

Vertical range Vertical segment of the Aggregate supply curve along which the economy is at full capacity.

Vicious circle of poverty A problem common to the less developed countries where their low per capita incomes are an obstacle to realizing the levels of saving and investment requisite to acceptable rates of economic growth.

Voluntary export restrictions The limitations by firms of their exports to particular foreign nations to avoid the erection of other trade barriers by the foreign nations.

Wage The price paid for Labor (for the use or services of Labor, *see*) per unit of time (per hour, per day, etc.).

Wage and salary supplements Payments made by employers of Labor into social insurance and private pension, health, and welfare funds for workers; and a part of the employer's cost of obtaining Labor.

Wage guidepost A government exhortation that wages (*see*) in all industries in the economy should increase at an annual rate equal to the rate of increase in the Average product (*see*) of Labor in the economy.

Wage-price controls A Wage-price policy (*see*) which legally fixes the maximum amounts Wages (*see*) and prices may be increased in any period.

Wage-price guideposts A Wage-price policy (*see*) which depends on the voluntary cooperation of Labor unions and business firms.

Wage-price inflationary spiral Increases in wage rates which bring about increases in prices and in turn result in further increases in wage rates and in prices.

Wage-price policy Government policy that attempts to alter the behavior of Labor unions and business firms to make their Wage and price decisions more nearly compatible with the goals of Full employment and a stable Price level.

Wage rate (*See* Wage.)

Wages The income of those who supply the economy with Labor (*see*).

Wealth effect (*See* Real balances effect.)

Welfare programs (*See* Public assistance programs.)

(The) "will to develop" Wanting economic growth strongly enough to change from old to new ways of doing things.

World Bank A bank which lends (and guarantees loans) to less developed nations to assist them to grow; formally, the International Bank for Reconstruction and Development.

World price The international price of a good or service, determined by world demand and supply.

World Trade Organization (WTO) An organization established in 1994 by GATT (*see*) to oversee the provisions of the Uruguay Round (*see*) and resolve any disputes stemming therefrom.